ESSAYS IN THE ECONOMIC HISTORY OF THE ATLANTIC WORLD

Written by one of the leading authorities on trade and finance in the early modern Atlantic world, these fourteen essays, revised and integrated for this volume, share as their common theme the development of the Atlantic economy, especially early British America and the Caribbean. They first establish the strengths and weaknesses of the sources available for understanding that economy and then exhibit by example how such materials can be put to use to analyze some of its key elements.

Topics treated range from early attempts in medieval England to measure the carrying capacity of ships, through the advent in Renaissance Italy and England of business newspapers that reported on the traffic of ships, cargoes, and market prices, to the state of the economy of France over the 200 years before the French Revolution and of the British West Indies between 1760 and 1790. Included is the story of the man who first tried to stop the American Revolution from happening and then tried to keep it from succeeding – using as his weapon trade statistics. Without their even knowing his name, Thomas Irving challenged and thwarted the likes of John Hancock, Samuel Adams, Alexander Hamilton, George Washington, and Thomas Jefferson.

John J. McCusker is the Ewing Hansell Distinguished Professor of American History and Professor of Economics at Trinity University, San Antonio, Texas. In his research and writing he concentrates on the economy of the Atlantic Rim in the seventeenth and eighteenth centuries. During the academic year 1996–1997 he was the Visiting Senior Mellon Scholar in American History, University of Cambridge, and the Helen Cam Visiting Fellow at Girton College, Cambridge.

ROUTLEDGE STUDIES IN INTERNATIONAL
ECONOMIC AND SOCIAL HISTORY
Edited by Mark Steele

1. ESSAYS IN THE ECONOMIC HISTORY OF THE ATLANTIC
WORLD
John J. McCusker

ESSAYS IN THE ECONOMIC HISTORY OF THE ATLANTIC WORLD

John J. McCusker

London and New York

First published 1997
by Routledge
11 New Fetter Lane, London EC4P 4EE

Simultaneously published in the USA and Canada
by Routledge
29 West 35th Street, New York, NY 10001

©1997 John J. McCusker

Typeset in Garamond by Florencetype Ltd, Stoodleigh, Devon

Printed and bound in Great Britain by TJ International Ltd, Padstow, Cornwall

British Library Cataloguing in Publication Data
A catalogue record for this book is available from the British Library
JK   *Library of Congress Cataloging in Publication Data*
McCusker, John J.
Essays in the economic history of the Atlantic world /
John J. McCusker
p.   cm.
Includes bibliographical references and index.
1. United States–Economic conditions–To 1865–.
2. Great Britain–Colonies–America–Economic conditions.
3. West Indies, British–Economic conditions.   4. North
America region–Economic conditions.   5. Economic
history.   I. Title.
HC104.M383   1997   97–5386
330.9182′ 1–dc21   CIP

ISBN 0–415–16841–4

For Anna

CONTENTS

FIGURES

FIGURES

TABLES

TABLES

ACKNOWLEDGMENTS

The author and publisher acknowledge with thanks the use of the following illustrations: fig. 4.1, Library of Congress, Washington, DC; figs 5.1, 6.4, 6.5, 6.7, 6.8, 6.10, 6.12, 6.15, 7.2 (a, b), Vereniging Het Nederlandsch Economisch-Historisch Archief, Amsterdam; figs 5.2, 10.1, 12.1, 12.4, 13.1, author; fig. 6.1, Gemeente Archief, Leiden; figs 6.2 (a, b), 8.2, Controller of HM Stationery Office, London; fig. 6.3, Archivio di Stato, Florence; fig. 6.6, Museum Plantin-Moretus, Antwerp; fig. 6.9, Chambre de Commerce et d'Industrie, Marseilles-Provence; Figs. 6.11, 6.13, 6.14, Università Commerciale Luigi Bocconi, Istituto di Storia Economica, Milan; fig. 7.1, House of Lords Record Office, Clerk of the Records, London; fig. 7.3 (a, b), Corporation of Lloyd's, London; fig. 7.4 (a, b), Bank of England, London; fig. 8.1, National Postal Museum, Smithsonian Institution, Washington, DC; fig. 9.1, A. M. T. Maxwell-Irving, Stirlingshire, Scotland; fig. 12.2, British Library, London; fig. 12.3, United Kingdom, Ministry of Defence, Hydrographic Office, Taunton, Somerset.

Quotations from and reproductions of unpublished Crown copyright materials in the Public Record Office, London, appear with the permission of the Controller of HM Stationery Office.

ABBREVIATIONS

Act of ...	in [Great Britain. Laws and Statutes.] *The Statutes of the Realm* (for the years prior to 1714, with the exception of 1642–1660*); Acts and Ordinances of the Interregnum* (for those years); *The Statutes at Large ... of Great Britain* (for the period from 1714 to 1806); or *The Statutes of the United Kingdom of Great Britain and Ireland* (for the years after 1806)
Add. MSS	Additional Manuscripts, in the British Library (BL)
Adm	Admiralty Records, in the Public Record Office (PRO)
AHR	*American Historical Review*
AN	Archives Nationales, Paris
AN-CAOM	Archives Nationales, Aix-en-Provence
AO	Exchequer and Audit Department Records, in the Public Record Office (PRO)
BL	British Library (formerly British Museum Library), London
BT	Board of Trade Records, in the Public Record Office (PRO)
C	Records of the Chancery, in the Public Record Office (PRO)
CO	Colonial Office Records, in the Public Record Office (PRO)
Customs	Board of Customs and Excise Records, in the Public Record Office (PRO)
E	Records of the Exchequer, in the Public Record Office (PRO)
EcHR	*Economic History Review*
FO	Foreign Office Records, in the Public Record Office (PRO)
HC	House of Commons
HCA	High Court of Admiralty Records, in the Public Record Office (PRO)
HLRO	House of Lords Record Office, London
HSP	The Historical Society of Pennsylvania, Philadelphia
JEcH	*Journal of Economic History*
KB	Records of the Court of King's Bench, in the Public Record Office (PRO)

Lambert	[Great Britain. Parliament. House of Commons.] *House of Commons Sessional Papers of the Eighteenth Century*. Edited by Sheila Lambert. 147 vols. Wilmington, Del., 1975
LC	Library of Congress, Washington
MM	*Mariner's Mirror: The Journal of the Society for Nautical Research*
NOSL	Naval Office Shipping List(s)
POE	Port of Entry
PRO	Public Record Office Documents, in the Public Record Office (PRO)
PRO	Public Record Office, London
PROB	Prerogative Court of Canterbury Records, in the Public Record Office (PRO)
SP	State Paper Office Records, in the Public Record Office (PRO)
Stevens Trans.	Benjamin Franklin Stevens Transcripts, in the Library of Congress (LC)
T	Treasury Office Records, in the Public Record Office (PRO)
W&MQ	*William and Mary Quarterly*

INTRODUCTION

The choice of my previously published works revised for presentation in this volume has been founded in three premises: the essays are favorites of mine; they were originally published in a variety of different places and benefit from being brought together; and they are ripe for revision – in that they are about subjects that I continue to explore. Obscure or not, being favorites of mine, I think them deserving of a broader audience. Worthy or not, because I persist in trying to perfect them if only for my own purposes, it makes good sense to present my updated and polished versions so as to continue to attract critical attention to them from colleagues who share my interests. Thus I am happy to offer these essays to new readers as well as old readers. I hope they will enjoy them and, perhaps, find some benefit in them.

I expect, for example, that readers will take as much pleasure in uncovering the career of Thomas Irving as I did. He certainly deserves a better appreciation for his ideas and his activities, if only because they so vividly illuminate an otherwise obscure corner of the eighteenth century. A champion of British mercantilism, he attempted, first, to stop the American Revolution and, failing that, to limit the economic impact of the emerging United States. Moreover, in his quietly subversive way, he had some success in his efforts. Thomas Irving was the nemesis of patriots like Alexander Hamilton but I doubt if Hamilton even knew Irving's name. I would have enjoyed introducing them and listening to their conversations as they shared information and exchanged ideas on such topics as the role of government in the economy. On most issues they seem more likely to have agreed than to have differed.

I flatter myself that Irving and Hamilton would also have agreed to share some interest in these essays. The central theme is one that engaged both men: the origins and development of the economy of early America within the context of the Atlantic World. Even those chapters that may seem less immediately connected to this theme are relevant to it. For instance, the chapter on medieval shipping has as its focus the contention between shippers and tax collectors over the measurement of the carrying capacity of ships, a matter of continuing concern to governments and shipowners – and economic historians – and a subject to which I return repeatedly (e.g., the subsequent chapter on tonnage measurement in the early modern period). The larger issue is how to understand the statistical data that contemporaries like Thomas Irving assembled about shipping and trade.

Once we are in better command of the data, then we can employ them in, for instance, analyzing the economies of early modern France and the British West Indies (see chapters thirteen and fourteen), economies in which international trade played an integral part. In addition to the substantive matters those two chapters discuss, they are, for me, exercises in how to turn seventeenth- and eighteenth-century statistics to the measurement of economic performance. That is, again, an issue that I continue to address, for the Thirteen Continental Colonies, for example, in essays on capital formation and investment in the shipping industry and on the real value of their export sector. The chapters on weights and measures and on foreign exchange negotiations are directly linked to my attempts to do a comparative analysis of the many different colonial economies in the Western Hemisphere. My investigations into the collection, compilation and communication of economic information, by post and through the business press, were the product of my curiosity about why and how people organized the dissemination of economic data and what that means for our use of those data. In the last quarter of the eighteenth century Thomas Irving oversaw the British government's analysis of much of the official economic data; he used – and, more importantly, he used cautiously and critically – the information to be found in, among other places, that same business press. He and I have read the same government records and the same business newspapers with the same eye and with many of the same purposes.

What I am about, then, is – in tandem with that quiet Scot – to establish on as firm a footing as possible some of the basic elements of the economic history of the centuries prior to the American and French Revolutions. The ultimate goal is straightforward: to understand better the economies out of which seventeenth- and eighteenth-century people carved for themselves lives of dignity and worth. And so they did, most particularly the colonial peoples of European ancestry – especially those who were slave owners, most especially *not* the enslaved. That the British colonists on the continent eventually chose to expend a fair portion of their considerable collective assets in a fight for their political independence is also an issue of some importance to me, both as a starting point (see chapter twelve) and a subject to which I have since returned (see chapter eleven). That Thomas Irving happened to have been involved here, too, is sheer serendipity. Far from a miscellaneous collection, these chapters move inexorably to where I am headed: a fuller understanding of the economy of the early modern Atlantic World.[1]

---

1 Or, as the editors' "Book Notes" in the *Journal of Economic History* (*JEcH*, XLI, [Sept. 1981], 668), said much more succinctly: "McCusker continues . . . putting the magnitudes of eighteenth-century commerce on a rock-firm base of evidence."

◆ ◆ ◆ ◆ ◆

The arrangement of the chapters in this book underscores the relationships about which I have just written. The essays are not in the order in which they were originally published but are, instead, grouped to complement each other, to reflect upon each other. Their original date of publication, while it is stated in the critical apparatus at the start of each chapter and in the bibliography, is less relevant than it might be otherwise because all of them have been carefully revised for inclusion here to reflect their mutual interdependence.

Every part of every essay has been subject to revision and to modification, to correction and to elaboration. The formulation and presentation of the arguments in each one have been reviewed and reconsidered. Outright mistakes of fact or language have been put right. Where I have interpolated words, numbers, dates, or other information that did not form part of the original text, I have regularly enclosed such matter in square brackets. This means, for instance, that in footnotes and in the bibliography, the bracketed material is not to be found on the title page of the article or book. All of the numerical data have been recompiled and recalculated. This last has had the result, especially in some tables, of changing occasionally not only an individual number but also some subtotals and totals. The effect for the author is embarrassing and cautionary. Others who have had the occasion to return to tabular work originally compiled by hand will know what I mean. To recompile everything using a computer and a spreadsheet program is to have powerfully reinforced my awareness that I am something less than perfect. I simply did not want to know that so much effort at checking and rechecking the original calculations still did not insure precision. Samuel Eliot Morison once wrote in comment upon a series of his own calculations: "Tabulated by the author, accuracy not guaranteed!"[2] Amen.

In addition to checking for and correcting mistakes, I have also taken some steps to improve matters. I have tried to keep up with the literature on the subjects in which I am interested. As a result, where relevant, I have sometimes made reference to a newer work that, in my opinion, significantly superseded something I had used early on. I have cited a more recent edition of an older work when the newer edition has incorporated substantive changes affecting the argument or the documentation of the argument. Something that I have changed throughout this volume is the mode of presentation in order to conform to a single set of stylistic conventions. Tables and notes, which perforce varied originally from instance to instance, have been regularized for consistency. In sum, the revision carried out here is less extensive than intensive. Nevertheless, the result is that all these essays have been

2   Morison, "The Commerce of Boston on the Eve of the Revolution," *Proceedings of the American Antiquarian Society*, n.s., XXXII (Apr. 1922), 39 n.

altered, to a greater or lesser degree, and I would prefer that readers make reference to these revised versions, as I will do myself – if only because I think my calculations are now correct! All these essays have benefited, I think, from this second chance to get things right.

♦ ♦ ♦ ♦ ♦

In this study, as in all others that deal with the early modern world, there needs to be some statement of the conventions employed to counter the confusion encountered in our investigation of the past and in its presentation to the present. For instance, I have adopted the usual accommodations to the welter of calendars that plagued the early modern Atlantic World, most especially the shift beginning in 1582 from the Julian Calendar ("Old Style") to the Gregorian Calendar ("New Style").[3] First, I have regularly reported dates as the writer recorded them – unless he or she simply made a mistake, which I then note and comment upon as well as correct. Thus, no matter how a person expressed a date, that is what is repeated herein – with only a minor modification. When the difference in dating because of different calendars is critical to an argument, I make a comment upon it either in the text or in a note.

Second, the new year is always taken as beginning on 1 January despite what may have been the practice of the author of a document. In Great Britain until 1752, the year ran from 25 March through 24 March; thus the day after 31 December 1740 was called 1 January 1740. The modification I mentioned enters here. When dating a document the writer of which used some day other than 1 January – say, 25 March – as the start of the new year, I record both years for the overlapping period (thus, what some contemporary writer designated 15 March 1740, I report as 15 March 1740/41). Many at the time actually employed the same device with the same purpose in mind, to minimize confusion.[4] I think it necessary to elaborate on these

---

3 While many parts of Europe adopted the new calendar that fall, Great Britain retained the old style until 1752. On the whole issue of the competing calendars in the early modern period, see John J. McCusker and Cora Gravesteijn, *The Beginnings of Commercial and Financial Journalism: The Commodity Price Currents, Exchange Rate Currents, and Money Currents of Early Modern Europe*, Nederlandsch Economisch-Historisch Archief, ser. III, no. 11 (Amsterdam, 1991), pp. 445–449, especially tables B.1 and B.2, and the sources cited there.

4 In doing so I follow the usual convention. An acceptable variation consistently converts dates to the modern mode. If I had followed this method, then a date that read 15 Mar. 1740 in the original document, I would have set down as 15 Mar. 1741.

An unusual and, for that reason potentially very troubling method that some employ is simply to retain the old style format (thus, 15 Mar. 1740 is reported as 15 Mar. 1740). Two works that do this are V[ernon] L. Skinner, Jr, *Abstracts of the Inventories of the Prerogative Court [of Maryland, 1718–1777]*, 17 vols ([Westminster, Maryland], 1988–1991), I, iii; and the *International Genealogical Index: IGI*, [2nd edn], 11,712 microfiche ([Salt Lake City, Utah], 1992) and the

procedures if only because I myself continue to be caught out by the vagaries of the calendar – as the sharp-eyed reader of both versions of chapter eight may detect.[5]

I have also adopted certain practices with regard to language that influence text and notes, bibliography and index, substance and presentation.[6] The Old English and Icelandic letter forms that approximate "th" – the runic thorn and the "ð" – are simply rendered "th". In addition I have dropped to the line all superscript letters. Thus I have transformed the word written "yᵉ" to the modern "the". Similarly I have transcribed the elongated or long-tailed version of the letter "s" as the modern form. Where people in the past used the letters "i" or "j" or the letters "u" and "v" interchangeably, I have quietly substituted the more modern spelling. I have recognized the Danish "å" as a double "a" and words using it are alphabetized accordingly. Similarly, words with Scandinavian diphthongs are alphabetized in the regular sequence; such words have not been separated out and treated idiosyncratically. I have handled German and Dutch words in the same way. Dutch surnames beginning with "van" and German surnames beginning with "von" have been alphabetized under the next word in the name; Belgian surnames beginning with "van" have been alphabetized under "van". Thus Johannes G. Van Dillen is indexed under "Dillen" and Herman Van der Wee under "Van der Wee."

projects associated with it. Not only is this an unnecessary reversion to a more confusing mode abandoned centuries ago but it is also most unwise and unacceptable especially in the latter instance because the choice of method (and its implications) is not anywhere made explicit and, thus, it is only discernible by comparing the *IGI* entries with the original records. The result for British and British colonial records is that vital events that occurred in the first quarter of each year through 1752 are effectively assigned to the previous year. For example, Arabella Castaing, the daughter of John Castaing, Sr, who was born on 24 Dec. 1699 and christened at St John's Church, Hackney, on 14 Jan. 1699/1700, has the latter event recorded in the *IGI* under 14 Jan. 1699, a year earlier than the actual date. In mid-summer 1700 she was six months old, not one year and six months. The correct date can be found by consulting the Transcript of Baptisms, 1545–1741 (MS 478/1), Parish Registers of St John at Hackney, Guildhall, London.

5   I am not alone. As Michael Harris, *London Newspapers in the Age of Walpole: A Study of the Origins of the Modern English Press* (London, 1986), p. 13, points out, such is the confusion caused by the changes in the English calendar that some of the newspapers in the Burney Collection in the British Library "have been put in the wrong sequence" in the bound volumes. This was despite the care that newspapermen themselves took to record the dating of events in either "veteri Stylo, [or] novo Stylo," as was observed and commented on by Richard Brathwait, *Whimzies: Or, a New Cast of Characters* (London, 1631), as in Allen H. Lanner, *A Critical Edition of Richard Brathwait's "Whimzies"* (New York, 1991, [Ph.D. diss., New York University, 1966]), p. 155.

6   In general, I have followed the "expanded" method of presenting quoted texts, as set out in Frank Freidel and Richard K. Showman, *Harvard Guide to American History*, rev. edn (Cambridge, Mass., 1974), I, 27–36.

Conventions concerning money are as I have set them down in an earlier study.[7] For instance, all values in this book originally expressed in twelve-based counting systems – such as British pounds sterling and Dutch gulden – have been regularly restated in new decimalized notation as more convenient for calculations. When necessary for purposes of comparison, values in the currencies of the colonies of Great Britain have been reduced to pounds sterling employing the rates of exchange set forth in that same book, sometimes supplemented by subsequent research. I have also had occasion to do the same thing with currencies of other countries. In addition, to make a point, I have once or twice stated the equivalent in modern terms of money values from the past.[8]

In the notes to each chapter I have acknowledged some of the help I received in organizing my research and presenting my findings. The institutions that supported my work, the people who aided me in gathering my materials or in gathering my thoughts are, of course, more numerous than I have mentioned or can mention. Colleagues and friends at several places where I have taught and studied have contributed to the development of my ideas in ways too complicated to contemplate. Some included in that list deserve special thanks which I express more fully where appropriate. I am grateful to them all for their unfailing kindnesses and I am pleased to have this chance to acknowledge it.

High on that special list are the several people with whom I have co-authored work that is either reproduced herein or is substantial to something that is presented herein: Cora Gravesteijn, Simon Hart, Russell R. Menard, and James C. Riley. I consider myself the continuing beneficiary of their counsel, their encouragement, and their friendship.

I and every other scholar at work in our age have been and continue to be warmly supported by more archivists and librarians than we will ever fully know. We are all aided by the interlibrary loan services, both the local library staff and the people at a distance who provide the materials we require and, more remotely still, those in North America who organized, perfected, and still compile the National Union Catalog based at the Library of Congress and who make what was once barely possible now eminently practical. There

---

7   John J. McCusker, *Money and Exchange in Europe and America, 1600–1775: A Handbook,* [2nd edn] (Chapel Hill, NC, [1992]).

8   Where I have done so, I have drawn upon John J. McCusker, *How Much Is That in Real Money? A Historical Price Index for Use as a Deflator of Money Values in the Economy of the United States* (Worcester, Mass., 1992); and McCusker, "How Much Is That in Real Money? A Historical Price Index for Use as a Deflator of Money Values in the Economy of the United States: Addenda et Corrigenda," *Proceedings of the American Antiquarian Society,* CVI (October 1996), 315–322. The latter incorporates the work of P. M. G. Harris, "Inflation and Deflation in Early America, 1634–1860: Patterns of Change in the British–American Economy," *Social Science History,* XX (Winter 1996), 469–505. I am very grateful to him for his permission to republish some of his data.

is a tendency, in this lamentably constrained time, for all things intellectual and artistic, for some to see a possible "income stream" in providing inter-library loan services – as well as access to libraries and archives. Such an attitude is to be deplored and denigrated as the antithesis of the spirit of the open exchange of ideas that rests at the heart of the life of the mind. Its votaries deserve to be relegated to the same level of the inferno as those who would charge admission to museums and art galleries. They all discriminate against an individual on the most irrelevant, regressive basis. Human society pays a fierce cost when it deprives itself of the best talent by stifling it, betraying its own best hope for the sake of a few pieces of silver.

I have been particularly well served by the special libraries in which I have worked and by the people who organized, maintained, and developed those collections: the Economisch-Historische Bibliotheek, Amsterdam; the Goldsmiths' Library, in the Senate House, University of London; the Kress Library of Business and Economics, in the Baker Library, Graduate School of Business Administration, Harvard University; and the Edwin R. A. Seligman Collection, Columbia University, New York. To these people, and to those who have worked to my benefit at all the other institutions listed in my bibliography, I am immensely grateful. That three out of these four special libraries are, for all practical purposes, now defunct as intellectual enterprises saddens me deeply. The books are still there – though just barely – but a fine library needs to be nurtured by the kinds of scholar-librarians who introduced me to each of these collections, especially Cora Gravesteijn of the EHB and Kenneth Carpenter and Ruth Rogers at the Kress. The living entity that was each of these libraries has died and they have become fossils of their former selves. As a consequence I am all the more thankful to these fine people and to many like them whom I have come to know at, for instance, the American Antiquarian Society, the John Carter Brown Library, the Bell Library, the Clements Library, the British Library, the Public Record Office, and, most particularly, the Library of Congress. They, too, labor under some threat at the end of a century that has expended an inordinate amount of its resources destroying rather than creating, and that, sadly, seems intent on perpetuating such fearful tendencies.[9]

Thus cautioned, we draw ever closer to those dear to us. Last place but highest place in this personal roll of honor is reserved for colleagues, friends, and family, who deserve more thanks than I am capable of rendering, for more things done on my behalf than I shall ever know. I cherish a rich circle of fine friends and close colleagues from whom I take inspiration and strength. You know who you are; I am deeply in your debt.

---

9. See, sadly, the announcement by the British Library of its intention to start charging readers' fees. It is the lead story in *The Times*, 30 Apr. 1997, p. 1.

Most especially I rejoice in my family. My wife, Ann Van Pelt, and I share five children, their spouses and "significant others," and three grandchildren – Brittany Escott Morgan, Dylan Michael Florance, and Tatum Alexandra Conner, each of whom, one way and another, is part of what seems at times a grand collective effort to cheer me on. Thank you all. I have dedicated the book to my wife, the linchpin of that loving family. She guides us all by being an example to us all of perfect love. Thank you, Anna.

Girton College, Cambridge
April 1997

1

GUIDES TO PRIMARY SOURCES FOR THE HISTORY OF EARLY BRITISH AMERICA

It should come as no surprise to historians of early British America that the resources for the subject are not only rich and diverse but also widely scattered.[1] In an era of cheap air fares and fast photocopies, this last characteristic creates less of a burden than in the days of George Bancroft or Charles M. Andrews – provided, of course, that we can first identify what we need to see. Fortunately, scholars have come forward with guides and handbooks that make such research both easier and potentially more comprehensive than in the past.

The purpose of this essay is to discuss a variety of published guides to primary materials – particularly manuscript materials – and to place them in the context of what had been done earlier. The exercise seems especially necessary because the major journals in American history no longer regularly review such guides as they appear. In addition, I hope that this notice will encourage the creation of more guides, since all students of the period benefit greatly from them. Many a fine book has been made possible by the existence of good guides to the sources. Preparing the best of these handbooks is as much an intellectual attainment as is the realization of any monograph based upon them.

A continuing point of reference in all such endeavors is the classic Carnegie Institution of Washington manuals produced early in the twentieth century under the direction of J. Franklin Jameson.[2] The Carnegie Institution guides

1   The original version of this chapter was published in *W&MQ*, 3rd ser., XLI (Apr. 1984), 277–295. Copyright © 1984 by the Institute of Early American History and Culture. This revision is presented here with the permission of the Institute of Early American History and Culture.

    I continue to be grateful for the help and support given me in the preparation of this chapter by Thomas R. Adams, Warren M. Billings, Kenneth E. Carpenter, Alison J. Cowden, Luca Codignola, Edward C. Papenfuse, and Jacob M. Price as well as the Institute of Early American History and Culture, Liberty Fund of Indianapolis, the National Endowment for the Humanities, the American Enterprise Institute, the Albert J. Beveridge Fund of the American Historical Association, the American Antiquarian Society, the American Philosophical Society, the University of Maryland, and the John Simon Guggenheim Memorial Foundation.
2   Lester J. Cappon, "'The Historian's Day' – From Archives to History," in *The Reinterpretation of Early American History: Essays in Honor of John Edwin Pomfret*, ed. Ray

and manuals dealt largely with manuscripts in European archives, but the latest fever seems to have worked its effect both here and abroad. Accordingly, some attention will be paid herein to guides to resources in this hemisphere, though the primary concern will be with the other side of the Atlantic. The intention is to notice all published guides to documentary resources for the study of pre-1800 British America.

There are, of course, other primary sources besides manuscripts. Historians of early British America are becoming increasingly aware of the breadth of

Allen Billington (San Marino, Calif., 1966), pp. 242–243. These volumes, in chronological order of publication, are: Luis Marino Perez, *Guide to the Materials for American History in Cuban Archives*, Carnegie Institution of Washington, Publication no. 83 (Washington, DC, 1907); William R. Shepherd, *Guide to the Materials for the History of the United States in Spanish Archives*, Carnegie Institution of Washington, Publication no. 91 (Washington, DC, 1907); Charles M. Andrews and Frances G. Davenport, *Guide to the Manuscript Materials for the History of the United States to 1783, in the British Museum, in Minor London Archives, and in the Libraries of Oxford and Cambridge*, Carnegie Institution of Washington, Publication no. 90 (Washington, DC, 1908); Carl Russell Fish, *Guide to the Materials for American History in Roman and Other Italian Archives*, Carnegie Institution of Washington, Publication no. 128 (Washington, DC, 1911); Charles M. Andrews, *Guide to the Materials for American History, to 1783, in the Public Record Office of Great Britain*, 2 vols, Carnegie Institution of Washington, Publication no. 90A (Washington, DC, 1912–1914); Marion Dexter Learned, *Guide to the Manuscript Materials Relating to American History in the German State Archives* (Washington, DC, 1912); Herbert E. Bolton, *Guide to Materials for the History of the United States in the Principal Archives of Mexico*, Carnegie Institution of Washington, Publication no. 163 (Washington, DC, 1913); David W. Parker, *Guide to the Materials for United States History in Canadian Archives*, Carnegie Institution of Washington, Publication no. 172 (Washington, DC, 1913); Charles O. Paullin and Frederic L. Paxson, *Guide to the Materials in London Archives for the History of the United States since 1783*, Carnegie Institution of Washington, Publication no. 90B (Washington, DC, 1914); Albert B. Faust, *Guide to the Materials for American History in Swiss and Austrian Archives*, Carnegie Institution of Washington, Publication no. 220 (Washington, DC, 1916); Frank A. Golder, *Guide to Materials for American History in Russian Archives*, 2 vols, Carnegie Institution of Washington, Publication no. 239 (Washington, DC, 1917–1937); David M. Matteson, *List of Manuscripts concerning American History Preserved in European Libraries and Noted in Their Published Catalogues and Similar Printed Lists*, Carnegie Institution of Washington, Publication no. 359 (Washington, DC, 1925); Herbert C. Bell, David W. Parker *et al. Guide to British West Indian Archive Materials, in London and in the Islands, for the History of the United States*, Carnegie Institution of Washington, Publication no. 372 (Washington, DC, 1926); and Waldo G. Leland, John J. Meng, and Abel Doysié, *Guide to Materials for American History in the Libraries and Archives of Paris*, 2 vols, Carnegie Institution of Washington, Publication no. 392 (Washington, DC, 1932–1943). All these were reprinted in the 1960s by the Kraus Reprint Corporation. Directly or indirectly they became the basis of later efforts to make copies of some of the documents they listed. For guides to the results of these efforts, see especially Grace Gardner Griffin, *A Guide to Manuscripts Relating to American History in British Depositories Reproduced for the Division of Manuscripts of the Library of Congress* (Washington, DC, 1946); Lester K. Born, *British Manuscripts Project: A Checklist of the Microfilms Prepared in England and Wales for the American Council of Learned Societies, 1941–1945* (Washington, DC, 1955); and [US, Library of Congress, Manuscript Division], *Manuscripts on Microfilm: A Checklist of the Holdings in the Manuscript Division [of the Library of Congress]*, by Richard B. Bickel (Washington, DC, 1975). Lawrence Henry Gipson built upon these guides and added to them in compiling *A Guide to Manuscripts Relating to the History of the British Empire, 1748–1776*, vol. XV of *The British Empire before the American Revolution* (New York, 1970).

published materials available to them. While lists of these other items are not the principal focus of this essay, they are guides to primary sources and many very worthwhile ones have appeared of late. Indeed, in large measure the historians' new awareness is the direct result of the preparation of such guides.

It seems strange to think that only in the last fifty years have historians generally been able to make full use of newspapers published in the Thirteen Continental Colonies. Clarence S. Brigham's guide to early newspapers,[3] the microform collections based on the Brigham guide,[4] and the Cappon and Duff index to the *Virginia Gazette*[5] have all been published since World War II. Much the same point can be made about the books and pamphlets published in the colonies during the seventeenth and eighteenth centuries. Charles Evans's *American Bibliography*, finally completed in 1959, has already been supplemented, extended into the nineteenth century, and made the basis of a microform edition of the works Evans listed.[6]

Materials published in Europe have also become more easily accessible. Several catalogues and bibliographies have been compiled that have become the stimulus for microform reproduction projects similar to the one based on the Evans bibliography. The two classic catalogues of early English language publications – Pollard and Redgrave's *Short-Title Catalogue . . . 1475–1640* and Wing's *Short-Title Catalogue . . . 1641–1700* – are the proto-types for the "Eighteenth-Century Short Title Catalogue," which continues its progress. It has recently been renamed the "English Short-Title Catalogue"

3 Brigham, *History and Bibliography of American Newspapers, 1690–1820*, 2 vols (Worcester, Mass., 1947). See also Brigham, "Additions and Corrections to *History and Bibliography of American Newspapers, 1690–1820*," *Proceedings of the American Antiquarian Society*, n.s., LXXI (Apr. 1961), 15–62. There is an interleaved, annotated copy of the book incorporating additions and corrections at the American Antiquarian Society, Worcester, Mass.
4 Individuals and firms have used Brigham to help assemble in microform nearly complete runs of many early American newspapers. They are most easily located using [US, Library of Congress, Cataloging Publications Division], *Newspapers in Microform, United States, 1948–1972* (Washington, DC, 1973), and the annual supplements to this volume.
5 Lester J. Cappon and Stella F. Duff, *Virginia Gazette Index, 1736–1780*, 2 vols (Williamsburg, Va., 1950). This is the only published index of a colonial newspaper. It is based on a microfilm edition of the newspaper similar to the ones mentioned in n. 4 of this chapter. There are other indexes, however. For instance, the Newspaper and Current Periodical Reading Room of the Library of Congress has a carbon copy of a typewritten index to the *Georgia Gazette* (Savannah), 1763–1776, that was done as a WPA project in the 1930s. See the *General Index to the Contents of Savannah, Georgia, Newspapers, 1763–1799*, 10 vols ([Savannah, 1937]). For other newspaper indexes, see Anita Cheek Milner, *Newspaper Indexes: A Location and Subject Guide for Researchers*, 3 vols (Metuchen, NJ, 1977–1982).
6 Evans, *American Bibliography: A Chronological Dictionary of All Books, Pamphlets and Periodical Publications Printed in the United States of America, 1639–1800*, 14 vols (Chicago, New York, and Worcester, Mass., 1903–1959); Roger P. Bristol, *Supplement to Charles Evans' American Bibliography* (Charlottesville, Va., 1970); Ralph R. Shaw and Richard H. Shoemaker, *American Bibliography. A Preliminary Checklist for 1801–1819*, 22 vols (New York, 1958–1966); and Shoemaker *et al.*, *Checklist of American Imprints [1820–1875]*, in progress (New York and Metuchen, NJ, 1964 to date).

("EngSTC") to reflect a widening of the inclusiveness of its database, which is commercially available on-line over the network. There are microform editions of the works listed in both Pollard/Redgrave and Wing, and the first units of microfilm of the eighteenth-century portion of the "EngSTC" have appeared. As was the case with Pollard and Redgrave and with Wing, the impact of the latest segment of the "EngSTC" will be felt both as a research tool and as the *agent provocateur* of new research and analysis.[7]

All three catalogues just mentioned try to include everything published in any language in the British Isles and all English language publications in Europe and the British colonies during their respective periods. Although there are no similar projects for materials in other languages, some valuable guides to such publications have been prepared on other bases. From the European perspective, much that had to do with the colonies was economic, broadly speaking, and thus collections of economic literature from the period frequently contain a great deal that concerns early British America. Another microfilm project has made available the holdings of the Kress Library of Business and Economics at Harvard University and the Goldsmiths' Library at the University of London. It is based on the published catalogues of both libraries[8] and is supplemented by a combined catalogue of its own.[8] John

---

7   A[lfred] W. Pollard and G[ilbert] R. Redgrave, *A Short-Title Catalogue of Books Printed in England, Scotland, & Ireland And of English Books Printed Abroad, 1475–1640*, 2nd edn, rev. and enl., ed. W[illiam] A. Jackson, F[rederic] S. Ferguson, and Katharine F. Pantzer, 3 vols (London, 1976–1991); Donald [G.] Wing, *Short-Title Catalogue of Books Printed in England, Scotland, Ireland, Wales, and British America and of English Books Printed in Other Countries, 1641–1700*, 2nd edn, rev. and enl., ed. John J. Morrison *et al.*, 3 vols (New York, 1972–1988). The completed part of the "EngSTC" is available in two early microfiche versions – *The Eighteenth Century Short Title Catalogue: The British Library Colections*, ed. R[obin] C. Alston, 113 microfiche (London, 1983); and *The Eighteenth Century Short Title Catalogue*, [2nd edn, rev.], 220 microfiche (London, 1990) – on a computer disk – *ESTC on CD-ROM: The Eighteenth Century Short Title Catalogue* (London, 1992) – and in a continuously updated version on-line in the United States through the Research Library Information Network (RLIN) and in Great Britain and other countries through the British Library's BLAISE-LINE. See John Bloomberg-Rissmann, "Pre-1701 Records in the English Short-Title Catalogue: A Description and Explanation," *Factotum: Newsletter of the XVIIIth Century STC*, XXXVIII (Feb. 1994), 3–5. See also R[obin] C. Alston and M[ervyn] J. Jannetta, *Bibliography, Machine Readable Cataloguing and the ESTC: A Summary History of the Eighteenth Century Short Title Catalogue* (London, 1978); [Becky Morton], *ESTC: An Eighteenth-Century Short Title Catalog*, Research Libraries Group 82–42 (Stanford, Calif., 1982); British Library News, LXXVII (July–Aug. 1982), 1; and John Bloomberg-Rissman, *Searching ESTC on RLIN*, Factotum, Occasional Paper 7 ([London], 1996). The microform edition of selected items based on this project by Primary Source Media (formerly Research Publications Inc.), *The Eighteenth Century*, in progress (Woodbridge, Conn., 1982 to date), will, unfortunately, reproduce only about 40 percent of the 18th-century items.

8   [Harvard University, Graduate School of Business Administration, Baker Library, Kress Library of Business and Economics], *Catalogue, with Data upon Cognate Items in Other Harvard Libraries*, 5 vols (Boston 1940–1967); [London, University, Goldsmiths' Company's Library of Economic Literature], *Catalogue of the Goldsmiths' Library of Economic Literature*, by M[argaret B. C.] Canney *et al.*, 5 vols (Cambridge, Eng., and London, 1970–1995); and *Goldsmiths'-Kress Library of Economic Literature: A Consolidated Guide*

Eliot Alden and Dennis Channing Landis have published a fine example of the bibliographer's art, *European Americana*, that seeks to identify, describe, and locate copies of anything printed in Europe that even so much as mentioned the Western Hemisphere.[9] Two bibliographies very carefully compiled by Thomas R. Adams have offered many new insights into the pamphlet literature that appeared on both sides of the Atlantic during the American Revolution.[10] The publication of the catalogues of the major national libraries has made it much easier for researchers to locate copies of

to ... *the Microfilm Collection*, 9 vols (Woodbridge, Conn., 1976–1989). Compare R[obert] D[enis] Collison Black, *A Catalogue of Pamphlets on Economic Subjects Published between 1750 and 1900 and Now Housed in Irish Libraries* (Belfast and New York, 1969); and C[ora] Gravesteijn, J[acobus] J. Seegers, and R[iekie] van Sijtveld-Verhoeven, *Handel in Theorie en Pratijk. Katalogus betreffende werken gepubliceerd voor 1830 aanwezig in de Economisch-Historische Bibliotheek, Amsterdam* (Amsterdam, 1981). Supplemental to these volumes are L[aurence] W. Hanson, *Contemporary Printed Sources for British and Irish Economic History, 1701–1750* (Cambridge, Eng., 1963), and Henry Higgs, *Bibliography of Economics, 1751–1775* (Cambridge, Eng., 1935). Stanley H. Palmer, *Economic Arithmetic: A Guide to the Statistical Sources of English Commerce, Industry, and Finance, 1700–1850* (New York, 1977) is, in effect, a specialized, annotated index to the Goldsmiths'-Kress collection.

9   Alden and Landis, European Americana. *A Chronological Guide to Works Printed in Europe Relating to the Americas, 1493–1776 [i.e., 1750]*, 6 vols (New York, 1980–1995). One of the many glories of these volumes is their comprehensive indexes that identify both the usual things (names, places, subjects) and also the printers. This makes them very much more usable for bibliographical purposes. See also Gravesteijn, Seegers, and van Sijtveld-Verhoeven, *Handel in Theorie en Pratijk*, pp. 122–155.

10 Adams, *American Independence, the Growth of an Idea: A Bibliographical Study of the American Political Pamphlets Printed between 1764 and 1776 Dealing with the Dispute between Great Britain and Her Colonies* (Providence, RI, 1965), and *The American Controversy: A Bibliographical Study of the British Pamphlets about the American Disputes, 1764–1783* (Providence, RI, 1980). Compare James E. Mooney, "Loyalist Imprints Printed in America, 1774–1785," *Proceedings of the American Antiquarian Society*, n.s., LXXXIV (1975), 105–128, and as reprinted in Gregory Palmer, *A Bibliography of Loyalist Source Material in the United States, Canada, and Great Britain* (Westport, Conn., 1982), pp. 885–997. Unfortunately the entries in Mooney are not picked up in the index to the Palmer volume.

None of these guides lists the periodical literature or newspapers published in Europe, the Kress *Catalogue* and the third volume of the *Catalogue of the Goldsmiths' Library* being only limited exceptions to that statement. We very much need a guide, similar to Brigham, for newspapers published in Europe during the 17th and 18th centuries. One that emphasizes newspapers important for the history of British America – such as the *Nouvelles Extraordinaires de Divers Endroits* (Leiden), popularly known as the *Gazette de Leyde* – would be especially welcome. So would a parallel volume for newspapers published in the Western Hemisphere outside of the British colonies on the continent. For a start toward this last objective, see Waldo Lincoln, "List of Newspapers of the West Indies and Bermuda in the Library of the American Antiquarian Society," *Proceedings of the American Antiquarian Society*, n.s., XXXVI (1926), 130–155. For a necessarily limited start toward the former objective, see John J. McCusker and Cora Gravesteijn, *The Beginnings of Commercial and Financial Journalism: The Commodity Price Currents, Exchange Rate Currents, and Money Currents of Early Modern Europe*, Nederlandsch Economisch-Historisch Archief, ser. III, no. 11 (Amsterdam, 1991). See also [British Library, Newspaper Library], *Catalogue of the Newspaper Library, Colindale*, 8 vols (London, 1975). For the *Gazette de Leyde*, see Jeremy D. Popkin, *News and Politics in the Age of Revolution: Jean Luzac's "Gazette de Leyde"* (Ithaca, [NY], [1989]).

the items cited in these several guides and handbooks.[11] No scholar can fail to benefit from the help such works offer.[12]

Authors of guides to archives and libraries usually take either a thematic or an institutional approach. The Carnegie Institution manuals were organized thematically; they discussed the documents available for American history, place by place. Other guides describe collections in one archive or library. Neither arrangement provides a guide organized perfectly for historians, but both can lighten the work of the researcher. Indeed, most modern manuals merely supplement rather than replace the Carnegie Institution guides. Thus we are not in a position of trading new lamps for old; to see our way clearly, we need both.

The principal European repositories of manuscripts dealing with British America are in the nations that colonized the New World. Great Britain is the first in any such list, but we would be silly to ignore France or Spain. There is a surprising amount in archives in Germany and Italy. Archives in The Netherlands and Denmark can be searched profitably for specific topics. Of late, effective guides have been published to many of the archives in these countries.

The archives and libraries of the United Kingdom have always – and quite rightly – been the starting point for the historian of early British America. Four books in the Carnegie Institution series dealt with British archives: Charles M. Andrews on the holdings of the Public Record Office (PRO) to 1783; Andrews and Frances G. Davenport on the manuscript collections of the British Museum (now the British Library [BL]) plus some other London repositories and some of the libraries of Oxford and Cambridge; Charles O. Paullin and Frederic L. Paxson on London archives for the period after

11 See [Paris, Bibliothèque Nationale de France, Département des Imprimés], *Catalogue général des livres imprimés de la Bibliothèque Nationale: Auteurs [à 1959]*, 231 vols in 232 pts (Paris, 1897–1981); [US, Library of Congress], *A Catalogue of Books Represented by Library of Congress Printed Cards*, 167 vols (Ann Arbor, Michigan, 1942–1946); and [British Library, Department of Printed Books], *The British Library General Catalogue of Printed Books to 1975*, 360 vols (London, 1979–1987). There are either supplements or antecedents or both to all three of these printed catalogues. By the mid-1990s the catalogues of the latter two libraries were searchable either on-line or on CD-ROMs or both, thus transforming research in both of them. We may hope that it will not be long before we have a similar facility for searching the catalogues of the Bibliothèque Nationale de France and one search engine that will suffice for a simultaneous search of them all. For the Bibliothèque Nationale de France, see Annick Bernard, *Guide de l'utilisateur des catalogues de livres imprimés de la Bibliothèque Nationale* (Paris, 1986).
   For all (or almost all) libraries in the United States and Canada, compare [US, Library of Congress], *National Union Catalog, Pre-1956 Imprints*, 754 vols ([London], 1968–1981).

12 There are other types of primary sources to which some worthwhile guides have been published. One of them is maps. See [GB, PRO], *America and the West Indies*, vol. II of *Maps and Plans in the Public Record Office* (London, 1975); and John R. Sellers and Patricia Molen van Ee, *Maps and Charts of North America and the West Indies, 1750–1789: A Guide to the Collections in the Library of Congress* (Washington, DC, 1981). The high level of scholarly work that such guides make possible is epitomized by Lester J. Cappon *et al.*, *Atlas of Early American History: The Revolutionary Era, 1760–1790* (Princeton, NJ, 1976).

1783; and Herbert C. Bell and David W. Parker on collections in London and the West Indies relating to the Caribbean colonies.[13]

The great value of these four works was compromised to a degree by deficiencies that the compilers themselves were the first to point out. The most severe limitation is that they concentrated almost exclusively on London, within London on the BL and the PRO, and within the PRO on only the more apparent and more accessible record groups. One of the first projects of the British Association for American Studies (BAAS) after World War II was to try to obviate these deficiencies by preparing a guide to materials for the whole of United States history in all British and Irish archives. That guide, compiled and edited by Bernard R. Crick and Miriam Alman, along with its supplements, served the post-war generation of historians of early America very well indeed.[14] It not only revealed the existence of notable collections in university, county, and city archives outside London, but it also alerted the archivists at those institutions to the significance of their collections for early Americanists. All of this has been reinforced for both groups by John W. Raimo's revision of the Crick and Alman guide, also completed under the auspices of the BAAS.[15]

We run the risk of seeming ungrateful to Andrews and his collaborators, to Crick and Alman, and to Raimo if we point out what still remains to be done, since they have done so much so well. Yet an essay designed to help historians find their way must point out what even the brightest beacons leave poorly illuminated. Ironically, in view of the observation made above about the Carnegie Institution series, the chief limitation of the new BAAS guides concerns their treatment of the major London repositories, particularly the PRO. For the materials that Andrews described, the BAAS guides add nothing. For materials accessioned since Andrews saw the collections, the discussions in the BAAS guide are neither as broad nor as thorough as the comparable coverage in the Carnegie Institution volumes. For instance, both

---

13 Cited in n. 2 of this chapter. An early piece by J[ohn] Franklin Jameson is still a serviceable supplement to this series: "Guide to the Items Relating to American History in the Reports of the English Historical Manuscripts Commission and Their Appendices," in American Historical Association, *Annual Report for the Year 1898* (Washington, DC, 1899), pp. 611–708. It needs to be brought up to date.

14 Crick and Alman, *A Guide to Manuscripts Relating to America in Great Britain and Ireland* (London, 1961); Crick, "First List of Addenda to a Guide to Manuscripts Relating to America in Great Britain and Ireland," *Bulletin of the British Association for American Studies*, n.s., V (Dec. 1962), 47–63; Crick, "Second List of Addenda to a Guide to Manuscripts Relating to America in Great Britain and Ireland," ibid., VII (Dec. 1963), 55–64; and [Dennis Welland], Crick, and Naomi Connelly, "Third List of Addenda to a Guide to Manuscripts Relating to America in Great Britain and Ireland," ibid., XII–XIII (1966), 61–77. A great many of the records described in Crick and Alman are available in microform copies as part of the series sponsored by the BAAS and distributed by Microform Ltd, *British Records Relating to America*, in progress (East Ardsley, Wakefield, West Yorkshire, Eng., 1963[?] to date).

15 Raimo, *A Guide to Manuscripts Relating to America in Great Britain and Ireland* (Westport, Conn., 1979).

Crick and Alman and Raimo omit any consideration of the British colonies in the Caribbean.[16] But the major problem with the treatment of the PRO materials in the BAAS guides is their failure, however understandable, to fill in the gaps left by Andrews and those who worked with him.[17]

The value of the PRO for early British American history cannot be overestimated, yet it is underutilized and its potential is not fully recognized, largely because of the lack of adequate guides and manuals. The most obvious collection, the Colonial Office Records, is so important to early British American history as to justify the kind of help that only complete calendaring offers. Yet the rate of publication of the *Calendar of State Papers, Colonial* seems now to have slowed to one volume every twenty-five years.[18] For the period after 1739 Andrews and Bell and Parker are of limited usefulness; the BAAS guides offer nothing more. K. G. Davies has only whetted our

16 As if the studies of Charles M. Andrews himself were not enough to demonstrate the wisdom, indeed the necessity, of considering the West Indies in any discussion of early British America, one would have hoped that the equally broad-ranging ripostes of his critics would have driven the lesson home. See Stephen Saunders Webb, *The Governors-General: The English Army and the Definition of the Empire, 1569–1681* (Chapel Hill, NC, 1979). Compare Gipson, *Guide to Manuscripts Relating to the History of the British Empire.* Yet one can still find major attempts at synthesis on such subjects as the origins and development of the relationships between the mother country and the colonies that ignore roughly half of the colonies. See Richard S. Dunn's review of *English America and the Restoration Monarchy of Charles II: Transitional Politics, Commerce, and Kinship,* by J[ack] M. Sosin, *AHR,* LXXXVII (Oct. 1982), 1150–1151. "Early British America" in this book comprises all of the English (later British) colonies in the Western Hemisphere.

17 The Virginia Colonial Records Project has attempted this but with an obvious geographical limitation. Its "Survey Reports" are guides to the photocopies collected over the years. They can be used at the Colonial Williamsburg Foundation Library, Williamsburg, Va.; the Library of Virginia, Richmond; and the Alderman Library, University of Virginia, Charlottesville. See Julian P. Boyd, "A New Guide to the Indispensable Sources of Virginia History," *W&MQ,* 3rd ser., XV (Jan. 1958), 3–13, and *The British Public Record Office: History, Description, Record Groups, Finding Aids, and Materials for American History, with Special Reference to Virginia,* Special Reports 25, 26, 27, and 28 of the Virginia Colonial Records Project, Virginia State Library Publications, no. 12 (Richmond, Va., 1960). North Carolina has sponsored a similar project but one limited to repositories in Great Britain. See Robert J. Cain, *Preliminary Guide to the British Records Collection,* Archives Information Circular, no. 16 (Raleigh, NC, 1979). For their time, the BAAS guides offered better coverage of the additions to the British Library's Department of Manuscripts because the ongoing catalogue of the library's manuscripts is slow to appear. The most recent supplement is [British Library, Department of Manuscripts], *The British Library Catalogue of Additions to the Manuscripts, New Series, 1986–1990,* 3 vols (London, 1993). There is also a consolidated index in one alphabetical sequence to all of the separate collections of manuscripts in the British Library that were acquired prior to 1950. [British Library, Department of Manuscripts], *Index of Manuscripts in the British Library,* 10 vols (Cambridge, Eng., 1984–1985).

18 [GB, PRO], *Calendar of State Papers, Colonial Series, America and West Indies [1574–1739],* by W[illiam] Noel Sainsbury *et al.,* in progress (London, 1860 to date). To date 45 vols (in 46 pts) have appeared. Vol. XLIV was a supplement to vol. XIV, an addendum for 1688–1696; the newest vol., for the year 1739, appeared in 1994.
  Historians of early British America have used these volumes uncritically, sometimes treating calendar entries as if they were the complete text, and collections of transcripts of documents as if they exhausted an archive. By definition, calendars are only synopses of documents, synopses that may not mention topics of concern to a particular researcher;

appetite with his fine calendar of this record series for the Revolutionary War period.[19] Even Davies, one man after all, chose to omit some germane Colonial Office files and to exclude altogether any West Indian records. (How can one deal with the American Revolution and ignore the Caribbean?)[20]

Similar things can be said about the Treasury Office Records, which are second only to the Colonial Office Records in their utility for the historian of early British America. While there are calendars prepared for the Treasury Office records covering their earlier years, there is only a very limited calendar/index to them and then only for part of the time after the full, published calendars stop.[21] In addition to these records, there are great bodies of documents for which Andrews and his co-workers are still our sole recourse

they are aids to research, not substitutes for the documents themselves. Just as the compilers of calendars and indexes have to be selective, so those who organize the copying of documents are forced to make compromises that can affect the ability of other historians to use what they have done. Most efforts to transcribe or photostat documents for the study of colonial history have been organized on a state or local basis, sometimes with the help of government funds. (See, for example, those of Virginia and North Carolina mentioned in n. 22 of this chapter. Compare the earlier project sponsored by South Carolina: Helen Craig Carson, *Records in the British Public Record Office Relating to South Carolina, 1663–1782* [Columbia, SC (1973)].) While the results are still helpful and should not be ignored, these projects left out a great deal by design. The careful historian, having found something in a calendar or a collection of transcripts, must check it in the original – and cite both sources. The careful historian, failing to find something in a calendar or a collection of transcripts, cannot assume that it is not in the original document or elsewhere in the repository. Early printed calendars – and copying projects based on them – systematically omitted materials now considered significant to historians, especially economic historians. See John J. McCusker, *Money and Exchange in Europe and America, 1600–1775: A Handbook,* [2nd edn] (Chapel Hill, NC, [1992]), pp. 119–120, n. 13. See also Charles M. Andrews, *The Colonial Period of American History,* 4 vols (New Haven, Conn., 1934–1938), IV, 18, n. 2, 139, n. 6; and Carson, *Records Relating to South Carolina,* pp. 6–7. Compare Rupert C. Jarvis, "The Sources of Transport History: Sources for the History of Ships and Shipping," *Journal of Transport History,* III (Nov. 1958), 215, who found "the indexing . . . the fullness and [the] adequacy" of the various PRO calendars "most uneven"; and Paul H. Smith, review of *Documents of the American Revolution, 1770–1783, Colonial Office Series,* ed. K[enneth] G. Davies, *AHR,* LXXXVI (Dec. 1981), 1146–1147.

19 *Documents of the American Revolution, 1770–1783 (Colonial Office Series),* ed. K[enneth] G. Davies, 21 vols (Shannon, Ireland, 1972–1981).

20 For references to some of the more important Colonial Office materials from the Caribbean during the period of the American Revolution, see Bell, Parker, *et al., Guide to British West Indian Archive Materials,* passim; George F. Tyson, Jr., and Carolyn Tyson, *Preliminary Report on Manuscript Materials in British Archives Relating to the American Revolution in the West Indian Islands* (St Thomas, US Virgin Islands, 1974); and George F. Tyson, *A Guide to Manuscript Sources in United States and West Indian Depositories Relating to the British West Indies during the Era of the American Revolution* (Wilmington, Del., 1978).

The many citations in this book to materials in the PRO are referenced according to a particular format; they involve abbreviations that are keyed in the table at the beginning of the book and in the bibliography at its end. The PRO organizes individual documents ("pieces") into "boxes" (which may, in reality, consist of papers gathered into bundles or bound into volumes); boxes are grouped into classes. Thus "HCA 30/733/10, fol. 1r, PRO" refers to a class, H[igh] C[ourt of] A[dmiralty Records] 30," and, within that class, to box 733, piece 10. The additional references are to the precise folios (or, alternatively, pages) within the piece, in this instance to folio one, recto.

– the War Office, the Admiralty Office, the State Paper Office – and still larger classes that, as they themselves noted, they never even examined for the purposes of their guides.[22] And then there are the collections that have been added to the PRO since the Carnegie Institution people worked there. The BAAS guides notice some but not all of these. For instance, Raimo never mentions the Prerogative Court of Canterbury records. Until we have adequate guides, the time necessary to explore the PRO will still be considerable, even for a circumscribed subject.

Despite all these shortcomings, the Crick and Alman and the Raimo guides represent a significant advance over the manuals prepared for the Carnegie Institution because of their inclusion of British and Irish repositories outside London, Oxford, and Cambridge. So successful were the BAAS guides in this regard that they induced others to supplement or extend their coverage. Some prepared more detailed guides and manuals that describe the general collections of a particular repository with readily apparent early American connections. Among them are guides to the collections of Anglican church records dealing with the colonies and guides to special libraries such as that in Rhodes House.[23] Others have sorted through larger collections to identify

21 The last of the published calendars appeared in 1969: [GB, PRO], *Calendar of Treasury Papers Preserved in Her Majesty's Public Record Office, 1557–1728*, by Joseph Redington, 6 vols (London, 1868–1899), [GB, PRO], *Calendar of Treasury Books and Papers, Preserved in Her Majesty's Public Record Office, 1729–1745*, by William A. Shaw, 5 vols (London, 1898–1903), and [GB, PRO], *Calendar of Treasury Books Preserved in Her Majesty's Public Record Office*, by William A. Shaw, in progress (London, 1904 to date). Typescript versions of a calendar continuing the second of these three – in reality simply a calendar of the T 1 series – are available in the PRO and have been published on a limited basis: [GB, PRO], *Treasury Board Papers (T. 1/319–364): Descriptive List and Index, Mainly 1745–1755*, List and Index Society, [Publications], vol. 120 ([London], 1975), *Treasury Board Papers (T. 1/365–388): Descriptive List and Index, Mainly 1756–1758*, List and Index Society, [Publications], vol. 125 ([London], 1976), and *Treasury Board: Papers, 1759–1764 (T 1/389–436), with an Index to T 1/429–436*, List and Index Society, [Publications], vol. 240 ([London], 1990).

22 Andrews mentions the records of the Chancery, the Exchequer, and the Court of King's/Queen's Bench (*Guide to the Materials for American History, to 1783, in the Public Record Office*, I, 12). One can most easily get an idea of what else is in the PRO by looking at the printed catalogue of its collections [GB, PRO], *Guide to the Contents of the Public Record Office*, 3 vols (London, 1963–1968), and the newer [GB, PRO], *Current Guide* [3rd edn], 27 microfiche (London, 1996). All of the class lists to those records can be found in [GB, PRO], *Kew Lists: The Microfiche Edition*, 3, 483 microfiche ([London, 1988]) and [GB, PRO], *Kew Lists: Microfiche Supplement, 1987–1991*, 278 microfiche ([London, 1991]). An example of the records that Andrews omitted (through no fault of his own; the records became available for public inspection only in the middle of the 20th century) is a whole class of Chancery Records – the Chancery Masters' Exhibits, C 103–116 and C 171, PRO – that contain the papers of individual people and firms, many of which had some connection with early British America. See the partial listing of this class: [GB, Court of Chancery], *Chancery Masters' Exhibits*, List and Index Society, [Publications], vols 13–14, 2 vols (London, 1966). In addition, see Henry Horwitz, *Chancery Equity Records and Proceedings, 1600–1800: A Guide to Documents in the Public Record Office*, Public Record Office Handbook 27 (London, 1995).

23 Some of the relevant records of the Anglican church are listed in William Wilson Manross, *The Fulham Papers in the Lambeth Palace Library. American Colonial Section: Calendar and*

items of special interest to Americanists. Among these are the lists of American manuscripts in the Scottish Record Office and in the Cornwall Record Office to take the two geographical extremes.[24]

There are also a good many guides that answer in a systematic way the need posed by the modern, lamentable omission of the West Indies from compilations on early British America. Fortunately, Latin Americanists include the Caribbean in their sphere of interest, and manuals such as Peter Walne's *Guide to Manuscript Sources for the History of Latin America and the Caribbean in the British Isles* do not neglect the British West Indies.[25] In addition, an increasing number of works locate materials relevant to the history of a

Indexes (Oxford, 1965*); Calendar of Letters from Canada, Newfoundland, Pennsylvania, Barbados and the Bahamas, 1721–1793, Preserved at the United Society for the Propagation of the Gospel*, List and Index Society [Publications], special ser., vol. 5 (London, 1972); and William Wilson Manross, *S.P.G. Papers in the Lambeth Palace Library: Calendar and Indexes* (Oxford, 1974). For Rhodes House, see *Manuscript Collections (Excluding Africana) in Rhodes House Library, Oxford*, by Louis B. Frewer (Oxford, 1970), and *Manuscript Collections (Africana and non-Africana) in Rhodes House Library, Oxford: Supplementary Accessions to the End of 1977, and Cumulative Index*, by Wendy S. Byrne (Oxford, 1978). Given Bristol's many colonial connections, Elizabeth Ralph's *Guide to the Bristol Archives Office* (Bristol, 1971) – now called the Bristol Record Office – and *Guide to the Archives of the Society of Merchant Venturers of Bristol* ([Bristol, 1988]) are of great interest. See also Maurice F. Bond, *Guide to the Records of Parliament* (London, 1971).

24 See [Edinburgh, Scottish Record Office], *List of American Documents in the Scottish Record Office* (Edinburgh, 1976), which is only a supplement to [Edinburgh, Scottish Record Office], *Source List of Manuscripts Relating to the U.S.A. and Canada in Private Archives Preserved in the Scottish Record Office*, List and Index Society [Publications], special ser., vol. 3 (London, 1970); and [Cornwall County and Diocesan Record Office], *The United States of America: Maps, Letters, Diaries*, Handlist no. 1 (Truro, Eng., 1981). As general guides to British archives, see [GB, Historical Manuscripts Commission], *Record Repositories in Great Britain: A Geographical Directory*, 9th edn, rev. (London, 1991); and Janet Foster and Julia Sheppard, British Archives*: A Guide to Archive Resources in the United Kingdom*, 3rd edn ([London, 1995]). A similar volume for Ireland is Seamus Helferty and Raymond Refaussé, *Directory of Irish Archives*, 2nd edn ([Blackrock, Co. Dublin, 1993]). See also Richard J. Hayes, *Manuscript Sources for the History of Irish Civilization*, 11 vols (Boston, 1965); it is largely a pastiche from such works as the Carnegie Institution guides.

25 Walne, *A Guide to Manuscript Sources for the History of Latin America and the Caribbean in the British Isles* (London, 1973). What Walne does for Great Britain and Ireland, other volumes in the same series do for elsewhere in Europe. Although not all the volumes say so explicitly, they had their beginnings as part of a project under the general direction of the International Council on Archives with the support of UNESCO. They are all part of "Ser. A: Latin America" of the Guide to the Sources of the History of the Nations. "Ser. B: Africa" has eleven vols of a parallel nature. Listed in chronological order of publication, the vols in Ser. A are [Spain, Dirección General de Archivos y Bibliotecas], *Guía de fuentes para la historia de Ibero-América conservadas en España*, 2 vols (Madrid, 1966–1969); Jean Baerten and Léone Liagre, *Guide des sources de l'Histoire d'Amérique Latine conservées en Belgique* (Brussels, 1967); Magnus Mörner, *Fuentes para la historia de Ibero-América [conservadas en] Escandinavia*, trans. Ester Pastor Lopez (Stockholm, 1968); M[arius] P. H. Roessingh, *Guide to the Sources in the Netherlands for the History of Latin America* (The Hague, 1968); Lajos Pásztor*, Guida delle fonti per la storia dell'America Latina negli archivi della Santa Sede e negli archivi ecclesiastici d'Italia*, Collectanea Archivi Vaticani, 2 (Vatican City, 1970); [Gerhard Schmid] *Übersicht über Quellen zur Geschichte Lateinamerikas in Archiven der Deutschen Demokratischen Republik* (Potsdam, 1971); Renate Hauschild-Thiessen and Elfriede Bachmann, *Führer durch die Quellen zur Geschichte*

particular island or group of islands, usually both in the British Isles and at home.[26] Worthy of being singled out is Jerome S. Handler's *Guide to Source Materials for the Study of Barbados History* because of its informed, intelligent annotations, its inclusiveness, its locations of extant copies, its full index, and its regular supplements. The book is a model of its kind, prepared by a scholar who has actually used most of the items listed.[27]

Fortunately one major resource that has been underutilized in the past by historians of eighteenth-century British America has recently become much more accessible. While scholars have long known of the existence of the House of Commons sessional papers – the printed reports and accounts generated for the use of Parliament – their unavailability to anyone not in London and their daunting mode of citation have combined to deter all but the most intrepid. The massive bibliography of all sessional papers that Sheila Lambert compiled makes them very much simpler to find and use.[28]

All of the separately printed sessional papers were originally published.[29] They are sometimes referred to as the "Papers Printed by order of the House

Lateinamerikas in der Bundesrepublik Deutschland, Veröffentlichungen aus dem Staatsarchiv der Freien Hansestadt Bremen, vol. 38 (Bremen, 1972); George S. Ulibarri and John P. Harrison, *Guide to Materials on Latin America in the National Archives of the United States* (Washington, DC, 1974); Elio Lodolini, *Guida delle fonti per la storia dell'America Latina esistenti in Italia*, Pubblicazioni degli Archivi di Stato, LXXXVIII (Rome, 1976); and [France, Archives Nationales], *Guide des sources de l'histoire de l'Amérique latine et des Antilles dans les archives françaises* (Paris, 1984). All of these volumes (except the ones on Italy, the Vatican, and France) have been reprinted in a microfiche edition by Inter Documentation Co. (Zug, Switzerland, 1978). While the amount in each volume concerning the British West Indies varies considerably, there is something pertinent in each. Note that there is no volume for Portugal and that the one for the United States is devoted to the National Archives only.

26 Helen Rowe, *A Guide to the Records of Bermuda* (Hamilton, Bermuda, 1980); Philip Cash, Shirley Gordon, and [Diane] Gail Saunders, *Sources of Bahamian History* (London, 1991); K[enneth] E. Ingram, *Sources of Jamaican History, 1655–1838: A Bibliographical Survey with Particular Reference to Manuscript Sources*, 2 vols (Zug, Switzerland, 1976 [M. Phil. thesis, University of London, 1970]); M[ichael] J. Chandler, *A Guide to Records in Barbados* (Oxford, 1965); E[dward] C. Baker, *A Guide to Records in the Leeward Islands* (Oxford, 1965), and *A Guide to Records in the Windward Islands* (Oxford, 1968); J[ean]-C. Nardin, "Les Archives anciennes de la Grenade," *Revue Française d'Histoire d'Outre-Mer*, XLIV (1962), 117–140; Tyson and Tyson, *Preliminary Report on Manuscript Materials in British Archives*; Tyson, *Guide to Manuscript Sources in United States and West Indian Depositories*. See also *Report of the Caribbean Archives Conference Held at the University of the West Indies, Mona, Jamaica, September 20–27, 1965* (n.p. [Kingston, Jamaica (?)], 1965).

27 Handler, *A Guide to Source Materials for the Study of Barbados History, 1627–1834* (Carbondale, Ill., 1971); and Handler, *Supplement to "A Guide to Source Materials for the Study of Barbados History, 1627–1834"* (Providence, RI, 1991). The latter is an amalgamation of Handler and Samuel J. Hough, "Addenda to *A Guide to Source Materials for the Study of Barbados History, 1627–1834,*" *Journal of the Barbados Museum and Historical Society*, XXXVI–XXXVIII (1980–1987), 172–177, 279–285, 385–397, 82–92, 296–307, 107–116.

28 Lambert's bibliography is in the first two volumes of [GB, Parl., Commons], *House of Commons Sessional Papers of the Eighteenth Century*, ed. Sheila Lambert, 147 vols (Wilmington, Del., 1975).

29 For a discussion of the changing procedures in their production, see H[ugh] Hale Bellot, "Parliamentary Printing, 1660–1837," *Bulletin of the Institute of Historical Research*, XI (Nov. 1933), 85–98.

of Commons." Until the nineteenth century, however, there was no move to collect and preserve the many items produced by the Parliamentary printers. A few reports were selected and reprinted in the *Reports from Committees of the House of Commons, Re-Printed by Order of the House*[30] but this eighteenth-century effort – sometimes called the First Series – was far from complete. Soon after the beginning of the next century Charles Abbot, the Speaker of the House of Commons from 1802 to 1817, directed Luke Hansard to assemble a collection of Parliament's printed papers. Hansard gathered multiple copies of as many as he could find and bound the collected papers covering the years 1731 to 1800 into four 110-volume sets. Three sets were kept in Parliament to be used there; a fourth set was delivered to the library of the British Museum. Hansard grouped 963 "Bills" (in thirty volumes), 174 "Reports" (in eighteen volumes), and 1,032 "Accounts and Papers" (in sixty-two volumes) in rough chronological sequence. His efforts have been called the Second Series.[31]

Sheila Lambert's work supersedes both the First Series and Hansard's Second Series for two reasons. To begin, her bibliography is a much more complete compilation of the sessional papers just because of the way in which she organized it. It lists in chronological order all of the papers that Parliament ordered to be produced, indicates whether and how they were afterwards printed, and specifies if and where she has located copies of those printed. She found a considerably larger number than did Hansard. Second, she organized the collecting and reprinting – in 145 volumes – of all of the available papers.[32] To each of the items reprinted she assigned a sequential serial number and so indicated that number in her bibliography.[33] Then, much to the delight of scholars who would use her edition, she even included a rudi-

30 [GB, Parl., Commons], *Reports from Committees of the House of Commons, Re-Printed by Order of the House*, 15 vols ([London], 1773–1803). This included only reports from 1715 to 1801; there is a general index in one volume.

31 Parliamentary papers after 1801 were organized by session, although the three-fold divisions into "Bills," "Reports," and "Accounts and Papers" was maintained within each sessional period. A fourth category of "Commission Reports" was added later and, after 1870, certain papers came to be called Command Papers and were assigned a serial number in a series that transcended the sessional arrangement of the other papers.

32 Both the Second Series and the post-1801 sessional papers have been available in microform since the 1950s. While Lambert's printed volumes replace the microform edition of the former, the latter is still of great value. By making these materials much more widely accessible for the first time, they constituted a significant contribution to the scholarship on early British America. For the preparation of the microform edition, see Edgar L. Erickson, "The Sessional Papers," *Library Journal*, LXXVIII (1 Jan. 1953), 13–17; and Erickson, "The Sessional Papers: Last Phase," *College and Research Libraries*, XXI (Sept. 1960), 343–358.

33 Any bill, report, account, or paper published as part of the series known collectively as the House of Commons sessional papers is best treated as a separate bibliographical entity produced as part of one of the three sub-series. Information about its place in one of the three series conventionally assumes a regular format, much like that accorded an item that is part of any other series. After the title of the item and before the place and date of publication, the location of the item within the series is indicated in the following fashion depending on to which of the three sections it belongs:

mentary index to the contents of the printed papers. There is much to be found of importance for the history of early British America in the sessional papers of the British Parliament – which will be even more apparent when someone undertakes to index them thoroughly.

◆ ◆ ◆ ◆ ◆

For the researcher into the history of early British America, the Carnegie Institution guides to European continental archives have strengths and weaknesses in many ways like those of the British manuals: they concentrate on the obvious collections and they are now out of date. To state this is to alert historians to the opportunities inherent in the existence of much more material than those guides discussed and to alert archivists to the need for supplemental guides. The need was illustrated sharply by the Koenig and Mayer listing of manuscripts in European repositories for the study of the American Revolutionary War that was based, almost exclusively, on references extracted from the old Carnegie guides. Barely more than a scissors-and-paste

- If it is to be found in the "First Series," reference is made to where in the volumes of the published *Reports from Committees*, it appears, e.g.:
  [GB, Parl., Commons], *A Report from the Committee Appointed to Enquire into the Original Standards of Weights and Measures in This Kingdom, and to Consider the Laws Relating Thereto* [London, 1758], as printed in [GB, Parl., Commons], *Reports from Committees of the House of Commons, Reprinted by Order of the House*, 15 vols (London, 1773–1803), II, 434 [Lambert 2293].
  In this instance the volume and page numbers are to the reprinted version.
- If it is to be found in the "Second Series," then the reference appears:
  [GB, Parl., Commons], *Report of the Lords of the Committee of [the Privy] Council . . . [for] Trade and Foreign Plantations . . . Concerning the Present State of the Trade to Africa*, HC Sessional Papers to 1801, Accounts and Papers, vols XXVI, no. 646a, 6 pts [Lambert 4132] ([London, 1789]).
  The reference to "Accounts and Papers" and the volume number in roman numerals are to the organizational structure and the number of the volume in the four 110-volume sets collected by Hansard – the Abbot Collection – and, most particularly, in the surviving set deposited in the British Library.
- If the item is to be found in the series that continues down to the present, then the reference appears, for example, thus:
  [GB, Parl., Commons, Select Committee on the High Price of Gold Bullion], *Report, Together with Minutes of Evidence, and Accounts, from the Select Committee on the High Price of Gold Bullion*, HC Sessional Papers, 1810, vol. III (Reports) ([London, 1810]), p. 36.
  In the series information, the year, denoting the session, is followed by the volume number for that session, the type of paper, and, when appropriate, the number of the paper. If the item is also a Command Paper, a parenthetical denotation of this fact will follow the number of the paper (e.g., "[Cmd. 8706]").

These conventions have been adopted in the notes to this book but with a significant addition. Each of the items published as part of the First Series and the Second Series that is reprinted in Lambert will also be given the serial number she assigned to it so that it can easily be located in her edition. This is all the more important because the Official Publications Library of the British Library has removed the volumes of the Abbot Collection from the open shelves in the State Papers Room and replaced them with the Lambert edition. There is a concordance available for use in the room.

job, it understates dramatically what is actually available.[34] Fortunately, more adequate guides for some countries have begun to appear.

The best of the newer guides, by far, is the multi-authored *Guide des sources de l'histoire des États-Unis dans les archives françaises*, a bountiful bicentennial present from French archivists to American historians. This work not only contains descriptions of the holdings of the Archives Nationales and related national archival collections but also surveys the departmental and municipal archives (the latter much less thoroughly than the former). Although the book deals with the history of the United States through the first third of the twentieth century, much of it concentrates on the period of the Ancien Régime. It includes the Caribbean for the years before 1815. Omitted completely, however, are documentary collections in repositories outside the public archival system, including the Bibliothèque Nationale de France. The *Guide* is made more serviceable by incorporating references to published and unpublished lists and calendars for each archive. It is made less usable – indeed, it is almost crippled – by the absence of any index and by an unsatisfactory table of contents. Consequently, the volume's arrangement of local archives by *département* will try the patience of all but the few non-residents of France who will know to look under Gironde to find Bordeaux or under Bouches-du-Rhône for Marseilles.[35]

It will be worth the effort to search this handbook, however, because French archives are far richer than the old Leland-Meng-Doysié guide would suggest. In the Archives Nationales, the *Archives Ministérelles Anciennes* of the *Fonds des Colonies* parallels the Colonial Office Records in the PRO. (These materials, formerly in the Archives Nationales, Paris, are now in the Centre des Archives d'Outre-Mer, Aix-en-Provence.) Just as the latter have reports of what the French were doing at Saint-Domingue, in Canada, and elsewhere, so also do the former have the latest news about Jamaica and New

---

34 W[illiam] J. Koenig and S[ydney] L Mayer, *European Manuscript Sources of the American Revolution* (London and New York, 1974). Compare the entries in the several guides listed in n. 2 of this chapter and in Gipson, *Guide to Manuscripts Relating to the History of the British Empire*.

35 Madeline Astorquia *et al.*, *Guide des sources de l'histoire des États-Unis dans les archives françaises* (Paris, 1976). This is particularly helpful because it takes into account the Caribbean through 1815 and thus neatly complements the French volume in the series of Latin American guides cited in n. 25 of this chapter. See also [France, Archives Nationales], *Les Archives Nationales: État général des fonds*, ed. Jean Favier, 5 vols (Paris, 1978–1988); and *États des inventaires*, ed. Jean Favier, 4 vols (Paris, 1985–1994). Some 800 of these finding aids have been reproduced in a microfiche edition by Chadwyck-Healey France: *Les Inventaires des Archives Nationales*, 8,388 microfiche (Paris, 1989). The best source for the Bibliothèque Nationale is still Leland, Meng, and Doysié, *Guide to Materials for American History in the Libraries and Archives of Paris, I: Libraries*, [Paris, Bibliothèque Nationale de France, Département des Manuscrits], *Catalogue général des manuscrits français*, in progress (Paris, 1886 to date), is the catalogue of the basic collection, the original Fonds Français and the newer, ongoing Nouvelles Acquisitions Françaises. There is much about colonial matters indicated in Joël Félix, *Économie et finances sous l'Ancien Régime: Guide du chercheur, 1523–1789* (Paris, [1994]).

York and elsewhere. The Archives Nationales is slowly publishing calendars of some of these records. Many of the current generation of calendars have been compiled in whole or in part by Étienne Taillemite, the Inspecteur Général des Archives de France. They are beautifully done, full of references to British America, with only the occasional omission of an index to make them perfect.[36] One hopes for the appearance of more such volumes.

There are, of course, many other classes of records in the Archives Nationales that relate to early British America.[37] One is particularly worth mentioning because it is readily accessible to historians in the Western Hemisphere. The French government moved quickly during the American Revolution to establish consular officials in the port cities of the United States. Their reports home were frequent and occasionally voluminous, and sometimes involved a retrospective element for comparative purposes. There is much about pre-war conditions in some of these reports. They have been microfilmed for the Library of Congress and a detailed published calendar (with an index!) has been compiled by Abraham P. Nasatir and Gary Elwyn Monell. Where I have had occasion to check, however, the calendaring has not always been carefully accomplished.[38]

The amount of material in the archives of Germany and Italy for the

36 [France, Archives Nationales], *Inventaire analytique de la correspondance générale avec les colonies: Départ, Série B*, ed. Étienne Taillemite (Paris, 1959); *Inventaire de la série Colonies C8: Martinique (Correspondance à l'arrivée)*, ed. Étienne Taillemite, Odile Krakovitch, and Michele Bimbenet[-Privat], 3 vols (Paris, 1967–1984); *Inventaire des archives Colonies, sous-série C14: Correspondance à l'arrivée en provenance de la Guyane Française*, ed. C. Bougard-Cordier *et al.*, 2 vols (Paris, 1974–1977); *Inventaire des archives Colonies [sous-série C13]: Correspondance à l'arrivée en provenance de la Louisiane*, ed. Marie-Antionette Menier Étienne Taillemite, and Gilberte de Forges, 2 vols (Paris, 1976–1984). The most complete guide to the Fonds des Colonies, available both in the Archives Nationales, Paris, and in the Centre des Archives d'Outre-Mer, Aix-en-Provence, is still Pierre de Vaissière [and Yvonne Bézard], "Répertoire numérique provisoire du fonds des Archives Colonies conservé [es] aux Archives Nationales" (unpublished typescript, 1914).

37 Perhaps the most important is the Fonds de la Marine, Séries Anciennes. For a sampling of their contents, see [France, Archives Nationales], *Inventaire des archives de la Marine, Sous-série B7 (Pays étrangers, commerce, consulats) déposée aux Archives Nationales*, ed. Étienne Taillemite and Philippe Henrat, 6 vols (Paris, 1964–1980).

38 Nasatir and Monell, *French Consuls in the United States: A Calendar of Their Correspondence in the Archives Nationales* (Washington, DC, 1967). Historians have largely ignored the reports of foreign consuls resident in a nation's ports as a source of information on subjects as diverse as the economy and the arts. See the series of articles devoted to "Consular Reports: A Rich but Neglected Historical Source" [ed. Theodore C. Barker], *Business History*, XXIII (July 1981), 265 ff. The richness of such materials can be sampled in the "Letters of Phineas Bond, British Consul at Philadelphia, to the Foreign Office of Great Britain, 1787–[1794]," ed. J[ohn] Franklin Jameson, American Historical Association, *Annual Report for the Year 1896*, 2 vols (Washington, DC, 1897), I, 513–659; American Historical Association, *Annual Report for the Year 1897* (Washington, DC, 1898), pp. 454–568; and in *Die Berichte des ersten Agenten Österreichs in den Vereinigten Staaten von Amerika, Baron de Beelen-Bertholff an Die Regierung der Österreichischen Niederlande in Brüssel, 1784–1789*, ed. Hanns Schlitter, Fontes Rerum Austriacarum/Œsterreichische Geschichts-Quellen, Zwiete Abtheilung: Diplomataria et Acta, XLV. Band, Zweite Hälfte (Vienna, 1891).

historian of British America is much smaller than in those of France or Great Britain, but some of it is surprisingly rich. It is also much more difficult to get at because archival holdings in the two countries are greatly dispersed. (There was no central government in eighteenth-century Germany or Italy, and therefore no central repository of government documents that gave rise to central archives comparable to the Archives Nationales or the PRO.) As a result, Carl Russell Fish dealt almost exclusively with Rome in his guide, and Marion D. Learned touched on only some of the German states.[39] For what used to be called "West Germany," Learned's book is superseded by the eleven-volume *Americana in deutschen Sammlungen*, a detailed description of materials for all of American history in the archives of the states of the Federal Republic of Germany.[40] For Italy, we are also fortunate in having a new calendar of American materials in the Propaganda Fide archives, records abounding with references to early America but in an archive traditionally difficult to use. This new calendar, running to several volumes, was prepared by Luca Codignola of the University of Genoa for the Public Archives of Canada and St. Paul University of Ottawa.[41] The remainder of Italy is almost terra incognita for the historian of early British America.[42]

What about the rest of Europe? William R. Shepherd's *Guide to the Materials for the History of the United States in Spanish Archives* has yet to be replaced. It needs to be. Shepherd surveyed only the three major Spanish archives – Archivo Histórico Nacional, Madrid; Archivo General de Indias,

39 For both, see n. 2 of this chapter.
40 [Dietrich Gerhard, Egmont Zechlen, and Erich Angermann], *Americana in deutschen Sammlungen (ADS): Ein Verzeichnis von Materialien zur Geschichte der Vereinigten Staaten von Amerika in Archiven und Bibliothek der Bundesrepublik Deutschland und West-Berlin*, 11 vols in 5 pts (n.p. [Heidelberg (?)], 1967). This volume obviously does not consider what was then in East German archives. Learned, *Guide to the Manuscript Materials for American History in the German State Archives*, had surveyed such records. Compare [Schmid], *Übersicht über Quellen zur Geschichte Lateinamerikas in Archiven der Deutschen Demokratischen Republik*. There is a useful sampling of other sources in Ulrike Skorsetz and Janine Micunek, *Guide to Inventories and Finding Aids at the German Historical Institute, Washington, D.C.*, Reference Guides of the German Historical Institute, Washington DC, no. 5 (Washington, DC, 1995).
41 Luca Codignola, *Calendar of Documents Relating to French and British North America in the Archives of the Sacred Congregation "de Propaganda Fide" in Rome, 1622–1799*, 6 vols (Ottawa, Ontario, 1983); and Codignola, *Guide to Documents Relating to French and British North America in the Archives of the Sacred Congregation "de Propaganda Fide" in Rome, 1622–1799* (Ottawa, Ontario, 1991). Fortunately for historians of the rest of British America, Canadians have a broad view of what is important to them in their early history, and this calendar will include much of use to those whose primary focus is south of the border. Compare Fish, *Guide to the Materials for American History in Roman and Other Italian Archives*, pp. 119–195, and Pásztor, *Guida della fonti per la storia dell'America Latina negli archivi della Santa Sede e negli archivi ecclesiastici d'Italia*, pp. 329–338. Contrast Finbar Kenneally *et al.*, *United States Documents in the Propaganda Fide Archive: A Calendar*, 9 vols (Washington, DC, 1966–1982), which lists almost nothing for the pre-1775 era.
42 See Fish, *Guide to the Materials for American History in Roman and Other Italian Archives*, passim, and Pásztor, *Guida della fonti per la storia dell'America Latina negli archivi della Santa Sede e negli archivi ecclesiastici d'Italia*, passim.

Seville; and Archivo General de Simancas, Valladolid – and omitted numerous other archives and libraries.[43] Nor has anyone improved upon Albert B. Faust's guide to Swiss and Austrian archives or, to my knowledge, on Frank A. Golder's guide to Russian archives – at least for the subject of early British American history.[44] The projected volumes in the Carnegie Institution series for The Netherlands and Sweden did not appear.[45] For them and for the rest of continental Europe there are no guides to early American materials, though Portugal, Denmark, and Belgium would certainly repay attention.[46]

43 Compare [Spain, Dirección General de Archivos y Bibliotecas], *Guía de fuentes para la historia de Ibero-América conservadas en España.* See also Ingram, *Sources of Jamaican History,* II, 998–1004, and José Tudela de la Orden, *Los manuscritos de América en las bibliotecas de España* (Madrid, 1954). Note the collection of *Documentos relativos a la independencia de Norteamérica existentes en archivos españoles,* 11 vols in 14 pts (Madrid, 1976–1985).
44 For Faust and Golder, see n. 2 of this chapter. For the former Soviet Union, see Patricia K. Grimsted, *Archives and Manuscript Repositories in the USSR: Moscow and Leningrad* (Princeton, NJ, 1972), and *Archives and Manuscript Repositories in the USSR: Estonia, Latvia, Lithuania, and Belorussia* (Princeton, NJ, 1981). See most especially Patricia Kennedy Grimsted [*et al.*], *Archives in Russia, 1993: A Brief Directory – Part 1, Moscow and St. Petersburg,* ed. Patricia Kennedy Grimsted [*et al.*] (Washington, DC, [1993]). This is a significant advance over the first of her guides largely because, of the changes as she notes (ibid., A-7), in the names of many of the institutions included.
45 They were planned. Andrews, *Guide to the Materials for American History, to 1783, in the Public Record Office of Great Britain,* I, iv. In their stead, for The Netherlands, see Engel Sluiter, "The Dutch Archives and American Historical Research," *Pacific Historical Review,* VI (Mar. 1937), 21–35. To help bring Sluiter's references up to date, see Roessingh, *Guide to the Sources in the Netherlands for the History of Latin America;* and W[illem] Ph. Coolhaas, *A Critical Survey of Studies on Dutch Colonial History,* ed. G. J. Schutte, Koninklijk Instituut voor Taal-, Land- en Volkenkunde, Bibliographical ser., no. 4, 2nd edn, rev. (The Hague, 1980); and, especially, the *Overzichten van de archieven en verzamelingen in de openbare archiefbewaarplaatsen in Nederland,* ed. L. M. Th. L Hustinx *et al.,* 14 vols (Alphen aan den Rijn, 1979–1992). The volumes in this splendid series supersede the older but still useful *De Rijksarchieven in Nederland: Overziect van de inhoud van de rijksarchiefbewaarplaatsen,* ed. L[ouis] P. L. Pirenne, 2 vols (The Hague, 1973).
    Special attention should be paid to the records of the Amsterdam notaries public – the Notariële Archieven, 1578–1895, Gemeente Archief, Amsterdam – which contain a variety of materials relating to the history of early Dutch (and British) America. See in this regard the "English Translations of Notarial Documents Pertaining to North America in the Gemeente Archief, Amsterdam," Rockefeller Archive Center, Pocantico Hills, North Tarrytown, NY. See also the "Dutch Documents Taken from the Notarial Archives of Holland Relating to the Fur Trade and Cod Fisheries of North America," collected, trans. and ed. by Jan Kupp, unpublished typescript, 18 vols, C. 433, McPherson Library, University of Victoria, Victoria, British Columbia; and Jan Kupp, "Dutch Notarial Acts Relating to the Tobacco Trade of Virginia, 1608–1653," *W&MQ,* 3rd ser., XXX (Oct. 1973), 653–655. (The Amsterdam Notariële Archieven are also the basis of the research reported in chapter five of the present book.) Also in the Gemeente Archief are the Archives of the Holland Land Company, 1789–1869. See Wilhelmina C. Pieterse, *Inventory of the Archives of the Holland Land Company Including the Related Amsterdam Companies and Negotiations Dealing with the Purchase of Land and State Funds in the United States of America,* 1789–1869, trans. Sytha Hart (Amsterdam, 1976).
    For Sweden, see Mörner, *Fuentes para la historia de Ibero-América [conservadas en] Escandinavia,* trans. Pastor Lopez, pp. 1–98.
46 For Belgium, see Baerten and Liagre, *Guides des sources de l'histoire d'Amérique Latine conservées en Belgique.* For Denmark, see Mörner, *Fuentes para la historia de Ibero-América [conservadas en] Escandinavia,* trans. Pastor Lopez, pp. 99–105. For some of the relevant

The Carnegie Institution also published guides to resources for American history in Canada, Mexico, and Cuba.[47] Little has been produced to supplement them. One should take note, however, of the *Dictionary of Canadian Biography*, the first four volumes of which extend through 1800, with a separate index volume for these four.[48] This is a distinguished reference work which deserves to be more widely known for the breadth and depth of its scholarship. Its bibliographies constitute a guide to the sources on early America – not only British and French but also Canadian.

Two thematic guides to sources have lately appeared that cover archives both inside and outside the United States. The first of these, by K. E. Ingram, sifts the various collections in archives in the United States and Canada for manuscripts relating to the Caribbean.[49] Although Ingram visited only some of the places mentioned, relying for the others on sometimes very old archival guides and thus missing some significant items, this is a most helpful study. It identifies numbers of interesting collections and annotates them insightfully. One is reminded of the Handler book noted above, though that guide is both broader in scope because it lists published as well as manuscript materials and narrower because it concentrates exclusively on Barbados.

The second guide organized around a major theme is the *Bibliography of Loyalist Source Materials in the United States, Canada, and Great Britain*, sponsored by the Program for Loyalist Studies. Established twenty-five years ago under the direction of Robert A. East, the program tried to search every appropriate repository and to examine every possible collection. The surveys for Canada and the United States published in this volume had already been printed in the Proceedings of the American Antiquarian Society, as had the two very valuable appendixes. It is handy, I suppose, to have them reprinted in a volume with the new surveys of British and Irish archives, if only to have them all together and served by a unified index to (almost) everything.[50]

In the past couple of decades a number of repositories in the United States have produced catalogues of value to historians of early British America. Noteworthy among these are the American Antiquarian Society and the

---

records of the Danish West Indies in Rigsarkivet, Copenhagen, see J[ohannes] O. Bro-Jørgensen and Aa[ge] Rasch, *Asiatiske, vestindiske og guineiske handelskompagnien*, [Denmark, Rigsarkivet], Vejledende Arkivregistraturen, XIV (Copenhagen, 1969). I would be happy to learn of an introduction to Portuguese records similar to the ones discussed in this chapter.

47 See n. 2 of this chapter.

48 *Dictionary of Canadian Biography*, ed. George W. Brown *et al.*, 13 vols (Toronto, 1966–1991).

49 K[enneth] E. Ingram, *Manuscripts Relating to Commonwealth Caribbean Countries in United States and Canadian Repositories* (St Lawrence, Barbados, 1975). See also Tyson, *Guide to Manuscript Sources in United States and West Indian Depositories*. As a supplement to both – and to Ingram's other work – see Ingram, *Sources for West Indian Studies: A Supplementary Listing, with Particular Reference to Manuscript Sources* (Zug, Switzerland, 1983). See also Charles Gehring, *A Guide to Dutch Manuscripts Relating to New Netherland in United States Repositories* (Albany, NY, 1978).

50 Palmer, *A Bibliography of Loyalist Source Material*. See n. 10 of this chapter.

Massachusetts Historical Society – for which there are published versions of their card catalogues[51] – as well as the Baker Library of Harvard University's Graduate School of Business Administration, the New-York Historical Society, the American Philosophical Society, the Historical Society of Pennsylvania, the City Archives of Philadelphia, the Maryland Historical Society, the William L. Clements Library of the University of Michigan, and the Henry E. Huntington Library – for which we have fully edited catalogues.[52] Given the scope and complexity of their holdings, we will never have complete guides to the manuscript collections of the major national archival repositories – the National Archives,[53] and the Library of Congress – despite their best

51 See *Catalogue of the Manuscript Collections of the American Antiquarian Society*, 4 vols (Boston, 1979); and *Catalog of Manuscripts of the Massachusetts Historical Society*, 7 vols (Boston, 1969). One begins any search for particular manuscripts in United States archives by turning, first, to Philip M. Hamer, *A Guide to Archives and Manuscripts in the United States* (New Haven, Conn., 1961), and then to [US, Library of Congress, Descriptive Cataloging Division], *The National Union Catalog of Manuscript Collections*, 29 vols (Ann Arbor, Mich., Hamden, Conn., and Washington, DC, 1962–1994). There are two cumulative indexes to the latter item, both published by Chadwyck-Healey, Inc.: *Index to Personal Names in the National Union Catalog of Manuscript Collections, 1959–1984*, 2 vols (Alexandria, Va., 1988); *and Index to Subjects and Corporate Names in the National Union Catalog of Manuscript Collections, 1959–1984*, 3 vols (Alexandria, Va., 1994). Chadwyck-Healey has announced the inclusion of all twenty-nine volumes in a soon-to-be-released CD-ROM publication entitled *Archives USA* (Alexandria, Va., forthcoming). The same company has begun a project to reproduce on microfiche the unpublished finding aids to manuscript collections in North America and the British Isles: *National Inventory of Documentary Sources in the United States*, in progress (Teaneck, NJ, 1983 to date); *National Inventory of Documentary Sources in the United Kingdom and Ireland*, in progress (Cambridge, Eng., 1984 to date); and *National Inventory of Documentary Sources in Canada*, in progress (Alexandria, Va., 1991 to date). By rough count so far, the ongoing project totals nearly 27,000 microfiche. Since 1992 it has been served by an "Index to NIDS" on CD-ROM that is updated twice a year. Also useful is Donald L. DeWitt, *Guides to Archives and Manuscript Collections in the United States: An Annotated Bibliography* (Westport, Conn., [1994]).

52 Robert W. Lovett and Eleanor C. Bishop, *Manuscripts in Baker Library: A Guide to Sources for Business, Economic, and Social History*, 4th edn (Boston, 1978); Arthur J. Breton, *A Guide to the Manuscript Collections of the New-York Historical Society* (Westport, Conn., 1972); Whitfield J. Bell, Jr., and Murphy D. Smith, *Guide to the Archives and Manuscript Collections of the American Philosophical Society*, Memoirs of the American Philosophical Society, LXVI (Philadelphia, 1966); *Guide to the Manuscript Collections of the Historical Society of Pennsylvania*, 3rd edn (Philadelphia, 1991); John Daly, *Descriptive Inventory of the Archives of the City and County of Philadelphia* (Philadelphia, 1970; with supplements, 1972, 1973, 1980); Avril J. M. Pedley, *The Manuscript Collections of the Maryland Historical Society* (Baltimore, 1968); Richard J. Cox and Larry E. Sullivan, *Research Collections of the Maryland Historical Society: Historical and Genealogical Manuscripts and Oral History Interviews* (Baltimore, 1981); Arlene Phillips Shy and Barbara A. Mitchell, *Guide to the Manuscript Collections of the William L. Clements Library*, rev. edn (Boston, 1978); Mary Robertson, *Guide to American Historical Manuscripts in the Huntington Library* (San Marino, Calif., 1979).

53 See the [US, National Archives and Records Administration], *Guide to Federal Records in the National Archives of the United States*, by Robert B. Machette *et al.*, 3 vols (Washington, DC, 1995). This is complemented for historians of early British America by [US, National Archives and Records Administration], *A Guide to Pre-Federal Records in the National Archives*, by Howard H. Wehmann, ed. Benjamin L. De Whitt (Washington, DC, 1989).

efforts, although the recent three-volume guide issued by the National Archives is most impressive and immensely useful. We can only hope that an equivalent catalogue of the manuscripts in the Library of Congress will soon be published[54] and that it will combine the erudition of Andrews and Davies, the thoroughness of Brigham and Raimo, the focus and insight of Handler, and the bibliographical skills of Alden and Adams. May it also be blessed with a good index.

54 Until there is a new complete catalogue of the manuscript collection, several published and unpublished guides are available that cover most of the division's holdings. Besides the old [US, Library of Congress, Manuscript Division], *Handbook of Manuscripts in the Library of Congress* (Washington, DC, 1918) and its supplements, there is a very helpful partial listing in the work of John R. Sellers, Gerard W. Gawalt, Paul H. Smith, and Patricia Molen van Ee, *Manuscript Sources in the Library of Congress for Research on the American Revolution* (Washington, DC, 1975). It includes references to materials from European archives available as microfilm, photocopies, or transcripts in the Manuscript Division. Most unfortunately new management has rescinded an older policy that made the microfilms available on interlibrary loan. Hundreds of the Division's collections are, of course, listed in the *National Union Catalog of Manuscript Collections*. Important listings of microform and photocopied materials in the Library of Congress are in the Griffin and Bickel guides (see n. 2 of this chapter). Of great utility also to historians of early British America, though infrequently used – perhaps because of a somewhat misleading title that implies inclusion of materials from only a later period – is the mammoth collection, in 1,700 reels, of the *Records of the States of the United States of America: A Microfilm Compilation*, comp. William Sumner Jenkins ([Washington, DC], 1949). The guides to the collection are William Sumner Jenkins and Lillian A. Hamrick, *A Guide to the Microfilm Collection of Early State Records* ([Washington, DC], 1950), and Jenkins, *A Guide to the Microfilm Collection of Early State Records: Supplement* ([Washington, DC], 1951).

Two "in-house" multi-volume guides and a continually updated list of collections are the basic finding aids to the division's 10,000 plus collections. The "Dictionary Catalog of Collections," 4 vols (unpublished computer printout, 1986), contains a short description of each of those collections, ordered by the titles of the collections; the "Reference Index for the Dictionary Catalog of Collections," 3 vols (unpublished computer printout, 1983), has not only a personal name index but also a place name and subject index. I wish to thank Dr Jacqueline A. Goggin, formerly of the Manuscript Division, and Dr Gerald W. Gawalt for help in understanding these guides. There is also a typescript of a valuable catalogue of the Papers of Peter Force which, I hope, will someday be completed and published. The initial draft is available as a finding aid to the collection. This is also the place to indicate the need for a concordance for the Neil Jamieson Papers, 1757–1789, a collection frequently cited by historians of early British America. Late in the 1970s the papers were completely and arbitrarily rearranged, and, while there is an in-house register of the collection available to researchers, there is no relationship between the old numbering scheme and the current order of the papers; this makes a concordance a necessity. No such concordance is available, however.

2

THE WINE PRISE AND MEDIEVAL MERCANTILE SHIPPING

The earliest history of the English customs on imported wines, the "prise," or "prisage," offers some valuable clues to the nature of the mercantile shipping of the period.[1] Wine prisage, which originated in "the arbitrary requisitions of the Crown to relieve its necessities, real or imaginary," was first formulated, in so far as extant sources indicate, about the year 1130 in a London regulation of the merchants of Lower Lotharingia or Lorraine.[2] The regulation distinguished between two levels of appropriation, assessing one variety of ship at a higher rate than another, the ceol at three tuns of wine, the hulc and other ships at two tuns.

> And if it is a ceol, they [the sheriff or the chamberlain] shall take two tuns below the mast and one before, the best for as much as they sell the mean. And the mean for as much as they sell the worst. And if it is a hulc or other ship, one tun before and another behind, the best for as much as they sell the mean. And the mean for as much as they sell the worst.[3]

1 The original version of this chapter was published in *Speculum: A Journal of Medieval Studies*, XLI (Apr. 1966), 279–296. Copyright © 1966 by the Medieval Academy of America. Copyright © renewed 1994 by John J. McCusker. I want to acknowledge a particular debt of gratitude for the quiet support given in the publication of this essay by Frederic C. Lane who, as I learned only later, championed it to the editor of the journal. His anonymous suggestions improved it; his intervention assured its appearance.
2 Hubert Hall, *A History of the Custom-Revenue in England from the Earliest Times to the Year 1827*, 2 vols (London, 1885), II, 90.
3 The text is in Add. MS 14252, fols 99v–100r, BL, and has been printed in Mary Bateson, "A London Municipal Collection of the Reign of John," *English Historical Review*, XVII (July 1902), 500.

> E si co est chiel, il prendrunt deus tonels bas le tonge. e un deuant le meillur pur al altretant. cum lom uendra le meein. E le meein pur altretant cum lom uendra le peiur. E si co est hulk. u altre nef. un tunel deuant e altre deriere. le meillur pur altretant cum lum uendra le meien. Et le meen pur altretant. cum lom uendra le peiur.

> Bateson identified "another unprinted version" of this law in "Guildhall MS., 'Liber Ordinationum' . . . " (ibid., p. 495). This is the manuscript by that name, dated ca. 1300, now in the Corporation of London Records Office, London. This same repository contains still a third rendition of the text in the Liber Custumarum, ca. 1324; it has been printed

The standard authors have always presumed that the criterion for the differentiation was the comparative sizes of the types of ships specified but, because there is little known of either of these ships, this hypothesis has been merely an untested assumption.[4] Documents as close in time to this regulation as the fourteenth century suggest that the ceol was a smaller ship than the hulc, thus making the law appear a study in reverse logic. Closer investigation reveals two related phenomena: at the beginning of the twelfth century the ceol was larger than the hulc; and that during the same century a change took place in these two vessels. It was a time of growth in the size of the hulc and one of diminution (or, at least, stabilization) in the size of the ceol.[5] There is, furthermore, a possibility that the wine prisage might have had something to do with this change. If the prisage did not in reality add impetus to the change, it did at least reflect the fact that a change in the relative size of the ceol and the hulc had taken place.

Early mercantile regulations, as they reflect the change in the size of the ceol and the hulc, went through three successive stages. An example of the first – an apparent recognition of their coeval roles in trade – is the first

in *Munimenta Gildhallae Londoniensis: Liber albus, liber custumarum, et liber horn*, ed. Henry Thomas Riley, [Rolls Series, no. 12], 3 vols in 4 pts (London, 1859–1862), II, pt i, p. 62, and in Hansisches Urkundenbuch, ed. [Johann Mathias] Konstantin Höhlbaum, K[arl] Kunze, and W[alther] Stein, 11 vols (Halle a.S. and Leipzig, 1876–1939), III, 91. Höhlbaum was the sole editor of the first three volumes. See also Neil R. Ker, "*Liber Custumarum*, and Other Manuscripts Formerly at the Guildhall," *The Guildhall Miscellany,* [I] (no. 3, Feb. 1954), 37–45. See also Hugo Deadman and Elizabeth Scudder, *An Introductory Guide to the Corporation of London Records Office* ([London, 1994]), pp. 9–10.

The date of the regulation was established by Höhlbaum *et al.*, op. cit., III, 388–390, and Bateson, op. cit., p. 495, in disagreement with Riley, op. cit., II, pt i, xxxv–xxxvi, who estimated it to have been a century later.

The translation offered here borrows heavily from that of Norman Scott Brien Gras, *The Early English Customs System: A Documentary Study of the Institutional and Economic History of the Customs from the Thirteenth to the Sixteenth Century* (Cambridge, Mass., 1918), p. 37, and Bateson's notes, op. cit., p. 496. Compare Martin Weinbaum, *London unter Eduard I. und II.: Verfassungs- und Wirtschaftsgeschichtliche Studien*, Vierteljahrschrift für Sozial- und Wirschaftsgeschichte, Beihften 28–29, 2 vols (Stuttgart, 1933), II, 18–38. Note Walther Vogel's defense of the translation of *tonge* as "mast" in his *Geschichte der deutschen Seeschiffahrt . . . von der Urzeit bis zum Ende des XV. Jahrhunderts* (Berlin, 1915), p. 111, n. 1.

For a discussion of the origin of the wine prisage, see Gras, op. cit., pp. 37–47. The King is, by the very statement of the regulation, purchasing his wine at below the market price and, in this way, is levying a tax on imports, Gras's opinion to the contrary notwithstanding; ibid., p. 41.

4 Gras, *Early English Customs*, pp. 39–41; Stephen Dowell, *A History of Taxation and Taxes in England From the Earliest Times to the Year 1885*, 2nd edn, rev., 4 vols (London, 1884), I, 17, 78–79; Hall, *History of the Custom-Revenue*, II, 96; William Stubbs, *The Constitutional History of England in Its Origins and Development*, 3rd edn, 3 vols (Oxford, 1883), II, 547–548. Paul Heinsius made the same assumption in "Dimensions et caractéristiques des 'Koggen' hanséatiques dans le commerce Baltique," in [Colloque International d'Histoire Maritime, 3rd., 1958, Paris], *Le Navire et l'économie maritime du Nord de l'Europe du Moyen Âge au XVIIIe siècle*, ed. Michel Mollat (Paris, 1960), p. 8.

5 As the modern dictionary meanings of keel and hulk attest to this change, it has been decided, for the sake of clarity, to use the older spellings of ceol and hulc to designate the pre-thirteenth-century forms of these two vessels.

extant mention of the two together. It is to be found in a law dating from about the year 1000 assessing the payment of groundage, a harbor duty. Ceol and hulc were rated together at 4d. (1.6p) apiece or eight times more than a very small ship and four times that of an intermediate vessel.[6] In the second stage, specified by the wine prisage of 1130, an apparent difference in the size of the two types was recognized, presumably the ceol being capable of carrying more than the hulc. By the beginning of the thirteenth century, in what N. S. B. Gras has called the third phase of the prisage or *recta prisa*,[7] a new mode of assessment had been developed. All references to ceol and hulc had disappeared and the distinction became one simply of a ship's capacity in tuns of wine.[8] For some reason the older distinction of the second stage was no longer used and seems to have become outmoded. Recognizable provisions of the regulation of 1130 continue to be written into the newer formulations,[9] but the basis of the tax was altered from the type of vessel to its capacity. This would seem to suggest that, whereas previously the type of ship had been *prima facie* indicative of capacity, this had ceased to be the

6   These so-called Billingsgate tolls are translated and printed in [GB, Laws and Statutes] *Die Gesetze der Angelsachsen*, ed. and trans. F[elix] Liebermann, 3 vols (Halle a.S., 1903–1916), I, 232–237, in a longer form than in either *Hansisches Urkundenbuch*, ed. Höhlbaum, I, 1–2, and II, 380–381, or Gras, *Early English Customs*, pp. 153–154, who reprinted Höhlbaum's second version. Gras, in dating his entry from the last third of the eleventh century, apparently did not accept Höhlbaum's earlier text that assigned it to the years between 991 and 1002. He also seems not to have been aware of Liebermann's printing of this text or of his suggestion that these tolls are from early in the reign of Ethelred II (978–1016). Liebermann's book does not appear in Gras's bibliography. By contrast, Robertson accepts Liebermann's dating and translates the text: [GB, Laws and Statutes], *The Laws of the Kings of England from Edmund to Henry I*, ed. and trans. A[gnes] J. Robertson (Cambridge, Eng., 1925), pp. 70–71 (Act of 4 Ethelred II).

7   Gras, *Early English Customs*, p. 38.

8   At first the new law determined three levels of collection: if a ship carried nine tuns of wine or less, no prise was assessed; if between ten and nineteen tuns, one tun was taken as the prise; if twenty tuns or over, two tuns were collected, but no more than that, no matter how large the cargo. Compare [Matthew] Hale, "Concerning the Customs of Goods Imported and Exported," pt iii of his "Treatise in Three Parts," in *A Collection of Tracts Relative to the Law of England*, ed. Francis Hargrave (Dublin, 1787), pp. 117–120, with several examples. Two more examples of this formulation of the prise can be found, one in the Liber Albus in *Munimenta Gildhallae Londoniensis*, ed. Riley, I, 247–248, and another in Gras, *Early English Customs*, p. 159. See also Stubbs, *Constitutional History of England*, II, 547–548, and Hall, *History of the Custom-Revenue*, II, 95–96. In 1303, the wine prise was commuted to a money payment of 2s. (10p) per tun of wine and continued to be collected into the early nineteenth century. [GB, Commissioners for Taking, Examining and Stating the Public Accounts], *The Reports of the Commissioners Appointed to Examine, Take, and State the Public Accounts of the Kingdom*, ed. William Molleson and John Lane, 3 vols (London, 1783–1787), III, 17–18, 225–226.

9   The tun of wine endured as the unit of customhouse measure (as distinguished from wine measure); and prisage law, as had the regulation of 1130, "everywhere distinguishes the cargo before and behind the mast"; Bateson, "London Municipal Collection," p. 496. Hale concurs in "Concerning the Customs of Goods," in *Collection of Tracts*, ed. Hargrave, p. 120. See also Thomas Madox, *The History and Antiquities of the Exchequer of the Kings of England . . .* , 2nd edn, 2 vols (London, 1769), I, 765.
    For examples of the continued use of this distinction, see *British Borough Charters*, 1042–1216, ed. Adolphus Ballard (Cambridge, Eng., 1913), p. 235 (Dublin, 1192); [GB,

case. The ceol and the hulc seem to have changed in size enough during the twelfth century to have warranted a change in the prisage laws.

What little information exists on the nature of the ceol and the hulc would confirm that the change in the wine prisage regulations occurred at the same time as a change in the size of these ships. The hulc originated as a small sailing vessel used in local river and coastal trade. It was simply rigged, probably having no more than the almost universal single mast stepped amidships setting a square sail.[10] The earliest references to the ceol show it to have been distinctly different both in its mode of propulsion – it could use both oar and sail – and in its size – it was considerably larger than the hulc. The ceol mentioned in the regulation of 1130 appears to have been a large model of the Scandinavian long ship adapted to commerce.[11]

◆ ◆ ◆ ◆ ◆

The difference in type between hulc and ceol resembles most strongly a distinction fundamental to all Western maritime development, one that can be traced as far back as 2000 BC and that the Venetians maintained in the early Renaissance.

From the time of the Phoenicians, ships had been divided into long ships and round ships. Long ships were equipped with oars, round ships were dependent entirely on sails, so that in general this distinction was the same as that between oarships and sailing vessels, and that between warship and merchantmen.[12]

PRO], *Calendar of Documents Preserved in France Illustrative of the History of Great Britain and Ireland . . . A.D. 918–1206*, by J[ohn] Horace Round (London, 1899), p. 36 (Rouen, 1199); Hale, op. cit., p. 117 (London, 1234); Madox, op. cit., I, 770 (Cinque Ports, 1278); and those quoted in Hall, *History of the Custom-Revenue*, II, 96n., one dating from 1245 and the other from the reign of Queen Elizabeth I.

10 See the discussion later in this chapter.

11 See the discussion later in this chapter. For a more recent and intriguing variation on my reading of the evidence, see Roald Morcken, *Langskip, knaar or kogge: Nye synspunkter på sagatidens skipsbygging i Norge og Nordeuropa*, 2nd edn, rev. (Bergen, 1983).

12 Frederic Chapin Lane, *Venetian Ships and Shipbuilders of the Renaissance* (Baltimore, 1934), pp. 2–3. See also, Romola Anderson and R[oger] C. Anderson, *The Sailing-Ship, Six Thousand Years of History*, [new edn] (New York, 1963), pp. 28–29, 48. Compare, in general, Richard W. Unger, *The Ship in the Medieval Economy, 600–1600* (London, [1980]).

The Greeks regularly distinguished between ναῦσ μακρά and στρογγύλη ναῦσ. Herodotus, *Historiae*, I, 163; Xenophon, *Hellenica*, V, i, 21; Theophrastus, *Historia plantorum*, V, vii, 1. Sometimes they talked instead in terms of ναῦσ μακρά and ὁλκάς. Appianus, of Alexandria, "De Bellis Civilibus," II, 54, in *Appiani historia Romana*, ed. Ludwig Mendelssohn, 2 vols (Leipzig, 1879–1881), II, 20, n. 11. Latin writers kept this same dichotomy between warships and merchantmen, calling the former *navis longa* and the latter *navis oneraria*; Caesar, *De bello Gallico*, IV, 22. See the discussion of this distinction by Johannes Guiliemus Schefferus in his "De varietate navium dissertatio," in Jacobus Gronovius, *Thesaurus Graecarum antiquitatum . . .*, 12 vols in 13 pts (Leiden, 1697–1702), XI, 771–772.

The differences between the Phoenician warship and merchant ship of 700 BC and between the Athenian war and merchant vessels of 500 BC are readily apparent in figs 10 and 11 of plate 2, and figs 17 and 18 of plate 4 in Cecil Torr, *Ancient Ships* (Cambridge,

The relevance of this distinction becomes pronounced when we realize that, the territory of the Veneti was one of the places where the Phoenicians used to come for tin, and Cornwall was another. There must have been plenty of opportunity for both Veneti and Britons to examine Phoenician ships, and after once grasping the principles of strong wooden shipbuilding they would have gone on building in the same way after the Phoenicians had disappeared.[13] Both Caesar and Tacitus testify in their descriptions of the ships of the Northern European tribes that they apparently did just so, the former's great detail indicative of his surprise and interest.[14] Their contact with Roman shipbuilding methods at the beginning of the Christian era would thus seem only to have strengthened patterns with which the peoples of Northern Europe were already familiar.[15] The ceol and the hulc, while

Eng., 1894). Note that with the ancients the variation was not so much one of the shape of the hull as it was motive power and function.

Jacques Heers discusses these two historically distinct forms of vessels as indicative, in a later era, of two kinds of traffic in the Mediterranean. Heers, "Types de navires et spécialisation des trafics en Méditerranée à la fin du Moyen Âge," in [Colloque International d'Histoire Maritime, 2nd, 1957, Paris], *Le Navire et l'économie maritime du Moyen Âge au XVIIIe siècle principalement en Méditerranée*, ed. Michel Mollat (Paris, 1958), pp. 107–117, especially p. 109.

13 Anderson and Anderson, *The Sailing-Ship*, pp. 62 (quotation), 64–65. Compare Sven Axel Anderson, *Viking Enterprise*, Columbia University Studies in History, Economics and Public Law, no. 424 (New York, 1936), pp. 24, 61–62. Concerning the Phoenician trade with Western Europe, see P. Bosch-Gompera, "Ph[ax]eniciens et Grecs dans l'Extrême-Occident," *La Nouvelle Clio: Revue Mensuelle de la Découverte Historique*, III (Oct.–Dec. 1959), 282–283; Richard Henning, *Terrae Incognitae: Eine Zusammenstellung und kritische Bewertung der wichtigsten vorcolombischen Entdeckungsreisen an Hand der darüber vorliegenden Originalberichte*, 2nd edn, rev., 4 vols (Leiden, 1944–1950), I, 96–107; and the discussion in Donald [B.] Harden, *The Phoenicians* (London, 1962), pp. 170–171, and the map on pp. 172–173. See also Fridtjof Nansen, *In Northern Mists: Arctic Exploration in Early Times*, trans. Arthur G. Chater, 2 vols (London, 1911), I, 21–42, 241–248.

14 Caesar, *De bello Gallico*, III, 13, reported the ships to have been less deep than his and with tall bows and sterns in order the better to sail out into the stormy Channel. They were stoutly built and used strong sails of skins or leather. Tacitus, *Germania*, XLIV, described the ships of the Suiones (Scandinavians) as propelled exclusively by oars, double-ended, and capable of being rowed in either direction. See Christian Karl Barth, *Teutschlands Urgeschichte*, 2 vols (Bayreuth and Hof, 1817–1820), II, 288–291; A[ugustin] Jal, *Archéologie navale*, 2 vols (Paris, 1840), I, 121–126; and George H. Boehmer, "Prehistoric Naval Architecture of the North of Europe," in *Report of the United States National Museum . . . of the Smithsonian Institution for . . . 1891*, vol. II of the *Annual Report of the Board of Regents of the Smithsonian Institution . . . for . . . 1891*, [US, Congress, 52nd Cong., 1st Sess., House Miscellaneous Documents, vol. no. 44, doc. no. 344, pt ii, Serial Set no. 3002] (Washington, DC, 1892), pp. 553–554. The ships that the army of Germanius used in AD 15 were both sailing ships and oared vessels, sharp prowed, wide decked, and had flat bottoms; Tacitus, *Annales*, II, 23. A modern edition of the Jal dictionary has been underway for the last quarter-century. See A[ugustin] Jal, *Nouveau glossaire nautique*, new edn, [ed. Michel Mollat], in progress (Paris and The Hague, 1970 to date).

15 Anderson and Anderson, *The Sailing-Ship*, p. 62. The indirect influence of the example of the Phoenicians and others upon Northern European shipbuilding practices seems not to have been the only way in which these peoples had knowledge of ships and the sea.

representing adaptations to local conditions and materials, grew from a much older tradition influenced directly by Mediterranean practices: hence the similarities in the configurations of these vessels and those of the Mediterranean. The twelfth-century ceol and hulc appear to have been long ship and round ship respectively.

The post-twelfth-century world saw a remarkable change in the mercantile shipping of Northern Europe with the development of large sailing vessels and all that went with them. Less often mentioned, but also occurring at this time, was the disappearance from these same waters of the large oared merchant vessel. Within two centuries the only trace that can be found of the ceol and the hulc are two vessels similar in name only. The fourteenth-century hulk was a ship whose very name connoted unusually large size,[16] while the keel of the Tyne and Newcastle varieties resembled, in its dependence on both oars and sail for motive power, the ceol in miniature.[17] In size the two had precisely traded places.

◆ ◆ ◆ ◆ ◆

Saxon folklore states that they were originally seafaring men themselves and there is both linguistic and historical evidence to lend credence to these traditions. We are told that the tribe was originally part of the army of Alexander the Great and that, at his death, they all set out in their ships, landing near the mouth of the Elbe River, where they met and conquered the Thuringians using their single-edged swords or "sax" (in the language of the Thuringians), whence they got their name. [Jakob Ludwig Karl Grimm and Wilhelm Karl Grimm], *Deutsche sagen,* ed. Herman [Friedrich] Grimm, 3rd edn, 2 vols in 1 pt (Berlin, 1891), pp. 410–413; *Das Annolied,* XXI, lines 321–346, ed. Max Roediger, in *Monumenta Germaniae historica ... scriptorum qui vernacula lingua usi sunt: Deutsche Chroniken und andere Geschichtsbucher des Mittelalters,* vol. I, pt ii (Hanover, 1895), p. 122; Widukind, von Korvey, *Widukindi rei gestae Saxonicae,* I, c. 2–7, ed. Georg Waitz, in *Monumenta Germaniae historica ..., scriptores rerum Germanicorum* (Hanover, 1839), III, 417–419. In the light of this tradition it is interesting to note that "ceol" was a Saxon word and that the ships in which this migration of the Saxons is said to have taken place were called, in the 12th century, *kelen.* [Eike, von Repgow], *Sachsenspiegel: Landrecht,* III, 44, 2, ed. Karl August Eckhardt, *Monumenta Germaniae historica ..., fontes juris Germanici antiqui,* n.s., vol. I, pt i, 2nd edn (Göttingen, [1955]), pp. 230–231. See the discussion later in this chapter of the Greek κέλης. Moreover, Tacitus, *Germania,* IX, talks of the worship by part of the Suevi (Saxons) of Isis, the Egyptian goddess of motherhood and fertility, which he notes as obviously being a "peregrino sacro." The specific object of this worship was "in modum liburnae," that is, fashioned like a *liburna* or light galley (see the discussion later in this chapter). The Roman *liburna* and the Greek κέλης resembled each other greatly. Concerning this worship, see Jakob [Ludwig Karl] Grimm, *Teutonic Mythology,* ed. and trans. James Steven Stallybrass, 4 vols (London, 1882–1888), I, 105, 257–265.

16 [Hazel] Dorothy Burwash, *English Merchant Shipping, 1460–1540* (Toronto, 1947), pp. 135–136. See also *The Oxford English Dictionary: Being a Corrected Re-Issue ... of A New English Dictionary on Historical Principles,* ed. James A[ugustus] H[enry] Murray *et al.,* 10 vols in 13 pts (Oxford, 1933), V, 441.

17 The keel is discussed by, among others, Burwash, *English Merchant Shipping,* pp. 139–140; G[eoffrey] S. Laird Clowes, *British Fishing and Coastal Craft: Historical Review and Descriptive Catalogue* (London, 1937), pp. 15–17, 21, 24, 28; and H. R. Viall, "Tyne Keels," *MM,* XXVIII (Apr. 1942), 160–162.

Hulc was a name of ancient origin and into the twelfth century AD it seems always to have been predicated of a small merchant ship. The Greek ὁλκάς (holkas) was a ship of burden, apparently, so the name would indicate, one that could be pulled along.[18] The widespread use of the word, practically unchanged over distance or time in a variety of tongues, argues strongly for a continuity in function as well, but what form it took, in Northern Europe in the Middle Ages, no one has said. An Anglo-Saxon vocabulary of the eleventh century offers minimal help by translating the Latin *liburna* as hulc.[19] The *liburna* gained fame and acceptance in the Roman Empire after the battle of Actium in 31 BC was supposedly won for Augustus by the timely intervention of his Liburnian auxiliaries in their powerful yet easily handled ships.[20] It was the ideas of manageability and maneuverability that the language attached to the word *liburna*,[21] and it was in this sense that the name must have been applied to the Northern European hulc.[22] Jal recorded that the hulc was at first a simple small coasting and river boat[23] apparently widely used in what is today Northern France and the Low Countries. It would seem, from the meaning of its name in the Germanic tongues, to have developed from nothing more than a hollowed-out log.[24]

18 Herodotus, *Historiae*, III, 135, VII, 25, 137; Thucydides, *De bello Peloponnesiaco*, VII, 7. The ὁλκός (holkos) was an instrument that dragged or hauled and the ὁλκοί (holkoi [plural of holkos]) were specifically machines for hauling ships on land. Compare ἕλκω, to drag or to draw. See Thucydides, op. cit., III, 15, for ὁλκοί, and Herodotus, op. cit., II, 154. For the ὁλκάς, see also n. 12 of this chapter.

19 Printed in Thomas Wright, *Anglo-Saxon and Old-English Vocabularies*, 2nd edn, ed. Richard Paul Wülcker, 2 vols (London, 1884), I, 287. Compare ibid., I, 181. See Torr, *Ancient Ships*, pp. 16–17; and Heinrich Schnepper, *Die Namen der Schiffe und Schiffsteile in Altenglischen: Eine kulturgeschichtlich-etymologische Untersuchung* (Kiel, 1908), pp. 18, 43–44.

20 Vegetius, who wrote at the end of the 4th century AD, tells this story; *Flavi Vegeti Renati epitoma rei militari*, IV, 33, ed. Carl Lang, 2nd edn (Leipzig, 1885), p. 151. He described the ship as a quinquereme (ibid., IV, 37, p. 153), hardly to be thought of as a light, fast sailing ship. Nevertheless G[eoffrey] S. Laird Clowes, *Sailing Ships: Their History and Development as Illustrated by the Collection of Ship-Models in the Science Museum*, 5th edn (London, 1932), pt i, p. 20, notes that:

> an interesting suggestion which [h]as recently been put forward is that the additional power of a Roman quinquereme was obtained by applying a second man to each of the oars of the two upper tiers of a trireme, and that this ... arrangement ... was responsible for the great improvement in speed and lightness of the Liburnian galleys of the last century B.C. over their predecessors.

See also Schefferus, "De varitate navium," pp. 782–783; Lionel Casson, *The Ancient Mariners: Seafarers and Sea Fighters of the Mediterranean in Ancient Times* (New York, 1959), pp. 201, 213–214; and R[oger] C. Anderson, Oared *Fighting Ships from Classical Times to the Coming of Steam* (London, 1962), pp. 31–36.

21 Caesar, *De bello civili*, III, 9; Tacitus, *Germania*, IX.

22 Joseph Bosworth, *An Anglo-Saxon Dictionary*, ed. T[homas] Northcote Toller, 4 vols (Oxford, 1882–1898), p. 565.

23 Jal, *Archéologie navale*, I, 126–128. See also Fréderic Godefroy, *Dictionnaire de l'ancienne langue française et tous ses dialectes du IXe au XVe siècle*, 10 vols (Paris, 1881–1902), IV, 532.

24 A[ugustin] Jal, *Glossaire nautique: Répertoire polyglotte de termes de marine anciens et modernes* (Paris, 1848), pp. 828, 831, 837. Compare Pliny the Elder, *Naturalis Historia*, XVI, 76.

Higher sides were added, and a sail, and the river boat ventured out to sea.[25] Its employment in the English wine trade would have been a natural extension of its coasting duties, while a further increase in size to be better able to navigate the Channel was a logical step as well. In Northern Europe the hulc continued to grow to form a part of the maritime tradition from which sprang the trading vessels of the late Middle Ages.[26] In the twelfth century, however, it seems clear that this transformation was just beginning.

In the prisage regulation of 1130 the distinction is stated in terms of the ceol and the "hulc u altre nef," and this suggests the motive power of the hulc. The nef or "*navis* is a sailing ship, pure and simple."[27] In other words, the nef or navis depended on the wind to fill its sail or sails and to move it along, and it thus had no oars or only the sweeps common to all sailing ships. The inclusion of the hulc as another ship would substantiate the implicit assumption of Jal that the hulc was primarily dependent on the wind, especially since, as shown above, a distinction on the basis of motive power was a continuing one.[28] The hulc, then, in the twelfth century, would appear to have been a small sailing ship, with a high bow and stern and single square sail rigged to a mast amidships. The precise difference between the hulc and the other sailing ships is not readily apparent, although there is good reason to believe that the hulc was already larger than the more local coastal vessels as it would have had to have been to cross the Channel.[29]

The identification, in the later Middle Ages, of the hulk with the Hanseatic merchant ship, the cog,[30] suggests some profitable considerations about the relationship between the hulc and other continental vessels of its period. The Rhine, the Lorrainers' river route to the North Sea, opened out onto it

---

25 See Vogel, *Geschichte der deutschen Seeschiffahrt*, pp. 111–112.

26 Jal, *Archéologie navale*, I, 129, and his reference to Pieter Marin, *Groot Nederdiutsch en Fransch Woordenboek . . . Grand dictionnaire hollandais & français*, 3rd edn (Dordrecht and Amsterdam, 1752). Compare Paul Heinsius, "Dimensions . . . des 'Koggen'," pp. 7–19, and his *Das Schiff der hansischen Frühzeit*, Quellen und Darstellungen zur Hansischen Geschichte, n.s., vol. XII, 2nd edn, rev. (Cologne, 1986), pp. 212–225.
     An indication of this growth is to be found in the use of modifying adjectives of size with hulc during the centuries immediately following. For instance, see the expanded version of Vegetius, *De Rei Militari*, translated into English in 1408, in which the writer inserted in bk 4, chap. 39, a list of ships including "hevy hulkes." Royal MS 18 A. XII, fol. 119r, and as noted in [Galfridus], *Promptorium parvulorum sive clericorum, lexicon anglo-latinum princeps . . .*, ed. Albert Way, Royal Historical Society, Camden Society, [o.s.], nos 25, 54, 89, 3 vols (London, 1843–1865), I, 252, n. 5. There are examples of a similar contemporary usage in French; Godefroy, *Dictionnaire de l'ancienne langue française*, IV, 532.

27 F[rederick] W. Brooks, *The English Naval Forces, 1199–1272* (London, [1932]), p. 71. See Jal, *Glossaire nautique*, p. 1061. Compare Heers, "Types de navires," p. 109.

28 Brooks, *English Naval Forces*, p. 71.

29 The groundage duty of the year 1000 would suggest such a difference in size. See the discussion earlier in this chapter.

30 Heinsius noted that the two words were often used interchangeably; "Dimensions . . . des 'Koggen'," p. 19, and *Das Schiff der hansischen Frühzeit*, p. 202. See also A[nton] W. Brøgger and Haakon Shetelig, *The Viking Ships: Their Ancestry and Evolution*, [trans. Katherine John] (Oslo, [1951]), p. 237.

through the territory of the Frisians.[31] These people were for several centuries *the* merchants of Western Europe, the *gens durissima maritima*.[32] Although they declined in importance after the tenth century, their period of decline was coextensive with that of the rise of the Rhenish Germans. In many ways the Frisians lived on in the Lorrainer, for the Lorraine merchants did not fail to learn from the past masters. In these ways, at least, the Frisians have been seen to be the forerunners of the Hanseatic merchants.[33] The earliest and perhaps the most distinctive of the Frisian characteristics, and the one that gave them preeminence in trade, was their mastery of the sea.[34] Part of this mastery stemmed from the special type of ship that they evolved and that was particularly well suited to commerce – the cog.[35] Not much is known in detail

31 Hermann Bächtold, *Der norddeutsche Handel im 12. und beginnenden 13. Jahrhundert,* Abhandlungen zur Mittleren und Neueren Geschichte, vol. XXI, ed. Georg v[on] Below, Heinrich Finke, and Friedrich Meinecke (Berlin and Leipzig, 1910), pp. 31, 137–142, 225–239. Compare H[enri] Pirenne, "Un Grand Commerce d'exportation au Moyen Âge: Le vins de France," *Annales d'Histoire Économique et Sociale,* V (May 1933), 231–232; and Vogel, *Geschichte der deutschen Seeschiffahrt,* pp. 103 ff.
32 The influence of the Frisian trader on early medieval history has not often been fully appreciated. For the best 20th-century discussion in English, see Dirk Jellema, "Frisian Trade to 1100" (Ph.D. diss., University of Wisconsin, 1951), and the article based on that dissertation, "Frisian Trade in the Dark Ages," *Speculum,* XXX (Jan. 1955), 15–36. Compare Hans Wilkens, "Zur Geschichte des niederländischen Handels im Mittelalter," *Hansische Geschichtsblätter,* XIV (1908), 295–356, and XV (1909), 125–203; Elis Wadstein, "Friserns och forntida handelsvägar i Norden," *Götesborgs Kungl[ig] Vetenskaps- och Vitterhets-samhälles Handlingar,* 4th ser., XXI–XXII (1918–1919), 1–[25]; and, especially, Barbara [C.] Rohwer, *Der friesische Handel im frühen Mittelalter* (Leipzig, 1937).
33 Jellema, "Frisian Trade to 1100," pp. 143–144, and Siegfried Mews, *Gotlands Handel und Verkehr bis zum Auftreten der Hansen (12. Jahrhundert)* (Berlin, 1937), p. 27. Compare Rohwer, *Der friesische Handel,* pp. 83–102 passim.
     This is a logical development when it is appreciated that the Frisians had long maintained mercantile control over the Rhine and that even as late as the 12th century they still had colonies of merchants in the cities of the Rhine valley; H[uibert] A. Poelman, *Geschiedenis van den Handel van Noord-Nederland gedurende het Merowinginsche en Karolingische Tijdperk* (The Hague, 1908), pp. 70–71. According to Jellema, op. cit., p. 74, Frisian control over the trade of the Rhine "was the basis of their prosperity." Compare Bächtold, *Der norddeutsche Handel im 12. und 13. Jahrhundert,* pp. 30–31; and Rohwer, op. cit., p. 16: "Das Rückgrat des friesischen Handels war der Rhein ..."
34 They were well known as the best sailors. Vogel, *Geschichte der deutschen Seeschiffahrt,* pp. 89–90. The word "Frisian" in fact became synonymous with "sailor"; L[eslie G.] Whitbread, "The 'Frisian Sailor' Passage in Old English Gnomic Verses," *Review of English Studies,* [o.s.], XXII (1946), 215–219. This passage can be found most easily in *Maxims I,* lines 94–106, *The Exeter Book,* ed. George Philip Krapp and Elliott Van Kirk Dobbie, vol. III of *The Anglo-Saxon Poetic Records: A Collective Edition,* ed. George Philip Krapp and Elliott Van Kirk Dobbie (New York, 1936), p. 160.
35 The best discussion of the cog is that by Ole Crumlin-Pedersen, "Cog-Kogge-Kaag: Træk af en frisisk skibstypes historie," *Årbog Handels- og Søfartsmuseet på Kronborg,* [XXIV] (1965), 81–144. He describes the remains of several that archaeologists have found. Compare the discussions in Poelman, *Geschiedenis van den Handel van Noord-Nederland,* pp. 156–160, and Vogel, "Zur nord- und westeuropäischen Seeschiffahrt im früheren Mittelalter," *Hansische Geschichtsblätter,* [XXXV] (1907), 190–191, and Vogel, *Geschichte der deutschen Seeschiffahrt,* pp. 93–94. See also Crumlin-Pedersen, "En Kogge i Roskilde," ibid., *Årbog Handels- og Søfartsmuseet på Kronborg,* [XXV] (1966), 39–57; and *Die Hanse-Kogge von 1380,* ed. Klaus-Peter Kiedel and Uwe Schnall (Bremerhaven, 1982).

about their ships, even this name being a matter of controversy among scholars,[36] but there is every reason to believe that the Lorrainers in their borrowings from the Frisians adopted their ship as well. The cog of the Hanseatic cities made its first recorded appearance in the sources of the late twelfth and

That it was a distinctly different type is attested to by the passage from the Anglo-Saxon Chronicle that tells that the ships built by King Alfred were neither Danish nor Frisian; *The Anglo-Saxon Chronicle: According to the Several Original Authorities*, ed. and trans. Benjamin Thorpe, [Rolls Ser., no. 23], 2 vols (London, 1861), I, 176–177 (896). Something of its distinctiveness and its flexibility can be appreciated in two contemporary accounts of the ship. In the "Life and Miracles of St Goar," the ship of the Frisian merchant is described as being moved upstream on the Rhine by means of ropes by which it was pulled along from the shore. The passage would seem to date from the last quarter of the 8th century and the ship mentioned might only have been a small version of the cog, but the value of a ship that could be towed when the wind died down or the river became tricky and dangerous can easily be understood. Wandalbert, of Prüm, *Vita [et miracula] Sancti Goaris,* c. 32, 33, in *Patrologiae cursus completus . . . series Latinae,* ed. J[acques] P[aul] Migne, 221 vols in 222 pts (Paris, 1844–1864), CXXI, cols 667–668.

When St Anskar sailed from Cologne in 826, he was accompanied by King Harold of Denmark who left his own ship, presumably an open Viking long ship, for that of St Anskar because of the comfortable accommodations it offered in the form of two closed cabins – "duae mansiunculae." St Anskar's ship had been given him at Cologne, and was most likely a Frisian cog. Rimbert, *Vita Anskari auctore Rimberto,* c. 7, ed. G[eorg] Waitz, *Scriptores rerum Germanicarum in usum scholarum ex Monumentis Germaniae historicis recusi,* [vol. 55] (Hanover, 1884), p. 29. Compare Poelman, op. cit., pp. 157–158, and Vogel, *Geschichte der deutschen Seeschiffahrt,* p. 94.

A certain adaptability and the existence of enclosed cabin spaces aboard ship mark the Frisian vessel. This second characteristic finds reinforcement in the etymology of the word cog (kogge) as Vogel outlines it (ibid., p. 93, n. 4) when he tells us that it meant a "gewölbtes Gefäß" – a closed container. It is this same characteristic that helps us to identify as a ship of Frisian design, the thing that is depicted in a 10th-century Anglo-Saxon riddle. The vessel is decked over and has a hatchway in the center of the deck. See [Franz Eduard Christoph] Dietrich, "Die Räthsel des Exeterbuchs: Würdingung, Läsing und Herstellung," *Zeitschrift für Deutsches Altertum,* XI (1859), 469–470. This is riddle no. 32 in *The Exeter Book,* ed. Krapp and Dobbie, pp. 196–197, 339.

The Frisian ships were portrayed on some of their coins. Sune Lindqvist, "Birkamynten," *Fornvännen: Meddelanden från K[ungliga] Vitterhets Historie och Antikvitets Akademien,* XXI (1926), 307–334, illustrates those found at the major Frisian Baltic port of Birka (Björkö, Sweden). See figs 205–208, 214, on p. 310, and fig. 217, p. 311. See also the Frisian coins from Duurstede and Quentovic that are described and illustrated in [Jean] Maurice Prou, *Les Monnaies carolingiennes* (Paris, 1896), p. 11, nos 63 (plate II) and 64, and p. 30, no. 187 (plate V), and the references listed by Crumlin-Pedersen, "Cog-Kogge-Kaag," pp. 121–122, and his illustrations in fig. 22. For a comparison of these with the long ship as represented on coins of that same era, see Lindqvist, op. cit., figs 205 and 215, p. 310.

36 Vogel, *Geschichte der deutschen Seeschiffahrt,* pp. 93–94, calls it a cog because he found this word used in a variety of forms in 9th- and 10th-century documents in reference to the ship of the Frisians. As such, Vogel is merely the most elaborately supported position of the numerous authors who say the same thing. For these others, see the summary of their statements contained in Heinsius, *Das Schiff der hansischen Frühzeit,* pp. 5 ff., who says, quite dismissively, that they are all wrong (ibid., pp. 69–71). He argued the same position in "Dimensions . . . des 'Koggen'," pp. 22–23. His challenge is weak and unconvincing, however. See also Rohwer, *Der friesische Handel in Frühen Mittelalter,* pp. 35–38; Vogel's review *of Die Entwicklung der wichtigsten Schiffstypen bis ins 19. Jahrhundert,* by Bernard Hagedorn, *Hansische Geschichtsblätter,* XX (1914), 374–375; [Johann Heinrich] Dietrich Schäfer, *Die Hansestädte und König Waldemar [IV] von Dänemark: Hansische Geschichte bis 1376* (Jena, 1879), p. 301; and, especially, the comments on Heinsius's

early thirteenth centuries,[37] and all indications point to the conclusion that it was, again, as in many things Hanseatic, an adaptation from the earlier Frisian model.[38] It seems entirely likely, therefore, that the hulc of the Lorraine merchants mentioned in the wine prise regulation was the early twelfth-century version of the Frisian–Hanseatic merchant ship, the cog.[39]

paper by [Louis] Guilleux La Roërie, in *Le Navire et l'économie maritime du Nord de l'Europe*, ed. Mollat, pp. 20–21. (For the author of these comments, a distinguished writer on maritime matters but one about whom there is some bibliographical confusion, see H[ilary] P. Mead, "Obituary: Captaine de Corvette de Reserve Louis Guilleux," *MM*, XLVII [May 1961], 160.) B[ernard] H. Slicher van Bath, "The Economic and Social Conditions in the Frisian Districts from 900 to 1500," *Afdeling Agrarische Geschiedenis Bijdragen*, XIII (1965), 124–125, gives Heinsius rather equivocal support but Crumlin-Pedersen, "Cog-Kogge-Kaag," pp. 82–85, dismisses Heinsius's ideas as utterly untenable.

37 According to Heinsius, *Das Schiff der hansischen Frühzeit*, p. 71. Compare Heinsius, "Dimensions . . . des 'Koggen'," pp. 9–10, where he cites the word as first appearing in an early German glossary that he dates to that period and that is printed in *Die althochdeutschen Glossen*, ed. [Emil] Elias [von] Steinmeyer and Eduart Sievers, 5 vols (Berlin, 1879–1922), III, 163. Steinmeyer and Sievers argued, however, that this glossary could have been produced any time after the year 1007 (ibid., p. 712).

38 Vogel, "Zur nord- und westeuropäischen Seeschiffahrt," p. 191, and *Geschichte der deutschen Seeschiffahrt*, pp. 93–94, and Brøgger and Shetelig, *Viking Ships*, [trans. John], pp. 236–237.

39 The conclusion can only be stated as "likely" because the evidence as presented is simply circumstantial. Two further points can be made that are also suggestive of this relationship but that still fail to take this hypothesis out of the realm of probability – although one of great probability.

The mark of the cog as a closed, cabined vessel helps to explain, if the cog and the hulc are the same type of ship, another use of the Anglo-Saxon word "hulc." Throughout this period "hulc" not only denoted the ship but meant as well "hut," "shed," or "cabin" (Bosworth, *Anglo-Saxon Dictionary*, ed. Toller, p. 565). It would seem that the two meanings shared a common word because they shared a common connotation – the idea of enclosed, protected space, be it on land or sea. This dual use of the word duplicates exactly that of the German word "kogge" that Vogel said also meant both the ship and a closed container. See the discussion above in n. 35 of this chapter.

Again, the mark of the cog as a towable vessel adds weight to our argument. Vogel states, *Geschichte der deutschen Seeschiffahrt*, pp. 111–112, that the hulc of the wine prise regulation was indigenous to the Rhine valley. He makes a great deal of its ability to be towed up-river and he tentatively suggests that it might well have evolved from the Rhenish towboat of Roman times. As we have already seen the Frisian merchant's ship being towed up the Rhine, the identity of cog and hulc seems all too apparent. For Roman river craft, see Lionel Casson, "Harbour and River Boats of Ancient Rome," *The Journal of Roman Studies*, LV (pts i and ii, 1965), 31–39, esp. plate III, 2. See also Hermann Aubin, "Der Rheinhandel in römischer Zeit," *Bonner Jahrbücher: Jahrbücher des Vereins von Altertumsfreunden im Rheinlande*, CXXX (1925), 1–37. Compare the vessel shown in plate 5, "Carriage of wine on the Douro, c. 1780," of H[arold] E. S. Fisher, *The Portugal Trade: A Study of Anglo-Portuguese Commerce, 1700–1770* (London, 1971), between pp. 78–79.

Vogel, however, unequivocally denies any such possibility and announces that "der 'hulc' [ist] ursprünglich . . . deutlich vom friesische 'Koggen' unterschieden," arguing that the hulk was distinguished from the cog up to the early 14th century and that only in the Hanse era did the two become identified (op. cit., p. 112). As evidence for this contention he cites an instance in 1315 in which the Frisian and the Lower Rhenish naval contributions to the war effort of William III of Holland were called by different names – the former's ships, cogs, the latter's, hulks. The very possible explanation that these names might well have been local words for the same ship goes unanswered and, apparently, unappreciated. He offers no other evidence.

If the hulc of the wine prise was the twelfth-century cog, what then was the ceol? It is just possible that its nature can also be established by comparing what we know of it with other vessels in the contemporary mercantile world.

The many occurrences of the word "ceol" in reference to a ship in Anglo-Saxon literature leave little doubt that the vessel so denoted was an oared ship of the Viking type. This is especially true of the examples from prose writings, but even most poetic usages of the word are sufficiently specific to support explicitly this contention.

All the accounts of the original arrival of the Saxons in Britain in AD 449 call the ships of Hengest and Horsa either ceols or long ships. The vernacular Peterborough or Laudian manuscript of the Anglo-Saxon Chronicle, cited as "E," records the coming of the Saxons in three "ceolom hider to Brytene." The Cottonian manuscript, designated as "F," translates this phrase as three "langan scipan."[40] Gildas, who set down his account within two centuries of the event, obviously had reference to an old tradition when he very neatly made explicit the equating of long ship and ceol implied in the two versions of the Anglo-Saxon Chronicle by telling his readers that the invaders crossed the seas "tribus, ut lingua eius exprimitur, cyulis, nostra [lingua] longis navibus."[41] Nennius and William of Malmesbury, writing closer in time to 1130, used ceol in a variety of instances but with the same meaning of "long ship" being consistently apparent.[42]

The word ceol occurs even more frequently in Anglo-Saxon poetry than it does in prose, but here again the long ship can almost always be seen as the ship mentioned. The ship of Beowulf is called a ceol and the context provides sufficient clues to identify it with the Viking-type long ship. Once, for instance, the ship is beached in typical long ship fashion, and on another occasion the shields are described as set over the bulwarks as the Vikings are known to have done.[43] The Anglo-Saxon *Andreas*, based on the apocryphal *Acts of St Andrew*, refers continually to the ship in which Andrew is sailing as a ceol, but enough features of it are mentioned to recognize it as a long

40 *The Anglo-Saxon Chronicle*, ed. Thorpe, I, 19, 21 (449).
41 *Gildae sapientis de excidio et conquestu Britanniae, ac flebili castigatione in reges, princips, et sacerdotes epistola*, v. 23, in *Chronica Minora Saec. IV. V. VI. VIII.*, ed. Theodor Mommsen, vol. XIII of *Monumenta Germaniae historica . . ., auctores antiquissimi* (Berlin, 1898), III, pt i, p. 38. *The Old English Version of Bede's Ecclesiastical History of the English People*, ed. and trans. Thomas Miller, Early English Text Society, nos 95, 96, 110, 111, 4 vols (London, 1890–1898), I, 15 [12], pp. 50–51, has "thrim myclum scysum."
42 Nennius, *Historia Brittonum . . .*, c. 19, 20, 31, 37, 38, in *Chronica minora saec. IV. V. VI. VIII.*, ed. Theodor Mommsen, vol. XIII of *Monumenta Germaniae historica . . ., auctores antiquissimi* (Berlin, 1898), III, pt i, pp. 162, 171, 177, 180; William of Malmesbury, *Willelmi Malmesbiriensis monachi de gestis regum Anglorum libri qunique: Historiae novellae libri tres*, I, v, xvi, ed. William Stubbs, [Rolls Ser., no. 90], 2 vols (London, 1887–1889), I, 8, 19.
43 See lines 38, 238, 1806, and 1912 of *Beowulf*, in *Beowulf and Judith*, ed. Elliott Van Kirk Dobbie, vol. IV *Anglo-Saxon Poetic Records*, ed. Krapp and Dobbie (New York, 1953), pp. 4, 10, 55, 59.

ship.[44] The same can also be said of the ceol mentioned in *The Whale*; it is, at least, described in the same terms as the ship of Andrew.[45] Other poems employ the word as well.[46] Poetic usage is not so vital to the argument as is prose usage, however, because of the potential in poetry of a less precise, poetical license in the use of words. Nevertheless, even if all of the instances cited here from the poetry of the period were vague and valueless, which they are not, the contention could still stand on the very pointed occurrences of ceol in prose literature alone. The ship denoted by the usage of the Anglo-Saxon word "ceol" was clearly a long ship of the Scandinavian variety.

The ceol of the wine prisage regulation was a merchantman, however, and, therefore, appears to have been a Viking-type long ship adapted for mercantile use. The resulting suggestion of a deviation from the historic distinction between merchant ship as round ship and long ship as warship tends to question the accuracy of the interpretation of the evidence offered above. Yet, archaeological discoveries over the last century and a half support Scandinavian literary evidence that there did, in fact, exist a commercial variant on the Viking long ship. The *hafskip*, or "ocean ship," the generic name for this variant, maintained the general characteristics of the *langskip*, but possessed distinct differences.[47] Its most important quality, greater

---

44 *Andreas,* lines 222, 253, 256, 273, 310, 349, 361, 380, 450, 555, 854, 899, in *The Vercelli Book,* ed. George Philip Krapp, vol. II of *Anglo-Saxon Poetic Records,* ed. Krapp and Dobbie (New York, 1932), pp. 9–13, 14, 18, 26, 28.

45 *The Whale,* line 17, in *The Exeter Book,* ed. Krapp and Dobbie, p. 172.

46 See, Cynewulf's *Christ,* lines 851 and 862, *The Seafarer,* line 5, *Maxims I,* line 96, and *The Riddles,* no. 3, line 28, no. 18, line 4, no. 33, line 2, from *The Exeter Book,* ed. Krapp and Dobbie, pp. 26–27, 143, 160, 182, 189, 197; and Cynewulf's *Elene,* line 250, in *The Vercelli Book,* ed. Krapp, p. 72. "Ceol" can also be found in *The Meters of Boethius,* lines 11, 23, and 60, in *The Paris Psalter and the Meters of Boethius,* ed. George Philip Krapp, vol. V of *Anglo-Saxon Poetic Records,* ed. Krapp and Dobbie (New York, 1932), pp. 185, 193–194; and in *Maxims II,* line 24, in *The Anglo-Saxon Minor Poems,* ed. Elliott Van Kirk Dobbie, vol. VI of *Anglo-Saxon Poetic Records,* ed. Krapp and Dobbie (New York, 1942), p. 56. Compare, as well, the instances of its appearance in the contemporary glossaries assembled in Wright, *Anglo-Saxon and Old English Vocabularies,* ed. Wülcker, I, 12, 203, 205, 276, 363.

47 For a comparison of the *langskip* and the *hafskip*, see Vogel, "Zur nord- und westeuropäischen Seeschiffahrt," pp. 180–186. The three best examples of the *langskip* still in existence were uncovered from burial mounds in Scandinavia within forty years of one another: the Tune ship in 1867, the Gokstad ship in 1880, and the Oseberg ship in 1904. The three standard works on these ships are N[icolay] Nicolaysen, *Langskibet fra Gokstad ved Sandefjord/The Viking-Ship Discovered at Gokstad in Norway,* [trans. Thomas Krag] (Oslo, 1882); Haakon Shetelig, *Tuneskibet: [Skibsfundet paa nedre Haugen paa Rolvsøy, 1867],* Norske Oldfund, vol. II (Oslo, 1917); and *Osebergfundet,* ed. A[nton] W[ilhelm] Brøgger *et al.,* 5 vols (Oslo, 1917–1928). Most convenient and yet obviously authoritative is Brøgger and Shetelig, *Viking Ships,* [trans. John], pp. 104–183. The best pictorial compilation is Thorlief Sjøvold, *Vikingeskipne: En kort orientering on Tuneskipet, Gokstadskipet og Osebergskipet* ([Oslo, 1952]).

For the seminal study of medieval Scandinavian shipping and the source, directly or indirectly, of much of what has been written since, is N[icolaï] E. Tuxen, "De Nordiske Langskibe," *Aarbøger for Nordisk Oldkyndighed og Historie,* [2nd ser., I] (1886), pp. 49–134.

seaworthiness, was pointedly reflected in its name. Broader of beam than the *langskip*, drawing more water, and having a higher freeboard, the *hafskip* was much the better sailer in the open seas of the North Atlantic.[48] As with the *langskip*, the *hafskip* was clinker-built, double-ended, and had a large square sail hoisted on a yard on the mast amidships. By purpose and by design it was not primarily an oared vessel but on occasion, as in port and in helping the vessel to go about, its few oars on the small raised decks fore and aft were necessary and could be manned with effect. The cargo was stowed in the open hold in the center of the ship between these decks.[49] The earliest type of *hafskip*, the biggest in size, and the one most widely employed was the *knörr* (pl. *knerrir*).[50] It was in this ship that the Vikings sailed on their journeys of colonization and trade, as many of their settlements testify by their name: Knarrarsund, Knarrarnes, Knörr, Knarravath, and Knarareyrron on the Icelandic coast being several examples.[51] Every indication suggests that

48 A case in point would be the *hafskip* that outsailed three *langskip* in *Haralds Harthratha Saga*, xlv, in *Sögur Magnúsar konúgs Góda, Haralds konúngs Hardráda ok sona hans,* [ed. Thorgier Gudmundsson and Rasmus Kristian Rask], vol. VI of *Fornmanna Sögur, eptir gömlum handritum útgefnar ath tilhutun hins konúngliga Norræna fornfrætha félags,* 12 vols (Copenhagen, 1825–1837), p. 249. Compare G[eoffry] J. Marcus, "The Evolution of the Knörr," *MM,* XLI (May 1955), 119.

49 The *hafskip* is described by Vogel, "Zur nord- und westeuropäischen Seeschiffahrt," pp. 184–186, and p. 184, n. 1. See also Tuxen, "De Nordiske Langskibe," pp. 71–75 and elsewhere. Compare G[eoffry] J. Marcus, "The Navigation of the Norsemen," *MM,* XXXIX (May 1953), 112-113; Marcus, "The Evolution of the Knörr," p. 117; and Marcus, "The Norse Emigration to the Faeroe Islands," *English Historical Review,* LXXI (Jan. 1956), 60. See in addition the description in *Egils Saga Skallagrímssonar,* XVII, xiii–xv, ed. Finnur Jónsson, vol. III of *Altnordische Saga-Bibliothek,* ed. Gustaf Cederschiöld, Hugo Gering, and Eugen Mogk (Halle a.S., 1894), p. 53.
    Note the two obvious points of contrast with the hulc: the closed versus the open hold for carrying cargo; and the absence versus the presence of oars to supplement the sail as a source of motive power. The question of the function of the oars on board the *hafskip* has been discussed by several authors, with Marcus arguing (in the works just cited) that they were rarely used and Brøgger and Shetelig (*Viking Ships,* [trans. John], p. 236) emphasizing the essentially oared nature of the *hafskip*. See also, Vogel, loc. cit., and Tuxen, op. cit., pp. 110–111. The present writer would agree with Brøgger and Shetelig and with Tuxen that the important point is not whether the oars were in use rarely or frequently but that the crew would have had to have been at least of a size sufficient to row them. On both these matters, see the discussion below.

50 Vogel, "Zur nord- und westeuropäischen Seeschiffahrt," pp. 183–184; Tuxen, "De Nordiske Langskibe," p. 72; Brøgger and Shetelig, *Viking Ships,* [trans. John], pp. 234–235.
    The other type of *hafskip* contemporary with the *knörr* was the *byrding*. It was smaller than the *knörr* and was employed more in coastal waters, size seeming to having been the significant difference. See Vogel, op. cit., p. 184, n. 1, and Brøgger and Shetelig, op. cit., p. 236.

51 All of these names are found in the sagas; several survive in one form or another are still in use in modern Iceland. The identification of these several localities with their modern equivalents was accomplished by P[eter] E. Kristian Kålund, *Bidrag til en historisk-topografisk Beskrivelse af Island,* 2 vols (Copenhagen, 1877–1882), I, 178, 385, 413, 466, II, 123, 133 (there were two Knarrarnes). Compare Knarrevik, referred to by Færøyvik, "Leivder av eit kaupskip på Holmen, Bergenhus," p. 33.
    The often repeated (but groundless) statement that it was the *langskip* that sailed on these trips has been most effectively dispatched by Marcus, "Navigation of the Norsemen,"

the ceol of the wine prisage was a type of *hafskip*, most likely a *knörr*. The presumptive evidence of common development, appearance, and function is compelling if not conclusive.

Until relatively recently only scattered references in the Northern saga supplied any indication as to the precise nature of the *hafskip*. In the past sixty years archaeologists have completely changed this picture by uncovering the remains of several Scandinavian merchantmen. Seven of these can be mentioned but they vary in their state of preservation and the amount of detail that they supply to the archaeologist and the historian. There is, moreover, in one or two cases, a question as to their distinct mercantile character. The argument in most instances where there is doubt hinges both on the size of the remains and on certain peculiarities of construction.[52] As a group, these ships span the period from AD 800 to 1200, from the origin of the *hafskip* to its decline.

The hafskip is thought to have originated in the late eighth or early ninth century.[53] The Äskekärr ship, which comes from roughly this same period, would thus appear to be an example of the earliest form of this type. It was found at Äskekärr, on the Gäta River, in Sweden in 1933 and it measured about fifty-two and one-half feet (16 m) in length.[54] The ship discovered in Eltang Vig off Kolding Fjord Jutland, Denmark, has been shown to have been built in the tenth or early eleventh century. It was over thirty-nine feet long (12 m).[55] The two best preserved examples of the *hafskip* were found with several other ships in Roskilde Fjord, Zealand, Denmark, in 1957, and were recovered from the fjord floor almost intact in the summer of 1962. Ships I and III were unquestionably merchant vessels and they were both built in the first half of the eleventh century. Ship I, the larger of the two, was fifty-four feet (16.5 m) long, while Ship III measured nearly forty-four feet (13.5 m) in length. The open cargo space between the covered decks

---

p. 113, "Norse Emigration to the Faeroe Islands," p. 60, and "The Greenland Trade-Route," *EcHR*, 2nd ser., VII (Aug. 1954), 73–74.

52 See the discussions of the individual ships later in this chapter as well as Carl V. Sølver, "Rabaekroret," *Årbog Handels- og Søfartsmuseet på Kronborg*, [III] (1944), 108–118. An abridged translation of this article appeared as "The Rabaek Rudder," *MM*, XXXII (Apr. 1946), 115–120.

53 Vogel, "Zur nord- und westeuropäischen Seeschiffahrt," pp. 185, 182, n. 2. Compare Tuxen, "De Nordiske Langskibe," pp. 72, 75; and Marcus, "Evolution of the Knörr," pp. 119–120.

54 [Knut] Philibert Humbla, "Båtfyndet vid Äskekärr," *Göteborgs och Bohusläns Fornminnes Förenings Tidskrift*, 1934, pp. 1–21, and H. Thomasson, "Äskekärrsbåtens ålder," ibid., pp. 22–34. For purposes of comparison, the three long ships mentioned in n. 47 of this chapter measured in length as follows: Gokstad ship, 75ft. 6in. (23 m); Tune ship, 65 ft. 6in. (20 m); Oseberg ship, 72 ft. (22 m).

Olaf Olsen and Ole Crumlin-Pedersen, "The Skuldelev Ships: A Preliminary Report on Underwater Excavations in Roskilde Fjord, Zealand," *Acta Archeologia* [Copenhagen], XXIX (1958), 171–174, discusses several of the mid-20th century ship finds.

55 Sigvard Skov, "Et middelaldert skibsfund fra Eltang Vig," *Kuml: Årbog for Jysk Arkaeologisk Selskab*, [II] (1952), 65–83, and Olsen and Crumlin-Pedersen, "The Skuldelev Ships," p. 172 and n. 14.

fore and aft of Ship III was thirteen feet (4 m) long.[56] The date of the Galtabäck ship, uncovered at Galtabäck, near Varberg, Halland, Sweden, has been a matter of some controversy but radiocarbon analysis of the cattle-hair oakum used as caulking for the ship places it definitely in the eleventh or early twelfth century. The Galtabäck ship was some forty-six feet (14 m) long and the man who originally wrote about its discovery and helped in its initial reconstruction, Philbert Humbla, declared it a *byrding*.[57] On the other hand, the early twelfth-century merchantman dug up at Bergen, Norway, in 1948, was pronounced definitely a *knörr* by the author who told of its unearthing.[58] Although this is the ship closest in time to the ceol of the wine prisage regulation, little more than a few boards remain of the Bergen ship and we cannot learn much from it. The youngest of the *hafskip* to have been found is also the smallest. Ship I of those excavated at Kalmar, Sweden, in 1934, is thought to date from the middle of the thirteenth century and was only thirty-six feet (11 m) long. It is the least like the *hafskip* of the saga literature and might well have been a *busse*, the *hafskip* variety that is known to have displaced the *knörr* around this period, although Harald Åkerlund, the man who worked most on its restoration, thought it to have been a cog.[59] The former possibility is thought by this writer to be the more likely.

All totaled, these ships form a remarkable record of early Northern merchant shipping and they nicely complement the information in the sagas. The fact of their undeniable identification with the one English ship pictured

---

56 Olsen and Crumlin-Pedersen, "The Skuldelev Ships," pp. 161-175; Olsen and Crumlin-Pedersen, "The Viking Ships in Roskilde Fjord," *MM*, XLIX (Nov. 1963), 300–302; and Olaf Olsen and Ole Crumlin-Pedersen, "The Skuldelev Ships (II): A Report of the Final Underwater Excavations in 1959 and the Salvaging Operation in 1962," *Acta Archeologia* [Copenhagen], XXXVIII (1967), 73–174. See also Olaf Olsen, "Die Kaufschiffe der Wikingerzeit in Lichte des Schiffsfundes bei Skuldelev im Roskilde Fjord," *in Die Zeit der Stadtgründung im Ostseeraum,* [ed. Mårten Stenberger], Acta Visbyensia I: Visby-Symposiet für Historiska Vetenskapen, 1963 (Visby, 1965), pp. 20–34. Compare [Denmark, Nationalmuseet], *Vikingeskibene i Roskilde Fjord* (Copenhagen, 1963), and Eugene H. Palatsky, "Danish Viking Ships," *Expedition: The Bulletin of the University Museum of the University of Pennsylvania*, IV (Winter 1962), 40–43.
    On the basis of the interpretation suggested by Bernard Færøyvik, the 12th-century *knörr* described in chap. 14 of the *Kristni saga* as having "vij rúm ok XX" ("7 spaces and 20") measured about 69 ft. (21 m) long and had a cargo space between its two raised decks that was nearly 46 ft. (14 m) in length, which seems rather too long. See Færøyvik, "Leivder av eit kaupskip på Holmen, Bergenhus," *Bergens Sjøfartsmuseum Årshefte 1948*, p. 33, and the *Kristni saga* from *Biskupa Sögur, gefnar út af hinu Íeslenzka Bókmentafélagi,* [ed. Jón Sigurthsson and Guthgrandur Vigfússon], 2 vols (Copenhagen, 1856–1878), I, 30. In this regard, see Brøgger and Shetelig, *Viking Ships,* [trans. John], p. 187.
57 [Knut] Philbert Humbla and Lennart von Post, "Galtabäcksbåten och tidigt båtbyggeri i Norden," *Göteborgs Kungl[ig] Vetenskaps- och Vitterhets-samhälles Handlingar*, 5th ser., pt A: Humanistiska Skrifter, VI (1937), 1–148; Harald Åkerlund, "Galtabäcksbåtens ålder och härstamning," *Göteborgs och Bohusläns Fornminnes Förenings Tidskrift*, 1942, pp. 22–49; H. G[ote] Ostlund, "Stockholm Natural Radiocarbon Measurements I," *Science*, CXXVI (13 Sept. 1957), 496.
58 Færøyvik, "Leivder av eit kaupskip på Holmen, Bergenhus," pp. 12–43.
59 Harald Åkerlund, *Fartygsfynden i den forna hamnen i Kalmar* (Uppsala, 1951). Compare Brøgger and Shetelig, *The Viking Ships,* p. 236; Marcus, "Evolution of the Knörr," p. 122.

in the Bayeux Tapestry places the hafskip irrefutably in the English experience,[60] as does the one appearance in Anglo-Saxon of the word cnear, for *knörr*.[61] No doubt is left that the ceol of the wine prisage regulation was a *hafskip*, most likely a *knörr*.

Such a variation on the traditional roles of long ship and round ship was not unique to Northern waters and an analogous situation is to be found in the Mediterranean. Most interestingly the analogy is a very strong one, extending to not only function but origin and name as well. Isidore of Seville, in the seventh century, wrote that the ceol was the same as the Greek κέλης and the Latin *carina* and that all three were light fast ships, having one or two banks of oars.[62] The κέλητες were small, fast vessels built primarily for speed and were found in wide use during the last five centuries before the Christian era.[63] The parallel and perhaps interdependent development of both words, ceol and *carina*, is indicative of the relationship between the two ships. Jal mentions, but does not commit himself to accepting, the Greek κάρα, meaning, literally, "head," as the origin of the word *carina*, signifying the main member of a ship, the keel.[64] *Carina* was used metonymically to

60 Tuxen, "De Nordiske Langskibe," pp. 75–77, suggested this correspondence with only his literary evidence to guide him. The similarity between the merchant ships uncovered since World War II and that pictured in the Bayeux Tapestry confirms his early opinion. See also Vogel, "Zur nord- und westeuropäischen Seeschiffahrt," p. 189. Compare Bernard S. Bachrach, "On the Origins of William the Conqueror's Horse Transports," *Technology and Culture*, XXVI (July 1985), 505–531. The definitive work on the tapestry itself is by Frank Stenton, *et al.*, *The Bayeux Tapestry: A Comprehensive Survey*, 2nd edn (London, 1965). See also N[icholas] P. Brooks and H. E. Walker, "The Authority and Interpretation of the Bayeux Tapestry," *Anglo-Norman Studies: Proceedings of the Battle Conference*, I (1978), 1–34. Compare the illustrations in David M. Wilson, *The Bayeux Tapestry: The Complete Tapestry in Colour* ([London, 1985]). The English ship – that in which Harold made his journey to France and back – is shown in several views in the tapestry (see plates 5, 6, 7). This has led many writers to assume that more than one ship is portrayed.

61 In the metrical account of the Battle of Brunanburh (Bromborough, Cheshire [?]) in the Anglo-Saxon Chronicle, the word "*cnear*" appears twice in reference to the ships of the Norse king of Dublin. The writer obviously tried to render in his own language a word foreign to him. The verse appears in four versions of the Chronicle, in texts "A," "B," "C," and "D"; *The Anglo-Saxon Chronicle*, ed. Thorpe, I, 204–207 (937). See Schnepper, *Namen der Schiffe und Schiffsteile im Altenglischen*, p. 46.

62 "Celoces, quas Graeci κέλητας vocant, id est veloces biremes vel triremes, aglies ad ministerium classis aptae. Ennius (Ann. 478): Labitur uncta carina per aequora cana celocis." *Isidori hispalensis episcopi etymologiarum sive originum libri XX*, XIX, i, 22, ed. W[allace] M. Lindsay, 2 vols (Oxford, [1911]), II, 2. Isidore of Seville's quotation from Quintus Ennius is, in fact, the source of this line from Ennius's now lost "Annals." *See Ennianae poesis reliquiae iteratis curis*, Liber Increta, XVII (478), ed. John Vahlen [2nd edn] (Leipzig, 1903), p. 86.

63 Schefferus, "De varitate navium," pp. 773 ff. See also Emil Luebeck, *Das Seewesen der Griechen und Römer*, 2 vols (Hamburg, 1890–1891), I, 29; and Torr, *Ancient Ships*, pp. 108–110. For examples, compare Herodotus, *Historiae*, VIII, 94, and Thucydides, *De bello Peloponnesiaco*, I, 53, IV, 9, VIII, 38.

64 Jal, *Archéologie navale*, II, 482–483, and *Glossaire nautique*, p. 425. Isidore of Seville wrote (*Etymologiarum . . .*, XIX, ii, 1, ed. Lindsay, II, 7) that "Carina a currendo dicta, quasi carrina," an idea he seems to have derived from an earlier writer. Jal, *Archéologie navale*, II, 452, 482–483, argues, somewhat obtusely, that this could not have been the case as the Greek κάρα preceded in time the Latin *currio*.

mean the entire ship as early as the second century BC, but just when it came to be applied to a particular type of ship is unknown.[65] Whether one accepts a similar synecdochic extension of the original meaning of ceol from the limited sense of the main longitudinal member of a ship – the keel – to the ship itself under the influence of the Latin word *carina*,[66] or the direct transference of the Greek word κέλης into their parlance by the migrating Saxons or others,[67] the close association of the two is evident.[68]

The *carina* as a ship type was still to be found in the twelfth-century Mediterranean world with a function apparently the same as the Northern European *hafskip* or ceol. The twelfth-century *carina* was a large oared vessel with a single sail at midships and sufficient height and beam to allow it to pass at a distance for a merchantman. It was employed both for military logistics and for trade, though initially its use seems to have been more for the former purpose.[69] As such it can be seen as a predecessor of the fourteenth-century Venetian "great galleys," suggesting that the Venetian development of these ships came earlier than has been previously supposed.[70] Originally, the *carina* seems to have been a warship enlarged and altered for the purposes of military supply. Its use as a commercial carrier followed later.

The similarity in origin between *knörr* and *carina* is thus striking, for the *knörr* also began as a modified long ship or *langskip* used to support Viking

65 Quintus Ennius used "*uncta carina*" in the sense of an especially swift ship (see n. 62 of this chapter). "*Uncta*" literally has reference to the caulking of a ship's timbers, rendering his meaning here a bit obscure; *Ennianae poesis reliquiae iteratis curis*, Liber XIV, ii (386), and Liber Increta, xvii (478), ed. Vahlen, pp. 70, 86. See also *The Annals of Quintus Ennius*, Liber XIV, iii, and Liber . . . Fragmenta, XCIV, ed. Ethel Mary Stewart (Cambridge, Eng., 1925), pp. 54, 73. Vergil has two parallel uses: *Aeneid*, IV, 398, and VIII, 91. See too, Vergil, *Aeneid*, II, 23, and *Georgics*, I, 303, 360.

66 *Oxford English Dictionary*, ed. Murray *et al.*, V, 658, suggests a metonymical equivalence between *carina* and ceol, the former word preceding and influencing through translation the usage of the latter in a part-for-the-whole attributive correspondence.

67 See n. 15 of this chapter.

68 The etymological derivation of the word ceol through the Greek γύαλον to the Indo-European root "geu," meaning "to curve" or "to bend," seems best in all particulars to fit the timber rather than the ship. This being so, the jump from timber to ship, which remains unexplained by such a derivation, is probably interpreted best in the way suggested above. For this derivation, see also Schnepper, *Namen der Schiffe und Schiffsteile im Altenglischen*, p. 43, and Alois Walde, *Vergleichendes Wörterbuch der indogermanischen Sprachen*, ed. Julius Pokorny, 3 vols (Berlin and Leipzig, 1927–1932), I, 556.

69 Jal, *Archéologie navale*, I, 411–414, II, 482–483. Three of the most valuable contemporary accounts of the *carina* are: Albert, of Aix (Albertus Aquensis), *Liber Christianae expeditionis pro ereptione, emundatione et restitutione sanctae hierosolymitanae ecclesiae*, [ed. Paul Meyer], Liber IX, ix, in *Historiens occidentaux: Recueil des historiens des Croisades* (Paris, 1879), IV, 595; William of Tyre, *Historia rerum in partibus transmarinis gestarum a tempore successorum Muhumeth usque ad annum Domini MCLXXIV*, [ed. Arthur Auguste Beugnot and A. Langlois], Liber XII, xxii, in *Historiens occidentaux: Recueil des historiens des Croisades* (Paris, 1844), vol. I, pt i, 546; and Laurence of Verona, *De Bello Balerico sive rerum in Majorica Pesanorum ac de eorum triumphano Pisis habito anno salutis 1115*, Liber I, *in Patrologiae cursus completus . . . series Latinae*, ed. Migne, CLXIII, col. 516.

70 For the Venetian "great galleys," see Lane, *Venetian Ships*, pp. 7, 13–34.

expeditions.[71] The later use of the *carina* for purposes of trade saw it ideally suited to certain mercantile functions and – as the great galley – it carried perishable products, specialty items of great value but small bulk, and pilgrim passengers around the Mediterranean. Where speed and reliability were important, the *carina* could be profitably employed. Bulk shipments went in the cheaper to operate but less dependable merchantmen.[72] The *knörr*, by contrast, declined rapidly in importance in northern waters, and was replaced by the more traditional merchant ship, the round ship. The reasons for this are many but can perhaps most easily be seen when it is appreciated that the cargoes upon which the *carina* throve were not available in quantity in Western Europe. Bulk shipments predominated and bulk shippers were what owners built and merchants used.[73] The open cargo area of the *knörr* compared unfavorably with the closed cabins of the hulk-cog; the flexibility of the *knörr* unfavorably with that of its rival.[74] Whereas the *knörr* had pretty much reached the limits of its practical size for its type of construction, the hulk-cog, as we have seen, could be and was greatly expanded in capacity. Especially important, the cost of operation per unit of cargo volume decreased as the size of the hulk-cog increased. The number of crew needed to man the larger hulks was little more than that needed for the smaller. On the *knerrir* this was not true, as they required a crew proportionate to their cargo capacity.[75] There had to be at least enough men to row the oars when they needed rowing and the number of oars necessary to be effective grew as the ship grew. Destroyed, as a result, were both the advantage to increased size and the incentive to increase it. Especially after the introduction of the stern rudder and refined rigging in the thirteenth century, the hulk-cog grew to enormous proportions.[76] The *knörr* as an ocean-going vessel completely disappeared.[77]

In the London wine trade, the Lorraine merchants at least could have found in the prisage regulation an added reason for using hulcs and other ships instead of ceols, and for increasing the size of their ships, since the

---

71 Marcus, "Evolution of the Knörr," pp. 116–117.
72 Lane, *Venetian Ships*, pp. 13–29 passim.
73 P[eter] H. Sawyer, *The Age of the Vikings* (London, [1962]), p. 78, and n. 20, p. 229. Compare Marcus, "The Greenland Trade-Route," p. 74, n. 4, and the sources he cited.
74 Bertil Almgren, "Vikingatåg och vikingaskepp," *Tor: Meddelanden från Institutionen för Nordisk Fornkunskap vid Uppsala Universitet*, VIII (1962), 195. Compare Brøgger and Shetelig, *The Viking Ships*, pp. 237–239.
75 Tuxen, "De Nordiske Langskibe," pp. 110–111; Brøgger and Shetelig, *The Viking Ships*, pp. 236–237.
76 Anderson and Anderson, *The Sailing-Ship*, pp. 83–84, 85–97.
77 Marcus, "Evolution of the Knörr," p. 122, logs one exception, the Greenland passage. By contrast oared long ships continued to be used as vessels of war in Western European waters into the modern era. See also J. T. Tinniswood, "English Galleys, 1272–1377," *MM*, XXXV (Oct. 1949), 276–315; Anderson, *Oared Fighting Ships*, pp. 42–51 ff. The reasons for the disappearance of the *knörr* from Northern waters are strikingly similar to those given by Lane, *Venetian Ships*, pp. 26–31, for the replacement of the "great galleys" by round ships in the Mediterranean at a somewhat later date.

wine prise originally favored the hulc over the ceol by assessing the former at less than the latter regardless of the size of the cargo. In theory, a ceol carrying the same number of tuns as a hulc, or even fewer, would still pay an extra tun prisage. The *recta prisa* also included implicit inequalities. By setting as its top duty two tuns of wine on all ships bringing in twenty tuns or more, it discriminated in favor of the larger vessels. The larger the ship, the smaller the rate of tax effectively levied.

Presuming that merchants and shipbuilders would react to the stimuli contained in these regulations, one would have expected the hulc to have increased in size after 1130 and to have continued to grow after 1200 while the ceol should have disappeared from the wine trade within the century. This is, as we have seen, what did happen, but whether the wine prise can be identified as an effective cause of these developments is impossible to say, for we possess no direct evidence to substantiate such a hypothesis. If it had any effect, it was probably that of speeding up changes already in progress for the other reasons suggested previously. This being so, there is an interesting parallel here with the effects that later taxing measures calculated on the cargo capacity of a ship had upon shipbuilding practices in subsequent centuries.[78] Nevertheless, if the wine prise did not bring on these alterations, it certainly did reflect them. The twelfth century witnessed such changes in the ships used in the trade that taxation measures based on distinctions applicable in 1130 were no longer relevant in 1200. No more could the assessment be on the type of ship, for the type was no longer indicative of the same things it had once been – cargo capacity, in particular. The law had to be altered as a result.

Twelfth- and early thirteenth-century wine prisage regulations bore a direct relationship to the merchant shipping of the era. They cannot be construed as initiating the far-reaching changes in ship construction focused in this time period. Whether these regulations had the effect of accelerating the

---

78 For an extreme example of this, see Nicolaas Corneliszoon Witsen, *Aeloude en heden-daagsche Scheeps-bouw en bestier . . .* (Amsterdam, 1671), p. 160, where he discusses a trade treaty that ambiguously specified the measurement of cargo capacity and thus gave rise to a ship in the shape of an hour-glass. In the 20th century, Ernest W. Blocksidge, *Hints on the Register Tonnage of Merchant Ships*, 2nd edn (Liverpool, 1942), p. v, enunciates what is apparently an ageless rationale for designing "a ship [so] as to obtain every possible concession."

The results have not always been seaworthy, however. The unstable depth of late 18th-century English merchantmen arose, it has been argued, because the legal calculation of capacity computed the depth of a ship at one-half the breadth instead of measuring it. Owners and builders were induced thereby to ignore the reasonableness of the traditional proportions and build ships deeper in relation to their breadth than had been considered safe in order to gain the untaxed additional capacity. See C[harles] Ernst Fayle, "Shipowning and Marine Insurance," in *The Trade Winds: A Study of British Overseas Trade during the French Wars, 1793–1815*, ed. C[yril] Northcote Parkinson (London, [1948]), p. 34; Basil Lubbock, "Ships of the Period and Developments in Rig," in ibid., p. 94; and Parkinson, "The East India Trade," in ibid., pp. 145–146. Compare Gerald S. Graham, "The Ascendancy of the Sailing Ship," *EcHR*, 2nd ser., IX (Aug. 1956), 78.

processes of innovation remains a moot question. That they reflected these changes by requiring internal alterations in their formulation is clear to see. Such suggestive indication of the interaction between taxing regulations and ship construction had been heretofore unappreciated for so early a period.

3

THE TONNAGE OF
SHIPS ENGAGED IN BRITISH
COLONIAL TRADE DURING
THE EIGHTEENTH CENTURY

Economic historians studying the British Empire in the seventeenth and eighteenth centuries have made considerable use of shipping statistics in their discussions of imperial trade.[1] Many of them have attempted to establish more precisely the character of the basic measure of shipping, the ton. The major difficulty plaguing such attempts centers in the fact that, as shall be made clear below, there were effectively three tonnage figures applicable to each vessel. In terms of numbers of tons, a shipowner of England or one of its colonies loaded a greater cargo on board his vessel (cargo tonnage) than he had contracted for with the shipbuilder (measured tonnage). He then registered his vessel and paid the port duties it incurred at a still smaller figure (registered tonnage). The differences are significant enough to create havoc with the work of anyone who fails to appreciate fully the size of such differences and their ramifications. With the sure knowledge that statements about the importance of shipping and trade rest on a very insecure basis until we know more about tonnage, the following is offered as an attempt at clarification.

Part of the problem that the economic historian has in sorting this out is chronological in origin. "Tonnage" is a technical term that, as defined in the eighteenth century, bears only a nebulous relationship to current similar measures. "Displacement tonnage," for instance, is a modern measure of the weight of a vessel or, more precisely, of the weight of the water displaced by that vessel. None of the measures for the earlier period has anything to do with a vessel's weight, however. "Gross registered tonnage" and "net registered tonnage" are modern measures of the cubic capacity of a vessel in feet. The first of these is a latter-day relation to what in the eighteenth century was called "measured tonnage," but its computation today is considerably more carefully done and refined than it was two centuries ago.

---

1   The original version of this chapter was published in *Research in Economic History*, VI (1981), 73–105. Copyright © 1981 by the JAI Press Inc. This revision is presented here with the permission of the publishers of the volume.

"Net registered tonnage" approaches, at least in theory, what an eighteenth-century shipowner knew as "registered tonnage." "Deadweight capacity tonnage" is a modern measure of net cargo capacity. Again a crude parallel exists between it and what shipowners and merchants once knew as cargo tonnage or "tons captain's measure," in the words of Henry Laurens, merchant of Charleston.[2]

Henry Laurens and his contemporaries were not noted for semantic precision. Thus another problem for twentieth-century historians stems from the use of terms. The three adjectives employed in these pages to qualify and, thereby, in the interests of clarity, to distinguish kinds of tonnage in the eighteenth century are faithful to the contemporary meaning of the word in its separate contexts but they are not used in necessarily the same way by other students of the subject, nor do they exhaust the possible qualifiers. A definition of terms is essential. "Cargo tonnage" denotes a vessel's actual carrying capacity with reference to the number of cargo tons of goods freighted on board a vessel. This is Laurens's "tons captain's measure" and reflects the interest of the master and owners of a vessel in what it could "burthen," using a favorite eighteenth-century word, but it is not necessarily its "tons burthen" because that phrase was often applied in situations where the figures were only a legal fiction. "Measured tonnage" denotes the size of a vessel as calculated on a standard formula. It is the same as "shipwright's" or "carpenter's" tonnage, phrases that indicate the origin of the formula in the construction and the buying and selling of vessels.[3] These phrases also indicate that this was a real measurement, not an estimate, taken by the shipwright as he built the vessel and accepted as such by the buyer who could quite easily have checked the shipwright's measurements while the vessel was still on the stocks. This measurement was the basis on which the builder

2 Henry Laurens, at Charleston, to Isaac Wheeler, at St Christopher, 3 Nov. 1755, *The Papers of Henry Laurens*, ed. Philip M. Hamer *et al.*, in progress (Columbia, SC, 1968 to date), II, 5. Concerning tonnage measurement in general, see A. van Driel, *Tonnage Measurement: Historical and Critical Essay* (The Hague, 1925). Concerning displacement tonnage and its use in measuring the relative sizes of naval vessels, see Jan Glete, *Navies and Nations: Warships, Navies and State Building in Europe and America, 1500–1860*, Acta Universitatis Stockholmiensis: Stockholm Studies in History, vol. 48 (Stockholm, [1993]). See also John J. McCusker, "Colonial Tonnage Measurement: Five Philadelphia Merchant Ships as a Sample," *JEcH*, XXVII (Mar. 1967), 82–91.

3 Gerald G. Beekman, at New York, to James Edward Powell, at Georgia, 30 May 1755, *The Beekman Mercantile Papers, 1746–1799*, ed. Philip L. White, 3 vols (New York, 1956), I, 249. In a letter to the Admiralty dated Deptford, 1 Jan. 1690/91, Robert Castell, Hr. Barham, Jonas Shist, and F. Harding, attested that 'their Majesties Ship the Dreadnought ... [measured] Eight hundred ffifty one Tuns & 8/10,' having measured it according to "the rule of Shipwrights Hall." Add. MS 22183, fol. 190r, BL. "Castell" was probably Robert Castle, the scion of the important London shipbuilding firm. Just at the end of the American Revolution, Robert Morris, Superintendent of Finance, had occasion to explain "carpenters tonnage" at great length to the French Minister to the United States, Anne-César-Henri, comte de la Luzerne, in a letter dated Philadelphia, 4 Oct. 1782, *The Papers of Robert Morris, 1781–1784*, ed. E[dgar] James Ferguson *et al.*, in progress (Pittsburgh, 1973 to date), VI, 493–495.

calculated how much he charged the buyer. "Registered tonnage" denotes a vessel's legal tonnage, the tonnage at which a vessel was initially registered and the figure that appeared, copied from the certificate of registration, in all official records relating to that vessel, including Customs documents and the colonial Naval Office shipping lists (NOSL).[4]

The existence of three ways of referring to a vessel's tonnage in the eighteenth century carries no necessary implication; they could as easily all have been the same as all have been different. Yet the question of sameness or difference – and, if different, by how much – certainly should arise. In an attempt at an answer, there have been several modern comparisons of measured and registered tonnage. Their results are summed up herein and some new material added (see tables 3.1 and 3.2). But there has been no attempt until now to discover the relationship between cargo tonnage and measured tonnage. The results of this test are also discussed herein. While the data base for all these tests is very small indeed, the complete randomness of the data for present purposes argues strongly that we have an adequate sample from which to generalize, albeit, as always, cautiously.

◆ ◆ ◆ ◆ ◆

The point of tonnage measure was to formulate a standard shorthand designation of the carrying capacity of a vessel in terms of a common unit.[5] Comparative tonnage figures permitted shipowners and merchants to purchase or to hire vessels best suited to their needs. In so far as we can trace the origins of tonnage measures, the cask of wine (or "tun") appears to have become the English unit of measure sometime after the middle of the twelfth century in connection with an early tax on imported wine, the wine

4   Registered tonnage, as an element of the ship's certificate of registration, is more a characteristic of vessels employed in the colonial trade of the empire after 1696. Before 1696, and for vessels that never ventured into the colonial trade, there was no need until much later in the 18th century to have a certificate of registration. Thus the regularity and consistency of a vessel's registered tonnage was not necessarily characteristic of the pre-1696 period nor of shipping engaged in British coastal commerce or the trade from Britain to the Continent. See Rupert [C.] Jarvis, "Ship Registry – to 1707," *Maritime History*, I (Apr. 1971), 29–45, and Jarvis, "Ship Registry – 1707–86," *Maritime History*, II (Sept. 1972), 151–167. Compare John Lyman, "Register Tonnage and Its Measurements," *American Neptune*, V (July, Oct. 1945), 223–234, 311–325, and Lyman, "Carpenter's Measurement," *American Neptune*, XXIII (Apr. 1963), 141–142. See also McCusker, "Colonial Tonnage Measurement," pp. 82–91.
5   Paul Gille, "Jauge et tonnage des navires," in [Colloque International d'Histoire Maritime, 1st, 1956, Paris], *Le Navire et l'économie maritime du XVe au XVIIIe siècles*, ed. Michel Mollat (Paris, 1957), pp. 85–100; Frederic C. Lane, "Tonnages, Medieval and Modern," *EcHR*, 2nd ser., XVII (Dec. 1964), 213–233; Michel Morineau, *Jauges et méthodes de jauge anciennes et modernes*, Cahiers des Annales, no. 24 (Paris, 1966); J[ohn] H. Parry, "Transport and Trade Routes [1300–1700]," in *The Economy of Expanding Europe in the Sixteenth and Seventeenth Centuries*, ed. E[dwin] E. Rich and C[harles] H. Wilson, vol. IV of *The Cambridge Economic History of Europe* (Cambridge, Eng., 1967), pp. 218–219; and Jean-Claude Hocquet, "Tonnages ancien et moderne: Botte de Venise et tonneau anglais," *Revue Historique*, no. 570 (Apr.–June 1989), 349–360.

prise or prisage.[6] The inconvenience involved in trying to count the actual number of wine casks on board a vessel and the inadequacy of impression-istic comparisons between vessels led, in the late sixteenth century, to the formulation of a crude mathematical equation to compute tonnage.[7] The formula, enshrined as such things become, maintained its crudity over a long period during which the vessels themselves underwent a considerable refine-ment. The result was that measured tonnage, which all agree in the seven-teenth century overstated cargo capacity, had, by the mid-eighteenth century, become a considerable understatement of the cargo capacity of merchant vessels.[8]

We can best picture for ourselves what had happened if we think of the hull of the vessel as encased in a large rectangular box. The length of the box is the length of the ship's deck; the width of the box is the vessel's breadth at its widest point; and the depth of the box is the ship's depth from the deck to the keel. It is immediately obvious to our mind's eye that, because of its streamlined shape, the vessel's hull does not fill the box. The propor-tion between the space that the ship does occupy and the whole of the box (or block) is called by modern naval architects its "block coefficient." The more streamlined the vessel, the lower its block coefficient, and vice versa. Vessels with a low block coefficient – with, therefore, a sharper bow, narrower hull and a more rounded stern – travel through the water with less resistance and are, therefore, faster sailers. At the same time they carried less cargo than a vessel of the same basic dimensions but with a higher block coefficient, that is a vessel whose bow was bluffer, whose hull was fuller, and whose stern was squarer.[9] The tonnage formula in use in the British Empire from the

6 John J. McCusker, "The Wine Prise and Medieval Mercantile Shipping," *Speculum: A Journal of Medieval Studies*, XLI (Apr. 1966), 279–296 – revised as chapter two of the present book; Ernest W. Blocksidge, *Hints on the Register Tonnage of Merchant Ships*, 2nd edn (Liverpool, 1942), pp. 1–2. There were ways to measure a vessel other than in terms of its cargo. "From the Viking Age onwards, probably still earlier, the measure of a ship was how many 'rooms' it had – that is, the number of spaces between cross beams." A[nton] W. Brøgger and Haakon Shetelig, *The Viking Ships: Their Ancestry and Evolution* [trans. Katherine John] (Oslo, [1951]), p. 187.

7 Westcott [S.] Abell, *The Shipwrights' Trade* (Cambridge, Eng., 1948), pp. 38–39; David W. Waters, *The Art of Navigation in Elizabethan and Early Stuart Times*, 2nd edn, rev. (Greenwich, Eng., 1978), p. 296; William Salisbury, "Early Tonnage Measurement in England," *MM*, LII (Feb., May, Nov. 1966), 41–51, 173–180, 329–340, LIII (Aug. 1967), 251–264, and LIV (Feb. 1968), 69–76; [Hazel] Dorothy Burwash, *English Merchant Shipping, 1460–1540* (Toronto, 1947), pp. 88–97; and M[ichael] Oppenheim, *A History of the Administration of the Royal Navy, and of Merchant Shipping in Relation to the Navy from 1509 to 1660* (London and New York, 1896).

8 Ralph Davis, *The Rise of the English Shipping Industry in the Seventeenth and Eighteenth Centuries* (London, 1962), pp. 7, 74, 372, and Ralph Davis, "The Organization and Finance of the English Shipping Industry in the Late Seventeenth Century" (Ph.D. diss., University of London, 1955), pp. 471–481.

9 The concept of block coefficient is explained and illustrated in Howard I. Chapelle, *The Search for Speed Under Sail, 1700–1855* (New York, 1967), p. 43. Hans Szymanski, *Deutsche Segelschiffe: Die Geschichte der hölzernen Frachtsegler an den deutschen Ost- und Nordseeküsten, vom Ende des 18. Jahrhunderts bis auf die Gegenwart*, Veröffentlichungen

late sixteenth century computed measured tonnage on the basis of a vessel's length, breadth, and depth but without reference to its block coefficient. So long as all merchant ships maintained roughly comparable block coefficients, measured tonnage by formula served its comparative purpose well enough. But the history of British and colonial ship design over the two centuries from 1600 to 1800 witnessed a trend to bluffer, rounder merchant vessels with increasingly greater block coefficients.[10]

Meanwhile, governments had discovered in a vessel's tonnage a relatively simple and equitable basis for collecting a whole range of maritime taxes and duties. Lighthouse fees, harbor dues, wharfage tolls, and the like, all came to be charged at a rate per ton.[11] From the beginning, merchants and shipowners had been able to gain the point that such duties, to be fair, should be charged on the vessel's estimated cargo tonnage. A petition of London merchants in a memorial to the Commissioners of the Customs in 1707 was arguing established precedent when it stated that: "When we report our ships att [sic] custom house, the Trinity house duties, and mostly the duties collected for Dover Peere are in proportion to the Tunnage we bring."[12]

In the pre-1700 era ships carried a smaller number of tons of cargo than the number of tons they measured and, as a consequence, the practice had grown up to discount measured tonnage before collecting duties calculated on a vessel's tonnage.[13] Nevertheless, late in the seventeenth century, when it became necessary to specify the basis of the tonnage figure to be entered on a vessel's certificate of registration, Parliament stipulated measured tonnage, effectively disallowing the traditional discounting. Had this change been realized, it would have resulted in the collection of harbor duties and the like based on the full measured tonnage. It would have increased the amount payable by as much as 50 percent. Fortunately for shipowners and merchants, precedent overruled Parliament and in most places the figure for

des Instituts für Meereskunde an der Universität Berlin, Neue Folge B: Historisch-volks-wirtschaftliche Reihe, Heft 10 (Berlin, 1934), p. 15, has drawings of the hulls of three three-masted sailing ships that, even though they have the same basic dimensions, have three different block coefficients (*Volligkeitskoeffizient*) measuring 0.74, 0.54, and 0.36. Glete, *Navies and Nations*, II, 527–530 and after, employs the concept of block coefficient to estimate in modern terms (displacement tonnage) the sizes of older naval vessels in order to compare the relative strength of various nations' naval forces. While everything hinges on whether he has guessed correctly any given ship's block coefficient, his method is certainly an ingenious way to address the problem of the different methods by which nations measured the size of ships.

10 Parry, "Transport and Trade Routes," pp. 211–213. See the discussion later in this chapter. This development was, at least in part, a response to the existence of the formula that made it easier for governments to tax vessels based upon the tonnage so calculated. Vessels came to be designed to carry the greatest cargo at the least taxable size. See McCusker, "Wine Prise."

11 McCusker, "Colonial Tonnage Measurement," p. 86.

12 Petition, endorsed as received 13 June 1707, CO 5/1315, pt ii, fol. 341r, PRO.

13 See, e.g., the letter of Col. Robert Rich, at Barbados, to John Ogilby, 31 May 1670, as printed in John Ogilby, *America: Being the Latest and Most Accurate Description of the New World* (London, 1671), p. 380.

tonnage entered on the certificate of registration was adjusted to reflect the traditional discounting of measured tonnage.[14]

In the meanwhile, however, by 1700 design changes had increased the block coefficient of vessels, and cargo tonnage had come to equal measured tonnage. The premise for the original discounting procedure had been overtaken by the progressively increasing fullness of late seventeenth-century vessels. Over the eighteenth century cargo tonnage continued to increase relative to both measured tonnage and registered tonnage. Vessels came to carry a larger number of tons of cargo than the number of tons in either their bills of sale or their certificates of registration. It was plain for all to see. In 1746 Governor William Mathew of the Leeward Islands commented about the ships that called at Antigua that "their tonnage by their registers . . . are generally much less than they carry."[15]

We can appreciate these relationships somewhat better if we look to actual vessels. This is more easily said than done because by far the greatest number of tonnage figures for eighteenth-century vessels available to historians are the legally recorded registered tonnage figures. Copied from the certificate of registration, the registration tonnage of a vessel followed it through its history from document to document like a faithful dog. But it is extremely difficult to discover either a vessel's measured tonnage or its cargo tonnage. To find a vessel's measured tonnage, we must either uncover its dimensions and calculate its measured tonnage for ourselves (using the appropriate formula) or depend on a contemporary who did so himself, such as the vessel's builder. A search for cargo tonnage presents even greater problems. Still, we do have some basis for comparisons.

To begin with we can ask: What was the difference, if any, between the registered tonnage and the measured tonnage of English and colonial vessels in the eighteenth century? Recall that, by law, the two were supposed to be identical since the legally prescribed formula for computed registered tonnage was the same one used by builders and owners. Table 3.1 demonstrates that, at least in twenty-five instances of vessels registered in the port of Philadelphia prior to 1775, the two figures were not identical but instead were quite dissimilar. When swearing the oath at registration, the owners understated their vessels' tonnages by from 6.2 percent to 70 percent of its measured tonnage. In terms of the total tonnages of these vessels, the difference between registered and measured tonnage was 43.4 percent of the latter. If we round this figure down somewhat to 40 percent, it means that we could estimate the measured tonnages of these vessels by multiplying their registered tonnages by 166⅔ percent. Eighteenth-century authorities stated that

14 McCusker, "Colonial Tonnage Measurement."
15 Gov. Mathew, at Antigua, to Commissioners for Trade and Plantations, 15 Apr. 1746, CO 152/25, fol. 194. There are copies of this report in the Shelburne Papers, 1665–1797, vol. 45, William L. Clements Library, University of Michigan, Ann Arbor; and in the Reports on the State of the British Colonies, 1721–1766, King's MS 205, BL.

throughout the empire, this "correction factor" averaged 150 percent. Among such commentators the most authoritative was Thomas Irving, who, from 1786 to 1800, was the Inspector-General of Imports and Exports of Great Britain. Before the Revolutionary War he had held a similar post in North America under the American Board of Customs at Boston, where he had also been the Register of Shipping.[16] Scholarly research tends both to confirm Irving's statement and the Philadelphia data supplied in table 3.1 and at the same time to indicate that insufficient attention had been paid to differences from port to port.[17]

The fact is that, although the discounting procedure was widespread in Great Britain and the colonies, neither its universality nor the regularity of the size of the discount can be assumed. It was, after all, an extra-legal convention. Variations in discounted tonnage stemmed from two causes. First,

16 See Irving's testimony before the Commissioners for Trade and Plantations in 1784 in BT 5/1, p. 165, PRO. For Irving, see John J. McCusker, "Colonial Civil Servant and Counter-Revolutionary: Thomas Irving (1738?–1800) in Boston, Charleston, and London," *Perspectives in American History*, XII (1979), 314–350 – revised as chapter nine of the present book.

17 A point well made by Christopher J. French, "Eighteenth-Century Shipping Tonnage Measurements," *JEcH*, XXXIII (June 1973), 434–443. New British registration procedures in force after 1786 effectively required that vessels be entered at full measured tonnage. Act of 26 George III, c. 60 (1786). See also Rupert C. Jarvis, "The Sources of Transport History: Sources for the History of Ships and Shipping," *Journal of Transport History*, III (Nov. 1958), 221. French carefully compared the pre-1785 and post-1786 registered tonnages for sixty-three vessels and determined a difference between the old registered tonnage and the new measured-registered tonnage of 34 percent for the group. A similar, contemporary analysis of the effect of the new law upon the shipping owned at Scarborough yielded a difference of 29 percent. Endorsed "Ships and Men belonging to Scarborough, 1787," Custom House, Scarborough, 11 May 1787, BT 6/189, PRO. There are a few instances where the available data from other ports allow us to make the same kind of comparisons of the relationship between measured and registered tonnage. The ship *Concord* of London (?) measured a fraction over 700 tons; it was registered at 500 tons, a difference of 29 percent. James Claypoole, at London, to Benjamin Furly, at Rotterdam, London, 13 Mar. 1682/83, in *James Claypoole's Letter Book, London and Philadelphia, 1681–1684*, ed. Marion Balderston (San Marino, Calif., 1967), p. 196. The ship *Susannah* of London sailed regularly between there and South Carolina in the years around 1740. It was registered at 100 tons, but Andrew Pringle, the brother of the owner, described it as of "about one hundred and eighty tons burthen," a difference of 44 percent. Pringle, at Charleston, SC, to Gedney Clarke, at Barbados, 13 Mar. 1741/42, in *The Letterbook of Robert Pringle, 1737–1745*, ed. Walter B. Edgar, 2 vols (Columbia, SC, 1972), I, p. 336; entries dated 2 Oct. 1739, 1 Apr. 1740, and 29 Dec. 1740, Adm. 68/197, fols 106r, 128r, 155r, PRO. The ship *Endeavor* of London, built at Rotherhithe in 1739, measured 200½ tons; it was registered at 150 tons, a difference of 25 percent. Mercantile Papers of Thomas Newson, bundle labeled "Papers belonging to Ship Endeavor, No. 86," re *Newson's Estate*, C 104/79, pt i, PRO; entry dated 11 Mar. 1739/40, Adm. 68/197, fol. 124, PRO. The snow *Providence* of Boston, built at Providence, RI, in 1739, measured about 130 tons; it was registered at Boston, 6 Feb. 1743/44, at 90 tons, a difference of 31 percent. Papers of the Snow *Providence*, HCA 32/142, PRO. The brigantine *Gregg* of New York, built in the colonies, measured at least 90 tons; it was registered at New York, 21 Nov. 1757, at 50 tons, a difference of 44 percent. Papers of the Brigantine Gregg, HCA 42/68, PRO. The sloop *Curaçao Packet* of New York, built at New York in 1760 or 1761, measured 60 tons; it was registered there in 1761 at 35 tons, a difference of 41.7 percent. Papers of the Sloop *Curaçao Packet*, HCA 42/59, PRO.

Table 3.1 Measured and registered tonnage compared, Philadelphia, 1709–1775

Vessel's name (year built)	Registered tonnage	Measured tonnage	Percentage difference $[(2) - (1)] \div 2$	Source
	(1)	(2)	(3)	(4)
Tucker (1709)	150	160	6.2	a
Dove (1719)	40	78	48.7	b
Mary (1725)	2	4	50.0	c
Diligence (1730)	60	104	42.3	d
Charming Molly (1733)	40	85	52.9	e
Frederica (1736)	30	62	51.6	f
Mary (1742)	100	143	30.1	g
Wilmington (1743)	130	300	56.7	h
Tetsworth (1748)	200	266	24.8	i
Diamond (1749)	30	100	70.0	j
Sally (1750)	70	131	46.6	k
Friendship (1751)	50	140	64.3	l
Severn (1755)	80	150	46.7	m
Severn (1756)	70	200	65.0	n
Carrington (1757)	100	170	41.2	o
Somerville (1757)	120	230	47.8	p
Rebecca (1761)	80	175	54.3	q
Hero (1762)	200	520	61.5	r
Two Brothers (1770)	130	182	28.6	s
Commerce (1771)	140	225	37.8	t
Lovely Lass (1773)	120	274	56.2	u
Union (1774)	150	170	11.8	v
Sally (1774)	200	288	30.6	w
Black Prince (1774)	200	300	33.3	x
Lord Camden (1775)	200	296	32.4	y
Totals	2,692	4,753	43.4	

Notes and sources:
(a) NOSL, POE York River, Va., 25 Mar. 1725 to 25 Mar. 1726, CO 5/1442, fol. 23, PRO.
(b) Ibid.
(c) Ibid.
(d) Alexander Wooddrop Account Books, 1719–1734, vol. II, fol. 393, LC; John J. McCusker, "Ships Registered at the Port of Philadelphia before 1776: A Computerized Listing" (unpublished computer printout, 1970), no. 99. References are to serial numbers assigned to the ships' registers. This compilation is based primarily on the Ship Register Books of the Province of Pennsylvania, 1722–1776, HSP. See John J. McCusker, "The Pennsylvania Shipping Industry in the Eighteenth Century" (unpublished typescript, 1972).
(e) Letters of John Reynell, at Philadelphia, to Lawrence Williams, 14 Nov. 1734, and 1 Mar. 1734/35, John Reynell Letter Book, 1734–1737, pp. 5, 9, 19, Coates and Reynell Papers, 1702–1843, HSP; McCusker, "Ships Registered at the Port of Philadelphia," no. 8097.
(f) Robert Ellis, at Philadelphia, to Gov. James Oglethorpe, 13 Sept. 1736, Robert Ellis Letter Book, 1736–1748, p. 3, HSP; McCusker, "Ships Registered at the Port of Philadelphia," no. 163.
(g) Daniel Flexney, at London, to John Reynell, at Philadelphia, 18 June 1740, 8 Aug. 1740, and 16 Sept. 1741, and Charles West, at Philadelphia, to Reynell, 8 Oct. 1740, John Reynell Papers, 1729–1783, HSP; Reynell Day Book, 1741–1745, entry for 8 June 1742, and Reynell Ledger C, 1741–1758, p. 74, Coates and Reynell Papers; McCusker, "Ships Registered at the Port of Philadelphia," no. 345.
(h) "Journal of William Black, 1744," ed. R[obert] Alonzo Brock, *Pennsylvania Magazine of*

History and Biography, I (July 1877), 247; McCusker, "Ships Registered at the Port of Philadelphia," no. 407.

(i) E[lias] B[land], at London, to Reynell, 21 Aug. 1746, Reynell Papers; Reynell Day Book, 1748–1752, for 27 Apr. 1748, and Reynell Ledger D, 1745–1767, p. 51, Coates and Reynell Papers; McCusker, "Ships Registered at the Port of Philadelphia," no. 588. See also Harrold E. Gillingham, "Some Colonial Ships Built in Philadelphia," *Pennsylvania Magazine of History and Biography*, LVI (Apr. 1932), 156–186, and John Lyman, "A Philadelphia Shipbuilding Contract of 1746," *American Neptune*, V (July 1945), 243, who printed a document said to be in his own possession.

(j) Hugh Davey and Samuel Carson, at Philadelphia, to Messrs Arthur Vance, Andrew Gregg, and William Caldwell, 29 June 1749, 21 Nov. 1749, and 14 Sept. 1750, Davey and Carson Letter Book, 1745–1750, fols 91, 97, 121, LC; McCusker, "Ships Registered at the Port of Philadelphia," no. 683.

(k) Account for building the snow *Sally*, from William Carter and Cornelius Stout, Philadelphia shipbuilders, to James Burd, at Philadelphia, 30 Mar. 1750, Miscellaneous Items, 1708–1757, Burd–Shippen Papers, 1708–1792, American Philosophical Society, Philadelphia; McCusker, "Ships Registered at the Port of Philadelphia," no. 695.

(l) Papers of ship *Armistad*, Add. MS. 36212, fols 15–20, BL; McCusker, "Ships Registered at the Port of Philadelphia," no. 822.

(m) Thomas Willing, at Philadelphia, to Thomas Willing, at London, 6 Oct. 1755, Willing and Morris Letter Book, 1754–1761, p. 134, HSP; McCusker, "Ships Registered at the Port of Philadelphia," no. 1055.

(n) Thomas Willing, at Philadelphia, to Messrs Mayne and Co. at Lisbon, 19 June 1756, Willing and Morris Letter Book, p. 204; McCusker, "Ships Registered at the Port of Philadelphia," no. 1083.

(o) Thomas Willing and Robert Morris, at Philadelphia, to Codrington Carrington, at Barbados, 26 Aug. 1757, and to Thomas Willing, at London, 1 Oct. 1757, Willing and Morris Letter Book, pp. 320, 357; McCusker, "Ships Registered at the Port of Philadelphia," no. 1165.

(p) Samuel Morris, Jr, at Philadelphia, to [David Barclay and Sons, at London], 2 Apr. 1759, Samuel Morris, Jr, Letter Book, 1757–1763, William Henry Russell Collection of Morris Family Papers, 1684–1935, Eleutherian Mills Historical Library, Greenville, Wilmington, Delaware; McCusker, "Ships Registered at the Port of Philadelphia," no. 1255.

(q) Samuel Morris, Jr, and Israel Morris, at Philadelphia, to Capt. Patrick Dennis, master of the brigantine *Rebecca*, at New York, 31 Aug. 1761, Morris Letter Book, Morris Family Papers; McCusker, "Ships Registered at the Port of Philadelphia," no. 1492.

(r) Joshua Humphreys Note Book, 1719–1832, p. 240, Humphreys Papers, 1682–1835, HSP; McCusker, "Ships Registered at the Port of Philadelphia," no. 7179.

(s) John and Peter Chevalier "Day Book 1770–1783]," entry for 16 Jan. 1771, John and Peter Chevalier Day Book and Journals, 1757–1783, HSP; McCusker, "Ships Registered at the Port of Philadelphia," no. 2080.

(t) John Ross to John Paul Jones, Nantes, 1 Sept. 1778, John Paul Jones Manuscripts, 1775–1783, Peter Force Papers, LC; John J. McCusker, "Colonial Tonnage Measurement: Five Philadelphia Merchant Ships as a Sample," *JEcH*, XXVII (Mar. 1967), 89; McCusker, "Ships Registered at the Port of Philadelphia," no. 2149.

(u) Draughts of HMS *Lightning* (formerly HMS *Sylph*), Deptford Yard, 2 Jan. 1777, Admiralty Sailing Navy Draughts, ZAZ 5568, 5569, 5570, Department of Ships' Plans and Technical Records, National Maritime Museum, Greenwich, London; *Lloyd's Register of Shipping . . . 1776* ([London, 1776]), ship L-292; McCusker, "Ships Registered at the Port of Philadelphia," no. 2355.

(v) Chevalier "Day Book," entry for 23 Sept. 1774; McCusker, "Ships Registered at the Port of Philadelphia," no. 2469.

(w) Entry for 1 Nov. 1774, Wharton and Humphreys Shipyard Accounts, 1773–1795, p. 17, Humphreys Papers; McCusker, "Ships Registered at the Port of Philadelphia," no. 2486.

(x) John J. McCusker, "The Tonnage of the Continental Ship *Alfred*," *Pennsylvania Magazine of History and Biography*, XC (Apr. 1966), 227–232; McCusker, "Ships Registered at the Port of Philadelphia," no. 2498. Compare entry dated 19 July 1775, Adm. 68/203, fol. 132r, PRO.

(y) Draughts of HMS *Vulcan* (formerly HMS *Lord Camden*), Plymouth, May 1778, Admiralty Sailing Navy Draughts, ZAZ 5258, 5608, 5609; McCusker, "Ships Registered at the Port of Philadelphia," no. 2518.

because of some regional differences in the basic formula, the measured tonnage of any given vessel could vary slightly from port to port.[18] Two vessels of the same dimensions registered in two different ports might therefore have different measured tonnages even before each was discounted. In 1748 Hugh Davey and Samuel Carson, Philadelphia merchants, told a correspondent of theirs, Andrew Armour, in the island of St Christopher, that he was foolish to have a ship built at New York:

> There measure greatly differ[s] from ours, vessels built there will measure several tons more than vessels of the same dimensions does here so that what is paid by building there is merely imaginary.[19]

This was the case with the snow *Diamond*, the property of John Erving of Boston. Owned and registered there, it measured 152 tons at that port. The wardens appointed to measure it at New York for the Royal Navy in 1762 calculated its size at only 133 tons, however.[20] Thus even the same percentage discount from measured tonnage could, in a different port, result in a somewhat different registered tonnage (see table 3.2). Moreover, the average percentage of that discount could and did vary considerably from one port to another over time.

18 Compare, for instance, the tonnage formulas in use in Barbados, New Hampshire, Massachusetts, Rhode Island, Connecticut, New York, Pennsylvania, and Virginia: [Barbados, Laws and Statutes], Acts, *Passed in the Island of Barbados. From 1643 to 1762, Inclusive*, ed. Richard Hall and Richard Hall (London, 1764), pp. 135, 156–157; New Hampshire Provincial Deeds, vol. VI, no. 51, New Hampshire Historical Society, Concord, NH, and as printed in George A. Nelson, "A Contract to Build a Sloop in 1694," *American Neptune*, II (Oct. 1942), 338; L[awrence] W. Jenkins, "Contract to Build a Brigantine ... 1750," *American Neptune*, XXI (June 1961), 15; [Massachusetts (Colony), Laws and Statutes], *The Acts and Resolves, Public and Private, of the Province of the Massachusetts Bay* [ed. Abner Cheney Goodell *et al.*], 21 vols (Boston, 1869–1922), I, 164–165, 207–208, 275; M[arion] V. Brewington, "A Boston Shipbuilding Contract of 1747," *American Neptune*, V (Oct. 1945), 328, printed from a document in the collections of the Bostonian Society; Howard M. Chapin, *Rhode Island Privateers in King George's War, 1739–1748* (Providence, RI, 1926), p. vii; G[eorge] Andrew[s] Moriarty, "Articles of Agreement, 1747," *The Mariner: The Quarterly Journal of the Ship Model Society of Rhode Island*, VII (Jan. 1933), 10–11; [Connecticut (Colony)], *The Public Records of the Colony of Connecticut*, ed. James Hammond Trumbull and Charles Jeremy Hoadly, 15 vols (Hartford, Conn., 1850–1890), VI, 147; [New York (Colony), Laws and Statutes], *Laws of New York, from the Year 1691 to [1762]*, [ed. William Livingston and William Smith, Jr], 2 vols (New York, 1752–1762), I, 223; [Pennsylvania, Laws and Statutes], *Statutes at Large of Pennsylvania from 1682 to 1801*, ed. James T. Mitchell and Henry Flanders, 18 vols (Harrisburg, Pa., 1896–1915), III, 166–167, V, 354, VI, 375–376; Jonathan Dickinson, at Philadelphia, to J[onathan] Gale, [at Jamaica], Philadelphia, 7 June 1718, Letter Book of Jonathan Dickinson, p. 198, Library Company of Philadelphia Collection, HSP, and Joshua Humphreys Note Book, 1719–1832, pp. 17–18, Joshua Humphreys Papers, 1682–1838, HSP; [Virginia (Colony), Laws and Statutes], *A Collection of All the Acts of Assembly, Now in Force, in the Colony of Virginia,* [ed. John Halloway *et al.*] (Williamsburg, Va., 1733), pp. 171, 243. See also John Lyman, "Early Tonnage Measurement in England," *MM*, LIV (May 1968), 114.
19 Letter, 29 July 1748, Davey and Carson Letter Book, 1745–1750, fol. 70, LC.
20 John Watts, at New York, to John Erving, at Boston, 7 June 1762, 1 July 1762, and 11 Jan. 1763, in *Letter Book of John Watts, Merchant and Councilor of New York, January 1,*

Table 3.2 Measured and registered tonnages compared: samples from three studies

Sample	Number of cases (1)	Total registered tonnage (2)	Total measured tonnage (3)	Percentage difference ([(3) – (2)] ÷ (3)) (4)
Philadelphia (1709–1775)				
Vessels registered (a)	25	2,692	4,753	43.4
Virginia (1725)				
Vessels entering (b)	75	5,754	8,937	35.6
Jamaica, Grenada,				
and Antigua (1785–1787)				
Vessels Entering (c)	63	14,078	18,884	25.5
Mean of three sample				
percentage differences			34.8%	

Notes and sources:
(a) Philadelphia Vessels Registered. table 3.1, above.
(b) Virginia Vessels Entering. NOSL, POE York River, Va., 24 Mar. 1724/25 to 25 Mar. 1726, CO 5/1442, fol. 23, PRO; NOSL, POE South Potomac, Va., 25 Mar. 1725 to 25 Dec. 1726, CO 5/1442, fols 16, 17, 26, 44., PRO. The number of cases used here differs from that employed in Christopher J. French, "Eighteenth-Century Shipping Tonnage Measurements," *JEcH*, XXXIII (June 1973), p. 434, table 5, in that my sample does not include second entries of the same vessel. Both French's figures and mine vary from those presented by Gary M. Walton, "Colonial Tonnage Measurements: A Comment," *JEcH*, XXVII (Sept. 1967), 392–397, because of the mistakes that Walton made in transcription and compilation and that French pointed out and corrected in "Eighteenth-Century Shipping Tonnage Measurements," p. 443, n. 27. Note as well that all three tabulations do not take into account the twelve vessels for which the clerk of the Naval Office recorded only one of the two tonnage figures.
(c) Jamaica, Grenada, and Antigua Vessels Entering. French, "Eighteenth-Century Shipping Tonnage Measurements," pp. 434–439, table 1.

1762–December 22, 1765, [ed. Dorothy C. Barck], Collections of the New-York Historical Society, LXI (New York, 1928), pp. 61, 65, 114. The difference referred to might not have been so much a regional variation as a function of the snow's being hired to the Royal Navy, if the case of the ship *Oliver* is relevant. David Ochterlong, the *Oliver*'s supercargo, wrote from New York, on 7 June 1761, to one of the owners and the ship's husband, William Wallaby of London, to say that it had entered into pay as a transport as of 25 May:

> but she measured farr short of what she did when in service before, but its all owing to the method of measureing here, for she really dont measure what she was paid for when built. She only measures about 260 tons . . . and when in the service before was allow'd for 311 tons but her measureing so much then was owing to my good friends which I now want.

Papers of the Ship *Oliver*, *Williamson* v. *Wallaby*, C 110/186, pt ii, bundle D, no. 7, PRO. A snow was a type of large, two-masted, 17th- and 18th-century sailing vessel, rigged with two lower sails on the mainmast, one a square mainsail attached, as usual, to a spar, and the second a fore-and-aft mainsail attached to a small mast stepped just behind the mainmast and secured to it. See William Falconer, *An Universal Dictionary of the Marine . . .*, [4th edn], [London, 1780], p. 271.

Table 3.3 Relationship between the registered tonnage of vessels and the percentage difference between their measured and registered tonnages

Range of registered tonnages	Philadelphia (1709–1775) Registered Vessels (1)	West Indian Series (1785–1787) London registered vessels (2)	Outport registered vessels (3)	Virginia Series (1725) London registered vessels (4)	Outport registered vessels (5)	Colonial registered vessels (6)
0–50	56.3% (6)				48.0% (10)	54.2% (20)
51–100	46.6% (7)		43.0% (3)	23.1% (2)	33.7% (14)	33.5% (17)
101–150	35.0% (7)	45.6% (3)	44.0% (11)	37.9% (2)	17.7% (1)	6.2% (1)
151–200	36.5% (5)	38.2% (3)	30.5% (6)	25.3% (3)	19.7% (2)	16.5% (2)
201–150		28.1% (4)	34.0% (7)	33.3% (1)		
251–300		8.3% (5)				
301–350		11.2% (9)				
351–400		8.4% (2)				
Weighted average	43.4%	19.0%	37.6%	29.8%	34.8%	37.1%
Mean of six weighted averages		33.6%				

Notes and sources:
The first number in each pair (e.g. 46.6) is the mean of the percentage differences between the measured and registered tonnages of the ships in that range (e.g., between 51 and 100 registered tons); the number in parentheses (e.g., 7) is the numbers of vessels in the sample. The weighted average was calculated in the same way as the total "percentage difference" in table 3.1, that is, the figure was computed by totaling the registered and measured tonnages of all vessels involved and computing the percentage difference between the totals. In other words, the number at the foot of column (2), "19.0", reports the percentage difference between the total measured tonnage (18,884) and the total registered tonnage (14,078) of the 26 vessels in that set. The average is thus weighted by the tonnages of the vessels.
  Column (1). From table 3.1 of this chapter.
  Columns (2) and (3). Christopher J. French, "Eighteenth-Century Shipping Tonnage Measurements," *JEcH*, XXXIII (June 1973), pp. 441–443, tables 3 and 4. I have corrected a mistake in calculation in French's table 3 for tonnage range "51–100" by reference to his table 2, op. cit., p. 440.
  Columns (4), (5), and (6). NOSL, POE York River, and POE South Potomac, Va., 25 Mar. 1725 to 25 Mar. 1726, CO 5/1442, fols 16, 17, 23, 26, 44, PRO.

Table 3.3 shows that the percentage of the discount was, to some extent, also dependent on the size of the vessel. This size-related difference, first pointed out by Christopher J. French, seems to have been the case throughout the empire.[21] Since all of the "average" discount figures are obviously weighted by the size of the vessels in the sample, those ports that registered smaller vessels will have a larger mean discount and those ports at which the vessels averaged a somewhat larger size will have a smaller mean discount.

One can only guess why this variation occurred. Since the whole practice of discounting operated as a silent agreement between shipowners and the

21 French, "Eighteenth-Century Shipping Tonnage Measurements."

Customs authorities, there might have been an equally tacit willingness not to allow discounting to become too flagrant. Recall that a variety of harbor, wharfage, and lighthouse dues were prorated on a vessel's registered tonnage. A discount of 50 percent on a four-ton vessel meant a considerably smaller *absolute* reduction in fees paid than the same percentage reduction on a 400-ton vessel. Thus Governor Charles Knowles of Jamaica complained in 1753 of

> the shortness of Tunnage of Ships and Vessels mentioned in their Registers, many not expressing half the burthen [i.e., measured tonnage] of the Ship whereby the Powder Duty here is greatly lessened, as well as the light House money in England, and other Dutys arising upon Tunnage.

He continued by arguing that "a reasonable Indulgence on this head I apprehend may be proper, but it is carried much beyond that now."[22] Perhaps it was in an attempt to be "reasonable" that we can find the origins of the size-related differential in the discount.

Even greater differences in the discount can be detected. For instance, there are a few (a very few) instances in which vessels registered at a British port and later re-registered at Philadelphia showed a new registered tonnage reduced by as much as half of the old registered tonnage. These cases number no more than five or six (out of over 3,000) and all were for vessels originally registered in Great Britain. The example of one brigantine built at Swansea in Wales in 1754 and registered there at seventy tons is a good one. It was later sold and re-registered three times: once was at St Christopher as the *Princess Mary* on 10 June 1758; the second was on 9 September 1758, as the *Captain Granville* at Philadelphia. Both times the tonnage was given as seventy tons. Then the brigantine's new owners registered it once again, at Philadelphia, as the *Success*, on 20 December 1758; that time its registered tonnage was given as thirty-five tons.[23] One possibility is that the *Princess Mary*'s original registered tonnage was, indeed, its measured tonnage, as the law stipulated, and that its Philadelphia owners were the first ones to invoke the usual discount. Perhaps at Swansea there was no discount at all. Certainly there was none in Virginia.

22 Knowles to Commissioners for Trade and Plantations, Jamaica, 10 Jan. 1753, CO 137/25, pt ii, fol. 308, PRO.
23 John J. McCusker, "Ships Registered at the Port of Philadelphia before 1776: A Computerized Listing" (unpublished computer printout, 1970), nos 1222–1246–1303–1407, 1829–2028–2194, 2160–2542. References are to serial numbers assigned to the ships' registers. This compilation is based primarily on the Ship Register Books of the Province of Pennsylvania, 1722–1776, HSP. See John J. McCusker, "The Pennsylvania Shipping Industry in the Eighteenth Century" (unpublished typescript, 1972). Copies of both of these works of mine have been been deposited in the HSP. See also, John J. McCusker, "Sources of Investment Capital in the Colonial Philadelphia Shipping Industry," *JEcH*, XXXII (Mar. 1972), 148 – revised as chapter eleven of the present book.

The case of Virginia was anomalous, perhaps unique, in the colonies. Yet what the Virginians did is understandable: they taxed the unrepresented, a practice later Virginians would deplore under different circumstances. The rationale for discounting tonnage centered upon the savings for shipowners of at least part of the duties mentioned by Governor Knowles. Those duties were payable upon entering into and clearing from a port. On the one hand, where local port authorities answered to a constituency made up of shipowners, pressure would be considerable to keep the net sum payable as low as possible by allowing a large discount. On the other hand, in a place where there were relatively few shipowners, there would be little or no pressure for discount from measured tonnage and perhaps some pressure in the opposite direction in order to maximize the revenue from the duty. This was what happened in Virginia. In 1705 the Virginia House of Burgesses enacted a revenue bill that collected a duty of 1s. 3d. (6.25p) sterling per ton on vessels entering the colony's ports. The law stipulated that tonnage be full measured tonnage computed using the formula set forth in the English Act of 1694.[24] Given that most of the vessels that entered the colony's ports were owned in England, the plantation owners of Virginia were quite happy taxing London shipowners to the fullest extent possible.

Equally unhappy were the London shipowners. Nor were they shy about expressing their displeasure. In a series of petitions, they argued at length to all who would hear them that the Virginia law was unfair because such fees and duties had traditionally been assessed at a discount from measured tonnage.[25] But Virginians counterattacked and found on their side worthy allies, the Commissioners of the Customs, who agreed, not surprisingly, that measured tonnage was the best basis for collecting duties. The London merchants won the first skirmish and succeeded in having the law of 1705 disallowed on the technical grounds that the law (and formula) of 1694 had been superseded by another law (and formula) in 1695. But they lost the war. In 1710 the House of Burgesses merely reenacted the law with the newer

---

24 [Virginia, Laws and Statutes], *The Statutes at Large; Being a Collection of All the Laws of Virginia*, ed. William Waller Hening, 13 vols (Richmond, Va., 1809–1823), III, 345. The Virginia legislature's adoption of the Parliamentary formula of 1694 was a conscious one. See the "Memorial of the Merchants & Owners of Ships Trading to Virginia" [at London], to the Commissioners for Trade and Plantations, endorsed as received 13 May 1707, CO 5/1315, pt ii, fols 274r, 340r, PRO. Compare the Act of 5 and 6 William and Mary, c. 20, sec. ix (1694).

25 See their petitions and other relevant papers in CO 5/1315, pt ii, PRO, and CO 5/1362, PRO. Compare the entries in [GB, Commissioners for Trade and Plantations], *Journal of the Commissioners for Trade and Plantations [1704–1782]*, 14 vols (London, 1920–1938), I, passim, printing CO 391/9, pp. 332–394 and elsewhere, PRO. Some mention of the dispute is made in Arthur Pierce Middleton, *Tobacco Coast: A Maritime History of Chesapeake Bay in the Colonial Era* (Newport News, Va., 1953), pp. 236, 412. See also the letter from the Commissioners of the Customs to the Commissioners for Trade and Plantations, 5 May 1719, and the reply of the same date, CO 388/21, pt i, fol. 90, PRO, and CO 389/27, p. 166, PRO. See the Act of 6 and 7 William and Mary, c. 12, sec. x (1695).

1695 formula.[26] Virginia tonnage duties continued to be collected on full measured tonnage down to the American Revolution.[27] Virginians protected and thereby promoted their own shipping industry by exempting from the duty vessels wholly owned by residents of the colony.

One result of this Virginia tonnage duty law was that vessels registered there often if not always were registered at full measured tonnage. The Virginia Naval Office shipping lists for the ports of York River and South Potomac for 1725 and 1726, which were used for table 3.2 and table 3.3, list both the registered and measured tonnage of each vessel that entered these ports. For most of the Virginia-registered vessels in these lists, the clerk of the Naval Office either set down only the registered tonnage (apparently aware that this was, in fact, the same as the measured tonnage), or he entered the same number in both columns. Perhaps more to the point, when vessels previously registered at Virginia were re-registered at Philadelphia, their tonnage figures were reduced. The new registered tonnages of these vessels reflected an average discount of 37.8 percent over the old figures.[28] For Virginia, at least, the discounting from measured tonnage cannot be assumed.

Even Pennsylvania, despite its large constituency of shipowners and shippers, was not immune to the temptation to collect greater revenue by disregarding the traditional discounting from measured tonnage. In 1758, in the midst of the Seven Years War, the Pennsylvania legislature passed a law to collect a duty on vessels entering the colony. The text of the law stipulated that the duty be assessed "for every ton . . . according to the measure" of the vessel, not according to the tonnage in its register.[29] Legislators and merchants alike recognized that the law would collect a greater revenue more quickly on this basis and the latter were upset. Thomas Willing and Robert Morris, the great Philadelphia mercantile partnership, called it "a cursed act" but they

26 *Statutes at Large . . . of Virginia*, ed. Hening, III, 344, 490–495.
27 Again, the choice of the formula was a deliberate one. CO 391/19, p. 394, PRO. Trying to put as good a face on the situation as he could, the Governor called use of the new formula "the only practicable way in this Country where the Ships cannot be laid dry in order to their mensuration." Letter from Alexander Spotswood, at [Williamsburg], Va., to Commissioners for Trade and Plantations, 6 Mar. 1710/11, in *The Official Letters of Alexander Spotswood, Lieutenant-Governor of the Colony of Virginia, 1710–1722*. ed. R[obert] A. Brock, Collections of the Virginia Historical Society, n.s., vols I and II, 2 vols (Richmond, Va., 1882–1885), I, 49. Compare Spotswood to Commissioners of the Customs, 28 July 1711, ibid., I, 97. The law contained no clause limiting its duration and I can find no repeal of it or any new law superseding it; it seems to have remained in effect throughout the colonial period. See, for instance, Spotswood, at [Williamsburg], Va., to Commissioners for Trade and Plantations, 7 Mar. 1717/18, ibid., II, 269. It also seems not to have been reenacted by the state legislature, however. See Edmund Berkeley, Jr, "The Naval Office in Virginia, 1776–1789," *American Neptune*, XXXIII (Jan. 1973), 29.
28 McCusker, "Ships Registered at the Port of Philadelphia," nos 1713–1812–2285–2329–2446, 1716–1876, 1958–1980, 1963–2014, 2284–2348.
29 *Statutes at Large of Pennsylvania*, ed. Mitchell and Flanders, V, 352–355. The law, or at least the same formula, seems still to have been in effect in 1790. See n. 31 of this chapter.

paid as obligated.[30] They could hardly do otherwise since the purpose of the duty was to purchase and fit out a provincial ship-of-war to protect the colony's trade. Nevertheless it is clear from the merchants' reaction that a duty collected upon the measured tonnage of a vessel was going to be more than one collected upon the same vessel's registered tonnage. And it is equally clear that this was a change from the usual practice of effectively allowing a discount in the duty payable by discounting the gross size of that upon which the duty was assessed.

As far as the relationship between registered tonnage and measured tonnage is concerned, we have learned several things. They were not equal, despite the provisions of the laws of 1694 and 1695. Empire-wide, the average difference between them probably approached the figure suggested at the time by Thomas Irving: registered tonnage equaled two-thirds of measured tonnage. This difference, tied to the size of vessels, varied on the average from port to port, just as the average size of vessels registered varied from port to port. At Philadelphia, for instance, registered tonnage averaged close to three-fifths of measured tonnage. Moreover, the discounting procedure was not a universal practice. Vessels registered at Virginia were regularly registered at their measured tonnage and so also, it seems, were some of the vessels that were registered at the smaller British ports. Given all of these qualifications, it is still possible to estimate the measured tonnage of vessels at one and a half times their registered tonnage – following Irving's suggestions. But the exceptions are enough to argue for further research and some caution in applying this correction. The outstanding instance where such a correction is warranted is in any gross comparison of shipping activity before and after the period 1780–1790, during which decade both Great Britain and the United States adopted and enforced new tonnage regulations that, in effect, substituted measured for registered tonnage.[31]

30 Thomas Willing and Robert Morris, at Philadelphia, to Codrington Carrington, at Barbados, 30 May 1758, Willing and Morris Letter Book, 1754–1761, p. 410, HSP.
31 McCusker, "Colonial Tonnage Measurement," 91; French, "Eighteenth-Century Shipping Tonnage Measurements," p. 436. Not every writer has understood the implications of this change. See, for instance, C[harles] Ernst Fayle, "Shipowning and Marine Insurance," in *The Trade Winds: A Study of British Overseas Trade during the French Wars, 1793–1815*, ed. C[yril] Northcote Parkinson (London, [1948]), p. 26.
   The British Consul resident at Philadelphia in the 1780s compared the effects of these new tonnage laws and calculated that the "different modes of admeasurement here and in England" resulted in different figures for the same vessel. "Brit[ish] admeasurement . . . is less than the American about 12 percent." Phineas Bond, at Philadelphia, to Duke of Leeds, 10 Nov. 1789, FO 4/7, PRO, and as printed in "Letters of Phineas Bond, British Consul at Philadelphia, to the Foreign Office of Great Britain, 1787–[1794]," ed. J[ohn] Franklin Jameson, American Historical Association, *Annual Report for the Year 1896*, 2 vols (Washington, DC, 1897), I, 640. At least for a while, the state of Pennsylvania continued to use the older formula: "the mode of calculation and measurement, under the act of congress, makes a difference of 12½ percent. above the carpenter's measurement and the mode prescribed by the act of the assembly of this state." Joseph Erwin, ["Present State of the Trade and Navigation of Pennsylvania"], *American Museum*, VIII (Sept. 1790), 118. Compare n. 29 of this chapter.

◆ ◆ ◆ ◆ ◆

Any interest in the ratio between measured (or registered) tonnage and cargo tonnage is almost purely academic because, however much individuals in the eighteenth century were interested in the cargo capacity of a vessel, they rarely if ever related it to a vessel's measured tonnage.[32] One reason for this is that cargo tonnage in relationship to measured tonnage kept increasing over the years before 1780. Another reason is that cargo tonnage had as much to do with the cargo as it did with the vessel. Increasingly vessels were constructed for specific trades. But this specialized construction meant that a ship that could stow 200 cargo tons of tobacco might be able to carry only half that number of cargo tons of another commodity. As one man had put it two centuries earlier, "no owner nor shypmaster can hable [i.e., vouch for] any shyppe for her burden . . . untill she be tryed uppon the Sea" – one simply could not determine a vessel's cargo capacity without first loading it.[33]

Our interest in discovering the average relationship between measured tonnage and cargo capacity for eighteenth-century vessels owes its origins to the economic historian's search for information about trade. The tonnage of vessels sailing between ports during this period is an accepted, if questionable, surrogate for the volume and, with less justification, the value of goods traded

32 For an especially informative exception to this rule, see the series of letters concerning the brigantine *Swift* that the Philadelphia firm of James and Drinker sent to Nehemiah Champion at Bristol, 20 Dec. 1756, 28 June 1757, 13 July 1757, Abel James and Henry Drinker Letter Books, 1762–1786, vol. I, pp. 63–64, 127–128, 144–145, Henry Drinker Papers, 1756–1869, HSP. The brigantine measured about 130 tons but they were able to register it "at 65 Tons which was as low as we could make it." (Compare McCusker, "Ships Registered at the Port of Philadelphia," no. 1147, which shows the brig *Swift* registered on 11 July 1757 at 60 tons.) For the vessel's first voyage James and Drinker loaded the *Swift* with a cargo of "about 60 Tons of our Tonnage." They explained the *Swift*'s diminished cargo capacity by reason of its design as an armed vessel; it had two 6-pounders and ten 4-pounders. "We think if she was to be fully Laden without Guns etc. as we Load our Vessels she would carry 70 Tons and with 2 Decks 90 Tons." Obviously, as an armed vessel, presumably intended to serve as a privateer during the Seven Years War, it must also have been built for speed and, therefore, had a low block coefficient. Compare the statement quoted below about the ship *Sidney*, "a remarkable fast sailer."

See in this regard the discussions of how to determine the relationship between measured tonnage and cargo tonnage in Edmund Bushnell, *The Complete Ship-Wright . . . Teaching the Proportions Used by Experienced Ship-Wrights*, 5th edn (London, 1688), pp. 50–51; and William Sutherland, *The Ship-Builders Assistant: or, Some Essays Towards Compleating the Art of Marine Architecture* (London, 1711), pp. 85–106.

33 Statement by John Sherewood, deponent in an Admiralty suit, Dec. 1541, HCA 13/4, fol. 284, PRO. See also G[eoffrey] V. Scammell, "English Merchant Shipping at the End of the Middle Ages: Some East Coast Evidence," *EcHR*, 2nd ser., XIII (no. 3, 1961), 331–332. Compare the statement of two Pennsylvania merchants in 1768: "We shall know for certainty next trip how much the [sloop] *America* can carry." Samuel and Jonathan Smith, at Philadelphia, to Nathaniel Homes, 19 Mar. 1767 [*sic* for 1768], Samuel and Jonathan Smith Letter Book, 1765–1770, Peter Force Papers, LC. At Jamaica in the 1780s the owners of one trading vessel demonstrated its cargo capacity by loading it with casks of pork, beef, and flour. See the "Memorial of the Merchants and Traders of the Town of Kingston," read 7 Dec. 1789, BT 6/76, PRO.

between the ports. Modern studies, multiplying tonnage times freight costs per ton, have yielded estimates of shipping earnings in these same trades. When we do not have records of cargoes carried, we have had to settle for surrogates, despite such obvious potential difficulties as partially loaded vessels, disparately valued cargoes, and the increasing "fullness" (or block coefficient) of British and colonial merchantmen. The last of these three difficulties, and, to a lesser extent, the first of them, can be offset if we can establish the average ratio between the cargo and capacity of merchant vessels and their registered tonnages.

Ralph Davis, the historian of England's shipping industry, argued that cargo tonnage in the seventeenth century was something less than measured tonnage (and, therefore, something close to registered tonnage). The earliest discounting procedure discussed above, wherein registered tonnage was originally established at a percentage less than measured tonnage, grew out of an appreciation of this difference. Davis went on to say that his "generalization was becoming doubtful by 1700; the two figures (cargo tonnage and measured tonnage) were coming together, so that by 1700 many ships carried as much as they measured, and by 1775 most carried more than they measured."[34] As he pointed out elsewhere, this trend had as its basis the introduction into English shipbuilding of the elements of design that characterized the Dutch *fluijt*, the block coefficient of which was greater than any other contemporary vessel.[35] The colonists recognized the *fluijt*'s advantages, as did their English counterparts, and they tended to build similar vessels, although not without some variation.[36] Thus we can find suggestions of a development occurring in the shipping of North America by 1775 similar to that described by Davis: vessels came to carry more than they measured. This is certainly the cause of

34 Davis, *Rise of the English Shipping Industry*, p. 372.
35 Davis, *Rise of the English Shipping Industry*, pp. 48–50 and elsewhere. Compare Parry, "Transport and Trade Routes," pp. 211–213. The special qualities of the *fluijt* are discussed in Bernard Hagedorn, *Die Entwickelung der wichtigsten Schiffstypen bis ins 19. Jahrhundert*, Veröffentlichungen des Verein für Hamburgische Geschichte, vol. 1 (Berlin, 1914), pp. 102–118; Kristof Glamann, *European Trade, 1500–1700*, trans. Geoffrey French ([London, 1971]), pp. 30–31; and Richard W. Unger, *Dutch Shipbuilding before 1800: Ships and Guilds* (Assen and Amsterdam, 1978), pp. 35–38.
36 See, e.g., William Fitzhugh, at Stafford County, Va., to Thomas Clayton, at Liverpool, 26 Apr. 1686 in *William Fitzhugh and His Chesapeake World, 1676–1707: The Fitzhugh Letters and Other Documents*, ed. Richard Beale Davis, Virginia Historical Society, Documents, vol. 3 (Chapel Hill, NC, 1963), p. 226. American-built vessels were "not so flat bottomed as those of G[reat] Britain, Holland and Sweden and are somewhat fuller than those of France," according to William Bingham, Collector of the Customs at Philadelphia, in a letter to Alexander Hamilton, [at Philadelphia], [25 Nov. 1789], in *The Papers of Alexander Hamilton*, ed. Harold C. Syrett *et al.*, 26 vols (New York, 1961–1979), V, 554. Compare the similar statements by Joseph Whipple, the Collector at Portsmouth, NH, in a letter to Hamilton, 19 Dec. 1789, ibid., VI, 22; and by Richard Graydon, one of the Haven-Masters of the port of Dublin, 7 Mar. 1774, [Ireland (Eire), Parl., Commons], *The Journals of the House of Commons of the Kingdom of Ireland, 1613–1776*, 19 vols (Dublin, 1753–1776), XVII, 428–429. As Graydon put it, given that the river bottom near the customhouse in Dublin is stony and uneven, "no American built ship, or others of sharp Construction, can come up to the Custom-house, as they will not take the Ground."

Governor James Glen's efforts in 1749, when, in reply to questions from the Commissioners for Trade and Plantations about the trade of the colony, he calculated, "the quantity of tonnage [of vessels clearing South Carolina] computed from their cargoes [and] not taken from their registers."[37] And it explains the somewhat exaggerated claims of John Williams, the Inspector-General of the Customs in North America, that "vessels by their Cargoes are of four times the Burthen they are Registered at."[38]

Fortunately, as with measured tonnage, it is possible to assemble sufficient data for a limited test of the relationship between registered tonnage and cargo tonnage. Basically what is done is to convert actual cargoes known to have been laden on board several vessels into the total number of cargo tons they equaled and to compare each vessel's cargo tonnage with its registered tonnage. This is, in fact, the way contemporaries, such as Governor Glen, measured cargo tonnage; they viewed a vessel's cargo tonnage in terms of actual cargoes.[39] Appropriately, it is contemporary commentators who provide us with the necessary conversion ratios, called, then and later, "stowage factors."

As far as merchants and shipowners were concerned, the "ton" of cargo varied with each commodity and depended on both the commodity's weight and its size. The optimum cargo for a vessel not only filled up the vessel's cargo space, essentially its hold, but also weighed it down so that it floated in the water at its best sailing depth, at its load water line. A vessel the cargo space of which was filled with a commodity the specific density of which was less than water failed to settle to its load water line, and the master of the vessel had to add ballast before setting sail or he would encounter great difficulty in handling his ship as it would ride too high out of the water. It would be too buoyant. Reciprocally, a vessel the cargo of which had a specific density greater than water settled to its load water line well before the cargo space was fully occupied. It would not be buoyant enough. Overloading it made it hard to manage at sea. Indeed loading its hold full risked sinking it at dockside. The freight ton, the basic unit of measure, was conceived of as occupying forty cubic feet, supposedly the cubic space taken up by four

---

37 Enclosure in Glen to Commissioners for Trade and Plantations, Charleston, 31 May 1749, CO 5/461, fol. 84, PRO. There is a copy of this report, identified as the "Answers from James Glenn, Governor of South Carolina, to Queries from the Lords Commissioners for Trade and Plantations," 1749, MS 114, Palaeography Room, Senate House, Library, University of London. Glen's report was also printed as [James Glen], *A Description of South Carolina, Containing Many Interesting and Curious Particulars* (London, 1761).

38 Extract from report of Williams, [at New York], to [American Board of Customs, at Boston], 22 Dec. 1768, enclosed in letter of the Commissioners of the American Board of Customs, [at Boston], to the Treasury, 18 Aug. 1774, T 1/505, fol. 292, PRO. For Williams and his reports, see Joseph R. Frese, "The Royal Customs Service in the Chesapeake, 1770: The Reports of John Williams, Inspector General," *Virginia Magazine of History and Biography*, LXXXI (July 1973), 280–318. Williams made a habit of exaggerating. McCusker, "Colonial Civil Servant and Counter-Revolutionary," pp. 323–324 (see n. 22 of chapter nine of this book).

39 See also Thomas Irving's comments and calculations of 1784 as presented in testimony before the Commissioners for Trade and Plantations, BT 5/1, p. 159, PRO.

hogsheads of wine, the specific density of wine being about the same as that of water.[40] In fact, the gross cargo ton occupied more like sixty-six cubic feet, allowing for the containers and the empty spaces between them,[41] and, in 1706, Trinity House defined it as seventy-two cubic feet.[42]

Unless one carried wine, it was necessary, obviously, for the master of the vessel to work at balancing a cargo so as both to fill the vessel's hold and to maintain it at its load water line. The latter consideration kept the ship afloat; the former consideration, by ensuring optimum returns on any voyage, kept the shipowner in business. Colonel Samuel Martin, Sr, the doyen

40 G[eorge] Moorsom, "On the New Tonnage-Law, as Established in the Merchant Shipping Act of 1854," *Transactions of the [Royal] Institution of Naval Architects*, I (1860), 133; Robert White Stevens, *On the Stowage of Ships and Their Cargoes*, [1st edn] (Plymouth and London, 1858), p. 15; Gille, "Jauge et tonnage des navires," p. 88. The freight ton of lumber and "bale goods of all kinds" was 40 cu. ft. at Philadelphia, Boston, and New York. *Statutes at Large of Pennsylvania*, ed. Mitchell and Flanders, V, 402; Henry Lloyd, at Boston, to John Freare, at Victualler General's Office, Halifax, 9 Sept. 1765, Henry Lloyd Letter Book, 1765–1767, p. 161, Manuscripts and Archives Department, Baker Library, Graduate School of Business Administration, Harvard University, Boston, Mass.; [New York (City), Chamber of Commerce], *Colonial Records of the New York Chamber of Commerce, 1768–1784; with Historical and Biographical Sketches*, ed. John Austin Stevens, Jr (New York, 1867), p. 142. Compare Burwash, *English Merchant Shipping*, p. 95; and Richard Hayes, *The Negociator's Magazine*, 9th edn, rev., ed. Benjamin Webb (London, 1764), p. 210.

Where we can determine the volume of the quantity of commodities for which we have stowage factors (see table 3.5), the net freight ton did average close to 40 cu. ft.

Volume of 1 Freight Ton of Selected Commodities
Of liquids, 1 freight ton equaled 252 gal. or 33.7 cu. ft.
Of sugar. 1 freight ton equaled 22 cwt. or 34.7 cu. ft.
Of wheat, 1 freight ton equaled 40 bu. or 49.8 cu. ft.
Of salt, 1 freight ton equaled 22 bu. or 39.8 cu. ft.
Of coal, 1 freight ton equaled 36 bu. or 42.4 cu. ft.
Mean volume of 1 freight ton = 40.1 cu. ft.

The gallon was the English wine gallon of 231 cu. in.; the bushel was the Winchester bushel of 2,150.42 cu. in. See table 3.5, nn. (c) and (f). For the volume of a cwt. of 18th-century muscovado sugar, see John J. McCusker, *Rum and the American Revolution: The Rum Trade and the Balance of Payments of the Thirteen Continental Colonies, 1650–1775*, 2 vols (New York, 1989 [Ph.D. diss., University of Pittsburgh, 1970]), II, 847.

41 Richard Steele and Joseph Gillmore, *An Account of the Fish-Pool: Consisting of a Description of the Vessel so Call'd* . . . (London, 1718), p. 17; Moorsom, "On the New Tonnage-Law," p. 135; Lane, "Tonnages, Medieval and Modern," p. 219.

42 See the report signed by the Master and Wardens of Trinity House, London, 30 Mar. 1706, Post Class 1/4, pp. 6–7, Post Office Archives, Post Office Archives and Records Centre, London. Compare John Haskell Kemble, "England's First Atlantic Mail Line," *MM*, XXVI (Apr. 1940), 196–197. In contrast, in the early 19th century, the East India Company allowed only 50 cu. ft. to the gross freight ton for such goods as cotton, flax, hemp, indigo, and "Lacquered and China-Ware." Charles Hardy, *A Register of Ships, Employed in the Service of the Honourable the East India Company, from the Year 1760 to 1810* . . . , [2nd edn], rev. and enl., edn Horatio Charles Hardy (London, 1811), Appendix, pp. 139–140.

of the Antigua sugar planter community during the third quarter of the eighteenth century, typified these concerns in a letter to some business associates in 1761. He was ordering a cargo of coal sent to him but he worried about the possible under-utilization of the vessel's cargo capacity. "You will observe," he wrote to Messrs Codrington and Miller of London, "that as coals are too heavy a loading to full [sic] up a ship, it will be to our profit to fill her up with oats and any other light commodity."[43] In established staple trades, such considerations worked to generate a commerce in complementary commodities such as: the export of fish from Iceland to Kingston-upon-Hull in which the ships were ballasted "with great coble stone . . . the which . . . pavid al the [streets in the] town";[44] the grain trade between Amsterdam and Italy that, in return, brought marble as ballast to The Netherlands and made Amsterdam the "marble emporium" of Northern Europe;[45] or the elaborate intercolonial trade in iron between Maryland and Virginia that supplied iron bars for export as ballast in tobacco ships from ports of both colonies.[46]

Freight rates in the organized, established trades were collected on the basis of the cargo ton and, in the more sophisticated mercantile centers, tables

43   Samuel Martin, at Antigua, to Messrs Codrington and Miller, at London, 30 July 1761, Add. MS 41349, fol. 113, BL. The freight ton of coal, at 2,880 lb., was 880 lb. or 44 percent heavier than the freight ton of wine. See table 3.5. On Martin, see R[ichard] B. Sheridan, "Samuel Martin, Innovating Sugar Planter of Antigua, 1750–1776," *Agricultural History*, XXXIV (July 1960), 126–139.

44   *The Itinerary of John Leland in or about the Years 1535–1543*, ed Lucy Toulmin Smith, 5 vols (London, 1907–1910), I, 50. Compare P. C. Buckland and Jon Sadler, "Ballast and Building Stone: A Discussion," in *Stone: Quarrying and Building in England, AD 43–1525*, ed. David Parsons ([Chichester, Sussex, 1990]), pp. 114–125.

45   D[avid] W. Davies, *A Primer of Dutch Seventeenth Century Overseas Trade* (The Hague, 1961), pp. 41–42.

46   Much about this trade is detailed in the letters of William Lux, merchant of Baltimore, in the William Lux Letter Book, 1763–1768, New-York Historical Society, New York City, and as edited in Pamela [B.] Satek, "William Lux of Baltimore, 18th-Century Merchant" (M.A. thesis, University of Maryland, 1974). See Davis, *Rise of the English Shipping Industry*, pp. 179–180, 290. See also the suggestion that, "if the vessel be light, you may dispose of as much rough rice as will fill the hollows in stowage of the casks" in which the finished rice was to be shipped. Letter from Henry Laurens, at Philadelphia, to John Lewis Gervais, at Charleston, 6 Sept. 1778, Henry Laurens Papers, 1747–1801, XI, p. 305, South Carolina Historical Society, Charleston.
      As one might imagine, the freight of non-staple goods was less clearly established and open to variations and negotiation. In 1744 George Maxwell, of the London firm of Lascelles and Maxwell, found it necessary to bargain hard with shipowner Daniel Flexney about the freight charges for twenty copper stills and worms that the firm was shipping on order to Samuel McCall in Philadelphia. Maxwell finally convinced Flexney to accept £40 rather than to be "paid freight according to measure for those bulky goods," which would have been more than the charge by weight. Lascelles and Maxwell wrote to McCall to explain all of this and then commented that "the freight of stills and worms and coppers to Jamaica was always rated according to measure but to Barbados by weight, but now in time of war it may become otherwise." Letter dated London, 10 Sept. 1744, Lascelles and Maxwell Letter Book, 1743–1746, fol. 196, Wilkinson and Gaviller, Ltd, Papers, vol. II, as transcribed in Richard Pares Papers, Box IV, Rhodes House Library, University of Oxford.

were published that equated the precise quantity of each commodity that was equal to one cargo ton. All cargo tons cost the same to ship; the quantity of cargo varied. The East India Company and the Levant Company prepared tables of these equivalents – or stowage factors – in the seventeenth century.[47] The city state of Venice and the Spanish Casa de la Contración de las Indias also maintained statements of such ratios.[48] The relatively new Chamber of Commerce of New York City published a similar set of stowage factors in 1773 (see table 3.5). With certain and somewhat significant exceptions, we can presume that the stowage factors in use at New York were roughly the same as those used elsewhere in the colonies.

The major exceptions to any such presumption are the two staple export trades in sugar and tobacco from the British West Indies and the Chesapeake Bay region. In the early years of these trades, shippers computed the freight ton for these commodities in the same way as they did for all other commodities. In the seventeenth century, when the hogsheads of both sugar and tobacco still contained about 500 pounds each, it became customary to allow four hogsheads to the freight ton without regard for their actual weight. The result was, of course, that both sugar planter and tobacco planter sought to ship more and more tobacco in each hogshead; the "hogshead" of tobacco doubled in size over the century before 1775; the "hogshead" of sugar almost quadrupled at some islands during the same period. Naturally shipowners

47 Davis, *Rise of the English Shipping Industry*, p. 180, referred to a list issued by the East India Company but cited no examples. See Hardy, *Register of Ships, Employed in the Service of the Honourable the East India Company*, [2nd edn], ed. Hardy, Appendix, pp. 139–142. The General Court of the Levant Company, meeting on 10 Mar. 1662/63, established a three-page list of the number of hundredweight and pounds equal to a freight ton for each of numerous commodities carried in its trade between England and Aleppo. SP 110/67, pp. 17–19, PRO. For instance, in the latter list, the freight ton of opium weighed 14 cwt., 7 lb.; in the former list, 14 cwt. Others are specified in table 3.5. These conventions were not new to the 17th century. See [GB, High Court of Admiralty], *Select Pleas in the Court of Admiralty [1390–1602]*, ed. Reginald G. Marsden, Selden Society Publications, vols 6 and 11, 2 vols (London, 1894–1897), I, p. 126: "35 butts wynes wich goith for fyeftey tons ladinge" (1544). Nevertheless, how much of any one commodity equaled a freight ton could be the subject of negotiation – and dispute. See, e.g., the freight contract, dated 18 Sept. 1609, Notariële Archieven, 1569–1895, CXVI, fols 221r–221v, Gemeente Archief, Amsterdam, and as calendared in E[lly] M. Koen *et al.*, "Notarial Records relating to the Portuguese Jews in Amsterdam," *Studia Rosenthaliana: Tijdschrift voor Joodse Wetenschap en Geschiedenis in Nederland*, IV (Jan. 1970), 110.
48 Frederic C. Lane, "Stowage Factors in the Maritime Statutes of Venice," *MM*, LXIII (Aug. 1977), 293–294; Manuel Carrera Stampa, "The Evolution of Weights and Measures in New Spain," [trans. Robert S. Smith], *Hispanic American Historical Review*, XXXIX (Feb. 1949), 13, and the works he cites: [Spain, Laws and Statutes], *Recopilación de layes de los Reynos de las Indias*, 4 vols (Madrid, 1681), IV, fols 52–53; and Rafel Antúnez y Acevedo, *Memorias históricas sobre la legislación y gobierno del comercio de los españoles con sus colonias en las Indias occidentales* (Madrid, 1797), pp. 164–169. See also Joseph de Veitia Linage, *Norte de la contratación de las Indias Occidentales* (Seville, 1672), pp. 189–193; I[rene] A. Wright, "The Coymans Asiento (1685–1689)," *Bijdragen voor Vaderlandsche Geschiedenis en Oudheidkunde*, 6th ser., I (nos 1–2, 1924), 31; Pierre Chaunu, "La Tonelada espanole aux XVIe et XVIIe siècles," in [Colloque International d'Histoire Maritime, 1st, 1956, Paris], *Le Navire et l'économie maritime du XVe au XVIIIe siècles*, ed. Michel Mollat (Paris,

were aware of what was happening and they compensated for this by charging commensurate freight rates calculated especially for these commodities when shipped respectively from the Chesapeake and the Caribbean.[49]

Using the table of stowage factors in table 3.5, it is possible to work backwards from the records of cargoes carried on board certain vessels and to estimate crudely their cargo capacity. The letters of John Reynell, merchant of Philadelphia, provide an example in the cargo freighted on board the ship *John and Anna* to Jamaica in 1734: 62,247 hogshead staves, 5,288 hogshead headings, and 188 bars of iron weighing 80.1.3 hundredweight.[50] From table 3.5, we learn that the staves occupied 159.6 freight tons, the headings 12.6 tons, and the iron 4 tons. While the *John and Anna* was registered at 80 tons, it could carry at least 176 tons of cargo.

Table 3.4 presents the results of this and similar calculations in eighteen separate instances for fifteen different vessels over the fifty years prior to the Revolutionary War. The mean difference between the registered and cargo tonnage of the vessels in these eighteen instances was 106 percent. The cases of the *Friendship*, the *City of Derry*, and the *Black Prince* exhibit the major flaw in this method and the one hinted at above in the case of the *John and Anna*: we cannot be sure how much of a vessel's cargo capacity any given cargo utilized. Obviously, at the lower figure for each of these three vessels,

1957), pp. 71–81. Compare Horace Doursther, *Dictionnaire universel des poids et mesures anciens et modernes* . . . (Brussels, 1840), pp. 544–560.

49 For tobacco, see John M. Hemphill, II, "Freight Rates in the Maryland Tobacco Trade, 1705–1762," *Maryland Historical Magazine*, LIV (Mar. 1959), 39–40; and Middleton, *Tobacco Coast*, pp. 101, 116–117. Compare: "Vessels built in our state for the tob[acc]o business are generally constructed for the stowage of that article and a ship of 200 [measured] tons ought to carry 400 hogshead" or about 200 freight tons of tobacco (compare table 3.5, n. [n]). The quotation is in a letter from John Fitzgerald, the Collector of the Customs, at Alexandria, Va., to Alexander Hamilton, undated but written late in Oct. 1789, *Papers of Alexander Hamilton*, ed. Syrett, V, 491–492. Compare Fitzgerald's letter with the petition of Micajah Perry and other London merchants to the Commissioners for Trade and Plantations, undated but enclosed in the Commissioners for Trade and Plantations to the Commissioners of the Customs, 14 May 1707, CO 5/1315, pt ii, fol. 342r, PRO: "a ship of 400 Tunn will not bring above half so many tuns of Tobacco." Tobacco ships regularly carried other cargo as well; from Virginia to England this was usually pig or bar iron that sometimes went as ballast in the hold (see also n. 46 of this chapter). For sugar, see McCusker, *Rum and the American Revolution*, II, 784–796, and Davis, *Rise of the English Shipping Industry*, pp. 282–284. In July 1772, reflecting just these pressures, London shipowners raised the freight rates for sugar shipped from the West Indies to Great Britain by 14 percent, from 3s. 6d. sterling to 4s. (20p) per cwt. Meeting, July 1772, Minutes of the Committee of the West India Merchants, vol. I, fols 39r–40v, West India Committee Records, University of the West Indies Library, St Augustine, Trinidad. A comparison between New York stowage factors of the 1770s, from table 3.4, and of the 1850s, from Stevens, *On the Stowage of Ships*, p. 28, reveals that the quantity of a commodity said to equal a freight ton of 40 cu. ft. had dropped considerably, effectively raising the costs of freight. Thus comparisons of freight rates over time can only be made with considerable caution.

50 John Reynell, at Philadelphia, to Richard Deeble, at Plymouth, England, 2 May, and 1 July 1734, and Reynell to Samuel Dicker, 25 June 1734, in John Reynell Letter Book, 1729–1734, Coates and Reynell Papers, 1702–1843, HSP.

Table 3.4 Cargo tonnage and registered tonnage of colonial-built vessels compared, 1729–1774

Vessel's name (year built)	Registered tonnage (1)	Cargo tonnage (2)	Percentage difference (3)	Source (4)
Friendship (1723)	100	270	+170	a
Friendship (1723)	100	224	+124	b
Torrington (1729)	50	66	+32	c
Delaware (1730)	40	67	+68	d
John and Anna (1734)	80	176	+120	e
America (1740)	60	114	+90	f
Tetsworth (1748)	200	288	+44	g
City of Derry (1748)	48	128	+167	h
City of Derry (1748)	48	103	+115	i
Success (1748)	100	146	+46	j
Diamond (1749)	30	68	+127	k
Severn (1755)	80	211	+164	l
Mary Harriott (1764)	120	461	+284	m
Back River (1765)	30	62	+107	n
Sidney (1766)	180	227	+26	o
Rose Island (1766)	200	385	+93	p
Black Prince (1774)	200	529	+165	q
Black Prince (1774)	200	327	+64	r
Totals	1,866	3,852	+106	

Notes and sources:

The "percentage difference" in column (3) is calculated as the figure in column (2) less the figure in column (1) divided by the figure in column (1). The mean of the eighteen "percentage differences" in column (3) is 111 percent; the same mean, omitting the lower of each of the three duplicate cases, is 113 percent.

(a), (b) Freights from Massachusetts to Barbados and Barbados to England in 1723. Samuel Weekes, at Boston, to Isaac Hobhouse, at Bristol, 17 Jan. 1722/23; John Davis, at Boston, to Hobhouse, 18 Jan. 1722/23; Crump and Hazell, at Barbados, to Hobhouse 25 Mar. 1723, Isaac Hobhouse Letters, 1722–1736, fols 13–14, 15, 38, Jeffries Collection, vol. XIII, Avon County Reference Library, Bristol, England, and as printed (somewhat imperfectly) in *The Trade of Bristol in the Eighteenth Century*, ed. W[alter] E. Minchinton, Bristol Record Society, Publications, vol. 20 (Bristol, 1957), pp. 93–95, 95–6, 97–98. Registered tonnage estimated at roughly two-thirds of measured tonnage (153 tons).

(c) Freight from Philadelphia to Plymouth, England, 1730. John J. McCusker, "Ships Registered at the Port of Philadelphia before 1776: A Computerized Listing" (unpublished computer printout, 1970), no. 61; John Reynell's Journal, p. 10, as printed in Harrold E. Gillingham, "Some Colonial Ships Built in Philadelphia," *Pennsylvania Magazine of History and Biography*, LVI (Apr. 1932), 162–163. References in the former source are to serial numbers assigned to the ships' registers. This compilation is based primarily on the Ship Register Books of the Province of Pennsylvania, 1722–1776, HSP. See John J. McCusker, "The Pennsylvania Shipping Industry in the Eighteenth Century" (unpublished typescript, 1972).

(d) Freight from Philadelphia to Plymouth, 1730. McCusker, "Ships Registered at the Port of Philadelphia," no. 96; John Reynell's Journal, [p. 46], as printed in Gillingham, "Some Colonial Ships Built in Philadelphia," p. 165.

(e) Freight from Philadelphia to Jamaica, 1734. See the letters cited in n. 50 of this chapter; McCusker, "Ships Registered at the Port of Philadelphia," no. 8119.

(f) Freight from Maryland to Bristol, 1754; McCusker, "Ships Registered at the Port of Philadelphia," no. 523; Thomas Willing, at Philadelphia, to James Campbell, 15 June 1754, and to John Parks, 15 Oct. 1754, Willing and Morris Letter Book, 1754–1761, pp. 1, 31, HSP.

(g) Freight from Philadelphia to Jamaica, 1748. McCusker, "Ships Registered at the Port of Philadelphia," no. 588; table 3.1, n. (i); John Reynell's Journal, p. 169, as printed in Gillingham, "Some Colonial Ships Built in Philadelphia," pp. 183–184.

(h), (i) Freights from Philadelphia to Madeira, 1748, and to Ireland, 1749. McCusker, "Ships Registered at the Port of Philadelphia," no. 601; Hugh Davey and Samuel Carson, at Philadelphia, to Messrs Arthur Vance & Co., 21 July 1748, and to Thomas Parkinson, Robert Parkinson, etc., 29 Nov. 1749, Davey and Carson Letter Book, 1745–1750, fols 79, 102–105, LC.

(j) Freight from Philadelphia to Ireland, 1750. McCusker, "Ships Registered at the Port of Philadelphia," no. 646; Davey and Carson, at Philadelphia, to John McConnell and Richard Beatson, 2 Mar. 1749/50, Davey and Carson Letter Book, fol. 115, LC.

(k) Freight from Philadelphia to Ireland, 1750. McCusker, "Ships Registered at the Port of Philadelphia," no. 683; Davey and Carson, at Philadelphia, to Messrs Vance, Gregg, and Caldwell, 29 June and 21 Nov. 1749, 14 Sept. 1750, Davey and Carson Letter Book, fols 91, 97, 121, LC.

(l) Freight from Philadelphia to Lisbon, 1755. McCusker, "Ships Registered at the Port of Philadelphia," no. 1055; Thomas Willing, at Philadelphia, to Mayne, Burns and Mayne, at Lisbon, 16 Sept. 1755, and to Thomas Willing, at London, 6 Oct. 1755, Willing and Morris Letter Book, pp. 127, 134, HSP.

(m) Freight from Piscataqua, NH, to Jamaica, 1765. "Invoice of the Cost and Outfit of the Ship *Mary Harriott* . . .," 25 Mar. 1765, Business Papers of James Lynde, *Fleming* v. *Lynde*, C 110/163, PRO; NOSL, POE Piscataqua, 5 Jan. to 5 Apr. 1765, CO 5/969, fol. 30r, PRO; NOSL, POE Kingston, Jamaica, 25 Dec. 1764 to 25 Mar. 1765, and 25 June to 25 Sept. 1765, CO 142/18, fols 122v–123r, 145v–146r, PRO; *Lloyd's Register of Shipping . . . 1764* ([London, 1764]), ship *Mary Harriott*; *Lloyd's Register of Shipping . . . 1768* ([London, 1768]), ship M-191; meeting, 1 Jan. 1771, Minutes of the Committee of the West India Merchants, vol. I, fols 15v–16r, West India Committee Records, University of the West Indies Library, St Augustine, Trinidad.

(n) Advertisement, *Maryland Gazette* (Annapolis), 11 July 1765; NOSL, POE Annapolis, Maryland, entered outwards, 15 Feb. 1765, Annapolis Port of Entry Record Books, 1756–1775, MS. 21, Maryland Historical Society.

(o) Statement of cargo capacity in John Smith and Sons to Council of Safety for Maryland, Baltimore, 4 Dec. 1775, Letter Book of John Smith and Sons, 1775–1784, Smith Letter Books, 1774–1821, MS. 1152, Maryland Historical Society, Baltimore; NOSL, POE Annapolis, Maryland, entered outwards, 6 Dec. 1773 and 1 June 1774, and entered inwards, 9 May 1774, POE Annapolis Port of Entry Record Books.

(p) Advertisement, *South Carolina Gazette* (Charleston), 9 June 1766; registration, Charleston, 3 Apr. 1766, "Ship Registers in the South Carolina Archives, 1734–1780," ed. R. Nicholas Olsberg, *South Carolina Historical Magazine*, LXXIV (Oct. 1973), 261–262.

(q), (r) Freights from Philadelphia to Bristol, 1774, and to London, 1775. McCusker, "Ships Registered at the Port of Philadelphia," no. 2498; table 3.1, n. (x); William Bell Clark, *Gallant John Barry, 1745–1803: The Story of a Naval Hero of Two Wars* (New York, 1938), pp. 41–49, based upon "The Journal of the *Black Prince*," formerly in the "W. Horace Hepburn Private Collection, Philadelphia," and afterwards, reputedly, among the private papers of Barry Hayes Hepburn of Philadelphia.

they were not fully laden. We can never know, therefore, whether any given cargo measured in this way represents a full or only a partial load. If we take only the upper figures of those three vessels as the measure of cargo capacity, then the average percentage difference for the fifteen vessels is 110.7 percent. Moreover, it is certain that some colonial-built vessels were purposely built with a low block coefficient. The ship *Sidney*, with the lowest percentage difference in this sample, was known as just such a vessel; it had a reputation as "a remarkable fast sailer."[51] Still, in so far as this sample is representative of all colonial-built ships, we are moved to the conclusion that cargo capacity

51 See table 3.4, n. (o). There was besides registered, measured, and cargo tonnage, still a fourth, and potentially different set of tonnage figures, the tonnages in the several early volumes of *Lloyd's Register of Shipping* ([London, 1764, and after]). The evidence about tonnage in these registers is somewhat confusing but it would appear on average that the Lloyd's tonnage figures were based on the surveyors' visual estimates of vessels' measured tonnages. Thus the tonnage figure for a vessel as given in *Lloyd's Register* was not another, fourth way of calculating tonnage but merely an estimate of measured tonnage. The length of the keel, a critical factor in computing measured tonnage, could not be ascertained with any accuracy when a vessel was afloat, thereby allowing for considerable error in any such estimate by the agents of Lloyd's. Seven vessels for which we have data in tables 3.1 and 3.4 can also be traced in the several *Lloyd's Register* to demonstrate this hypothesis.

Comparison of tonnage figures

Vessel	Registered tonnage (1)	Measured tonnage (2)	Cargo tonnage (3)	Lloyd's tonnage (4)
Hero	200	520	(690)	350
Commerce	140	225	(300)	200
Mary Harriott	120	216	461	200
Lovely Lass	120	274	(360)	250
Sally	200	288	(380)	350
Black Prince	200	300	530	380
Lord Camden	200	296	(390)	400
Totals	1,180	2,119	3,111	2,130

Notes and sources:
See table 3.1, nn. (r), (t), (u), (w), (x) and (y), and table 3.4, nn. (m) and (r). Compare with *Lloyd's Register of Shipping . . . 1764* ([London, 1764]), ships *Hero* and *Mary Harriott*; *Lloyd's Register of Shipping . . . 1768* ([London, 1768]), ship N-191; and *Lloyd's Register of Shipping . . . 1776* ([London, 1776]), ships C-311 (H-373), L-292, S-134 (S-161), L-254. The figures in parentheses in column (3) are estimates of cargo tonnage computed at one-third more than measured tonnage (column [2]).

The compilation and printing of *Lloyd's Register* served the needs of the insurers and ship brokers of London who depended fundamentally on up to date accurate information about the nature and condition of the ships of the empire. The original handbook was the product of the Society of Underwriters established in 1760 to publish it. By 1775 the society had appointed regular reporters, called "surveyors," at twenty-seven of the major ports of the British Isles (London, twenty-one English and Scottish ports, and five Irish ports). In preparation for the 1776 revision, the society charged each surveyor to report on every vessel engaged in overseas trade that had entered his port from 1772 through the autumn of 1775; collected and compiled, this information was the basis of the 1776 volume. See [West India Planters and Merchants, London], *Considerations on the Present State of the Intercourse between His Majesty's Sugar Colonies and the Dominions of the United States of America,* [ed. James Allen] ([London, 1784]), pp. 52–53; George Blake, *Lloyd's Register of Shipping, 1760–1960,* ([London, 1960]), pp. 4–7; Jarvis, "Sources of Transport History: Sources for the History of Ships and Shipping," pp. 212–234; E[dward] K. Haviland, "Classification Society Registers from the Point of View of the Maritime Historian," *American Neptune,* XXX (Jan. 1970), 9–10; Joseph A. Goldenberg,

was at least twice registered tonnage.[52] While this is not quite as much as John Williams contended in 1768, it is enough that colonial shipowners could share in the satisfaction of the owners of the *Friendship*: "We shall pay the builder for nigh 153 tons but she will burden a vast deal more."[53]

◆ ◆ ◆ ◆ ◆

In conclusion, it is apparent that we cannot talk simply about "tonnage" in the pre-Revolutionary War period. If we are interested in the payments of and revenue from harbor or lighthouse dues, registered tonnage meets our purposes well enough, although the Pennsylvania Act of 1759 is an exception, and there were others. If we are interested in the buying, the selling, or the leasing of ships, or if we are comparing pre- and post-1780s tonnage figures, we must talk in terms of measured tonnage and, perhaps, correct one set of data to accommodate this discussion.[54] If we are interested in the carrying trade, shipping earnings, the changing productivity of shipping, or the utilization of cargo capacity, then cargo tonnage is the measure to employ. From the admittedly imperfect data base used for this essay, one might expect to find that the registered tonnage, measured tonnage, and cargo tonnage of colonial vessels maintained a ratio of roughly two registered tons to three measured tons to four cargo tons. In other words, a ship that was registered at 100 tons measured 150 tons, and could carry 200 tons of cargo.

"An Analysis of Shipbuilding Sites in *Lloyd's Register* of 1776," *MM*, LIX (Nov. 1973), 419–435; and Jacob M. Price, "A Note on the Value of Colonial Exports of Shipping," *JEcH,* XXXVI (Sept. 1976), 704–724.

52 The *Friendship* and the *Mary Harriott* were built in New England. As a subset, their combined cargo tonnage (at the larger cargo tonnage for the *Friendship*) averaged +232 percent of their registered tonnage. Omitting these two and the *Rose Island* (built in South Carolina), and the *Back River* and the *Sidney* (both Maryland built), the ten remaining vessels were Pennsylvania built and their cargo capacity on the same basis averaged +102 percent.

53 Samuel Weekes, at Boston, to Isaac Hobhouse, at Bristol, Isaac Hobhouse Letters, 1722–1736, fols 13–14, Jeffries Collection, vol. XIII, Avon County Reference Library, Bristol, England, and as printed (somewhat imperfectly) in *The Trade of Bristol in the Eighteenth Century*, ed. W[alter] E. Minchinton, Bristol Record Society, Publications, vol. 20 (Bristol, 1957), p. 94. Compare Joseph and William Russel, at Providence, RI, to Aaron Lopez, [at Newport, RI], 19 Jan. 1786, in *Commerce of Rhode Island, 1726–1800*, [ed. Worthington Chauncey Ford], *Collections of the Massachusetts Historical Society*, 7th ser., vols IX–X, 2 vols (Boston, 1914–1915), I, 219. Shipbuilders, aware of the trend to more "burthensome" vessels, moved to require bonuses for constructing ships that they felt were "unproportionable to the builder." Henry Lloyd, at Boston, to John Lloyd, 9 May 1765, Henry Lloyd Letter Book, p. 61.

54 See D. P. Lamb, "Volume and Tonnage of the Liverpool Slave Trade," in *Liverpool and the African Slave Trade, and Abolition: Essays to Illustrate Current Knowledge and Research*, ed. Roger [T.] Anstey and P[aul] E. H. Hair, Historic Society of Lancashire and Cheshire, Occasional Series, vol. 2 ([Liverpool], 1976), pp. 105–107 and elsewhere. Contrast the treatment of tonnage by Lawrence A. Harper, *The English Navigation Laws: A Seventeenth-Century Experiment in Social Engineering* (New York, 1939), p. 9, and by Merrill Jensen, *The New Nation: A History of the United States during the Confederation, 1781–1789* (New York, 1950), pp. 214–218.

Table 3.5 Colonial stowage or load factors: commodity equivalents of one cargo ton

Commodity	Stowage factor
Beef, in casks	8 barrels,[a] 22 hundredweight[b]
Beer, in casks	252 gallon[c]
Beeswax	22 hundredweight
Bread, in bulk	12 hundredweight[e]
in bags or casks	11 hundredweight
[Bricks	20 hundredweight][d]
Butter	22 hundredweight
Candles	22 hundredweight
[Cattle	one-fifth count][d]
Chocolate	22 hundredweight
Coal	36 bushels[f]
Cocoa	22 hundredweight
Codfish, dried, in bulk	20 hundredweight
dried, in casks	22 hundredweight[b]
wet	8 barrels
Coffee	22 hundredweight
Cotton	7 hundredweight[g]
Dye woods	20 hundredweight
Fish, wet	8 barrels
Flaxseed	32 bushels[h]
Flour	22 hundredweight[i]
Furs and pelts, in bales	40 cubic feet
in casks	20 cubic feet
Fustic	20 hundredweight
Grains, in bulk	40 bushels
in casks	32 bushels
Ham	[8 barrels],[a] 22 hundredweight
Hides, dried	by the pound[g]
Honey	22 hundredweight
[Horses	one-fifth count][d]
Indian corn, in bulk	40 bushels
in casks	32 bushels
Indigo	22 hundredweight
Iron, bar and pig	20 hundredweight
Lard, hogs	22 hundredweight
Logwood	20 hundredweight
Lumber (see Timber)	
[Men and women	one-half count][j]
Molasses, in casks	252 gallons
Oil, in casks	252 gallons
Pease, in casks	32 bushels
Pitch	8 barrels
Pork	8 barrels,[a] [22 hundredweight]
Potash [and Pearl ash]	22 hundredweight
Rice	22 hundredweight[k]
Rum	252 gallons
Salt, in casks	32 bushels
Sarsaparilla	by the pound[g]
Soap	22 hundredweight

70

Commodity	Stowage factor
Starch	22 hundredweight
Staves (see Timber)	
Sugar	22 hundredweight
Tallow	22 hundredweight
Tar	8 barrels
Timber, square	480 board feet[l]
mahogany	480 board feet[l]
oak plank	480 board feet[l]
pine boards	480 board feet[l]
staves, barrel	870 count[m]
[staves, butt	120 count][m]
staves, hogshead	390 count[m]
staves, pipe	280 count[m]
headings	420 count[m]
hoops	380 count[m]
shingles	1,030 count[m]
Tobacco	22 hundredweight[b, n]
[Tongues	8 barrels, 22 hundredweight][a]
Turpentine	8 barrels[o]
[Vinegar	252 gallons][p]
Wheat, in bulk	40 bushels[q]
in casks	32 bushels
Wine	252 gallons
Wood (see Timber)	
[Wool	9 hundredweight][r]

Notes and sources:
Almost all of the stowage factors in this table come directly from the report of a committee of the New York Chamber of Commerce submitted on 5 Nov. 1771. [New York (City), Chamber of Commerce], *Colonial Records of the New York Chamber of Commerce, 1768–1784; with Historical and Biographical Sketches,* ed. John Austin Stevens, Jr (New York, 1867), pp. 141–142. See also, ibid., pp. 40, 44, 138; and *New-York Gazette; and the Weekly Mercury,* 27 Jan. 1772. Compare the mid-19th-century table for New York in Robert White Stevens, *On the Stowage of Ships and Their Cargoes,* [1st edn] (Plymouth and London, 1858), p. 28. Additional stowage factors, inserted in square brackets, have been added from the sources indicated. For information about colonial weights and measures and the contents of casks, see Helen Louise Klopfer, "Statistics of the Foreign Trade of Philadelphia, 1700–1860" (Ph.D. diss., University of Pennsylvania, 1936), pp. 14–111, and John J. McCusker, *Rum and the American Revolution: The Rum Trade and the Balance of Payments of the Thirteen Continental Colonies, 1650–1775,* 2 vols (New York, 1989, [Ph.D. diss., University of Pittsburgh, 1970]), II, 768–878; McCusker, "Weights and Measures in the Colonial Sugar Trade: The Gallon and the Pound and Their International Equivalents," *W&MQ,* 3rd ser., XXX (Oct. 1973), 599–624 – revised as chapter 4 of the present book; McCusker, "Correction," *W&MQ,* 3rd ser., XXXI (Jan. 1974), 164; and McCusker, "Les Équivalents métriques des poids et mesures du commerce colonial aux XVIIe et XVIIIe siècles," *Revue Française d'Histoire d'Outre-Mer,* LXI (no. 3, 1974), 349–365. The material from the last two of these items has been incorporated into the revisions of chapter 4 of the present book.
(a) One researcher summed up her investigation of the trade in beef, pork, ham, and tongue at Philadelphia in the colonial period by taking barrels of these meats as containing of 220 lb. and "tierces . . . as the equivalent of two barrels." Klopfer, "Statistics of the Foreign Trade of Philadelphia," pp. 96–101 (quotation, p. 99). Compare Arthur Harrison Cole, *Wholesale Commodity Prices in the United States, 1700–1861* (Cambridge, Mass., 1938), II, x. Given that all four weighed the same per barrel in the Philadelphia trade, tongue, which does not appear in the New York list, is treated here as having the same stowage factor as the other three meats.

Table 3.5 continued

(b) The cwt. weighed 112 lb. in Maryland and northward and 100 lb. in Virginia and southward except for tobacco and codfish, which were bought and sold at 100 lb. to the cwt. everywhere; McCusker, "Weights and Measures" – revised as chapter 4 of the present book. Hundredweight, here abbreviated "cwt.," was expressed in a distinctive notation, e.g., 211.1.24, which indicates 211 cwt., 1 quarter, 24 lb. For the "long" cwt., the quarter obviously equaled 28 lb.

(c) The gallon used in the colonies was the English wine gallon of 231 cu. in. McCusker, "Weights and Measures." Although some colonies at first adopted both the English wine gallon and the English ale gallon (282 cu. in.), the subsequent confusion forced at least one of them, Pennsylvania, to enact the use of the wine gallon alone for all liquids. McCusker, "Weights and Measures"; [Pennsylvania, Laws and Statutes], *Statutes at Large of Pennsylvania from 1682 to 1801*, ed. James T. Mitchell and Henry Flanders, 18 vols (Harrisburg, Pa., 1896–1915), II, 221–222.

(d) Bricks and livestock were two important colonial exports not included in the Chamber of Commerce list. An estimate of 20 cwt. per cargo ton puts bricks in a class with iron, the dye woods, and dried bulk codfish. An estimate of 5 freight tons each for cattle and horses presumes that they occupied approximately twice the space allotted per soldier on Royal Navy transports. See n. (j) of this table. For discussion of the size of colonial draft animals, see Lewis Cecil Gray, *History of Agriculture in the Southern United States to 1860*, Carnegie Institution of Washington, Publication no. 430, 2 vols ([Washington, DC], 1933), I, 202–205, and Max George Schumacher, *The Northern Farmer and His Markets during the Late Colonial Period* (New York, 1975 [Ph.D. diss., University of California, Berkeley, 1948]), pp. 19–20.

(e) Two sizes of bread cask were especially popular at Philadelphia in the 18th century, the barrel and the tierce. In the quarter-century prior to the Revolutionary War, the barrel of bread contained 140 lb. (1.1.0 cwt.) and the tierce of bread contained 280 lb. (2.2.0 cwt.). Klopfer, "Statistics of the Foreign Trade of Philadelphia," pp. 45–46. Bread was freighted from England to Newfoundland in the 1780s at 12 bags (of 1 cwt. each) to the ton. Testimony of Andrew Buchanan, clerk of the Naval Office at POE St John's, BT 5/2, fol. 202, PRO.

(f) The bushel of coal used at Philadelphia during the colonial period was the standard Winchester bushel of 2,150.42 cu. in. See Klopfer, "Statistics of the Foreign Trade of Philadelphia," pp. 22–23. A chaldron of coal in the colonies is thought to have equaled 36 bushels and 2,880 lb. [US, Department of Commerce, Bureau of the Census], *Historical Statistics of the United States: Colonial Times to 1970*, 2 vols (Washington, DC, 1975), II, 1159. "A load of cole" in Pennsylvania measured "144 bushels." John Relfe, "Estimate on Pennsylvania Furnaces," in a letter from Relfe, at Philadelphia, to Nicholas Brown and Co., at Providence, RI, undated but in reply to a letter from the company to Relfe dated 21 May 1765, Brown Papers, P-H6, Calendared, vol. I, John Carter Brown Library, Brown University, Providence, RI, and as mentioned in James B. Hedges, *The Browns of Providence Plantations*, 2 vols (Cambridge, Mass., 1952–1968), I, 129. Thus the load was the equivalent of 4 chaldrons, 11,520 lb., or about 103 cwt. The London chaldron of coal measured 2,987 lb.; the Newcastle chaldron (after the 1680s), nearly twice as much, or 5,956 lb. For the weights and measures used in the British coal trade, see John U. Nef, *The Rise of the British Coal Industry*, 2 vols (London, 1932), II, 367–378.

(g) Cotton, sarsaparilla, and dried hides were to "be rated by the pound," apparently the subject of negotiation between freight owner and shipowner on every occasion. For the last two, about all we can do is presume that 20 cwt. equaled 1 freight ton. If we agree with Ralph Davis, *The Rise of the English Shipping Industry in the Seventeenth and Eighteenth Centuries* (London, 1962), pp. 178–179, that "West Indian [and North American?] cotton before the invention of the powerful bale presses was packed at a density which gave it no more than a third the weight of water," then 7 cwt. equaled 1 freight ton. At a meeting of the General Court on 10 Mar. 1662/63, the Levant Company set the freight ton of cotton wool at 9.0.5 cwt. SP 110/67, pp. 17–19, PRO. The East India Company rated cotton at 50 cu. ft. to the freight ton. Charles Hardy, *A Register of Ships, Employed in the Service of the Honourable the East India Company, from the Year 1760 to 1810 . . .*, [2nd edn], rev. and enl., ed. Horatio Charles Hardy (London, 1811), Appendix, p. 139. Compare Paul W. Gates, *The Farmer's Age:*

Agriculture, 1815–1860, vol. III of *The Economic History of the United States*, edited by Henry David *et al.* (New York, [1962]), pp. 283–284.

(h) There were regularly 7 Winchester bushels of flaxseed to the hogshead. Klopfer, "Statistics of the Foreign Trade of Philadelphia," pp. 68–76. Compare [G.B., Parl., Commons (1766)], *The Examination of Doctor Benjamin Franklin, before an August Assembly, Relating to the Repeal of the Stamp Act* (Philadelphia, 1766), p. 131, and as printed in *The Papers of Benjamin Franklin*, ed. Leonard W. Labaree *et al.*, in progress (New Haven, Conn., 1959 to date), XIII, 147, question no. 113; Samuel and Jonathan Smith, at Philadelphia, to Nathaniel Holmes, 5 Dec. 1767 [*sic* for 1768], Samuel and Jonathan Smith Letter Book, 1765–1770, Peter Force Papers, LC; and Gerald G. Beekman, at New York, to Adam Schoales, at Londonderry, 27 Dec. 1755, and 16 Jan. 1758, and to John and David Ross, at Newry, 16 Jan. 1760, *The Beekman Mercantile Papers, 1746–1799*, ed. Philip L. White, 3 vols (New York, 1956), I, 270, 321, 350.

(i) Two sizes of flour casks dominated the Philadelphia industry in the 18th century; both were called the flour barrel. One contained 224 lb. (2 cwt. or 8 quarters) of flour on the average; the other, known as the 7/4 ("seven-quarter") barrel, contained 196 lb. (1.3.0 cwt. or seven quarters). The larger barrel seems, from Klopfer's research, to have been more popular from 1700–1715 and again after 1740 while the 7/4 barrel appears as the preferred cask between 1715 and 1740. Klopfer, "Statistics of the Foreign Trade of Philadelphia," pp. 34–43. Compare Cole, *Wholesale Commodity Prices in the United States*, II, x; and the testimony of Thomas Irving, 30 Mar. 1784, BT 5/1, p. 96, PRO. The change from the middle of the 1740s seems to have been the effect of a new law in Maryland and the widespread adoption for a variety of trades of a barrel capable of containing 31½ gallons. Klopfer, "Statistics of the Foreign Trade of Philadelphia," pp. 69, 71. Flour from the Middle Colonies sold at Bristol in sacks or bags of 2.2.0 cwt. Richard Champion, at Bristol, to Willing and Morris, at Philadelphia, 28 July 1774, in *The American Correspondence of a Bristol Merchant, 1766–1776: Letters of Richard Champion*, ed. G[eorge] H. Gutteridge, University of California, Publications in History, vol. XXII, no. 1 (Berkeley, Calif., 1934), 23–24.

(j) That is, one person per 2 cargo tons. This is the rate at which forty vessels carried Irish immigrants to the Thirteen Continental Colonies, 1771–1774: one person per registered ton. Derived from data in R[obert] J. Dickson, *Ulster Emigration to Colonial America, 1718–1775*, Publications of the Ulster-Scot Historical Society, no. 1 (London, 1966), pp. 62–63. Compare the Pennsylvania laws of 1750 and 1765 regulating the size of vessels that carried passengers to the colony. See *Statutes at Large of Pennsylvania*, V, 94–97, VI, 432–440. During the Seven Years War, the Admiralty contracted for troop transports at the rate of 2⅔ cargo tons (two measured tons) per soldier; this was to include some space for baggage. Enclosure in Lt John Hutchinson, at Portsmouth, to Navy Board, 11 Jan. 1762, Adm. 106/257, PRO, and Admiralty to Navy Board, 12 Jan. 1762, Adm. 2/230, fol. 374, PRO, both as printed in *The Siege and Capture of Havana, 1762*, ed. David Syrett, Publications of the Navy Records Society, CXIV (London, 1970), 6. In both the 17th and 18th centuries, slave shipowners thought of two-thirds of a cargo ton (one-half of a measured ton) as the optimum rate per slave. See K[enneth] G. Davies, *The Royal African Company* (London, 1957), p. 194; and *Documents Illustrative of the History of the Slave Trade to America*, ed. Elizabeth Donnan, Carnegie Institution of Washington, Publication no. 409, 4 vols ([Washington, DC], 1930–1935), II, 583, n. 2. The Act of 28 George III, c. 54 (1788), sought to reform conditions on slave ships by requiring a rate no smaller than 8/10 of a cargo ton (6/10 of a measured ton) per slave on ships up to 201 measured tons and 1⅓ cargo tons (one measured ton) for larger ships. That law refers to tonnage as "set forth in the . . . certificate of the registry of . . . [the] vessel," as measured by the rule in the Act of 26 George III, c. 60 (1786); see n. 17 of this chapter. (The law was later amended by the Act of 39 George III, c. 80 [1799].) According to data collected by Herbert S. Klein, "The English Slave Trade to Jamaica, 1782–1808," *EcHR*, 2nd ser., XXXI (Feb. 1978), 29, ships in the trade after the enactment of the 1788 law conformed to its provisions, but just barely. At an average during 1791–1799 of 1.4 slaves per measured ton, ships carried slaves at a rate of 1.05 per cargo ton; during 1800–1808 this improved to 1⅓ cargo tons per slave (one measured ton). (His data for the years 1782–1788 span the years during the change in tonnage measurement and thus are subject to some confusion.) Contrast James G. Lydon, "New York and the Slave Trade, 1700 to 1774," *W&MQ*, 3rd ser., XXXV (Apr. 1978), 384, n. 26, who thoroughly confused the issue. See also the Act of 43 George III, c. 56 (1803).

Table 3.5 continued

(k) The barrel of rice at Philadelphia contained an average of 450 lb. between 1730 and 1740 and 250 lb. after 1768; the tierce of rice there contained about 550 lb. Klopfer, "Statistics of the Foreign Trade of Philadelphia," pp. 99, 101–104. The barrel of rice exported from Charleston in 1767–1771 averaged 527 lb. Ledger of Imports and Exports, British North America, 1768–1772, pp. 54, 142, 198, 201, Customs 16/1, PRO. Compare *Historical Statistics of the United States*, II, 1163–1164. Recall, from note (b), above, that the cwt. of rice varied in weight, north to south. It weighed 100 lb. at Charleston and 112 lb. at Philadelphia. From Klopfer, "Statistics of the Foreign Trade of Philadelphia," pp. 68, 77–78, we learn that bagged goods measured 1.5 bushels. Since the bushel of rice weighed 65 or 66 lb. – *American Husbandry* (1775), ed. Harry J. Carman, Columbia University Studies in the History of American Agriculture, no. 6 (New York, 1939), p. 278; J[ohn] F. D. Smyth, *A Tour in the United States: Containing an Account of the Present Situation of that Country . . .*, 2 vols (London, 1784), II, 68 – the bag of rice must have held about 100 lb. Thus the pre-Revolutionary War barrel at Philadelphia held about 4 bushels or 2½ bags.

(l) New York and Philadelphia merchants accepted cut timbers at 40 cu. ft per freight ton. *Colonial Records of the New York Chamber of Commerce*, ed. Stevens, p. 142; and *Statutes at Large of Pennsylvania*, ed. Mitchell and Flanders, V, 402. The traditional English "load" of lumber, at 50 cu. ft, was the equivalent of 600 American board feet according to Robert Greenhalgh Albion, *Forests and Sea Power: The Timber Problem of the Royal Navy, 1652–1862*, Harvard Economic Studies, XXIX (Cambridge, Mass., 1926), 9. But see Davis, *Rise of the English Shipping Industry*, p. 182, n. 2, where the load of timber is said to have been 1.2 freight tons; and Henry Laurens, at Charleston, to Isaac Wheeler, at St Christopher, 3 Nov. 1755, *The Papers of Henry Laurens*, ed. Philip M. Hamer *et al.*, in progress (Columbia, SC, 1968 to date), II, 5, where Laurens equates "1,000 feet of lumber board measure" with "two tons" of freight and calls this "the common way of estimating the tonnage" of lumber.

(m) The New York merchants, "because of the great irregularity of staves brought to this market," thought it better to accept them by the thousand rather than by the freight ton. And this despite a mutual agreement overseen by the Chamber of Commerce in Sept. 1760 to regulate the size of staves and other wood exports. *Colonial Records of the New York Chamber of Commerce*, ed. Stevens, pp. 57–58, 141–142. Other colonies tried to settle the matter by legislation, among which Pennsylvania's law of 21 Apr., 1759, provides the basis for the figures here. *Statutes at Large of Pennsylvania*, ed. Mitchell and Flanders, V, 401. The count per freight ton given here is the average round number of each size that occupied 40 sq. ft computing their individual volume on the measurements from that law and from the New York agreement and taking, where possible, the mean count of the two. Where either specification set a range, calculations were based on the maximum in order to impart a downward bias to the result. Compare Stevens, *On the Stowage of Ships*, p. 18. On the whole subject, see Arthur L. Jensen, "The Inspection of Exports in Colonial Pennsylvania," *Pennsylvania Magazine of History and Biography*, LXXVIII (July 1954), 275–297; and Newton B. Jones, "Weights, Measures, and Mercantilism: The Inspection of Exports in Virginia, 1742–1820," in *The Old Dominion: Essays for Thomas Perkins Abernethy*, ed. Darrett B. Rutman (Charlottesville, Va., 1964), pp. 122–134. Note that the "thousand" – frequently abbreviated with the Roman numeral "M" – equaled 1,200 staves, headings, and hoops but only 1,000 shingles. Klopfer, "Statistics of the Foreign Trade of Philadelphia," pp. 24–31; BT 5/1, p. 96, PRO. Compare similar modes of counting involving the "hundred." Ronald Edward Zupko, *A Dictionary of Weights and Measures for the British Isles: The Middle Ages to the Twentieth Century*, Memoirs of the American Philosophical Society, CLXVIII (Philadelphia, 1985), pp. 190–192.

(n) Klopfer, "Statistics of the Foreign Trade of Philadelphia," pp. 102, 104–109, found hogsheads of tobacco averaging about 850 lb. before the mid-1730s and 1,000 lb. thereafter. Over the years 1769–1772, tobacco hogsheads exported from Maryland contained an average of 1,004 lb. and, from Virginia, 1,079 lb. Customs 16/1, pp. 45, 154, 192, 237, PRO. Compare Gray, *History of Agriculture in the Southern United States*, I, 219–223.

(o) The barrel of turpentine contained 31½ gallons, Cole, *Wholesale Commodity Prices in the United States*, II, x. It "ought to weigh" 321 lb. according to Joshua Humphreys Note Book, 1719–1832, p. 161, Joshua Humphreys Papers, 1682–1835, HSP. The entry reads "321 Ct." but it is clear that the writer meant the abbreviation for lb. and not for cwt.

(p) Vinegar is assumed to have been classed with rum, oil, wines, and other liquids.

(q) Davis, *Rise of the English Shipping Industry*, p. 185, estimated 5½ quarters to the cargo ton. He cited [G.B., Parl., Commons], *Journals of the House of Commons*, in progress (London, 1742 to date), XXIII, 492 [*sic*, for 495]. The statement there is that "a ship of 70 tons may be stowed . . . if loaded for wheat, about 380 or 400 quarters," which works out to 5.6 quarters per ton. At 8 bushels per quarter – Zupko, *Dictionary of Weights and Measures for the British Isles*, pp. 337–340 – 5.5 quarters per ton would mean about 44 bushels of wheat to the cargo ton. "Fine Doncaster wheat [weighed] . . . 60 lb. the bushel" (ibid., p. 495), so, by these measures, the freight ton of wheat weighed 2,640 lb. Compare Zupko, op. cit., pp. 55–60.

(r) Richard Hayes, *The Negociator's Magazine*, 4th edn (London, 1739), p. 210.

4

WEIGHTS AND MEASURES IN THE COLONIAL SUGAR TRADE

The gallon and the pound and their international equivalents

So wir hetten einen Glauben
Gott und Grechtigkait vor Augen,
Ein Ehl, Gewicht, Maß, Müntz, oñ Gelt
So stünd es wol in dieser Welt.

René Budel[1]

Great Britain has gone metric. The United States must do so also, sooner or later, finally following the urgings of such early leaders as Thomas Jefferson. Before the end of the twenty-first century, the use of the metric system will

---

1 René Budel, *De monetis, et re numaria* . . . (Cologne, 1591), [p. xi]. Budel quoted this as an ancient and venerable saying ("vetus est et elegans dictum") and translated it, some-what loosely, as "Una fides, pondus, mensura, moneta sit una, Et status illasus totius orbis erit." Whereas his interpretation suggests that one faith, one system of weights and measures, and one money would render the world whole, his dictum in fact stipulates that the acceptance of one creed, one god, and one law is the prerequisite for any universal system of weights and measures, numbering, and money. This chapter incorporates an argument that, in practice, commerce is a unifying force, at least with regard to weights and measures.

The original version of this chapter was published in *W&MQ*, 3rd ser., XXX (Oct. 1973), 599–624. Copyright © 1973 by the Institute of Early American History and Culture. This revision is included here with the permission of the publishers of the journal. It incorporates additional material from John J. McCusker, "Correction," *W&MQ*, 3rd ser., XXXI (Jan. 1974), 164; and from McCusker, "Les Équivalents métriques des poids et mesures du commerce colonial aux XVIIe et XVIIIe siècles," *Revue Française d'Histoire d'Outre-Mer*, LXI (no. 3, 1974), 349–365.

In its first form the essay prophesied that the change in the United States would take place before the end of the 20th century. Such a miserable effort at prognostication under-scores the wisdom in the adage that should have encouraged this shoemaker to stick to his last. Even still, I was not alone in my enthusiasm: *A Metric America: A Decision Whose Time Has Come* (Washington, DC, 1971).

I continue to be grateful for the help and support given me by Kenneth E. Carpenter, then curator of the Kress Library of Business and Economics, and the Institute of Early American History and Culture, the Council on Research in Economic History, the Smithsonian Institution, the General Research Board of the University of Maryland, and the American Philosophical Society.

no doubt have become universal. Economic historians wish that this had happened centuries ago because one of their most perplexing problems arises, in the words of James Madison, from "the inconveniency of . . . using different and arbitrary weights and measures."[2] This essay suggests solutions to some of the problems created by the disparate weights and measures employed in the sugar trades during the seventeenth and eighteenth centuries with the intention of reducing somewhat such "inconveniencies" for those who study the economy of the period.

◆ ◆ ◆ ◆ ◆

Weights and measures have varied by place, time, and substances measured. Such differences were not defined only by national borders, for the nations of Europe used internally several schemes of measurement. Their New World colonies usually, although not always, followed the practice of the capital city of the mother country. Thus, in order to determine the measure employed in the colonies, it is necessary to ascertain the measure regularly applied to a particular commodity or type of commodity in each mother country. Additional complexities result from the fact that during the two centuries after 1600 some of the original colonial standards were supplanted as a result of pressures from colonists of other nations who, either by their presence in a colony or by their commercial dealings with a colony, induced the adoption of "foreign" measures.

The potential for confusion occasioned by the varieties and changes of weights and measures justifies the presentation of findings merely for one trade and three related commodities, together with an indication of sources to which the economic historian may repair for additional information. At the very least, a clearer comprehension of colonial weights and measures, and their interrelationships, should help to correct and in the future to prevent some of the more glaring errors that are too often encountered in studies of colonial economic history, when, for instance, as happens all too frequently, an author translates the word for a foreign measure but fails to work out its equivalent.[3]

---

2   "Next to the inconveniency of speaking different languages, is that of using different and arbitrary weights and measures." Madison at [Montpelier], Orange [Co.], Va., to James Monroe, 28 Apr. 1785, in *The Papers of James Madison*, ed. William T. Hutchinson *et al.*, in progress (Chicago, 1962 to date), VIII, 273. On Madison as "Jefferson's principal collaborator" in his 1790 report on the subject, see *The Papers of Thomas Jefferson*, ed. Julian P. Boyd *et al.*, in progress (Princeton, NJ, 1950 to date), XVI, 602–675 (quotation, p. 607). On Great Britain's progress towards metrification, see R[obert] D. Connor, *The Weights and Measures of England* (London, 1987), pp. 289–307. Compare Julian Hoppit, "Reforming Britain's Weights and Measures, 1660–1824," *English Historical Review*, CVIII (Jan. 1993), 82–104. The key pieces of modern legislation are the two Weights and Measures Acts: Act of Elizabeth II, c. 31, 1963; and Act of Elizabeth II, c. 77, 1976.

3   Ward Barrett, *The Sugar Hacienda of the Marquesses del Valle* (Minneapolis, Minn., 1970), passim, seems consistently to have mistaken the Castilian *libra* (0.4601 kg) for the avoirdupois lb. (0.4536 kg). As a result, his discussion of production per acre is not in

A particularly striking instance of confusion concerns the ton as a unit of weight. The instance is striking because the confusion is widespread, even shadowing the work of so careful a scholar as Richard B. Sheridan who, in his monograph on the colonial sugar industry, leaves his readers wondering which of several possible tons he employed and how – or even if – he converted to his standard the different units that confronted him.[4] Still today there are different "tons" in use for buying and selling sugar: the net or short ton (2,000 pounds or 907 kilograms) common to the United States; the gross or long ton (2,240 pounds or 1,016 kilograms) used in the United Kingdom and the British West Indies; and the metric ton (2,205 pounds or 1000 kilograms), the ton of the metric world and the statistical ton for international purposes.[5] The long ton is 12 percent larger than the short ton. The reader might argue that the margin for error in dealing with seventeenth- and eighteenth-century economic data is at least 10 percent anyhow, so why the fuss? The rejoinder seems obvious: 10 percent is an unacceptable

terms of lb. per acre but *libras* per acre (pp. 48–49). The English translation of François Chevalier's *La Formation des grands domaines au Mexique: Terre et société aux XVIe–XVIIe siècles*, Travaux et Mémoires de l'Institut d'Ethnologie de Paris, no. 56 (Paris, 1952), published as *Land and Society in Colonial Mexico: The Great Hacienda*, trans. Alvin Eustis, ed. Lesley Byrd Simpson (Berkeley and Los Angeles, 1966), quietly turns metric tons (1,000 kg) into American short tons (907 kg). See also P[ieter] J. van Winter, *Het aandeel van den Amsterdamschen handel aan den opbouw van het Amerikaansche gemeenebest*, Werken Uitgegeven door de Vereenignig het Nederlandsch Economisch-Historisch Archief, nos 7 and 9, 2 vols (The Hague, 1927–1933), passim, who regularly translated avoirdupois lb. into Dutch *ponden* (0.4941 kg), the word but not the measure.

4   Richard [B.] Sheridan, *The Development of the Plantations to 1750; An Era of West Indian Prosperity, 1750–1775*, Chapters in Caribbean History, I (Barbados, 1970), passim. Compare the confusion created by the acceptance and repetition of a statement like the one that the *quintal* used in the Portuguese trade "corresponded" to the English cwt. The Portuguese *quintal* for the sugar and rice trades weighed 58.8 kg; the English cwt. weighed 50.8 kg in England and most of the Thirteen Continental Colonies and 45.4 kg in South Carolina and the Caribbean (see later in this chapter and table 4.4). Compare C[harles] R. Boxer, "English Shipping in the Brazil Trade, 1640–65," *MM*, XXXVII (July 1951), 204, n. 1; H[arold] E. S. Fisher, *The Portugal Trade: A Study of Anglo-Portuguese Commerce, 1700–1770* (London, 1971), p. 17, n. 6; and *The Papers of Henry Laurens*, ed. Philip M. Hamer *et al.*, in progress (Columbia, SC, 1968 to date), III, xxi.

    One must beware, as well, of mixing up the ton weight with the shipping ton; they were, and are still, two completely different measures. Frederic C. Lane, "Tonnages, Medieval and Modern," *EcHR*, 2nd ser., XVII (Dec. 1964), 213–233, and John J. McCusker, "The Tonnage of Ships Engaged in British Colonial Trade during the Eighteenth Century," *Research in Economic History*, VI (1981), 73–105 – revised as chapter three of the present book. Compare Jean-Claude Hocquet, "Tonnages ancien et moderne: Botte de Venise et tonneau anglais," *Revue Historique*, no. 570 (Apr.–June 1989), 349–360.

5   All conversions of older weights and measures made in the text and tables of this chapter – and this book – will be to their metric equivalents (kilograms [kg] and liters). For the ton in the sugar trade, see Otis P. Starkey, *Commercial Geography of Barbados*, Indiana University Department of Geography, Technical Report no. 9 ([Bloomington, Ind.], 1961), p. 16; and [UN, Food and Agricultural Organization], *The World Sugar Economy in Figures . . . 1880–1959*, Commodity Reference Ser., 1 ([Rome, 1961]). Two very valuable general reference books are Stephen Naft and Ralph de Sola, *International Conversion Tables*, rev. and enl., ed. P[hilip] H. Bigg, (London, [1965]); and [UN, Statistical Office], *World Weights and Measures: Handbook for Statisticians*, [rev. edn] (New York, [1966]).

margin of error. We might suffer it in colonial data, but we should work to reduce it. We certainly ought not to compound it by introducing ourselves a further margin of error of the same order. With difficulty, colonial merchants accommodated themselves to the diversity of weights and measures in international and transatlantic commerce, most regularly and effectively by re-weighing and re-measuring the goods they traded.[6] (See figure 4.1.[7]) So must we attempt a similar accommodation.[8]

Sugar, molasses, and rum illustrate some of the basic problems to be faced. Weights and measures, we are told, varied with the commodity traded. Sugar was and is still sold by weight. Originally treated as a rare spice, it was traded in smaller quantities than today when the wholesale unit for sugar is the ton. Rum was traded by liquid measure. Molasses was sold sometimes by liquid measure and sometimes by weight.

◆ ◆ ◆ ◆ ◆

Early modern Europe inherited its basic unit of weight from the Roman Empire. The pound, the *livre*, and the *pfund* have a common ancestor in the *libra*. By the sixteenth century, after more than a millennium of fragmentation, most areas had evolved their own variants from the ancient standard. As table 4.1 indicates, even though they were all of the same order of magnitude, the range of differences was great, in excess of 20 percent. Nor were these differences always or precisely recognized. Jean Pierre Ricard failed understandably to detect a difference of less than 1 percent when he wrote that "la livre de Paris est égal à la livre d'Amsterdam."[9] Other "authorities"

---

6 Thus they took care to keep their weighing and gauging equipment uniform and in good order. See *Select Cases in the Mayor's Court of New York City, 1674–1784*, ed. Richard B. Morris, American Legal Records, vol. II (Washington, DC, 1935), p. 34. Scales in 16th-century Mexico differed from one another by only 2 percent according to a deposition in a 1586 dispute over the weight of sugar sold. Archivo del Hospital de Jesús, legajo 208, expediente 7, Archivo General de la Nación, Mexico City, as cited in Barrett, *Sugar Hacienda*, p. 23, a reference that I have been unable to trace. Compare [Mexico, Archivo General de la Nación], "Inventario del Archivo del Hospital de Jesús" [by C. Emilio Quintanar], *Boletín del Archivo General de la Nación*, VII (Oct.–Dec. 1936), 606. Compare n. 24 of this chapter.

7 The Bible is rich in texts for which this is an appropriate illustration. The one for which it is the occasion is Prov. 16:11 "Honest balances and scales are the Lord's; all the weights in the bag are his work." See also, among others, Lev. 18:35–36; Deut. 25:13–15; Prov. 11:1; Prov. 20:10; Prov. 20: 23; Ezek. 10–11. Of a different flavor is Dan. 5:27. Compare this illustration with those discussed in Richard Vieweg, *Mass und Messen in kulturgeschichtlicher Sicht*, Beiträge zur Geschichte der Wissenschaft und der Technik, Heft 4 (Wiesbaden, 1962). See also the Vermeer painting of a *Woman Holding a Balance* (ca. 1664), actually money scales, with its obviously theological implications, she standing in front of a picture of *The Last Judgment*. [Arthur K. Wheelock, Jr, *et al.*], *Johannes Vermeer*, [ed. Arthur K. Wheelock, Jr] (Washington, DC, [1995]), pp. 140–145.

8 In this regard see the essays in *Les Anciens Systèmes des mesures: Projet d'enquête métrologique – Table ronde du 17 octobre 1981* ([Paris, 1982]) and *Introduction à la métrologie historique*, ed. Bernard Garnier, J[ean]-C[laude] Hocquet, and D[enis] Woronoff (Paris, 1989), especially those by Paul Butel and Pierre Jeannin.

9 Ricard, *Le Négoce d'Amsterdam* (Amsterdam, 1722), p. 508.

Figure 4.1 The balance and the steelyard. The illustration pictures the two means
of weighing commercial goods common in the eighteenth century: the unequal
arm balance or steelyard in the foreground to the left ("Fig. I") and the equal
arm balance or scale in the background at the right ("Fig. II"), the former
utilizing the mechanical advantage of the lever. For a detailed discussion of these
considerations see Bruno Kisch, *Scales and Weights: A Historical Outline*, Yale
Studies in the History of Science and Medicine, no. 1 (New Haven, Conn.,
1965). Note the merchant's marks on the bales of goods.

Source: The source of the illustration is German, the practice universal. Johann J. Scheuchzer,
Kupfer-Bible, in welcher de Physica Sacra, oder Beheiligte Natur-wissenschaft derer in Heil.
Schrifft Vorkommenden Natürlichen Sachen . . . , 4 vols in 6 pts. (Augsburg and Ulm,
1731–1735), IV, opp. p. 754, Plate DLXXIX.
Courtesy of the Library of Congress, Washington, DC.

stated that the English (and Irish) pound was the same as the Scottish pound
although the latter could actually have been 8.7 percent larger.[10]

The case of Scotland is especially perplexing. The Act of Union of 1707

10 See Richard Hayes, *The Negociator's Magazine*, 4th edn (London, 1739), p. 212; [Richard]
Rolt, *A New Dictionary of Trade and Commerce* (London, 1756), s.v. "Measure"; Thomas

Table 4.1 Metric equivalents of the basic units of commercial weight in eighteenth-century Western Europe

Country (locality)	Unit	Equivalent (kilograms)
DENMARK	pund	0.4960
THE NETHERLANDS		
Amsterdam	pond	0.4941
Rotterdam	pond	0.4941
GERMANY		
Hamburg	pfund	0.4844
FRANCE		
Paris	livre	0.4895
Nantes	livre	0.4895
Bordeaux	livre	0.4895
Marseilles	livre	0.4084
SPAIN	libra	0.4601
PORTUGAL	árratel	0.4590
GREAT BRITAIN		
England	pound	0.4536
Scotland, pre-1707	pound	0.4935
Scotland, post-1707	pound	0.4536
Ireland	pound	0.4536

Notes and sources:
Denmark: The *pund* of Copenhagen. Astrid Friis and Kristof Glamann, *A History of Prices and Wages in Denmark, 1660–1800* (London, 1958), p. 132, and Poul Thestrup, *The Standard of Living in Copenhagen, 1730–1800 Some Methods of Measurement*, Københavns Universitet, Institut for Økonomisk Historie, Publikation no. 5 (Copenhagen, 1971), pp. 123–124. Compare [Mathieu] Tillet, *Essai sur le rapport des poids étrangers avec le marc de France . . .* (Paris, 1766), p. 33, which implies 0.4945 kg in comparison with the Parisian *livre*; *De Koopman, of Bijdragen ten Opbouw van Neerlands Koophandel en Zeevaard* (Amsterdam), I (no. 16, [17 Dec. 1766]), 124, which implies 0.4879 kg in comparison with the Amsterdam *pond*; and Horace Doursther, *Dictionnaire universel des poids et mesures anciens et modernes . . .* (Brussels, 1840), p. 219, who says 0.4994 kg. Tillet's paper was reprinted in the *Histoire de l'Académie Royale des Sciences . . . avec les Mémoires de Mathématique et de Physique [pour 1767]* [Paris, 1770], "Mémoires," pp. 350–408. It was also translated into Italian with an appendix comparing the weights and measures of Florence: *Saggio sul rapporto dei pesi stanieri con il marco di Franco . . .* (Florence, 1769). See also [Louis Paul Abeille and Mathieu Tillet], *Observations de la Société Royale d'Agriculture sur l'uniformité des poids et des mesures* [Paris, 1790]). For the dating of the issues of *De Koopman*, see H[ajo] Brugmans, "De Koopman: Mercurius als Spectator," *Jaarboek van het Genootschap Amstelodamum*, X (1912), 65, 67–68, n.
The Netherlands, Amsterdam, and Rotterdam: Doursther, op. cit., p. 213; W[inand] C. H. Staring, *De Binnen- en Buitenlandsche Maten, Gewichten en Munten*, ed. R. W. van Wieringen, 4th edn (Schoonhaven, [1902]), p. 91; and J[an] J. Reesse, *De Suikerhandel van Amsterdam van het begin der 17de eeuw tot 1894*, 2 vols (Haarlem, 1908–1911), I, Bijlage C, lxxxii. For the towns of all the Seven United Provinces, see K. M. C. Zevenboom and D[irk] A. Wittop

Bond, *A Digest of Foreign Exchanges* (Dublin, 1795), p. 146. This discussion concerns itself exclusively with commercial weight or, for England, the avoirdupois lb. The English also used another lb. called the apothecary or troy lb. (0.3732 kg) to weigh drugs, jewels, and precious metals. Ronald Edward Zupko, *A Dictionary of Weights and Measures for the British Isles: The Middle Ages to the Twentieth Century*, Memoirs of the American Philosophical Society, CLXVIII (Philadelphia, 1985), 322–326. See also Ronald Edward Zupko, *British Weights and Measures: A History from Antiquity to the Seventeenth Century* (Madison, Wis., 1977); and Connor, *Weights and Measures of England*.

Table 4.1 continued

Koning, *Nederlandse gewichten: Stelsels, ijkewezen, vormen makers en merken*, Rijksmuseum voor de Geschiedenis der Natuurwetenschappen te Leiden, Mededeling no. 86 (Leiden, 1953), pp. 179–183. See also, for Utrecht, F[rans] Ketner, "Bijdrage tot de kennis van de Utrechtse maten en gewichten," *Bijdragen en Medelingen van het Historisch Genootschap*, LXVI (1948), 192.

Germany, Hamburg: Doursther, op. cit., p. 223. Compare Tillet, op. cit., p. 41, which implies 0.4843 kg in comparison with the French *livre*, and *De Koopman* (Amsterdam), I (no. 16, [17 Dec. 1766]), 124, which implies 0.4842 kg in comparison with the Amsterdam *pond*. The *marc* of Cologne, equal to one-half *pfund*, while also used at Hamburg, was more common to the rest of Germany. According to Doursther, op. cit., pp. 218, 248–249, the *pfund* weighed 0.4675 kg. Three of the standard weights of Cologne sent to Emperor Leopold I of the Holy Roman Empire in 1703 were checked in the 19th century and found to weigh 0.4675 kg, 0.4677 kg, and 0.4681 kg, or an average of 0.4678 kg. [Austria, Handels-Ministerium], *Über das Verhältnis des Bergkrystall-Kilogrammes, welches bei Einführung des metrischen Maasses und Gewichtes das Urgewicht in Österreich bilden soll, zum Kilogramme der Kaiserlicher Archive in Paris . . .* (Vienna, 1870), pp. 101–103.

France, Paris: P[atrick] Kelly, *The Universal Cambist and Commercial Instructor*, 2nd edn, 2 vols (London, 1835), I, 133; Doursther, op. cit., pp. 221, 228; Henri Hauser, *Recherches et documents sur l'histoire des prix en France, de 1500 à 1800* (Paris, 1936), pp. 31, 89, 94; and Ronald Edward Zupko, *French Weights and Measures before the Revolution: A Dictionary of Provincial and Local Units* (Bloomington, Ind., 1978), pp. 97–100. George Graham's notes on weights that he laid before the council meeting of the Royal Society of London, 21 June 1742, in comparison with the English lb. avoirdupois, imply a French *livre* equal to 0.4896 kg. Add. MS. 6180, fol. 183v, BL, and as printed in Hubert Hall and Freida J. Nicholas, *Select Tracts and Table Books Relating to English Weights and Measures [1100–1742]*, Royal Historical Society, Camden, 3rd ser., no. 41, *Camden Miscellany*, vol. XV (London, 1929), p. 40. Other contemporaries suggest that the *livre* weighed 0.4941 kg when they equate it with the Amsterdam *pond*. See, for instance, Jean Pierre Ricard, *Le Négoce d'Amsterdam . . .* (Amsterdam, 1722), p. 508; Wyndham Beawes, *Lex Mercatoria Rediviva; or the Merchant's Directory* (London, 1752), p. 877; *De Koopman* (Amsterdam), I (no. 16, [17 Dec. 1766]), 125.

France, Nantes: Hauser, op. cit., p. 483. *De Koopman* (Amsterdam), I (no. 16, [17 Dec. 1766]), 125, implies 0.4892 kg in comparison with the Amsterdam *pond*. Doursther, op. cit., p. 227, says 0.4944 kg.

France, Bordeaux: Prior to the middle of the 16th century, Bordeaux had a local *livre*; after the 1560s this was slowly replaced by "la livre poids de marc," the *livre* of Paris. "Il est permis de penser que les anciennes mesures de poids restèrent plus longtemps encore en usage dans les campagnes du Bordelais," said J[ean] A. Brutails, "Recherches sur l'équivalence des anciennes mesures de la Gironde," *Actes de l'Académie des Sciences, Belles-Lettres et Arts de Bordeaux* (1911), p. 133. Nevertheless, as Brutails contends (ibid., pp. 131–135), and as a contemporary commercial newspaper states – *Le Négociant, ou, Annonces et Avis Divers sur le Commerce* (Paris), 3 May 1762 – "le poids de Bordeaux est le même que celui de Paris" in all major mercantile matters. Compare Kelly, op. cit., I, 46, and Doursther, op. cit., p. 216, both of which say 0.4944 kg, and *De Koopman* (Amsterdam), I (no. 16, [17 Dec. 1766]), 123, which implies 0.4941 kg in comparison with the Amsterdam *pond*. The *quintal* at Bordeaux measured 101 *livres* or 49.4401 kg according to Brutails, op. cit., pp. 135, 152. The Bordeaux commodity price current stated otherwise in pricing a long list of goods per *quintal* "qui est de 100 l." which, at 0.4895, equaled 48.95 kg. *Pris au Commerce qui ce Fait à Bordeaux*, 14 Feb. 1634. For this newspaper, see John J. McCusker and Cora Gravesteijn, *The Beginnings of Commercial and Financial Journalism: The Commodity Price Currents, Exchange Rate Currents, and Money Currents of Early Modern Europe*, Nederlandsch Economisch-Historisch Archief, ser. III, no. 11 (Amsterdam, 1991), pp. 153–158 (fig. 10.1).

France, Marseilles: "La livre poids de Marseille, est égale à 408431,44076505 [milligrammes]" (or 0.4084 kg). The *quintal* was 100 *livres*. P. Debures, *Tableau complet des poids et mesure anciennement en usage à Marseille et à Paris, comparés avec les poids et mesure de la République* (Marseilles, An XI [1802–1803]), pp. 81–88 (quotation, p. 83). Compare *De Koopman* (Amsterdam), I (no. 16, [17 Dec. 1766]), 124, which implies 0.4002 kg in comparison with the Amsterdam *pond*; Doursther, op. cit., p. 226, who says 0.4095 kg; and Zupko, op. cit., p. 100, who says 0.4079 kg. The Marseilles commodity price current regularly called attention to the difference between the *livre* of Paris and that of Marseilles. See, for instance, the *Prix Courant des Marchandises à Marseille*, 25 Nov. 1722, 10 July 1723: "120 liv. de Marseille sont 100 liv. poids de Marc." Compare the *Prix-Courant au Comptant, des Marchandises sur la Place de Marseille*, 10 Germinal, an VI [30 Mar. 1798]; and *Prix Courant Général de Marchandises* (Marseilles), 3 July 1810. For this newspaper, see McCusker and Gravesteijn, op. cit., pp. 363–369 (compare fig. 27.1, p. 365).

Spain: The *libra* of Spain, equal to two *marcas* of Castile. Kelly, op. cit., I, 65, 322; Doursther, op. cit., pp. 218, 220–221, 249; Earl J. Hamilton, *American Treasure and the Price Revolution in Spain, 1501–1650*, Harvard Economic Studies, vol. XLIII (Cambridge, Mass., 1934), pp. 175–177; Earl J. Hamilton, *War and Prices in Spain, 1651–1800*, Harvard Economic Studies, vol. LXXXI (Cambridge, Mass., 1947), p. 229; and Huguette Chaunu and Pierre Chaunu, *Séville et l'Atlantique (1504–1650)*, 8 vols in 11 pts. (Paris, 1955–1960), I, 271. *De Koopman* (Amsterdam), I (no. 16, [17 Dec. 1766]), 125, implies 0.4660 kg in comparison with the Amsterdam *pond*. The Spanish *arroba* of 25 *libras* equaled 11.5023 kg. For the conversion of the weights and measures of the Spanish provinces into those of Castile, see *Reducción completa y recíproca de las monedas, pesos y medidas de Castilla con las de Cataluña, Aragón, Valencia, Mallorca, Navarra y otras provincias: Con una adición de valor de varias monedas estrangeras* (Barcelona, 1823), pp. 328–368 and passim.

Portugal: The Portuguese *árratel* equaled two *marcos*. Kelly, op. cit., I, 212; Doursther, op. cit., p. 229; Vitorino [de] Magalhães Godinho, *Prix et monnaies au Portugal, 1750–1850* ([Paris], 1955), pp. 16, 80. Tillet, op. cit., p. 43, implies 0.4587 kg in comparison with the Parisian *livre*; *De Koopman* (Amsterdam), I (no. 16, [17 Dec. 1766]), 124, implies 0.4660 kg in comparison with the Amsterdam *pond*. The Portuguese *arroba* used in the sugar trade was of 32 *arráteis* and equaled 14.6867 kg. See, for instance, Dierick Ruiters, *Toortse der Zee-vaert* (1632), ed. S[amuel] P. l'Honoré Naber, Werken Uitgegeven door de Linschoten-Vereeniging, VI (The Hague, 1913), p. 33; J[an] D. H[er]l[ein], *Beschryvinge van de Volk-Plantinge Zariname*, [2nd edn] (Leeuwarden, 1718), p. 77; *Le Négociant, ou, Annonces et Avis Divers sur le Commerce* (Paris), 25 Apr. 1762; Tillet, op. cit., p. 43; Robert Southey, *History of Brazil*, 3 vols (London, 1810–1819), III, 900; Kelly, op. cit., I, 212; Doursther, op. cit., p. 28. Compare, however, Herman Wätjen, *Das holländische Kolonialreich in Brazilien: Ein Kapital aus der Kolonialgeschichte des 17. Jahrhunderts* (Gotha, 1921), p. 234, n. 3, p. 276, n. 5, and p. 315, where he equates the *arroba* with "28 Pfund." He was close, if he is to be taken literally, for 28 modern German *pfund* equal 14.0 kg, but he has confused some who thought he meant 28 Portuguese *arráteis* or 12.8509 kg.

Great Britain, England: This is the English avoirdupois lb., the standard today in both Great Britain and the United States. [U.N., Statistical Office], *World Weights and Measures: Handbook for Statisticians*, [rev. edn] (New York, [1966]), pp. 2, 97. Tillet, op. cit., p. 45, implies 0.4535 kg in comparison with the Parisian *livre*. *De Koopman* (Amsterdam), I (no. 16, [17 Dec. 1766]), 124, implies 0.4472 kg in comparison with the Amsterdam *pond*; Kelly, op. cit., I, 220, says 0.4535 kg. Doursther, op. cit., pp. 214, 225, says, 0.4535 kg and 0.4536 kg.

Great Britain, Scotland: A[lex] J. S., Gibson and T[homas] C[hristopher] Smout, *Prices, Food and Wages in Scotland, 1550–1780* ([Cambridge, Eng.], 1995), pp. 366–368. Compare Ronald Edward Zupko, *A Dictionary of Weights and Measures for the British Isles: The Middle Ages to the Twentieth Century*, Memoirs of the American Philosophical Society, vol. CLXVIII (Philadelphia, 1985), p. 324; and Zupko, "The Weights and Measures of Scotland before the Union," *Scottish Historical Review*, LVI (October 1977), 134. In both places he indicates that it is the equivalent of 493.517 grams. See also *De Koopman* (Amsterdam), I (no. 16, [17 Dec. 1766]), 124, which implies 0.5100 kg in comparison with the Amsterdam *pond*, Doursther, op. cit., p. 260, which says 0.4924 kg; and Ronald Edward Zupko, *A Dictionary of English Weights and Measures from Anglo-Saxon Times to the Nineteenth Century* (Madison, Wis., 1968), pp. 113, 136, where the numbers work out to 0.4931 kg.

Great Britain, Ireland: Ireland, perforce, has shared England's measures of weight, despite some indications to the contrary. Walter Harris, "Of the Weights and Measures Used in Ireland; and of Denomination Given to Lands There," in *The Whole Works of Sir James Ware Concerning Ireland*, trans. and ed. Walter Harris, 3 pts in 2 vols (Dublin, 1739–1745), II, 223; Patrick Kelly, *Metrology; or An Exposition of Weights and Measures, Chiefly Those of Great Britain and*

Table 4.1 continued

France (London, 1816), p. 116. This was not the effect of "Poyning's Law" of 1495 as Harris and Kelly claim, and it was only partly the effect of another law passed later that same year. See Irish Acts of 10 Henry VII, c. 4 (1495), and 10 Henry VII, c. 22 (1495), in [Ireland (Eire), Laws and Statutes], *The Statutes at Large, Passed in the Parliaments Held in Ireland from . . . 1310 . . . to . . . 1800*, [ed. James Goddard Butler], 20 vols (Dublin, 1786–1801) I, 44, 56–57. A later act is more to the point: see Irish Act of 4 Anne, c. 14 (1705), entitled "An Act for regulating the weights used in this kingdom . . ." Ibid., IV, 102–108. Equally incorrect was George Clerk, Member of Parliament and Lord of the Admiralty, when he testified before a Parliamentary inquiry in May 1823 that Ireland as well as Scotland had "a different system . . . of weights . . . from that in force in England." [G.B., Parl., Lords, Select Committee Appointed to Consider the Petition of the . . . City of Glasgow . . .], *Report from the Select Committee of the House of Lords Appointed to Consider the Petition of the . . . City of Glasgow Taking Notice of the Bill Entitled "An Act for Ascertaining and Establishing Uniformity of Weights and Measures etc."*, HC, Sessional Papers, 1824, vol. VII (Reports), no. 94. [London, 1824], p. 10.

abolished the Scottish system of weights and measures. By law, at least, goods were to be traded throughout Great Britain using English measures.[11] Yet the Scot has never taken kindly to the Sassenach, and the question whether to comply fully with the Act of Union is still debated today. Thus for at least a century after 1707, Scotland employed two systems of measurement. Internal trade utilized the old Scottish measures, and the courts of law defended this practice. But the Customs and Excise, administered from London, collected duties and compiled statistics of trade using English measures.[12] The wholesale trade in sugar, tied to customhouse measure,

11 According to the Act of Union, 6 Anne, c. 11, sec. 17 (1706). The compilation of English weights and measures promised in William [H.] Beveridge, *Prices and Wages in England from the Twelfth to the Nineteenth Century* (London, 1939), p. lix, although never published, is available as an index file and related materials, Boxes S 4 to S 6, Beveridge Wages and Prices Collection, British Library of Political and Economic Science, Manuscript Department, London School of Economics and Political Science, University of London. A finding aid to the collection is available in the Manuscript Department. See G. A. Falla, "A Catalogue of the Papers of William Henry Beveridge, 1st Baron Beveridge" (unpublished typescript, 1981).

12 [John Swinton], *A Proposal for Uniformity of Weights and Measures in Scotland, by Execution of the Laws Now in Force* (Edinburgh, 1779), passim; Henry Mackay, *An Abridgment of the Excise-Laws, and of the Customs-Laws Therewith Connected, Now in Force in Great Britain* (Edinburgh, 1779), pp. 45–52; testimony of George Clerk, 28 May 1823, [GB, Parl., Lords, Select Committee Appointed to Consider the Petition of the . . . City of Glasgow . . .], *Report from the Select Committee of the House of Lords Appointed to Consider the Petition of the . . . City of Glasgow Taking Notice of the Bill Entitled "An Act for Ascertaining and Establishing Uniformity of Weights and Measures etc."*, HC Sessional Papers, 1824, vol. VII (Reports), no. 94. [London, 1824], p. 10; Patrick Kelly, *Metrology; or, An Exposition of Weights and Measures, Chiefly Those of Great Britain and France . . .* (London, 1816), pp. 90–112; J[ames] M. Henderson, *Scottish Reckonings of Time, Money, Weights and Measures*, Historical Association of Scotland, [Pamphlets], n.s., no. 4 ([Edinburgh], 1926), pp. 5–8, 13–14. For the origins of Kelly's work in a 1797 letter from John Sinclair to the Bank of England, see *The Correspondence of the Right Honourable Sir John Sinclair, Bart., with Reminiscences of the Most Distinguished Characters Who Have Appeared in Great Britain, and in Foreign Countries, during the Last Fifty Years*, [ed. John Sinclair], 2 vols

weighed sugar by the English pound or, more precisely, by the English "hundredweight."[13]

As the basic units of weight differed from place to place, so too did the compound units. The usual and quite ancient multiple of the pound was the "hundred," called frequently the "quintal" and more fully the "hundredweight" (abbreviated "cwt." or "Ct." in eighteenth-century accounts). The hundredweight usually but not always equaled 100 times the basic unit. Thus "un quintal de sucre brut" at Nantes weighed 100 times 0.4895 kilogram, or 48.95 kilograms. But for Portugal the *quintal* equaled 128 *arráteis* (58.75 kilograms), and in seventeenth-century England there were at least three hundredweights in use for various commodities. The first of these weighed 100 pounds (45.36 kilograms) and was the oldest measure, equivalent to four quarters (of twenty-five pounds each) or to eight stone (of twelve and one-half pounds each). This "short" hundredweight sometimes called the hundred subtle, was used for the sale of spices, drugs, and other fine-grained or powdery commodities. By common practice the seller allowed the buyer an extra four pounds, known as the "tret," to compensate for the loss or "garble" that inevitably occurred in the buying and selling of what were thus designated garbled commodities. It followed that any transaction involving them was a garbled transaction.

The second important hundredweight, a newer measure of Plantagenet origin, weighed 112 pounds (50.80 kilograms) and equaled four quarters (of twenty-eight pounds each) or eight stone (of fourteen pounds each). Such coarser goods as groceries and salt were sold by this "gross" or "long" hundredweight. In fact all commodities, both fine and coarse, were first weighed by the long hundredweight, and "all fine commodities [were] afterwards reduced to the suttle hundred" for resale purposes. The long hundredweight was the

(London, 1831), I, 440–441. An important corrective to a blind reliance on what the statutes ordered is explicit in Ian Levitt and [Thomas] Christopher Smout, "Some Weights and Measures in Scotland, 1843," *Scottish Historical Review*, LVI (Oct. 1977), 146–152. Compare A[lex] J. S., Gibson and T[homas] C[hristopher] Smout, *Prices, Food and Wages in Scotland, 1550–1780* ([Cambridge, Eng.], 1995), pp. 365–375.

13 Kelly, *Metrology*, pp. 91–92. For an argument that the Scottish Customs officers used English weights and measures from the time of the Union because of the active control of the Scottish Board from London, see John J. McCusker, *Rum and the American Revolution: The Rum Trade and the Balance of Payments of the Thirteen Continental Colonies, 1650–1775*, 2 vols (New York, 1989 [Ph.D. diss., University of Pittsburgh, 1970]), II, 983, n. 1. Accounts of Scottish sugar merchants indicate unequivocally that sugar paid freight charges and assessed duties, and was bought and sold all by the same weight, the English cwt. of 112 lb. avoirdupois (50.80 kg). See, e.g., Sales Book of William MacDowall, 1729–1732, MS 8800, Houston Papers, 1729–1798, National Library of Scotland, Edinburgh; "Alexander Houston & Company's Sale Book no. C," 1775–1779, MS 8799, Houston Papers; and Accounts and Papers Relating to the South Sugar House, Glasgow, Collections Deposited by Messrs Tods, Murray, and Jamieson, W.S., GD. 237/139, Miscellaneous Gifts and Deposits, Scottish Record Office, Edinburgh. Compare William Gordon, The *Universal Accountant and Complete Merchant*, 3rd edn (Edinburgh, 1770), I, 49: "In Scotland, the excise and breweries use the English measures; but the retailer and victuallers in the country use the Scotch pint."

one used by the Customs and Excise. The third hundredweight, called the stannary hundred, weighed 120 pounds (54.43 kilograms) and, as its name indicates, was used almost exclusively for tin in Cornwall.[14] In the old British Empire both of the first two hundredweights were used in the sugar trade.

By the middle of the seventeenth century, the "great hundred" of 112 pounds had become established as the standard hundredweight for the English sugar trade of the mother country but this was not quite the case in its colonies. The English colonists on the North American continent from Maryland north did as they did at home and bought and sold sugar by the great or long hundredweight.[15] From Virginia south, through the Carolinas

14 For these cwt., see Gerard de Malynes, *Consuetudo vel Lex Mercatoria; or the Ancient Law-Merchant* (London, 1622), p. 22; Lewes Roberts, *The Merchants Mappe of Commerce . . .,* [1st edn] ([London], 1638), [2nd pagination], p. 239 (quotation); Jonas Moore, *A New Systeme of the Mathematicks*, 2 vols (London, 1681), I, 11–12; Zupko, *Dictionary of Weights and Measures for the British Isles*, pp. 192–197. For the use of the gross or long cwt. by the Customs and Excise, see Acts of 21 James I, c. 33 (1623), and 12 Charles II, c. 4 (1660). Compare [GB, Laws and Statutes, Customs], *The Rates of Merchandise . . . As They are Rated and Agreed on by the Common House of Parliament . . . Saturday July 28. 1660* (London, 1660), pp. 22, 49. At an earlier period sugar seems to have been grouped with pepper, cinnamon, and other spices, and weighed 13½ lb. to the stone or 108 lb. to the cwt., but I have seen no commercial evidence of such usage in the 17th and 18th centuries. See Moore, *Systeme of Mathematics*, I, 12, and Zupko, loc. cit. Compare [GB, Laws and Statutes], *A Collection in English, of the Statutes Now in Force, Continued from the Beginning of Magna Carta . . . Until . . . [1610]* (London, 1615), fol. 464v (ca. 1300); Michael Dalton, *The Countrey Justice, Containing the Practice of the Justices of the Peace,* 5th edn (London, 1635), p. 149. One finds the occasional reference to the thousand-weight or ten cwt. See, e.g., "Commodities which this island produceth," enclosure in letter of Gov. Thomas Modyford, at Jamaica, to Henry Bennet, Earl of Arlington, Sec. of State, 23 Sept. 1670, CO 138/1, p. 81, PRO; H. John Overing, at Newport, RI, to [Nicholas Brown and Co., at Providence, RI], 25 May 1770, Brown Papers, L+A 60–82 M, John Carter Brown Library, Brown University, Providence, RI. Compare Zupko, op. cit., pp. 408–409.

15 Arthur Harrison Cole, *Wholesale Commodity Prices in the United States, 1700–1861* (Cambridge, Mass., 1938), II, x, 73. Compare Patrick Kelly, *The Universal Cambist, and Commercial Instructor,* [1st edn], 2 vols (London, 1811), I, 11.
      The use of the short cwt. of 100 lb. for tobacco and codfish, commodities for which the mother country employed the long cwt., seems to have been universal in the Thirteen Continental Colonies. Cole, op. cit., I, x. For the tobacco trade, see also William Fitzhugh, at Stafford County, Va., to Ralph Smith, at Bristol, 22 Apr. 1686, and to Thomas Clayton, at Liverpool, 26 Apr. 1686, in *William Fitzhugh and His Chesapeake World, 1676–1707: The Fitzhugh Letters and Other Documents,* ed. Richard Beale Davis, Virginia Historical Society, Documents, vol. 3 (Chapel Hill, NC, 1963), pp. 176, 181; Lt. Gov. Alexander Spotswood, at [Williamsburg], Va., to Commissioners for Trade and Plantations, 7 Mar. 1717/18, in *The Official Letters of Alexander Spotswood, Lieutenant-Governor of the Colony of Virginia, 1710–1722,* ed. R[obert] A. Brock, Collections of the Virginia Historical Society, n.s., vols I and II, 2 vols (Richmond, Va., 1882–1885), II, 269; Isaac Norris, at Philadelphia, to John Clarke, May 1731, Isaac Norris Letter Books, Norris Family Papers, 1705–1860, HSP; and the correspondence of Petersburg, Va., tobacco factor Roger Atkinson, in the Roger Atkinson Letter Book, 1769–1776, Alderman Library, University of Virginia, Charlottesville. The Norris letter is quoted, in part, and other examples are cited, in Helen Louise Klopfer, "Statistics of the Foreign Trade of Philadelphia, 1700–1860" (Ph.D. diss., University of Pennsylvania, 1936), pp. 18–19.
      Thus I am at a loss to explain why Marylander Charles Carroll told John Hamburg, merchant of London, in a letter of 15 June 1728, that tobacco was weighed by the "grosse

and Georgia,[16] and across the Caribbean, from Jamaica to Barbados, the short hundredweight of 100 pounds was the standard unit in the sugar trade.[17]

Hundred's at the Scale here." "Extracts from Account and Letter Books of Dr. Charles Carroll, of Annapolis," *Maryland Historical Magazine*, XVIII (Sept. 1923), 230. By contrast, Maryland case law attests to the regular use of the short cwt. of 100 lb. in the tobacco trade there. See, for instance, the evidence in the case of *Sawyer* v. *Gibbs* (1680), *Archives of Maryland*, ed. William Hand Browne *et al.*, in progress (Baltimore, 1883 to date), LXIX, 300–309.

Equally a mystery to me is why the long cwt. appears as the regular unit of measure in the Virginia tobacco trade conducted by Jacob van Cortlandt, the New York merchant. See, e.g., the entries for Mar. 1764 and 19. Dec. 1767, in his Journal C, 1764–1772, fols 11r, 193v, Van Cortlandt Account Books, 1700–1875, New York Public Library, New York City.

The use of the long cwt. in New England in the 1650s explains the illusory anomaly commented upon by the editors of the published letter from George Halsall, at Boston, to John Winthrop, Jr., at New London, 27 Apr. 1654, *Winthrop Papers*, ed. Malcolm Freiberg *et al.*, in progress (Boston, 1929 to date), VI, 376, and n. 1.

16   The general use of the short cwt. as the standard for all trades in Virginia, North Carolina, South Carolina, and Georgia was widely recognized. See, e.g., Kelly, *Universal Cambist*, I, 11. Compare some of the references in the previous note. Mercantile records make it clear that the likes of rice and sugar were traded at South Carolina by the cwt. of 100 lb. See the *Papers of Henry Laurens*, ed. Hamer *et al.*, passim (e.g., for rice, II, 489, for sugar, II, 370, 409). Compare the sale of rice from the Newington Plantation, 1702–1707, as recorded in the Daniel Axtell Account Book, 1699–1707, Massachusetts Historical Society, Boston, as explicated in Alexander Moore, "Daniel Axtell's Account Book and the Economy of Early South Carolina," *South Carolina Historical Magazine*, XCV (Oct. 1994), 299; and the discussion by the various collectors of the Customs of the provisions in the "Act to provide more effectively for the collection of the duties imposed by law on goods . . . imported into the United States," sec. 35, provoked by Alexander Hamilton's "Circular" letter of 13 May 1791. *The Papers of Alexander Hamilton*, ed. Harold C. Syrett *et al.*, 26 vols (New York, 1961–1979), VIII, 340–341 and passim. The reference is to [US, Laws and Statutes], *The Statutes at Large of the United States of America*, ed. R[ichard] Peters *et al.*, 17 vols (Boston, 1845–1873), I, 166 (4 Aug. 1790).

17   Although there are only a few textual indications of this situation for the West Indian colonies, it is easy to detect from an examination of British West Indian plantation records or of commercial documents, especially shipping invoices. For the sale of sugar on St Christopher, 1719–1721, see the Alexander Wooddrop Account Books, 1719–1734, LC; for Antigua, see Col. Samuel Martin, at Antigua, to Charles Batho, 7 Aug. 1766, Add. MS 41350, fol. 29, BL. A convenient series of invoices that serve this purpose are those transcribed into the books of the Royal African Company, 1673–1743, T 70/936 to T 70/961, PRO. At least two islands specified the short cwt. as the legal cwt.: [Barbados, Laws and Statutes], *Acts and Statutes of the Island of Barbados . . .* , [ed. John Jennings] (London, [1654]), p. 73, and [Nevis, Laws and Statutes], *Acts of Assembly Passed in the Island of Nevis, from 1664 to 1739, Inclusive* (London, 1740), pp. 7–8. For Barbados, see also Lewes Roberts, *The Merchants Map of Commerce . . .*, 3rd edn, rev. (London, 1677), p. 61; for the Leeward Islands, see also [Robert Robertson], *A Detection of the State and Situation of the Present Sugar Planters of Barbadoes and the Leeward Islands* (London, 1732), p. 47, and his *A Supplement to the Detection . . .* (London, 1732), p. 3. In addition, see Hayes, *Negociator's Magazine* (1739), p. 214; John Mair, *Book-keeping Methodiz'd; or A Methodical Treatise of Merchant-Accompts, According to the Italian Form*, 5th edn (Edinburgh, 1757), p. 238; J[oseph] Massie, *Calculations and Observations Relating to an Additional Duty upon Sugar* ([London], 1759), p. 1, and his *A State of the Exports to and Imports from the British Sugar Colonies* ([London, 1760]), p. 1.

While it is clear that Jamaica also used the short cwt. for the trade in sugar, there is an intriguing anomaly. Both shipping invoices and plantation accounts indicate unequivocally that sugar was measured by the short cwt. for all commerce. See, e.g., the Royal

Thus sugar shipped from the islands was measured there by the short hundredweight; the same sugar when sold at London, Bristol, or Glasgow was measured by the long hundredweight. The possible confusion thus created carries over into the still larger unit, the ton, as we have already seen. The duality seems to have been unique, however, to the English sugar trade; all other colonies of European nations used the same quintal as their mother countries.[18]

Molasses presents an even stickier problem. Almost everywhere save the British colonies molasses was sold by weight, and the documents speak of

African Company invoices cited above (e.g., T 70/939, pp. 5, 217, PRO, T 70/958, p. 51, PRO, or T 70/959, p. 44, PRO). Compare the Spring Plantation Accounts, Jamaica, 1719–1724, 1747–1776, in Spring Plantation Papers, The Woolnough Papers, Ashton Court Papers, AC/WO 16(7), 16(27), Bristol Record Office, Bristol, England, and the Amity Hall Plantation Records, Goulburn Papers, Surrey Record Office, Kingston-upon-Thames, England. See also Patrick Browne, *The Civil and Natural History of Jamaica* (London, 1756), p. 16. Nevertheless, the accounts, dated Port Royal, Nov. 1750, presented to the Jamaican House of Assembly on 21 Nov. 1751 used *both* the long and the short cwt. in what has to have been a conscious, if fraudulent, attempt to maximize the yield from the valuation of sugars offered in payment of loans. Multiplying the stated number of cwt. by 112 lb. each inflated the total amount of sugar present; dividing the total amount of sugar by 100 lb. per cwt. inflated the number of cwt. then to be priced at so many shillings per cwt. There is no comment on this sleight of hand in the minutes of the assembly but it can scarcely have gone unnoticed. [Jamaica, Assembly]. *Journals of the Assembly of Jamaica from January 20th, 1663–4 ... [to 1826]*, 15 vols (Jamaica, 1795–1829), IV, 322–323. Compare the use of the long cwt. in [Jamaica, Laws and Statutes], *Acts of Assembly Passed in the Island of Jamaica; From the Year 1681, to the Year 1769*, 2 vols (St Jago de la Vega, 1769–1771), I, 318.

    Samuel Ricard, *Traité général du commerce . . .*, rev. edn [ed. Tomás Antonio de Marien y Arrospide], 2 vols (Amsterdam, 1781), II, 137, indicated the use of "le quintal de 100 lb, poids de la Jamaïque, & des autres Isles anglaises."

18 Sugar in the Danish West Indies and in Denmark and Norway was bought, sold, and taxed by the *centner* of 100 *pund*. Waldemar C. Westergaard, *The Danish West Indies under Company Rule (1671–1754), with a Supplementary Chapter, 1755–1917* (New York, 1917), pp. 213, 317; Astrid Friis and Kristof Glamann, *A History of Prices and Wages in Denmark, 1660–1800* (London, 1958), pp. 133–134; and Jean Louise Willis, "The Trade between North America and the Danish West Indies, 1756–1807, with Special Reference to St Croix" (Ph.D. diss., Columbia University, 1963), pp. 66–67, 78, and elsewhere. The Dutch West Indies followed the same practice (one *centenaar* equaled 100 *ponden*). J[an] J. Reesse, *De Suikerhandel van Amsterdam van het begin der 17de eeuw tot 1894*, 2 vols (Haarlem, 1908–1911), I, Bijlage G, cxxi–cxxiii. The French West Indies used the *quintal* of 100 *livres*. Guy Josa, *Les Industries du sucre et du rhum à la Martinique (1639–1913)* (Paris, 1931), passim. Compare Jean Boizard, *Traité des monoyes, de leurs circonstances et dépendances* (Paris, 1692), p. 274. In the Spanish colonies the *quintal* equaled four *arrobas* of twenty-five *libras* each. Manuel Carrera Stampa, "The Evolution of Weights and Measures in New Spain" [trans. Robert S. Smith], *Hispanic American Historical Review*, XXXIX (Feb. 1949), 13. Compare Jean-Claude Hocquet, "Pesos y medidos y la historia de los precios en México: Algunas consideraciones metodológicas," [trans. Ana Claudia Morales Viramontes], in *Los precios de alimentos y manufacturas novohispanos*, ed. Virginia García Acosta [Mexico City, 1995], pp. 72–85. Brazil's *quintal* equaled four *arrobas* of thirty-two *arráteis* each. See table 4.1. Compare Frédéric Mauro, *Le Portugal et l'Atlantique au XVIIe siècle (1570–1670): Étude économique* (Paris, 1960), p. lvii. For all of these, see also Horace Doursther, *Dictionnaire universel des poids et mesures anciens et modernes . . .* (Brussels, 1840), pp. 457–460.

hundredweight and ton.[19] Thus the equivalents in table 4.1 come into play in these instances. But in the British West Indies and British North America planters and merchants treated molasses as a liquid and bought and sold it by liquid measure.[20] At this point the equivalents set out in table 4.2 are more applicable, as well as the comments made hereafter about the use of English liquid measures in the colonies of the other European nations. The

19   English Customs regulations reinforced English mercantile practice and English Customs officers collected duties on molasses on the same basis as that on which it was bought and sold, the long cwt. For an interesting instance of mercantile practice that involved the man who published the London commodity price current, see John Day, *The Modest Vindication of John Day of London, Merchant* (London, 1646), p. 7. As for statute law, see, for England and Wales, Act of 12 Charles II, c. 4 (1660). Compare Irish Act of 4 Anne, c. 14 (1705), entitled "An Act for regulating the weights used in this kingdom . . . ," in [Ireland (Eire), Laws and Statutes], *The Statutes at Large, Passed in the Parliaments Held in Ireland from . . . 1310 . . . to . . . 1800* [ed. James Goddard Butler], 20 vols (Dublin, 1786–1801) IV, 103. Thus English and Irish molasses import statistics are in cwt.: Customs 2/1 to 2/10, PRO, Customs 3/1 to 3/80, PRO, Customs 15/1 to 15/104, PRO, and Add. MS 4579, BL. Wholesale prices in England also reflect the sale of molasses by weight. See any of the contemporary price-currents cited in J[acob] M. Price, "Notes on Some London Price-Currents, 1667–1715," *EcHR*, 2nd ser., VII (Dec. 1954), 240–250; and John J. McCusker and Cora Gravesteijn, *The Beginnings of Commercial and Financial Journalism: The Commodity Price Currents, Exchange Rate Currents, and Money Currents of Early Modern Europe*, Nederlandsch Economisch-Historisch Archief, ser. III, no. 11 (Amsterdam, 1991), pp. 291–352. Compare the records of sales by the Royal African Company, e.g., T 70/84, fol. 50, PRO, T 70/86, fols 43, 94, PRO; the records of purchases made by the Hudson's Bay Company, e.g., entry dated 5 Feb. 1734/35 in the Minute Book of the Governor and Committee, Section A, Class 1, vol. 144, fol. 72v, Hudson's Bay Company Archives, Provincial Archives of Manitoba, Winnipeg, Manitoba, Canada; and the prices cited in [London, Sugar Refiners], *Epitome of the Sugar Trade* ([London, 1781]), [p. 2].
        Sale by weight was also the European practice, at home and in the colonies – at least some of the time. "Syroop, koomt in Vaten, de bruine Inlandse, zo wel als de Franse en Hamburger, word by de 100 [ponden] verkogt." *De Koopman, of Bijdragen ten Opbouw van Neerlands Koophandel en Zeevaard* (Amsterdam), I (no. 24, [ca. 16 Feb. 1768]), 195. (For the dating of the issues of this serial, see H[ajo] Brugmans, "De Koopman: Mercurius als Spectator," *Jaarboek van het Genootschap Amstelodamum*, X (1912), 65, 67–68, n.) See also N[icolaas] W. Posthumus, *Inquiry into the History of Prices in Holland*, 2 vols (Leiden, 1946–1964), I, 142–146, and Henri Hauser, *Recherches et documents sur l'histoire des prix en France de 1500 à 1800* (Paris, 1936), pp. 483, 494 495. Plantation accounts of Saint-Domingue also measured molasses by weight, at least as late as 1774. G[abriel] Debien, "Comptes, profits, esclaves et travaux de deux sucreries de Saint-Domingue (1774–1798)," *Revue de la Société d'Histoire et de Geographie d'Haïti*, XV (Oct. 1944), 21–22. Twenty years later some molasses was being sold on Saint-Domingue by liquid measure. G[abriel] Debien, *Plantations et esclaves à Saint-Domingue*, Université de Dakar, Faculté des Lettres et Sciences Humaine, Publication de la Section d'Histoire, no. 3 (Dakar, Senegal, 1962), p. 150. Mexican planters also sold molasses by weight. Barrett, *Sugar Hacienda*, pp. 61–62.
20   While this was true in North America apparently from the very beginning of the trade with the West Indies, there is just the hint that on one or two of the English West Indian islands molasses was accounted by weight in the earliest decades of the rum trade. For the former point see, e.g., *The Letter Book of Peleg Sanford of Newport, Merchant (later Governour of Rhode Island), 1666–1668*, ed. Howard M. Chapin (Providence, RI, 1928), pp. 57, 67, 70, 72. Documentation of the continued use of liquid measure for molasses in North America is so ubiquitous as to make additional references pointless. At St Christopher, however, some molasses exported to England was invoiced by the (short?) cwt. in 1700. CO 390/6, fol. 52r, PRO.

Table 4.2 Molasses, weight per unit of liquid measure, 1690–1927

		Weight in	
Date	*Description*	*Pounds per gallon*	*Grams per liter*
1690	Molasses, English Caribbean Colonies	11.11	1331.3
1725	Treacle, England	10.50	1258.2
1737	Molasses, St Christopher	11.00	1318.1
1747	Molasses, England	11.20	1342.1
1761–1793	Molasses [Treacle], England	11.25	1304.0
1781	Molasses, Grenada	10.79	1292.9
1785–1789	Molasses, Philadelphia	10.00	1198.3
1790	Molasses, St Christopher	9.75	1168.3
1793	Molasses [Treacle], Jamaica	7.00	838.8
1836	Molasses, [Louisiana]	11.48	1375.6
1849	Molasses, Louisiana	12.00	1437.9
1927	Blackstrap Molasses, Cuba	11.64	1394.8
Median		11.06	1324.7

Notes and sources:
Omitting the 1793 number as obviously erroneous, the median of the eleven remaining values is 1,331 grams per liter; the mean is 1,315 grams per liter.

1690. [Dalby Thomas], *An Historical Account of the Rise and Growth of the West India Collonies* (London, 1690), p. 15.

1725. George Smith, *A Compleat Body of Distilling . . .* (London, 1725), p. 88.

1737. "Some Observations . . . by a Planter of St Christopher," *Barbados Gazette* (Bridgetown), 22 Oct. 1737, as reprinted in *Caribbeana: Containing Letters and Dissertations . . . Chiefly Wrote by Several Hands in the West Indies,* [ed. Samuel Keimer] (London, 1741), II, 242.

1747. "Observations on the Duty on Molasses-Spirits," Report by the Commissioners of the Excise, London, 18 Mar. 1746/47, T 1/325, fol. 26, PRO.

1761–1793. The Memorandum Book of Messrs John Cooke and Co., 1761–1793, entitled "Observations, upon Brewing, Fermentation, and Distillation," fols 4, 16, and passim, Add. MS. 39683, BL.

1781. [Charles Casaux], *Essai sur l'art de cultiver la canne et d'en extraire le sucre* (Paris, 1781), p. 397.

1785–1789. Tench Coxe, *A View of the United States of America . . .* (Philadelphia, 1794), p. 78.

1790. Joshua Peterkin, *A Treatise on Planting, from the Origin of the Semen to Ebulliotion with a Correct Mode of Distillation . . .*, 2nd edn, rev. (Basseterre, St Christopher, 1790), p. 91.

1793. Bryan Edwards, *The History, Civil and Commercial, of the British Colonies in the West Indies,* 2 vols (London, 1793), II, 463: "raw sugar, if refined in the colonies, [would] yield the planter 448 lb. [of molasses] being equal to 64 gallons." Edwards is plainly mistaken as a gallon of water weighs 8 lb.

1836. [Jean-Baptiste(?)] Avequin, "Suite du mémoire sur la canne d'Otaïti et la canne à rubans," *Journal de Chimie Médicale, de Pharmacie, de Toxicologie, et Revue des Nouvelles Scientifiques Nationales et Etrangères,* 2nd ser., II (1836), 135.

1849. Charles L. Fleischmann, ["Report on Sugar Cane and Its Culture in Louisiana"] in [US, Patent Office], *Annual Report of the Commissioner of Patents, for the Year 1848,* [US, Congress, 30th Cong., 2nd Sess., House Executive Documents, no. 59] (Washington, DC, 1849), p. 312.

1927. Carl F. Snyder and L[ester] D. Hammond, *Determination of Weight per Gallon of Blackstrap Molasses,* US, Department of Commerce, National Bureau of Standards, *Technologic Papers,* XXI, no. 345. (Washington, DC, 1927), p. 411. They reprinted a synopsis of their paper in *The [Louisiana] Planter and Sugar Manufacturer,* LXXIX (1 Oct. 1927), 268. Compare Frederick J. Bates *et al., Polarimetry, Saccharimetry and the Sugars,* US, Department of

Commerce, National Bureau of Standards, Circular C 440 (Washington, DC, 1942), p. 252, and Carl F. Snyder and L[ester] D. Hammond, *Weights per United States Gallon and Weights per Cubic Foot of Sugar Solutions*, US, Department of Commerce, National Bureau of Standards, Circular C 457, rev. edn (Washington, DC, 1946), pp. 6–7.

Honey in England is said to weigh 12 lb. per gallon. See Smith, op. cit., p. 88; and *The Compleat Compting-House Companion; or, Young Merchant and Tradesman's Sure Guide . . .* (London, 1763), p. 46.

problem falls at the junction of these two systems: how much did a given volume of molasses weigh?

The answer to this question is not a simple one. There were different types of molasses and their weight varied with the percentage of water in any given batch.[21] Properly, "molasses" is the drainage from the first manufacture of raw crystalline sugar, called muscovado sugar in the British West Indies and *sucre brut* in the French islands. Raw muscovado sugar could be and was subjected to several further stages of processing, and at each stage more liquid was expressed. In the islands the most frequently performed secondary processing resulted in *sucre terré* or clayed sugar. Contemporaries warned each other against confusing the drainage from this processing and that from the initial manufacture, a warning we must heed as well. "You are always to have regard to the difference between muscovado-sugar molasses, and clay'd sugar molasses," cautioned William Belgrave in his book about Barbados.[22] The final processing, usually performed in Europe, was the refining of sugar, an operation to which sugar could be subjected several times, resulting in single-, double-, or triple-refined sugar. Again there was drainage, a kind of molasses more widely called "syrup" and, in Great Britain, "treacle." All of these "molasses" varied in quality, "muscovado-sugar molasses" being more bitter, thinner, and lighter, refined sugar treacle being sweeter and somewhat thicker and heavier.[23]

21 These distinctions and their impact are discussed throughout McCusker, *Rum and the American Revolution*.
22 *A Treatise upon Husbandry or Planting* (Boston, 1755), p. 26. The distinction Belgrave made is an old and continuing one. Compare [Christophe(?) de Quélus], *Histoire naturelle du cacao et du sucre* [corr. and ed. Nicolas Mahudel] (Paris, 1719), p. 190, n. a: "On distingue les sirops en gros et fins . . ." For the probable author (perhaps "de Caylus"), who died at Cayenne in French Guiana in 1683 after fifteen years of government service in the colony, see [France, Archives Nationales], *Inventaire analytique de la correspondance générale avec les colonies: Départ, Série B*, ed. Étienne Taillemite (Paris, 1959), p. 305. Already by 1668, those who dealt with Barbados sugar were making the distinction between "muscovado mallaces" and other kinds. Peleg Sanford, at Newport, RI, to William Sanford, at Barbados, 28 Dec. 1668, *Letter Book of Peleg Sanford*, ed. Chapin, p. 70. Compare Myer Lynsky, *Sugar Economics, Statistics, and Documents* ([New York], 1938), p. 42.
23 According to a statement in *Vervolg van den Surinaamschen Landman* (Paramaribo), ed. Anthony Blom, No. 5 (15 Jan. 1802), p. 71, "die malassie . . . is dunder en wateriger als de Hollandsche syroop" – it was thinner and more watery. Compare Richard Pares, *Yankees and Creoles: The Trade between North America and the West Indies before the American Revolution* (London, 1956), pp. 124–125.

The resolution of these differences in answer to the question "How much did a volume of molasses weigh?" is made even more difficult because there are few contemporary references to the subject. We are forced to rely, in part, on modern analyses of molasses, which might not necessarily reflect eighteenth-century experience. Still, the essential agreement of the several figures gathered in table 4.2 does support a contention that, in the eighteenth century, a liter of molasses weighed about 1⅓ kilograms.

◆ ◆ ◆ ◆ ◆

The European heritage of the Roman *libra* found little parallel in the units of liquid measure. As table 4.3 shows, the basic European liquid measures present a far greater diversity than do the measures of weight. The Irish pint, the smallest of these, was less than half the size of the Parisian *pinte* and hardly one-quarter the size of the pre-1707 Scottish pint. Moreover, within nations there seems to have been even greater divergence of liquid measure than of weights. England itself had two gallons, one for beer and ale, the other for wine, oil, and other liquids, including rum.[24] Nevertheless, as James Loftus, the Gauger of Customs, testified in 1758: "they have but one gallon,

---

24 From the time of Queen Elizabeth I the English ale gallon (and beer gallon) measured 282 cubic inches or 4.6212 liters. Zupko, *Dictionary of English Weights and Measures*, pp. 69–70; Zupko, *Dictionary of Weights and Measures for the British Isles*, pp. 162–163. Compare Doursther, *Dictionnaire universel des poids et mesures*, p. 155. Although the English colonies regularly adopted both the wine and the ale gallon, the consequent confusion resulted in at least one of them legislating the ale gallon out of existence. After 1706 ale and beer were sold in Pennsylvania by wine measure. [Pennsylvania, Laws and Statutes], *Statutes at Large of Pennsylvania from 1682 to 1801*, ed. James T. Mitchell and Henry Flanders, 18 vols (Harrisburg, Pa., 1896–1915), II, 221–222; Klopfer, "Statistics of the Foreign Trade of Philadelphia," pp. 21–22. It is in an instance such as this that the approach of someone like Klopfer shows itself so very much superior to that of the likes of Zupko. The latter simply rehearsed what the statute books said and what commentators on them thought; Klopfer researched how business was actually conducted.

It is also only in actual mercantile transactions that we can recognize such anomalies as the two slightly different bushels used for grain measure in the trades of the neighboring colonies of Maryland and Pennsylvania. Since much Maryland grain was sold in Pennsylvania, this difference caused considerable confusion and some rancor until, in 1774, the Common Council of the City of Philadelphia investigated and sorted out the cause of the problem, an old standard half-bushel measure, made of copper, that "appears to have received some injury, not being now circular, and bulging out at the bottom." Since this was the standard from which copies used in trade were made, and since the defects in the standard meant that Marylanders were being cheated, they complained mightily. The Common Council set out to have a new measure, "to contain the exact and legal measure according to the Act of Parliament," cast in bronze. It was delivered to the Common Council on 28 Nov. 1774. See the entries under various dates from Mar. through Nov., Common Council, Minutes, 1704–1776, vol. III, Record Group 120.1, City Council Records, Archives of the City of Philadelphia, Department of Records, Philadelphia. The problem had been around for some time. Two decades earlier, Philadelphia merchant Thomas Willing explained to his correspondent Hall Caile (Caillé [?]) that "your measure is less by a pint than ours here w[hi]ch occasion[s] [the] short measure" about which Caile had protested. Letter dated 3 June 1756, Willing and Morris Letter Book, 1754–1761, pp. 195–196, HSP. If Willing was accurate, the difference, one pint in a bushel, was something less than 2 percent.

Table 4.3 Metric equivalents of the basic units of commercial liquid measure in eighteenth-century Western Europe

Country (locality)	Unit	Equivalent (Liters)
DENMARK	*pot*	0.9661
THE NETHERLANDS		
Amsterdam	*pint*	0.6063
Rotterdam	*pint*	0.6397
GERMANY		
Hamburg	*nößel*	0.4522
FRANCE		
Paris	*pinte*	0.9313
Nantes	*pinte*	1.0000
Bordeaux	*pot*	2.2648
Marseilles	*pot*	1.0573
SPAIN	*quartillo*	0.5043
PORTUGAL		
Lisbon	*quartilho*	0.3446
Faro	*quartilho*	0.3556
Oporto	*quartilho*	0.5225
Viana	*quartilho*	0.5125
GREAT BRITAIN		
England	pint	0.4732
Scotland, pre-1707	pint	1.6944
Scotland, post-1707	pint	0.4732
Ireland	pint	0.4457

Notes and sources:

Denmark: The *pot* equaled 4 *paegle* (0.2415 liters); 2 *potter* equaled a *kande* (1.9322 liters) and 8 *potter* or 4 *kander* equaled a *viertel* (7.7290 liters). W[inand] C. H. Staring, *De Binnen-en Buitenlandsche Maten, Gewichten en Munten*, ed. R. W. van Wieringen, 4th edn (Schoonhaven, [1902]), p. 22. Compare P[atrick] Kelly, *The Universal Cambist and Commercial Instructor*, 2nd edn, 2 vols (London, 1835), I, 77, who equates the *viertel* with 7.7268 liters; ibid., II, 234–237, where the *viertel* is 7.726 liters; and Horace Doursther, *Dictionnaire universel des poids et mesures anciens et modernes . . .* (Brussels, 1840), p. 574, who equates the *viertel* with 7.728 liters and 7.487 liters. See also Astrid Friis and Kristof Glamann, *A History of Prices and Wages in Denmark, 1660–1800* (London, 1958), pp. 120, 132.

The Netherlands, Amsterdam: One *aam* (155.22 liters) equaled 4 *ankers* (38.805 liters), 8 *steêkan* (19.4025 liters), 21 *viertels* (7.3914 liters), 64 *stoopen* (2.4253 liters), 128 *mengels* (1.2126 liters) and 256 *pinten*. Staring, op. cit., I, 10, who equates the *aam* with 155.20 liters; ibid., II, 235–237, where he equates the *steêkan* with 19.403 liters (and, therefore, the *aam* with 155.224 liters); and Doursther, op. cit., p. 5, who equates the *aam* with 152.34 liters and, after Kelly, with 155.20 liters. According to Doursther, op. cit., p. 506, the *steêkan* of brandy at Amsterdam measured 18.76 liters. Compare Jan Pieter Dobbelaar, *De branderijn in Holland tot het begin der negentiende eeuw* (Rotterdam, 1930), p. 20. On that basis the *pint* equaled 0.5862 liters.

The Netherlands, Rotterdam: One *aam* (153.5328 liters) equaled 4 *ankers* (38.3832 liters), 60 *stoopen* (2.5589 liters), 120 *kannen* (1.2794 liters), and 240 *pinten*. Doursther, op. cit., pp. 7, 429. For Utrecht, see F[rans] Ketner, "Bijdrage tot de kennis van de Utrechtse maten en gewichten," *Bijdragen en Medelingen van het Historisch Genootschap*, LXVI (1948), 193–194 – the Utrecht *pint* equaled 0.8630 liters.

Germany, Hamburg: One *ahm* (144.7 liters) equaled 20 *stübken*. One *stübken* (3.6175 liters) equaled 2 *kannen*, 4 *quartiers*, or 8 *nößel* (0.4521875 liters). Kelly, op. cit., I, 171. Compare Doursther, op. cit., p. 509; Fritz Verdenhalven, *Alte Maße, Münzen und Gewichte aus dem deutschen Sprachgebiet* (Neustadt an der Aisch, 1968), pp. 42, 49. See also Jürgen Elert Kruse, *Allgemeiner und besonders Hamburgischer Contorist* (Hamburg, 1753), [pt i], p. 114.

Table 4.3 continued

France, Paris: One *velte* (7.4505 liters) equaled 4 *pots* (1.8626 liters), 8 *pintes*, and 16 *chopines* (0.4657 liters). Kelly, op. cit., I, 133, and Doursther, op. cit., pp. 429, 439, 570.

France, Nantes: One *velte* (6.0 liters) equaled 3 *pots* (2.0 liters) and 6 *pintes*. Doursther, op. cit., pp. 438, 570.

France, Bordeaux: One *velte* (7.5286 liters) equaled roughly 3½ *pots*. The first lesser unit of the *pot* was the *demi-pot* (1.1324 liters). Some documents mention a *pinte locale* (1.056 liters). J[ean] A. Brutails, "Recherches sur l'équivalence des anciennes mesures de la Gironde," *Actes de l'Académie des Sciences, Belles-Lettres et Arts de Bordeaux* (1911), pp. 117–130. Doursther, op. cit., pp. 49, 437, 570, 573, equates the *pot* with 2.1640 liters and the *velte* with 7.54 liters, while Kelly, op. cit., I, 47, implies a *velte* equal to 7.1853 liters and a *pot* equal to 2.0903 liters. Compare Théophile Malvezin, *Histoire du commerce de Bordeaux depuis les origines jusqu'à nos jours*, (Bordeaux, 1892), III, 109, who says that, in the 18th century, the *velte* measured 7.61 liters and the *pot* 2.28 liters.

France, Marseilles: The *pot* equaled 1.0573 liters. P. Debures, *Tableau complet des poids et mesure anciennement en usage à Marseille et à Paris, comparés avec les poids et mesure de la République* (Marseilles, An XI [1802–1803]), pp. 73–81 (esp. p. 80B). Compare Doursther, op. cit., pp. 142, 280, 438, 446, 570, 573, who said that the *pot* equaled 1.0667 liters at Marseilles. Ronald Edward Zupko, *French Weights and Measures before the Revolution: A Dictionary of Provincial and Local Units* (Bloomington, Ind., 1978), pp. 142, 180, who says that the *pot* equaled 1.067 liters and the *velte* equaled 7.54 liters at Marseilles.

Compare, in general, V[ictor] Dauphin, "Tableau des mesures ou expressions de mesures usitées en Anjou avant l'introduction du système métrique," *Revue d'Histoire Économique et Sociale*, XIX (no. 1, 1931), 77–96, and Charles Leroy, "Mesures de capacité en usage en Haute-Normandie aux XVIIe et XVIIIe siècles," *Bulletin de la Société Libre d'Émulation, du Commerce et de l'Industrie de la Seine-Inférieure* (1936), pp. 49–97, and (1937), pp. 155–218.

Spain: The Spanish standard was the wine *arroba* of Toledo. The *arroba* (16.137 liters) equaled 4 *quartillas* (4.0342 liters), 8 *azumbres* (2.0171 liters), and 32 *quartillos*. Doursther, op. cit., p. 29. See also [Spain, Laws and Statutes], *Informe de la imperial ciudad de Toledo al real, y Supremo Consejo de Castilla, sobre inqualácion de pesos y medidas en todos los reynos, y senorias de S[u] Mag[estad] segun las layes*, [ed. Andrés Marcos Burriell] ([Madrid], 1758), pp. 340–341. Compare Kelly, op. cit., I, 322, who says 16.073 liters; Earl J. Hamilton, *American Treasure and the Price Revolution in Spain, 1501–1650*, Harvard Economic Studies, vol. XLIII (Cambridge, Mass., 1934), p. 171, and Earl J. Hamilton, *War and Prices in Spain, 1651–1800*, Harvard Economic Studies, vol. LXXXI (Cambridge, Mass., 1947), pp. 229–230, who says 16.13 liters.

Portugal, Lisbon: The *almude* (16.54 liters) equaled 2 *alqueires*, *cantaros*, or *potes* (8.27 liters), 12 *canadas* (1.3783 liters), 24 *meias-canadas* (06892 liters), and 48 *quartilhos*. Kelly, op. cit., I, 212, 215; Doursther, op. cit., p. 13. Staring, *De Binnen- en Buitenlandsche Maten*, ed. Wieringen, p. 49, says 16.741 liters; Vitorino [de] Magalhães Godinho, *Prix et monnaies au Portugal, 1750–1850* ([Paris], 1955), p. 16, says 16.8 liters.

Portugal, Faro: The *almude* (17.04 liters) had the same constituents as at Lisbon. Doursther, op. cit., p. 13. Kelly, op. cit., I, 215, implies an *almude* of 17.03 liters in comparison with the English wine gallon.

Portugal, Oporto: The *almude* (25.08 liters) had the same constituents as at Lisbon. Kelly, op. cit., I, 215, in comparison with the English wine gallon; Doursther, op. cit., p. 13.

Portugal, Viana: The *almude* (24.6 liters) had the same constituents as at Lisbon. Kelly, op. cit., I, 215, in comparison with the English wine gallon; Doursther, op. cit., p. 13.

Great Britain, England: The English wine gallon of 231 cu. in. (3.7854 liters) equals 4 quarts (0.9464 liters) and 8 pints. The newer, post-1825 British imperial gallon equals 4.5461 liters or 1.2 wine gallons. Stephen Naft and Ralph de Sola, *International Conversion Tables*, rev. and enl., ed. P[hilip] H. Bigg (London, [1965]), pp. 17–18; *World Weights and Measures*, pp. 2, 97. For John Quincy Adams' history of the wine gallon and his discussion of its increase in size, see [US, Department of State], *Report of the Secretary of State, upon Weights and Measures*, [by John Quincy Adams], [US, Congress, 16th Cong., 2nd Sess., Senate Documents, vol. no. 4, doc. no. 119, vol. 4, Serial Set no. 45] (Washington, DC, 1821), pp. 22–43. Although the legal standard kept at Guildhall in London in the late 17th century measured only 224 cu. in. (3.6707 liters), the mercantile gallon, based on the Act of 12 Henry VII, c. 5 (1496), was the gallon of 231 cu. in. from at least that date. See [Samuel Starling], *A Discovery of the True Standard-Gallon of England* (London, 1658); [Samuel Starling], *The Cry of the Oppressed by Reason of False Measures: or, A Discovery of the True Standard-Gallon of England* . . . (London, 1659); and John Ward, *The Young Mathematicians Guide: Being a Plain and Easy Introduction to the Mathematicks*, 6th edn, rev. (London, 1734), pp. 34–35. Ward's citation is to J[ohn] W[ybard], *Tactometria. seu, Tetagmenometria. Or, the Geometry of Regulars* . . . (London, 1650), pp. 288–290. Compare Patrick Kelly, *Metrology; or An Exposition of Weights and Measures, Chiefly Those of Great Britain and France* (London, 1816), pp. 38–39, and Ronald Edward Zupko, *A Dictionary of English Weights and Measures from Anglo-Saxon Times to the Nineteenth Century* (Madison, Wis., 1968), p. 71.

Great Britain, Scotland: Prior to the Act of Union – and after Union for internal purposes – Scots employed their own system of liquid measures. One Scottish gallon (13.6679 liters) equaled 8 pints (also called the "jug" or "stoup") or 16 choppines (0.8542 liters). Kelly, op. cit., I, 234–237; Doursther, op. cit., pp. 155, 428; J[ames] M. Henderson, *Scottish Reckoning of Time, Money, Weights, and Measures*, Historical Association of Scotland [Pamphlets], n.s., no. 4 (Edinburgh, 1926), p. 13; and Ronald Edward Zupko, *A Dictionary of Weights and Measures for the British Isles: The Middle Ages to the Twentieth Century*, Memoirs of the American Philosophical Society, vol. CLXVIII (Philadelphia, 1985), pp. 90–91, 165, 300–302. See also [John Swinton], *A Proposal for Uniformity of Weights and Measures in Scotland, by Execution of the Laws Now in Force* (Edinburgh, 1779), p. 30, who implies 1.6994 liters in comparison with the English wine gallon. Compare A[lex] J. S., Gibson and T[homas] C[hristopher] Smout, *Prices, Food and Wages in Scotland, 1550–1780* ([Cambridge, Eng.], 1995), pp. 368–370.

Great Britain, Ireland: This is the ancient Irish (and English) gallon of 217.6 cu. in. (3.5658 liters) equal to 4 quarts (0.8915 liters). Irish Acts of 28 Henry VI, c. 3 (1450); 13 and 14 George III, c. 47 (1773–1774); and 26 George III, c. 35 (1786): in [Ireland (Eire), Laws and Statutes], *The Statutes at Large, Passed in the Parliaments Held in Ireland from . . . 1310 . . . to . . . 1800*, [ed. James Goddard Butler], 20 vols (Dublin, 1786–1801) I, 35, X, 635–645, XIII, 840–841. Compare Kelly, *Metrology*, p. 117; Kelly, op. cit., I, I94; II, 234–237; Doursther, op. cit., p. 155. See also the testimony of John Archer, the Inspector of Imports for the Excise, 31 May 1823: "in the present excise the Irish Gallon is 217 and six-tenths cubic inches, and we have to reduce each cask to English measure (231) before we can make any comparison." [G.B., Parl., Lords, Select Committee Appointed to Consider the Petition of the . . . City of Glasgow . . .], *Report from the Select Committee of the House of Lords Appointed to Consider the Petition of the . . . City of Glasgow Taking Notice of the Bill Entitled "An Act for Ascertaining and Establishing Uniformity of Weights and Measures etc.,"* HC, Sessional Papers, 1824, vol. VII (Reports), no. 94. [London, 1824], p. 25. For the history of the Irish gallon, see Adams in *Report of the Secretary of State*, pp. 22–27 and elsewhere.

viz. the wine gallon, at the Custom-house."[25] Ireland, which shared the pound with England, had its own gallon. The Netherlands had at least two different *pint* measures; Portugal, four.

The transatlantic migration of these differences compounded an already complex situation. As with the measures of weight, so in liquid measures did the colonies tend to follow the examples of their mother countries. But which example? The British colonies patterned themselves on London; the French on Paris; the Danish on Copenhagen; the Dutch on Amsterdam; the Spanish on Castile and Toledo; and the Portuguese on Lisbon (see table 4.4). Yet

25 [GB, Parl., Commons], *A Report from the Committee Appointed to Enquire into the Original Standards of Weights and Measures in This Kingdom, and to Consider the Laws Relating Thereto* [London, 1758], as printed in [GB, Parl., Commons], *Reports from Committees of the House of Commons, Reprinted by Order of the House*, 15 vols (London, 1773–1803), II, 434 [Lambert 2293].

Table 4.4 Metric equivalents of the basic units of weight and liquid measure
employed in eighteenth-century colonial trade

Colonies	Unit	Equivalent
DENMARK	*pund*	0.4960 kg
West Indian Islands	*centner*	49.6000 kg
	pot	0.9661 liters
	gallon	3.7854 liters
THE NETHERLANDS		
West Indian Islands	*pond*	0.4941 kg
Surinam, Essequibo and	*centenaar*	49.4090 kg
Demerara, Berbice	pint	0.6063 liters
	gallon	3.7854 liters
FRANCE		
West Indian Islands	*livre*	0.4895 kg
Cayenne	*quintal*	48.9506 kg
Louisiana	*pinte*	0.9313 liters
Quebec	gallon	3.7854 liters
SPAIN		
West Indian Islands	*libra*	0.4601 kg
New Spain	*arroba*	11.5023 kg
Spanish South America	*quintal*	46.0093 kg
	quartillo	0.5042 liters
PORTUGAL	*árratel*	0.4590 kg
Brazil	*arroba*	14.6867 kg
	quintal	58.7469 kg
	quartilho	0.3446 liters
GREAT BRITAIN		
Thirteen Continental Colonies	pound	0.4536 kg
Nova Scotia	long hundredweight	50.8023 kg
Newfoundland	short hundredweight	45.3593 kg
Caribbean Colonies	gallon	3.7854 liters

Notes and sources:
The presumption is always that weights and measures followed the flag unless we have evidence
to the contrary. See the text of this chapter.
Danish colonies: Samuel Ricard, *Traité général du commerce . . .*, rev. edn, [ed. Tomás Antonio
de Marien y Arrospide], 2 vols (Amsterdam, 1781), II, 132; P[atrick] Kelly, *The Universal
Cambist and Commercial Instructor*, 2nd edn, 2 vols (London, 1835), I, 367, states that the
Danish West Indian Islands used the weights and measures of Copenhagen. Of the three
Danish islands, only St Croix provides any evidence to indicate the use of other than Danish
measures. And we have that evidence best in the repeated attempts by the colony's government to enforce the use of Danish measures. The epitome of these attempts was the *placat*
or proclamation of the island's council, the *Secrete Raadet*, 17 May 1756, esp. section 22. See
Placat Bog, St Croix, 1744–1791, pp. 71–72, Generalguvernørens Arkiv, Dansk-Vestindiske
Lokalarkiver, Rigsarkivet, Copenhagen. As a similar proclamation of 6 Apr. 1773 showed, the
prime concern was for goods imported into the island from foreign places. It ordered that
they "i den tilkonmende Tild [*sic*] bliver solgt efter Dansk Vægt" (shall in future be sold by
Danish weight). Placat Bog, pp. 185–187, Generalguvernørens Arkiv; and as published in
Royal Danish American Gazette (Christiansted, St Croix), 17 Apr. 1773, Københavns
Universitets-bibliotek, Fiolstræde. Compare still later attempts at enforcement announced in
Royal Danish American Gazette, 28 Aug. 1773, and 4 Sept. 1773. The result was that the
merchants, many of whom were Englishmen, used a variety of measures, some of which were

English. The most flagrant example of this was the use of the English wine gallon for the export trade of molasses and rum – flagrant because the government itself so used it. See, e.g., the Danish West Indian Customs valuations for molasses in *skillings* per gallon from the Customs Journals for Christiansted, 1757–1762, and Fredericksted, 1760 and 1763, Records of the Government of the Virgin Islands, 1672–1950, Record Group 55, National Archives, Washington, DC, and as discussed in Jean Louise Willis, "The Trade between North America and the Danish West Indies, 1756–1807, with Special Reference to St Croix" (Ph.D. diss., Columbia University, 1963), pp. 64–67; and the government's advertisement in *Royal Danish American Gazette*, 23 July 1777, and 9 Aug. 1777, to buy rum "for His Majesty's store house in Christiansted and exportation for Copenhagen" at so much per gallon. Peter Lotharius Oxholm, *De Danske Vestindiske Øers: Tilstand Henseende til Population, Cultur og Finance-Forfatning* (Copenhagen, 1797), p. 38n., found it necessary to inform his Danish readers that "en gallon er 4 potter" – one adds, approximately.

Dutch colonies: In Apr. 1625 the Dutch West India Company ordered the use of Amsterdam "ghewichte, elle ende maete" in those places under its jurisdiction. *Documents Relating to New Netherland, 1624–1626, in the Henry E. Huntington Library*, trans. and ed. A[rnold] J. F. van Laer (San Marino, Calif., 1924), pp. 116–117. As one result, the measure of weight was the Amsterdam *pond* everywhere except on the island of Curaçao, which used one weighing 0.5313 kg, and Dutch St Martin, which used the French *livre* of 0.4895 kg. Ricard, *Traité général du commerce . . .*, rev. edn, [ed. Marien y Arrospide], II, 82 (Curaçao), 203 (Surinam), 232 (St Eustatius); Kelly, op. cit., I, 365; Horace Doursther, *Dictionnaire universel des poids et mesures anciens et modernes . . .* (Brussels, 1840), pp. 219, 221, 226, 232. See also N. J. van Suchtelen, "Maten en gewichten in Suriname," *De Surinaamse Landbouw*, X (1962), 215. Compare [Surinam, Laws and Statutes], *Plakaten, ordonnantiën en andere wetten, uitgevaardigd in Suriname, 1667*, ed. J[acobus] Th. de Smidt and T. van der Lee, West Indisch Plakaatboek, no. 1, Werken der Vereniging tot Uitgaaf der Bronnen van het Oud-Vaderlandsche Recht, 3rd ser., no. 24, 2 vols (Amsterdam, 1973), I, 140–141, 154–155, II, 1011–1012. In practice at Curaçao, in at least one instance, the Amsterdam *pond* was the one used. See the entry dated 4 Apr. 1721, Journal, 1714–1723, fol. 212r, Nathan Simson Papers, *Isaac v. DeFriez*, C 104/13, pt ii, PRO. Sixteen bags of snuff brought to London from Curaçao "weying 2726 lb Curaçao W[eigh]t makes here 2971 lb." At St Eustatius the law specified the use of "Hollands gewigt" (1798). [Netherlands Antilles, Laws and Statutes], *Publikaties en andere wetten betrekking hebbende op St Maarten, St Eustatius, Saba, 1648/1681–1816*, ed. J[acobus] Th. de Smidt and T. van der Lee, West Indisch Plakaatboek, no. 3, Werken der Stichting tot Uitgaff der Bronnen van het Oud-Vaderlandse Recht, no. 4 (Amsterdam, 1979), p. 377.

As for liquid measure, there is no suggestion that the colonies used anything but the Amsterdam standard except for their trade in molasses and rum. Here again the presence of large numbers of English sugar planters and the regular trade with the English colonies in English vessels induced the use of the wine gallon. Even internal rum and molasses accounts were kept in gallons at Essequibo and Demerara. See the governors' correspondence with the Zeeland Chamber of the West India Company, 1686–1792, for various examples of its use, CO 116/18 to CO 116/68, PRO. For a specific instance, see Laurens Storm van's Gravesande, at Rio Essequibo, to [Zeeland Chamber], 27 Sept. 1763, CO 116/33, no. 215, p. 4, PRO. A 1739 excise tax on rum ("*kiltum*") served in taverns in Curaçao collected the duty per "*galon*." [Netherlands Antilles, Laws and Statutes], *Publikaties en andere wetten alsmede de oudste resoluties betrekking hebbende op Curaçao, Aruba, Bonaire*, ed. J[acobus] Th. de Smidt, T. van der Lee, and J[acob] A. Schiltkamp, West Indisch Plakaatboek, no. 2, Werken der Stichting tot Uitgaff der Bronnen van het Oud-Vaderlandse Recht, no. 2, 2 vols (Amsterdam, 1978), I, 185. See also, ibid., I, 211 (1740), 283 (1752), and II, 413 (1782). Compare the gallon's use in the export trade of Surinam as recorded by Anthony Blom, *Verhandeling van den Landbouw in de Colonie Suriname* (Amsterdam, 1787), p. 80; J[ohannes] van den Bosch, *Nederlandsche Bezittingen in Azia, Amerika en Afrika* (The Hague, 1818), II, 204, n. 43; and Marten D. Teenstra, *De Landbouw in de Kolonie Suriname* (Groningen, 1835), II, 159, 164n. These references – and a more modern one – argue for a certain confusion, at least for one author, Blom, who, in reference to Surinam, stated (op. cit., p. 80) that "een galon is twee gewoone stoopen" or 4.8506 liters, a difference of +28.1 percent. Teenstra, op. cit., p. 164n., equated "de gallon [met] 6–14/19 Amsterdamsche pinten" or 4.08 liters, a difference of +7.9 percent. A more recent guide, W[inand] C. H. Staring, *De Binnen- en Buitenlandsche Maten, Gewichten en Munten*, ed. R. W. van Wieringen, 4th edn (Schoonhaven, [1902]), p. 20, stated

Table 4.4 continued

that both Surinam and Curaçao used the "Englesch gallon," which is the equivalent of "6 pint van 0.6 L." or 3.6 liters, a difference of – 4.9 percent. See also Suchtelen, "Maten en gewichten in Suriname," p. 215, where he said that the unit of liquid measure was "het oude Engels gallon (3,6 l)." Blom, ibid., quoted the price of molasses at Surinam in *stuivers* per *pul* or jug; he equated the *pul* with five *stoopen* or 12.1265 liters. Suchtelen, op. cit., p. 215 explained that: "Voor de rum, dram en melasse welke vroger belangrijke uitvoerprodukten waren had man omstreeks 1874 als inhoudmaat de pul. Deze was 3 Engelse gallon van 3,6 l" or 10.8 liters. Blom's statements are not internally consistent; nor is either of his two implied equivalencies for the *stoop* close to the Amsterdam measure. On St Eustatius a 1793 regulation priced rum and "siroop" in stuivers per gallon. *Publikaties . . . op St. Maarten, St. Eustatius, Saba*, ed. De Smidt and Van der Lee, p. 360.

French colonies: The French colonies used the weights and measures of Paris almost without exception. Ricard, *Traité général du commerce . . .*, rev. edn, [ed. Marien y Arrospide], II, 139; [Médéric L. É.] Moreau de Saint-Méry, *Loix et constitutions des colonies françaises de l'Amérique sous le vent*, 6 vols (Paris, [1784–1790]), I, 120, 139; IV, 9–14; Moreau de Saint Méry, *Description topographique, physique, civile, politique et historique de la partie française de l'isle Saint-Domingue*, rev. edn, ed. Blanche Maurel and Étienne Taillemite, 3 vols (Paris, 1958), I, 16; Kelly, op. cit., I, 364; Doursther, op. cit., pp. 217, 219, 223, 225, 226, 228, 229, 428. At Martinique, in 1665, "on adopta pour les liqueurs la quarte de Paris et tous les autres mesures de cette ville." The *quart* or *pot* of Paris equaled two *pintes* or 1.8626 liters. Prior to that date the colonists had used a somewhat larger *pot*. Louis-Philippe May, *Histoire économique de la Martinique (1635–1763)* (Paris, 1930), pp. 130–131, 162–163 (quotation, p. 162). He cited the "réglement de 1675," Fonds des Colonies, C8B 1, AN-CAOM. The change gave rise to continuing concerns. See the report by Charles de Courbon, comte de Blénac, the Governor General of the French West Indies, at Martinique, to Jean-Baptiste Colbert, at Paris, 28 Jan. 1678, Fonds des Colonies, C8A 2, fols 50 et seq., AN-COAM. Doursther, op. cit., p. 438, says that Guadeloupe, Martinique and their dependencies – Les Îles du Vent – used a *pot* that measured 1.8926 liters (*pinte* equaled 0.9463). Note, also, the mistaken suggestion that the French West Indian *velte* equaled 7.61 liters, a mistake consequent upon a misreading of an admittedly imprecise secondary account. Françoise Thesée, "Sur deux sucreries de Jacquezy (nord de Saint-Domingue), 1778–1802," in [Congrès National des Sociétés Savantes, 92nd, 1967, Strasbourg and Colmar, France, Section d'Histoire Moderne et Contemporaine], *Actes du Quatre-Vingt-Douzième Congrès National des Sociétés Savantes*, 3 vols (Paris, 1970), II, 274, n. 36; and Dieudonné Rinchon, *Pierre-Ignace-Liévin Van Alstein: Captaine négrier, Gand 1733-Nantes 1793*, Mémoires de l'Institut Français d'Afrique Noire, no. 71 (Dakar, Senegal, 1964), pp. 19, 177. The only exception was the use of the English wine gallon with reference to the export of molasses and rum from Saint-Domingue to the English North American colonies in the 1760s and 1770s. "Tableau général des différentes denrées importées et exportées au Môle St Nicholas," Saint-Domingue, 1768–1770, Fonds des Colonies, C9A 138, bound following letter no. 65, AN-CAOM; "État général de l'importation et de l'exportation étrangères faites en 1772," Môle St Nicholas, Fonds des Colonies, C9A 142, AN-CAOM; *Observations des négocians de Bordeaux, sur l'arrest du Conseil, du 30 Août 1784, qui a été connu à Bordeaux le 20 Novembre* (Paris, 1784), pp. 48–49. This last source confuses the issue once again by defining the "galon" as containing "a peu près quatre pots de notre mesure" (ibid., p. 48), or 9.0592 liters. One rather suspects that the author meant Parisian *pintes* (and thus 3.7252 liters) rather than Bordeaux *pots*, as in Samuel Ricard, *Traité général du Commerce . . .*, 4th edn, rev. (Amsterdam, 1721), p. 36. After the American Revolution, the gallon was also used to price molasses and rum at Martinique. See, e.g., *Gazette de la Martinique* (Saint-Pierre), 19 June 1788.

With regard to measures of weight, the differences between the *livre* of Paris used in the colonies and those of Marseilles and Havre were matters of continuing concern and comment among people involved in the sugar trade. That of Paris (0.4895 kg.) was 20% larger than that of Marseilles (0.4084 kg.) while that of Havre (0.5287 kg.) was 8% larger than the *livre* of Paris. See, for the latter, *Avis Divers et Petites Affiches Américaines* (Au Cap, Saint-Domingue), 26 June 1765; for the former, the letter from M. Boussé, at Marseilles, to M. Tourrès, at Au Cap, 20 Oct. 1757, quoted in Philippe Chassaigne, "L'Économie des îles sucrières dans les conflits maritimes de la seconde moitié du XVIIIème siècle: L'exemple de Saint-Domingue," *Histoire, Économie et Société*, VII (no. 1, 1988), 101–102.

The measures in use in Louisiana "are all of French origin," according to M. Bouchon, the "Surveyor General of the state of Louisiana," in his statement "respecting weights and measures in Louisiana before its cession to the United States," sent from New Orleans, 9 Oct. 1820, to Secretary of State John Quincy Adams. [U.S., Department of State], *Report of the Secretary of State, upon Weights and Measures*, [by John Qunicy Adams], [U.S., Congress, 16th Cong., 2nd Sess., Senate Documents, vol. no. 4, doc. no. 119, vol. 4, Serial Set no. 45] (Washington, DC, 1821), pp. 224–225. "It does not appear that the Spanish weights and measures have ever been used." See also the ordinance of 1 Apr. 1715 and the arrêt of 19 July 1725, both of the Conseil Supérieur de la Louisiana, in Fonds des Colonies, A23, fols 6r, 59v, AN-CAOM.

Spanish colonies: From the earliest times the Spanish colonies were to have as their standard the weights and measures of the mother country, the *marca* of Castile and the *quartillo* of Toledo. M[anuel] O[rozco] y B[erra], "Medidas y pesos en la republica Mexicana," in *Diccionario universal de historia y de geografía . . . sobre las Americas en general y especialmente sobre la republica Mexicana*, 10 vols (Mexico, 1853–1856), V, 206–214; Manuel Carrera Stampa, "The Evolution of Weights and Measures in New Spain" [trans. Robert S. Smith], *Hispanic American Historical Review*, XXXIX (Feb. 1949), 2–24; Carrera Stampa, "El sistema de pesos y medidas colonial," *Memorias de la Academia Mexicana de la Historia*, XXVI (Jan.–Mar. 1967), 1–37. Compare Ricard, *Traité général du commerce . . .*, rev. edn, [ed. Marien y Arrospide], II, 179; Kelly, op. cit., I, 254, and Doursther, op. cit., pp. 223, 233, 453. Carrera Stampa, "Evolution of Weights and Measures," [trans. Smith], p. 10, makes the point that there were some local variations from the standard (compare Stephen Naft and Ralph de Sola, *International Conversion Tables*, rev. and enl., ed. P[hilip] H. Bigg [London (1965)], p. 33) and then goes on to say that "in foreign commerce and in the contraband trade foreign weights and measures crept in, and such units as the English gallon, pint, bushel and sack are encountered frequently." Compare Manuel Salustio Fernández, *Instrucción breve sencilla sobre el sistema métrico decimal . . .*, 2nd edn (Santiago, [Chile], 1859), pp. 46–48, and Cecilio A. Robelo, *Diccionario de pesas y medidas Mexicanas, antiguas y modernas . . .* (Cuernavaca, Mexico, 1908), pp. 1–18. This *galón* measured from 3.5 liters to 5.0 liters according to Carrera Stampa, "Evolution of Weights and Measures" [trans. Smith], p. 15, arguing again more a use of word than the measure. [Francisco de Arango y Parreño], *Resultan grandes perjuicios de que en Europa se haga la fabricación del refino* (Havana, [1796]), p. 6, n. (d), states that, in Cuba, "un gallon equivale a 4 botellas nuestras poco más o menos." This would suggest a Cuban *botella* equal to about 0.95 liters. Pelayo González de los Rios, *Prontuario del sistema legal de pesas, medidas y monedas, o sea el sistema metrico decimal . . .* (Havana, 1862), p. 35, said that "1 litro es igual a . . . 1⅓ botellas comunes." One *botella*, then, equaled 0.75 liters. Hans-Joachim v[on] Alberti, *Mass und Gewicht: Geschichtliche und tabellarische Darstellungen von den Anfängen bis zur Gegenwart* (Berlin, 1957), p. 355, found the Colombian *botella* equal to 0.7 liters. The *botija* of molasses used in Puerto Rico in the 1780s, as indicated by Pedro Tomás de Córdoba, *Memorias geográficas, históricas, económicas y estadisticas de la isla de Puerto-Rico*, 6 vols ([Puerto Rico], 1831–1838), I, 159, III, 15, was more likely the large cask rated by Carrera Stampa, "Evolution of Weights and Measures" [trans. Smith], p. 14, at 435 liters (114.9 gals.). Compare F[rancisco] A. López Dóminguez, "Origin and Development of the Sugar Industry in Porto Rico," *The [Louisiana] Planter and Sugar Manufacturer*, LXXIX (23 July 1927), 63. See also Manuel Lobo Cabrera, *Monedas, pesas y medidas en Canarias en el siglo XVI* (Las Palmas, 1989).

Portuguese colonies: In general in Brazil, the weights and measures were those of Lisbon. Ricard, *Traité général du commerce . . .*, rev. edn, [ed. Marien y Arrospide], II, 58; Kelly, op. cit., I, 48, 212n.; and Doursther, op. cit., pp. 217, 249, 439, 453. Nevertheless, at Rio de Janeiro, one late nineteenth-century writer noted that the standard container for liquids, especially rum and other spirits, was the pipe which contained 132 English wine gallons or 499.66 liters. At Bahia, the pipe of rum measured 518.87 liters, or "72 canadas . . . di Bahia" equal, each *canada*, at about 7.2 liters, to roughly 5.2 *canadas* of Lisbon. At Pernambuco the *canada* equaled 6.06496 liters. Angelo Martini, *Manuale di Metrologia: Ossia Misure, Pesi e Monete in Uso Attualmente e Anticamente Presso Tutti i Popoli* (Turin, 1883), pp. 51, 518, 580.

With regard to Portugal's other overseas possessions, T[homas] Bentley Duncan, *Atlantic Islands: Madeira, the Azores and the Cape Verdes in Seventeenth-Century Commerce and Navigation*

Table 4.4 continued

(Chicago, [1972]), pp. 259–262, makes the point that, in law and in practice these islands used the weights and measures of Lisbon. He then states that the *árratel* equaled 458.938 grams and the *quartihlo*, 0.397 liters. Compare Kelly, op. cit., I, 246–247, who indicates that the *quartihlo* measured 0.369 liters at Madeira.

English colonies: The distinction between the English Caribbean colonies and the English Continental Colonies comes from the difference in the cwt. described above in this chapter. All of these measures were English in origin. For typical colonial laws enacting English weights and measures into colonial use, see [Massachusetts (Colony), Laws and Statutes], *The Acts and Resolves, Public and Private, of the Province of the Massachusetts Bay*, [ed. Abner Cheney Goodell *et al.*], 21 vols (Boston, 1869–1922), I, 69–70; [New York (Colony), Laws and Statutes], *The Colonial Laws of New York from the Year 1664 to the Revolution*, [ed. Robert C. Cumming], 5 vols (Albany, N.Y., 1894), I, 64–65, 95, 98, 555; [Pennsylvania, Laws and Statutes], *Statutes at Large of Pennsylvania from 1682 to 1801*, ed. James T. Mitchell and Henry Flanders, 18 vols (Harrisburg, Pa., 1896–1915), II, 86–87, 88–90; *Archives of Maryland*, ed. William Hand Browne *et al.*, in progress (Baltimore, 1883 to date), II, 279–281; [Virginia, Laws and Statutes], *The Statutes at Large; Being a Collection of All the Laws of Virginia*, ed. William Waller Hening, 13 vols (Richmond, Va., 1809–1823), I, 331, 473, II, 89–90, IV, 406–407; [Jamaica, Laws and Statutes], *Acts of Assembly Passed in the Island of Jamaica; From the Year 1681, to the Year 1769*, 2 vols (St Jago de la Vega, 1769–1771), I, 318–319; [Barbados, Laws and Statutes], *Acts and Statutes of the Island of Barbados*, [ed. John Jennings] (London, [1654]), pp. 125–126.

this rule had some significant exceptions, among which the example of Saint-Domingue is especially instructive. On the one hand, the colony shipped its sugar to France, as it was obliged to do, and measured its sugar exports in *quintaux*. On the other hand, the planters sold their molasses to the British North American colonies and measured it diversely. At the plantation they weighed their molasses in *quintaux*, but in their external trade they treated it as a liquid and measured it sometimes in *pintes* and sometimes in English wine gallons. They even framed their export regulations to collect a duty in *livres tournois* per gallon.[26] Similarly, the Dutch at Surinam and Essequibo, the Danes on St Croix, and even the Spaniards in Mexico used the gallon, on occasion, as the liquid measure for molasses and rum.[27] The occasion most frequently came in their dealings with British North American merchants and ship captains.

26 See n. 19 of this chapter and table 4.4.
27 See table 4.4. For French measures in an English colony, see the survival of the Parisian *minot* (39.025 liters) in the grain trade of English Quebec after 1763. Guy Carleton's testimony before the Commissioners for Trade and Plantations in early 1784, BT 5/1, p. 17, PRO – there is a copy of this volume in the Liverpool Papers, Add. MS 38388, BL; Letter Book of Lawrence Ermatinger, Montreal, 1770–1778, passim, Lawrence Ermatinger Papers, 1765–1789, Ermatinger Estate Papers, 1758–1874, MG 19 A2, Public Archives of Canada, Ottawa; Doursther, *Dictionnaire universel des poids et mesures*, pp. 282–283. Compare similar survivals of Dutch measures in early New York, English measures in Tobago, and Spanish measures in Trinidad. Herbert Alan Johnson, *The Law Merchant and Negotiable Instruments in Colonial New York, 1664 to 1730* (Chicago, 1963), pp. 8, 59, n. 18; "État du produit de l'Îsle de Tabago ... ," Fonds des Colonies, C10E 1, AN-CAOM; Jean-Claude Nardin, *La Mise en valeur de l'Isle de Tabago (1763–1783)* (Paris,

Thus it appears that the exigencies of commerce were at the root of pressures toward uniformity of measures. Completely compatible national and international systems of measurement waited upon legal formulation, but the directions taken by the law reflected the pragmatic needs of the merchant.[28] The examples of the colonies suggest this; the international adoption of the metric system over the past two centuries confirms the suggestion. It is certainly the demands of commerce which are the fundamental source of the drive which has moved Great Britain and will move the United States into the world of metric measurement.

1969), pp. 227–245; and *Trinidad Almanac and Commercial Register for 1840* (Trinidad, 1840), p. 62. For the persistence of French weights and measures in Louisiana through periods of ownership by Spain and the United States, see the statement "respecting weights and measures in Louisiana," by Claude Nicholas Bouchon, the "Surveyor General of the State of Louisiana," sent from New Orleans, 9 Oct. 1820, to Secretary of State John Quincy Adams. [US, Department of State], *Report of the Secretary of State, upon Weights and Measures,* [by John Quincy Adams], [US, Congress, 16th Cong., 2nd Sess., Senate Documents, vol. no. 4, doc. no. 119, vol. 4, Serial Set no. 45] (Washington, DC, 1821), pp. 224–225.

28 Compare similar conclusions reached by Eli F. Heckscher, *Mercantilism,* trans. by Mendel Shapiro. 2nd edn, rev. edn E[rnst] F. Söderlund, 2 vols (London, [1955]), I, 110–118; and by Witold Kula in his masterful study, *Miary i ludzie* (Warsaw, 1970), pp. 204–213.

5

THE RATE OF EXCHANGE ON AMSTERDAM IN LONDON, 1590–1660

Co-authored with Simon Hart[1]

Fundamental to the commercial and financial relations between England and The Netherlands was the rate of exchange between their two currencies. Modern studies have increased our understanding of the negotiation of bills of exchange and the exchange rate for several places in Europe during the sixteenth, seventeenth, and eighteenth centuries.[2] These have opened up to more detailed examination a variety of topics concerned with both the internal and external economic history of the several countries involved. Important additions to the data base, especially when they extend it backward into the early modern period, expand the scope of such exploration significantly. This is particularly true when the additions concern such a critical period in the history of England and of the United Provinces as the years 1590 through 1660.

1   The original version of this chapter was published in *The Journal of European Economic History*, VII (Winter 1979), 689–705. Copyright © 1979 by the Banco di Roma. This revision is presented here with the permission of the publishers of the journal. The co-author of this essay was Simon Hart, formerly the archivist of the Gemeente Archief, Amsterdam. I continue to be grateful for his help and his encouragement.

2   There are graphs showing the Bruges–London rate, 1388–1411, and the Antwerp–London rate, 1315–1588, in Herman van der Wee, *The Growth of the Antwerp Market and the European Economy (Fourteenth–Sixteenth Centuries)*, 3 vols (The Hague, 1963), III, nos 32 and 33. Van der Wee did not publish his data but he has shared some of them with John D. Gould and, based on them and on other data uncovered by his own researches, Gould, in *The Great Debasement: Currency and the Economy in Mid-Tudor England* (Oxford, 1970), p. 89, compiled his table 9 showing the London–Antwerp rate, 1544–1563. John J. McCusker, *Money and Exchange in Europe and America, 1600–1775: A Handbook*, [2nd edn] (Chapel Hill, NC, [1992]), pp. 52–55, relied almost exclusively for his data before 1660 on N[icolaas] W. Posthumus, *Inquiry into the History of Prices in Holland*, 2 vols (Leiden, 1946–1964), I, 590–591, who, in turn, took his figures from the published commodity price currents of Amsterdam. A full list of the newspapers that Posthumus used, of additional copies found since he did his work, and of other, similar materials, giving the location of surviving copies of them all, is in John J. McCusker and Cora Gravesteijn, *The Beginnings of Commercial and Financial Journalism: The Commodity Price Currents, Exchange Rate Currents, and Money Currents of Early Modern Europe*, Nederlandsch Economisch-Historisch Archief, ser. III, no. 11 (Amsterdam, 1991). Compare the wider range of sources and data employed in Jürgen Schneider *et al.*, *Währungen der Welt*, 11 vols in 14 pts (Stuttgart, 1991–1997).

While it should be obvious that the rate of exchange by itself will not answer the many questions about these years that have attracted the attention of economic historians, new data are always welcome. Indeed the absence of information about exchange rates, and thus the lack of insights that series like the ones presented below could offer, has explicitly been lamented by writers on such subjects as the depressed state of the English economy during the early 1620s. Barry Supple's is the most detailed of such analyses. Based on the evidence available to him, he expected that the unfavorable English balance of trade over those years drove the rate of exchange down.[3] Yet the data in table 5.1 show just the reverse to have been the case: the pound sterling bought more rather than fewer *gulden* (in English, guilders) each year from 1619 through 1625. This information does not on its own negate Supple's work, of course. What it might merely be saying is that the guilder was in even worse shape than the pound, that the Dutch balance of payments (because of the renewal, in 1621, of the Spanish–Dutch War) was even worse than the English, the depression in Amsterdam even worse than in London. All that these new data can do is suggest new ideas worth investigating – and, additionally, facilitate the comparative aspects of such research by allowing for the conversion of values from one currency to another.

◆ ◆ ◆ ◆ ◆

A rich source of new data on exchange rates in early modern Europe is the records of notaries public. Perhaps the best collection of such records is that of Amsterdam. The Notariële Archieven (Notarial Archives) in the Gemeente Archief, Amsterdam, though incomplete still contain approximately 25,000 volumes covering the years 1578–1895.[4] Among the large variety of documents that Amsterdam notaries copied into their record books

---

3   Our reference is to Supple, *Commercial Crisis and Change in England, 1600–1642: A Study in the Instability of a Mercantile Economy* (Cambridge, Eng., 1959), pp. 94–96, and elsewhere. See also J[ohn] D. Gould, "The Trade Depression of the Early 1620s," *EcHR*, 2nd ser., VII (Aug. 1954), 81–88.

4   For the period of this chapter, 1590–1660, there are approximately 2,500 volumes of notarial records. The entire collection runs about 3,000 meters of shelf space (nearly two miles). *De archieven in Amsterdam*, ed. J. H. van den Hoek Ostende, P. H. J. van der Laan, and E. Lievense-Pelser, vol. VIII of *Overzichten van de archieven en verzamelingen in de openbare archiefbewaarplaatsen in Nederland*, ed. L. M. Th. L Hustinx *et al.* (Alphen aan den Rijn, 1981), pp. 25–26, 78.

    One of the authors of this chapter, Simon Hart, retired in 1976 as the Director of the Gemeente Archief. Both he and McCusker wish to acknowledge the cooperation of the subsequent Director, Mevr. Drs. Wilhelmina Chr. Pieterse. These data were identified and extracted during the course of a systematic inventory of the contents of the Notariële Archieven. Hart also thanked Mevr. A. Bosma and those who assisted her in that project. McCusker expresses his appreciation to Mevr. Drs. C. Gravesteijn, formerly the librarian of the Economisch-Historische Bibliotheek, Amsterdam, for her many good offices and to the Committee on Research in Economic History of the Economic History Association for helping to fund research trips to Amsterdam.

    Hart made extensive use of the Notariële Archieven for his article "Amsterdam Shipping and Trade to Northern Russia in the Seventeenth Century," *Mededelingen van de*

were the protests for non-payment of bills of exchange drawn against Amsterdam merchants. An integral part of each protest was a verbatim copy of the text of the bill itself. It was the custom during this period that London bills on Amsterdam record in their text the rate at which they were drawn.[5] Extracted, copied, and compiled for the years 1591 through 1660, these rates of exchange become the basis of the tables in this chapter. As such they supplement printed materials found elsewhere and thus constitute the beginnings of a series that now can run from the late sixteenth century to the present.[6]

The bill of exchange drawn in London on Amsterdam was a convenient means of transferring funds from the one country to the other. In the standard manner the bill of exchange involved four participants. A merchant in London (the payer) who wanted to send money to someone in Amsterdam (the payee) approached another merchant in London (the drawer) and asked him to order his own correspondent in Amsterdam (the drawee) to make the required payment. The drawer's instructions were sent through the post to the payee in Amsterdam by means of a signed document written according to a standard formula: a bill of exchange. The drawee, following those instructions, gave the payee in Amsterdam a sum in Dutch currency for which the payer in London had given the drawer a sum in English currency. The ratio

Nederlandse Verenining voor Zeegeschiedenis, XXVI (Mar. 1973), 5–30, 105–116, and there printed 40 examples of the rate of exchange at Archangel on Amsterdam, 1606–1710, from the protests of bills of exchange. This has been translated as "Amsterdamse scheepvaart en handel op Nord-Rusland in de zeventiende eeuw," and printed in Hart, *Geschrift en Getal: Een keuze uit de demografisch-, economisch- en sociaal-historische studiën op grond van Amsterdamse en Zaanse archivalia, 1600–1800*, Hollandse Studiën, 9 (Dordrecht, 1976), pp. 267–314. There are other, similar notarial record collections in other city archives in The Netherlands. See, for instance, H. E. van Gelder, *Notarieele Protocollen van 1597 tot 1811, opgenomen in het Archiefdepot der Gemeente's-Gravenhage* (The Hague, 1911). See also Alice [C.] Carter, "The Dutch Notarial Archives," *Bulletin of the Institute of Historical Research*, XXVI (May 1953), 86–91. The Middelburg notarial records were destroyed in World War II. For a general introduction to the kinds of documents to be found in the notarial records, see A. Fl. Gehlen, *Notariële Akten uit de 17e en 18e eeuw: Handleiding voor gebruikers*, Werken der Stichting tot Uitgaaf der Bronnen van het Oud-Vaderlandse Recht, no. 12 (Zutphen, 1986).

5   This was not always the case. See McCusker, *Money and Exchange*, p. 124n. The other major source of quotations of the exchange rate – besides the bills of exchange themselves and published commodity price currents such as those discussed in McCusker and Gravesteijn, *Beginnings of Commercial and Financial Journalism* – is the correspondence of merchants. See, e.g., the rate at Rotterdam on London included regularly at the foot of Brian Ball's letters of 1641 to George Warner, at London, printed from SP 46/84, PRO, in Joan Thirsk and J[ohn] P. Cooper, *Seventeenth Century Economic Documents* (Oxford, 1972), pp. 497–499.

6   The three tables in this chapter have been compiled so as to be compatible with tables 2.7, 2.8, 2.9, and 5.1 in McCusker, *Money and Exchange*, pp. 52–55, 56–57, 58–60, 305–312. Table 2.9 can be extended by going to *The Course of the Exchange* (London) and its continuation, *The Stock Exchange Daily Official List* (London). For these two newspapers, see McCusker and Gravesteijn, *Beginnings of Commercial and Financial Journalism*, pp. 311–322. Table 2.7 can be extended through 1914 by reference to Posthumus, *History of Prices in Holland*, I, 606–638.

between the two sums of money in the two different countries, expressed in terms of their national moneys of account, was the rate of exchange.[7]

Our London payer in the above example probably proceeded through an exchange broker who operated on the Royal Exchange in the building that Thomas Gresham constructed in the 1560s.[8] The broker acted as an intermediary between drawer and payer, blunting the competitive disadvantage that either would have been under in initiating any such transaction. The market was more efficient for his presence because the rate of exchange was the result of bargaining and as such was subject to a variety of short-term and long-term pressures among which the changing balance of payments between the two countries was usually the most important.[9] Since we have

7   The explanation in this paragraph (and in much that follows) is available in a more highly articulated form in McCusker, *Money and Exchange*, passim. The distinction between a money of account and a real money is an important one; it is discussed in that book and in all contemporary treatises. The pound sterling was the money of account of England; the *pond Vlammsch* was the money of account of The Netherlands. See McCusker, op. cit., pp. 31–36, 42–45. The real money in use in both countries – the coins people used in their daily business – were English shillings and Dutch guilders.

The most authoritative contemporary English language discussion of the negotiation of bills of exchange is Gerard de Malynes, *Consuetudo vel Lex Mercatoria; or the Ancient Law-Merchant*, which was first published in London in 1622, was reprinted in 1629 and 1639, and had a second and third edition in 1656 and 1686. There is a manuscript of a French translation of the 1622 edition among the papers of Jean-Baptiste Colbert, Mélanges de Colbert, MS 34, Bibliothèque Nationale de France, Paris. According to Raymond [A.] de Roover, "On the Authorship and Dating of 'For the Understanding of the Exchange,'" *EcHR*, XX (Apr. 1967), 150, n. 1, Malynes was almost certainly "a Fleming whose real name was Geraart van Mechelen, which he translated into French." Compare Jean Meuvret, "Manuels et traités à l'usage des négociants aux premières époques de l'âge moderne," *Études d'Histoire Moderne et Contemporaine*, V (1953), 22. As was typical of such books during this period, Malynes borrowed heavily from others; one important source, especially appropriate for any investigation of the London–Amsterdam exchange, was a Dutch work. Originally published by (and perhaps authored by) Harman Janszoon Muller, this book, *Tresoir van de Maten van Gewichten van Coorn, Lande, van Elle ende natte Mate, Oock van de Gelde en Wissel . . .* (Amsterdam, 1590), was subsequently reprinted in 1615, 1647, and 1668 to our knowledge, and perhaps more frequently; the title varied slightly each time. Herman van der Wee thinks that "the author was probably an Antwerper." "Monetary, Credit and Banking Systems," in *The Economic Organization of Early Modern Europe*, ed. E[dwin] E. Rich and C[harles] H. Wilson, vol. V of *The Cambridge Economic History of Europe* (Cambridge, Eng., 1977), p. 328.

Appropriately, Wyndham Beawes, *Lex Mercatoria Rediviva; or, the Merchants Directory* (London, 1751, and numerous subsequent editions) is the standard 18th-century authority. See also Paul Einzig, *The History of Foreign Exchange*, 2nd edn, rev. (New York, 1970).

8   Raymond [A.] De Roover, *Gresham on Foreign Exchange: An Essay on Early English Mercantilism with the Text of Sir Thomas Gresham's Memorandum for the Understanding of the Exchange* (Cambridge, Mass., 1949), p. 8. The only flaw in this otherwise very fine book is De Roover's attribution of the memorandum to Gresham; most seem now to agree that Gresham was not its author. See M[ary] Dewar, "The Memorandum 'For the Understanding of the Exchange': Its Authorship and Dating," *EcHR*, 2nd ser., XVIII (Apr. 1965), 476–487; Daniel R. Fusfeld, "On the Authorship and Dating of 'For the Understanding of the Exchange'," *EcHR*, XX (Apr. 1967), 145–150; Gould, *Great Debasement*, pp. 161–164.

9   Another was the par of exchange based upon the comparative legal valuations in the two countries given to the same amount and the same quality (fineness) of precious metal.

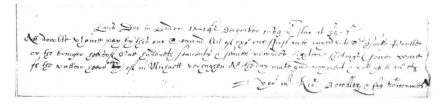

Figure 5.1 Bill of exchange drawn in London on Middelburg, 1609. See the text for a transcription of the text of this bill of exchange.
Photograph by A. J. Looyenga. Courtesy of the Vereniging Het Nederlandsch Economisch-Historisch Archief, Amsterdam.

little other information on this subject during the era, the exchange rate series presented here will, other things being equal, reflect some of the changes in the Anglo-Dutch balance of payments. It will do so more reliably because of the smoothing in the fluctuations of the exchange rate implicit in the workings of exchange brokers.

The bill of exchange had a set format; as an example, here is the text of one (see figure 5.1):

> Laus Deo in London le 14th December 1609 100 li star[ling] at 35s-7d Att dowble uzerance pay by this our seacond bill of ex[chang]e our first nott payed unto Sir Isacke Poulle or the bringer hereof One hundreth seaventy & seaven powndes eighteene shillings and fower pence for the vallew heere rec[eive]d of Mr Michael Verhaghen. Att the day make good payment & putt ytt to acco[unt] etc.
>
> Your M[ast]rs Rich[ar]d Bowdler & F[ranci]s Gre[e]nowes[10]

("The equality of silver, expressed by different denominations of coins, constitutes what is usually called the par of exchange betwixt any two countries." [Joseph Harris], *An Essay upon Money and Coins*, 2 vols in 1 pt [London, 1757–1758], I, 115.) In 1590 the par of exchange was 33 *schellingen* 6 *grooten* (33.50 *schellingen*) per pound sterling. *Tresoir van de Maten van Gewichten*, p. 156. Compare De Roover, op. cit., pp. 129–131, 136. According to M[atthijs] v[an] Velden, *Fondament vande Wisselhandeling* (Amsterdam, 1629), p. 117, in the late 1620s par was 33 *schellingen* 4 *grooten* (33.33 *schellingen*). Compare De Roover, loc. cit. In 1700 par was 37 *schellingen* 0⅗ *grooten* (37.05 *schellingen*) according to Samuel Ricard, *Traité général du commerce . . .* , [1st edn] (Amsterdam, 1700), pp. 379–380.

10 *Wissels uit de 17e, 18e, en 19e Eeuw, Collectie Jozef Antoon Lodewijk Velle, 1400–1925*, Economische-Historische Archief, Internationaal Instituut voor Sociale Geschiedenis, Amsterdam. While this bill was in fact sent to George Morgan and Isaac Greenowes in Middelburg, it duplicated the format of bills drawn on Amsterdam and has the advantage as an illustration for this discussion of being in English. The authors wish to thank Prof. James S. Cockburn for help with the transcription of this bill of exchange. See also the text of the bill printed in *Tresoir van de Maten van Gewichten*, pp. 148–149; and the 1611 and 1650 bills illustrated and discussed in De Roover, *Gresham on Foreign Exchange*, pp. 123–127, and fig. III. For Bowdler, Greenowes (especially), and Morgan, see the overseas business papers of Lionel Cranfield as calendared in [GB, Historical Manuscripts Commission], *Calendar of the Manuscripts of . . . Lord Sackville . . .*, ed. A[rthur] P. Newton and F[rederick] J. Fisher, 2 vols (London, 1940–1966), II, passim (e.g., pp. 168, 210).

There are in this example one or two things worth commenting upon. The rate of exchange at the top, "35s-7d" is the sum in Dutch currency to be paid for each pound sterling, here 35 *schellingen* and 7 *grooten vlaamsch*. There were 12 *grooten* per *schelling*, and 40 *grooten* or 3⅓ *schellingen* per *gulden* or *florijn* (in English, the guilder). In the tables, these values, originally expressed in twelve-based counting systems, have been restated in decimalized notation as more convenient for calculations. The "uzerance" (usance) of the bill specified the customary period after sight at the end of which a bill was to be paid. In the Amsterdam–London trade, one usance equaled one calendar month and "att dowble uzerance" signified, obviously, two months.[11] What this all meant is that Poulle could reasonably have expected to collect 177 *ponden* 18 *schellingen* and 4 *grooten vlaamsch* (or 1,067½ *gulden*) sometime shortly after 14 February 1609/10 old style, 4 February 1610 new style, provided the payer accepted the bill.

Not all bills of exchange drawn in London on Amsterdam were accepted and paid. The drawee in Amsterdam could refuse to honor the bill of exchange, most frequently because the drawer had insufficient funds to his credit on the drawee's books. If, when the payee presented the bill for acceptance, the drawee said no, then the payee instituted a formal protest. The central document in these proceedings, itself called the protest, was sent back to the payer in London, there to be filed with the appropriate authorities in an attempt to get the drawer to repay the money given him there. Before sending the original protest on to London, the prudent payee made certain that a copy was first inscribed into the book of one of Amsterdam's notaries.

Between 1592 and 1660, 556 London bills of exchange entered the Amsterdam notarial records as protested. These are the ones of which we have a surviving record and the ones used for this study (table 5.1). But they are only a fraction of all such London bills because the Notarial Archives are not complete for all notaries for all years. And, of course, protested bills made up only a small part of all bills drawn in London on Amsterdam. These warnings are but the most important caveats to be entered in any discussion of the data. The impact of all of this is to force us to use these and similar data with caution. The potential problems will be treated below. Suffice it to say that none of these problems is severe enough to stop the reader from doing the most obvious calculations based upon the rates of exchange here compiled, i.e., converting a sum in one currency into its equivalent in the other. Table 5.3 below makes this a bit easier by giving on an annual basis the number of guilders equal to £100 sterling between 1590 and 1660 (see also the chart in figure 5.2).

Using the rates only of protested bills might result in a distorted picture if we have reason to believe that the rates were somehow related to the fact of protest. If, for instance, there was reason to believe that bills that had

---

11 *Tresoir van de Maten van Gewichten*, p. 146.

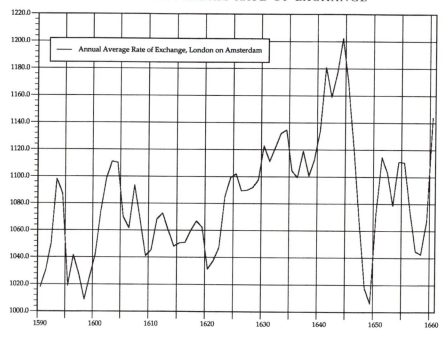

Figure 5.2 Annual average rate of exchange, London on Amsterdam, 1590–1660. (In gulden or florijns banco per £100 sterling.)
Source: Table 5.3.
Courtesy of the author.

been sold at a "cheap" rate were more prone to being protested, the drawer being somehow less secure financially, then this would indicate a bias in the rates quoted here. But where we have the opportunity of comparing these data with data drawn from other sources, there is no suggestion of such a pattern (see table 5.2). We are reasonably safe in the inference that the rates of protested bills of exchange were representative of the going rate at the time they were drawn.

There are, however, other factors that could influence and perhaps distort these data. A bill of exchange once received through the post by the payee was presented by him to the drawee who, willing to pay the bill, marked it as accepted. Accepted did not mean paid, however, and the reason was the obvious one: some time had to be allowed for the drawee to assemble the money. The time to be allowed to pass was a combination of the usance mentioned above and a small, additional period of grace. Thus even "at sight" bills were not in fact paid the very day presented. The usance or sight stipulated in the bill was an object of negotiation between payer and drawer and the difference in price between one period and another was effectively the difference in the interest payable at the going rate on a loan of that duration. The bills in the notarial records ranged in usance from "at sight" to three usances plus four days, about ninety-five days. There is a clear pattern of lengthening usance over the seventy-year span we are dealing with; one usance was the mode until 1612 and two usances afterwards.[12]

It is difficult to decide how to account for differences in usance when compiling the rates of exchange. In theory we would expect the rate in London to have risen as the usance increased.[13] The payer in London who waited longer for his money to be paid at Amsterdam should have received more *schellingen* per pound sterling than the payer who had a shorter wait. Yet differences in usance were not the only reason why one bill cost more or less than the next one.[14] Indeed the several cross-pressures on the rate of exchange could resolve themselves in either direction. In our data we have eleven instances of bills drawn within two days of one another; all other things being equal, the rates at which they were drawn should have varied directly with the usance. Yet it worked that way less than three-quarters of the time. In the remaining instances some other factor intervened to cause the payer and the drawer to agree to a rate that we would not otherwise have expected.

What this means in practice is that it would be rash to compute much less to implement any systematic "correction" based on the implicit premise that exchange rates varied only with the usance.[15] We have not attempted to reduce all rates to the same usance. We have simply averaged together all the rates available to us to arrive at the monthly and annual means in the following tables. Basically, then, we think of our data as showing the usual commercial rate of exchange in London or Amsterdam. Our feeling in adopting this convention is that, during this period, fluctuations in the rate of exchange caused by factors other than usance were at least as important as differences based on usance. We risk smoothing out too much of the former by presuming to correct only for the latter without knowing for certain what it was that caused any particular variation in the rate of exchange.[16]

12 Before 1612 more than two-thirds of all bills were drawn at one usance; afterwards some 70 percent were drawn at two usances. The change is sudden and sharp but we know of no reason for it. Nor does there appear to have been any equivalent change at Amsterdam, at least in the rates as quoted by Posthumus, *History of Prices in Holland*, I, 586, 590–592. See also De Roover, *Gresham on Foreign Exchange*, p. 109.

13 "The exchange rate for bills payable at double usance was always above the rate for usance bills . . ." De Roover, *Gresham on Foreign Exchange*, p. 149.

14 Probably the most important of these factors was the reputation of the drawer and the drawee for honesty and financial soundness. It is clear that some individuals were willing to pay more than the going rate for bills they were certain would be paid. It is equally clear that a market existed, presumably at less than the going rate, for bills the pedigree of which was uncertain or even doubtful. McCusker, *Money and Exchange*, pp. 12, 122, 159, 180.

15 Contrast Gould, *Great Debasement*, p. 88, who reduced the rates of all bills not drawn at sight by an annual rate of 10 percent.

16 This is one difference between rates derived from actual transactions and those quoted, in a later period, by foreign exchange dealers. Edward J. Perkins could indeed state with some certainty concerning the rates quoted by dealers after 1878 that "the price differ-

A final point may be made, saved until last because of its importance. In 1609 the *Wisselbank van Amsterdam* was established as the first exchange bank in Northern Europe. All exchange transactions were cleared through it and it performed other functions as well. Starting in 1624, a difference began to develop between "bank money" (*banco*), the money of exchange, and current money, the money of the marketplace.[17] The difference between the two, called the *opgelt* or the agio was expressed as the percentage premium paid in current money to equal a given sum in bank money. An agio of 5 percent meant that one had to give 105 guilders in current money to get 100 guilders in bank money. There are only a few quotations of the agio before 1660; they suggest a usual rate of between 1 percent and 4 percent with a high of at least 10 percent in the mid-1640s.[18] For the economic historian, this means in practice that Dutch commodity prices must first be reduced from current money to bank money before they can be converted into sterling and vice versa.

What we have then is a fairly satisfactory series giving some monthly and complete annual figures of the rate of exchange in London between English currency and the exchange or bank money of Amsterdam from 1590 through 1660. It complements and supplements other published series in that it compares well with an expanded series of the rate at Amsterdam (published here as table 5.2) and links up with a series of the rate in London that begins with 1660 and carries on through 1775. As a result we are able to trace the fluctuations in the London–Amsterdam rate of exchange for nearly 200 years – and beyond.

ence between a 60-day bill and the more expensive short [3-day or sight] bill represented solely the interest component." See Perkins, "Foreign Interest Rates in American Financial Markets: A Revised Series of Dollar–Sterling Exchange Rates, 1835–1900," *JEcH*, XXXVIII (June 1978), 396. Even so, the firm the records of which he examined, "for reasons not fully understood," never bought bills at the quoted rates (ibid., 409). L[ance] E. Davis and J[onathan] R. T. Hughes, working on a series for earlier in the same century, decided that their data before 1831 were such as not to allow them to correct for differences in usance. See "A Dollar–Sterling Exchange, 1803–1894," *EcHR*, 2nd ser., XIII (Aug. 1960), 56. Data in McCusker, *Money and Exchange*, passim, were compiled in much the same way as they were for this chapter, but with the difference that, when they were so plentiful as to have more than one quotation for the same date, a preference was always shown for rates with the shortest usance.

17 G[errit] van der Wal, *Rekeneenheid en Ruilmiddel* (Helder, 1940), pp. 75–87. Compare Posthumus, *History of Prices in Holland,* I, lvii–lx, cx.

18 In 1629 Van Velden, *Fondament vande Wisselhandeling,* p. 3, talked of "eenighe differenite . . . van 1/4 a 1/2 ten hondert tusschen loopend' ghelt en Wissel-ghelt . . . de aggio . . ." See also McCusker, *Money and Exchange*, pp. 43–44, and table 2.6, pp. 46–51. What Frank C. Spooner, *International Economy and Monetary Movements in France, 1493–1725* (Cambridge, Mass., 1972), p. 69, called "the agio on converting into bank money" was really an interest rate. See (his source) J[ohannes] G. van Dillen, *Bronnen tot de geschiedenis der Wisselbanken (Amsterdam, Middelberg, Delft, Rotterdam),* Rijks Geschiedkundige Publicatiën, 59–60, 2 vols (The Hague, 1925), II, 949–950, n.

Table 5.1 Rate of exchange: London on Amsterdam, 1590–1660 (*Schellingen Banco* per £1 sterling)

Year	Jan.	Feb.	Mar.	Apr.	May	June	July	Aug.	Sept.	Oct.	Nov.	Dec.	Average
1590					33.93								33.93
1591											34.33		34.33
1592									35.00				35.00
1593		36.17					36.00	36.08	36.92	37.12			36.60
1594				36.33		36.33		36.62	36.08	36.50		35.63	36.23
1595	35.00	34.33			34.63		33.33	33.50	34.58		33.81		33.97
1596		34.58			34.33	34.50		35.00	33.83	35.00	35.33		34.71
1597	34.67					34.17			33.82				34.24
1598						33.63							33.63
1599				33.75						35.00	35.00		34.19
1600	34.25	34.67	34.25		34.83				34.67		35.08		34.73
1601	35.00	35.50		35.50							36.67		35.81
1602				36.58	36.58	36.54					36.67		36.61
1603	36.00	37.00					37.00		37.25	39.17	37.50	37.50	37.03
1604	37.17		37.00				36.96		36.00	36.83			37.01
1605		36.00	35.50	35.46	35.67		35.25	35.75					35.66
1606	34.83	35.03		35.38			35.75					35.50	35.39
1607	36.83	36.17		36.13	36.33				36.33		36.71		36.44
1608	36.17			36.58	36.42			35.42	35.08		34.50		35.60
1609			34.04	34.75	34.96	34.27	34.67			35.83	35.83		34.70
1610			34.75		35.50	34.67						35.00	34.85
1611	35.08	35.08			35.63				36.00	37.00		34.67	35.60
1612		35.83		36.00	35.50				35.46	35.92			35.76
1613	35.17								35.37		35.58	35.00	35.33
1614	34.83		34.67	34.67				34.83		35.71	35.00	35.00	34.94
1615	34.94	35.42			34.75							35.17	35.02
1616	35.04	34.92	34.83	34.75	34.96	35.17	35.00	35.13	35.25	35.00	35.17	35.19	35.03
1617	35.22	35.25	35.25	35.25	35.28	35.31	35.33	35.58	35.83	35.53	35.22	34.92	35.33

Table 5.1 continued

Year	Jan.	Feb.	Mar.	Apr.	May	June	July	Aug.	Sept.	Oct.	Nov.	Dec.	Average
1618		35.50	35.67	35.67	35.58		35.33				35.75	35.58	35.56
1619	35.67	35.58	35.50	35.75		35.54	35.53	35.51	35.50	35.33	34.92	34.50	35.41
1620	34.08		34.42		35.50					34.67		34.33	34.38
1621	34.29	34.33		34.50		34.08				34.63			34.58
1622		34.00	34.00					35.58		35.52			34.91
1623					35.50		35.75		35.67	36.75		36.96	36.16
1624	36.92		36.75				36.17	36.17	36.42		37.00		36.64
1625			36.50	36.50			36.48			37.00	36.92		36.74
1626		36.58	36.58	35.58	36.88				36.67				36.31
1627							36.67		36.17		36.00		36.33
1628	36.50	36.35	36.21	36.33	36.25	36.17	36.08	36.22	36.63	36.58	36.83	36.83	36.39
1629	36.50	36.42	36.33	36.17	36.00	36.46		36.88	36.36	36.50	36.75	37.00	36.59
1630	37.00	37.08	37.25	37.17	37.33	37.17	36.92		36.83	36.92	37.00	36.67	37.43
1631	36.50	36.67	37.00	36.88	36.75	36.58	36.88	37.17	37.50	37.83	38.17	37.75	37.05
1632	37.33	37.42	36.50	37.00	37.50	37.44	37.39	37.33	37.54	37.75	37.42	37.38	37.39
1633	37.67	37.50	37.42	37.50	37.67	37.69	37.72	37.75	38.00	38.25	37.72	37.69	37.73
1634	37.78	37.75	37.58	37.75	38.17	38.03	37.89	37.75	37.83	38.00	37.83	37.81	37.82
1635	37.33	37.58	37.67	37.50	37.14	36.78	36.42	36.38	36.33	36.29	37.75	37.54	36.81
1636	35.81	35.58	35.58	35.67	36.17	37.00		37.22	37.33	37.39	36.25	36.03	36.65
1637	36.92		37.00		37.32	37.00	37.11			37.83	37.44	37.50	37.30
1638				36.67				36.58	36.67		36.58		36.69
1639	36.33	37.17	36.67	37.33	36.75	37.58				37.33		36.33	37.09
1640		37.25	37.29	37.29						38.13			37.79
1641			39.75					40.17	39.17		38.92	39.50	39.36
1642	38.63	38.63		38.42	38.79					38.50		38.58	38.64
1643		38.42		40.17	40.42		39.42	39.00	39.00	40.00		38.50	39.22
1644	40.42	40.58	40.40	39.17			39.42			40.25		40.08	40.07
1645		39.83	39.00		38.92	38.75	38.63	38.50					38.97

Year	Jan.	Feb.	Mar.	Apr.	May	June	July	Aug.	Sept.	Oct.	Nov.	Dec.	Average
1646	36.42		38.17	37.75		37.33	37.42	37.33			36.79	36.25	37.40
1647		35.92			35.58	35.58				35.33	35.42	34.00	35.56
1648	33.83			33.33	33.17	32.50				35.33	35.42	34.00	33.92
1649				33.29	33.00		33.25	34.25			33.75		33.55
1650	34.25	34.08	34.42					35.33	35.67	36.67	37.50	38.42	35.76
1651	37.50	37.88	37.50				36.67			37.25		37.08	37.15
1652	37.42	37.17			36.92	36.67	36.33				37.00	36.33	36.77
1653	36.25		35.92	35.67				36.83	35.92	36.17			35.96
1654	37.17		37.06			37.08		37.08			37.08	37.13	37.04
1655	37.00					36.86				37.21			37.02
1656	36.50	36.46	36.42	36.17	35.42	35.56	35.71	35.56	35.42	35.54	35.67	35.42	35.82
1657	*35.17*	*34.67*	*34.83*	*34.79*	*34.40*	*34.00*	*34.79*	*34.90*	*35.00*	*34.96*	*34.92*	*35.58*	34.83
1658	34.67	35.00	34.92	34.75	34.58	34.67	34.75	34.79	34.83	34.75	34.67	34.75	34.76
1659	34.67	34.58	34.75	34.58	34.67	34.83	35.67	35.50	36.83	37.17	37.08	36.50	35.57
1660	37.67	37.50	37.67	38.19	38.25	38.29	38.33	37.92	38.09	38.27	38.67	38.75	38.13

Notes and sources:

1590: *Tresoir van den Maten van Gewichten van Coorn, Lande, van Elle ende natte Mate, oock van den Gelde en Wissel* ... (Amsterdam 1590), pp. 148–149.

1591–1660: Notariële Archieven, 1569–1895, Gemeente Archief, Amsterdam. See the discussion in this chapter.

The data in these tables were compiled in ways comparable to the methods used in John J. McCusker, *Money and Exchange in Europe and America, 1600–1775: A Handbook.* [2nd edn] (Chapel Hill, NC, [1992]). They were assembled according to the date of the bill of exchange; the bills, drawn in London, were dated there in the English fashion according to the old Julian calendar and they are here grouped in the same order. The United Provinces had adopted the new Gregorian calendar in 1583. Prior to Feb. 1600 there was nine days' difference between the two calendars; in the 17th century there were ten days. When there was more than one rate available for a given month, a mean was calculated for each third of the month (1–10, 11–20, 21–31) and then a monthly mean computed. The exchange rate between The Netherlands and England was quoted in terms of however many Dutch *schellingen* were required per pound sterling. There were 12 *grooten* per *schelling*, and 40 *grooten* or 3⅓ *schellingen* per *gulden* or *florijn* (in English, the guilder). In these tables, such values, originally expressed in a twelve-based counting system, have been restated in decimalized notation as more convenient for calculations. Figures in italics are straight-line interpolations based on the figures for the preceding and following months. Annual averages are the mean of the twelve monthly figures, but, when they were fewer than twelve monthly figures, the year was first divided into its four quarters and quarterly averages calculated from the available monthly figures. Annual averages are then the mean of the available quarterly averages. The idea in all of this is to avoid weighting the averages by what has simply chanced to survive.

Table 5.2 Rate of exchange: Amsterdam on London, 1593–1623 (*schellingen banco* per £1 sterling)

Year	Jan.	Feb.	Mar.	Apr.	May	June	July	Aug.	Sept.	Oct.	Nov.	Dec.	Average
1593									35.58	35.79			35.69
1594													
1595	33.67					32.17					32.25		32.69
1596													
1597							33.58						33.58
1598													
1599													
1600					33.75					33.42			33.42
1601											34.13	34.17	33.95
1602													
1603					35.83								35.83
1604		36.25											36.25
1605			34.35		34.52	34.67							34.61
1606				34.50			34.63		35.33				34.73
1607					35.58							35.42	35.50
1608	35.58									34.42			35.00
1609		33.67							34.33		34.67		34.10
1610					34.33	33.75							34.33
1611													
1612													
1613													
1614		34.00											34.00
1615		34.08											34.08
1616													
1617													
1618													
1619			34.84					35.00				34.67	34.76
1620													

Year	Jan.	Feb.	Mar.	Apr.	May	June	July	Aug.	Sept.	Oct.	Nov.	Dec.	Average
1621				33.50									33.50
1622					33.83								33.83
1623							34.83						34.83

Notes and sources:
1593–1623: Notariële Archieven, 1569–1895, Gemeente Archief, Amsterdam.
1609, 1619: N[icolaas] W. Posthumus, *Inquiry into the History of Prices in Holland*, 2 vols (Leiden, 1946–1964), I, 590.
The data in the Notariële Archieven come from official statements made by brokers or merchants about the current rate of exchange at Amsterdam, usually in connection with a protest. The dates are the dates of the attestation and are usually close to or the same as the date of the entry of the protest. The rates are compiled as were those for table 5.1.

Table 5.3 Annual average rate of exchange, London on Amsterdam, 1590–1660 (*gulden* or *florijns banco* per £100 sterling)

Year	Rate	Year	Rate
1590	1017.92	1626	1089.38
1591	1029.90	1627	1089.79
1592	1050.00	1628	1091.82
1593	1097.92	1629	1097.71
1594	1086.87	1630	1122.92
1595	1018.96	1631	1111.35
1596	1041.41	1632	1121.56
1597	1027.08	1633	1132.01
1598	1008.75	1634	1134.55
1599	1025.69	1635	1104.24
1600	1041.98	1636	1099.51
1601	1074.17	1637	1119.10
1602	1098.44	1638	1100.63
1603	1111.04	1639	1112.78
1604	1110.21	1640	1133.75
1605	1069.79	1641	1180.83
1606	1061.67	1642	1159.17
1607	1093.28	1643	1176.56
1608	1068.13	1644	1202.24
1609	1041.09	1645	1169.24
1610	1045.42	1646	1122.03
1611	1068.13	1647	1066.67
1612	1072.66	1648	1017.50
1613	1060.00	1649	1006.46
1614	1048.21	1650	1072.78
1615	1050.65	1651	1114.58
1616	1051.01	1652	1103.13
1617	1059.93	1653	1078.75
1618	1066.88	1654	1111.15
1619	1062.29	1655	1110.68
1620	1031.25	1656	1074.58
1621	1037.29	1657	1045.00
1622	1047.34	1658	1042.81
1623	1084.86	1659	1067.08
1624	1099.17	1660	1144.00
1625	1102.11		

Notes and sources:
These figures are the annual averages from table 5.1 multiplied by a factor of 30. For instance, given that in November 1591 34.33 *schellingen* equaled £1, then £100 equaled 3433 *schellingen*. At 3⅓ *schellingen* to 1 *gulden*, 3433 *schellingen* equaled 1029.90 *gulden*. The same result can be achieved more easily by multiplying 34.33 times 30 (since 100 ÷ 3⅓ = 30).

6

THE ITALIAN BUSINESS PRESS
IN EARLY MODERN EUROPE

This chapter has three purposes. It seeks, first, to introduce the early financial and commercial newspapers that were published in Italy over the two-and-a-half centuries prior to the 1780s; second, to instill an enthusiasm for them that may translate into a willingness to help identify and locate additional examples of these newspapers; and, finally, to justify both enterprises by explaining why these early newspapers are worth our attention. In treating the origins and development of the business press in sixteenth-, seventeenth- and eighteenth-century Italy the essay will proceed in three stages: it begins by describing and illustrating the types of business newspapers that were published in Italy; then, it discusses the publication histories of these newspapers; and finally, it explores the economic importance of these newspapers not only for contemporaries but also for those like us who study the period.[1]

In accomplishing these objectives, the chapter addresses one of the larger themes of which any discussion of the "history of the book" must be a part. Anyone interested in the subject quickly appreciates that printers did not live by books alone. There existed another category of "literature" that publishers published and printers printed: what people in the world of bibliography call "serials." One type of serial is the newspaper.[2] This essay discusses the first kind of newspaper, the business newspaper. For complex reasons the history

1   The original version of this chapter was published in *Produzione e Commercio della Carta e del Libro, secc. XIII–XVIII,* ed. Simonetta Cavaciocchi, Istituto Internazionale di Storia Economica "F. Datini," Pubblicazioni, ser. II, no. 23 (Prato, 1992), pp. 797–841. Copyright © 1992 by the Istituto Internazionale di Storia Economica "F. Datini," Prato. This revision is presented here with the permission of the Istituto Internazionale di Storia Economica "F. Datini." Unfortunate difficulties during the copyediting introduced into the original published version of this essay several significant errors; they have been silently corrected here.

2   Otto Groth, *Die Zeitung: Ein System der Zeitungskunde (Journalistik),* 4 vols (Mannheim, 1928–1930), I, 22–90, argued that, for a publication to be deemed a newspaper, it had to be (a) issued periodically; (b) duplicated mechanically; (c) available to anyone willing to pay for it; (d) broad in the news that it reported; (e) general in the audience to which it appealed; (f) timely in its reporting; and (g) produced by an established, ongoing enterprise.

   The commercial and financial newspapers discussed in this chapter fall short of Groth's criteria in several ways. First, and most particularly, they were not the general purpose

117

of the early newspaper has traditionally dealt exclusively with what can be called the "general purpose newspaper" or, perhaps, the "political newspaper." There is an extensive historical literature that has traced the origins and development of the "general purpose newspaper." Most agree that it had its start in the early seventeenth century.[3]

The first newspapers were in fact more specialized newspapers, the clientele for which was the business community (see table 6.1).[4] Publishers were publishing them, printers were printing them, and businessmen were already

newspaper about which Groth wrote. They were narrow, specialized newspapers, a subset of the genre "newspaper" but newspapers nonetheless in the same way that financial and commercial newspapers published in our own time are so considered. Second, while they were for the most part reproduced mechanically, some were only partly printed. I argue that is an unimportant distinction in the time when they were being published. Finally, some of the newspapers discussed herein were issued less frequently than once a week, Groth's minimum level of periodicity. Again, for early modern Europe, this seems less significant. They were certainly regular and periodical. I think that "early business newspapers" describes them neatly and accurately. Compare Eric W. Allen, "International Origins of the Newspaper: The Establishment of Periodicity in Print," *Journalism Quarterly*, VII (Dec. 1930), 307–319, who based his analysis on Groth's criteria but employed a more subtle and historically sensitive perspective when discussing early newspapers. See also Anthony Smith, *The Newspaper: An International History* (London, 1979), pp. 9–13 and elsewhere.

3   The early "political newspaper" in fact took several different forms called, even then, by several different names. Their common feature was that they conveyed political news (in contrast to early business newspapers that published business news). For an insightful overview of this subject, see, again, Allen, *International Origins of the Newspaper*, pp. 307–319. Compare Ludwig Salomon, *Allgemeine Geschichte des Zeitungswesens* (Leipzig, 1907); Georges [J.] Weill, *Le Journal: Origines, évolution et rôle de la presse périodique* (Paris, 1934); Else Bogel, Elger Blühm *et al.*, *Die deutschen Zeitungen des 17. Jahrhunderts*, 3 vols (Bremen, 1971–1985), passim; and Smith, *The Newspaper: An International History*.
     For a discussion of the traditional treatment of the business press in the standard histories of newspaper publication, see John J. McCusker, *European Bills of Entry and Marine Lists: Early Commercial Publications and the Origins of the Business Press* (Cambridge, Mass., 1985), pp. 8–13, 33–34.

4   The German economist Paul Jacob Marperger, *Anleitung zum rechten Verstand und nußbarer Allerhand so wohl gedrucker als geschreibener ... Zeitungen oder Avisen* [Leipzig(?), n.d. [1726(?)], pp. 4–7, carefully distinguished among five types of "Zeitungen oder Avisen" ("Nouvellen," "Couranten," "Gazettes," "Realtiones," "Journals") and then went on to note that, in the larger commercial centers, there were also published weekly commodity price currents and exchange rate currents (ibid., p. 7). He added that, in some places, merchants in "See-Städten" also had available "die Schiffer-Listen und Notifications-Zettel." Marperger is the only contemporary author I have found who made note of all four types of early business newspaper (see table 6.1) and included them in a discussion of newspapers generally. Compare [Kaspar von Stieler], *Zeitungs-Lust und Nutz: oder, derer so genanten Novellen oder Zeitungen, wirkende Ergetzlichkeit ...* (Hamburg, 1695), pp. 24–29 and elsewhere. Marperger referred his readers to other of his recent publications for more information about commodity price currents and exchange rate currents. He would seem to have meant his *Erläuterung der Hamburger und Amsterdamer Waaren-Preiß-Couranten* ([Dresden, 1725]); and his *Erläuterung der Holländischen und sonderlich der Amsterdamer Waaren-, Geld- und Wechsel-Preiß-Couranten* ([Dresden, 1726]). For more information on Marperger and these works, see Hannelore Lehmann, "Paul Jacob Marperger (1656 bis 1730), ein Vergessener Ökonom der deutschen Frühaufklärung: Versuch einer Übersicht über sein Leben und Wirken," *Jahrbuch für Wirtschaftsgeschichte*, [XI] (no. 4, 1971), 125–157.

demanding and consuming them early in the sixteenth century, well before the "general purpose newspaper" appeared. In the words of Ugo Bellocchi, "L'esigenza dell'informazione economica è dunque all'origine del giornalismo."[5] Both business and political newspapers coexisted in the seventeenth century but, in the early eighteenth century, editors and publishers began to combine them into one, much more modern-looking newspaper. As we all know, the typical newspaper of the late twentieth century testifies to that tradition. Political newspapers have a section of business news and business newspapers have a section of political news. The difference between *The Times* of London and *The Financial Times* is one only of degree.

Despite the very early introduction of printing into Italy, the first solid evidence of the publication there of a business newspaper is the surviving copies of the Piacenza exchange rate current and the Venetian commodity price current from the 1580s (for the latter, see figure 6.1).[6] Within a decade we have unmistakable references to the weekly "listre di cambi, et mercanti" of Florence, although the earliest known extant copies date only from the next century (see figure 6.3).[7] Nevertheless there must have been earlier currents published in Italy, perhaps commodity price currents published at Florence or Venice, probably exchange rate currents issued at the quarterly fairs. Indeed it is likely that the business press had its origins in Italy. If this assertion is correct, then Italy is the home of all newspaper publishing.

However strongly held a belief, the evidence to support these statements is almost exclusively inferential. It is grounded in the contention that the Antwerp commodity price current of ca. 1540, the first known business newspaper, had Italian antecedents.[8] There are two reasons for thinking so. The

---

5 Bellocchi, *Storia del Giornalismo Italiano*, 8 vols (Bologna, 1974–1980), III, 18.
6 John J. McCusker and Cora Gravesteijn, *The Beginnings of Commercial and Financial Journalism: The Commodity Price Currents, Exchange Rate Currents, and Money Currents of Early Modern Europe*, Nederlandsch Economisch-Historisch Archief, ser. III, no. 11 (Amsterdam, 1991), pp. 393–420.
7 McCusker and Gravesteijn, *Beginnings of Commercial and Financial Journalism*, pp. 189–200. See also Maria Augusta Morelli [Timpanaro], "Gli inizi della stampa periodica a Firenze nella prima metà del XVII secolo," *Critica Storia: Bollettino dell'Associazione degli Storici Europei*, VI (May 1968), 288–323. Compare Maria Augusta Morelli [Timpanaro], *Delle prime gazette fiorentine* (Florence [1963]), to which Morelli's article is, in part, a correction; and Bellocchi, *Storia del Giornalismo Italiano*, II, 37–40, 118, 126. The records that discuss the Florence commodity price current are those generated by the petition for and grant of the right to publish it. For the context of that process, see Berta Maracchi Biagiarelli, "Il privilegio di stampatore ducale nella Firenze Medicea," *Archivio Storico Italiano*, CXXIII (no. 3, 1965), 304–370.
8 These arguments are developed in McCusker and Gravesteijn, *Beginnings of Commercial and Financial Journalism*, passim; and John J. McCusker, "The Role of Antwerp in the Emergence of Commercial and Financial Newspapers in Early Modern Europe," in *La Ville et la transmission des valeurs culturelles au bas Moyen Âge et aux temps modernes – Die Stade und die Übertragung von kulturelles Werten im Spätmittelalter und in die Neuzeit – Cities and the Transmission of Cultural Values in the Late Middle Ages and Early Modern Period*, Gemeentekrediet van België/Crédit Communal de Belgique, Collection Histoire, no. 96 (Brussels, 1996).

first is language. There is every indication that the language of the business newspapers published at Antwerp was Italian from the beginning. Indeed the language of almost all the early business newspapers was Italian, no matter where they were published. This continued to be the case, even at some places where Italian was not the local language, down into the eighteenth century. The Antwerp exchange rate current was published in Italian until the 1750s. In the words of Pietro Rota: "Ecco i fatti: . . . la lingua italiana fu la lingua ufficiale per molto tempo dei negozi di cambio."[9] The wide-spread and persistent use of the Italian language in these business newspapers supports the proposition that they were an Italian invention.

The second reason to think that the business press had its origins in Italy is

Figure 6.1 Venice. Commodity price current, 3 June 1588.
Courtesy of the Gemeente Archief, Leiden.

9   Pietro Rota, *Storia delle banche* (Milan, 1874), p. 63.

more compelling. The format of the earliest printed, published commodity price currents duplicated almost precisely the format used by fourteenth- and fifteenth-century Italian merchants for the private, handwritten reports they sent home from various posts abroad in which they listed commodity prices, exchange rates, and the like.[10] Even though these reports were essentially inter-office memoranda and were not meant for public distribution, they were clearly something more than randomly prepared lists of merchants' selling prices.[11]

All known copies of these early manuscript *listini dei prezzi* followed the same standardized format and included a wide range of commodities. The copy-clerks followed the standard format so carefully that they frequently copied the name of a commodity even when they were unable to enter a price for it. From places as widely separated geographically as Damascus and London and as far apart in time as 1383 and 1430, they were remarkably consistent. It is even more remarkable that the earliest printed, published commodity price currents later used essentially the same format. Someday someone will discover the links between the two by finding copies of late fifteenth-century or early sixteenth-century commodity price currents pub-lished at, say, Venice or Florence. Nevertheless the widespread and persistent use of the same format for the commodity price current, carried over from the age of script to the age of print, further supports the proposition that these business newspapers were first published in Italy.

While the dating of these earliest newspapers to within a century of the invention of moveable type printing may at first seem surprising, upon reflec-tion it is quite understandable. Indeed one may wonder just how long it took European merchants and printers to get together to use the printing press to disseminate market information on a regular, consistent basis. Certainly businessmen in Europe had been collecting and sharing such infor-mation for a very long time before the 1540s. Data on local commodity prices, foreign exchange rates, and international shipping were and are the stuff of private business communications. The use by Italian merchants of a manuscript "form" to collect and distribute commodity prices had a very early history, as was mentioned above. The limited "publication" of the exchange rates at the financial fairs of Southern Europe was as regular a

---

10 There are several examples of these lists in the Archivio Datini, filza 1171, Archivio di Stato, Prato. See Guido Pampaloni, *Inventario sommario dell'Archivio di Stato di Prato* (Florence, 1958), pp. 62–84. Federigo Melis, *Documenti per la storia economica dei secoli XIII–XVI*, Istituto Internazionale di Storia Economica "F. Datini," Pubblicazioni, Ser. I: Documenti, no. 1 (Florence, 1972), pp. 38–39, 298–321 (documents number 86–94), discusses and reproduces fourteen such lists dated between 1383 and 1430.

11 One may contrast them with the usual reports of the same kind of information. See, for instance, the letters sent in the 13th century from the Champagne fairs to the Siennese firm of Andrea Tolomei. Adolf Schaube, "Ein italienischer Coursbericht von der Messe von Troyes aus dem 13. Jahrhundert," *Zeitschrift für Social- und Wirtschaftsgeschichte*, V (1897), 248–308. For these fairs, see Robert-Henri Bautier, "Les foires de Champagne: Recherches sur une évolution historique," *Recueils de la Société Jean Bodin pour l'Histoire Comparative des Institutions*, V (1953), 97–147.

Table 6.1 Catalogue and description of the types of early commercial and financial serial publications that appeared in Europe before the end of the eighteenth century

Catalogue

A Publications that reported on the local economy ("currents"):
  1 Commodity price currents:
    • General price currents
    • Specialized price currents
  2 Foreign exchange rate currents
  3 Money currents
  4 Stock exchange currents
B Publications that reported on overseas trade and shipping:
  1 Bills of entry
    • General bills
    • Specialized ("small") bills
  2 Marine lists
C Publications that combined two or more of the elements from categories A and B:
  1 Exchange rate current/stock exchange current
  2 Exchange rate current/marine list
  3 Exchange rate current/stock exchange current/marine list

Description

A Local market publications or "currents"
1 Commodity price currents
Published the local currency prices of goods offered for sale in a specific market. The general commodity price currents included the prices of a broad range of goods; the specialized price currents were limited to particular kinds of commodities, e.g., cloth, grain, sugar, imported colonial goods, etc. The general commodity price current also usually listed a few exchange rates and sometimes insurance rates and money rates.
2 Foreign exchange rate currents
Published the going rates on the local exchange or bourse for bills of exchange against a list of cities in other countries. Bills of exchange are negotiable instruments for the transfer of funds, usually to another country. They were similar to modern bank checks but were drawn on funds held by individuals or businesses rather than on funds held by banks.
3 Money currents
Published the value in the local money of account of a variety of foreign and domestic coins and, sometimes, gold and silver bullion. As this implies, even domestically minted coins sometimes fluctuated in value against the local money of account.
4 Stock exchange currents
Published the prices at which shares of stock, bonds, and government securities were traded on the local market.
B Overseas trade and shipping publications
1 Bills of Entry
Published lists of commodities that had been entered into the local customhouse books as being off-loaded and imported or as being loaded on board for export.
2 Marine Lists
Published lists of ships entering into or clearing from various ports, particularly the port at which the list was published but sometimes other domestic and foreign ports also.

C Combined publications

As economies grew more complex and business publishing became more sophisticated and competitive, some publishers produced newspapers that incorporated more than one of the elements in categories A and B. Modern business newspapers and the business sections of modern political newspapers combine everything distinguished above.

Notes and sources:
An earlier version of this table appeared in John J. McCusker and Cora Gravesteijn, *The Beginnings of Commercial and Financial Journalism: The Commodity Price Currents, Exchange Rate Currents, and Money Currents of Early Modern Europe*, Nederlandsch Economisch-Historisch Archief, ser. III, no. 11 (Amsterdam, 1991), pp. 31–33. See also John J. McCusker, *European Bills of Entry and Marine Lists: Early Commercial Publications and the Origins of the Business Press* (Cambridge, Mass., 1985), pp. 10–12.

feature of these events as was the *conto,* the ritual occasion at which the rates were settled. Nevertheless printing did introduce a difference by making it possible to publish such information on a wider, more regular, and, therefore, more commercial basis. Periodic publications organized by a local businessman, usually operating under license from some authority, simply became more feasible with the advent of printing.[12]

The critical question is why merchants chose to start publishing information that, held privately, may have afforded them commercial advantage. News of a ship's sailing, a fall in a price, the arrival of a cargo of goods: these could all be considered business secrets and were worth a considerable amount to an individual firm. The decision to publish this information must have been taken when members of the business community in a particular place understood that henceforth it would be more to their advantage to publish such information than to keep it private any longer. Take the example of exchange rates or commodity prices generated on the local exchange. Eventually businessmen appreciated that, since everyone working on the exchange already knew this information, they might as well publish it, sell the publication, and profit from the enterprise. It seems likely that a similar impulse drove the publication of the first exchange rate current at some exchange fair where those in attendance bought multiple copies to mail to their contacts abroad. More powerful reasons to publish commercial and financial information arose from the sense that doing so helped to increase business by advertising the existence of a service or the availability at a particular market of a range of goods at competitive prices. Information also

12 Thus I would argue that the important change came with the publication of business news, a development that was merely facilitated by the printing press. The turning point was the decision to publish and not the decision to print. In this emphasis I am somewhat at odds with the thrust of the work of scholars like Elizabeth Eisenstein who, in her book *The Printing Press as an Agent of Change: Communications and Cultural Transformation in Early Modern Europe,* 2 vols (Cambridge, Eng., 1979), argues that the printing press caused such changes. Compare Anthony T. Grafton, "The Importance of Being Printed," *Journal of Interdisciplinary History,* XI (Autumn 1980), 265–286.

increased the efficiency of businesses by diminishing risk and helping with planning. The result was the emergence of more productive business operations with consequences that will be treated more fully below.[13]

So obviously did these early business newspapers fill a need that, once established, their publication proliferated rapidly. Before the end of the sixteenth century there were commodity price currents and exchange rate currents published across Western Europe. Venice and Florence – as well as Amsterdam, Hamburg, and Frankfurt – had their commodity price currents; Piacenza, Lyons, and Antwerp had exchange rate currents; London, its bills of entry. The first marine list made its appearance sometime within the next hundred years. By the 1690s, at London – which was, with Amsterdam, the leading commercial and financial center of late seventeenth- and early eighteenth-century Europe[14] – several different business newspapers were produced every week. Merchants in each of these places subscribed to these newspapers and sent them to overseas correspondents on a regular basis. Provision for the business press had been made in merchant law and in mercantile practice. The postal services and the taxing authorities had taken note of them and governments in many places had made decisions to encourage them as part of larger promotional efforts to support their business communities. Merchants abroad had begun to expect and to demand them of their metropolitan colleagues. Well before the middle of the seventeenth century the business press had become part of the essential fabric of European commercial and financial life.

The information in table 6.2 summarizes what can be said about the publication of these newspapers in early modern Italy. Before the end of the eighteenth century three of the four basic types of commercial and financial newspaper were being published in Italy during the business week: the bills of entry; the commodity price current; and the exchange rate current.[15]

---

13 See John J. McCusker, "The Business Press and Transaction Costs in Early Modern Europe, 1530–1775" (paper presented at the conference on "The Rise of Merchant Empires: Changing Patterns of Long-Distance Trade, 1360–1750," Center for Early Modern History, University of Minnesota, 1987). Compare Douglass C. North, "Transaction Costs in History," *Journal of European Economic History*, XIV (Sept.–Dec. 1985), 557–576.

14 Compare Jonathan I. Israel, "The Amsterdam Stock Exchange and the English Revolution of 1688," *Tijdschrift voor Geschiedenis*, CIII (1990), 412–440.

15 There is no known evidence of the publication of a marine list anywhere in Italy during this period, although it is possible that one or more may have been published there. Nevertheless, see [Jean François Bourgoing], *Nouveau Voyage en Espagne, ou tableau de l'état actuel de cette monarchie ... depuis 1782 jusqu'à présent*, 3 vols (Paris 1789), III, 187, who presented data compiled from the Cadiz marine list and then noted that similar newspapers were published "chaque semaine comme dans toutes les grandes places commerçantes de l'Europe." I am very grateful to R. G. Hare of High Wycombe, Buckinghamshire, who told me of this reference.

Table 6.2 Commercial and financial newspapers published in Italy prior to 1775

BERGAMO – exchange rate current
  [Corso del Cambio,] Bergamo. 1750–1751. Weekly (Wednesdays).
BOLOGNA – exchange rate current
  Pretij de' Cambij seguiti in Bologna. 1628–1686. Weekly (Tuesdays).
BOLZANO – commodity price current and exchange rate current
  Nota de prezzi di Mercanzie . . . in Fiera . . . di Bolgzano. 1631–1675. Quarterly.
  Prezzi di Cambi, corsi in Fiera . . . Bolzano. 1655–1775 and after. Quarterly.
FLORENCE – commodity price current and exchange rate current
  [Corso de Pretii de Mercantie] in Fiorenza. 1598–1660. Weekly (Tuesdays).
  [Corso del Cambio] Firenze. ca. 1626–1774. Twice weekly (Wednesdays and
    Saturdays to 1746; Tuesdays and Saturdays after 1750).
GENOA – commodity price current and exchange rate current
  In Genova. Prezzi correnti in questa Piazza delle sottonotate Mercantie. 1667.
    Weekly (Saturdays) [?]
  [Corso del Cambio] in Genova. 1619–1775 and after. Weekly (Saturdays).
LEGHORN – commodity price current, exchange rate current, and bills of entry
  Prezzi Correnti delle Seguenti Mercanzie, Livorno. 1627–1775 and after. Three
    times a week (Mondays, Wednesdays, and Fridays).
  [Corso del Cambio] Livorno. 1663–1775 and after. Three times a week
    (Mondays, Wednesdays, and Fridays).
  [Manifesto del Carico] Livorno. 1667–1775 and after. Weekly (Fridays).
    Beginning in the 1750s, if not earlier, the Friday edition of the exchange rate
    current was published as an appendix to the weekly bills of entry.
NAPLES – exchange rate current
  [Corso de' Cambij,] Napoli. 1627–1775 and after. Weekly (Thursdays to 1662;
    Saturdays 1770 and after).
NOVI – exchange rate current
  Prezzi de Cambij fatti in pagamenti di fiera . . . fatta in Novi. 1625–1685. Quarterly.
  Prezzi de Cambij fatti in pagamenti di fiera . . . fatta in Rapallo. 1658–1755. Quarterly.
  Prezzi de Cambij fatti in pagamenti di fiera . . . fatta in Santa Margherita.
    1712–1722. Quarterly.
  Prezzi de Cambij fatti in pagamenti di fiera . . . fatta in Sestri Levante.
    1627–1672. Quarterly.
PIACENZA – exchange rate current
  Prezzi de' Cambij fatti in pagamenti di fiera . . . fatta in Piacenza. 1581–1691.
    Quarterly.
VENICE – commodity price current and exchange rate current
  Corso di Mercanzie, Venezia. 1585–1775 and after. Weekly (Fridays).
  [Corso del Cambio] Venetia. 1623–1775 and after. Weekly (Fridays to about
    1759; Saturdays from about 1764 on).
VERONA – exchange rate current
  Prezzi de Cambi Posti Nella Fiera de Verona . . . . 1631–1638. Quarterly.

Notes and sources:
John J. McCusker and Cora Gravesteijn, *The Beginnings of Commercial and Financial Journalism: The Commodity Price Currents, Exchange Rate Currents, and Money Currents of Early Modern Europe*, Nederlandsch Economisch-Historisch Archief, ser. III, no. 11 (Amsterdam, 1991), and as supplemented by subsequent research. Compare John J. McCusker, *European Bills of Entry and Marine Lists: Early Commercial Publications and the Origins of the Business Press* (Cambridge, Mass., 1985).
  The titles specified are the ones used by the publisher at the very end of the period indicated. Such titles were sometimes different from a title used earlier in the publication's history. The portion of any title placed in brackets has been supplied, if only for descriptive purposes, based on the style and language in use later, at the same place, and in use at the same time, in other places.
  There is some indication that such newspapers were published at other places in Italy during this period but not enough information has yet to be assembled and analyzed to add such cities to this list.

A "bills of entry" was a newspaper that published lists of commodities imported and exported at a particular port of entry.[16] In 1678, the English author John Vernon, described this kind of newspaper in the following words:

> By a Custom-house Bill is meant a sheet of paper that comes out every day (except Holy days); in which Paper there is set down all the Goods by themselves that are Imported; and all them that are Exported by themselves; and there is put the Place they are Imported from, the Merchant's Name that Imports them, and the quantity of Goods; and so for the Exportation of Goods.[17]

This succinctly yet accurately describes the form and the content of the Leghorn bills of entry (see figure 6.2), a newspaper that was published in an unchanging format from 1667, if not earlier, down through to 1775 and after.[18] Lacking both title and imprint, and almost any other identifying mark except the city name, the Leghorn bills of entry shows itself to have been a newspaper only when one has located enough copies to establish its regularity and periodicity. Beginning in 1771, the following statement appeared at the end of the listings: "V. L'Avvocato Brignole Cancell[iere] di Sanità." Note that it was entirely printed. Very little else is known about it although it seems, in a way remarkably similar to the history of the London bills of entry, to have been a published version of data collected systematically over a much longer period.[19] Moreover, it appears to have been the only newspaper of this type published at an Italian port.

> The *Correspondance Maritime de Bordeaux* and *Lloyd's List* of London were marine lists. They are what Marperger called *Schiffer-Listen*. See McCusker, *European Bills of Entry*, pp. 52–64, 73, and n. 4 of this chapter.
>
> McCusker and Gravesteijn, *Beginnings of Commercial and Financial Journalism*, p. 261, n. 3, corrects the error in McCusker, *European Bills of Entry*, pp. 65–66, where the Leghorn bills of entry is mistakenly described as a marine list. For European marine lists in general, see ibid., pp. 52–75.

16 This is what were called in French *Manifestes des Marchandises* and what Marperger titled, *Notifications-Zettel*. See McCusker, *European Bills of Entry*, pp. 66–73, and n. 4 of this chapter.

17 J. Vernon, *The Compleat Comptinghouse: or, The Young Lad Taken from the Writing School, and Fully Instructed, by Way of Dialogue, in All the Mysteries of a Merchant* (London, 1678), p.197.

18 McCusker, *European Bills of Entry*, pp. 65–66; McCusker and Gravesteijn, *Beginnings of Commercial and Financial Journalism*, p. 261, n. 3. Compare Elena Gremigni, *Periodici almanacchi livornesi secoli XVIIe–XVIIIe*, [Quaderni della Labronica no. 69] (Livorno, 1996). Many of the known extant copies of the Leghorn bills of entry survive in the Public Record Office, London; they were sent home by the English consuls stationed at Leghorn. Gigliola Pagano de Divitis alerted me to the location of many of them and I am grateful to her for her help.

19 There appears to have been some relationship between these published bills of entry and the *portate* compiled at Leghorn in the 16th and 17th centuries, though precisely what is still not clear. For a description and analysis of the *portate*, see Fernand [P.] Braudel and Ruggiero Romano, *Navires et marchandises à l'entrée du port de Livourne (1547–1611)* (Paris, 1951). See also Cesare Ciano, *La sanità marittima nell'età medicea*, Biblioteca del "Bollettino Storico Pisano," Collana Storica, no. 15 ([Pisa, 1976]), p. 23, n. 6, and elsewhere; and Gremigni, *Periodica livornese*, passim.

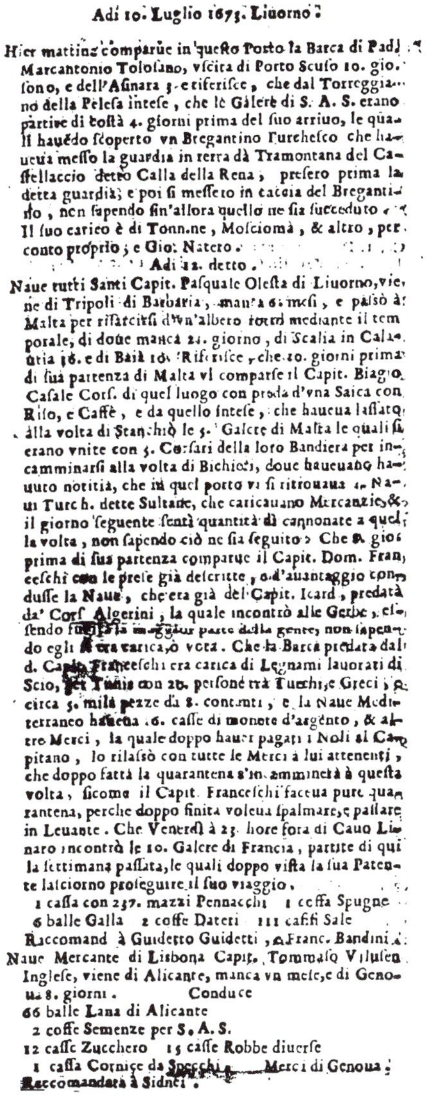

Adi 10. Luglio 1673. Liuorno.

Hier mattina comparùe in questo Porto la Barca di Padj.
Marcantonio Tololano, vícita di Porto Scuſo 10. gio.
ſono, e dell'Aſinara 3. e tiferiſce, che dal Torreggia-
no della Peleſa inteſe, che le Galère di S. A. S. erano
pàrtite di coſtà 4. giorni prima del ſuo arriuo, le quali hauèdo ſcoperto vn Bregantino Turcheſco che haueua meſſo la guardia in terra dà Tramontana del Ca-
ſtellaccio detto Calla della Rena, preſero prima la
detta guardià; e poi ſi meſſero in caccia del Bregantino, nen ſapendo fin'allora quello ne ſia ſucceduto.
Il ſuo carico è di Tonn.ne, Moſciomà, & altro, per
conto próprio; e Gio: Natero.

Adi 12. detto.

Naue tutti Santi Capit. Paſquale Oleſta di Liuorno, viene di Tripoli di Barbària, man'a 6. meſi, e paſsò à
Malta per rifarcirſi d'vn'albero totro mediante il tem-
porale, di doúe manca 24. giorno, di Scalia in Cala-
bria 16. e di Baſk 10. Riferiſce, che 10. giorni prima
di ſua partenza di Malta vi comparſe il Capit. Biagio
Caſale Corſ. di quel luogo con preda d'vna Saica con
Riſo, e Caffè, e da quello inteſe, che haueua laſsato
alla volta di Stanchiò le 5. Galère di Malta le quali ſi
erano vnite con 5. Corſari della loro Bandiera per in-
camminarſi alla volta di Bichiett, doue haueuano ha-
uuto notitia, che in quel porto vi ſi ritrouaua 1. Na-
ui Turch. dette Sultane, che caricauano Mercanzie &
il giorno ſeguente ſentì quantità di cannonate a quella volta, non ſapendo ciò ne ſia ſeguito. Che a gior-
prima di ſua partenza comparue il Capit. Dom. Fran,
ceſchi con le preſe già deſcritte, o d'auantaggio con-
duſſe la Naue, che era già del Capit. Icard, predata
da' Corſ. Algerini, la quale incontrò alle Gerbe, eſ-
ſendo fuggita la maggiur parte della gente, non ſapendo egli ſe tra carica, ò vota. Che la Barca predata dal
d. Capit. Franceſchi era carica di Legnami lauorati di
Scio, per Tunis con 28. perſone trà Turchi, e Greci; à
circa 5. mila pezze dà 8. contanti; e la Naue Medi-
terraneo haueua 16. caſſe di monete d'argento, & altre Merci, la quale doppo hauer pagati i Noli al Capitano, lo rilaſsò con tutte le Merci à lui attenenti,
che doppo fatta la quarantena s'inammincia à queſta
volta, ſicome il Capit. Franceſchi faceua pure quarantena, perche doppo finita voleua ſpalmare, e paſſare
in Leuante. Che Venerdì à 25. hore fora di Cauo Li-
naro incontrò le 10. Galère di Francia, partite di qui
la ſettimana paſſata, le quali doppo viſta la ſua Paten-
te laſciorno proſeguire il ſuo viaggio.

1 caſſa con 237. mazzi Pennacchi   1 ceſſa Spugne
6 balle Galla   2 coffe Dateri   111 caſſi Sale
Raccomand à Guidetto Guidetti, a Franc. Bandini.
Naue Mercante di Lisbona Capit. Tommaſo Viluſen
Ingleſe, viene di Alicante, manca vn meſe, e di Genoua 8. giorni.   Conduce
66 balle Lana di Alicante
2 coffe Semenze per S. A. S.
12 caſſe Zucchero   15 caſſe Robbe diuerſe
1 caſſa Corniçe da Specchi ___ Merci di Genoua.
Raccomandata à Sidnei.

Figure 6.2a Leghorn. Bills of Entry, 14 July 1673 (obverse).
By permission Controller of HM Stationery Office.

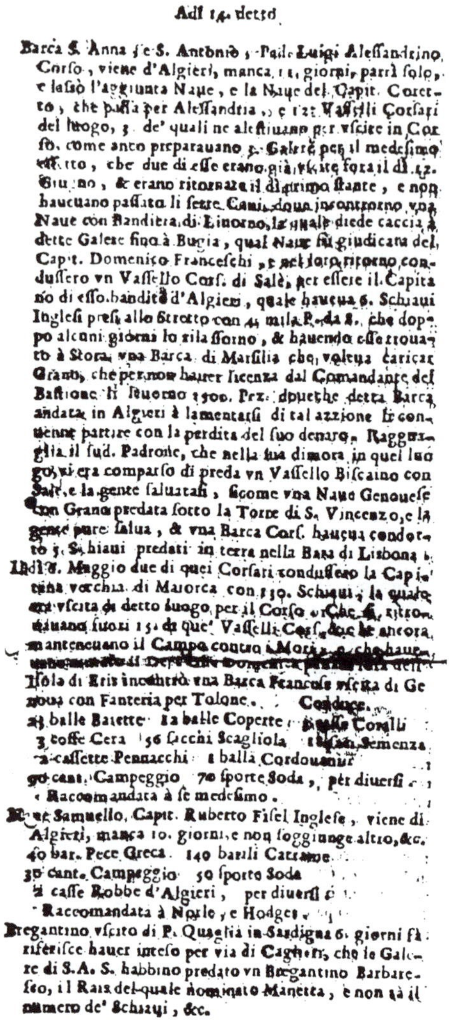

Adi 14. detto

Barca S. Anna e S. Antonio, Padr. Luigi Alessandrino Corso, viene d'Algieri, manca 11. giorni, parrà solo, e lasciò l'aggiunta Naue, e la Naue del Capit. Coretto, che passa per Alessandria, e 12. Vasselli Corsari del luogo, 3. de' quali ne allestiuano per vscire in Corso, come anco preparauano 5. Galere per il medesimo effetto, che due di esse erano già vscite fora il dì 12. Giugno, & erano ritornate il dì primo stante, e non haueuano passato li sette Capi, doue incontrorno vna Naue con Bandiera di Liuorno, la quale diede caccia à dette Galere fino à Bugia, qual Naue fu giudicata del Capit. Domenico Franceschi, e nel loro ritorno condussero vn Vassello Cors. di Salè, per essere il Capitano di esso bandito d'Algieri, quale haueua 6. Schiaui Inglesi presi allo Stretto con 44 mila P. da 8. che doppo alcuni giorni lo rilassorno, & hauendo esse trouato à Stora vna Barca di Marsilia che voleua caricar Grano, che per non hauer licenza dal Comandante del Bastione li presero 1500. Pez. doue che detta Barca andata in Algieri à lamentarsi di tal azzione li conuenne partire con la perdita del suo denaro. Raggualglia il sud. Padrone, che nella sua dimora in quei luogo vi era comparso di preda vn Vassello Biscaino con Sale, e la gente saluatasi, siccome vna Naue Genouese con Grano predata sotto la Torre di S. Vincenzo, e la gente pure salua, & vna Barca Cors. haueua condotto 5. Schiaui predati in terra nella Baia di Lisbona.
Adì 8. Maggio due di quei Corsari condussero la Capitana vecchia di Maiorca con 130. Schiaui, la quale era vscita di detto luogo per il Corso, e che si ritrouauano fuori 15. di que' Vasselli Cors. e che ancora mantenevano il Campo contro i Mori, e che haue-[illegible] dell' Isola di Eris incontrò vna Barca Francese vscita di Genoua con Fanteria per Tolone. Conduce.
23 balle Baiette 12 balle Coperte [illegible] Coralli
3 coffe Cera 56 sacchi Scagliola 1[illegible] Semenza
2 cassette Pennacchi 1 balla Cordouani
90 cant. Campeggio 70 sporte Soda, per diuersi
Racoomandata à se medesimo.
[illegible] Samuello, Capit. Ruberto Fisel Inglese, viene di Algieri, manca 10. giorni, e non soggiunge altro, &c.
40 bar. Pece Greca 140 barili Cattame
30 cant. Campeggio 50 sporte Soda
2 casse Robbe d'Algieri, per diuersi
Raccomandata à Noyle, e Hodges.
Bregantino vscito di P. Quaglia in Sardigna 6. giorni fà riferisce hauer inteso per via di Caglieri, che le Galere di S.A.S. habbino predato vn Bregantino Barbaresco, il Rais del quale nominato Manetta, e non sà il numero de' Schiaui, &c.

Figure 6.2b Leghorn. Bills of entry, 14 July 1673 (reverse). By permission Controller of HM Stationery Office.

The second of the three kinds of business newspapers published in Italy, the commodity price current, set down lists of commodities and the wholesale prices at which they sold on the local market. John Vernon had words for it, also: "A Price-Current, is a small piece of Paper that is printed in most Places where a trade is used, that specifies what all manner of Goods are worth; and that is so printed once every week, and sent by one Merchant

Adi 9. Dicembre 1606. In Firenze.	
Roma	ſc.90.17.6
Napoli	d.135.8
Venezia	d.80.5
Ancona . . ∻ .	ſc.115.10
Lione	c.94.18
Biſenzon.	c.108
Piſa	ſc.106.18
Anuerſa . . ∻ .	g.117.10
Milano . . . ∻	f.
Siuilia . . . ∻	m.
Fiera di Spagna	m.
Rea di buo.ſlap.	l. 72.16
Che t mi ſi canuto	l.49
detto ordinario	l.45.10
Pepi leuāt.	d.27.25.25
zaferano noſtral.	l.42 — cont.
zucher dl verzino	d.16.10.17.
detto ſecondo	d.15.10.
Maſcauati	d.10.10.11
Cannelle inteſe	d.37.10
Grofani	16 — cont.
Cera bianca	d.27.10.28
meſſine	l.23 10
tonde	l.
piane	l.
Reggie	l.
Saponare ∹ . ∻.	l.24.10
Santa Lucie	l.24.10
ſermone	l.26.15.27.10
Rafini di molina	ſc
Seconda, terza	ſc.
Rafin. de cordoua	ſc.
Meze conche	ſc.
Rafini di ſegouia	ſc.
Seconda. terza	ſc.
Rafini di toledo	ſc.
Seconda. terza	ſc.
Rafini di ſeretta	ſc.
Seconda	ſc.
Rafi. vil'a caſtina	ſc. — cont
Seconda	ſc. cont.
Rafini d'i concha	ſc.
Seconde	ſc.
Rafini di granata	ſc.
Rafini di Soria	ſc.
second	ſc.

Figure 6.3 Florence. Commodity price current, 9 December 1606. Courtesy of the Archivio di Stato, Florence. Su concessione del Ministero per i Beni Culturi e Ambientali.

to another."[20] The earliest extant copies of the Venetian commodity price current, the oldest one known, establish its significance at several levels (see figure 6.1). It was organized in the same format as the fifteenth-century price lists that were discussed earlier in this essay. Moreover, that very same format was used by the earliest known commodity price currents published elsewhere in Europe, specifically at Amsterdam and, importantly, even earlier, at Antwerp.[21] Thus, the Venetian commodity price current appears to have been both a link with the late medieval past and a harbinger of the future.

There are other characteristics of the Venetian commodity price current that are worthy of remark. Although it had a full title, there was no imprint. This is the case with most of these early newspapers. Note as well that the Venetian commodity price current included as the last section at the bottom of the last column a list of foreign exchange rates. From this one may infer that there was no separate exchange rate current published at Venice in the 1580s and 1590s. Although that inference no longer holds true later, it accurately characterizes the situation during the early years of the publication of these newspapers.

The Venetian commodity price current invites comparison with the one published at Florence (see figure 6.3). Even though it is essentially the same kind of newspaper, there are some significant differences. They are similar in that both lack a title and an imprint. But the list of commodities for which prices are quoted is much shorter in the Florentine newspaper and

20 Vernon, *Compleat Comptinghouse*, p. 196. Compare: "Price Current. A weekly account published in London, of the currant value of most commodities." Edward Hatton, *The Merchant's Magazine: or, Trade-Man's Treasury*, [2nd edn] (London, 1697), p. 236.
21 See McCusker, "Role of Antwerp."

the order of exchange rates and commodity prices is the reverse of the Venetian commodity price current. Note, too, that the Florentine newspaper is completely printed.

By contrast, the Venetian commodity price current is a combination of printed and handwritten material. Many of the earliest business newspapers appeared in the same way. The list of commodities or city names was printed and the prices or the rates of exchange were inserted by hand with pen and ink. Later many came to be completely printed. And, indeed, at least two Italian business newspapers – the Florentine commodity price current and the Venetian exchange rate current – the earliest known surviving copies of which are completely printed, later reverted to a partly printed, partly handwritten presentation. They are newspapers nonetheless simply because they fulfill every other defining characteristic of newspapers. It would be unreasonable to contend that either the commodity price current of Florence or the Venetian exchange rate current, which were clearly business newspapers for over a century, became something else later merely because they ceased to be completely printed. They were all business newspapers from the first.

The third and last of the early Italian business newspapers that concern us here is the exchange rate currents, which published the rates at which foreign bills of exchange sold on the local market. The bill of exchange was the premier negotiable instrument in the overseas trade and finance of the Western world during the entire period from the late Middle Ages down into our own century. Joseph Harris called them "substitutes for bullion."[22] Obviously, knowing the rates at which they sold was critical to success in the world of international trade and finance.[23]

It seems clear from the history of the Italian exchange rate currents that they had their origins in the financial fairs of Southern Europe, fairs that were dominated by Italian merchant and banking houses even when they were held outside Italy. At all such financial fairs, a high point was the negotiation of the rates of exchange at which transactions done at the fair would be settled. Called the *conto*, this negotiation was a formal occasion during which representatives of the major mercantile firms involved in the fair met to settle the rates of exchange by bargaining amongst themselves.[24] However

---

22 [Joseph Harris], *An Essay upon Money and Coins*, 2 vols in 1 pt (London, 1757–1758), I, 120.

23 In testimony to which stand the numerous handbooks on foreign exchange practice published at the time. One example, especially apposite to the present discussion, is Pompeo Baldasseroni, *Leggi e costumi del cambio che si osservano nelle principali piazze d'Europa e singolarmente in quella di Livorno* (Pescia, 1784).

24 For contemporary discussions of the *conto* and the usual progress of events at the fairs, see, among others, Tommaso Buoninsegni, *De i cambi: Trattato risolutissimo et utilissimo, nel quale con molta brevità, & chiarezza si dichiarano i modi hoggi, usitati ne i cambi* (Florence, 1573), fols 21r–v; Sigismund Scaccia, *Tractatus de commerciis, et cambio* (Rome, 1619), pp. 180–183; Lewes Roberts, *The Merchants Mappe of Commerce* ... , [1st edn] ([London], 1638), [3rd pagination], pp. 34–35; Raffelle della Torre, *Tractatus de cambiis* ([Genoa, 1641]), p. 8; Gio[vanni] Domenico Peri, *Il Negotiante*, [3rd (?) edn], 4 vols in

it may sound, the exercise was far from an arbitrary imposition; it was simply a reconciliation of the buying and selling that had gone on at the fair. The same thing took place weekly at Venice. "On fixe le cours des changes tous les vendredis de chaque semaine, lorsqu'il n'est pas un jour de fête. Les Banquiers, Négocians & Courtiers s'assemblent à Rialto; ils en établissent le cours, qui reste fixé jusqu'au vendredi suivant."[25] The exchange brokers in the *conto* behaved in much the same way that, in our own time, representatives of the five major gold trading firms meet twice daily in London to "fix" the price of bullion.[26]

Once determined by these merchants, the exchange rates were then reported to the chancellor of the fair who had the responsibility of broadcasting this information. Originally he did so by displaying and distributing handwritten lists of the rates agreed on; multiple copies of these lists were prepared by clerks in his employ.[27] As a way both of lessening his need for

1 pt (Venice, 1682), I, 94–96. See also Hieronymus da Luca, *Tractato de Cambi e de Marchi per Lione* (Florence, 1517); and Fabiano Chiavari, *Tractatus de Cambijs* (Rome, 1557). This last work is frequently catalogued under the name "Fabiano, Genuensis" or "Fabiano, Genovese" rather than under the author's full name. The book was first published in 1555. For the author, see David Aurelius Perini, *Bibliographia Augustiniana cum Notis Biographicis: Scriptores Itali*, 4 vols (Florence, [1929–1938]), I, 225–226. Compare the discussion of the *conto* in Richard Ehrenberg, *Das Zeitalter der Fugger: Geldkapital und Creditverkehr im 16. Jahrhundert*, 2 vols (Jena, 1896), I, 74–78, 131, 230–236; P[aul] Huvelin, *Essai historique sur le droit des marchés & des foires* (Paris, 1897), pp. 568–577. For references to the conto at Antwerp, see Herman van der Wee, *The Growth of the Antwerp Market and the European Economy (Fourteenth–Sixteenth Centuries)*, 3 vols (The Hague, 1963), II, 366–367. The most extensive modern treatment of the subject runs throughout José-Gentil da Silva, *Banque et crédit en Italie au XVIIe siècle*, 2 vols (Paris, [1969]).

25 Jean Michel Benaven, *Le Caissier italien, ou l'art de connoitre les monnoies actuelles d'Italie . . .*, 2 vols ([Lyons], 1787–1789), I, 203. Compare, for Genoa, ibid., p. 248: "Les changes se reglent ordinairement les vendredis & samedis; mais à cause du retard trop ordinaire des courriers, ils se reglent presque toujours le samedi."

26 *The London Gold Market* ([London], 1980), p. 4. See also "London Gold Market Reopened for First Day's Trading Since '39," *The New York Times*, 23 Mar. 1954, pp. 35, 37; "London Gold Price Is Fixed at 4-Year High," *The New York Times*, 6 Aug. 1965, pp. 33, 35; "Gold fixers who fly the flag," *The Times* (London), 8 Sept. 1982, p. 1. See also the testimony in 1810 before the famous Bullion Committee by Aaron Asher Goldsmid, partner in Mocatta and Goldsmid, one of the five legendary London bullion brokerage houses. [GB, Parl., Commons, Select Committee on the High Price of Gold Bullion], *Report, Together with Minutes of Evidence, and Accounts, from the Select Committee on the High Price of Gold Bullion*, HC Sessional Papers, 1810, vol. III (Reports) ([London, 1810]), pp. 35–38, 38–43, 55–58, 65. Compare the picture of the assembled brokers meeting in the "Kursnoteringsværelset" (the exchange rate quotation room) in Johannes Werner, *Børsen: En Fremstilling i Billeder og Text af Københavns Børsbygnings Historie, 1619–1915* (Copenhagen, 1915), p. 156.

27 Da Silva, *Banque et crédit en Italie*, I, 81. See also, ibid., pp. 68–69. The Chancellor of the Genoese fairs kept the record of the exchange rates fixed at the conto. See Stefano Bianco, *Proportioni della quantità' discreta ridotte in prattica* (Naples, 1653); and José-Gentil da Silva and Ruggiero Romano, "L'Histoire des changes: Les foires de 'Bisenzone' de 1600 à 1650," *Annales: Histoire, Sciences Sociales*, XVII (July–Aug. 1962) 715–721. Compare, for Florence, the source cited by Mario Bernocchi, *Le monete della Repubblica Fiorentina*, Arte e Archeologia, Studi e Documenti, vols V–VII, XI, 4 vols (Florence, 1974–1978), IV, vi–vii.

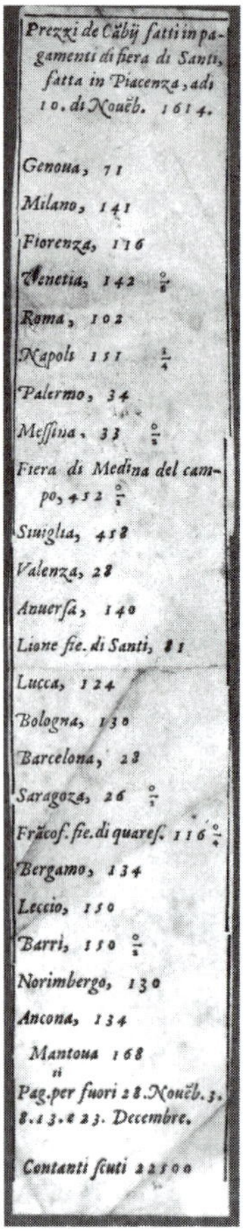
Prezzi de Cãbij fatti in pagamenti di fiera di Santi, fatta in Piacenza, adi 10. di Nouẽb. 1614.

Genoua, 71
Milano, 141
Fiorenza, 116
Venetia, 142 0/8
Roma, 102
Napoli 151 1/4
Palermo, 34
Messina, 33 0/2
Fiera di Medina del campo, 452 0/2
Siuiglia, 458
Valenza, 28
Anuersa, 140
Lione fie. di Santi, 81
Lucca, 124
Bologna, 130
Barcelona, 28
Saragoza, 26 0/2
Frãcof. fie. di quares. 116 0/4
Bergamo, 134
Leccio, 150
Barri, 150 0/2
Norimbergo, 130
Ancona, 134
Mantoua 168
Pag. per fuori 28. Nouẽb. 3. 8. 13. e 23. Decembre.

Contanti scuti 22500

Figure 6.4 Piacenza. Exchange rate current, 10 November 1614.
Photograph by A. J. Looyenga. Courtesy of the Vereniging Het Nederlandsch Economisch-Historisch Archief, Amsterdam.

copy clerks and of increasing the number of copies available for sale – as a way, thereby, of decreasing the cost of and of increasing the revenue for running the fair – some chancellor of some fair turned to the printing press. If this hypothesis is correct, then it was he who organized the printing and sales of the first exchange rate current, the *listini di cambi*.[28] It seems likely that the first of the published exchange rate currents were the product of the Lyons fairs, the creature of the merchant-bankers of Florence.[29]

While we have some indication that exchange rate currents were published at the Lyons fairs from the middle of the sixteenth century, the first known extant

28 Even though some scholars have known of these *listini di cambi*, they have not thought to consider them exchange rate currents in the way in which they are dealt with in this chapter. See, for instance, the treatment of them in Da Silva, *Banque et crédit en Italie*, II, 8–9 and elsewhere. Da Silva, ibid., II, 9, made the point that merchants returning from the fairs frequently retained a copy of the *listini di cambi* among their own records of the proceeding of the fairs, in their account books, the *scartafaci*. We know that merchants also bought extra copies to send to their colleagues abroad because many of them survive in collections of mercantile correspondence, received from some colleague abroad.

29 Unless, of course, they were first published at Antwerp for which there is some evidence that they appeared there as early as the 1540s. See McCusker, "Role of Antwerp."

For the exchange rate currents of Lyons, see McCusker and Gravesteijn, *Beginnings of Commercial and Financial Journalism*, pp. 353–362. Discussed in that chapter (ibid., pp. 361–362, n. 20) is evidence that an exchange rate current was published at Lyons at least as early as 1558. Compare Ehrenberg, *Das Zeitalter der Fugger*, II, 22–23; Hermann [P.] Bode, *Die Anfänge wirtschaftlicher Berichterstattung in der Presse: Eine volkswirtschaftliche Studie als Beitrag zur Geschichte des Zeitungswesens* (Pforzheim, 1908), pp. 8–10, especially n. 36. An 18th-century writer contended that the Italian bankers introduced into the Lyons fairs many practices from Bolzano. Le Sieur Bouthillier, *Le Banquier françois. Ou, la pratique des lettres de change suivant l'usage des principales places de France*, 2nd edn, rev. (Paris, 1727), p. 93. Whether they had anything to do with the publication of the exchange rate current we do not know.

My guess is influenced, in part, by what we know of the history of printing and publishing at Lyons during the last half of the 15th century. See Charles Perrat, "Barthélemy Buyer et les débuts de l'imprimerie à Lyon," *Humanisme et Renaissance*, II (1935), 103–121, 349–387; Lucien [P. V.] Febvre and Henri-Jean Martin, *The Coming of the Book: The Impact of Printing, 1450–1800*, trans. David Gerard, ed. Geoffrey Nowell-Smith and David Wootton (London, 1976), pp. 117–120; René Fédou, "Imprimerie et culture: La vie intellectuelle à Lyon avant l'apparition du livre, " and Jacqueline Roubert,

copy comes from the Easter Fair at Piacenza, 26 May 1581.[30] While it had a full title, it was not entirely printed; the first known extant copy that was entirely printed is from the All Saints' Fair, 12 November 1605 (compare figure 6.4).[31] Despite the change in the fairs from Genoese to Florentine control after 1621, later exchange rate currents published at Piacenza retained all of these characteristics.[32] The only alteration in their appearance was the addition of an imprint at the foot of the page beginning some time before 1628. The imprint simply indicated the name of the *cancelliere* (chancellor) of the fair. This had the impact, probably intended, of emphasizing the authenticity and, therefore, the reliability of the information published therein. The imprint also served to tell people where copies could be purchased. The exchange rate currents from the Bolzano "Fiera [di] Mezza Quares[ima]" of 1756 pictured in figure 6.5 and from Verona, dated 4 November 1633, in figure 6.15, display similar characteristics.[33]

More than one contemporary observer and later writer has commented that the bourses or exchanges of Europe functioned in effect as year-long fairs.[34] The same imperatives that suggested the wisdom of publishing the market information produced at the fairs seem to have provoked those who controlled the urban exchanges. The foreign exchange brokers of Genoa, Florence, Naples, Venice, and elsewhere appear to have been the ones in each of their cities who organized the collection and publication of the exchange

"La Situation de l'imprimerie lyonnaise à la fin du XVIIe siècle," in *Cinq études lyonnaises*, ed. H[enri]-J[ean] Martin, Histoire et Civilisation du Livre, no. 1. (Geneva and Paris, 1966), pp. 9–25, 77–111; and Eisenstein, *Printing Press as an Agent of Change*, I, 179, 404–405, 410.

30 Archivo Simón Ruiz, caja 203, no. 471, Archivo Histórico Provincial y Universitario, Universidad de Valladolid, Valladolid, Spain. See also McCusker and Gravesteijn, *Beginnings of Commercial and Financial Journalism*, pp. 387–392.

31 Archivio Fiere de' Cambi, 10, Archivio di Stato, Parma, Italy. Frank C. Spooner alerted me to the exchange rate currents in this collection and I am grateful to him for his help.

32 Compare the exchange rate currents published at the Novi fairs and at the Verona fair. McCusker and Gravesteijn, *Beginnings of Commercial and Financial Journalism*, pp. 379–386, 421–426.

33 See McCusker and Gravesteijn, *Beginnings of Commercial and Financial Journalism*, pp. 143–151, 421–426. The Bolzano exchange rate current was reprinted in a contemporary manual of foreign exchange practices. See Johann Caspar Herbach, *Europäische Wechselhandlung . . . auch eine General-Wechsel-Reduction* (Nuremberg, 1757), p. 11.

34 In Florence "there always is a market" according to the city's chronicler Giovanni Villani. Villani made this statement in explanation of why the 14th-century attempt to create a fair at Florence had failed. Villani, *Croniche . . . dopo la confusione della torre di Babello insino all' a 1338*, as quoted (in translation) in *Medieval Trade in the Mediterranean World*, ed. Robert S. Lopez and Irving W. Raymond (New York, 1955), p. 80, n. 21, but without a citation. This chronicle was first published at Venice in 1537. I have checked the best modern edition – Villani, *Cronica*, 8 vols in 4 pts (Florence, 1823) – but I have been unable to trace this quotation, whether through my own fault or the fault of this edition I am not sure. Compare the characterization of "il mercato di Rialto" at Venice as functioning as an international fair "tutti i giorni dell'anno." Gino Luzzatto, "Vi furono fiere a Venezia?", *Recueils de la Société Jean Bodin pour l'Histoire Comparative des Institutions*, V (1953), 278.

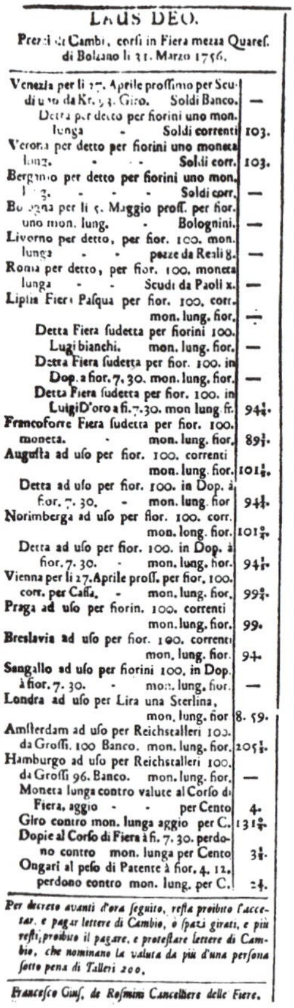

LAUS DEO.

Prezzi de' Cambi, corsi in Fiera mezza Quaref. di Bolzano li 31. Marzo 1756.

Venezia per li 27. Aprile proffimo per Scudi uno da Kr. 93. Giro. Soldi Banco.	—
Detta per detto per fiorini uno mon. lunga - Soldi correnti	103.
Verona per detto per fiorini uno moneta lung. - - - Soldi corr.	103.
Bergamo per detto per fiorini uno mon. lung. - - - Soldi corr.	—
Bologna per li 5. Maggio proff. per fior. uno mon. lung. - Bolognini.	—
Livorno per detto, per fior. 100. mon. lunga - - pezze da Reali 8.	—
Roma per detto, per fior. 100. moneta lunga - - Scudi da Paoli x.	—
Lipsia Fiera Pafqua per fior. 100. corr. mon. lung. fior.	—
Detta Fiera fudetta per fiorini 100. Luigi bianchi. mon. lung. fior.	—
Detta Fiera fudetta per fior. 100. in Dop. a fior. 7. 30. mon. lung. fior.	—
Detta Fiera fudetta per fior. 100. in LuigiD'oro a fi. 7. 30. mon lung fr.	94¼.
Francoforte Fiera fudetta per fior. 100. moneta. - mon. lung. fior.	89½.
Augufta ad ufo per fior. 100. correnti mon. lung. fior.	101½.
Detta ad ufo per fior. 100. in Dop. à fior. 7. 30. - mon. lung. fior	94¼.
Norimberga ad ufo per fior. 100. corr. mon. long. fior.	101¾.
Detta ad ufo per fior. 100. in Dop. à fior. 7. 30. - mon. lung. fior.	94½.
Vienna per li 27. Aprile proff. per fior. 100. corr. per Caffa. - mon. lung. fior.	99¾.
Praga ad ufo per fiorin. 100. correnti mon. lung. fior.	99.
Breslavia ad ufo per fior. 100. correnti mon. lung. fior.	94.
Sangallo ad ufo per fiorini 100. in Dop. à fior. 7. 30. - mon. lung. fior.	—
Londra ad ufo per Lira una Sterlina, mon. lung. fior	8. 59.
Amfterdam ad ufo per Reichstalleri 100. da Groffi. 100 Banco. mon. lung. fior.	205½.
Hamburgo ad ufo per Reichstalleri 100. da Groffi 96. Banco. mon. lung. fior.	—
Moneta lunga contro valute al Corfo di Fiera, aggio - - per Cento	4.
Giro contro mon. lunga aggio per C.	131¾.
Dopie al Corfo di Fiera à fi. 7. 30. perdono contro mon. lunga per Cento	3½.
Ongari al pefo di Patente à fior. 4. 12. perdono contro mon. lung. per C.	2¼.

Per decreto avanti d'ora feguito, refta proibito l'accettar, e pagar lettere di Cambio, ò fpazi girati, e più refti proibito il pagare, e proteftare lettere di Cambio, che nominano la valuta da più d'una perfona fotto pena di Talleri 200.

Francefco Giuf. de Rofmini Cancelliere delle Fiere.

Figure 6.5 Bolzano. Exchange rate current, 31 March 1756.
Photograph by A. J. Looyenga. Courtesy of the Vereniging Het Nederlandsch Economisch-Historisch Archief, Amsterdam.

rate currents.[35] They probably operated through the agency of the officers of the brokers' guild or, later, those who controlled the bourse. The basis for these assertions is largely the way in which the exchange rate currents later came to be published elsewhere in Europe. The presumption is that Northern Europeans not only borrowed the idea of the exchange rate current from Italians but also imitated the way in which its publication was organized. Although there is almost no direct evidence of who, in fact, published the exchange rate currents of the Italian cities, in the instance of Florence the earliest licenses to do so were sought by and awarded to a foreign exchange broker, thus lending some support to the hypothesis just enunciated.

The weekly or twice weekly exchange rate currents of seventeenth-century Italy are all very similar in their appearance. (See the ones from Venice, pictured in figure 6.6, Naples, in figure 6.13, and Verona, in figure 6.15.) Almost none of them had a title; indeed, the same was true in the eighteenth century. Some had an imprint; some did not. Some were completely printed; some were not. (Compare figure 6.6, figure 6.13, and figure 6.15 with the exchange rate currents from Bologna and Novi in figure 6.11 and figure 6.14.) But all consisted in the simple parallel lists of city names and numbers. Lacking title and obvious indication of the nature of their contents, their function has not always been clear. They have never before been identified – except, perhaps, by Paul Jacob Marperger – as financial newspapers.[36]

The Italian exchange rate currents of eighteenth-century Italy are even closer to one another in their appearance than were those of the seventeenth century. By the second third of the eighteenth century none of these weekly newspapers was fully printed – except one version of that of Leghorn – but they retained in every other way the character of the exchange rates currents

35 McCusker and Gravesteijn, *Beginnings of Commercial and Financial Journalism*, pp. 213–222, 189–200, 371–377, 393–420.
36 See n. 4 of this chapter.

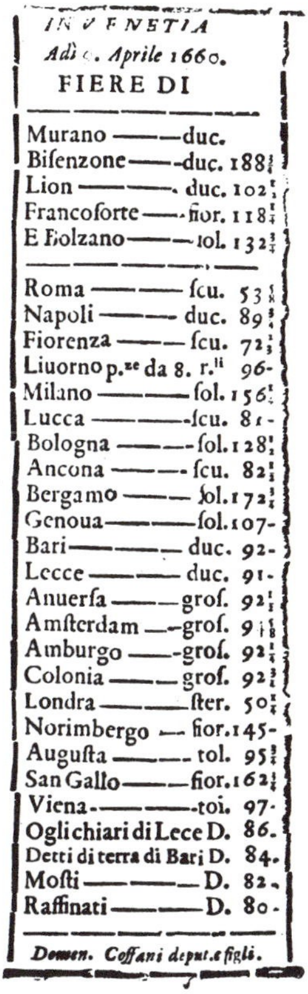

```
IN VENETIA
Adì 9. Aprile 1660.
FIERE DI

Murano ———duc.
Bifenzone———duc. 188½
Lion ———. duc. 102½
Francoforte———fior. 118½
E Bolzano———tol. 132½

Roma ———— fcu. 53½
Napoli ——— duc. 89½
Fiorenza ——— fcu. 72½
Liuorno p.ᵉ da 8. r.ˡⁱ 96-
Milano ———— fol. 156½
Lucca ———fcu. 81-
Bologna ———fol.128½
Ancona ——-. fcu. 82½
Bergamo ——— fol.172½
Genoua——————fol.107-
Bari——————— duc. 92-
Lecce ——— duc. 91-
Anuerfa———grof. 92½
Amfterdam —-grof. 9¼
Amburgo ——-grof. 92½
Colonia ——— grof. 92½
Londra———fter. 50½
Norimbergo —- fior.145-
Augufta——— tol. 95½
San Gallo———fior.162½
Viena.————toi. 97-
Oglichiaridi Lece D. 86.
Detti di terra di Bari D. 84.
Mofti———D. 82-
Raffinati———D. 80-

Domen. Coffani deput.e figli.
```

Figure 6.6 Venice. Exchange rate current, 9 April 1660.
Courtesy of the Museum Plantin-Moretus, Antwerp.

of the seventeenth century – and they added something new. What they all now included were small engraved vignettes showing various sights of the city. These city scenes were printed at the top of the page, under the dateline; beneath them were the usual lists of cities. The exception at Leghorn was the edition of the exchange rate current that was appended on Fridays to the weekly bills of entry published there.

For some cities, like Bergamo and Florence, the same scene was employed throughout the period for which we have examples; for others there were several scenes used either successively or interchangeably. Most of the scenes pictured have been identified but a few still remain in doubt. The one used at Florence was a view as from the west of the city. In the immediate foreground is a seated female figure with crown and scepter; just behind her is the Arno River and the walls of the city; above and behind the walls can be seen the towers of several of Florence's more notable buildings, from left to right, the Cappella dei Principi, the Cattedrale di Santa Maria del Fiore with its Campanile, the Bargello, and the Palazzo Vecchio (see figure 6.7; compare the view of Bergamo in figure 6.10). One of the several scenes used on the Genoa exchange rate current showed the Borsa on the Piazza Banchi, the location where the exchange brokers met to conduct their business (see figure 6.8). In an analogous fashion, and no doubt with the same point in mind, one of the scenes used on the exchange rate current of eighteenth-century Venice pictured the Campo San Giacomo di Rialto, the Piazza dei Mercanti, that city's center of trade and finance (see figure 6.9). By contrast, the Leghorn exchange rate current underscored the size, safety, and efficiency of its harbor (see figure 6.12). Many of those done for the Venetian exchange rate current remind the untutored eye of the city scenes painted in a far more sophisticated fashion by Canaletto. All reflect the eighteenth-century interest in such art work, here done in miniature.[37]

37 I am grateful to A. J. Looyenga for his help with these vignettes. He is preparing a comparative study of them. See his "Business and Urban Scenery: Illustrations in Eighteenth-Century Commercial Newspapers" (unpublished paper, in progress). Compare Guiliano Briganti, *The View Painters of Europe*, [trans. Pamela Waley] (London, 1970). For the Venetian vignettes, see also Pietro Zampetti, *I vedutisti veneziana del Settecento* (Venice,

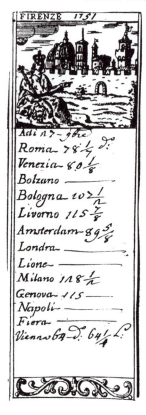

Figure 6.7 Florence. Exchange rate current,
27 November 1751.
Photograph by A. J. Looyenga. Courtesy of the
Vereniging Het Nederlandsch Economisch-
Historisch Archief, Amsterdam.

Just as the civic pride implicit in the incorporation of city scenes at the top of the exchange rate currents suggests to us, the publication of these early commercial and financial newspapers was important to the Italian economy. These newspapers were economically noteworthy at two levels: both as a business itself and as a service to other businessmen.

Even though these newspapers first developed as offshoots of the businesses that they served, they quickly became important enterprises in their own right. Businessmen continued to publish these newspapers because they made a profit from their publication.[38] Certainly they behaved as if they were engaged in profitable enterprises as when, for instance, they made the effort to obtain, to maintain, and to extend their monopolies. The same behavior is apparent from the buying and selling of such rights. The families that controlled the publication of the Florentine and Venetian currents – respectively, the Gigli and the Coffani (see figure 6.6) – expended considerable effort to obtain and to maintain their licenses over an extended period. The value of the monopoly for the publication of the London bills of entry rose in worth four-fold over the century-and-a-half from the 1660s to the 1820s. It follows

1967); and Katharine Baetjer and J. G. Links, *Canaletto* (New York, 1989). Baetjer and Links note that *vedutista*, like Canaletto, "did not find favor with academicians" (ibid., p. 274). It is for that reason, I presume, only one of the artists who drew and engraved these scenes identified himself, Isidoro Frezze of Naples. See McCusker and Gravesteijn, *Beginnings of Commercial and Financial Journalism*, p. 372. For Frezze, see Emmanuel Bénézit, *Dictionnaire critique et documentaire des peintres, sculpteurs, dessinateurs et graveurs de tous les temps et tous les pays*, rev. edn, 10 vols ([Paris], 1976), IV, 524.

38 "*The Wall Street Journal* does not provide this information [about prices] out of altruism or because it recognizes how important it is for the economy. Rather, it is led to provide this information by the very price system whose functioning it facilitates. It has found that it can achieve a larger and more profitable circulation by publishing these prices." Milton Friedman and Rose [D.] Friedman, *Free to Choose: A Personal Statement* (New York and London, 1980), p. 16. Compare Michael Harris, *London Newspapers in the Age of Walpole: A Study of the Origins of the Modern English Press* (London, 1986), p. 176, where he notes that the inclusion of such "tabular material" in general purpose newspapers beginning in the 1720s had become "a useful selling point."

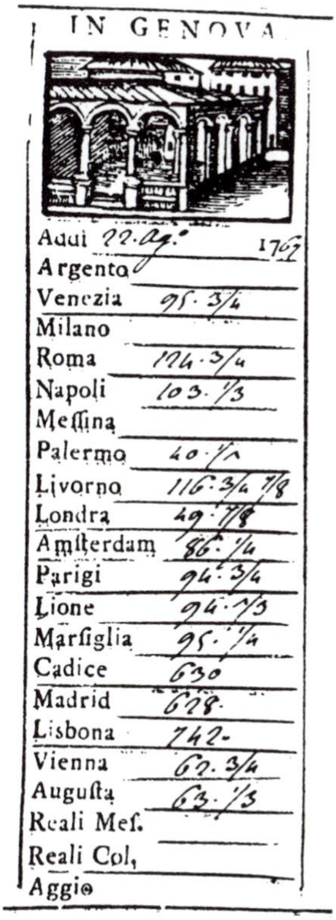

IN GENOVA

Aaui 22.24.	1767
Argento	
Venezia	95·3/4
Milano	
Roma	174·3/4
Napoli	103·1/3
Messina	
Palermo	40·1/2
Livorno	116·3/4 7/8
Londra	49·7/8
Amsterdam	86·1/4
Parigi	94·3/4
Lione	94·1/3
Marsiglia	95·1/4
Cadice	630
Madrid	678
Lisbona	742
Vienna	60·3/4
Augusta	63·1/3
Reali Mes.	
Reali Col.	
Aggio	

Figure 6.8 Genoa. Exchange rate current,
22 August 1767.
Photograph by A. J. Looyenga. Courtesy of the
Vereniging Het Nederlandsch Economisch-Historisch
Archief, Amsterdam.

that the publishers would be careful in the exercise of these rights and avoid actions – such as the publication of misinformation, either through design or carelessness – that might drive away customers or put their license at risk. We have evidence to confirm this conclusion.

Equally was this business enterprise important to those whom the publishers employed, especially the printers of these newspapers. The modern distinction between printers and publishers is, of course, not always applicable to the business of publishing in the seventeenth and eighteenth centuries. Frequently a printer was the one who by himself organized the entire production of a published work. The determining factor seems to have been who owned and distributed what came off the presses. Nevertheless, where we have enough information to make a determination, such distinctions appear to have operated in a modern way with regard to the publication of the early commercial and financial newspapers. The publishers or their deputies saw to the preparation of the text and the sale of the printed copies. They hired printers to do the printing.

The printing of these newspapers involved numerous individuals over the three centuries under question. Where we can identify them – and it has not been possible to identify more than two of them in Italy[39] – most printers seem to have been satisfied enough with their employment to have retained long-term connections with their newspapers. We can establish this directly from the records of publication and, less directly and not altogether quite so certainly, from such evidence as the continuity in the typefaces and ornaments used. This satisfaction implies a profitability in the arrangements for the printers. Indeed, such long-term contractual arrangements must have been very important to printers. Books may have been beautiful works of art that

39 The 1664 Bolzano commodity price current recorded in the imprint the name of the printer: "Per Carlo Ghirardi., Typogr. Arciduc." In the 1680s and 1690s the imprint of the Piacenza exchange rate current read "Piacenza nella Stampa Ducale del Bazachi." McCusker and Gravesteijn, *Beginnings of Commercial and Financial Journalism*, pp. 144, 388. I have not been able to trace Carlo Ghirardini (Gherardini?) nor il signor Bazachi elsewhere.

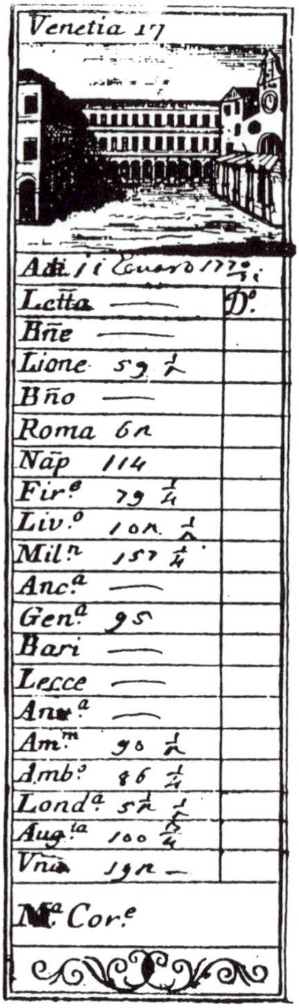

Figure 6.9 Venice. Exchange rate current, 11 January 1771. Photograph by A. J. Looyenga. Courtesy of the Chambre de Commerce et d'Industrie, Marseilles-Provence.

immortalized great printers like William Caxton (ca. 1421–1491) of London, Christophe Plantin (1514–1589) of Antwerp, and Aldus Manutius (1450–1515) of Venice, but such staples as government printing, job printing, and the printing of serials – like the newspapers discussed herein – kept many a smaller print shop in business.

The printing and publication of these newspapers was also important to individual businessmen and to the economy as a whole. Put most simply, these early commercial and financial newspapers distributed business news more efficiently than it had been promulgated in the past. It was more efficient because newspapers diffused information about developments in the economy more widely, more quickly, more regularly, and more reliably than did earlier modes of distribution. Businessmen were aware from the first of the important potential for their affairs of each of these factors. The financial press quickly became a power in its own right.[40]

Wider distribution of business news created more business. All of these newspapers served an implicit advertising function. They announced the availability of ships, insurance, and freight; they told readers where and at what price they could buy commodities and bills of exchange. Perhaps there is no better example of this than the way in which the English East India Company and the Dutch East India Company used the London and the Amsterdam commodity price currents. One thing that drove both companies in their trade with the East was the need to find things other than silver that they could use in trade there. Beginning as early as the 1670s, each company sent out copies of the local commodity price currents to try to generate increased business by telling people what was available and

---

40 Compare Wayne Parsons, *The Power of the Financial Press: Journalism and Economic Opinion in Britain and America* (Aldershot, Hampshire, 1989). See also H. J. Hoes, "Voorgeschiedenis en ontstaan van het *Financieele Dagblad*, 1796–1943," *Economisch- en Sociaal-Historisch Jaarboek*, XLIX (1986), 1–43; and David Kynaston, *"The Financial Times": A Centenary History* (London, 1988).

Bergamo Anno 1750		
Adi ~18bre	L.	D.
Per le Fiere di	S.	S.
Lione		
Bolzano in mta. L.		
Detto in Valute		10¾
Lipſia in Cor.		
Detta in Dop.		
Francfort in monet.		
AD USO		
Venezia Banco		104
Detta in Cor.		
Amſterdam banc.		89
Auguſta in Cor.		108
Detta in Dop.		
Detta in mta.		
Vienna in cor.		107
Milano		216
Roma in mta.		
Livorno		194
Genova Banco		
Detta in cor.		
Napoli		
Hamburg		
Londra		
Pariggi		
Genevra		

Figure 6.10 Bergamo. Exchange rate current, 21 October 1750.
Photograph by A. J. Looyenga. Courtesy of the Vereniging Het Nederlandsch Economisch-Historisch Archief, Amsterdam.

at what price. In an earlier era, the merchants of Venice obviously engaged in similar activity in Northern Europe. It is because of these activities that we can find large numbers of the commodity price currents of Venice in archives in The Netherlands and large numbers of the Amsterdam commodity price current in archives in Indonesia. Individual merchants, large companies, and the entire economy benefited from the increased business in commodity exports, freight contracts, insurance sales, and financial transactions engendered by these newspapers.

Quicker distribution of business news meant that businessmen could react more rapidly to changes in market conditions. Being the first to learn of a change in circumstances gave a businessman considerable competitive advantage. Filled with information gathered, published, distributed, and sent off in the post all in the same afternoon or evening, these business newspapers spread the news of prices and the rest much more quickly than in the past. The trend toward more frequent publication over the two centuries before 1780 reflected this push for an ever more rapid broadcasting of the most recent news. Merchants and traders always and everywhere rightly put great premium on having the "freshest advices."

Greater regularity in the distribution of business news meant considerably greater efficiency in the conduct of business. Produced and available at the same time on the same day of the week, week in and week out, these business newspapers provided information in routine ways that earlier modes never came close to duplicating. Knowledge of the trends in prices, exchange rates, shipping, and insurance, allowed merchants to make shrewd, authoritative choices about the best course of action. Planning replaced guessing. And one could be assured that, if necessary, next week's newspapers would permit an alteration of direction in the light of updated information. It would be there, regular as clockwork. One could count on it.

More reliable distribution of business news meant an introduction of greater certainty into the conduct of business. Reports of ships arriving and

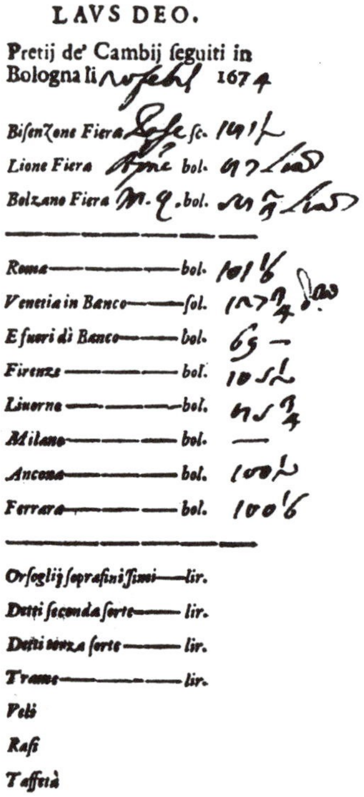

LAVS DEO.

Pretij de' Cambij feguiti in
Bologna li ~~febl~~ 1674

Bifenzone Fiera ~~...~~ fc. 141 ½

Lione Fiera ~~...~~ bol. 97 ...

Bolzano Fiera ~~...~~ bol. ...

Roma ———————— bol. 101 ½

Venetia in Banco ————— fol. 177 ...

E fuori di Banco ———— bol. 65 —

Firenze ———————— bol. 10 ...

Liuorno ———————— bol. ...

Milano ———————— bol. —

Ancona ———————— bol. 100 ...

Ferrara ———————— bol. 100 ⅙

Orfoglij foprafinißimi —— lir.

Detti feconda forte ——— lir.

Detti terza forte ———— lir.

Trame ——————— lir.

Veli

Rafi

Taffetà

Figure 6.11 Bologna. Exchange rate current, 20 February 1674.
Photograph by A. J. Looyenga. Courtesy of the Università Commerciale Luigi Bocconi, Istituto di Storia Economica, Milan.

departing had traditionally been passed on by other ship captains during the time they were in port. But such news sometimes never reached the party most concerned. Reports of prices and exchange rates sent on by some individual involved in the deal benefited considerably from the corroboration offered by the data published in a commodity price current or an exchange rate current. Business newspapers provided an independent, objective source of information. That everyone could rely on the business news published in the business press lent an element of certitude where before one could legitimately have had some doubts. Businessmen did not have to be in attendance on the Exchange every day; they no longer had to be quite so cautious about those with whom they dealt at a distance. Modes of business could be somewhat different than they had been, given the reliable reporting of business news in the business press.

However significant their impact on the affairs of individual businessmen, the effect of these developments on the entire economy was even more important. Greater individual productivity obviously created a potential for a more productive economy as a whole. Yet the collective impact of these changes was more than simply additive; they helped stimulate an expansion in the scope, in the scale, and in the efficiency of all economic activity. Transaction costs fell. These effects were especially significant to the regional Italian economies of early modern times as they struggled to find and maintain a role for themselves within a newly competitive environment.

Businessmen who had access to news from more markets, more quickly, more regularly, and more reliably than others could more easily expand their horizons. They could and did begin to extend themselves beyond local and regional customers and sources of supply and to stretch their reach abroad. A rise or fall in the price of goods somewhere else could be taken advantage of by the merchant who had hard information about what was happening. Merchants had always tried to weigh the comparative advantages of buying and selling in one market as opposed to another, but with the advent of business newspapers they had readily at hand the data necessary to do so

Figure 6.12 Leghorn. Exchange rate current, 24 January 1752.
Photograph by A. J. Looyenga. Courtesy of the Vereniging Het Nederlandsch Economisch-Historisch Archief, Amsterdam.

efficiently and profitably. It now became possible to buy in one market, ship to another, and transfer proceeds to a third in ways not likely before. A rise or a fall in the rate of exchange induced a similar calculation. The technical word for all this is, of course, arbitrage. Commercial and financial arbitrage dealings made for more efficient and more profitable markets. And, just as arbitrage transactions permitted a considerably wider scope for the businessman with access to the latest business news, so also did they widen the scope of the economy of which these businesses were a part.

The changes in the economy of Europe that were induced in part by the rise of the business press also influenced the scale of economic operations. It is clear now that the eighteenth century witnessed an increasing consolidation of the major trades into the hands of a smaller number of firms.[41] Economies of scale were one result. Obviously this development depended in part on the diminished risk to large-scale enterprises that resulted from the more efficient dissemination of business news. In turn, the scale economies of larger businesses made them and the economy of which they were a part more efficient, more profitable, and more powerful.

These developments had important consequences for the Italian economy. Much has been made of the decline of the Italian city states during the seventeenth and eighteenth centuries. Let us remind ourselves, however, that the economic decline was a relative one. Even after the center of world trade and finance had shifted out of the Mediterranean and into the North Atlantic world, much was still going on in Florence, Genoa, Milan, and Venice. Indeed, the beginning of the publication of information about markets, prices, and exchange rates may have been an early and prescient response by entrepreneurially minded Italian merchants to their changing fortunes. The business newspapers of these Italian cities may then be testimony both to the relative decline of these economies and to their continued vigor.

41 Jacob M. Price and Paul G. E. Clemens, "A Revolution of Scale in Overseas Trade: British Firms in the Chesapeake Trade, 1675–1775," *JEcH*, XLVII (Mar. 1987), 1–43; Kenneth [J.] Morgan, *Bristol and the Atlantic Trade in the Eighteenth Century* (Cambridge, Eng., 1993), pp. 157–160.

A 17 Settembre 1637 In Napoli	
Noui	158
Verona	158 $\frac{1}{2}$
Roma	157
Firenze	121 $\frac{1}{8}$
Venetia	90
Messina	107
Palermo	181
Cosenza	99
Montelione	99 $\frac{1}{2}$
Bari	98 $\frac{1}{4}$
Lecce	98 $\frac{1}{4}$
Aquila	98 $\frac{1}{4}$
Salerno	99 $\frac{1}{2}$
Fogia	
Lanciano	

Figure 6.13 Naples. Exchange rate current, 17 September 1637.
Photograph by A. J. Looyenga. Courtesy of the Università Commerciale Luigi Bocconi, Istituto di Storia Economica, Milan.

Commercial and financial markets continued to function at a high level, high enough not only to stimulate a demand for a business press but also to support a business press that displayed a certain style. The combination of substance and style still distinguishes much that is noteworthy in the Italian world. The commercial and financial newspapers of the region helped to perpetuate and to convey the continuing economic success of early modern Italy.

In closing, it is important to appreciate why these commercial and financial newspapers are significant for economic historians, too. They are important simply as a source of data about prices, exchange rates, shipping, and the rest. But they are not merely another source of such data. Given the essential character of these newspapers and what has been recounted about the way in which they were produced and published, it must be said that the data in them have to be assigned a particular primacy.

Take commodity prices, for instance. There are several sources for commodity prices over the centuries before the 1780s. Merchants' records, especially letters and accounts, have traditionally been accepted as the best of these sources if only because they more accurately reflect the market price. But the thoughtful economic historian will tell you that such prices in merchants' records potentially suffer from several defects, especially for the purposes to which they are frequently put, namely the construction of price series.[42]

Their chief fault is that we cannot be certain about the terms of the deal of which a particular price might be the only surviving testimony. One concern is the very nature of the transaction. Was it to be consummated immediately or was it to be completed at some future time? In other words, was the price recorded a cash price or, since the account was to be settled weeks or months later, did the price reflect an unstated charge for credit that both parties knew about but had no reason to record? As another example,

42 See, in this regard, John J. McCusker, "Price History: The International Context, Old and New" (paper presented at the conference on "Wage and Price History: The View from the Nordic Countries," Institutt for Økonomisk Historie, Universiteit i Bergen, 1988).

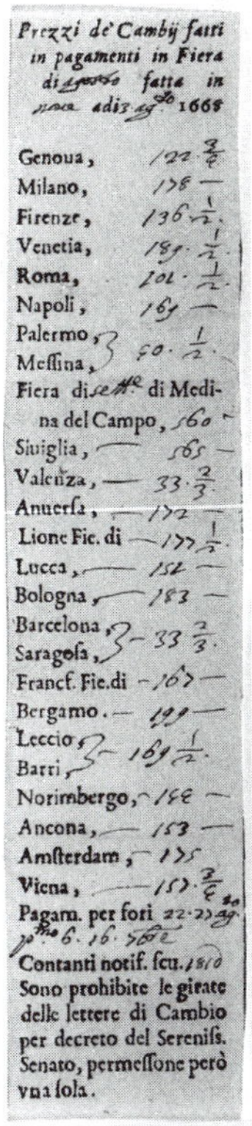

Prezzi de' Cambij fatti
in pagamenti in Fiera
di *** fatta in
**** adis *** 1668

Genoua,   *122 ⅖*
Milano,   *138 —*
Firenze,   *136 ½.*
Venetia,   *185 ¼.*
Roma,   *202 ½.*
Napoli,   *184 —*
Palermo,   ⎫
Meſſina,   ⎬ *50 ¼*
Fiera di *** di Medi-
na del Campo, *160*
Siuiglia,   *165*
Valeñza, — *33 ⅔.*
Anuerſa, — *172*
Lione Fie. di — *177 ½.*
Lucca, — *112*
Bologna, *183 —*
Barcelona, ⎫
Saragoſa, ⎬ *33 ⅔.*
Francf. Fie. di —*163 —*
Bergamo. — *101*
Leccio, ⎫
Barri, ⎬ *164 ½.*
Norimbergo, *168 —*
Ancona, — *153 —*
Amſterdam, — *135*
Viena, — *153 ⅖.*
Pagam. per fori *22-23 ½*
p.*** 6. 16 ſ ½.*
Contanti notif. ſcu. *1810*
Sono prohibite le gieate
delle lettere di Cambio
per decreto del Serenifs.
Senato, permeſſone però
vna ſola.

Figure 6.14 Novi. Exchange rate current, 3 August 1668.
Photograph by A. J. Looyenga. Courtesy of the Università
Commerciale Luigi Bocconi, Istituto di Storia
Economica, Milan.

did the two different prices that we see entered into an account book on the same day for the same commodity represent two different types of transactions – one for cash, another for credit – or did they reflect differences in the quality of the commodity sold? And then there is the problem of special prices for special customers or long-term institutional prices that reflect many forces at work besides the simple market forces. The impact of such considerations multiplies when one tries to link together prices from several different kinds of documents over an extended period of time. Price series based on such records can run into significant difficulties and may even distort the historical record.

All these warnings need not cause us to despair. They are enunciated here only to underscore the elegance of the data published in the commodity price currents. Published commodity prices are, by the very fact of their publication, more consistent and more reliable than those found elsewhere.[43]

Data derived from these commercial and financial newspapers can be considered consistent because the prices were quoted in the same way always – or, at the least, for very long periods of time. More importantly, any changes in the way they were quoted were noted in the source itself. Indeed, such prices were frequently referred to as being "the market price." This was particularly the case in contemporary discussions involving variations from "the market price" because of deviations from the market standard to take into account credit costs or differences in quality.

Data derived from these commercial and financial newspapers can be considered reliable because the publications were always produced under some form of scrutiny. Great care was taken in the collection of the data and in its publication. These newspapers were considered so important to each of the branches of business that they served that they were overseen, one way or another, by the business community. Rarely did publishers of any of these newspapers fall shy of the expected norm. When they did, their peers were quick to act to restore the balance. Contemporaries trusted the data published in them to be a completely accurate reporting of the market price simply

43 Similar problems concerning data series of exchange rates, shipping information, and statements about goods imported and exported are offset in much the same way.

because it was published; so may we. Where we have business newspapers it is no longer necessary to resort to surrogates for market prices; published price data were and are the market prices.[44]

Figure 6.15 Verona. Exchange rate current, 4 November 1633. Photograph by A. J. Looyenga. Courtesy of the Vereniging Het Nederlandsch Economisch-Historisch Archief, Amsterdam.

44 The only problem with all of this is that we do not have enough copies of many of these newspapers to make up series from which to derive long runs of data. Thus this chapter ends with a plea that readers notice and report any copies that they come across in their own research. Reports of hundred-year runs would be especially welcome but the location of any single number folded up in some merchant's letter will be happily acknowledged. A photocopy would be helpful. A full reference is a necessity. I will respond by collating such references and making them available on a reciprocal basis. Interested readers are invited to write the author at Trinity University, Department of History, San Antonio, Texas 78212.

7

THE BUSINESS PRESS IN
ENGLAND BEFORE 1775

Europe after about 1530 witnessed an explosion of business newspapers. Time has muffled the report. Before the end of the sixteenth century – and, therefore, well before the beginnings of what may be called the "political newspaper" – commercial and financial newspapers were being published in more than a half-dozen cities.[1] Amsterdam, Hamburg, Frankfurt, Rotterdam, Middelburg, and Venice had their commodity price currents; Antwerp its exchange current; London its bills of entry. This is a conservative accounting

1   The original version of this chapter was published in *The Library: Transactions of the Bibliographical Society*, 6th ser., VIII (Sept. 1986), 205–231. Copyright © 1986 by the Bibliographical Society. This revision is presented here with the permission of the Bibliographical Society.
    This chapter reports on continuing research into the history of European commercial and financial newspapers that has already resulted in several papers, articles, and two published books. The last two need to be specified more fully because, in the interests of economy, citations will be made to them in lieu of lengthy notes to the original sources: John J. McCusker, *European Bills of Entry and Marine Lists: Early Commercial Publications and the Origins of the Business Press* (Cambridge, Mass., 1985); John J. McCusker and Cora Gravesteijn, *The Beginnings of Commercial and Financial Journalism: The Commodity Price Currents, Exchange Rate Currents, and Money Currents of Early Modern Europe*, Nederlandsch Economisch-Historisch Archief, ser. III, no. 11 (Amsterdam, 1991). This chapter draws upon and adds to the materials concerning England assembled in both of those books; most references made below to other materials are in addition to what appears in them.
    I continue to be grateful for the help and support given me by the members of the Bibliographical Society, London, and other scholarly audiences who allowed me the benefit of their critical responses to versions of this chapter: Seminar on the History of the Book, Widener Library, Harvard University; American Antiquarian Society; Seminar on Economic History, Universität Erlangen-Nürnberg; Seminar on Economic History, Universiteit i Bergen; Graduate Seminar in Economic History, University of Exeter; Seminar in the Economic and Social History of Pre-Industrial England, Institute of Historical Research, University of London; Department of History, University of Minnesota; Annual Meeting of the Social Science History Association, Chicago, Ill.; and the Washington, DC, Area Economic History Seminar. I am also grateful to the American Council of Learned Societies, the National Endowment for the Humanities, the American Enterprise Institute, the American Antiquarian Society, the American Philosophical Society, the American Historical Association, the University of Maryland, the John Simon Guggenheim Memorial Foundation, and the Council for International Exchange of Scholars for a Fulbright Western European Research Fellowship.

since it is quite likely that additional research will add both to the number of cities in such a list and to the variety of newspapers published in each.

Additional research is called for because very few copies of these newspapers survive and there is little contemporary mention of them. So few survive because they were instantly ephemeral; the news in one of them was immediately superseded by the news published in the next number. Thus there was no reason to keep them; they were quickly discarded. Some of their characteristics – such as the lack of a title – makes accessioning into a library's collections the few that have survived almost impossible. Contemporaries made little mention of them because they were so common within the circle of those who used them as to be hardly worthy of comment. Everyone knew what a commodity price current was. And, to complete the circle, the lack of surviving copies renders almost unintelligible what little contemporaries did say about them.

Additional research is justified by the significance of these early business newspapers. They had importance as a source of economic information for contemporaries and they continue to have importance as a source of economic information for historians of the economy of the early modern Atlantic world. Indeed, given the published and therefore public nature of the information they broadcast, these early business newspapers are a uniquely valuable source. This essay has as its purpose to sum up what we know about the origins of the English business press so as to provide a starting point for all who would pursue the subject further.

◆　◆　◆　◆　◆

It is appropriate to begin this exposition by defining terms. Table 7.1 distinguishes between two broad types of early commercial and financial newspapers. The first type – the "current," to adapt a word in use at the time – published information produced by the local market. This information was essentially price data: the price of commodities; the price of foreign bills of exchange; the price of money; and the price of investments. Thus publishers produced "commodity price currents," "exchange rate currents," "money currents," and "stock exchange currents." The second type of newspaper published information about shipping and trade. The "bills of entry" recorded the shipment of commodities into and out of ports; the "marine list" published information about the arrivals and departures of cargo vessels. These two types are called "A" and "B" not only to group them and to designate the groups simply but also because doing so permits us to establish a category "C" to allow for the eventual incorporation into a single newspaper of more than one of the originally separate kinds of publication.

By defining what these newspapers were, we are better able to describe them and to distinguish them from what they were not. These were all newspapers in the classic, even modern meaning of that word. They were printed and published on a frequent, regular basis, as a commercial venture, for sale

Table 7.1 The types of early commercial and financial serial publications that appeared in Europe before 1775

A **Publications that reported on the local market ("currents"):**
  1 Commodity price currents:
    • General price currents
    • Specialized price currents
  2 Exchange rate currents
  3 Money currents
  4 Stock exchange currents
B **Publications that reported on overseas trade and shipping:**
  1 Bills of entry:
    • General bills
    • Specialized ("small") bills
  2 Marine lists
C **Publications that combined two or more of the elements from categories A and B:**
  1 Exchange rate current/stock exchange current
  2 Exchange rate current/marine list
  3 Exchange rate current/stock exchange current/marine list

Notes and sources:
This table is an adaptation of table 6.1 (q.v.).

to a paying public. An editor or publisher employed individuals who gathered the desired information. The editor assembled the information into a consistent format and sent the copy to a printer who set and printed the newspaper. It was then sold about town both to regular subscribers and to occasional purchasers. The newspaper appeared as a serial; that is, it was printed and distributed regularly, usually weekly, on the same day of the week, at the same time of the day. The publisher expected to make a profit over his costs, which many times included not only the sums owed to the people he employed but also charges involved in obtaining and keeping the license under which he operated.

Consequently there are several things that these newspapers were not. Most emphatically they were not the same as the lists of rates or prices that one merchant sent privately to another merchant, frequently as an addition to or insert in a letter. It is necessary to distinguish between a "price current" and a list of "prices current," the former public and published, the latter personal and private. Published information reported the doings on the exchange and in the market; private correspondence was one step removed from the market, no matter how dependent upon it the information may have been. By the eighteenth century many merchants had begun to use printed or partly printed forms to distribute to their correspondents lists of their own buying and selling prices. At the same time bankers had begun to use similar forms to tell their correspondents about exchange rates and stock prices. This is a key point because some of the very earliest published commodity price currents and exchange rate currents of the sixteenth and seventeenth centuries *looked like* the printed forms of the eighteenth century: they were only partly printed with the data filled in by hand. Whatever the similarity in appearance, however, the distinction is essential. Lists prepared by individuals for occasional distribution to their own customers recording their own offering prices are fundamentally different from published newspapers. This present discussion deals only with the published newspapers.[2]

None of the developments discussed herein was peculiarly English. The earliest traceable commodity price current was published at Antwerp before 1540 although it may have been modeled upon an even earlier Italian commodity price current, possibly Venetian.[3] Antwerp was also the place of publication of the first known exchange rate current dating from as early as the 1580s, although it too may have started concurrently with the Antwerp commodity price current in the 1540s.[4] While the dating of these earliest newspapers to within a century of the invention of moveable type printing may at first seem surprising, upon reflection it is quite understandable. Business people across the ages have pushed at the frontiers of information technology.[5]

While printing came to England fairly quickly, the first indication of the publication there of a business newspaper is the suggestion somewhat after the fact that the London bills of entry had their origins in the 1580s. The earliest extant copies of an English commodity price current are ones from London dating to the first and second decades of the seventeenth century. Both the London bills of entry and the London commodity price currents were appearing regularly by the 1620s and 1630s: the former daily, the latter weekly. Over the next several decades other business newspapers began to be

---

2   This distinction is fundamental to this discussion and is developed at length in both of the books cited in the previous note; readers are asked to return there for a full exposition of the argument. The distinction – and, as part of it, the recognition that the publications discussed herein were newspapers – is part of a determination formally arrived at it the United States in the 1830s and 1840s that had to do with the rate of postage to be charged for sending commercial newspapers through the mails. The Post Office consulted the Department of Justice for an opinion. See the letter from the Attorney General, Hugh S. Legaré, to the Postmaster General, Charles A. Wickliffe, dated 18 Mar. 1842, in [US, Department of Justice], *Official Opinions of the Attorney General of the United States*, ed. Benjamin F. Hall *et al.*, in progress (Washington, DC 1852 to date), IV, 10–13 (4 Opinions of the AG 10–13). Wickliffe published the opinion: [US, Laws and Statutes], *Laws and Regulations for the Government of the Post Office Department* (Washington, DC, 1843), [2nd pagination], pp. 19–21, n.

3   John J. McCusker, "The Role of Antwerp in the Emergence of Commercial and Financial Newspapers in Early Modern Europe," in *La Ville et la transmission des valeurs culturelles au bas Moyen Âge et aux temps modernes – Die Stade und die Übertragung von kulturelles Werten im Spätmittelalter und in die Neuzeit – Cities and the Transmission of Cultural Values in the Late Middle Ages and Early Modern Period*, Gemeentekrediet van België/Crédit Communal de Belgique, Collection Histoire, no. 96 (Brussels, 1996).

4   McCusker and Gravesteijn, *Beginnings of Commercial and Financial Journalism*, pp. 85–110.

5   Compare the argument expressed by Edmond Dummer, the developer of a packet boat service, quoted at the head of chapter eight of this book.

produced. Merchants not only subscribed to them for their own enlightenment but also sent them to overseas correspondents on a regular basis. Provision had been made for them in government and in law. The postal service and the taxing authorities had taken note of them and decisions had been made to limit charges levied against them in order to encourage them as part of government's general promotional efforts for the English economy. Well before 1700 business newspapers had become an essential part of English commerce and finance.

♦ ♦ ♦ ♦ ♦

At the turn of the eighteenth century there were four basic types of commercial and financial newspaper published at London during the business week: the bills of entry; the commodity price current; the marine list; and the exchange rate current. It is now possible to sketch the history of each of them.

BILLS OF ENTRY

The "bills of entry" were newspapers that published lists of commodities imported and exported at a given port of entry. In 1678, John Vernon, writing in his book *The Compleat Comptinghouse: or, the Young Lad . . . Instructed . . . in All the Mysteries of a Merchant*, described the newspaper in the following words:

> By a Custom-house Bill is meant a sheet of paper that comes out every day, (except Holy days); in which Paper there is set down all the Goods by themselves that are Imported; and all them that are Exported by themselves; and there is put the Place they are Imported from, the Merchant's Name that Imports them, and the quantity of Goods; and so for the Exportation of Goods.[6]

Vernon's description highlights for us two important characteristics of the bills of entry: the source of the information published in them and the market for them. The information in the newspaper came directly from the records of the customhouse. The importer or exporter of any commodity had to enter the details of the shipment at the customhouse. The handwritten docu-

---

6   Vernon, *The Compleat Comptinghouse: or, The Young Lad Taken from the Writing School, and Fully Instructed, by Way of Dialogue, in All the Mysteries of a Merchant* (London, 1678), p. 197. There is a lengthy contemporary description of the London bills of entry. John Houghton, ["Custom-House Bills"], *Collection for Improvement of Husbandry and Trade* (London), [I] (no. 6, 27 Apr. 1692), [p. 1]. Houghton's own weekly newspaper, a mix of general political and economic news combined with sober editorials and advertisements, deserves a study by itself. For a start in that direction, see D[ermot] T. O'Rourke, "John Houghton (1645–1705): Journalist, Apothecary and F.R.S.," *Pharmaceutical Historian: Newsletter of the British Society for the History of Pharmacy*, IX (Apr. 1979), 2–3. McCusker, *European Bills of Entry*, pp. 22, 31–32, 36, table 2, table 3, and table 4, record the basic data about the publishing history of the London bills of entry.

ment recording these details was called the "bills of entry." It was on the basis of this document that the Customs assessed duties. Customhouse clerks made several copies of the entries inwards and outwards for the internal administration of the Customs. Two of those copies are of special interest to historians of the Customs. One copy was sent on to the Exchequer and became the basis of the port books; after the mid-1690s another was sent to the office of the Inspector-General of Imports and Exports where his clerks compiled the data into the large, annual ledgers of imports and exports. The customhouse bills of entry were the primary fiscal and statistical documents of the Customs.

The bills of entry were also of great importance to businessmen. Importers and exporters were interested in the information that the bills contained so as to keep track of what their competition was doing. Shopkeepers were interested in the information in order to find out where to buy wholesale the things they sold retail. By longstanding tradition, all could apply to the customhouse clerks for handwritten copies of summaries of the bills of entry. Someone thought to print and publish these summaries, apparently as early as the reign of Queen Elizabeth I. The venture was such a success that in 1619 King James I found ready buyers for the office of Clerk of the Bills in two of his courtiers, Alexander Foster and Richard Grimes.

While the monopoly granted by letters patent in 1619 extended to all the ports of England and Wales, the newspaper was published at first only at London, and the London bills of entry published lists of imports and exports only for that port. It appeared, as Vernon said, every day the customhouse was open, six days a week excepting only public holidays. It was a single-sheet publication, circumscribed in size and shape by the amount of information generated by a day's business (see figure 7.1). Thus it grew in size as the trade of the port of London grew. By the 1770s the newspaper was considerably larger than those of a century earlier. As it grew in size, it acquired other characteristics that we associate with the more modern newspaper but it consistently lacked any title or any printer's information or publisher's imprint.

In addition to the growth in size, there were other changes. At some time in the seventeenth century the publisher of the London bills of entry started issuing several shorter compilations – called "small bills" – besides the complete or "general bills." Of these "small bills," the import bills listed only goods imported; the grocers' bills, only groceries; the linen bills, only linens; and the wine bills, only wines. Later, in the 1730s or 1740s, provincial publishers, operating under license from the holder of the monopoly, began to publish bills of entry at Liverpool and Bristol. The same thing happened at Dublin as early as the 1690s;[7] at Hull beginning as early as 1753; and at many other British ports

7   See *A Weekly Account of Goods Imported Into, and Exported Out Of the Port of Dublin*, 5 Feb. 1696/97. It is said in the imprint to have been printed for Robert Rowan and

London, Imported March 26. 1662 | **Num. 1**

Ostend, Geo. Robinson, 1 case wro. silks
Tho. Lowe —142 | dz. bridges thred
John Weeks — 87
Dunkirk, Rich. Henshaw, 50
Dan Porteue —60 | 2 | dz. wrd bro. thr
Newport, Fra. Swiftfoot, 230 | 19
— and —1400 | l. Linnen yarn
Hambro, Court Berens, 1200
Hen. Haswell, 2340 | 6 | C. Ells Germ. cloth
Will. Robinson —28
Jer. Foreman — 11
Iam. Stephens — 20
Edw. Neithrop — 17 | 6 | C. ells pac.
John Hall — 11 | 18 | canvas
1000 ells sletia, 11 | C. ells Hessens
Geo. Smith —12 | 12 C. Ells sletia
— and —14 | C. Ells pac. canvis
Chr. Paulsanton, 13 | 65 quar. wheat
Tob. Rainmorter, 40 | dz. hogs bristles
Geo. Mation — 48 | 50 C. Anniseeds
John Vandermarsh, 1 bale Ferret silk
Dort, — and 130 l. Incle
Ben. St John, 2 fats hemp
Will. Walker, 105 dz. sword blades
Pet. Mathews, 21 pieces Rhenish wine
Warehouse Henry Martin, 100 Ells Linnen
Will. Johnson, 50 C. white starch
Porto, Char. Thorold, 11 chests sugar
Geo. Webb, 5 M Oranges & Lemons
Will. Fisher—3 | tons Oyle
Peter Ducane— | 90 | bags shoomack
Peter Hublon, 7 | 21 | 24 C. Argoll
John Hublon, 8 | 120 C. hayberries
Bilboa, Jacob Luce —4 | bags cloth wooll
Sir Rich. Ford 10

Roch., Nich. Thurman, 15 | C. Kid skins
Will. Carbonell, 30 | in the hair
Anth. Philp, 3 tons French spirits
Geo. Toriano, 35 tons Vinegar ten bran
Flushing, John Weeks, 540 Ells Linnen
Mar. Bichas, 140 Ells Tapistry with silk
John Cranenberg, 50 l. wro. silk
Harlem, —and— 81 | peces stripe canvis
John Brunnick, 74 | 13 dz. Incle
Morlex, Peter Ducane —60 | ps Lockrams
James Hublon —120
James Lordell —70
Rich. Bryant —33 | 5 | C. Ells Vit.
Isaac Hublon—55 | 2 | (canvas
John Selby —78
Henry Norton —51
Roan, — and 18 C. Ells Norm. canvas
Court Berens—8 | tons French wine
Ioh. Goodman, 4
Dan. Oniell—2
James Littleton, 110 M. Teazels
15 Bowrell Raines
Matth. Rundull, 17 doz. buckroms
Tho. Papillon, 60 Reams paper
Rotterd. Fra. Miller, 6 doz. Incle
Tho. Saunders, 750 l. Annotto
Tho. Hessell, 1 fatt Hemp
James Burkin, 95 buff, 37 losh hydes
Chr. Eilers —250 | quarters wheat
Jacob Jacobson, 240
Adr. Beyer, 12 C. bacon
Peter Delme, 1 bale fallowre
80 C. Hemp, 3 cask Argoll
Abra. Wessell, —5 bales | Madder
Geo. Morris, 7 ba. mull

Cadiz, Will. Justice, 1 | C. wt. Eleph. Teeth
Dan. Hart—25 | 7 Civit cats
25 C. cork, 30 wey salt
Cane, John Owen, 480 | Reams paper
James Garron, 120 | 14 | C. Ells Norm.
Wil Carbonel, 518 | 17 | (canvas
Bream, John Cawston, 1500 Ells Ozenbrigs
Burdeaux Fra Young, 6 | tons French wine
Sam. Beak, 10
Tho Fincham, 75 C. cork, 6 ton Rapes
183 C. common Turpentine
Dublin, Andr. Loyd, 60 quar. maule, 2 bar. wheat
Norway, John Hockenhull, 1200 Deals, 350 balks
& spars, 25 load timber, 100 peces Asp
Amsterd. James Burkin, 200 quarters wheat
John Vandermarsh, 30 C. Hemp
Midland. Adr. Bever, 6 bales madder
Deip, Matth. Bell, certain smal wares
Bayon, Peter Delavier, 25 tons Rozin
Virginia, Chr. Conyers, 32 hhds Tobacco
New-Eng. Rich. Draper, 36 beaver skins
Barbados John Highland, 3 cask sugar

Eight ships Entred Inwards

The Virgin of Deip, John Biner a Rochell
Olive Branch of London, Arth. Bartlet a Cadiz
Grace of Dunkirk, Tho. Pepper a Dunkirk
Society of London, Chr. Clark a New-England
Constant Frendship of Lond. Ra. Story | a Virg
Margaret of London, Rob Fox—
Bilboa Merchant of Plym, Io. Tawton ab Alicant
St. Anne of Lorwick, Jens Torson a Norway

Exported March 26. 1662.

Legorn, Edw. Radcliff, 200 serges
Sam. Chamlet—42 | C. Tinn
Nich. Corcellis, 45 | 22 Min. bayes, 25 sayes, 25 perp.
Andrew West—24 | long — | clothes
Ralph Lee, 4 dou. bayes | 3 | short | 45 sayes
Hambro, James Young —4 | 23
John Dickens —5715 | l. cotton wooll
Chr. Joyner —10500
John Bullock, 20 C. shott
Ostend, Abra. Sutton —18 | spanish clothes
John Mascall —9 | 1 Kerse
Rob. Deluna—15 | serges
Jos. Almond —22
Rotterdam, Barn. Terisbew, 15 | 3 spanish clothes
Sir Thomas Bludworth, 10 fodder Lead
Ben. Delawne—13 | tons copperis
St. Vallery, Geo. Cowart —10
Bremen, James Smith —10
John Parsons, 2 tons beer
Rich. Spencer, 20 C. Lead
Gerard Reyers, 57 | doz. worsted— | hose, 40 perpet.
2 single bayes— | 130 dz. woolen | 4 stroudwaters
Canary, John South —9 | 14 | serges, 17 Norwich stuffs
Middlebro, John Hendricks —40
John Perry, 50 doz woollen hose
Dan. Ingram, 8 C. Tinn
Will. Bretton, 12 C. Glew
Flushing, Jam. Brailesford 36 castors
Abr Sutton 9 spanish 8 long clothes 6 double bayes
5 Perpets 50 grad cottons
John Mascall, 1 Kerse, 6 long clothes
Innernes, Allex. Blaire 8 C. wro. Iron 4 C. haberdashery 9 C. shot
40 doz. shoos 1 C. copper 31 doz woollen cards
Spain, Nich Warren 4 spanish cloths
Mallego, Rich. Young 85 gallons strong waters

Bilboa, John Cooke —60 | Perpets
Will. Read —68
Tho. Talcot —12 | 9 | double bayes
Isa Delillers — | 18
Ra. Gilbraham — | 18
Will Martin — | 190 doz. woollen hose
Bridges, John baptista —60
Anth. Bussell — | 15 castors
Dansick, Nev. Larimore —53 | 18 short cloths
Rob. Brooke — | 58 Cade sprats
Ireland, Will Hidges —11 | 10 paire blankets 16 ruggs
Rob. Vaulx 2 C. Pewter 1 | C. wro. Iron
New-England, Abr. Jeson —15
Geo. Roche 3 cask latten wyre
John Turner 26 single 18 miniking bays 20 serges
5 C. haberdashery 8 goad cottons
54 kersies North dozens
John Harwood [illegible] doz. Irish hose 5 C. wro. Iron 20 C.
Cordage 3 C. Bookes 8 goad cottons
35 kersies north dozens
Venice, Rob. Bale [illegible] coney skins
Edw. Falcliff 5 C. red [illegible] 25 C. white lead
Will Batten 5 | fodder lead
Burdeaux, Tho Shaw 5 | 7 C. stubb Nailes
Sam Farr 9 kersies
Cadiz, Nich. Warren 48 doz. wost. hose 29 double bays
40 Norwich stuffs
Sir John Fredrick 300 | l. wrought silks
Lixa, Abr Wessell —28 | 5 | miniking bays
Pet. Ducane —18
John Hublon 41 double | bays
Madera, Geo. Boyce 6 double —
Deip, Jonath Ash 18 single—
France, Fra. Fenly 12 M. horne plates 5 M. Ox bones

Goods Exported by Certificate.

Bilboa, Arth. Ingram 380 | callicoes
Tho Fox — 380
Patient Trot 448 l. bermoodus tobacco
John Jefferies 3309 | l. Virginia tobacco
Ireland, Rob Vaulx —1029
Tho. White —100
Fra. Boys 10 C. hopps
Hambro, Tho Saunders 95 | l. raw silk
Amsterdam, Hugh Forth 460
Char. Marisco 16 butts malligo
John Brunnick 232 C. saltpeter
France, Leven. Altham 1800 l. goats haire
Cadiz, Geo Falldero 39 C. white 18 C. muscovad sugar
Cane, Hen. Rayner 500 India hides
Spain, John Mansell, 300 Ells Linnen
New-England, Will Williams 95 Ells Linnen, 400 Ells canvas,
8 cambrick, 7 Lockrams

Ostend, Peter Delavier, 280 cow hides
Iacob Lucey, 554 l. Indico, 434 Reams paper
77 bundles brown paper, 12 C. spanish wooll
Amsterdam, Iohn Bagnall, 774 l. Aloes Epatica, 1365 l. Aloes succotr.
762 l. Mirrha, 894 l. seedlack
Mallego, Iohn Chevall, 23 C. Ells Germany Linnen

Four ships Entred Out.

The Phenix, Rich. Brown for Rotterdam
The Ann, Henry Barnard for Newport
The Peter, Henry Dunfrey, for Ireland & Cape Deverd
The Dove, Iohn Iohnson for Ouins[illegible]

Two ships cleared Out.

The St Peter, Will. Certain for Deip
The Blackmore, David beck for Hambro

Figure 7.1 London. Bills of entry, 26 March 1662.
House of Lords Record Office, London. Courtesy of the Clerk of the Records.

beginning in the early nineteenth century.[8] Almost all of these newspapers continued to be published down until the start of World War II.

Although these newspapers were widely sold and well known to contemporaries, few copies have survived from before the end of the eighteenth century. Yet several hundred copies of the London bills of entry were printed and published every day in the seventeenth and eighteenth centuries; they were subscribed to not only by individual merchants but also by such institutions as the London coffee houses and government agencies; and contemporaries turned them to good use both inside and outside of government. The records of the publishers show print orders for the general bills of 260 in 1672, 350 in 1676, and 500 in 1798. In 1696 there were eleven bound volumes of the London bills of entry in the library of the Lords of Trade. John Houghton extracted information from the newspaper and reprinted it in his own periodical, *A Collection for Improvement of Husbandry and Trade*, in the 1680s and 1690s; Charles Whitworth used it for his *A Register of the Trade of the Port of London; Specifying the Articles Imported and Exported* begun in 1777; and several compilations appear to have been based upon it, beginning as early as one prepared under the direction of Lionel Cranfield during his term of service as Surveyor-General of Customs, 1613–1618.[9] Nevertheless for the period through 1775 there are no known extant copies

Nathaniel Yapp "at the Custom-House." Beinecke Rare Book and Manuscripts Library, Yale University, New Haven, Conn. Compare the number for 23 July 1767 discussed in McCusker, *European Bills of Entry*, pp. 49–51. While this newspaper is otherwise completely unknown, there is some mention in the literature of a Dublin "Custom-House Printing-House." *A Catalogue of the Bradshaw Collection of Irish Books in the University Library Cambridge,* [ed. Charles E. Sayle], 3 vols (Cambridge, Eng., 1916), I, 65; Robert Munter, *A Dictionary of the Print Trade in Ireland, 1550–1775* (New York, 1988), pp. 139–140, 241–242.

8 Compare Josiah Tucker, *Four Tracts, Together with Two Sermons, on Political and Commercial Subjects* (Gloucester, Eng., 1774), p. 199: "let any one cast his Eye over the Bills of Exports from London, Bristol, Liverpool, Hull, Glasgow, etc. etc." This is the first mention I have seen of an 18th-century Glasgow bills of entry. His statement obviously suggests that they were published in other ports, too.

9 G[eorge] N. Clark, *Guide to English Commercial Statistics, 1696–1782*, Royal Historical Society, Guides and Handbooks, no. 1 (London, 1938), p. xii; R[ichard] H. Tawney, *Business and Politics under James I: Lionel Cranfield as Merchant and Minister* (Cambridge, Eng., 1958), pp. 129–130; and Menna Prestwich, *Cranfield: Politics and Profits under the Early Stuarts – The Career of Lionel Cranfield, Earl of Middlesex* (Oxford, 1966), pp. 156–157, 177, 182. Compare John J. McCusker, "The Current Value of English Exports, 1697 to 1800," *W&MQ*, 3rd ser., XXVIII (Oct. 1971), 607–628 – revised as chapter ten of the present book (esp. n. 4). See also [Dudley Digges], *The Defence of Trade. In a Letter to Sir Thomas Smith Knight, Governour of the East-India Companie, &c. From One of that Societie* (London, 1615), pp. 42, [51]. In 1770 the government used the record in the bills of entry of goods being shipped to Virginia to counter the impact of the colonists' non-importation movement. The bills of entry showed that the colonists were continuing to import almost all of the supposedly prohibited articles. The Earl of Hillsborough, the Sec. of State for the Colonies, "(very naturally) took great advantage [of this information] when the Committee of Merchants waited on him with a Copy of the Petition to Parliament." Perkins, Buchanan and Brown, at London, to Thomas Adams, at Richmond, 9 Apr. 1770, Adams Family Papers, 1672–1792, Virginia Historical Society, Richmond.

of any of the "small bills" and only a few hundred of the general London bills of entry.[10]

In lieu of surviving copies, the best sources of information about the newspaper are the records concerning the monopoly on its publication, especially the papers of two of the patent holders. King Charles II granted the monopoly to Andrew King in 1660 and he and his heirs held it until 1722. In that year it passed to the Lewis family, who published the newspaper for the next century. King was a London merchant originally engaged in the Spanish trade; he was knighted and given the patent for services rendered to the Royalist cause during the Civil War. The Lewises of Harpton Court were an important Welsh landed family. Members of the family held local and national governmental offices throughout the period and included Thomas Lewis, Member of Parliament for New Radnor Boroughs, and Henry Lewis, Collector of Customs in the port of London.[11] After the 1620s the patent never strayed far from the hands of men involved in trade.

Government support of the monopoly greatly enhanced the value of the patent. The patent guaranteed the active, if sometimes reluctant assistance of the Customs authorities both in providing access to the requisite information and in denying it to others. It protected the patent holder from any competition from either inside or outside the Customs establishment. In the seventeenth century the customhouse clerks who had previously obtained some of their income from the production of handwritten copies of the bills of entry mounted repeated but regularly unsuccessful campaigns to keep the right to produce at least some copies of the bills.[12] In the eighteenth century the publishers of some provincial political newspapers tried to improve their competitiveness by

---

10 In addition to the four identified in McCusker, *European Bills of Entry*, p. 36, table 4, a further one, dated 26 Mar. 1662, has been found in "House of Lords [Main] Papers, 28 Apr. 1662 to 1662 (Undated)," fol. 173, Main Papers, 19 May 1662, Sessional Papers, House of Lords, HLRO (see fig. 7.1), as have two lengthy series, one for the entire year 1669 and the other for the nineteen months from Aug. 1696 to Mar. 1698, both in the Beinecke Library. Compare Carolyn Nelson and Matthew Seccombe, *British Newspapers and Periodicals, 1641–1700: A Short-Title Catalogue of Serials Printed in England, Scotland, Ireland, and North America* (New York, 1987), pp. 171–180. Please note that the date of the first known number is 30 June 1660 (not 29 June). See also McCusker, *European Bills of Entry*, p. 37, fig. 2, for an illustration of the one dated 30 June 1660.
    All measurements of these early newspapers given in this chapter – and this book – are for the approximate size of the working surface (the type area plus any space allocated for insertions) at the widest point on either side of the sheet.
11 According to the Earl of Egmont (writing in 1729), "Mr. [Thomas] Lewis [was] a country gentleman, without place or pension, and one of the richest commoners in England." [GB, Historical Manuscripts Commission], *Manuscripts of the Earl of Egmont: Diary of Viscount Percival, Afterwards First Earl of Egmont*, 3 vols (London, 1920–1923), III, 337.
12 McCusker, *European Bills of Entry*, pp. 26–27 and n. 37, discusses this issue for the period after ca. 1660. We now know that such protests began almost immediately, as might well have been expected. See [London, Customhouse, Clerks], *An Abstract of the Grievances of the Poore Clerks of His Majesties Custome-house London, by Reason of Letters Pattents Lately Obtained for the Erecting of a New Office called the Office of the Clerke of the Bills* ([London, 1621]). There is a copy of this broadside in Guildhall Library, London. The petition was

obtaining and printing information about cargoes entered in at the custom-house for import or export. The battle was particularly fierce at Liverpool in the 1780s and early 1790s. Victory always went to the monopolist.

Government support involved more than defense of the monopoly, how-ever. The bills of entry – and, indeed, all of the newspapers discussed herein – were afforded special status in the mails. Instead of paying the usual postage rates, which were very high, newspapers paid nothing. They went free – free of postage, that is, but not quite free of any transportation costs. The car-riage of newspapers at fees to be arranged between publishers and themselves was a perquisite of the Clerks of the Roads, who administered the transport of the mails between the cities of England. Newspapers were, as a result, dis-tributed with the mails but at much less than the usual postage costs. As William, Lord Lowther, President of the Commissioners for Trade and Plantations, put it in 1835: "The principle of the Post-Office at its estab-lishment . . . was to afford advantage to trade and commerce. The direct rev-enue to be derived from the Post-Office was not the primary consideration."[13]

While all newspapers eventually came to share such treatment with regard to the post, government promotion of commercial newspapers went even further. When all other newspapers were brought within the scope of the Stamp Duty in 1712, business newspapers were exempted. The exemption extended to all the ones discussed in this chapter but the bills of entry were mentioned explicitly in the statute.[14] The distinction was based on the omission from business newspapers of any advertisements. One anomalous

presented to the House of Commons and debated in Mar. and Apr. 1621, as we learn from, among other sources, the notes of the debate kept by Thomas Barrington, MP. See [GB, Parl., 1621, Commons], *Commons Debates, 1621,* ed. Wallace Notestein, Frances Helen Relf, and Hartleys Simpson, 7 vols (New Haven, Conn., 1935), III, 1, 75, IV, 183, 212, VII, 347–348, 515–519. The text of the broadside is reprinted in those volumes (ibid., VII, 515–519). Compare the undated draft of a very similar but later petition in the Barrington Papers, Egerton MS 2651, fols 92r–v, BL, which was calendared in [GB, Historical Manuscripts Commission], *Seventh Reports of the Royal Commission on Historical Manuscripts,* 2 vols (London, 1879), I, 576. This petition is datable from internal evidence – the 1619 patent is said to have been obtained "about eight year since" – to around 1627. Earlier, in 1619, John Wolstenholme, one of the farmers of the Customs, had complained against the original patent and had been placed under house arrest. Letter of John Chamberlain, [at London], to Dudley Carleton, at The Hague, 1 Jan. 1619/20, SP 14/112, fol. 2r, PRO. Later in the 1620s the patent was transferred to Abraham Dawes. The Dawes patent, 30 Dec. 1628, C 66/2453, no. 4, PRO, recites the checkered history of the enterprise during the 1620s. See also Thomas Rymer, *Fœdera, conventiones, literæ, et cujuscumque generis acta publica, inter reges Angliæ,* 3rd edn, ed. Jean LeClerc and Paul de Rapin, 10 vols (The Hague, 1739–1745), VIII, pt iii, p. 25. Compare McCusker, *European Bills of Entry,* p. 22, table 2.

13 As quoted in McCusker, *European Bills of Entry,* pp. 34–35.
14 Act of 10 Anne, c. 19 (1712). Frederick Seaton Siebert, *Freedom of the Press in England, 1746–1766: The Rise and Decline of Government Controls* (Urbana, Ill., 1952), pp. 311, 314. Compare the 19th-century Act that reduced the stamp duties and which specifically exempted all of these kinds of newspapers: "Daily Accounts or Bills of Goods imported and exported . . . Papers containing any Lists of Prices Current, or . . . the Arrival . . . [of] Merchant Ships or Vessels, or any other Matter wholly of a Commercial Nature." Act of 6 and 7 William IV, c. 76, [last sec.] (1836).

result of this exemption is that studies of eighteenth-century English news-papers, which tend to be based on records created in the collection of the Stamp Duty, omit mention of almost all of these business newspapers.

The special status afforded the bills of entry – and, perhaps, the commodity price currents – included one other element that serves additionally to camou-flage them in the historical record. Until the very end of the seventeenth century the English government kept strict control of printing through a licensing procedure. It is not clear how and why it happened but the printer of the bills of entry was excused from this control, apparently by custom up to 1662, when the new "act for preventing the frequent abuses in printing" was brought in, and afterwards directly by proviso in that statute.[15] This exclusion would explain why these men are not picked up in the contem-porary lists of licensed printers. However inconvenient for historians, this exception served to cut printers' costs and, thereby, to promote the publica-tion of bills of entry still more.

The protection and promotion of the publication of the bills of entry had important implications for the significance of these newspapers both for the contemporary consumer and for the modern user. They served to enforce a certain care and caution in the gathering and presentation of the published data, which permitted merchants at the time and economic historians later to rely on their accuracy and consistency. At the very least, the grant of a monop-oly, by implying the possibility that it could be withdrawn, worked to prevent obvious misuse of the rights conferred. Only twice were the letters patent for the bills of entry withdrawn and the patent granted to others. It was done once in the time of the Commonwealth when the motives were purely political. On the other occasion it was withdrawn after complaints about the quality of the service rendered.[16] One expects that the lesson was not lost.

COMMODITY PRICE CURRENTS

The second of these four business newspapers, the commodity price current, published lists of commodities and the wholesale prices at which they sold

15 Act of 14 Charles II, c. 33, sec. xxii (1662). Aware of the probable consequences of the act for his enterprise, Andrew King, the patent holder, petitioned Parliament during the committee stage of the bill to have a clause inserted exempting his newspaper. See his petition and related materials in "House of Lords [Main] Papers, 28 Apr. 1662 to 1662 (Undated)," fols 167–173, Main Papers, 19 May 1662, Sessional Papers, House of Lords, HLRO. Although undated, King's petition (fol. 172) was written before 6 Mar. 1661/62, the date on which it was first read and considered in committee. See Committee Minute Books, I (1661–1664), pp. 166, 193, 231, 234, Records of Proceedings in Committees of the House of Lords, HLRO. In his petition King stated: "For the performing of the Printing work in this business there is, and alwais hath binn imployed a free printer, that is to say free of the Citty and of the Company of Stationers."
16 See "the humble petition of diverse Marchants and Tradesmen within the Cittie of London, and of the Clerkes of the Customhouse there" (1627), referred to above in n. 12 of this chapter.

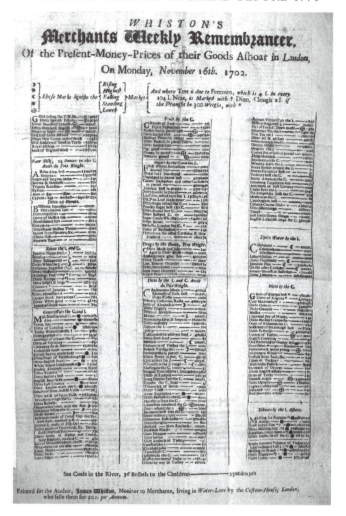

Figure 7.2a Whiston's Merchants Weekly Remembrancer, 16 November 1702 (obverse).
Courtesy of the
Vereniging Het Nederlandsch Economisch-Historisch Archief, Amsterdam.

on the local market. Writing roughly a century after it first appeared in England, Edward Hatton described it thus: "Price Current. A weekly account published in London, of the currant value of most commodities."[17] The earliest extant copies of the London commodity price current – four of them

---

17 Edward Hatton, *The Merchant's Magazine: or, Trade-Man's Treasury*, [2nd edn] (London, 1697), p. 236. Compare John Vernon: "A Price-Current, is a small piece of Paper that is printed in most Places where a trade is used, that specifies what all manner of Goods are

Figure 7.2b Whiston's Merchants Weekly Remembrancer, 16 November 1702 (reverse).
Courtesy of the
Vereniging Het Nederlandsch Economisch-Historisch Archief, Amsterdam.

dated between 1601 and 1614 – are not especially impressive.[18] They were only partly printed on two sides of a long, narrow sheet of paper (25 cm by 6 cm); the date and the prices were filled in by hand in pen and ink. Under a full title, *Pris des marchandises en Londres*, some ninety commodities were

worth; and that is so printed once every week, and sent by one Merchant to another."
Vernon, *Compleat Comptinghouse*, p. 196.

18 The most recent addition to this list, the one dated 5 Sept. 1601, was discovered in the overseas business papers of Lionel Cranfield, as calendared in [GB, Historical Manuscripts

crudely listed in alphabetical order. There was no imprint.[19] In these same years the *prijs-courantiers* of Amsterdam were producing a larger, completely printed, two-page list with title and imprint that gave the prices on the Amsterdam Exchange of many more commodities than did the considerably humbler publication emanating from London. Indeed if it were not that we possessed copies of more than one number published in the same format several years apart, legitimate doubt could be registered about whether these early examples were even a commodity price current. Nevertheless, by the 1630s London's commodity price current had come to rival that of Amsterdam and, by the end of the century, to better it (see figure 7.2). Viewed in this light, the history of the publication of the two cities' commodity price currents paralleled the changes in their comparative commercial and financial positions during the seventeenth century. (Table 7.2 records the basic data about the publishing history of the London commodity price currents down to 1775.)

An added reason to think that the earliest examples of the London commodity price current were a true published newspaper is the close control exercised at that period over all printing and publishing. Mention has already been made of this in connection with the history of the bills of entry. Printers were licensed; publishers of newspapers such as the bills of entry and commodity price currents sought grants of monopoly rights from the Crown and the City. Where extant copies of these publications fail us, it is the records of both the national and the local government that we can turn to learn what was happening. Thus, as at Amsterdam, all of the publishers of the London commodity price current that have been identified were licensed brokers. At Amsterdam they operated under cover of a city ordinance that not only granted them a monopoly to publish a commodity price current but also exercised strict control over it. Similar rights and obligations seem to have operated in London although, given the traditional tensions between

Commission], *Calendar of the Manuscripts of . . . Lord Sackville . . .*, ed. A[rthur] P. Newton and F[rederick] J. Fisher, 2 vols (London, 1940–1966), I, 43–44. As of Oct. 1995 it could no longer be located in the collection, now in the Centre for Kentish Studies (formerly the Kent County Archives Office), County Hall, Maidstone, Kent. Letter from Donald Gibson to the author, 10 Oct. 1995.

Note that the date for the third number of this newspaper given in table 7.2 differs from the date assigned it in McCusker and Gravesteijn, *Beginnings of Commercial and Financial Journalism*, p. 308. Compare, also, the dating in the original version of this chapter. Further research has convinced me that the usual day of publication was Thursday through 1669. Exceptions, like that of Friday, 9 Dec. 1614, occurred, but for explainable reasons. I suspect that, in 1614, Thursday, 8 Dec., was observed as a holy day; as a consequence the publishers produced the paper a day later. See John Dowden, *The Church Year and Kalendar* (Cambridge, Eng., 1910), pp. 52–56, 148–153; C[hristopher] R. Cheney, *Handbook of Dates for Students of English History, Royal Historical Society*, Guides and Handbooks, No. 4 (London, 1961), p. 55. Compare Castaing in the *Course of the Exchange* for 10 Apr. 1718: "Thursday . . . Tomorrow being Good Friday."

19 Although in the issue dated 15 Mar. 1610 the initials "M . . . M" appear in the top line along with the year. They may have been the initials of the publisher's name.

Crown and City, in a somewhat different way. In the seventeenth century the publishers sought and received grants of letters patent from the King to establish their monopoly.[20] They complied with City regulations about the price they charged – and were empowered to display the City's arms in the masthead of their newspaper as a result.[21] Presumably, too, the printers they employed fell within the Acts regulating printing. At least until the end of the century, ancient rights and privileges circumscribed what was possible.[22] It would have been impossible, therefore, to have sustained publication of an extra-legal *Pris des marchandises en Londres*.

Much of this changed during the two decades after 1680 when controls of the press were ended. Nothing testifies better to this change than the sudden proliferation of published business newspapers including several different commodity price currents. Yet the publishers continued to be licensed brokers and so were not without some constraints upon their actions. Indeed, there may have been even greater constraints than before, exercised this time by the need to satisfy their customers. Should one commodity price current prove to be unreliable, London merchants had others from which to choose, others to whom to give their custom. There is even a suggestion that one group of brokers later threatened to start a new commodity price current

20 See, e.g., the letters patent issued to John Day, 1 Nov. 1634, C 66/2650, no. 3, PRO. See also Rymer, *Fædera*, 3rd edn, ed. LeClerc and Rapin, VIII, pt iv, pp. 92–93. Compare the patent issued to Humphrey Brome, 7 Aug. 1660, C 66/2946, no. 9, PRO. Both Day (ca. 1595–1660) and Brome (ca. 1628–1667) were members of the Fishmongers' Company: Day apprenticed in 1614 and freed in 1621, Brome apprenticed to Day in 1647 and freed in 1655. Register of Freedom Admissions, 1614–1650 (MS 5576/1), pp. 5, 94, 411, Register of Freedom Admissions, 1650–1698 (MS 5576/2), p. 64, and Indexes to Freedom Admissions, 1592–1752 (MS 5587/1), s.v., Fishmongers' Company Archives, Archives of the City Livery Companies, Guildhall Library, London. In a tract that he authored in 1646, Day spoke of his "great imployment, as the sole printing of the Bills of Prices, to the advance of Trade, encreased of Custome, great benefit to the Merchants in generall, to the Honour of the Citie, and to the profit of the State many thousands pounds per annum." John Day, The *Modest Vindication of John Day of London Merchant* . . . (London, 1646), p. 4. The registered copy of Day's will is in PROB 11/300, fol. 167v–168r, PRO. It is dated 20 Aug. 1660. Just as he proclaimed, his newspaper was known and used by the London merchant community. "Here enclosed I send you one of John Day's bills of prices . . ." John Paige, at London, to William Clerke, at Tenerife in the Canary Islands, 17 July 1654, in *The Letters of John Paige, London Merchant, 1648–1658*, ed. George F. Steckley, London Record Society Publications, vol. XXI (London, 1984), p. 110. The registered copy of Brome's will is in PROB 11/325, fol. 232v–232r, PRO. It is dated 27 Oct. 1667. He died the next month. He does not appear to have been related to the London printer Henry Brome, fl. 1656–1681. Henry R. Plomer, *A Dictionary of the Booksellers and Printers Who Were at Work in England, Scotland and Ireland from 1641 to 1667* (London, 1968), p. 34.

21 See, e.g., the entries concerning John Day, 27 Feb. 1635/36, and Humphrey Brome, 27 Sept. 1660, in the Repertories of the Court of Aldermen, vol. L, fol. 129v–130r, and vol. LXVII, fol. 136v, Corporation of London Records Office, London. Compare Charles Welch, "The City Printers," *Transactions of the Bibliographical Society*, XIV: 1915–1917 (1919), 234, 236.

22 Compare the situation of the London bills of entry which, despite its privileged condition, was still subject to the oversight of the authorities. McCusker, *European Bills of Entry*, pp. 33–35.

to compete with an existing one with which there was some dissatisfaction. The visible hand of government was replaced by the invisible hand of the market as the agency that ensured due care in the publication of the London commodity price current.[23]

By the middle years of the 1690s there were four different commodity price currents being published at London (see table 7.2). They resembled one another in many ways. All were completely printed in two or three columns on both sides of a single sheet of paper. They all had proper titles and a full imprint at the foot of the second side (see figures 7.2a and 7.2b). They were all weekly newspapers and, in so far as we know, cost the same per copy to buy both individually and on a subscription basis. French, which seems to have been the language of the London commodity price current in its first decades, continued to be important throughout the period. In the 1690s one of the four was published exclusively in that language and the others had parallel French translations. Contemporary comments tend to confirm the impression that there was not much to distinguish among them, while contemporary records also reveal that merchants and others bought more than one of these newspapers if only because they appeared on different days of the week. In 1696 the Lords of Trade had on its library shelves bound volumes of some of these newspapers, including two of Samuel Proctor's and three of James Whiston's, having subscribed to them regularly over the years.[24]

The competition among the several publishers seems to have continued down at least into the 1720s but something happened at that point which is very difficult to explain. For some fifty years, between roughly 1725 and 1775, there are almost no known extant numbers of any London commodity price current. If it were not for the very occasional mention of the commodity price current in contemporary sources and the recent discovery of a short

23 Other publications – especially the more general, political newspapers – occasionally published commodity prices, as well as other bits of financial and commercial news; this became increasingly common as time went on. Michael Harris – in his magnificent study of the London press – *London Newspapers in the Age of Walpole: A Study of the Origins of the Modern English Press* (London, 1986), p. 176, calls them "a useful selling point." Lacking any official character, these utterances neither benefited from nor suffered from the effects of government promotion or regulation. One of the earliest of these was *The Mercury* (or, alternatively, *The City Mercury and The Country Mercury*). Copies of issues for 1667–1681 are at press mark C.40.l.1, BL, and in the Charles Burney Collection of Newspapers, vol. 75a, BL; SP 116/1, PRO, and SP 9/251/146, PRO; and the John Nichols Newspaper Collection, Bodleian Library, University of Oxford. See also J[acob] M. Price, "Notes on Some London Price-Currents, 1667–1715," *EcHR*, 2nd ser., VII (Dec. 1954), 242–243.

24 John J. McCusker, *Money and Exchange in Europe and America, 1600–1775: A Handbook*, [2nd edn] (Chapel Hill, NC, [1992]), p. 324, n. 1.; receipts for subscriptions, dated 21 May 1684, 26 Jan. 1688/89, 9 Feb. 1688/89, Apr. 1690, 30 Jan. 1690/91, 14 Feb. 1692/93, 27 Feb. 1693/94, 30 Jan. 1694/95, 26 July 1696, William Blathwayt Papers, 1631–1722, vol. XX, nos 3, 9–10, 13, vol. XLI, nos 4–6, Colonial Williamsburg Foundation Library, Williamsburg, Va.

run of the *London Price Current on The Royal Exchange* for 1754, one could easily have been convinced that there was no such newspaper published at London during those five decades. Why the number of commodity price currents published at London fell off so fast and so far after about 1720 and why one can find almost no copies from this period are questions for which there is as yet no satisfactory answer. *The London Price Current* published by William Prince began production in April 1776 and continued to be issued until nearly the end of the nineteenth century.[25]

Prince proclaimed in his masthead that the information he published was "regulated by near fifty eminent brokers, factors, and others."[26] His statement underscores the point made above about how important, in the name of accuracy and reliability, the exercise of some control over the newspaper was thought to be. Prince's invocation of nearly fifty prominent people as having some interest in and oversight of his enterprise is reminiscent of a similar pronouncement in the Amsterdam commodity price current almost two centuries earlier. The brokers who oversaw its publication (the *prijs-courantiers*) repeated in each number that it was "checked over by the five of us" – "Ghecorrigeert by ons vyven."[27] It also suggests the broad basis of support for the newspaper and hints at a possible reason for the decline over the years in the number of London commodity price currents that were published. Perhaps the London brokers, in uniting behind one such publication, had thereby forced any others into an untenable position: they had no backers and they had no customers. Despite the paucity of known copies, there appears to have been a London commodity price current printed and sold in the City from 1601 or before until 1775 and beyond.

Apparently there were no commodity price currents published in the provinces. The nearest thing to a provincial commodity price current of which mention has been found was a newspaper that combined a marine list and a list of commodity prices that appeared at Liverpool for a short while in the mid-1760s. It disappeared quickly, however, because, as one contemporary commentator put it, the commodity prices in it "proved often very incorrect."[28] The situation in England was analogous to that in the Low

---

25 McCusker and Gravesteijn, *Beginnings of Commercial and Financial Journalism*, p. 335, n. 30.
26 By 1788, according to Thomas Irving, Inspector-General of Imports and Exports of Great Britain, the London commodity price currents were being published by "Two different Societies of Brokers belonging to Lloyd's Coffee House." "Memorandum" to the "Supplement to Account No 10," in [GB, Parl., Commons], *Report of the Lords of the Committee of [the Privy] Council ... [for] Trade and Foreign Plantations ... Concerning the Present State of the Trade to Africa*, HC Sessional Papers to 1801, Accounts and Papers, vols XXVI, no. 646a, 6 pts [Lambert 4132] ([London, 1789]), pt iv: "Accounts." For Irving, see John J. McCusker, "Colonial Civil Servant and Counter-Revolutionary: Thomas Irving (1738–1800) in Boston, Charleston, and London," *Perspectives in American History*, XII (1979), 314–350 – revised as chapter nine of the present book.
27 McCusker and Gravesteijn, *Beginnings of Commercial and Financial Journalism*, p. 44, quoting from *Cours van Negotie* (Amsterdam), 23 Nov. 1609.
28 As quoted in McCusker, *European Bills of Entry*, p. 47.

Countries. The Amsterdam commodity price current had no competition because the Amsterdam market dominated the region.[29] In a parallel fashion, London wholesale prices – and, therefore, the London commodity price current – constituted the point of reference for all in England.[30]

The sudden burgeoning of newspaper publishing consequent upon the effective lifting of censorship controls in the 1680s and 1690s brought with it the establishment of two other English business newspapers. Intriguingly both of these newspapers continue to be published today, the first of them using once again its ancient title. They are *Lloyd's List*, a marine list, founded sometime before January 1692, and *The Course of the Exchange*, an exchange rate and stock exchange current, initially published in March 1697, the modern descendant of which is called the *Daily Official List*.

MARINE LISTS

A marine list published information about the arrival and departure of vessels at various ports at home and abroad. *Lloyd's List*, the first known marine list, was the work of one man, Edward Lloyd, the proprietor of a London coffee house. While it is one of the better known of England's business newspa-

29 See McCusker, "Role of Antwerp," for an elaboration of this argument.
30 Thus see the statement by one commentator at Newcastle upon Tyne in 1740: "London . . . governs the value of all grain in England." *Newcastle Journal*, 19 July 1740, as quoted in Jeremy [M.] Black, *The English Press in the Eighteenth Century* (London, 1987), p. 69. London's emergence by the 16th century as the "price-making center" for much of the English grain trade has been traced by Norman Scott Brien Gras, *The Evolution of the English Corn Market from the Twelfth to the Eighteenth Century*, Harvard Economic Studies, XIII (Cambridge, Mass., 1915), 95–129 (quotation, p. 123). Compare Peter J. Bowden, *Economic Change: Prices, Wages, Profits and Rents, 1500–1750*, vol. I of *Chapters from The Cambridge Agricultural History of England*, ed. Joan Thirsk (Cambridge, Eng., [1990]), pp. 33–35, 210–211, and elsewhere. One consequence was an empire-wide demand for these newspapers. See, for instance, Thomas Fitch, at Boston, to Thomas Crouch and Company, at London, 15 Mar. 1706/07, Thomas Fitch Letterbook, 1703–1711, p. 182, American Antiquarian Society, Worcester, Massachusetts; of James Logan, at Philadelphia, to John Askew, at London, 28 May 1713, James Logan, Copies of Letters Sent, 1712–1715, p. 113, Logan Papers, 1664–1871, Historical Society of Pennsylvania, Philadelphia. Aware of all this, we can better appreciate the significance in the early 18th century of the announcement in the pages of the *Boston News-Letter* that the editor had available for sale in his office copies of London newspapers, including the bills of entry and the commodity price currents (e.g., 30 July 1705, 10 June 1706). Compare the discussion in Ian K. Steele's immensely insightful study, *The English Atlantic, 1675–1740: An Exploration of Communication and Continuity* (New York, 1986), pp. 213–228 and passim. Concerning the availability of English newspapers generally in the colonies, compare David Cressy, *Coming Over: Migration and Communication between England and New England in the Seventeenth Century* (Cambridge, Eng., 1986), pp. 235–262, and Carolyn Nelson, "American Readership of Early British Serials," in *Serials and Their Readers, 1620–1914*, ed. Robin Myers and Michael Harris (Winchester, 1993), pp. 27–44.

According to Abbott Payson Usher, *The History of the Grain Trade in France, 1400–1710*, Harvard Economic Studies, IX (Cambridge, Mass., 1913), 45–125 and elsewhere, Paris had become the center of the French grain trade fully a century before London assumed that same role for England. Compare Gras, op. cit., p. 122. Both Usher and Gras were influenced in their analyses by the theories of Johann Heinrich von Thünen (1783–1850). See Thünen's *Der isolirte Staat in Beziehung auf Landwirtschaft und*

pers (if only because its continued publication has interested people in its early history), much about its origins has only recently been clarified as a result of the discovery of numerous very early numbers. Lloyd's marine list was pretty much what he described it as being in his early running title: a listing of *Ships Arrived at, and Departed from several Ports of England . . . [and] An Account of what English Shipping and Foreign Ships for England, I hear of in Foreign Ports*. It is no wonder then that someone, perhaps Lloyd or perhaps one of his successors as editor and publisher, shortened the title sometime between 1704 and 1741.[31]

The earliest numbers of *Lloyd's List* – if we may be permitted the anachronistic use of the shorter title – were printed on one side of a single sheet of paper. Like the London commodity price currents, it appeared weekly, for sale by subscription or to individual purchasers. Like them, too, and as distinct from the bills of entry, *Lloyd's List* had both a title and an imprint that spelled out who published it and where it could be purchased. In 1735 major changes were effected in the composition and issuance of the newspaper when it began to be published twice a week and when, with the marine list proper relegated to the second side of the sheet, the front page was given over to publishing other business news. That "other business news" was, in fact, a wholesale copying of the *Course of the Exchange*, about which more information can be found below (see figure 7.3; compare figures 7.4a and 7.4b). Obviously the editor of *Lloyd's List* sought to strengthen his competitive position by combining his marine list with an exchange rate and stock exchange current and changing the frequency of appearance to compete directly with the very successful *Course of the Exchange*. *Lloyd's List* continued to be published in much the same manner down through the next century – as it continues to be into our own.

Richard Baker, the editor of *Lloyd's List* in 1735 who instituted the changes just mentioned, was also Master of Lloyd's, the association of marine insurers, as had been his predecessors. Under Edward Lloyd's leadership, helped by his publication of his newspaper, the London marine insurance industry had coalesced around his coffee house. While the extent of that development was extraordinary, its nature was not. Many of the coffee houses of London were recognized gathering places for businessmen with specialized interests, and Lloyd's coffee house was a place where those concerned in shipping sought each other out. It was certainly these men who provided the facilities upon which Lloyd initially depended for the information he published, although

---

Nationalökonomie, oder Untersuchungen über den Einfluss, den die Getreidepreise, der Reichthum des Bodens und die Abgaben auf den Ackerbau ausüben, 3rd edn, ed. Hermann Schumacher-Zarchlin, 3 vols in 4 pts (Berlin, 1875).

31 McCusker, *European Bills of Entry*, pp. 56–57, table 7, records some of the basic data about the publishing history of the London marine list. See ibid., p. 54, fig. 5, for an illustration of the one dated 22 Dec. 1696. See also John J. McCusker, "The Early History of *Lloyd's List*," *Historical Research: The Bulletin of the Institute of Historical Research*, LXIV (Oct. 1991), 427–431.

Lloyd's LIST. Nº 848

TUESDAY, January 3. 1743

THIS List, which was formerly publish'd once a Week, will now continue to be publish'd every *Tuesday* and *Friday*, with the Addition of the Stocks Course of Exchange, &c.——Subscriptions are taken in at Three Shillings per Quarter, at the Bar of *Lloyd's* Coffee-House in *Lombard-Street*.
Such Gentlemen as are willing to encourage this Undertaking, shall have them carefully deliver'd according to their Directions.

LONDON, EXCHANGES On

Amst.	34	11
Ditto Sight	34	$8\frac{1}{2}$
Rott.	35	1
Antw.	35	6
Hamb:	33	9
Paris —		$32\frac{15}{16}$
Ditto at 2U		$32\frac{5}{8}$
Bourdeaux 2 Usance		$32\frac{1}{4}$
Cadiz——		$41\frac{5}{8}$
Madrid —		$41\frac{7}{8}$
Bilboa ——		$41\frac{3}{4}$
Leghorn —		$51\frac{5}{8}$
Genoa——		55
Venice——		52
Lisbon	5	6 $5\frac{7}{8}$
Oporto	5	$5\frac{5}{8}$
Dublin	8	
Agio of the Bank from Holland		5

Aids in the Excheq		*given for*	*Paid off*
19th 4 Ditto	1741	2000000	1878900
20th 4 Ditto	1742	2000000	1737000
——	1743	2000000	292000
Malt——	1741	750000	617715
Malt——	1742	750000	603921
Salt——	1735	500000	448000

Gold in Coin - - - -	per Oz	3	18	$8\frac{1}{2}$
Ditto in Barrs - - -		3	18	7
Ps of Eight: Pillar large - - -		0	5	$6\frac{1}{2}$
Ditto Small - -		0	5	$6\frac{1}{4}$
Mexico large - -		0	5	$6\frac{1}{2}$
Ditto Small - -		0	5	$6\frac{1}{4}$
Silver in Barrs - - -		0	5	$6\frac{1}{2}$

Annuities

14*l*. per Cent at $22\frac{1}{2}$ Years Purchase
1704 to 1708 Inclusive 24. ditto
$3\frac{1}{2}$ Salt Tallies $102\frac{3}{4}$
$3\frac{1}{2}$ per Cent. $104\frac{1}{4}$
3 per Cent. 98

Cochineal 15s od p. lb. *Dis.* oos p. C.

—*Price* of Stocks—	*Saturday*	*Monday*	*Tuesday*
Bank Stock - - - -	$147\frac{1}{4}$a$\frac{1}{2}$	$147\frac{1}{2}$	$147\frac{3}{4}$
East-India - - - - -		$198\frac{3}{4}$	199
South Sea - - - -		Shut	
Ditto Annuity Old	$114\frac{1}{8}$	$114\frac{1}{8}$	$114\frac{1}{4}$
Ditto—— New		Shut	
3 *per* Cent. 1726			
Annuity - 1731		Ditto	
Ditto—— 1742			
Ditto —— 1743	$101\frac{1}{4}$	$101\frac{1}{4}$	$101\frac{3}{8}$
Million Bank - - - -	118	118	118
Equivalent - - - - - -		Shut	
R. Aff. 100l paid in		Ditto	
L. Aff. 12l 10s p. in	$11\frac{3}{4}$	$11\frac{3}{4}$	$11\frac{3}{4}$
7 p. Cent Em. Loan			
5 per Cent. Ditto			
India Bonds, præm.	4l 18s	4l 18s	4l 17s a 14
N. Bank Circulation	3l 5s od	3l 10s od	3l 10s od
Lottery Tickets	16l	18l 10s a 20l	20l

India Stock Dividend will be paid the 27th of January—The Transfer Books Open the 19th ditto
S. Sea Stock Dividend will be paid the 7th of February—The Transfer Books Open the 3d ditto
New S. Sea Annuity Dividend will be paid the 31st of January—The Transfer Books the 26th ditto
Equivalent Opens the 11th of January.
Royal Assurance Opens the 24th of January.
3 per Cent. Annuities 1742 Open the 16th of Jan. ditto 1726 the 17th of Jan. ditto 1731 the 18th of Jan.
Navy and Victualling Bills to the 30th of June last are in course of Payment.

Printed by *Luke Hinde* in *George-Yard*, *Lombard-street*; Where BROKERS Catalogues, &c. are carefully printed with Expedition

Figure 7.3a Lloyd's List, 3 January 1743/44 (obverse). Courtesy of the Corporation of Lloyd's, London.

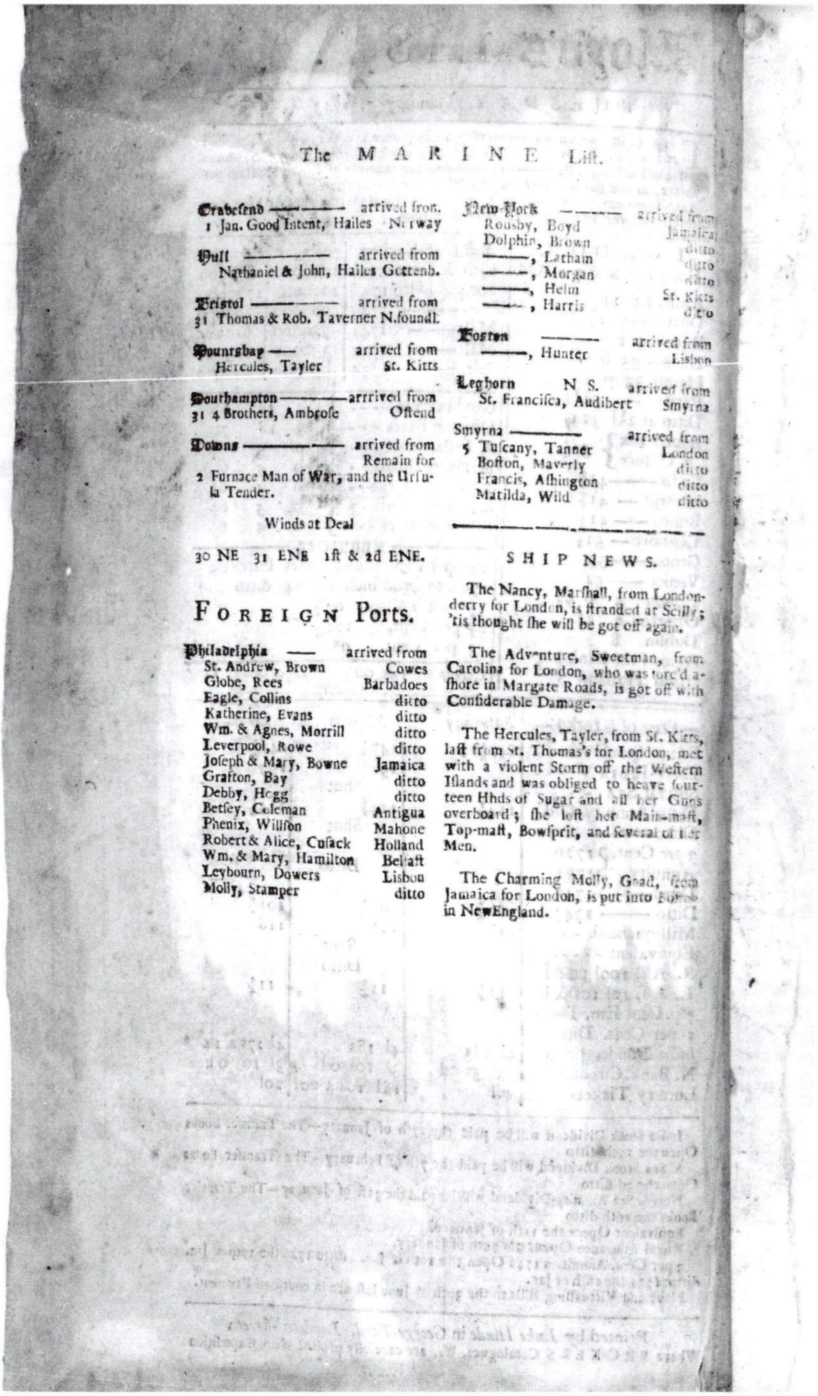

The MARINE List.

Gravesend — arrived from.
1 Jan. Good Intent, Hailes Norway

Hull — arrived from
Nathaniel & John, Hailes Gottenb.

Bristol — arrived from
31 Thomas & Rob. Taverner N.foundl.

Mountsbay — arrived from
Hercules, Tayler St. Kitts

Southampton — arrived from
31 4 Brothers, Ambrose Oftend

Downs — arrived from
Remain for
2 Furnace Man of War, and the Ursula Tender.

New-York — arrived from
Rousby, Boyd Jamaica
Dolphin, Brown ditto
—, Latham ditto
—, Morgan ditto
—, Helm St. Kitts
—, Harris ditto

Boston — arrived from
—, Hunter Lisbon

Leghorn N. S. arrived from
St. Francifca, Audibert Smyrna

Smyrna — arrived from
5 Tuscany, Tanner London
Bofton, Maverly ditto
Francis, Afhington ditto
Matilda, Wild ditto

Winds at Deal

30 NE 31 ENE 1ft & 2d ENE.

FOREIGN Ports.

Philadelphia — arrived from
St. Andrew, Brown Cowes
Globe, Rees Barbadoes
Eagle, Collins ditto
Katherine, Evans ditto
Wm. & Agnes, Morrill ditto
Leverpool, Rowe ditto
Joseph & Mary, Bowne Jamaica
Grafton, Bay ditto
Debby, Hogg ditto
Betfey, Coleman Antigua
Phenix, Willfon Mahone
Robert & Alice, Cufack Holland
Wm. & Mary, Hamilton Belfaft
Leybourn, Dowers Lisbon
Molly, Stamper ditto

SHIP NEWS.

The Nancy, Marfhall, from Londonderry for London, is ftranded at Scilly; 'tis thought fhe will be got off again.

The Adventure, Sweetman, from Carolina for London, who was forc'd afhore in Margate Roads, is got off with Confiderable Damage.

The Hercules, Tayler, from St. Kitts, laft from st. Thomas's for London, met with a violent Storm off the Weftern Iflands and was obliged to heave fourteen Hhds of Sugar and all her Guns overboard; fhe left her Main-maft, Top-maft, Bowfprit, and feveral of her Men.

The Charming Molly, Goad, from Jamaica for London, is put into Bofton in NewEngland.

Figure 7.3b Lloyd's List, 3 January 1743/44 (reverse).
Courtesy of the Corporation of Lloyd's, London.

he quickly set up a more elaborate and more formal network of accredited agents throughout the country to collect and pass on news about shipping. Since such news was of particular importance to those interested in marine insurance, they naturally gravitated to the source. Lloyd's coffee house quickly became the center for marine insurance brokers and underwriters, who then organized an association headed by a Master. Under Edward Lloyd the ownership of the coffee house and the publishing of the newspaper had been united in the same person. The association of marine insurers eventually took control of both coffee house and newspaper, probably sooner rather than later. The Master of the association quite naturally assumed the editorship of *Lloyd's List*. The parallel between the history of *Lloyd's List* and the London commodity price current, the publication of each eventually taken over, one way or another, by the association of professionals who dominated the businesses that the newspapers served, will be seen below to have been matched by the history of the newspaper that published the news from the Stock Exchange.

To guarantee the rapid reliable flow of information from his network of correspondents, the editor of *Lloyd's List* relied on a unique relationship with the Post Office. Letters from the newspaper's agents addressed to Lloyd's received favored treatment in the post: they traveled free of postage; they were sorted specially and conveyed with despatch; and they were held out for collection by a Lloyd's clerk once they arrived at London. For all of this the newspaper paid a set fee; it amounted to £200 a year by the 1780s.[32] But no other newspaper could avail itself of these services, at any price. Given what was said above about government's attitudes toward business newspapers, this can be simply viewed as another promotional device. We do not know when it first began but we do know that Lloyd moved his establishment from Tower Street to new premises in Lombard Street, near the General Post Office, just after Christmas in 1691, suggesting a new development in the relationship between Lloyd's and the Post Office. The initial number of *Lloyd's List* in the series from which we have the two earliest copies started immediately thereafter, in January 1692. It seems reasonable to presume that the newspaper had had its origins in the old coffee house in Tower Street sometime before that date.

Lloyd's List repaid these promotional efforts handsomely, both to the London business community and to government. As early as 1693 the Hudson's Bay Company had come to rely so greatly on "Mr Loyd the Coffee Man for his Intelligence of the Comp[an]ies Shipps" that the Governor and the committee of the company awarded him a gift of £3.[33] The Master of Lloyd's also made it his business to see that government was speedily apprised

---

32 Compare Kenneth Ellis, *The Post Office in the Eighteenth Century: A Study in Administrative History* (Oxford, 1958), p. 61.
33 As quoted in McCusker, *European Bills of Entry*, p. 55, n. 91. When adjusted for inflation £3 in 1693 is roughly the equivalent in 1997 of £250 sterling or $420.00.

of news that was of particular importance. Indeed one historian has concluded that, because of its maritime intelligence capability, during wartime *Lloyd's List* became in effect an arm of the Admiralty.[34]

These factors assume some significance for our understanding of the development and the importance of the newspaper. As with the other business newspapers, both institutional and commercial constraints operated to insure the completeness and the accuracy of what the editor inserted into his columns. Edward Lloyd's new newspaper could not have survived long unless he had exercised due care. The organization of accredited correspondents in all the major ports and the elaborate preferential arrangements with the Post Office that sped the flow of reports to Lloyd's office helped establish and maintain the reputation of the newspaper. Subsequent editors not only had Lloyd's example as their guide; they also had to answer to the association of marine insurers gathered under the name of Lloyd's. Later in the century, for several years after 1769, as a result of disputes between two groups of marine insurers, a second, rival *Lloyd's List* did appear. It was published alongside the older one until the dispute was settled and a single publication once again sufficed. One element in the continuing competition was the question of the quality of the paper's news coverage. So important to the marine insurance industry had *Lloyd's List* become that neither contending faction felt comfortable without its own newspaper.

EXCHANGE RATE AND
STOCK EXCHANGE CURRENTS

The fourth and last type of the early English business newspapers that concern us here is a variation on an exchange current. Exchange rate currents published the rates at which foreign bills of exchange sold locally. As Gerald de Malynes wrote in 1622, "exchange is the rudder of the ship of trafficke."[35] Without knowledge of the set of the rudder, merchants could not navigate well in the world of commerce. While John Castaing did not invent the exchange rate current, he did tailor it to his own time and place. As was noted above, the earliest known exchange current was published at Antwerp

---

34 R. P[atrick] Crowhurst, "The Admiralty and the Convoy System," *MM*, LVII (Nov. 1971), 167, n. 2. Compare C[harles] Ernst Fayle, "Shipowning and Marine Insurance," in *The Trade Winds: A Study of British Overseas Trade during the French Wars, 1793–1815,* ed. C[yril] Northcote Parkinson (London, [1948]), p. 45; and D[avid] E. W. Gibb, *Lloyd's of London: A Study in Individualism,* [2nd edn] (London, 1972), p. 13. See importantly in this regard the Letters from Lloyd's, 1793–1839, Adm. 1/3992–Adm. 1/3946, PRO. Intriguingly, the French government seems to have put *Lloyd's List* to a parallel use, that is, to keep track of English shipping! See Frank C. Spooner, *Risks at Sea: Amsterdam Insurance and Maritime Europe, 1766–1780* (Cambridge, Eng., 1983), p. 106. Whether and where there exists a file of the newspapers subscribed to, I have not yet been able to discover.

35 G. [de] Malynes, *Consuetudo, vel Lex Mercatoria; or the Ancient Law-Merchant,* [1st edn] (London, 1622), p. 60.

certainly by the 1580s, probably as early as the 1540s. Many others followed later. Castaing, a Huguenot who arrived in London from France in the 1680s and became a citizen in 1688, had his origins in a continental tradition where such newspapers were well known. A rising broker on the Royal Exchange, Castaing found himself caught up in the London of the 1690s amid a rapidly developing market for all kinds of business and government securities. He took advantage of this booming business to establish a newspaper. In his *Course of the Exchange* he published not only the rates of foreign exchange but also the prices of stocks and bonds. Castaing's was the first exchange rate and stock exchange current. (Table 7.3 records the basic data about the publishing history of the London exchange rate and stock exchange currents down to 1775.)

The first part of Castaing's twice weekly newspaper resembled all other exchange rate currents (see figures 7.4a and 7.4b). There he printed a list of European cities in one column and the price at which bills of exchange on those cities sold on the Royal Exchange. The rest of the page was taken up with information about the prices and conditions of sale of numerous forms of investment: company shares, company bonds, lottery tickets, annuities, and government securities. The *Course of the Exchange*, started by Castaing in March 1697, continued to be published well into the nineteenth century, in much the same format, always fully printed, always on one side of the sheet, headed by the title, footed by an imprint giving the names of the successive publishers. Published by the London Stock Exchange, and called the *Daily Official List*, it is still published today in a considerably expanded format.[36]

In January 1707 John Castaing, Jr, succeeded his father as publisher. Four years before his death in 1729, the younger Castaing started publishing the newspaper in partnership with his sister Arabella's husband, Edward Jackson. Sometime after Jackson's death in 1735 she remarried and, as Mrs Arabella Wharton, continued to be involved in the publication of the newspaper for at least forty-five years, always in partnership with a man who was a broker on the Exchange but, apparently, taking a leading publishing role in the business herself (see figure 7.4b).[37] In 1786, what had been the arrangement in fact for some time, was made explicit in the imprint for the first time when

36 After a long evolution from the form in which Castaing first issued it to that of a modern business newspaper with a size and shape like *The Wall Street Journal* and *The Financial Times*, the *Daily Official List* has recently changed again. It is still today nothing more than a list of exchange rates, stock prices, and the like. While it has no "editorial content," it is still published daily, registered as a newspaper. It is, however, somewhat bulkier than Castaing's newspaper. Measuring 30 cm by 21 cm, printed on both sides of the sheet, it numbers about 140 pages in length!

37 All of this is inferred from statements in the imprint of the newspaper. For example, the number dated 10 Jan. 1706/07 is the first in which the publisher's name reads "John Castaing Jun." See also Elizabeth A. Buckman, "Course of the Exchange, 1705–1888: Bibliographical Notes" (unpublished typescript, 1973). I wish to thank T. I. Bell, the Librarian of the Bank of England, for his consistent help with these materials. Compare

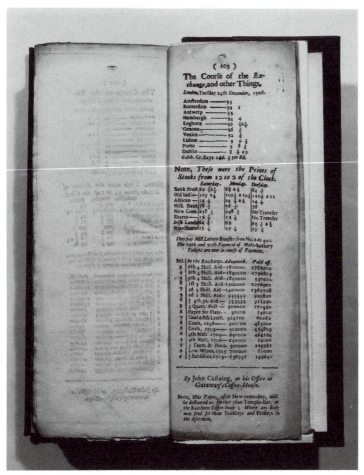

Figure 7.4a Course of the Exchange, 24 December 1706.
Courtesy of the Bank of England, London.

the newspaper was said to be "published . . . by Edward Wetenhall, Stock-broker, appointed by the unanimous vote of the gentlemen of the Stock-Exchange, October 30, 1786." In ways very similar to what had happened with *Lloyd's List*, Castaing's *Course of the Exchange*, long a de facto ward of the Royal Exchange if only because its publishers and many of its readers were licensed brokers, was taken formally into its custody.

the similarly involved history of the ownership of Lloyd's coffee house after the death of Edward Lloyd in 1713 as set out in Gibb, *Lloyd's of London*, p. 17. See also Charles Wright and C[harles] Ernest Fayle, *A History of Lloyd's from the Founding of Lloyd's Coffee House to the Present Day* (London, 1928), pp. 32–33, 67–72.

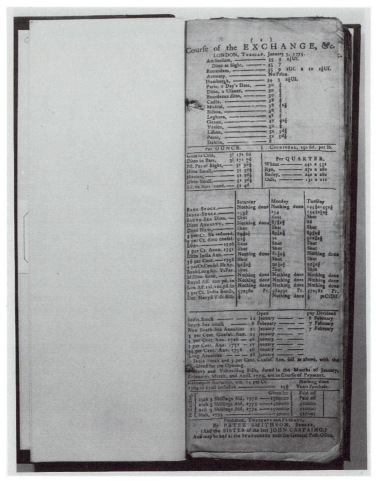

Figure 7.4b Course of the Exchange, 3 January 1775.
Courtesy of the Bank of England, London.

Castaing's *Course of the Exchange* had always had an excellent reputation and deservedly so. He and his successors organized the collection of his information carefully and published the compilation with due caution. Business was concluded on the walks of the Royal Exchange by mid-afternoon and Castaing's clerks then circulated among the various brokers noting down the latest prices for bills of exchange and shares of stock.[38] The newspaper was set – presumably from standing type – printed, and ready for distribution

38 Sometime between 1705 and 1715 the Royal Exchange extended by an hour the time it was open, from noon until three rather than two o'clock. See the issues of the *Course of the Exchange* for those years (e.g., 5 Jan. 1704/05, 7 Jan. 1714/15). Compare [Thomas]

170

within a matter of hours. Copies could be collected at the editor's office or, by arrangement, they would be delivered to subscribers.[39] When an error was made, Castaing took pains to correct it in the next number. Much about all this is available from a deposition in an Exchequer Court case of the 1740s during which the then current editor of the newspaper, Richard Shergold, was called upon to testify about the price of the South Sea Company's stock over that fateful year 1720. He brought along to court with him the bound office copy of the newspaper for that year, which was then admitted as evidence. In reply to a direct question, Shergold testified that the *Course of the Exchange* was "of good credit and esteem among the persons who usually bought and sold stocks."[40] Much the same could have been said about the other early business newspapers discussed in this essay.

Mortimer, *Every Man His Own Broker: or, A Guide to Exchange-Alley,* [5th edn] (London, 1762), pp. xiii–xiv.

39   There are extant two receipts for annual subscriptions to the *Course of the Exchange* for the years 1703 and 1706 in the name of John Knight and signed "J. Castaing." Each subscription cost 12s. sterling (60p). Exchequer Office, Clerks' Papers, E 219/448, PRO. The subscriber may well have been John Knight, MP (ca. 1686–1733), one time Treasurer of the Customs, director of the Bank of England, and member of the Court of Assistants of the Royal African Company. For Knight, see Romney Sedgwick, *The History of Parliament: The House of Commons, 1715–1754,* 2 vols (London, 1970), II, 191–192.

40   Deposition by Robert Shergold, 16 Nov. 1743, *Percival Lewis* v. *Jacob Sawbridge,* Depositions Taken Under Commission, E 134, 17 Geo. II, Michaelmas, no. 7, PRO. Compare the statement in 1810 before the famous Bullion Committee by Aaron Asher Goldsmid, partner in Mocatta and Goldsmid, one of the five legendary London bullion brokerage houses, to the effect that the prices for gold and silver reported in the newspaper could be relied upon because it was his firm that had. been supplying them to Castaing and his successors since the 1690s. [GB, Parl., Commons, Select Committee on the High Price of Gold Bullion], Report, *Together with Minutes of Evidence, and Accounts, from the Select Committee on the High Price of Gold Bullion,* HC Sessional Papers, 1810, vol. III (Reports) ([London, 1810]), p. 36.

In 1743, when Shergold made his deposition in a case before the Count of Exchequer, he took with him and offered up in evidence a bound volume of the newspaper for the year 1720. In its flyleaf, Charles Taylor, the Deputy Remembrancer of the court, duly noted that this volume had been produced as an exhibit, "marked with the Letter (A)." The volume, so inscribed, survives as the first in the set of volumes running from 1720–1755 in the British Library (press mark C. 108.ee.2). They are beautifully bound in maroon leather, gold tooled on the cover and spine, with gilt-edged pages. The volumes for 1698–1720 formerly in the Stock Exchange Library, London, and now in Guildhall Library, are similarly bound and may well have originally been part of the same set. In 1732, in Edward Jackson's will – PROB 11/672, fols 87r–88v, PRO – he bequeathed to the benefit of Arabella Wharton "the *Course of the Exchange* Books bound up from the year 1697 to the time of my decease provided I continue binding them annually as I [have] hitherto done." (He died in July 1735.) He instructed that they not be sold, however. It is highly likely that these are the very volumes that are now in the British Library and Guildhall Library – with the exception of the volume for 1697, the whereabouts of which I do not know. Also part of the estate was a picture of her brother, John Castaing, which I have not yet been able to locate.

Newspaper publishers seem regularly to have kept copies of their newspapers, a characteristic observed and commented upon in the early 17th century by Richard Brathwait who noted that the "corranto-coiner's" "librarie" consisted in little besides "his owne continuation." In *Whimzies: Or, a New Cast of Characters* (London, 1631), as in Allen H. Lanner, *A Critical Edition of Richard Brathwait's "Whimzies"* (New York, 1991, [Ph.D. diss., New York University, 1966]), p. 158.

Perhaps the best evidence of how successful and how valuable were these newspapers is the eager competitors they attracted. The *Course of the Exchange* seems to have been a particularly popular target. We have already seen how Richard Baker altered *Lloyd's List* in 1735 to the point that it became a near clone to Castaing's newspaper. Others did the same thing. For at least eight years from 1714 to 1722 John Freke published his *Prices of Stocks* at London. In the mid-1730s a newspaper appeared called *The London Course of the Exchange* that so mirrored Castaing's paper as to be virtually indistinguishable from it except for the added word in the title and the different names in the imprint. Imitation sprung from more than mere flattery. These newspapers served a growing clientele that was anxious for the latest news, the "freshest advices," about every aspect of the business world. They found paying customers for the news they printed both at home and abroad. They flourished and developed. Their success underscores for us how very important these newspapers were to the economy of seventeenth- and eighteenth-century Great Britain.

Table 7.2 The London commodity price currents, 1601–1775

1a TITLE (varies):   *The Prices of Merchandise in London*
    1601–1614   *Pris des marchandises en Londres*
    1649   *Pris courrant des Marchandises à Londres*
    1667–1696   *The Prices of Merchandise in London*
1b FREQUENCY OF PUBLICATION/DAY(S) OF THE WEEK PUBLISHED
    Weekly   Thursdays(?), 1601–1669
                  Wednesdays, 1671–1696
1c PUBLISHERS
    Unknown   1601–1614   William Bannister 1668–1669
    John Day   1632–1660   Robert Woolley   1671–1696
    Humphrey Brome 1660–1667
1d PRINTERS
    Not known.
1e EXTANT COPIES

1601,	5 September	1668,	1, 8, 15, 22, 29 October
1608,	30 April		5, 12, 19, 26 November
1610,	15 March		3, 10, 17, 24 December
1614,	9 December	1669,	25 March
1649,	15 November	1669,	1, 8, 22, 29 April
1667,	8 July		6, 13, 20, 27 May
1668,	7 May		10, 17, 24 June
1669,	1, 8, 15, 22, 29 July	1675,	14 April
	5, 12, 19, 26 August		18 August
	2, 9, 16, 23, 30 September		2 November
	7, 14, 21, 28 October		8 December
	4, 11, 18, 25 November	1676,	19 April
	2, 9, 16, 23 December		10 May
1671,	22 November		9 August
1672,	31 January	1677,	24 January

	14, 21 February		28 February
	27 March		12 September
	8, 22 May		17 October
	25 September		21 November
	6 November	1678,	9 January
	31 December	1679,	29 January
1673,	19 February	1680,	15 December
	6, 20 August	1681,	25 October
	8 October	1682,	21 June
	12 November		25 October
	3, 10 December	1683,	3 January
1674,	7 January	1684,	30 December
	25 March	1685,	30 December
	17, 24 June	1686,	12, 19 May
	15 July		14 July
	9, 23 December		25 October
1675,	27 January	1687,	11 May
	24 February	1697,	12 February
	17, 31 March		

2a TITLE (varies): *Whiston's Merchants Weekly Remembrancer, of the Present-Money-Prices of their Goods Ashoar in London*

1680–1686	*The Merchants Remembrancer*
1689–1707	*Whiston's Merchants Weekly Remembrancer, of the Present-Money-Prices of their Goods Ashoar in London*
1681–1696	*Le Mémorial des Marchands*
1708–1714	*Robinson's Merchants Weekly Remembrancer, of the Present-Money-Prices of their Goods Ashoar in London*

2b FREQUENCY OF PUBLICATION/DAY(S) OF THE WEEK PUBLISHED
Weekly   Mondays

2c PUBLISHERS
James Whiston   1680–1707
Francis Robinson 1708–1714

2d PRINTERS
Not known.

2e EXTANT COPIES

1680,	16 February	1683,	20 August
1681,	23 May		8 October
	4 July	1684,	15 December
	14 November	1685,	16 January
1682,	20 March		23 February
	8 June		13 April
1683,	12 February		28 September
	14 May		9, 23 November
1686,	11 January	1697,	1, 29 March
	28 June		5, 12, 26 April
1689,	17 June		6, 14 June
1691,	26 January		16, 23 August
1691,	26 October	1698,	17 January
1692,	25 January		7 March
1693,	3 April		4, 18 July
1694,	10 September	1699,	9 January
	19 November	1700,	2 September

173

Table 7.2 continued

1696,	23 March	1701,	17 November
	20 April	1702,	16 November
	13 July	1704,	28 August
	31 August	1707,	7 July
	12 November	1713,	23 March
	7 December		

3a TITLE (varies):   *Proctor's Price Courant: The Prices of Merchandise in London*
  1694–1706   *Proctor's Price Courant: The Prices of Merchandise in London*
  1696   *Prix Courant de S. Proctor*
  1717   *Proctor's Price-Courant Improv'd*
  1728–1731   *Proctor's Price-Courant Reviv'd*

3b FREQUENCY OF PUBLICATION/DAY(S) OF THE WEEK PUBLISHED
  Weekly   Thursdays

3c PUBLISHERS
  Samuel Proctor   1694–1731

3d PRINTERS
  D[aniel] Bridge   1717

3e EXTANT COPIES

1696,	28 February	1697,	5, 12, 19, 26 August
	3, 30 April		2, 9, 16, 23, 30 September
	21 May		7, 14, 21, 28 October
	11 June		4, 11, 18, 25 November
	24 September		2, 9, 16, 23, 30 December
	29 October	1698,	6, 13, 20, 27 January
	15, 26 November		3, 10, 17, 24 February
1697,	21 January		3, 10, 17, 24 March
	18 February		4 August
	18 March	1706,	17 January
	1, 8, 15, 22, 29 April		19 September
	6, 13, 20, 27 May	1717,	28 November
	3, 10, 17, 24 June	1731,	1 July
	1, 8, 15, 22, 29 July		

4a TITLE: *Prix courant de marchandises à Londres.*

4b FREQUENCY OF PUBLICATION/DAY(S) OF THE WEEK PUBLISHED
  Weekly   Thursdays

4c PUBLISHER
  Étienne Mahieu   1698–1721

4d PRINTERS
  Not known.

4e EXTANT COPIES

1699,	22 June	1717,	5 December
1715,	10 February		

5a TITLE: *Great Britain's Weekly Pacquet: Containing the Prices of Goods,*
               with their Neat Duties and Draw-Backs; And a Collection of
               Sundry Goods Imported and Exported Weekly. With An Account of
               News Foreign and Domestic

5b FREQUENCY OF PUBLICATION/DAY(S) OF THE WEEK PUBLISHED
  Weekly   Saturdays

5c PUBLISHER
  Thomas Hartwell 1716

5d PRINTERS
B. Mills	1717, January–March
S. Lee	1717, July

5e EXTANT COPIES

1716,	21 July	1717,	13, 27 July
	13 October		17 August
1717,	12 January		21 September
	23 February		5 October
	9, 23 March		28 December

6a TITLE: Unknown
6b FREQUENCY OF PUBLICATION/DAY(S) OF THE WEEK PUBLISHED
Weekly(?)	Unknown

6c PUBLISHER
Peter Fearon	1747

6d PRINTERS
Not known.
6e EXTANT COPIES
None known.

7a TITLE (varies): *The London Price Current*
1754	*London Price Current on The Royal Exchange*
1776–	*The London Price Current*

7b FREQUENCY OF PUBLICATION/DAY(S) OF THE WEEK PUBLISHED
Weekly	Thursdays, 1747–1756
	Fridays, 1776 and after

7c PUBLISHERS
Edward Taylor	1754
William Vaughan	1754
Benjamin Vaughan	1754
Mark Hudson	1754
William Prince	1776 (and after)

7d PRINTERS
Not known.
7e EXTANT COPIES

1754,	10, 17 24, 31 January	1754,	2, 16, 23 May
	7, 14, 21, 28 February		6, 13 June
	7, 14, 21, 28 March		4, 11 July
	4, 11, 25 April		1, 8, 22, 29 August
1754,	5 September	1779–1785,	All
1778,	30 January		

Notes and sources:
This table is an adaptation and expansion of John J. McCusker and Cora Gravesteijn, *The Beginnings of Commercial and Financial Journalism: The Commodity Price Currents, Exchange Rate Currents, and Money Currents of Early Modern Europe*, Nederlandsch Economisch-Historisch Archief, ser. III, no. 11 (Amsterdam, 1991), pp. 291–311. The added information is based on ongoing research into the subject (see, e.g., n. 18 of this chapter).

Note that the pre-1615 commodity price currents have been assigned numbers 9175z.5 and 9175z.10 in A[lfred] W. Pollard and G[ilbert] R. Redgrave, *A Short-Title Catalogue of Books Printed in England, Scotland, & Ireland And of English Books Printed Abroad, 1475–1640*, 2nd edn, rev. and enl., ed. W[illiam] A. Jackson, F[rederic] S. Ferguson, and Katharine F. Pantzer, 3 vols (London, 1976–1991), I, 411.

Table 7.3 The London exchange rate and stock exchange currents, 1697–1775

1a TITLE (varies):	*The Course of the Exchange*		
1697–1710	*The Course of the Exchange, and Other Things*		
1710–1741	*The Course of the Exchange, &c.*		
1741–1775	*Course of the Exchange, &c.*		

1b FREQUENCY OF PUBLICATION/DAY(S) OF THE WEEK PUBLISHED
TWICE WEEKLY   Tuesdays and Fridays

1c PUBLISHERS

John Castaing	1697–1707	Richard Shergold and Arabella Wharton	1735-1749
John Castaing, Jr	1707–1725	George Shergold and Arabella Wharton	1750–1763
John Castaing, Jr, and Edward Jackson	1725–1729	Peter Smithson and Arabella Wharton	1764–1779
Edward Jackson [and Arabella Jackson?]	1730-1735		

1d PRINTERS
Not known.

1e EXTANT COPIES
1698–1775,   All

2a TITLE: *Freke's Prices of Stocks, &c.*

2b FREQUENCY OF PUBLICATION/DAY(S) OF THE WEEK PUBLISHED
Twice weekly   Tuesdays and Fridays

2c PUBLISHERS
John Freke   1714–1722

2d PRINTERS
Not known.

2e EXTANT COPIES

1714,	26 March–31 December	1716,	27 November
1715,	All	1717–1721,	All
1716,	2 January–22 June	1722,	15 January–22 June

3a TITLE: *The London Course of the Exchange*

3b FREQUENCY OF PUBLICATION/DAY(S) OF THE WEEK PUBLISHED
Twice weekly   Tuesdays and Fridays

3c PUBLISHERS
Francis Viouja and Benjamin Cole   1736–1737
Francis Viouja   1739

3d PRINTERS
Not known.

3e EXTANT COPIES

1736,	27 April	1737,	16 September
	31 August	1738,	15 December
	22 October	1739,	14 December

Notes and sources:
This table is an adaptation of John J. McCusker and Cora Gravesteijn, *The Beginnings of Commercial and Financial Journalism: The Commodity Price Currents, Exchange Rate Currents, and Money Currents of Early Modern Europe*, Nederlandsch Economisch-Historisch Archief, ser. III, no. 11 (Amsterdam, 1991), pp. 321–322.

8

NEW YORK CITY AND THE BRISTOL PACKET

A chapter in eighteenth-century postal history

It being a certain Maxim that as Trade is the
producer of Correspond[en]ce so Trade is govern'd
& influenc'd by the certainty & quickness of
Correspondence.

Edmond Dummer[1]

Merchants have always been concerned about keeping abreast of market fluctuations. The mails convey such intelligence and it comes as no surprise that
businessmen have had a consistent interest in maintaining and improving
postal service. For seventeenth- and eighteenth-century English merchants
who had dealings with the colonies, a tenuous but normally effective line of
communication involved letter drops at taverns frequented by ship captains
who traded to particular areas. A ship's captain would collect letters there
and deliver them when he arrived, receiving a small sum for the carriage of
each letter. This worked well until war disrupted the system. Letters were
delayed if convoys had to be formed and letters were lost if ships were
captured.[2] The War of the Spanish Succession (1702–1713) saw a partial
solution to this problem when the British government, at the behest of the

1   Edmond Dummer, organizer of the first transatlantic packet service, in a letter to Sidney,
    First Earl of Godolphin, Lord High Treasurer, 15 Feb. 1706/07, T 64/89, p. 356, PRO.
        The original version of this chapter was published in *Postal History Journal*, XIII (July
    1968), 15–24. Copyright © 1968 Postal History Society of the Americas. Copyright ©
    renewed 1996 by John J. McCusker. This revision is presented here with the permission
    of the Postal History Society which awarded the original essay its gold medal as the best
    article to appear in the journal in 1968.
        I continue to be grateful for the help and support given me in the preparation of this
    chapter by Carl H. Scheele, then Associate Curator-in-Charge, of what was then the
    Division of Philately and Postal History and is now the National Postal Museum,
    Smithsonian Institution. Photographs are courtesy of the Division of Philately and Postal
    History, Smithsonian Institution. I am additionally thankful to Joseph Geraci of the
    National Postal Museum for his advice and assistance.
2   An example of the other kinds of problems that could occur under this system is found
    in the complaint by one London businessman who reported to his correspondent that his
    most recent "letters . . . being brought upon the [Royal] Exchange to deliver, it was not
    my fortune to be there, so that my letters were catched up" by someone else. John Paige,

Figure 8.1 Letter from New York City, May 1711. The cover sheet of a letter that
traveled on the second voyage of the Bristol-to-New York packet mail service.
The letter left New York City in May 1711 and arrived at London on 14 June.
Among its postal markings is the earliest use of a straight line hand stamp known
for North America.
Courtesy of the National Postal Museum, Smithsonian Institution,
Washington, DC.

merchants and to serve its own needs, established packet ship mail services
to speed communications. Improved were the already existing runs to the
European Continent; inaugurated were totally new packets to the Western
Hemisphere, first to the West Indies, later to North America, between Bristol
and New York.[3] The discovery of one piece of mail carried by the Bristol
packet sheds a bit more light on the service, its origins, its demise, and its

at London, to William Clerke, at Tenerife, Canary Islands, 20 Sept. 1650, in *The Letters
of John Paige, London Merchant, 1648–1658*, ed. George F. Steckley, London Record Society
Publications, XXI (London, 1984), 25. People learned to send second and third copies
of letters to offset such problems but the consequent delays in the receipt of important
information could be significant.

3   See, in general, Frank Staff, *The Transatlantic Mail* (London and New York, [1956]);
and Howard Robinson, *Carrying British Mail Overseas* (London, [1964]). For the broader
context of all of these developments, see especially Ian K. Steele, *The English Atlantic,
1675–1740: An Exploration of Communication and Continuity* (New York, 1986), particularly pp. 168–188.

more lasting implications. The letter itself becomes an important document in the postal history of the early eighteenth century.

Unfortunately the covering sheet of the letter in question lacks an explicit date (see figure 8.1). This difficulty, while tending to pervade the postal history of this period, is not insurmountable. The dates of the packet service, 1710 to 1713, suggest initial limits to any dating of the letter. Its postal markings provide added support to such a hypothetical dating. The identification of the writer of the letter and its recipient, the establishment of their relationship, and the uncovering of their dates of death, all meshing neatly with the other particulars, confirm the argument. As a result, this postal cover, of untraced provenance,[4] presumably unnoticed previously because of its lack of a date, can now be appreciated as both the earliest known example of a stamped post office marking in American history and as the first tangible evidence of the original packet service between Great Britain and North America.

◆ ◆ ◆ ◆ ◆

The cover itself offers little direct testimony concerning the questions asked of it. Addressed "To Mr Joseph Levy, Merchant in London," its obverse also indicates that it was assessed 2s. (10p) postage ("2/-") and that it went "per the Bristoll pakett."[5] The three letters of the alphabet just under the name of the vessel, "QDG," for "Que Dios Guarde," are a pious invocation asking God to protect the ship.[6] On the reverse, a black stamped marking designated New York City as the point of origin, a red wax seal served to close the letter (and to identify the writer), and a postal marking applied in London showed the day and the month the letter arrived at that city, 14 June. The year in which all this occurred is not apparent, but these bits of information are enough to date the cover to 1711. A closer look at these several elements not only explains the basis for this conclusion but also offers some insights into the packet service and its history.

The first transatlantic packet mail service linking England and the Western Hemisphere had its initial run in 1702. Edmond Dummer had earlier organized packets between England and cities on the European Continent in the

---

4   This cover sheet, and other 18th- and 19th-century pre-stamp covers, were given to the author as a boy by some now-forgotten member of a stamp club to which he then belonged. It is now among the collections of the National Postal Museum of the Smithsonian Institution (accession number 280593). It was on display in the Museum's "Rarities Gallery" in 1995.

5   Compare the markings on the letter illustrated in L[eonard] E. Britnor, *British West Indies Postal Rates to 1900* ([England], 1977), p. 13. The total reflects the rate for packet letters, 1s. 6d., plus 6d., the inland postal charge between Bristol and London. When adjusted for inflation, 2s. in 1711 is roughly the equivalent in 1997 of £7.00 sterling or $12.00.

6   The phrase in Latin is "quam Deus conservet" and, thus, the initials "QDC" are also found on such letters. Compare L[eonard] E. Britnor, *An Introduction to the Postal History of the West Indies*, British West Indies Study Circle, Paper no. 1 ([England], 1959), p. 7.

1690s and this new venture was his also.[7] The War of the Spanish Succession (known as Queen Anne's War in America) created an obvious need for such a service to continue close contacts with the colonies. Dummer struggled to maintain reasonably regular sailings between Falmouth and the islands of the West Indies until his unfortunate bankruptcy in 1711. The same cause was father to both the service and its failure, for the war saw too many of Dummer's ships captured at sea.[8] The Post Office, at this time still a branch of the Treasury, had tried to keep the service efficient – even to the point of supplying metal hand stamps to be used to designate the island from which the letters were sent[9] – but it did not see fit to keep Dummer solvent. Neither was there need to worry about replacing him because hostilities at sea ceased soon thereafter, and, in mid-summer of 1712, all packets were put back on a peacetime establishment even though no treaty was signed until the next April.[10] Packet service to the West Indies was only revived in 1745 when a new war again threatened mercantile and governmental lines of communication.[11]

Part of Dummer's original idea had called for a packet service between North America and the West Indies, there to link up with the English packet, but nothing ever came of this suggestion.[12] About this same time, 1704,

---

7 L[eonard] E. Britnor, "Edmund Dummer and His Packet Service." *B.W.I. Study Circle Bulletin*, no. 44 (Mar. 1965), pp. 2–7, 10–12. See also Britnor, *Introduction to the Postal History of the West Indies*, p. 8; Britnor, *The History of the Sailing Packets to the West Indies*, British West Indies Study Circle, Paper no. 5 ([England], 1973), pp. 3–15.

8 John Haskell Kemble, "England's First Atlantic Mail Line," *MM*, XXVI (Jan., Apr. 1940), 33–54, 184–198; Herbert Joyce, *The History of the Post Office from Its Establishment down to 1836* (London, 1893), pp. 78–82, 108–109; Staff, *The Transatlantic Mail*, pp. 28–31; and Robinson, *Carrying British Mail Overseas*, pp. 32–38. Dummer's ships also used other English ports on occasion, especially Plymouth. Account of West India packet service by Edmond Dummer, [July 1712], CO 137/9, no. 66 (i), PRO.

9 Letter of Robert Cotton and Thomas Frankland, the Postmasters-General, to Deputy Postmasters in Jamaica, Barbados, Antigua, St Christopher, Montserrat, and Nevis, 29 Nov. 1705, Post Class 48/1, p. 77, Post Office Archives, Post Office Archives and Records Centre, London: "We have caus'd stamps to be made for each place, and do by this mail send you two stamps for your island with which you are to stamp all letters."

10 Joyce, *History of the Post Office*, pp. 108–109, 173; [J. T. Dixon], "The Problem of Imperial Communications during the Eighteenth Century, with Special Reference to the Post Office" ([M.A. thesis, University of Leeds, 1964]), pp. 81–102; and Steele, *English Atlantic*, pp. 168–188.

11 Joyce, *History of the Post Office*, p. 459. For the later history of the packet service, see Staff, *Transatlantic Mail*, passim; Robinson, *Carrying British Mail Overseas*, passim; Arthur C. Wardle, "The Post Office Packets," *in The Trade Winds: A Study of British Overseas Trade during the French Wars, 1793–1815*, ed. C[yril] Northcote Parkinson (London, [1948]), pp. 278–290; and [Dixon], "Problem of Imperial Communications," passim.

12 Letter from [Dummer to Godolphin], 24 Feb. 1703/04, T 1/89, no. 81 (i), PRO. In 1702 one of Dummer's packets had made a round-trip voyage from Falmouth to New York. Staff, *Transatlantic Mail*, p. 118. This seems to have been a trial run advised by the Commissioners for Trade and Plantations when it approved Dummer's first proposals. Dummer had suggested one service to the West Indies. The Commissioners liked the idea of a packet service but thought three to be the optimum number: one to Antigua and Barbados, one to Nevis and Jamaica, and a third to the Thirteen Continental Colonies to be based near the Delaware Capes. Letter of the Commissioners for Trade and

English merchants began petitioning for a direct line to New York.[13] The Treasury found little justification for their demands and inquired rather sourly "whether the merchants intended to be at the charge?"[14] Pressure continued and at least three different plans for such a service were proposed in the next few years.[15] The last of these went to the Treasury late in 1709, presented by one William Warren.[16] The Treasury responded favorably and granted him a contract to set up a packet line.[17] Warren had a broadside printed

Plantations to Daniel Finch, Earl of Nottingham, Sec. of State, 22 June 1702, CO 318/3, no. 3, PRO. Early in 1705 Dummer issued an advertisement advising that correspondence intended for the mainland could be sent by way of his West India packet. Once in the islands, the letters would be dispatched by the first ship northward. A copy of the printed advertisement, dated 10 Feb. 1704/05, is in CO 323/5, fol. 213r, PRO.

13 The question of why New York and not Boston as the North American terminus of the mail line is probably best answered by its central location but another reason for its choice can be understood by remembering a basic difference in the mercantile orientations of the two cities. New England during this period was easily doing three times the volume of import trade from England that New York did. But, as Curtis P. Nettels pointed out, "the major part of the New England trade was probably carried on by the independent merchants of Boston who bought in England through agents; whereas the trade of New York seems to have been chiefly in the hands of London exporters operating through factors in the colony." Nettels, "England's Trade with New England and New York, 1685–1720," *Publications of the Colonial Society of Massachusetts*, XXVII (Transactions, 1930–1933), 326. Compare his, *The Money Supply of the American Colonies before 1720*, University of Wisconsin, Studies in the Social Sciences and History, no. 20 (Madison, Wis., 1934), pp. 73–74. The petition of the London merchants was read on 30 May 1704. It is in the PRO and is recorded in [GB, PRO], *Calendar of Treasury Papers Preserved in Her Majesty's Public Record Office, 1557–1728*, by Joseph Redington, 6 vols (London, 1868–1899), III (1702–1707), 267–268.

14 Petition, 30 May 1704, op. cit., p. 268; and William Smith, *The History of the Post Office in British North America, 1639–1870* (Cambridge, Eng., 1920), pp. 31–32.

15 Two were unsuccessful. One of these was made by Agnes Hamilton, the widow of the Deputy Postmaster-General of North America, Andrew Hamilton, and Robert West in 1706. Joyce, *History of the Post Office*, p. 116; and Wesley Everett Rich, *The History of the United States Post Office to the Year 1829*, Harvard Economic Studies, XXVII (Cambridge, Mass., 1924), 21. The other was a request by Jeffery Jefferys to have his ship *Eagle*, 180 tons, 14 guns, Capt. John Davison, designated a packet; the Treasury appears to have accepted a proposal from him for two trial runs. Smith, *History of the Post Office in British North America*, pp. 32–33; and Staff, *Transatlantic Mail*, p. 32. Staff (op. cit., p. 114) prints Jefferys' petition to the Treasury and dates it ca. 1707. It is in Post Class 1/3, pp. 126–127, Post Office Archives, and from its placement in the volume, should be dated considerably earlier than 1707. Jefferys' ship was at New York in the spring of 1704. *An Account of Her Majesty's Revenue in the Province of New York, 1701–1709: The Customs Records of Early Colonial New York*, ed. Julius M. Bloch (Ridgewood, NJ, [1966]), pp. xvi–xvii, 122–123, 127. Additional impetus came in the form of a strongly favorable report by William Blathwayt, writing in his capacity as one of the Commissioners for Trade and Plantations. He thought that sailings from the continent ought to be at the rate of eight times a year and the North American rendezvous towards the middle of the continent. His report, dated 6 Sept. 1707, is summarized in the *Calendar of Treasury Papers*, by Redington, III, 532–533.

16 His proposals and the letter of referral, dated 28 Dec. 1709, are in Post Class 1/4, pp. 137–138, Post Office Archives.

17 The conditions of Warren's contract are unknown but Dummer's 1705 contract had been for three years with an option for an additional two more if the war continued. Letter of Cotton and Frankland to William Lowndes, Sec. to the Treasury, 6 Nov. 1704, Post Class 1/3, pp. 236–238, Post Office Archives; Lowndes to the Postmaster General,

announcing a new monthly packet between Bristol and New York City and listing a scale of rates.[18] He began the service in the fall of 1710.

At least five, and perhaps seven packets left from Bristol in the next few years under Warren's contract (see table 8.1). The inaugural passage to New York City was made by Captain John Shorter in the brig *Royal Anne*. He left Bristol about the end of September and took fifty days out and twenty-eight more home. Shorter arrived back in Bristol early in January 1711. The second packet had left for New York only a few days earlier. There were three more sailings in 1711, the last one reaching its destination in March the year following. After each arrival in New York City, John Hamilton, the Postmaster for North America, placed an advertisement in *The Boston News-Letter* announcing the intended departure date of the packet for Bristol and enjoining all those interested to forward mail to New York to meet that deadline. In August 1711 he optimistically echoed Warren's broadside and proclaimed that "a Packet Boat will be ready to sail the last of every month for New York (Wind and Weather permitting)."[19] But the next year was the last for the packet ships, and even then there is doubt about the status of the ships that made the journey. It might have been that Warren realized what the increased number of merchant ship sailings reported in the Boston newspaper made quite apparent: with the ending of the war at sea in mid-1712, there was little need for a packet service. Letters went by the first ship. His contract was probably allowed to expire, or was broken, about this time. What voyages his ships now undertook were made as simple merchantmen. Packet service from England to New York was not revived until 1755 when the Falmouth packets were established during the Seven Years War with France.[20]

14 Nov. 1704, [GB, PRO], *Calendar of Treasury Books Preserved in Her Majesty's Public Record Office*, by William A. Shaw, in progress (London, 1904 to date), XIX, 412. If Warren's contract also ran for three full years, it would have been in effect from the fall of 1710 to the fall of 1713.

18 [William Warren], *Whereas the Queen has been Pleased to Direct, that a Monthly Correspondence be Established between this Kingdom, and Her Majesties Dominions on the Continent of America, by Packet-Boats, to Pass to, and from Bristol and New York* ... ([London, 1710]). There is a copy in the Department of Printed Books, BL (press mark: 816.m.10 [no. 60]). L[awrence] W. Hanson, *Contemporary Printed Sources for British and Irish Economic History, 1701–1750* (Cambridge, Eng., 1963), p. 146, no. 1389, dates it tentatively to 1711.

19 The *Boston News-Letter*, the oldest newspaper in the British colonies, kept a close watch on maritime affairs. News reports from New York and elsewhere recorded the entries into and clearances from these ports as a matter of course. As one might imagine, news of the packets received special coverage. The advertisements supplemented this. They are the basis for table 8.1. Compare Frank C. Bowen, *A Century of Atlantic Travel, 1830–1930* (Boston, 1930), p. 3; and Steele, *The English Atlantic*, pp. 314–315. Colonial merchants followed these comings and goings carefully. See. e.g., Thomas Fitch, at Boston, to John Crouch and Samuel Arnold, at London, 27 Nov. 1710, Thomas Fitch Letterbook, 1703–1711, p. 470, American Antiquarian Society, Worcester, Mass. Compare similar, later letters to other correspondents (ibid., pp. 503–505, 507, 509, 523).

20 Staff, *Transatlantic Mail*, p. 35.

Table 8.1 The Bristol–New York packet service: the ships and their sailings, 1710–1713

Ship and Captain	Left Bristol	Arrived New York	Left New York	Arrived Bristol
Royal Anne	[late Sep.]	[mid Nov.]	[early Dec.]	[early Jan.]
John Shorter	1710	1710	1710	1711
Bristol	28 Dec.	17 April	7 May	[6 June]
William Ball	1710	1711[a]	1711	1711
Royal Anne	9 March	6 May	13 June	11 July
John Shorter	1711	1711	1711	1711
Harley	14 July	18 Aug.	18 Sept.	[18 Oct.]
John Palmer	1711	1711	1711	1711
Harley	11 Dec.	29 Mar.	26 June	28 July
Joseph Palmer	1711	1712[b]	1712	1712
Edgley[c]	5 March	3 May	[?]	[?]
	1712	1712	1712	1712
Harley[d]	14 Oct.	30 Dec.	[?]	[?]
Joseph Palmer	1712	1712	1713	1713

Notes and sources:
All the data for table 8.1 are derived from the weekly issues of the *Boston News-Letter* for these years; the newspaper reported New York shipping news regularly. Dates in square brackets are supplied based on averages calculated from these data. The average number of sailing days between Bristol and New York was 57; between New York and Bristol, 29. Compare Ian K. Steele, *The English Atlantic, 1675–1740: An Exploration of Communication and Continuity* (New York, 1986), pp. 314–315. See also the reference to the arrivals and departures of the packet ships in the letters of Boston merchant Thomas Fitch, Thomas Fitch Letterbook, 1703–1711, pp. 470, 503–505, 507, 509, 523, American Antiquarian Society, Worcester, Massachusetts.
[a] Arrived at Charleston, SC, 24 Feb.; later went aground before reaching New York.
[b] On the coast from early Feb.; stormy weather prevented its arrival at New York.
[c] Went to Philadelphia, although its announced destination had been New York. There is no further mention of this ship.
[d] There is serious doubt if this voyage of the *Harley* was made as a packet ship. Despite an initial announcement of its impending arrival that called it a packet, no further mention of it did so. More significantly, the usual advertisements specifying arrangements for forwarding mail by post from Boston to sail on the packet do not occur at this time and even its departure from New York went unreported. On a still later trip with the same captain in 1715, the *Harley*, definitely was not the Bristol packet ship; it returned from New York to London.

The Bristol to New York packet undoubtedly received some impetus from the Act of 1710 that reorganized the postal services of the empire and set up the General Post Office independent of the Treasury.[21] Regulations for packet mail were included in the provisions of the Act and it specified a scale of rates considerably above those traditionally assessed on transatlantic mail carried by merchant ship captains. In contrast to 2d. or 3d. sterling per letter, the new rates charged 1s. 6d. (7.5p) for each sheet of paper in a letter. Central post offices were established in Great Britain and the colonies; New

---

21 Act of 9 Anne, c. 11. (1710). See Staff, *Transatlantic Mail*, p. 32; and Smith, *History of the Post Office*, pp. 18–24. Compare Smith's article, "The Colonial Post-Office," *AHR*, XXI (Jan. 1916), 267–268.

York City was chosen as the central office for all North America.[22] How much such a choice was influenced by New York City's role as the western terminus of the packet service is a moot point, but the two developments seem obviously interrelated.

What we have learned about the Bristol packet service is enough, in itself, to date the cover to the period 1710 to 1713 simply on the basis of the one marking on its obverse. The other markings, on both sides of the piece, affirm such a conclusion and refine it. As noted above, the letter was charged the postage rate for packet mail and was so marked. After arriving in Bristol, packet mail traveled by express to London. At its destination the London Post Office applied another postmark, a "Bishop Mark," so called after Henry Bishop its inventor, to each piece to record the date it arrived. The cover in question was so stamped as received on "Ju[ne] 14." "Bishop Marks" were in use as London receiving marks for six score years and more but, despite the obvious omission of any indication of the year, stylistic differences in the design of the hand stamp permit some distinctions in their dating. The one used on this cover began to be employed in 1673 and was last used in 1713.[23] Thus, from the "Bishop Mark" alone, we can only say with certitude that the cover reached London on 14 June in the year 1713 or before. Nonetheless, in conjunction with the data in table 8.1, this does contribute an important element to the analysis. Only the second sailing of the packet, that of the *Bristol* (Captain William Ball), left New York City in time to have had a letter reach London on 14 June.[24] The year was 1711. All other sailings arrived either too early in a particular year, or too late.

Of far greater interest, and of some potential difficulty to the posited dating, is the impression of the New York hand stamp on the reverse of the cover.[25] The Post Office apparently required Warren's packet service to designate the point of origin of the letters handled, just as they had Dummer's

22 Act of 9 Anne, c. 11, sec. iv. Compare Smith, *History of the Post Office*, p. 19, n. 1, and Smith, "Colonial Post-Office," p. 267, n. 37; and Britnor, *British West Indies Postal Rates to 1900*, pp. 6–7, 12–13, 18.

23 Robson Lowe, *Handstruck Postage Stamps of the Empire, 1680–1900*, 2nd edn (London, [1938]), pp. 244–257.

24 For evidence of another letter that traveled from New York City in the *Bristol*, Capt. Ball, and was received in London on 14 June 1711, see [GB, PRO], *Calendar of State Papers, Colonial Series, America and West Indies [1574-1739]*, by W[illiam] Noel Sainsbury *et al.*, 45 vols in 46 pts (London, 1860–1994), XXVI, 3. See also the letters of Samuel Sewall at Boston to William Ashurst at London, 30 April 1711, 21 May 1711, and 5 May 1712, Correspondence from Boston, 1677–1761 (MS 7955), New England Company Archives, Guildhall Library, London.

25 A black, straight-line marking, at its outside limits it measures 21 × 11 mm The top line ("NEW") is 17 mm long with the letters 4 mm high; the second line ("YORK") measures 21 mm long with its letters 5 mm in height; the space between the two words is 2 mm (see fig. 8.1).

The paper on which this letter was written is typical letter paper of the period, imported into England from Holland and exported thence to the colonies. It is watermarked "C & I H," the mark of the Zaandyk mill of Cornelis and Jan Honig that produced paper from 1675 to 1902. See W[illiam] A. Churchill, *Watermarks in Paper in Holland, England,*

West Indies service. They also seem to have supplied the same type metal[26] hand stamp; all are of similar configuration.[27] A real difficulty would arise if this marking proved to be an impression of a device known to have been used much later as well. It would be necessary to explain either a lengthy gap in the use of the marking or the failure to find any examples of its use during the intervening years, although the very infrequent sailings of the packets might help to solve the latter difficulty.

Neither explanation is needed for there are no other known examples of a marking made by this hand stamp. Even a cursory examination quickly establishes that this marking bears only a general resemblance to similar hand stamps used at New York after mid-century, rendering such discussions superfluous. The marking is unique. While it shares a two-line format with later devices used at New York, the hand stamp that made this marking differs distinctly from the others both in size, it is smaller, and in the form of most of the letters. Benjamin Franklin, who served as a Deputy Postmaster General of the colonies from 1753 to 1774, usually is credited with the introduction of these New York hand stamps as part of his important reforms of the colonial postal system. The earliest example of their use occurs on a cover sent from New York City to Colonel George Washington on 17 June 1756. Several types are known to have been employed until about 1772.[28] To resolve the similarity in the design of the earlier and later New York markings requires

France, etc., in the XVII and XVIII Centuries and Their Interconnection (Amsterdam, 1935), pp. 6, 15, 40, 54. There is no illustration of precisely this watermark, but see nos 87, 160, 179, 184, 408, 429, and 566 Any dating of the paper can, of course, tell us only when the paper was made and not when the letter was sent.

26 I say "metal" for three reasons. First, those issued for Dummer's service were metal. There is no reason to think that another kind would have been made for New York. Second and third, the marking has two of the characteristics of one made by a new metal stamp. It is poorly inked; but the impression is very clearly defined because of the deep impress made by the strike into the paper.

27 For examples, see the two line "BARBA / DOES" marking on two covers, ca. 1760, among the collections of the National Postal Museum of the Smithsonian Institution (accession number 280593). See, in this regard Cotton and Frankland to Deputy Postmasters, 29 Nov. 1705, as quoted in n. 9 of this chapter. Compare Lowe, *Handstruck Postage Stamps of the Empire*, pp. 33–34; Britnor, *History of the Sailing Packets to the West Indies*.

28 They are described and illustrated in *American Stampless Cover Catalog: The Standard Reference Catalog of American Postal History,* 3rd edn, ed. E[dward] N. Sampson *et al.* (North Miami, Fla., [1978]), pp. 150–152, and in earlier editions of the same work. Type A, designated there as "the earliest known handstamp used in America" (p. 151), is from the Washington cover. The section on New York City was edited by William H. Bauer (ibid., pp. 150–154). Compare Harry M. Konwiser, *United States Stampless Cover Catalogue* (Batavia, NY, 1936), pp. 3, 137. Konwiser's *Colonial and Revolutionary Posts: A History of the American Postal Systems, Colonial and Revolutionary Periods* (Richmond, Va., 1931), pp. 30, 66, illustrates the Washington letter, discusses its discovery, and calls it the earliest known marking. But later in his book (ibid., p. 72) Konwiser also illustrates Sampson Type A1 and dates it to 1711 (1771?). The Washington cover was found "in the archives of a government institution at Washington" by Delf Norona. See his "The Earliest American Postmark," *American Philatelist,* XLI (Aug. 1928), 725–726. Compare Robert F. Chalmers, "Straight Line Postal Markings," *American Philatelist,* XLII (Sept. 1929),

no more than to note that in both instances New York hand stamps were preceded by ones of the same format in the West Indies. The later New York hand stamp might simply have been patterned after those employed in the West Indies in the 1740s, in just the same way that, forty years before, the early hand stamp had been copied from the ones used for Dummer's service. The supposition can easily be made that the use of the 1710–1713 hand stamp ended with the termination of the service that had brought it into being.[29]

To satisfy ourselves still further about the appropriateness of assigning this cover to early in the second decade of the eighteenth century, it remains to identify Joseph Levy and his New York correspondent. While the latter man did not supply his full name to the reverse of the letter, he did seal it. The design of his seal encloses within a decorative scrollwork a crest mounting two fish in profile swimming in opposite directions. Above the crest are the two initials "NS" and it seems reasonable to assume that these are the initials of the owner of the seal and that it was he who wrote to Joseph Levy, merchant, of London. There is little point in regaling the reader with the details of several years' work in the archives. Suffice it to say the search for a New Yorker, presumably someone in business, most likely Jewish as Levy was, who corresponded with Levy, and who had these initials, eventually produced positive results. "NS" has been found.

Nathan Simson, born in Germany and bred in Holland and London, settled in New York City about the turn of the century. There he remained for over twenty years before he returned to England in mid-1722 to live in London until his death in the fall of 1725. He made his fortune in New York by dealing mostly in goods that he imported from Great Britain; he also imported slaves from Africa. Before his departure he had become an important figure in the community and had served it in both civil and religious capacities; he was elected constable in 1718 and in the 1720s was *parnas* or president of Congregation Shearith Israel. After his death, dissatisfied heirs challenged Simson's will in the English High Court of Chancery and, as a result, many of his mercantile papers, which were called by the Chancery as exhibits and never reclaimed, survive in the Public Record Office, London.[30] There, in full evidence, is ample testimony of his close relations with Joseph Levy.

781–791; V. W. Rotnem, "New York Straight Line Postmarks," *Collectors Club Philatelist*, XIII (Apr. 1934), 84–86; and Lowe, *Handstruck Postage Stamps of the Empire*, pp. 96–97. Sampson Type A measures 26 × 12.5 mm; Type A1, 24 × 12 mm; and Type B, 27.5 × 13 mm. All three have distinctive configurations in their lettering. The revised editions of the Sampson catalogue have ignored the findings presented in this chapter.

29 It was probably less than coincidental that packet service to New York was revived in 1755 and that hand stamp markings reappeared at roughly the same time.

30 The chief source for Simson and his affairs is this large collection, *Isaac v. DeFriez*, C 104/13–14, PRO. Some of these papers have been photostatted and microfilmed by the American Jewish Archives, Cincinnati, Ohio, the Director of which, Dr Jacob R. Marcus,

We know less of Joseph Levy than we do of Simson but he was the more prominent and certainly must have been the wealthier of the two. In 1712 he apparently loaned Prince Eugène of Savoy, famed Austrian statesman and general who had shared the victory at Blenheim with Marlborough, some £30,000, the modern equivalent (in 1997) of roughly £2,400,000 or $4,000,000, when adjusted for inflation.[31] It was at Joseph Levy's home that the renowned rabbinical authority of the day, Haham Zevi, stayed when he visited London from Hamburg in 1714. A London merchant who had long dealt in jewels and precious metals, Joseph was brother to Moses and Samuel Levy, merchants of New York, and acquaintances of Simson there.[32] Joseph Levy's younger son, Isaac, appeared as one of the executors of Simson's will and Simson called Isaac his nephew.[33] Depending on how the relationship

kindly made them available to the author. Published information concerning Simson is scattered. On his origin and early life, see Jacob R. Marcus, "The Oldest Known Synagogue Record Book of Continental North America, 1720–1721," in *In the Time of Harvest: Essays in Honor of Abba Hillel Silver on the Occasion of His 70th Birthday*, ed. Daniel Jeremy Silver (New York [1963]), pp. 228–229; and [J. J. Lyons], "Items Relating to the Simson Family, New York," *Publications of the American Jewish Historical Society*, XXVII (1920), 371 and n. While in England he anglicized his name to Simson from the Hebrew "Shimshon," meaning Samson. This accounts for the variations found: Simson, Simpson, and Samson. He became a citizen of Great Britain on 15 June 1713; C. 104/13, pt i, PRO. Concerning his life in New York, see Marcus, "Oldest Known Synagogue Record Book," passim; Marcus, *Early American Jewry*, 2 vols (Philadelphia, 1951–1953), I, 64, 163; *Documents Illustrative of the History of the Slave Trade to America*, ed. Elizabeth Donnan, Carnegie Institution of Washington, Publication no. 409, 4 vols ([Washington, DC], 1930–1935), III, 444, and 472, n. 6; *Select Cases in the Mayor's Court of New York City, 1674–1784*, ed. Richard B. Morris, American Legal Records, vol. II (Washington, DC, 1935), pp. 701–704; and "Wills of Early New York Jews [1704–1799]," ed. Leo Herskowitz, *American Jewish Historical Quarterly*, LV–LVI (Mar., Sept. and Dec. 1966), 330, n. 5, 342, n. 1, 339, n. 1, and 200, n. 1. Simson's Journal, 1714–1723, in the collection of his papers, establishes that he left New York sometime after 18 June 1722 and arrived in London before 21 Aug. that same year (C 104/13, pt ii, PRO). On Simson's own will, see Samuel Oppenheim, "Will of Nathan Simson, a Jewish Merchant of New York before 1722, and Genealogical Note Concerning Him and Joseph Simson," *Publications of the American Jewish Historical Society*, XXV (1917), 87–91. The registered copy of Simson's will is in PROB 11/605, fol. 281, PRO. It is dated 3 Aug. 1725 and was probated 24 Oct. 1725. Simson obviously died sometime during the intervening period. On the court case and its outcome, see the depositions taken in the summer of 1743 in Bills, Answers, and Depositions, E 112/1202, 16 & 17 Geo. II, Trinity, no. 1970, PRO; [GB, Court of Chancery], *Reports of Cases Argued and Determined in the High Court of Chancery, during the Time of Lord Chancellor Eldon*, comp. Francis Vesey and John Beames, 1st American edn, ed. Edward D. Ingraham, 3 vols in 2 pts (Philadelphia, 1822), I, 372, n. (a); and Albert M. Fridenberg, "The Simson Trust," *Publications of the American Jewish Historical Society*, XXVIII (1922), 246–248.

31 So stated Levy's obituary notice in the *Weekly Courant or, British Advertiser* (London), 14 Oct. 1721. See Matthias Levy, "Jews in the English Press," *The Jewish Chronicle* (London), 19 Aug. 1904, p. 20; and Cecil Roth, *The Great Synagogue, London, 1690–1940* (London, [1950]), pp. 27–28, 47, 52. For the occasion, see also Alfred Arneth, *Prinz Eugen von Savoyen*, [2nd edn], 3 vols (Vienna, 1864), II, 194–217.

32 "Wills of Early New York Jews," ed. Herskowitz, pp. 342–343, 347–351.

33 Oppenheim, "Will of Nathan Simson," p. 89. Arthur P. Arnold, "Anglo-Jewish Wills and Letters of Administration (Registered at the Principal Probate Registry, Somerset House, London)," in *Anglo-Jewish Notabilities: Their Arms and Testamentary Dispositions* (London,

Figure 8.2 Statement of account, London, 10 February 1717/18. A statement of account between Nathan Simson and Samuel Levy. This was written in the same handwriting as that used to address the letter in figure 8.1. Compare especially the words "To", "Levy", "p[e]r", and "London", and the letters "B" (in Bristol and Balance) and "J" (in Joseph and Jacob). The statement of account is among the Nathan Simson Papers, C. 104/13, Public Record Office, London. By permission Controller of HM Stationery Office.

was based, Nathan Simson and Joseph Levy might have been brothers-in-law. If not, their wives were sisters. Whether related or not, the two men must have known one another well before Simson left London. They carried on occasional business from as early as we have records until Joseph Levy died at six o'clock in the afternoon of Friday, 4 October 1721.[34]

Not only do Simson's papers demonstrate that he could have written the letter in question but a comparison of handwriting proves that he did write it (see figure 8.2). The hand that addressed this cover also wrote a variety of the documents now part of the collections of the Public Record Office, London, all of which date between 1703 and 1725.

1949), p. 178, noted the probate of a will of Isaac Levy in 1772. The Portsmouth family of engravers by the name of Levy had a son Isaac who died in 1795. Cecil Roth, "The Portsmouth Community and Its Historical Background," *Transactions of the Jewish Historical Society of England*, XIII (1932–1935), 161–162, 176; Alfred Rubens, "Early Anglo-Jewish Artists," *Transactions of the Jewish Historical Society of England*, XIV (1935–1939), 102–103; Albert M. Hyamson, "Plan of a Dictionary of Anglo-Jewish Biography," in *Anglo-Jewish Notabilities*, p. 40.

34 The papers in C 104/13–14, PRO, provide a reasonably full record of Simson's business affairs. The name of Joseph Levy can be found frequently among those papers. See particularly the Account Book, 1713–1719, and the Ledger 1714–1722, in C 104/13, pt i, PRO; the Journal, 1714–1723, in C 104/13, pt ii, PRO; and the Journal, 1718–1722, C 104/13, pt iii, PRO. In C 104/14, PRO, is a copy book of the letters that Simson sent and a great many letters that he received. More letters to him and a very few letters from him are in C 104/13, pt i. The latter are, as one should expect in a collection of this type, a rare item. The vast majority of the letters he sent would naturally have ended up elsewhere – as did the one here under examination. There are, therefore, no further

To summarize what has been said about the date of the letter, it is sufficient to note that it was sent from New York by a man who lived there between roughly 1703 and 1722 to a man in London who died in 1721. It was addressed in the same handwriting as other documents found in a collection of the sender's papers. It traveled by a mail service that existed from 1710 to 1713. Marked as received at the London Post Office on 14 June, there is only one voyage of the packet service upon which it could have traveled, the initial sailing of the packet ship *Bristol* in 1711. Administrative, philatelic, archival, and genealogical evidence unite to support the validity of the conclusion that this letter was sent from New York early in May of 1711.

Corollaries proceed from such a conclusion. The New York marking used on this cover is the oldest known North American postal marking produced by a hand stamp. Its use seems to have been tied to the packet service and it is not impossible that, for New York at least, this was solely the packet marking. Manuscript markings were employed again afterwards and, for overland and non-packet transatlantic mail, might well have been used concurrently with the hand stamp. This does not seem to have been the case at a later date. Franklin's contribution maintains its innovative aspect, therefore, for his hand stamp serviced inland mail too.

The letter traveled on precisely the business and precisely the route that the organizers of the packet service had intended. It linked English and colonial merchants and secured their communications during a time of war. London merchants, like Joseph Levy, had been the ones who had pressed for the packet. For Levy and Simson, and many more like them, the mails meant the continuation of their business but government, too, realized the need, and reaped the advantages of secure lines of communication with the Continental Colonies. For New York and the merchants of the colony, direct mail service to England meant economic advantage and seems to have had some role in the choice of the city as the site of the central post office. How much precedent meant when the packet service was later revived we can only guess, but the location of the administrative center for the post office there must surely have been an important determinant when it was reestablished there in the 1750s.[35] Thus, this lone example of the mail carried on board the Bristol packet serves to bring into sharp focus not only the existence of the service – until now not widely appreciated – but also the pressures that brought it into being and some of the ramifications it had for the Continental Colonies and the colonists.[36]

examples of the seal he used on this letter and no other letters with a marking like this one; at least the author's search uncovered none.

35   Robert Greenhalgh Albion, *The Rise of New York Port, 1815–1860* (New York, 1939), p. 6.

36   After the original essay was in the hands of the editor, the author learned of and was able to consult a copy of Kay Horowicz and Robson Lowe, *The Colonial Posts in the United States of America, 1606–1783* (London, 1967). Unfortunately it incorporated nothing of value for this present study. The authors ignored the Bristol packet, despite the mention of it by Bowen, by Staff, and by Robinson; the material on New York cancellations was, as they admitted, totally dependent on the 2nd edn of the *American Stampless Cover Catalog*.

9

COLONIAL CIVIL SERVANT AND COUNTER-REVOLUTIONARY

Thomas Irving (1738?–1800) in Boston, Charleston, and London

For the last two decades of the eighteenth century almost every officially compiled account of the trade of Great Britain and its empire bore the signature of Thomas Irving (1738?–1800).[1] A careful, astute, efficient administrator, Irving was one of many Scots employed in the British civil service. (See figure 9.1.) Since his early years included experience in Great Britain's North American colonies, aspects of his career offer considerable insight into a significant period of Anglo-American history. Among his many activities were an attempt at forestalling the American revolutionary movement from the vantage point of the customhouse in Boston and, later, at thwarting the emerging, post-war economic independence of the United States from a strategic post within the customhouse in London. His failure in the first enterprise fueled his ardor for the second, an effort in which he was indeed more successful.

The surviving personal details of Irving's life are sparse. He was the fourth son of William Irving of Gribton (ca. 1690–1774), a member of a strongly Jacobite strain of the Irvings of Dumfriesshire, and Katherine Menzies of Enoch; they had twelve children in all. The family estate, where Thomas Irving was presumably born, consisted of several hundred acres in the parish of Hollywood, about four miles northwest of the burgh of Dumfries.[2]

---

1   The original version of this chapter was published in *Perspectives in American History*, XII (1979), 313–350. Copyright © 1979 by the President and Fellows of Harvard College and afterwards transferred by assignment to the author. Copyright © 1995 by John J. McCusker. This revision is presented here with thanks to the original publishers and to the President and Fellows of Harvard College.

   I continue to be grateful for the help and support given me by the American Council of Learned Societies, National Endowment for the Humanities Research Fellowship at the American Enterprise Institute Center for Advanced Study, Washington, DC, and the Institute of Early American History and Culture, Williamsburg, Virginia.
2   All that we are ever likely to know about Thomas Irving of Gribton and the Irving family has been assembled by Alastair M. T. Maxwell-Irving of Stirlingshire, Scotland, in a model

Figure 9.1 Thomas Irving (1738?–1800). Small monochrome drawing.
Done just before his death on 13 July 1800.
Formerly in the possession of Mrs Isobel Irving of Wellwick, Wendover,
Buckinghamshire, England. Courtesy of A. M. T. Maxwell-Irving,
Stirlingshire, Scotland.

of genealogical research. He has been both kind and generous in placing the results of his efforts at the author's disposal and I am grateful for his help. Maxwell-Irving's study, "The Irvings of Dumfries (Senior Cadets of the Irvings of Bonshaw)" (unpublished typescript, 1968), is on deposit in the National Library of Scotland, Edinburgh, and Ewart Public Library, Dumfries. It is founded largely on family papers still in private hands and is itself the basis of the entry in [John] Bernard Burke, *Burke's Genealogical and Heraldic History of the Landed Gentry*, ed. Peter Townend, 18th edn, 3 vols (London, 1965–1969), II, 338–340. See also Maxwell-Irving's *The Irvings of Bonshaw: Chiefs of the Noble and Ancient Scots Border Family of Irving* (Bletchley, 1968), p. 32. His efforts, and some of my own – directed largely by the suggestions of Jacob M. Price of the University of Michigan – are the foundation of most of what is said in this chapter about Irving's family. See also John Beaufin Irving, *The Irvings, Irwins, Irvines, or Erinveines, or Any Other Spelling of the Name: An Old Scots Border Clan* (Aberdeen, 1907), pp. 84–86, 220, based in part on an article in the *Dumfries Courier*, 5 June 1877; and Burke, *Genealogical and Heraldic History of the Landed Gentry*, 6th edn, 2 vols (London, 1879), I, 856. For Gribton, see Francis H. Groome, *Ordnance Gazetteer of Scotland: A Survey of Scottish Topography, Statistical, Biographical, and Historical* (Edinburgh, 1886), II, 228, 273–274.

The miniature of Thomas Irving illustrated here as fig. 9.1 was supplied to me by Mrs Isobel Stuart Irving of Wellwick, Wendover, Buckinghamshire, England, the wife of Charles Maxwell Trelawny Irving. The inscription on the back of the miniature, said to be in the handwriting of Thomas's grandson James Corbet Irving, reads: "Thos. Irving, Esqr., taken a few hours before his death 13th July, 1800." Letter from C. M. Trelawny Irving, at Wellwick, to [A. M. T.] Maxwell-Irving, 6 Nov. 1962. Copy in the author's possession.

Thomas Irving's father and Thomas's brother James were among a handful of people in Dumfries who were cited as active supporters of Bonnie Prince Charlie in the rebellion of 1745.[3] Another brother, Charles, a naval doctor and something of an inventor, demonstrated a practical method for the desalination of sea water for which in 1772 Parliament granted him the rather spectacular sum of £5,000, the modern equivalent (in 1997) of roughly £320,000, more than $530,000.[4] In later life Thomas Irving frequently visited Edinburgh, on 3 April 1774 he and Marion Corbet, the daughter of a merchant and Provost of Dumfries burgh were married there, and it is possible that he attended school or worked there or at Glasgow while a young man.[5] Irving acquired learning

3   For father and son in The '45, see Herbert Maxwell, *A History of Dumfries and Galloway*, 2nd edn (Edinburgh, 1900), pp. 360–361; *A List of Persons Concerned in the Rebellion, Transmitted to the Commissioners of the Excise by the Several Supervisors in Scotland, in Obedience to a General Letter of the 7th May 1746 with a Supplementary List with Evidences to Prove the Same*, ed. Walter Macleod, Publications of the Scottish History Society, [1st ser.], vol. 8 (Edinburgh, 1890), pp. 142–145; and letter from W. C. at Dumfries to George Clerk at Durham, in W[illiam] A. J. Prevost, "Letters from Dumfries during the Jacobite Rebellion in 1745," Dumfriesshire and Galloway Natural History and Antiquarian Society, *Transactions and Journal of Proceedings*, 3rd ser., XL (1961–1962), 178 and n. 25.

4   The Admiralty had already granted him £300 in 1771. Secretary to the Admiralty to Charles Irving, 9 Oct. 1771, Adm. 2/731, PRO; [GB, Parl., Commons], *Journals of the House of Commons*, in progress ([London, 1742 to date]), XXXIII, 534, 600, 661–664, 714, 717, 740–741, 745; *The Annual Register . . . for the Year 1772* (London, 1773), "Chronicle," pp. 98, 212; Thomas Irving, at London, to Dr William Smibert, at Boston, 3 Mar. 1772, as referred to in Smibert to Dr Thomas Moffat, 8 Apr. 1772, in the papers of Dr Thomas Moffat, bundle labeled "Smibert to Moffat . . . 1767–1773," *Curgenven v. Peters*, C 106/193, pt i, PRO – hereafter cited as "Moffat Papers" (both physicians were friends of Irving; Moffat held the position of Comptroller of Customs at New London, Conn.); *Virginia Gazette* (Williamsburg), ed. Alexander Purdie and John Dixon, 20 May 1773; Constantine John Phipps, *A Voyage Towards the North Pole Undertaken by His Majesty's Command, 1773* (London, 1774), pp. 11, 28, 205–221; James Lind, *An Essay on the Most Effectual Means of Preserving the Health of Seamen in the Royal Navy*, new edn, enl. (London, 1774), pp. iv, 97–130; John Sinclair, *The Statistical Account of Scotland. Drawn Up from the Communications of the Ministers of the Different Parishes*, 21 vols (Edinburgh, 1791–1799), I, 35; Christopher [C.] Lloyd and Jack L. S. Coulter, *Medicine and the Navy . . . 1714–1815*, vol. III of J[ohn] J. Keevil, Christopher [C.] Lloyd and Jack L. S. Coulter, *Medicine and the Navy, 1200–1900* (Edinburgh and London, 1961), pp. 90–92, 313; *The Journals of Captain James Cook on His Voyages of Discovery*, ed. J[ohn] C. Beaglehole, 5 vols in 6 pts (Cambridge, Eng., 1955–1974), II, 10; P[atricia] K. Crimmin, "A Distilling Machine of 1772," *MM*, LII (Nov. 1966), 392; J. E. Roberts, "Distillation of Water at Sea," *MM*, LXIV (Nov. 1978), 299–300; J. A. Sulivan, "The Distillation and Purification of Water at Sea," *MM*, LXV (May, 1979), 161–162; and Ann Savours, "The Parliamentary Award of 1772 to Dr. Charles Irving for Salt Water Distillation at Sea," *MM*, LXXVI (Nov. 1990), 362–365.

5   Maxwell-Irving, "Irvings of Dumfries," pp. 72–73; *Register of Marriages of the City of Edinburgh, 1751–1800*, ed. Francis J. Grant, Publications of the Scottish Record Society, [o.s.], vol. 53, 1 vol. in 11 pts (Edinburgh, 1917–1922), p. 374. James Corbet (1709?–1762) was Provost of Dumfries, 1758–1760. William McDowall, *History of the Burgh of Dumfries, with Notices of Nithsdale, Annadale, and the Western Border*, 3rd edn (Dumfries, 1906), pp. 607–619, 868–869, and elsewhere. See also McDowall, *Memorials of St. Michael's, the Old Parish Churchyard of Dumfries* (Edinburgh, 1876), pp. 65–66. Marion Corbet Irving's father and her uncle Thomas Corbet were merchants and shipowners of Dumfries engaged in the Virginia trade. Some of their business papers, from the years

and sophistication somewhere and one might plausibly conjecture that this exemplar of the new, rationalized bureaucracy was early exposed to the ideas of Adam Smith but there is no direct evidence of this.[6]

Ties of blood and kinship were important to Thomas Irving.[7] His country credentials as a member of an ancient and noble landed family greatly assisted his early career. Through his mother's family, the Menzies of Enoch and Stenhouse, Irving was related to Charles Douglas, the third Duke of Queensberry, a favorite of King George III, and to others in Queensberry's political circle in Dumfries. John Douglas of Kelhead, a second cousin of Thomas's mother, was the Member of Parliament for Dumfries from 1741 to 1747, on Queensberry's interest. One observer called him "the chief director of his friend the Duke of Queensberry's country affairs and parliamentary interest in the county of Dumfries." Imprisoned in the Tower of London for two years because of his involvement in The '45, John Douglas was doubtless willing to look after the son and brother of like-thinking men and to recommend Thomas to Queensberry. In 1770 a colleague of Irving's in the Customs pointedly informed the Treasury, the fountain of patronage, that "the Duke of Queensberry is a friend of Mr. Irvings family and will probably make some appl[icatio]n on his behalf."[8]

1745 to 1762, are in the James Corbet Papers, 1745–1762, Court of Sessions Productions, CS 96/2147–2162, 4912–4193, Scottish Record Office, Edinburgh.

6   Smith was part of the same Douglas–Queensberry clientage network to which Irving belonged (see n. 8 of this chapter) and accompanied Henry Scott (1746–1812), later the fifth Duke of Queensberry, as his tutor on the Grand Tour; see *Dictionary of National Biography*, ed. Leslie Stephen and Sidney Lee, 63 vols (London, 1885–1901), s.v. One author has identified some of Irving's ideas as "Smithian." John Ehrman, *The Younger Pitt: The Years of Acclaim* (London, 1969), p. 503. And Adam Smith and Thomas's eldest brother and namesake were in the same class at the University of Glasgow, Smith having matriculated in his third year in 1737 and Irving in his fourth year in 1738. W[illiam] Innes Addison, ed., *The Matriculation Albums of the University of Glasgow from 1728 to 1858* (Glasgow, 1913), pp. xx, 18, 20. The first Thomas died soon thereafter and, as happened, William and Katherine named their next baby boy after their dead first son. Since Thomas's younger brother Joseph Irving of Borran, Kirkbean, was also born in the 1730s, our Thomas, arriving between the death of his eldest brother and the birth of this younger one, had to have been born in 1738 or very early in 1739. Maxwell-Irving, "Irvings of Dumfries," pp. 51, 92–93.

7   Unfortunately there is little about his early life or family in the single most important collection of materials relating to Irving, the various papers he prepared in support of his claim for compensation as a Loyalist *émigré*. See the Memorials and Supporting Documents Presented by Thomas Irving to the Loyalist Claims Commission, ser. I, 1786–1788, AO 12/51, fols 152v–164v, PRO. There are copies of the materials in Series I in the Transcripts of the Manuscript Books and Papers of the Commission of Enquiry into the Losses and Services of the American Loyalists, 1783–1790, New York Public Library, New York City. For related documents concerning Irving, see AO 13/130, fols 24–56, PRO. For a summary of his earlier case and the determinations made, under dates 27 May and 11 June 1783, see AO 12/99, fols 282r–283v, PRO. There is no other known collection of "Thomas Irving Papers." Compare, John Ehrman, *The British Government and Commercial Negotiations with Europe, 1783–1793* (Cambridge, Eng., 1962), pp. 12n.

8   For Irving's place in the Douglas–Queensberry patronage system, the establishment of which I owe in great measure to Jacob M. Price, see [John Anderson], "Douglas, Duke of Queensbury," in *The Scots Peerage*, ed. James Balfour Paul, 9 vols (Edinburgh,

Personal friendships, as well as family connections, played an influential role in Irving's life. At Boston, during his service in the colonies, he fell in with Charles Steuart, the Surveyor-General of the Customs in the Eastern-Middle District of America and later Cashier and Paymaster-General of the Customs in North America. Steuart had himself come out from Scotland in 1742 and had worked as a merchant at Norfolk until his diplomatic handling there of the potentially explosive "Spanish Affair" in 1762, during the Seven Years War, earned him his Surveyor-Generalship in 1765. Two years later he became the Cashier and Paymaster-General: offices that, after he returned home in 1769, he exercised through his deputy, Nathaniel Coffin.[9] By way

1904–1914), VII, 143–147, 150–151; Craufurd Tait Ramage, *Drumlanrig Castle and the Douglases: with the Early History and Ancient Remains of Durisdeer, Closeburn, and Morton* (Dumfries, 1876), pp. 93–94; and R[obert] C. Reid, "The Baronies of Enoch and Durisdeer," Dumfriesshire and Galloway Natural History and Antiquarian Society, *Transactions and Journal of Proceedings*, 3rd ser., VIII (1923), 153–171. For John Douglas (ca. 1708–1778), see Romney Sedgwick, *The History of Parliament: The House of Commons, 1715–1754*, 2 vols (London, 1970), I, 384, 618. The quotation about him is from a memorandum by Alexander Dick in *Curiosities of a Scots Charta Chest, 1600–1800, with the Travels and Memoranda of Sir Alexander Dick, Baronet, of Prestonfield, Midlothian Written by Himself*, ed. Margaret Alice Forbes (Edinburgh, 1897), p. 223. The quotation about Irving is in a letter from Joseph Harrison, [at London?], to Grey Cooper, at London, [1770], AO 12/51, fol. 161r, PRO, and AO 13/130, fol. 34v, PRO. Harrison, Collector of Customs at Boston, wrote this letter to Cooper, one of the joint Secretaries to the Treasury (1765–1782), soon after Harrison arrived back in England in 1770. See Harrison, at "Bawtry," to Irving, 7 Nov. 1783, AO 12/51, fol. 160r, PRO, and AO 13/130, fol. 28v, PRO. Irving's family, headed by his brother James, who became Laird of Gribton in 1773, was still considered to be firmly in the Queensberry camp fifteen years later. *View of the Political State of Scotland in the Last Century: A Confidential Report of the Political Opinions, Family Connections, or Personal Circumstances of the 2662 County Voters in 1788*, ed. Charles Elphinstone Adam (Edinburgh, 1887), pp. 97, 102. See also Lewis [B.] Namier and John Brooke, *The History of Parliament: The House of Commons, 1754–1790*, 3 vols (London, 1964), I, 476, II, 329, 332–333. Presumably it was the Duke of Queensberry to whom John Pownall, the Undersecretary of State for the Colonies, referred in his letter of introduction for Irving that he sent to Gov. Francis Bernard of Massachusetts: "Mr. Irving . . . who will wait upon you with this, has been particularly recommended to me by a friend." Letter, dated London, 23 Oct. 1767, Bernard Papers, vol. XI, p. 99, Jared Sparks Manuscripts, pt IV, Houghton Library, Harvard University, Cambridge, Mass. Given Pownall's own remarkable career, his recommendation was impressive in itself. For Pownall (1720–1795), in the words of Edmund Burke, "an able, intelligent, honest man, of remarkable probity," see Namier and Brooke, *House of Commons*, III, 315–316.

The Duke of Queensberry's patronage extended to writing the Loyalist Claims Commission on behalf of Alexander Irving, Thomas's younger brother, who accompanied him out to Boston in 1768, worked with him for a while there, and then moved to South Carolina where he set himself up as a planter in the vicinity of Georgetown, presumably near to his sister and brother-in-law, Winifred and Archibald Baird. Alexander, like his brother Thomas, was forced to leave the state in 1777. See his memorials to the commission dated 26 Dec. 1778 and 14 Feb. 1780, AO 13/70B, pt ii, fols 298r, 300r, 302r, PRO. See also nn. 10 and 63 of this chapter.

9 Steuart (1725–1797) deserves a full biography, the sources for which are readily available. See the Charles Steuart Papers, 1758–1798, MSS 5025–5046, Charters 3887, 4006, National Library of Scotland, Edinburgh; the Charles Steuart Letter Books, 1751–1763, HSP; the Charles Steuart Papers, 1762–1789, Colonial Williamsburg Foundation Library, Williamsburg, Va.; Steuart's memorial to the Loyalist Claims Commission, 26 Aug. 1789, AO 13/48, PRO; and the accounts of his office in AO 1/844/1137–1140, PRO, and AO

of Steuart, Thomas Irving not only had ties in the colonies to others like Coffin in the Customs bureaucracy but also to Steuart's Scottish merchant friends at Norfolk and elsewhere.[10] The two men maintained contact once Steuart was back in London, where he also proved helpful to Irving. Their friendship ended only with Steuart's death in 1797. Others among Irving's circle of acquaintances in London later in his life were John Baker Holroyd, Earl of Sheffield, the friend and editor of Edward Gibbon, and John Sinclair, Scottish MP, organizer and President of the Scottish Board of Agriculture, and the man who in the 1790s compiled the famous *Statistical Account of Scotland*.[11]

◆ ◆ ◆ ◆ ◆

3/305, PRO. See also [George Chalmers], ["Biographical Account of Charles Steuart, Esqr."], *Gentleman's Magazine*, LXVIII (May 1798), 442–444. The title supplied for this obituary is the one that Chalmers used to identify it in his own set of his collected works. George Chalmers, [*Works*], 26 vols in 8 pts ([London, 1777–1799]), III, [item 2], Division of Rare Books and Special Collections, LC. When Steuart arrived in England from Virginia in Nov. 1769, he had with him his black slave, James Somerset. Somerset later sued for his freedom, which was the occasion of the famous decision of Lord Chief Justice Mansfield in 1772. James Walvin, *Black and White: The Negro and English Society, 1555–1945* (London, 1973), pp. 117–131.

10 Thomas Irving was also associated by marriage with others in the Customs service. His youngest sister Winifred's first husband was Archibald Baird, Collector of Customs at Georgetown, SC, from 1740 until his death in 1777. Baird's memorial, 5 Mar. 1774, T 1/511, fols 204–205, PRO; Irving, *The Irvings*, p. 86; Maxwell-Irving, "Irvings of Dumfries," p. 52; Caroline T. Moore and Agatha Aimar Simmons, *Abstracts of the Wills of the State of South Carolina, 1670–1784*, 3 vols (Columbia, SC, 1960–1969), III, 264; George C. Rogers, Jr, *The History of Georgetown County, South Carolina* (Columbia, SC, [1970]), pp. 37–38, 48; Winifred [Irving] Baird, at Georgetown, SC, to Charles Steuart, 1 June 1778, in A[rchibald] Francis Steuart, "Letters from Virginia, 1774–1781," *Magazine of History*, III (Apr. 1906), 212–213; Steuart Papers, National Library of Scotland. His second cousin Ann Irving (1729?–1819) married David Blair (d. 1784), the Collector at Dumfries. Burke, *Landed Gentry*, ed. Townend, 18th edn, II, 338. Most importantly, Thomas Irving seems to have been related to Robert Menzies of Culterallers (d. 1769), the Inspector-General of Imports and Exports of Scotland, 1764–1769, whose family also came from Dumfries. Robert Menzies' father was Dr John Menzies, a physician there. Since it is likely that Irving had had some training and experience in the Customs service before 1767, we can speculate whether or not he might have worked as an assistant clerk in the Edinburgh office of his kinsman, the Scottish Inspector-General. (As such he would not have been carried upon the establishment.) This speculation has been provoked by Jacob M. Price, who also established the Dumfries connection of Robert Menzies. Personal communication, 31 July 1978, citing Robert Menzies Papers, Register House Records, Miscellaneous Bundles, RH 15/92/13, and Lanark Commissary Court Records, CC 14/5/18, Scottish Record Office, Edinburgh, and *The Register of Marriages for the Parish of Edinburgh, 1585–1750*, ed. Henry Paton, Publications of the Scottish Record Society, [o.s.], vols 27, 35, 2 vols in 11 pts (Edinburgh, 1905–1908), II, 330, 370.

11 For Sheffield (1735–1821), see n. 69 of this chapter. For Sinclair (1754–1835) – author of *The Statistical Account of Scotland*, 21 vols (Edinburgh, 1791–1799), see *The Correspondence of the Right Honourable Sir John Sinclair, Bart., with Reminiscences of the Most Distinguished Characters Who Have Appeared in Great Britain, and in Foreign Countries, during the Last Fifty Years*, [ed. John Sinclair], 2 vols (London, 1831), I, xvii–xxxiv; Rosalind Mitchison, *Agricultural Sir John: The Life of Sir John Sinclair of Ulbster, 1754–1835* (London, 1962); Namier and Brooke, *House of Commons*, III, 440–441; and n. 81 of this chapter. It was at a dinner party at John Sinclair's in Apr. 1790 that the brilliant American

The narrative of Thomas Irving's public life begins on 9 September 1767, the date of the warrant that appointed him Inspector-General of Imports and Exports and Register of Shipping of North America. This office had been established as part of the effort to tighten British control of the Thirteen Continental Colonies by reproducing in miniature at Boston the Customs establishment in London. Irving was thus part of the bureaucracy supervised by the Commissioners of the American Board of Customs. His job combined for the North American colonies two posts that were separate in London, the Inspector-General of Imports and Exports and the Register of Shipping. The former office oversaw the collection and compilation of the statistics of imperial trade, the latter supervised the registration of British vessels and compiled statistics concerning their employment.[12]

At Boston, Irving had to create the job from scratch. The Commissioners of Customs in London had sought to instruct him in his duties before he went out and even prepared samples of the required forms for his education.[13] But Irving altered both the forms and the substance of his position after he

---

diplomat Gouverneur Morris took Irving's measure and pronounced him "a statesman," although one "decidedly opposed to America." *The Diary and Letters of Gouverneur Morris, Minister of the United States to France . . .*, ed. Anne Cary Morris, 2 vols (New York, 1888), I, 315. Compare Charles R. Ritcheson, *Aftermath of Revolution: British Policy toward the United States, 1783–1795* (Dallas, 1969), p. 13.

12 Warrant, 9 Sept. 1767, T 28/1, p. 303, PRO. See also Treasury Board, meeting of 27 Aug. 1767, Minute Books, T 29/38, p. 459, PRO; and Thomas Bradshaw to Commissioners of the Customs, 28 Aug. 1767, announcing Irving's appointment, T 11/28, p. 145, PRO. For the establishment at Boston, reference should be had to Dora Mae Clark, "The American Board of Customs, 1767–1783," *AHR*, XLV (July 1940), 777–806. At one time Joseph R. Frese was at work on a book-length study of this body; I am in his debt for sharing with me some of the fruits of his research. The fullest discussion of the two London offices is still G[eorge] N. Clark, *Guide to English Commercial Statistics, 1696–1782*, Royal Historical Society, Guides and Handbooks, no. 1 (London, 1938), pp. 1–42, 45–51. See also Elizabeth Evelynola Hoon, *The Organization of the English Customs System, 1696–1786* (New York, 1938), pp. 116–119. Both positions were parts of the operations of the Customs which was itself part of the Treasury. The office of the Inspector-General was the antecedent of the modern Statistical Office of HM Customs and Excise. See Rupert C. Jarvis, "The Archival History of the Customs Records," *Journal of the Society of Archivists*, I (Apr. 1959), 245. We have no consolidated collection of Customs papers for this era, largely because of their destruction in the fire in the London customhouse in Feb. 1814. Edward [A.] Carson, *The Ancient and Rightful Customs: A History of the English Customs Service* (London, 1972), pp. 131–132. With minor exceptions, what papers do survive are now in the PRO. See nn. 16 and 24 of this chapter.

13 Commissioners of the Customs, at Custom House, London, to Lords of the Treasury, 26 Aug. 1767, T 1/459, fol. 140r, PRO. See also Treasury Board meeting of 26 Aug. 1767, T 29/38, p. 459, PRO. Some of their instructions might well have been based on a memorandum prepared by Henry Hulton, plantation clerk to the Customs Commissioners, 16 May 1765, about which the Commissioners thought highly enough to send it on to the Lords of the Treasury. T 1/442 fols 333–334, PRO. Hulton was later named as one of the Commissioners of the American Board of Customs. See *Letters of a Loyalist Lady: Being the Letters of Ann Hulton, Sister of Henry Hulton Commissioner of Customs at Boston, 1767–1776* (Cambridge, Mass., 1927); and "An Englishman Views the American Revolution: The Letters of Henry Hulton, 1769–1776," ed. Wallace Brown, *Huntington Library Quarterly*, XXXVI (Nov. 1972, Feb. 1973), 1–26, 139–151.

arrived. He was uniquely successful in bringing order and efficiency to the collection of American commercial statistics. Moreover, under his direction, these dispread data were consolidated into the first composite view of colonial commerce, a document that survives as the one-volume ledger of imports and exports of the North American colonies for the five years 1768–1772, known best by its classification in the Public Record Office, London: "Customs 16/1."

In 1770, in a report to the Commissioners of the American Board of Customs, Irving reflected on the state of the records before he had begun his reforms. Until he had reorganized things,

> accounts of imports and exports . . . were drawn out in a very confused, imperfect and inaccurate manner, the accounts of imports from Great Britain being entirely omitted by reason of the multiplicity of articles of which such cargoes generally consist, and the imports and exports to and from the neighbouring colonies (which commonly pass under the denomination of coasting trade) being seldom or ever inserted in the accounts and even such goods and commodities as were brought into account were not arranged in any order or method nor were the real quantity thereof ascertained with proper precision.[14]

After he had taken matters in hand, not only did he right all these wrongs, but he also introduced many innovations.

One of Irving's innovations involved the more systematic collection of information. The gathering of colonial trade data had started in the seventeenth century when Customs officials were first installed in each colonial "port" (i.e., Customs district or port of entry [POE]).[15] One of their responsibilities was to check the registry and the cargo of the vessels that cleared into and out of their ports in order to insure conformity with the Acts of Trade.[16] Each time a vessel came or went, the clerk of the Naval Office copied down the details of the ship and its cargo based on its registry certificate and manifests. He assembled the information quarterly and passed the completed compilation – the Naval Office shipping lists (NOSL) – to the colony's Governor who then sent them on to London. Sometime after Irving's assumption of office in May 1768, he directed the clerks of the Naval Office in all the colonial ports to dispatch them directly to his Boston office

---

14 Report, enclosed in Irving to American Board of Customs, Boston, 31 Jan. 1770, T 1/476, fol. 47r, PRO. Part of this report has been printed in Mary Alice Hanna, *Trade of the Delaware District before the Revolution* (Northampton, Mass., 1917), p. 285.

15 The best summary of the origins and functions of the clerks of the colonial Naval Offices is in Charles M. Andrews, *The Colonial Period of American History*, 4 vols (New Haven, Conn., 1934–1938), IV, passim. See also my own forthcoming study, *An Introduction to the Naval Office Shipping Lists* (in progress).

16 See, especially, the Acts of 12 Charles II, c. 4, and 14 Charles II, c. 11. Compare Lawrence A. Harper, *The English Navigation Laws: A Seventeenth-Century Experiment in Social Engineering* (New York, 1939), pp. 321–364.

in the customhouse.[17] Similar instructions were given to the Customs officers in those ports; he also told them to send him the duplicates of the ship registers issued in their ports.

With all of this information at hand, Irving and his assistants had the basis for producing their own yearly summaries of colonial trade. Before setting to work, however, they carefully scrutinized the shipping lists. One of Irving's office letter books survives; it testifies to his efforts to insure that these records were as complete and as accurate as could be. He badgered and threatened any who were recalcitrant and he questioned and cross-checked everything he found sloppy or suspect.[18] Such labors required his writing 700 letters in 1769 alone and the keeping of 250 ledgers.[19] Little if anything escaped his attention.

17 This is the date of "General Letter (No. 1)" over Irving's name in the Letter Book of the Inspectors-General of Imports and Exports and Register of Shipping in North America, 1768–1775, Customs 21/16, PRO.
     Irving had arrived at the end of Jan. *Massachusetts Gazette. And Boston News-Letter*, 4 Feb. 1768. The reference is to "Robert Irvine, the inspector of imports and exports" on board the brig *Abigail* after a cold passage of fourteen weeks; this suggests a departure from London the last week of Oct. 1767. (Irving carried with him a letter of introduction to Gov. Bernard dated 23 Oct.; it was endorsed as having been received 30 Jan. 1768 [see n. 8 of this chapter].) By contrast the Commissioners and some members of their staff, about twenty men altogether, had left London in mid-Sept. on board the ship *Thames* and arrived after a passage of six weeks on 4 Nov. 1767. They were greeted next day during the Bostonians' annual "Pope's Day" (Guy Fawkes Day) fête by signs pinned to twenty holiday dummies labeled "Liberty and Property and No Commissioners." [Hulton], *Letters of a Loyalist Lady*, p. 8; *Letters and Diary of John Rowe, Boston Merchant, 1759–1762, 1764–1779*, ed. Anne Rowe Cunningham (Boston, 1903), p. 145. See also the report of that day's events in [George Sackville], at London, to [John] Irwine, at Bath, 29 Dec. 1767, Germain Papers, 1683–1785, vol. 3, no. 64, fol. 136v, William L. Clements Library, University of Michigan, Ann Arbor, Mich.
18 See, e.g., Irving, at Boston, to Collector and Comptroller, at New York, 20 Jan. 1772, Customs 21/16, fols 28–29, PRO, in which he faults their carelessness. (Andrew Elliott was the Collector and Lambert Moore was the Comptroller.) Upon comparing the record of the clearance of the sloop *Sally* from the port of Philadelphia with the record of its entry in New York, Irving noted that the 28 hogsheads of rum and 2 casks of flour had been mistakenly entered as 28 hogsheads and 2 casks of flour. Irving did not imply fraud, though that may have been the case; rather he complained about a lack of due care.
19 Irving to American Board of Customs, 31 Jan. 1770, T 1/476, fols 46r–v, PRO. Very little of this material has come down to us. See Winslow Warren ["Loss of Boston Customs Records, 1776"], *Proceedings of the Massachusetts Historical Society*, XLIII (1909–1910), 423–428. Other than Customs 16/1, PRO, and the Letter-Book of the Inspectors-General, Customs 21/16, PRO, referred to above, there is not much else. Eleven miscellaneous accounts compiled in the Inspector-General's office survive as GB, Commissioners of the Customs in America, Customs Papers, 1765–1774, Massachusetts Historical Society, Boston. Three of them, nos 5, 6, and 7, are extracts from or duplicate parts of Customs 16/1, PRO. See also n. 27 of this chapter. There are also some of Irving's letters to the Collector of Customs at Philadelphia, John Swift, and some of Swift's responses, in Custom House Papers, 1750–1774, IX, fols 1084, 1101, 1102, 1104, and X, fols 1184, 1229, 1236, 1259, Custom House Papers, 1704–1789, HSP. See especially the "Directions in order to keep your books agreeable to the annex'd plan." It appears to have been an enclosure in Irving to the Collector and Comptroller of the Customs at Philadelphia, Boston, 26 Aug. 1768, Custom House Papers, IX, fols 1084, 1104, HSP. See also Alfred S. Martin, "The King's Customs: Philadelphia, 1703–1774," *W&MQ*, 3rd ser., V (Apr.

This is not to say that his data, as compiled in the Customs 16/1 ledger or preserved elsewhere, have no defects. For instance, despite all his letters, Irving never did get the officers at Port Royal, South Carolina, to send him even one of the quarterly reports that they were supposed to prepare. But according to Irving, this was "the only delinquent port in the continent."[20] There were other problems with the shipping lists and, therefore, with the ledger.[21] Since they recorded only the legally permitted trade, goods smuggled in or out did not appear in their pages. Sugar, molasses, and rum were the major smuggled imports and the quantities of these items recorded in the ledger are only a fraction of what really entered North American markets. Some tobacco was smuggled out.[22] Irving and other Customs authorities were

1948), 201–216. There are references to Irving and his reforms in the letters from William Smibert to Thomas Moffat, "Moffat Papers."

In addition to the reasons Warren offered (above), there is another explanation for the disappearance of these records. The London Custom House fire of 1814 mentioned in nn. 12 and 72 of this chapter destroyed not only all of the records generated in London that were stored there but also any from other ports that had been returned there, such as those brought home or sent home from abroad by Customs officers. Irving did just that; he brought home from Boston many such records. See his statement, in reference to his term as Inspector-General of Imports and Exports of North America, that "the books and papers of that office are still in my possession." Testimony, 5 Apr. 1791, [GB, Parl., Commons], *Minutes of the Evidence . . . Respecting the African Slave Trade*, HC Sessional Papers to 1801, Accounts and Papers, vol. XXXIV, no. 747 (3) [Lambert 4281] ([London], 1791), p. 265. Where they were when he spoke of them and what happened to them afterwards is not known but, if he or his son and successor, William Irving, deposited them with the Customs authorities prior to 1814, then they could have been lost in the fire.

20 Irving, at Boston, to Richard Halloway, Collector at Port Royal, SC, 16 Sept., 1769, Customs 21/16, fol. 11v, PRO; James Murray, at Boston, to Collector and Comptroller at Port Royal, SC, 12 Oct. 1774, Customs 21/16, fol. 32v, PRO. (Murray was Irving's successor; he took over in 1774. See n. 57 of this chapter.) Irving, at Boston, wrote the same thing to the Benedict Calvert, Collector at Patuxent, Maryland, 7 May 1770, Customs 21/16, fol. 20, PRO.

21 There are no figures for imports into any of the colonies from Great Britain for 1768 or 1772, for instance, and the data for Philadelphia are defective.

22 For the extent of the smuggling of sugar, molasses, and rum, see John J. McCusker, *Rum and the American Revolution: The Rum Trade and the Balance of Payments of the Thirteen Continental Colonies, 1650–1775*, 2 vols (New York, 1989 [Ph.D. diss., University of Pittsburgh, 1970]), passim. Concerning tobacco, in 1770 John Williams, the Inspector-General of the Customs in North America, estimated that about 80,000 hogsheads. were grown annually in Maryland and Virginia, of which only about 63,000 were legally exported. "The deficiency (being about 17,000 hogsheads) can be accounted for in no other way than that it is clandestinely carried away." Williams, at Boston, to American Board of Customs, 28 July 1770, T 1/476, fol. 259r, PRO, and as printed in Joseph R. Frese, "The Royal Customs Service in the Chesapeake, 1770: The Reports of John Williams, Inspector General," *Virginia Magazine of History and Biography*, LXXXI (July 1973), 315. Not only can one be skeptical of his estimate because of the recognized propensity of Customs officials to imagine smugglers behind every rock and tree, but also because he seems not to have allowed for any domestic consumption. In this regard, see Harper, *English Navigation Laws*, pp. 246–274 (esp. p. 262). Compare Andrews, *Colonial Period of American History*, IV, 240, n. 1: "Present-day conclusions are favorable to the idea that the colonists were not the inveterate smugglers that older writers, as well as some modern ones, have thought." See also n. 38 in chapter three of this book.

aware of these gaps, which they tried to repair and, more importantly for our purposes, for which they sought to compensate when compiling their data and basing arguments upon those compilations.[23] Modern historians, often following some of Irving's own suggestions, have continued these attempts.[24] As a result of Irving's efforts, eighteenth-century civil servants who collected and compiled the data were better able to understand the nature of their defects and thereby to correct for them. Twentieth-century scholars have been equivalently empowered.

We may well ask what it was that spurred Irving to reorganize on his own the collection and compilation of colonial trade data. He was later to do similar things as Receiver-General of the quit rents in South Carolina and, still later, on a grander scale, during a long career in London. His activity at Boston thus fitted a lifelong pattern of innovative assembly and analysis of financial and commercial information. More broadly, his behavior was characteristic of many Scots who joined the imperial civil service in the eighteenth century. Loyal, efficient, vigorous, industrious, public spirited, they worked hard at their jobs to please and impress their superiors. The reward sought and expected was advancement through the ranks to a higher position, larger salary, and greater prestige. Firm in their belief that they could serve the good of the public as well as their own through public office, many found that a term of service in the colonies moved their careers along more quickly. Yet the colonials, in North America at least, cared little for these professional administrators whose loyalties were clearly lodged in London just as the bureaucrats themselves someday expected to be. In the years after mid-century, especially in the colonial Customs service, this new type of professional civil servant came to predominate. Colonial and bureaucrat were bound to collide.[25]

23 See, e.g., Irving's testimony before the Commissioners for Trade and Plantations early in 1784, BT 5/1, PRO. There is a copy of this volume in the Liverpool Papers, Add. MS 38388, BL.

24 As one example, Irving appreciated that the colonists consistently registered their vessels at less than the full measured tonnage in order to diminish the impact of tonnage duties. He not only estimated how much the difference was, but also added it back when appropriate, in order to insure the comparability of data or the validity of an argument. See the account, dated Boston, May 11, 1771 [*sic*; 1772?], in John [Baker Holroyd], Lord Sheffield, *Observations on the Commerce of the American States*, 6th edn, enl. (London, 1784), p. 96; his testimony before the Commissioners for Trade and Plantations in 1784 in BT 5/1, p.165, PRO; and his letter to the Commissioners of the Land Revenues, London, Jan. 7, 1792, in [GB, Parl., Commons], *Journals of the House of Commons*, LXVII, 272–273, 356–357. See also John J. McCusker, "The Tonnage of Ships Engaged in British Colonial Trade during the Eighteenth Century," *Research in Economic History*, VI (1981), 73–105 – revised as chapter three of the present book.

25 For the Scots who ventured to the colonies, see Gordon Donaldson, *The Scots Overseas* (London, 1966); William R. Brock, *Scotus Americanus: A Survey of the Sources for Links between Scotland and America in the Eighteenth Century* (Edinburgh, 1982); and Alan L. Karras, *Sojourners in the Sun: Scottish Migrants in Jamaica and the Chesapeake, 1740–1800* (Ithaca, NY, [1992]). Stanley H. Palmer, *Economic Arithmetic: A Guide to the Statistical Sources of English Commerce, Industry, and Finance, 1700–1850* (New York, 1977), pp. 180, noted

Thomas Irving's efforts soon attracted considerable attention, both in the colonies and at home. His reforms pleased the Commissioners of the American Board of Customs, who wrote to London praising his work. In March 1770 they recommended him to the Lords of the Treasury, calling him "in all respects a good officer," and suggested that his salary be increased.[26] To demonstrate his abilities, the Commissioners sent along an early version of the ledger of imports and exports. Frederick, Lord North, First Lord of the Treasury and Prime Minister, was sufficiently impressed to keep it for himself; the volume remains among his papers to this day.[27]

It was not only in London that people were becoming aware of Irving's achievements. Each of his reforms served to tighten the control of the British government over American trade. Irving, as an efficient representative of the new Customs bureaucracy in North America, was helping to shape a pattern of administrative reform that many colonists perceived as an attempt to alter or annul their traditional privileges and rights. Some of the Customs men went even further and found in the stricter enforcement of legal minutiae an opportunity to make money from fees and fines. Oliver M. Dickerson has aptly described this last practice as "Customs racketeering."[28] Yet, just as all colonial merchants were not smugglers, neither were all Customs men racketeers. Such subtleties were lost upon both sides in the inflamed atmosphere of Boston during the crisis occasioned by the Townshend Revenue Act and the subsequent non-importation movement.[29]

the prominence of Scotsmen at this time in the collection and compilation of economic statistics, "whether because of the religious training or strong morality, the strenuous work-ethic or the educational system . . ." he confesses not to be able to discern. Compare Donaldson, op cit., p. 20, on the importance and quality of local education in Scotland.

26 American Board of Customs, at Boston, to Lords of the Treasury, 9 Mar. 1770, T 1/476, fols 45r–v, PRO. The Treasury increased his salary by £50 sterling, only half the recommended raise. Warrant, 16 July 1771, T 28/1, p. 370, PRO. The American Board of Customs did allow Irving the occasional extra sum for the hire of clerks. "List of Warrants issued by the Commissioners of His Majesty's Customs in America on Account of Incidental Expenses attending the Service," 10 Oct. 1769–10 Oct. 1770, T 1/471, fols 337–338, PRO.

27 Account of the Goods Imported into North America from Great Britain and Ireland, 1769, MS North c. 83 (SC 49488), Papers of Frederick, Lord North, 2nd Earl of Guildford, North Family Papers, Bodleian Library, Department of Western Manuscripts, University of Oxford. See also the Imports and Exports of North America, 1770, MS 1030, Department of Special Collections, Joseph Regenstein Library, University of Chicago, Chicago, Illinois. Both were signed by Thomas Irving.

28 Oliver M. Dickerson, *The Navigation Acts and the American Revolution* (Philadelphia, 1951). Joseph R. Frese has shown how the attempts by the American Board of Customs to "tidy up" two areas of customhouse administration – enforcing the payments of fees both for Customs certificates and for the support of the Royal Hospital for Seamen – caused considerable annoyance. Frese, "Some Observations on the American Board of Customs Commissioners," Massachusetts Historical Society, *Proceedings*, LXXXI (1969), 3–30; "The Greenwich Hospital Tax, Continued," *Essex Institute Historical Collections*, CVI (Jan. 1970), 46–53; and "Henry Hutton and the Greenwich Hospital Tax," *American Neptune*, XXXI (July 1971), 192–216.

29 Act of 7 George III, c. 46. The most convenient and authoritative overview of these events can be found in Merrill Jensen, *The Founding of a Nation: A History of the American*

Thomas Irving played an important if hitherto unappreciated role in the pre-Revolutionary crisis in the Thirteen Continental Colonies. A closer look at his actions shows him to have been one of the leaders in the drive by the Customs bureaucracy in Boston to discredit and destroy the non-importation movement. He may well have been motivated more by a positive regard for the laws of Parliament than by any strong negative reaction to the "patriots" of Boston. Still, his feelings about Bostonians must have been affected by the fact that they twice tried to do him bodily harm. In April 1768 and again the following June, the mob set upon him. The first time, a crowd of 200 people stoned and nearly sank a boat in which he and others had just departed from Long Wharf; the second time, again on Long Wharf, the mob attacked him, beat him, and dragged him through the streets.[30] Irving's clandestine scheme to discredit non-importation and, with it, the patriots' cause began soon thereafter and involved much of the Customs bureaucracy and loyalist Boston. The actions of Irving and his colleagues come close to being identifiable as a conspiracy, one that was supported at least after the fact by Lord North's government and that resulted in substantial rewards for the men involved, Irving included.[31]

Someone in the loyalist community in Boston hit upon the notion that the best way to disrupt non-importation was to show that the leading patriot merchants were cheating on their fellows and continuing to import goods from Great Britain. John Mein is usually given the credit for this scheme. Certainly he was the most visible participant. A Scot who came to Boston from Edinburgh in the fall of 1764, Mein and another Scot, John Fleeming, were the publishers of the *Boston Chronicle*, the largest newspaper in Boston,

---

Revolution, 1763–1776 (New York, 1968), pp. 334–372. See also Arthur Meier Schlesinger, *The Colonial Merchants and the American Revolution, 1763–1776*, Columbia University Studies in History, Economics and Public Law, vol. LXXVIII, no. 182 (New York, 1918), pp. 104–239.

30 Richard Reeve and Irving, at Boston, to American Board of Customs, at Boston, 18 Apr. 1768, T 1/465, fol. 72, PRO; Irving, at Boston, to American Board of Customs, 11 June 1768, T 1/465, fol. 130, PRO. There are copies of these depositions in the Liverpool Papers, Add. MS 38340, fols 214, 255, BL.

31 Isaiah Thomas, *The History of Printing in America* (1810), new edn, ed. Marcus A. McCorison (New York, 1970), p. 152, argued that a key figure, John Mein, "had unquestionably been encouraged, in Boston, as a partisan and an advocate for the measures of government." Schlesinger, *Colonial Merchants*, p. 160n., reads this as an inclination by Thomas toward "the contemporary opinion that Mein was in the pay of the government." Mein was indeed "in the pay of the government," but not directly, in the way Schlesinger's phrase would suggest. In other words, I do not think that the American Board of Customs Commissioners did anything more than take advantage of opportunities offered them to stir up trouble for the leaders of non-importation. Mein was in their pay as stationer and printer from spring 1769 and, I think, as nothing more – even if, after the fact, the Treasury did reimburse him for his costs (see n. 34 of this chapter). See John Mein, [at London], to the Lords of the Treasury, received 21 Mar. 1770, T 1/478, fol. 478r, PRO; "List of Warrants issued by the Commissioners of His Majesty's Customs in America on Account of Incidental Expenses attending the Service," 5 Apr.–10 Oct. 1771, T 1/482, fols 225–226, PRO. For what Dickerson makes of all this, see his *Navigation Acts*, p. 263, n. 81. I have been unable to trace his reference to "Mr. Irving from Scotland."

from December 1767 until its demise in June 1770. Beginning in August 1769, the *Boston Chronicle* published detailed copies of the manifests of cargoes imported by the leaders of the non-importers. John Hancock headed the list. Mein added an invective commentary upon the lives and habits of these men, only lightly screening their identities behind caustic pseudonyms. Hancock became "Johnny Dupe, a young man with long ears [and] a silly grin"; John Otis was "Counsellor Muddlehead"; and Sam Adams, "Samuel the Publican." Neither the name-calling nor the embarrassing revelations of their inconstancy was tolerated for long, and the mob was quickly unleashed upon Mein. He left town shooting – quite literally – on 17 November 1769, and was rewarded in London with a job writing propaganda for the North Ministry and a government pension.[32]

The newspaper pieces, both the cargo manifests and the satire, were soon reprinted in a book titled *A State of the Importations from Great-Britain into the Port of Boston, From the beginning of Jan. 1769 to Aug. 17th 1769* (Boston:

---

32 Mein's story has been told frequently. See Thomas, *History of Printing in America*, pp. 151–152; Schlesinger, Colonial Merchants, pp. 159–170; Charles M. Andrews, "The Boston Merchants and the Non-Importation Movement," *Publications of the Colonial Society of Massachusetts*, XIX (*Transactions*, 1916–1917), 227–230, 250–252; Arthur M. Schlesinger, "Propaganda and the Boston Newspaper Press, 1767–1770," *Publications of the Colonial Society of Massachusetts*, XXXII (*Transactions* 1933–1937), 411–416; John Eliot Alden, "John Mein, Publisher: An Essay in Bibliographic Detection," *Papers of the Bibliographical Society of America*, XXVI (1942), 199–214; and Alden, "John Mein: Scourge of Patriots," *Publications of the Colonial Society of Massachusetts*, XXXVI (*Transactions*, 1937–1942), 571–599. For another instance of Mein's contentiousness, see Catherine [S.] Menand, "Juries, Judges, and the Politics of Justice in Pre-Revolutionary Boston," in *The Law in America, 1607–1861*, ed. William Pencak and Wythe W. Holt, Jr. ([New York, 1989]), pp. 155–185.

Alden's second essay emphasized Mein's later career as a paid propagandist for the North ministry – he authored the "Sagittarius" letters – and ends the speculation about whether he ever returned to Boston. He did not. The chief reason for believing that Mein stayed on at, or later returned to Boston, is the continued appearance of the tracts associated with his name. Schlesinger, *Colonial Merchants*, p. 160n. See also Mein to Treasury, received 21 Mar. 1770, T 1/478, fols 478–479, PRO; "Extracts of a Letter from Mr Fleeming Printer at Boston to his Partner Mr John Mein now in London. Dated Castle William near Boston. July 1st 1770," Papers Relating to New England, vol. IV, fol. 5, Sparks Manuscripts, pt X; and John Mein, at London, to Lords of the Treasury, 1 July 1771, T 1/481, fols 62–63, PRO. Dickerson, *Navigation Acts*, p. 263, n. 81, inferred that Mein's inclusion in Lord North's list of those who received pensions (at £200 per year) was a reward for Mein's activities at Boston. The list included all those added between 1770 and 1782, however, and Mein's reward might just as easily have been for his later activities in London as for his earlier ones at Boston. *The Correspondence of King George the Third from 1760 to December 1783*, ed. John [W.] Fortescue, 6 vols (London, 1927–1928), V, 468.

The *Chronicle* ceased publication largely because, reacting to Mein's publishing of the manifests, some 700–800 subscribers canceled their orders for the newspaper. Mein to Treasury, received 21 Mar. 1770, T 1/478, fol. 478r, PRO. Among them was Nicholas Brown and Co. of Providence, RI. See Nicholas Brown and Co., at Providence, to Mein and Fleeming, at Boston, 16 Oct. 1769, Brown Papers, Correspondence-Miscellaneous, 1768–1769, John Carter Brown Library, Brown University, Providence, RI. I benefited in my understanding of Mein from a conversation with John Eliot Alden at Brown University in July 1975. I am grateful for his help.

Printed by Mein and Fleeming, 1769).[33] At least three and probably four further editions were printed in 1770. Only three of them survive in known copies, two of which are unique.[34] The 1770 editions all bore the same basic title, *A State of Importations From Great-Britain, Into the Port of Boston, From the beginning of January, 1770*; they differed only in their length. They all printed merely the cargo manifests: the first 1770 edition listed goods imported from 8 January through 5 May 1770; the second added an account of goods re-exported after January 1769; and the third added further manifests from the period 24 May through 29 June 1770.[35] There seems also to have been a fourth 1770 edition, judging from a reference to it in the *New-York Gazette and the Weekly Mercury* for 15 October 1770. The writer spoke of having "received [it] from the same authority"; it listed entries inward for 7 July through 14 August; there is no known extant copy of this edition. The three 1770 editions of which we have copies all used the same typeface as the 1769 edition, indicating that John Fleeming had continued to have a hand in publishing them after Mein had fled for his life.[36] But, as we might

33 John Mein signed the foreword. This is entry number 71 in Thomas R. Adams, *American Independence, the Growth of an Idea: A Bibliographic Study of the American Political Pamphlets Printed between 1764 and 1776 Dealing with the Dispute between Great Britain and Her Colonies* (Providence, RI, 1965), p. 54. The tract appears to have been published on 20 Nov. 1769. *Boston Chronicle*, 20 Nov. 1769. But see Cunningham, *Letters and Diaries of John Rowe*, p. 194. Mein stated that he "printed upwards of 4000 sheets of the principal importations and circulated them, gratis, over all America, from Florida to Nova Scotia; besides printing 500 copies of the whole, in a quarto pamphlet, one half of which he has, already, given away." Mein to Treasury, received 21 Mar. 1770, T 1/478, fol. 478v, PRO. There seem to be no surviving copies of the "4000 sheets," presumably a broadside printing of just the cargo manifests. Adams found only 9 copies of the tract in the 30 libraries he surveyed. Andrews, "Boston Merchants," p. 228n., appears to have seen a copy of the booklet "with an appendix of importations to January 1, 1770." Such an appendix was indeed advertised in the *Boston Chronicle* as forthcoming over about a ten-week period beginning 11 Dec. 1769, but there are no known copies. The copy of the pamphlet in Houghton Library (*AC7.M4771.769s), Harvard University, has this appendix, not printed, however, but handwritten.
34 Adams, *American Independence*, p. 64. The American Board of Customs paid Mein £28 14s. 3rd. (£28.71) "for paper and printing a state of the Importations for 1770 and Postage of Letters." T 1/482, fol. 225r, PRO.
35 For the complete titles and fuller bibliographical details, see entries 83a, 83b, and 83c in Adams, *American Independence*, p. 64. Compare entry number 11744 in Charles Evans, *American Bibliography: A Chronological Dictionary of all Books, Pamphlets and Periodical Publications Printed in the United States of America, 1639–1800*, 14 vols (Chicago, New York, and Worcester, Mass., 1903–1959), VI, 240. Evans's title appears to be a confused composite of the titles of the three 1770 editions. He added without attribution: "One hundred fifty copies of this pamphlet [*sic*] was distributed in Philadelphia." The *Pennsylvania Journal, and the Weekly Advertiser* (Philadelphia), June 28, 1770, reported the same information. The version referred to was probably the first 1770 edition which, given an appearance at Philadelphia late in June, was probably published at Boston in late May. The second 1770 edition seems to have been published on June 29 or 30 (see n. 36 of this chapter). Extracts from the third 1770 edition were printed in the *New-York Gazette and the Weekly Mercury*, 27 Aug. 1770, arguing for a publication date late in July or early in Aug.
36 Adams, *American Independence*, p. 64. On Sunday, 1 July 1770, Fleeming wrote to Mein (in London) telling him that the mob was so furious over the appearance of the latest

expect, the publisher's name did not appear on the title page, nor is there any claim to authorship anywhere in any of them, first to last.

The 1769 edition is commonly ascribed to Mein; for the others there is no acknowledged author. Mein was thought to have had some aid with his pieces of invective; it is certain that someone in the customhouse helped him out with the basic information.[37] Since there were apparently four more editions published after Mein left the country, someone else continued the project, perhaps his original collaborator. And since these later editions published cargo manifests, that collaborator must have had continued access to the Customs records. In fact, it seems likely that it was this individual who originated the whole scheme, since only someone familiar with the Customs records in the first place could have known that there was cheating going on. All such records passed through Thomas Irving's office as a matter of course.

One contemporary actually accused Irving of complicity in the affair. On 24 August 1769, soon after Mein began publishing the cargo manifests, John Hancock's store manager, William Palfrey, tried to defend his employer in a letter in the *Massachusetts Gazette*. Not only were reports of Hancock's importing forbidden goods spurious, he charged, but they were being "industriously propagated by the Inspector of Exports and Imports and his emissaries." In what can only have been a charade staged to mislead the Sons of Liberty, Irving sought to protect his innocence by berating the *Gazette*'s printer, Richard Draper, for publishing Palfrey's letter. Draper, a good Loyalist himself, played his part by then swearing the peace against Irving.

> When Irving made his appearance before the justices a vast number of the true sons collected themselves who when he came out of the [court] house, his'd laughed shouted and gave three huzzas to the hero, who had the resolution to attack a poor sick disabled printer.[38]

edition (probably the second 1770 edition) that the day before he had fled for safety to Castle William in Boston harbor. Fleeming to Mein, 1 July 1770, Papers Relating to New England, vol. IV, fol. 5, Sparks Manuscripts, pt X. See also Mein to Treasury, 1 July 1771, T 1/481, fol. 62v, PRO. The first 1770 edition, said the *Pennsylvania Journal, and the Weekly Advertiser* (Philadelphia), 28 June 1770, "is the work of the detestable Board of Commissioners [because] it is plain [that] it is printed by Mein and Fle[e]ming, their printers in Boston."

37 Schlesinger, "Propaganda and the Boston Newspaper Press," p. 415n., repeated allegations that "Mein was aided in his editorial labors by Samuel Waterhouse, a customs officer, and Joseph Green, a Boston wit of repute. He may also have had other helpers . . . [including] William Burch, one of the customs commissioners. . . ." The last was based on a statement implicating Burch in *Boston-Gazette, and Country Journal*, 11 Sept. 1769. See also *Boston Chronicle*, 1 June 1769.

38 Nathaniel Coffin, at Boston, to Charles Steuart, 11 Sept. 1769, Steuart Papers, MS 5025, fols 185–186, National Library of Scotland. For Draper, see Thomas, *History of Printing in America*, esp. pp. 143–145, 228–231. For Coffin, see the discussion of him earlier in this chapter. For the court case, see Menand, "Juries, Judges, and the Politics of Justice," p. 180, n. 8, and her reference to the case papers among the records of the Inferior Court of Common Pleas, Suffolk, in the Judicial Archives, Archives of the Commonwealth of

Although the ruse seems to have diverted the mob's attention from Irving, we now know that Palfrey was right. Irving was the originator of the scheme, the author of the first tract, with or without any help, and the sole author of the four subsequent editions. We have this on the best authority: Irving himself and a colleague at Boston in the customhouse. Joseph Harrison, the Collector of Customs of the Port of Boston, wrote Grey Cooper at the Treasury in 1770 giving Irving full credit for the whole affair. While "Mr. Mein (as the publisher) is highly deserving of the favour and protection of government" because of his part in the publication, Irving was the one behind it all.

> . . . as I was knowing to the forming of this plan of communicat[in]g to the public the true state of the Boston import[atio]ns I think it a piece of justice due to an absent person to inform you, and to desire the same may be communicated to my Lord North, that another gentleman Mr. Tho[ma]s Irving Inspector Gen[era]l of the Imports and Exports of America and Register of Shipping had *the prin[cipa]l hand in projecting and executing that useful plan* he being the person who with much labour and industry collected from the cocketts all the articles imported from Great Britain and by means of the entries at the Custom House *formed and digested a state of those accounts in a pamph[le]t* which he distributed at a very great risk over the Continent.[39]

Later, in 1779, Irving said the same things himself in a letter to the Secretary of State for the Colonies, Lord George Germain, and still later, in 1786, in a petition to the Loyalist Claims Commission, though by then this had become only one of many accomplishments in a long career. His 1786 statement that while at Boston he "undertook and at the hazard of his life executed a publication formed chiefly from the books of the customs" is sufficiently obscure to have passed unnoticed even in an era of increased interest in the Loyalists and their papers.[40]

The activities of Irving – and probably others – did not stop with Mein's flight nor did their antagonists retire quietly from the field. The efforts of the patriot party to maintain non-importation intensified in the fall of 1769

---

39 Emphasis added. Harrison, [at London?], to Cooper, at London, [1770], AO 12/51, fols 160v–161r, PRO, and AO 13/130, fol. 34v, PRO. Harrison sent Irving a copy of his letter in 1783 at which time he said that he had written it to Cooper "to inform him of the prin[cipa]l share you had in that publication." Harrison to Irving, 7 Nov. 1783, AO 12/51, fol. 160v, PRO.
40 Irving's memorial, Mar. 1786, AO 12/51, fol. 153r, PRO. The statement in Irving to Germain, London, 12 Aug. 1779, CO 5/176, fols 46–47, PRO, was more explicit:

> The nature of my office furnishing me with the best information on the subject, I made out a state of the imports &c into the different provinces which I caused to be secretly printed in a pamphlet, and distributed over the whole continent. This pamphlet by exposing the duplicity of the Bostonians, created a suspicion in the southern and middle provinces and soon broke up the whole scheme.

and the following winter and spring. But Boston could not hold the wall alone. Just as the Boston merchants had worked to secure New York City's and Philadelphia's cooperation in the non-importation movement, so did Irving seek to undermine it. As Inspector-General of Imports and Exports, he was in regular communication with Customs officials at both places. In letters to John Swift, the Collector at Philadelphia, he argued that the Boston non-importers were continuing to import considerable quantities of goods.[41] He also sent Swift copies of the various booklets to distribute there.[42] Two key communications discussed in the New York City press probably came from Irving.[43] It seems highly likely that he wrote to other places, too.

These letters and booklets had their effect. New York fell out first, early in June 1770. Arthur Schlesinger, Sr, has called attention to the impact of the "timely pamphlet" – Irving's second 1770 edition – on the vote taken there. Philadelphia broke next, in September, and the Boston merchants thereupon caved in as well. A meeting in Boston on 12 October 1770 ended non-importation. Though we would be wrong to attribute the outcome entirely to Irving, his demonstrations of the duplicity of leading Boston merchants did much to play upon the fears and jealousies of other merchants there and in the other Thirteen Continental Colonies. The cracks in the patriots' wall were not of his making, but Irving's paper wedges did split them wider and helped to bring it down.[44]

His contemporaries certainly believed that Thomas Irving deserved credit for ending non-importation. Joseph Harrison later wrote that he felt that "the principle share" Irving had "in that publication ... which in a great measure rendered abortive the intentions of the famous non-importation agreements."[45] In his earlier letter of 1770, he had told Grey Cooper that Irving's "publications respecting the importation at Boston were undoubtedly the occasion of disuniting the colonies."[46] If some Bostonians would have had their rebellion in 1770, and Irving helped to stop them, he had a hand in delaying the American Revolution.

---

41 See especially Irving, at Boston, to Swift, 5 June 1770, Custom House Papers, X, 1256-a, HSP.

42 Irving to Swift, 5 June 1770, ibid.; *Pennsylvania Journal and the Weekly Advertiser,* 28 June 1770. The "pamphlets are said to be brought here by one—M'D—n—d, third clerk of the board." The man seems to have been Thomas MacDonogh of New Hampshire who was the third clerk to the American Board of Customs. I am indebted to Joseph R. Frese for this identification.

43 *New-York Gazette and the Weekly Mercury,* 27 Aug., 15 Oct. 1770.

44 Schlesinger, *Colonial Merchants,* p. 225. Jensen, *Founding of a Nation,* pp. 362, 372, joins numerous others in ascribing the loss of Boston's leadership role to the confirmation of "the suspicion long held in other colonies that Bostonians were cheats and canting hypocrites" and the ending of non-importation to "the widespread conviction that the Bostonians were cheaters." Irving was the one who confirmed that suspicion and established that conviction. Even though his role has heretofore not been appreciated, it is Irving, not Mein, to whom is due whatever recognition those actions earned.

45 Harrison to Irving, 7 Nov. 1783, AO 12/51, fol. 160v, PRO.

46 Harrison to Cooper, [1770], AO 12/51, fol. 160v, PRO.

Irving's actions, however unrecognized by historians, did not go unrewarded by the North government. Although Irving continued at Boston for another year, his situation there grew increasingly precarious. He felt his life to be in danger.[47] By November 1771 he had determined to go home and was in the process of leaving Boston.[48] On 10 January 1772, the Treasury granted him a six months' leave of absence with salary, a leave later extended through the following eighteen months.[49] His next employment did not begin until January 1774.[50] In recognition of his efforts in Boston, he was appointed Receiver-General of the Quit Rents of South Carolina.[51]

While in London, Irving, ever the organizer, argued that imperial revenues could be increased if land rents were more efficiently collected in those colonies where they were due.[52] The key to such a plan was an accurate and

47 Irving's memorial, Mar. 1786, AO 12/51, fol. 153r, PRO.
48 Irving appointed William Barrell to act as his deputy while he was away. Charter 3887, [Boston], 13 Nov. 1771, Steuart Papers, National Library of Scotland. William Smibert wrote Thomas Moffat from Boston on 11 Nov. 1771, that Irving "is hastening for embarkation in a very short time – a week – I shall miss him much as a warm hearted friend." "Moffat Papers." Nathaniel Coffin wrote from Boston to Charles Steuart in London, 20 Nov. 1771, that "you'l receive this by my worthy friend Mr. Irving . . . as Irving is going home." Steuart Papers, MS 5027, fols 57r, 58r. The letters in the "Moffat Papers" further reveal that Irving had arrived in London by 3 Mar. 1772, when he wrote Smibert that a spate of poor health ("rheumatic fever, which threatened his lungs, but turned to diarrhea and inflammation of his bowels that had well nigh finished him," Smibert to Moffat, 8 Apr. 1772) had forced him to go to Scotland (Smibert to Moffat, 23 Nov. 1772); to Gribton, one imagines. Irving was indeed staying at Gribton again in 1773 for he conducted some family business at that time; his father was to die there the next year. Maxwell-Irving, "Irvings of Dumfries," pp. 52, 72. Later in 1773 he returned to London; he appeared before the Treasury Board at their meeting on 10 Dec. 1773, T 29/43, fol. 119v, PRO.
49 Warrants, 10 Jan. 1772, 5 Aug. 1772, T 28/1, pp. 309, 380, PRO.
50 Smibert wrote Moffat on 23 Aug. 1773, presumably having had another letter from Irving, that he "is still unsuccessful in his application for an encreas'd salary or further promotion, and it is thought [he] will return to us. It is a pity his merit is not sufficiently known and rewarded." "Moffat Papers."
51 Irving later wrote to the Loyalist Claims Commission that upon his return home "Lord North [had expressed] . . . to his friends his approbat[io]n of his conduct and his wish to provide for him in some other part of the world" and that "his appointment to the office of Receiver General of South Carolina . . . was meant by [the North] administration as a reward for his services." Irving's memorial, Mar. 1786, AO 12/51, fols 153r, 156v, PRO.
52 Irving's case, 27 May and 1 June 1783, AO 12/99, fol. 282r, PRO; and Irving's supplementary memorial, 9 Oct. 1787, AO 12/51, fol. 158r, PRO. In the latter he claimed that the idea had been given him by one of the joint secretaries to the Treasury (perhaps Grey Cooper). The quit rents of South Carolina were particularly known to be in need of reform. See Robert K. Ackerman, *South Carolina Land Policies* (Columbia, SC, 1977); Alan D. Watson, "The Quitrent System in Royal South Carolina" (Ph.D. dissertation, University of South Carolina, 1971); and Watson, "Placemen in South Carolina: The Receiver Generals [*sic*] of the Quitrents," *South Carolina Historical Magazine*, LXXIV (Jan. 1973), 18–30. See also Beverley W. Bond, Jr, *The Quit-Rent System in the American Colonies* (New Haven, Conn., 1919).
  For rumors of Irving's appointment to various other posts during this period, see *Virginia Gazette* (Williamsburg), ed. William Rind, 12 Dec. 1772, and *Virginia Gazette* (Williamsburg), ed. Purdie and Dixon, 20 May 1773. He is also at this time supposed

complete rent roll. Irving drew up a detailed manual incorporating his plan and presented it to government where it was well received. Promised the next available position as Receiver-General, he preferred to hurry the process a bit by buying his office from an incumbent, George Saxby, Receiver-General of South Carolina, for a one-time payment of £500 sterling and an annuity of £40 sterling.[53] On 1 February 1774, Irving received the usual appointment allowing him £70 sterling per year for expenses and 10 percent of all moneys collected.[54] The office was considered to be worth £500 sterling a year.[55] The Earl of Dartmouth, the Secretary of State for the Colonies, also named him to the council in South Carolina.[56] It was only then that Irving resigned

to have requested an exchange of posts with Charles Burdett, Collector of the Customs at St Augustine, East Florida, after 1767. Maxwell-Irving, "Irvings of Dumfries," p. 72. For Burdett, see Charles Loch Mowat, *East Florida as a British Province, 1763–1784*, University of California, Publications in History, vol. XXXII (Berkeley and Los Angeles, Calif., 1943), pp. 44, 163, 165. Burdett, at Gude Tulford, near York, recounted his experiences in the colonies in a memorial to Charles Watson-Wentworth, Marquis of Rockingham, the Prime Minister, 5 Apr. 1782, T 1/571, no. 268, PRO.

53 Irving's supplementary memorial, 9 Oct. 1787, AO 12/51, fols 158r–v PRO. Irving did not pay Saxby immediately but instead gave him an interest-bearing note; he attached to the memorial mentioned above an account of his payments against the note through Aug. 1787 (ibid., fol. 158v). As of 12 Sept. 1788 he was still paying the annuity to Mrs Saxby, whom he estimated then to be 58 or 60 years old. Irving's evidence of that date, AO 12/51, fols 164r–v, PRO. George Saxby was Receiver-General from 1742 to 1774; he had gone back home to London in 1772 because of ill health but he must have recovered somewhat for he was still alive in Jan. 1784. Ackerman, *South Carolina Land Policies*, pp. 112–113; Watson, "Quitrent System in Royal South Carolina," pp. 45–59 and passim; Irving's supplementary memorial, 9 Oct. 1787, AO 12/51, fol. 158v, PRO; Irving's evidence, 10 Oct. 1787, AO 12/51, fol. 163r, PRO.

54 Warrants, 1 Feb. and 2 Feb. 1774, T 28/1, pp. 235–236, 237, PRO; Irving's memorial, Mar. 1786, AO 12/51, fols 153r–v, PRO; Irving's evidence, 10 Oct. 1787, AO 12/51, fol. 162v, PRO. The warrant of 2 Feb. 1774 allowed him £70 for the hire of deputies, even though he later referred to it as salary.

55 In testimony on 10 Oct. 1787 Irving stated that "the office yielded to his predecessor [George Saxby] about £500 per annum." AO 12/51, fol. 163r, PRO. Compare the returns for the period 1735–1774 in Bond, *Quit-Rent System*, p. 346, n. 1. See also Saxby's account for the period 26 Mar. 1766–25 Mar. 1773, in T 1/504, fol. 36–37, PRO. "By a certif[icat]e from Mr Saxby the late Receiver General dated 23rd January 1784, whereby and by the rec[eip]t of the Dep[ut]y Auditor it appears that the p[er]centage from 26 March 1772, to 26 March 1783, amounted to £411 sterling which added to the salary w[oul]d make the emoluments to £480 per annum": so testified Irving, AO 12/51, fol. 163r, PRO. Compare Watson, "Quitrent System in Royal South Carolina," pp. 57–59.
   Irving, at London, petitioned the Treasury, 22 Feb. 1774, to be allowed to make bond in Great Britain, as had been customary, rather than in the colony, as the Treasury was trying to institute. T 1/511, fol. 200, PRO. His petition was allowed. The bond of his predecessor, George Saxby, in 1742, had amounted to £2,000 sterling. Watson, "Quitrent System in Royal South Carolina," p. 70 and n. 6.

56 Commissioners for Trade and Plantations, meeting of 14 Feb. 1774, CO 391/81, fol. 10v, PRO; Commissioners for Trade and Plantations to Crown, Whitehall, 21 Feb. 1774, CO 5/381, fols 383–384v, PRO; Lt. Gov. William Bull to Sec. of State, 1 Aug. 1774, CO 5/396, fols 46–47v, PRO; Irving's memorial, Mar. 1786, AO 12/51, fols 153r–v, PRO. As a member of the Council, Irving was also a member of the Court of Chancery. *Records of the Court of Chancery of South Carolina, 1671–1779*, ed. Anne King Gregorie, American Legal Records, VI (Washington, DC, 1950), 624, 625, and elsewhere.

the office of Inspector-General.[57] It was also only then, in the early spring of that year, in his mid-thirties, secure in his new position, that he and Marion Corbet were married. The new Receiver-General of South Carolina and his wife quickly set out for Charleston, arriving there in mid-July. He was soon established in an office in Orange Street close to the center of town.[58]

Irving's year in South Carolina was not fruitful – or so he later claimed. He spent almost his entire tenure as Receiver-General trying to repair defects in the collection of the quit rents, and he struggled to prepare a new tax roll for that purpose. Before he had finished, the Revolution had taken hold and he could not profit from his labors. He made himself so unpopular among the patriot party, especially for his support of the Governor in the Drayton affair, that, for his health, "he was advized to try the sea air." Irving betook himself to the Bahama Islands and, as a consequence, began an odyssey unparalleled in the history of the American Revolution.[59]

Irving's luck had run out. In March 1776, in its first fleet engagement, the new navy of the newly United States attacked and captured the forts and town of Nassau, the capital of the Bahamas. The American forces stormed ashore on Sunday, 3 March; by early the next morning, after a bloodless battle, they were in complete control. Within two weeks they had ransacked the place of all military stores, but thanks to the ineptness of their commander, Esek Hopkins, they lost what they had come for – gunpowder

---

57　Irving's supplementary memorial, 9 Oct. 1787, AO 12/51, fol. 158v, PRO. James Murray replaced him. *Virginia Gazette* (Williamsburg), ed. Purdie and Dixon, 13 Oct. 1774, dateline Boston, 22 Sept.; *Georgia Gazette* (Savannah), 2 Nov. 1774, dateline Boston, 22 Sept. For Murray – whose papers are in the Massachusetts Historical Society – see *Letters of James Murray, Loyalist*, ed. Nina Moore Tiffany and Susan I. Lesley (Boston, 1901). Charles Steuart managed Murray's affairs for him in London during the war (ibid., p. 265, n. 1) just as he seems to have done Irving's.

58　*Georgia Gazette* (Savannah), 10 Aug. 1774, dateline Charleston, 22 July; *South Carolina Gazette* (Charleston), 17 Sept. 1774.

59　For his time in South Carolina prior to the Revolutionary War, see his memorial, Mar. 1786, AO 12/51, fols 153v–155r, PRO (quotation, fol. 155r); Watson, "Quitrent System in Royal South Carolina," pp. 60–61, 88–89, 205; Watson, "Placemen in South Carolina," pp. 27–30. For the Drayton affair and its aftermath, see the evidence of Thomas Knox Gordon, former Chief Justice of South Carolina, 10 Oct. 1787, AO 12/51, fols 163r–v, PRO. It was Gordon who described Irving as "a most active and zealous servant of the Crown." John Drayton, *Memoirs of the American Revolution, from Its Commencement to the Year 1776, Inclusive; as Relating to the State of South-Carolina* (Charleston, 1821), II, esp. 17; and William M. Dabney and Marion Dargan, *William Henry Drayton and American Revolution* (Albuquerque, NM, 1962), pp. 40–64. Earlier in the year Irving's acquaintance Charles Burdett had fled from St Augustine to New Providence. See Burdett to Rockingham, Apr. 5, 1782, T 1/571, no. 268. Daniel Chamier, Jr, another friend of Irving's who had fled from Charleston to Florida before Irving decamped, later wrote to his father in Boston to say that Irving had since gone to "Providence Island, for recovery from a bilious complaint, and he will remain there for some time if he is wise." Chamier to Chamier, St Augustine, 3–4 Oct. 1775, Intercepted Letters, 1775–1781, vol. I, p. 245, Records of the Continental and Confederation Congresses and the Constitutional Convention, 1765–1821, Record Group 360, National Archives, Washington, DC.

for George Washington's army. Governor Montfort Browne of the Bahamas had managed to send it all away to St Augustine, East Florida, because Hopkins had failed to press his advantage and to blockade the port. Hopkins, out of spite, carried away three important prisoners: Governor Browne; Browne's secretary; and, as luck would have it, Thomas Irving, Receiver-General and member of the Council of South Carolina. Someone among Hopkins' forces had recognized Irving or his name and reported him to Hopkins as "a dangerous person."[60]

Irving's trials did not end until two years later. Hopkins carried him to Connecticut on board the flagship *Alfred*. In Connecticut, Irving remained a prisoner until late 1776, despite his pleas to Governor Jonathan Trumbull, his letters to the Continental Congress, the intercession of both William Campbell, the former Governor of South Carolina, and of General William Howe, and even an arrangement for an exchange of prisoners that had General Washington's personal approval.[61] Finally granted a parole, Irving was freed by the Continental Congress in January 1777 and soon thereafter rejoined his family in South Carolina.[62] He had been home only a short

---

60 Irving's memorial, Mar. 1786, AO 12/51, fols 155r–v, PRO (quotation, fol. 155r). See also John J. McCusker, "The American Invasion of Nassau in the Bahamas," *American Neptune*, XXV (July 1965), 189–217 – revised as chapter twelve of the present book – and McCusker, *"Alfred": The First Continental Flagship, 1775–1778*, Smithsonian Studies in History and Technology, no. 20 (Washington, DC, 1973). It is within the realm of the possible that among those who recognized Irving, one was John Paul Jones, then serving as First Lieutenant on board *Alfred*. Whether he knew Thomas Irving or not, Jones must surely have known Thomas's younger brother, Joseph Irving of Borran.

61 Irving's memorial, Mar. 1786, AO 12/51, fols 155r–v, PRO; Washington, at "Head Quarters," to Col. Samuel John Atlee, at New York, 25 Nov. 1776, AO 13/130, fol. 42r, PRO, and as printed in *The Writings of George Washington*, ed. John C. Fitzpatrick (Washington, DC, 1931–1944), VI, 297n.; Campbell to Howe, 29 Nov. 1777, AO 12/51, fol. 161r–v, PRO. Irving and the two other prisoners were taken first to New London, Conn., where the fleet anchored on 8 Apr. 1776 They were paroled for twelve months on 12 Apr. with the provision that they agree "peaceably to abide within the limits" of the town of Windham, Conn., whence they were taken under escort on 18 Apr. *Connecticut Gazette* (New London), 12, 19 Apr. 1776; parole, dated 12 Apr. 1776, Revolutionary I Series, 1763–1789, V, fols 430, 432a, Connecticut Archives, 1636–1820, Connecticut State Library, Hartford; minutes of Connecticut Council of Safety, 15 Apr. 1776, [Connecticut (Colony)], *The Public Records of the Colony of Connecticut*, ed. James Hammond Trumbull and Charles Jeremy Hoadly, 15 vols (Hartford, Conn., 1850–1890), XV, 261–263. On 8 May 1776, the Continental Congress established a committee of seven members "to consider the situation" of the prisoners. [US, Continental Congress], *Journals of the Continental Congress, 1774–1789*, ed. Worthington Chauncey Ford et al., 34 vols (Washington, DC, 1904–1937), IV, 334. Gov. Browne, with whom Irving was initially imprisoned, wrote later that, "I was sent to Norwich, Lebanon, Windham, and Hartford in Connecticut, and Lastly to Middletown where I did not experience the same hard usage I did at first, and at which place I remain'd till I was a few days ago exchanged." Browne, at New York, to George Germain, 5 Nov. 1776, CO 23/23, fols 107–109, PRO, and as printed in Malcolm Lloyd, Jr, "The Taking of the Bahamas by the Continental Navy in 1776," *Pennsylvania Magazine of History and Biography*, XLIX (Oct. 1925), 349–366.

62 *American Archives: . . . a Documentary History of . . . the North American Colonies; of . . . the American Revolution; and of the Constitution of the Government of the United States*

while, however, when he was caught up by the "Test Act" there and made a refugee once again.[63] Forced to fly under pain of death, he and his family took the first available vessel from Charleston to Europe, a small sloop bound for Spain. But this sloop was captured by a ship of the Royal Navy, HMS *Brune*, and taken to St Augustine, from where Irving and his family had to make their way to New York, then in British hands. He became ill, again, at New York and he and his family did not get to London until June or early July 1778.[64]

Upon his return to England, the government came forward again to support him. A Treasury pension or allowance of £200 sterling per year was granted him, retroactive to 5 January 1778.[65] When the decision was made to reinstate the government in South Carolina after the capture of Charleston by Henry Clinton, Irving was ordered to return. From his arrival in mid-1781 until the time of the final evacuation in December 1782, he was active not only as Receiver-General but also as a member of the important Board of Police, Charleston's *de facto* civilian government during the British occupation.[66]

..., ed. Peter Force, 9 vols ([Washington, DC, 1837–1853]), 4th ser., V, 867, 5th ser., III, 619, 791–792, 838, 899; [US, Continental Congress], *Journals of the Continental Congress, 1774–1789*, ed. Worthington Chauncey Ford *et al.*, 34 vols (Washington, DC, 1904–1937), VII, 9; *Letters of Delegates to Congress, 1774–1789*, ed. Paul H. Smith, in progress (Washington, DC, 1976 to date), V, 687–690.

63 The 13 Feb. 1777 "Ordinance for establishing an Oath of Abjuration and Allegience" required that "all the state officers of the King" swear the oath or "within sixty days ... be sent off from this state" to Europe or the West Indies. The state was to bear the cost. [South Carolina, Laws and Statutes], *The Statutes at Large of South Carolina*, ed. Thomas Cooper and David J. McCord, 10 vols (Columbia, 1836–1841), I, 135–136. In the late winter and early spring of 1777 committees visited suspected Loyalists to administer the oath; those who refused were banished. See *The Papers of Henry Laurens*, ed. Philip M. Hamer *et al.*, in progress (Columbia, SC, 1968 to date), XI, passim (e.g., p. 213 nn.). See also the similar stories of Thomas's brother Alexander and brother-in-law Archibald Baird (see nn. 8 and 10 of this chapter).

64 Irving's memorial, Mar. 1786, AO 12/51, fols 155r–v, PRO. For the log books of HMS *Brune*, 32 guns, Capt. James Ferguson, see Captains' Logs, Adm. 51/117, PRO, and Masters' Logs, Adm. 52/1619–1620, PRO.

65 Treasury Board, meeting of 5 Aug. 1778, T 29/47, fol. 150v, PRO; Irving to Germain, 12 Aug. 1779, CO 5/176, fols 46–47, PRO. See also Thomas Irving to Treasury, 24 Oct. 1780, Germain Papers, vol. 13, Clements Library; the copy in T 1/400, no. 180, PRO, is endorsed as having been read on 16 Nov. 1780. For the Treasury's reaction, see the minutes of the Board meeting, 16 Nov. 1780, T 29/49, fols 218v–219r, PRO. Irving estimated that between "the end of April 1775 when the collection of the Crown revenues ceased [in South Carolina] until his return to England in the year 1778," his expenses amounted to £1,500 sterling; his income was nil during the same period. Irving's memorial, Mar. 1786, AO 12/51, fol. 155v, PRO. Irving's old friend Charles Steuart drew on his personal account at Messrs Thomas Coutts and Co. for the sum of £75 on 12 Aug. 1778, in Irving's favor. Steuart Papers, MS 5037, fol. 39, National Library of Scotland. The allowance from the Treasury stopped in July 1780 upon his recall to South Carolina. Irving's case, May–June 1783, AO 12/99, fol. 282r, PRO. See also Sec. of State to Lt Gov. Bull, Whitehall, 6 July 1780, CO 5/408, p. 147, PRO.

66 For Irving's return to South Carolina, see George Germain, at Whitehall, to Irving, [17 July 1779], AO 12/51, fol. 161v, PRO, and as extracted in Irving, at Charleston, to Lt

We know little of Irving's activities during the first three years after his return to London in 1783. Again he had not been well in South Carolina,[67] a complaint we hear more frequently as he grew older, and perhaps illness helps to explain this gap in our knowledge of his life. Later, in the 1790s, he mentioned that he had spent some time in the past traveling on the Continent, a trip that might have occurred in these years, perhaps in 1785. He petitioned the Loyalist Claims Commission in May and June 1783 and then again in March 1786 and October 1787; he could easily have devoted a considerable portion of his time over these months to preparing such petitions and gathering the necessary supporting materials.[68]

Gen. Alexander Leslie, 31 Jan. 1782, PRO 30/55/35, no. 4092, PRO. This and items cited subsequently from this collection are part of the Sir Guy Carleton: British Army Headquarters Papers, 1747–1783, PRO 30/55, PRO. There are photostats of these papers in the Colonial Williamsburg Foundation Library, Williamsburg, Va., and the Manuscript and Archives Division, New York Public Library, New York City; transcripts in the Public Archives of Canada, Ottawa; and microfilms in the Manuscript Division, LC. See also Thomas De Grey, at London, to Irving, 30 July 1779, AO 12/51, fol. 162r, PRO; Grey Cooper to Irving, [1779?], AO 12/51, fol. 162r, PRO; and Treasury Board, meeting of 4 Aug. 1779, T 29/48, fol. 209v, PRO. Irving, and, apparently, most of the rest of the civil officers took two years to get to South Carolina; they came out together in a fleet that first stopped at Virginia. *Royal Georgia Gazette* (Savannah), 14 June 1781, dateline Charleston, 6 June. Once in South Carolina, Irving spent a good bit of his time trying to secure from the military authorities the right to some of the revenues that they had begun to collect for their own purposes in lieu of any civil government. See the series of letters in the Carleton/Headquarters Papers, PRO 30/55/34, nos 3928, 3929, PRO; PRO 30/55/35, nos 4091, 4092, 4098, 4101, PRO; PRO 30/55/37, nos 4248, 4249, 4250, PRO. Copies of some of these appear in T 1/571, nos 316–327, PRO, and in CO 5/105, fols 13–40, PRO. The records of the Board of Police are in CO 5/513–526, PRO. See George Smith McCowen, Jr, *The British Occupation of Charleston, 1780–82* (Columbia, SC, 1972), pp. 13–42. Irving's own summation of the events of the period can be found in his case, May–June 1783, AO 12/99, fol. 282r, PRO; and in his memorial, Mar. 1786, AO 12/51, fols 155v–156r, PRO. See also Mary Beth Norton, *The British-Americans: The Loyalist Exiles in England, 1774–1789* (Boston, 1972), pp. 109–111; Watson, "Quitrent System in Royal South Carolina," pp. 62–64.

67 Irving, at Charleston, to Steuart, at London, 20 Dec. 1781, Steuart Papers, MS 5040, fols 223–224, National Library of Scotland. He had been sick in bed on and off from 22 June until 2 Oct.

68 For the European trip, see the discussion later in this chapter. The first claim to the Loyalist Claims Commission resulted in the award of an allowance of £100 per year. AO 12/99, fols 282r–283v, PRO.

   Burke, *Landed Gentry*, ed. Townend, 18th edn, II, 338, reports that Irving was "King's Agent for W. Florida, 1772 ... King's Agent for Florida 1774, Gov. of Leeward (or Windward) Islands ca. 1780 ..." See also Irving, *The Irvings*, p. 86; and Maxwell-Irving, "Irvings of Dumfries," p. 72. My own researches confirm none of this. The standard authorities not only fail to indicate that Irving held any of these offices but also show other people in the offices at the stated times. See Cecil Johnson, *British West Florida, 1763–1783* (New Haven, Conn., 1943), p. 98n; Mowat, *East Florida*, p. 34; David P. Henige, *Colonial Governors from the Fifteenth Century to the Present: A Comprehensive List* (Madison, Wis., 1970). Most importantly, Irving himself made no mention of ever having held any of those positions in his presentations to the Loyalist Claims Commission; he was under an obligation to do so because he was supposed to show all of the sources of his income during the times for which he was making a claim for compensation. The Commission checked on such matters and the claimants knew it.

In the same period we can identify Irving's endeavors in the successful campaign to keep the commerce of the British Empire closed to the United States. After the ending of the Revolutionary War, many on both sides hoped that the Americans could continue to trade in the same old ways with Great Britain and its colonies, especially with the West Indies. Yet strong arguments against such a breach in the principles of mercantilism prevailed and a series of Orders in Council promulgated in July 1783 and afterwards forbade American merchants a role in the British West Indian trade. Discussions continued, however, and arguments were heard on both sides. The most effective public tract in defense of the Orders in Council was Lord Sheffield's *On the Commerce of the American States* which went through several editions in the mid-1780s. Irving supplied material for the book but, in my estimation, his contribution went well beyond the few tables identified with his name. Sheffield, who had no first-hand acquaintance with the workings of the American economy, obviously relied heavily on people who had, one of whom was Irving.[69]

Irving performed a parallel service for government and we are able to document that more satisfactorily. The debate over the Orders in Council continued in Parliament as well as in the popular press. Through the spring of 1784 the Commissioners for Trade and Plantations held hearings to gather information on the West Indian–North American trade. Irving appeared before the committee repeatedly in the role of expert witness, presented with detailed questions one week and asked to return the next with all the answers. His data and commentary appear regularly in the surviving records of the committee.[70] Moreover, much of his data and the points he made about

69 The first edition of Sheffield's book was entitled *Observations on the Commerce of the American States with Europe and the West Indies* (London, 1783); the 6th, enlarged edition (London, 1784) is the fullest version. See Herbert C. Bell "British Commercial Policy in the West Indies, 1783–93," *English Historical Review*, XXXI (July, 1916), 429–441; Ritcheson, *Aftermath of Revolution*, passim. The nature and the extent of the relationship between Sheffield and Irving are not clear, largely because neither man has left behind a collection of his papers. There is the suggestion that the two families were on quite friendly terms in the 1790s but how old that friendship was, again, we can really only guess. See *The Girlhood of Maria Josepha Holroyd (Lady Stanley of Aderley). Recorded in Letters of a Hundred Years Ago: From 1776 to 1796*, ed. J[ane] H. Adeane (London, 1896), p. 367. Nevertheless it does seem reasonable to suppose, given the range and depth of their shared interests, that they would have sought each other out early and often. For Sheffield, see Namier and Brooke, *House of Commons*, II, 43.

70 Irving testified several times between Mar. and May 1784 before the Lords of the Committee of the Privy Council Appointed for the Consideration of all Matters Relating to Trade and Foreign Plantations. (This body was, in everything but name, the old "Commissioners for Trade and Plantations"; and it is sometimes, but inaccurately, called the "Board of Trade," a name that only applies later in Britain's history. For an impassioned plea that we all use the more accurate name – a call with which I am in sympathy – see K. G. Davies in his "Introduction" to the most recent volume of [GB, PRO], *Calendar of State Papers, Colonial Series, America and West Indies [1574–1739]*, by W[illiam] Noel Sainsbury *et al.*, 45 vols in 46 pts [London, 1860–1994], XLV, xiv.) The record of their proceedings is in BT 5/1, PRO. (There is a copy of this volume in the Liverpool

them turn up again in the expanded sixth edition of Sheffield's extremely influential book. Clearly, Irving's was an important voice in the drive to maintain the integrity of the British imperial system. What else he did between 1783 and 1786 we have yet to discover, but his activities – perhaps in this one sphere alone – were enough to catch the attention of government and again to earn for him an appropriate reward.

Thomas Irving began the last and longest phase of his public career when on 5 January 1786, he was appointed Deputy Inspector-General of Imports and Exports of Great Britain. Three months later, on April 7, he was promoted to Inspector-General, and began, in the words of George Clark, "a new era" in that office.[71] Clark's assessment is justified not only by the reforms that Irving instituted in the work of his own agency but also by the more active role that he as Inspector-General undertook in government as a whole.

The traditional task of the Inspector-General and his staff was to collect and compile trade statistics. From the middle of the 1690s onward, the end product of those labors had been an annual summary ledger of England's imports and exports, the comparative values of which were used to strike the nation's balance of trade. One problem with the import–export ledgers as Irving found them was that they were organized basically by countries traded with; to extract information about specific commodities required considerable retabulation. Beginning with 1792, imports, exports, and re-exports were

Papers, Add. MS 38388, BL.) Additionally, Irving's own testimony has been copied into Liverpool Papers, Add. MS 38345, fols 136–152, BL. Compare ibid., fols 153–155. For the papers he presented to support his testimony, see BT 6/83, pts i and ii, PRO. See also Irving's "Observations on the Trade carried on between the W[est] Indies and America," [21 Feb. 1788], Add. MS 59238, fols 122–123, BL. Compare Ritcheson, *Aftermath of Revolution*, pp. 12–13, 21, 213, 221, 224, 345.

71 Clark, *Guide to English Commercial Statistics*, p. 32, and his citations to T 11/34, pp. 261, 389, PRO. Irving once testified that "the Title of the Office is, Inspector General of the Imports and Exports of Great Britain and the British Colonies" (28 Mar. 1797). See [GB, Parl., Commons, Committee of Secrecy], *Third Report from the Committee of Secrecy [on the Outstanding Demands on the Bank of England]*, [Lambert 4717] ([London], 1797), p. 105. On another occasion, speaking more freely, he called himself the "Inspector General of the Commerce of the Empire." [GB, Parl., Commons, Select Committee on Finance], *Fourth Report from the Select Committee on Finance. Collection of the Public Revenue. Customs* [Lambert 4759] ([London],1797), p. 140. The previous Deputy Inspector-General, John Tomkyns, retired with a pension of £100 paid out of Irving's salary. Irving later complained not only about that £100 deduction, but also about several others that reduced his new annual income from the office from a salary of £780 to £272 10s. (£272.50). Irving's evidence, 10 Oct. 1787, 18 Sept. 1788, AO 12/51, fols 162v, 164v, PRO. See also the statement by John Tomkyns, 26 May 1785, in [GB, Commissioners for Taking, Examining and Stating the Public Accounts], *The Reports of the Commissioners Appointed to Examine, Take, and State the Public Accounts of the Kingdom*, ed. William Molleson and John Lane, 3 vols (London, 1783–1787), III, 432–433. The suppression of the sinecure and, by implication, the appointment of an active Inspector-General, had been one of the recommendations of the fourteenth report, 30 Dec. 1785, of the commission appointed under the Act of 20 George III, c. 54 (1780). See *Reports of the Commissioners*, ed. Molleson and Lane, III, 99, 105. For the broader context of these reforms, see Ehrman, *Younger Pitt*, passim.

compiled both by commodity and by country in a new series of six annual volumes. This reform was certainly Irving's.[72]

A second major problem with the import–export ledgers involved the valuations assigned to commodities. The Customs officials in the various ports sent to London the quantities of each commodity imported and exported. Clerks in the office of the Inspector-General multiplied quantity by unit value and entered both the total quantity and the total value of each commodity. The grand totals of these values of exports and imports added up by country gave, supposedly, the balance of trade between England and the places with which it did business. The difficulty was that the unit values used by the clerks had not been changed since the early eighteenth century and no longer reflected current market prices. Consequently the annual ledgers were useless for striking an accurate balance of trade.[73]

Knowledgeable contemporaries recognized and criticized this deficiency in the government's figures. In *The Wealth of Nations*, Adam Smith stated that "the custom-house books, I think, it is now generally acknowledged, are a very uncertain criterion [of the value of trade], on account of the inaccuracy of the valuation at which the greater part of goods are rated in them."[74] Irving noted the same defect: "the arguments held both in and out of Parliament, and the voluminous writing of various authors upon the subject

72 For a discussion of the early ledgers and the data in them, see John J. McCusker, "The Current Value of English Exports, 1697 to 1800," *W&MQ*, 3rd ser., XXVIII (Oct. 1971), 607–628 – revised as chapter ten of the present book. At least one copy of each of the ledgers still survives for the years down through 1780 (with the exceptions of the years 1705 and 1712); the most complete set is designated Customs 3, PRO. We can only theorize about the changes in 1792 because the 1814 fire in the London Custom House apparently destroyed the last eleven years of the older one-volume series and as much as the first twenty years of some of the new, post-1792 six-volume series. Clark, *Guide to English Commercial Statistics*, p. 31, speculated on the loss of the last eleven vols of the Customs 3 series. See also [GB, Royal Commission on Public Records], *Report of the Royal Commission on Public Records Appointed to Enquire into and Report on the State of the Public Records and Local Records of a Public Nature of England and Wales*, [HC Sessional Papers, Cmd. 6361, 6395–6396, 7544–7546, 367–369] (London, 1912–1919), I, pt ii, p. 47n. The guess about the post-1792, six-volume arrangement is my own based on the existing volumes in the several series Customs 4, 5, 8, 9, 10, and 11, PRO. From 1772 on, as a supplement to the Customs 3 ledgers, the Inspector-General's office also prepared an annual volume of tables summarizing the year's shipping, commercial, and revenue statistics. This is the series Customs 17, PRO. Irving's intentions in his reforms of 1792 were summed up in his annual report dated 12 Dec. 1791, Customs 17/12, pp. 1–5, PRO. There is a copy of this volume, identified as the "State of the Navigation, Revenues and Commerce of Great Britain in the Year 1790," MS 140, Palaeography Room, Senate House, Library, University of London.

73 McCusker, "Current Value of English Exports," passim. See also Irving's "A few general Observations on the Trade between Great Britain and Portugal and Spain," Dec. 1789, Add. MS 34429, fols 196–199, BL; and his testimony, in Mar., 1797, included in the *Third Report from the Committee of Secrecy [on the Outstanding Demands on the Bank of England]*, pp. 153–154.

74 Adam Smith, *An Inquiry into the Nature and Causes of the Wealth of Nations* (1776), ed. R[oy] H. Campbell, A[ndrew] S. Skinner, and W[illiam] B. Todd, 2 vols (Oxford, 1976), I, 475–476.

of commercial balances, chiefly founded upon the accounts of the inspector-general's office, are made upon false data."[75] His efforts to deal with this problem were less successful than in other areas because there seems to have been considerable difficulty in collecting the required prices. Only in the late 1790s did the office begin to use current market prices, and not until many years later, during his son William's time as Inspector-General, were Irving's ideas about how to strike the balance of trade fully implemented.[76]

Thomas Irving's services went far beyond collecting better data. His experience and his command of information equipped him to express knowledgeable opinions on many policy matters. Accordingly, his views came to be solicited on nearly every branch of the trade and shipping of the empire. His responses to inquiries are to be found throughout the papers of the Commissioners for Trade and Plantations and other governmental agencies.[77] John Ehrman, who has studied this period closely, found that Irving expressed influential opinions on everything from imported Portuguese wine and the boom in trade with Russia to the dangers of overexpansion in the early

---

75 Customs 17/12, p. 4, PRO. Irving had to have been aware of Smith's opinions.

76 "Commercial Accounts of Great Britain," pp. 3–40, in [GB, Parl., Commons], *Accounts and Papers Relative to the Commerce, Revenue, and Expenditure of the Kingdoms of Great Britain and Ireland*, HC Sessional Papers to 1801, Accounts and Papers, vol. XLIX, no. 981 [Lambert 5010] ([London], 1800). Thomas Irving supervised the preparation of these accounts and sent them to William Pitt over his signature; they are dated 31 Mar. 1800. Pitt presented them to the House of Commons on 2 Apr. 1800. Phyllis Deane and W[illiam] A. Cole, *British Economic Growth, 1688–1959: Trends and Structure*, 2nd edn (Cambridge, Eng., 1962), pp. 43, 315, checked some of Irving's work and concluded that he was both "careful" and "remarkably accurate." See also Albert H. Imlah, *Economic Elements in the Pax Britannica: Studies in British Foreign Trade in the Nineteenth Century* (Cambridge, Mass., 1958), pp. 24–25. For William Irving, see n. 83 of this chapter.

77 See nn. 70, 79, and 80 of this chapter. As an example of an important report, presented by Irving (in 1791) but later published only anonymously, see the unsigned answers to three questions about the ownership of colonial shipping in BT 6/20, fols 269r–273v, PRO. The author did identify himself (ibid., fols 270v–271r) as a pre-war Inspector-General of Imports and Exports and Register of Shipping in America but, more to the point, we know for certain that he was Irving because it was to him that the Commissioners for Trade and Plantations submitted the questions on 10 Dec. 1790, BT 5/6, fol. 195, PRO. There is a copy of this volume in the Liverpool Papers, Add. MS 38393, BL.
   The data that Irving presented, which were considered significant enough by contemporaries to have been printed several times, become much more compelling because Irving compiled them. The committee to which Irving presented the material incorporated it into its published report (but, again, with no indication of its author). [GB, Commissioners for Trade and Plantations], *A Report of the Lords of the Committee of Privy Council, Appointed for All Matters Relating to Trade and Foreign Plantations, on the Commerce and Navigation between His Majesty's Dominions and the Territories belonging to the United States of America* ([London], 1791), pp. 31–33. The British government thought it important enough information to have suppressed the report, but not before Andrew Burnaby had a chance to extract some material from it, including the data referred to specifically here. Andrew Burnaby, *Travels through the Middle Settlements in North-America, In the Years 1759–1760 with Observations upon the State of the Colonies*, 3rd edn (London, 1790), p. 134. Thomas Jefferson also seems to have obtained a copy of the report; there is a précis of it in the Thomas Jefferson Papers, 1651–1856, LC, which was also edited and published. See [GB, Commissioners for Trade and Plantations], *Report of a Committee of the Lords*

1790s and the impact on the Customs reforms of William Pitt's attempts to make smuggling less attractive.[78] He appeared before the committee investigating the slave trade, played a part in discussions of Canadian–West Indian trade, testified before the committee looking into the Bank of England, formulated a plan for an extended free port system in the Caribbean, and commented on similar plans for the home ports.[79] In short, Irving was at the center of British governmental discussions on trade and commerce during the last fifteen years of the eighteenth century. John Ehrman has speculated that Irving may even have had the ear of the Prime Minister himself.[80]

We gain still another measure of the man from the evidence that he gave before the committee that examined British government finances in 1797. They had asked him to compare conditions at home and abroad. Irving was impressive. He cited conversations with men of affairs during his visit to

of the Privy Council on the Trade of Great Britain with the United States, January 1791, [ed. Worthington C. Ford] (Washington, DC, 1888), p. 16. "The Society of Ship-Owners of Great Britain" reprinted the original report several years later in their *Collection of Interesting and Important Reports and Papers on the Navigation and Trade of Great Britain, Ireland, and the British Colonies in the West Indies,* [comp. Nathaniel Atcheson] ([London], 1807), pp. 74–75. This, in turn, was the source of the still anonymous data reprinted in two contemporary American works: Adam Seybert, *Statistical Annals ... of the United States of America* (Philadelphia, 1818), p. 290; and Timothy Pitkin, *A Statistical View of the Commerce of the United States of America,* 2nd edn (New Haven, Conn., 1835), p. 345.

78 Ehrman, *British Government and Commercial Negotiations with Europe,* pp. 11n., 12n., 94n., 191, 206n., 207n.; Ehrman, *Younger Pitt,* pp. 163, 247, 326n., 382, 503.

79 For the slave trade, see his testimony, 5 Apr. 1791, *Minutes of the Evidence ... Respecting the African Slave Trade,* pp. 264–275. Compare *Remarks upon the Evidence given by Thomas Irving, Esq., Inspector General of the Exports and Imports to Great Britain before the Select Committee appointed to Take the Examination of Witnesses on the Slave Trade* (London, 1791). Many of the accounts relating to the slave trade prepared for Parliament in the 1780s and 1790s bore the signature of Thomas Irving. See, for example, "An Account of the Ships that have arrived from the Coast of Africa ... ," 10 June 1799, Main Papers, 10 June 1799, Sessional Papers, House of Lords, HLRO. Compare *Documents Illustrative of the History of the Slave Trade to America,* ed. Elizabeth Donnan, Carnegie Institution of Washington, Publication no. 409, 4 vols ([Washington, DC], 1930–1935), II, li. For the other topics, see CO 42/12, esp. fols 111r, 113r, 133r, 135–137, PRO, and Gerald S. Graham, *British Policy and Canada, 1774–1791: A Study in 18th Century Trade Policy* (London, 1930), pp. 92, 94; *Third Report from the Committee of Secrecy [on the Outstanding Demands on the Bank of England],* pp. 153–156, 164–165; Frances Armytage, *The Free Port System in the British West Indies: A Study in Commercial Policy, 1766–1792* (New York and London, 1953); and *Fourth Report from the Select Committee on Finance. Collection of the Public Revenue. Customs,* pp. 139–140. For Irving's comments on a variety of other subjects between 1784 and 1799, see: Add. MS 34427, fols 346–365, BL; Add. MS 34429, fols 190–199, BL; Add. MS 38218, fol. 271, BL; Add. MS 38225, fol. 346, BL; Add. MS 38345, fols 208–213, BL; Add. MS 38348, fols 75–76, BL; Add. MS 38354, fol. 114, BL; Add. MS 59238, fols 62–76, 91–123, BL; MS. 57, Beinecke Collection of Manuscripts, Hamilton College Library, Clinton, NY. See also George Chalmers, *Considerations on Commerce, Bullion and Coin, Circulation and Exchanges; with a View to Our Present Circumstances* (London, 1811), p. 168.

80 Ehrman, *British Government and Commercial Negotiations with Europe,* p. 191; Ehrman, *Younger Pitt,* pp. 326n., 503, 510. There are numerous letters and accounts from Irving in Pitt's papers. See, e.g., PRO 30/8/147, fols 237–254, PRO, and PRO 30/8/286, passim, PRO. Compare Morris, *Diary and Letters,* I, 315.

France and the Low Countries a few years earlier and called upon his extensive reading in the published materials about the finances of those nations. The Dutch "Government [has] never possessed any collective View of the Revenues," and there was also much reason for concern about the completeness and accuracy of the French government's figures. In Irving's eyes, these were shocking deficiencies in statecraft. One infers that he held both governments to have deserved the chaos that such sloppy bookkeeping had brought upon them. In contrast, the British system merited respect and trust from every citizen because income and expenses were accounted for down to the last farthing, "with a mathematical Accuracy."[81]

This is the theme that seems to have run through Irving's entire career – in North America on the eve of the Revolution and thereafter. Great Britain, in his view, offered to its subjects the best of all possible worlds. As he said with specific reference to the Acts of Trade:

> I feel it perfectly within the Province of my official Situation . . . to remark, that under the Operation of these great fundamental Laws (commonly called Navigation Acts) our Trade, our Navigation, our Revenues, and our Manufactures, have flourished beyond the example of all other Nations.[82]

He devoted his mature life to preserving the integrity of an imperial system founded upon the Navigation Acts. His personal contribution consisted in turning to the defense of the empire the records of imperial trade, records the integrity and trustworthiness of which he strove to maintain down to the last barrel of flour, "with proper precision," "with a mathematical accuracy."

◆ ◆ ◆ ◆ ◆

Though not a man of first rank among the public figures of his time, Irving was no mere functionary. He was an innovative and effective administrator within his sphere – and more. At Boston, risking limb and life, he stepped

---

81 *Fourth Report from the Select Committee on Finance. Collection of the Public Revenue. Customs*, pp. 36–37 (quotation, p. 37). Compare, ibid., pp. 139–140. See also J[ohn] E. D. Binney, *British Public Finance and Administration, 1774–92* (Oxford, 1962), p. 255. This was, of course, a favorite subject of Irving's friend John Sinclair, who wrote the standard contemporary work on it, *The History of the Public Revenue of the British Empire*, [1st edn], 3 vols (London, 1785–1790).

82 *Fourth Report from the Select Committee on Finance. Collection of the Public Revenue. Customs*, p. 140. Compare his celebration of "the great System of our Commercial Regulations" in the "Report by Mr. Irving, Inspector General of Imports & Exports, to the Commissioners of the Customs upon a Correspondence refer'd to him between the Officers of the Navy and the Civil Officers in the West Indies," in Add. MS 59238, fols 91–123, BL, and as quoted by Michael John Craton, "The Caribbean Vice Admiralty Courts, 1763–1815: Indispensable Agents of an Imperial System" (Ph.D. diss., McMaster University, 1968), p. 125, n. 24; and the tenor of his testimony in Apr. 1791 to the "Select Committee appointed to take Examination of Witnesses on the Slave Trade," as recorded in the *Minutes of the Evidence . . . Respecting the African Slave Trade*, pp. 264–275.

beyond his official duties to become a pamphleteer in defense of King and country. His tenure as Inspector-General of Imports and Exports in London marked the end of that position as a sinecure and the beginning of reforms that were to outlive Irving by several decades. One hopes that he would have been pleased by his obituary notice in *The Times*:

> Died . . . At his house, in Middle Scotland-yard, on Sunday last, after a long and severe illness, Thomas Irving, Esq., Inspector General of the Imports and Exports of Great Britain. To Mr. Irving's able and indefatigable exertions the Public have been much indebted for the excellent and correct system which now prevails in the arrangement of the National Accounts. His loss, therefore, cannot be more deeply regretted by His numerous Friends, who knew his worth and could appreciate his virtues, than it must be felt by the Government and the Country, in being deprived of the useful services of this intelligent and valuable Man.[83]

83 *The Times* (London), 15 July 1800, p. 3. Compare *The Gentleman's Magazine*: "In Scotland-yard, after a long and severe illness, Thomas Irving, esq., inspector-general of imports and exports of Great Britain; an office in which his talents were invaluable." ["Thomas Irving Obituary"], *Gentleman's Magazine*, LXX (Aug. 1800), 798. Thomas Irving's will is dated 3 June 1800. PROB 11/1345, fols 94v–96r, PRO. He died on 13 July.
   Bouts of ill health had plagued Irving throughout his life, while he was resident in North America and after. See, e.g., nn. 48, 67, of this chapter. In Apr. 1791 the "Select Committee appointed to take Examination of Witnesses on the Slave Trade," came to him at his house – in Middle Scotland Yard, off Whitehall, one presumes – to take his testimony because, as they acknowledged, he was "only lately recovered from a dangerous illness." *Minutes of the Evidence . . . Respecting the African Slave Trade*, pp. 264, 266.
   Irving and his wife had at least three children, only two of whom lived to adulthood. In 1781 Thomas wrote of "my little William and Libby," but the daughter whom he mentioned in his will was named Marion, after her mother, and was herself called a "little girl" in 1796. "Libby" – most likely a diminutive for Elizabeth – probably died in the 1780s, perhaps in London. Her younger sister, Marion, who was probably born near the end of the same decade, later married a London West Indian merchant named Furness whom I have been unable to trace. Maxwell-Irving, "Irvings of Dumfries," pp. 73–74; Irving, at Charleston, to Steuart, at London, 20 Dec. 1781, Steuart Papers, MS 5040, fols 223–224, National Library of Scotland; Irving's evidence ("His family . . . consists of a Wife and two Children"), 10 Oct. 1787, AO 12/51, fol. 162v, PRO; *Girlhood of Maria Josepha Holroyd*, ed. Adeane, p. 367; PROB 11/1345, fols 94v–96r, PRO.
   Son William, who died on 27 Aug. 1855 at age 78, had to have been conceived before Irving left Charleston for the Bahamas in the summer of 1775 and must, therefore, have been born in South Carolina in 1776. Death Certificate, Register of Deaths, Office of Population Censuses and Surveys, London. William Irving's will is dated 1 Mar. 1856. PROB 11/2227, fol. 176v, PRO. He succeeded his father as Inspector-General, taking over immediately despite his relative youth. He started work before the end of Oct. 1800. See William Irving, at Custom House, to the Earl of Liverpool, 20 Oct. 1800, Add. MS 38234, fol. 179, BL. See also *The Royal Kalendar; or, Complete and Correct Annual Register for England, Scotland, Ireland, and America for the Year 1800* (London, [1800]), p. 210; *Royal Kalendar . . . 1801* (London, [1801]), p. 255. Compare The *Court and City Register* (London, 1799), 2nd pagination, p. 211; *The Court and City Register* (London, 1800), p. 255. For the latter source, see Alizon M. Mathews, "Editions of the Court and City

Economic historians have particular cause to be indebted to Thomas Irving, because those talents bequeathed an invaluable corpus of statistical data with which to illumine a crucial half-century of Anglo-American economic history.

Register, 1742–1813," *Bulletin of the Institute of Historical Research*, XIX (1942–1943), 9–12. William Irving retained the position until his retirement, shortly before his death. Maxwell-Irving, "Irvings of Dumfries," p. 73. Together, father and son served as Inspectors-General for nearly seventy years.

10

THE CURRENT VALUE
OF ENGLISH EXPORTS,
1697–1800

Ever since Charles Whitworth first published his volume on the *State of the Trade of Great Britain* in 1776, scholars have used his figures to evaluate England's balance of trade with the rest of the world.[1] Among those most interested in this endeavor have been historians of colonial America who have related Whitworth's numbers to the changing fortunes of the Continental Colonies and, naturally, to the American Revolution.[2] They have not been alone, for England traded with the world, and others have used his data in discussions of the trade of Scandinavia, Southern Europe, Africa, and the East Indies.

1   Charles Whitworth, *State of the Trade of Great Britain in Its Imports and Exports . . . 1697 [to 1773]* (London, 1776). Despite the title, the volume presented data for England and Wales only. Two copies of the book exist with manuscript additions and corrections to 1801, one among the George Chalmers Collection in the Peter Force Papers, LC, and the other as BT 6/185, fols 1–167, PRO. A French translation, published by the government, appeared the following year: *Commerce de la Grande-Bretagne, et tableaux de ses importations progressives, depuis l'année 1697 jusqu'à la fin de l'année 1773* (Paris, 1777).
   The original version of this chapter was published in *W&MQ*, 3rd ser., XXVIII (Oct. 1971), 607–628. Copyright © 1971 by the Institute of Early American History and Culture. Copyright © re-registered 1987 by John J. McCusker.
   I continue to be grateful for the help and support given me in the preparation of the original essay by the Council on Research in Economic History, the Smithsonian Institution, the American Philosophical Society, and the Institute of Early American History and Culture.

2   An indication of their importance for colonial historians is the repeated instances in which the series for the Thirteen Continental Colonies has been extracted and printed separately. See Isaac Smith Homans, Jr, *An Historical and Statistical Account of the Foreign Commerce of the United States* (New York, 1857), pp. 7–8; Charles H. Evans, *Exports, Domestic and Foreign, from the American Colonies to Great Britain, from 1697 to 1789, Inclusive. Exports, Domestic, from the United States to All Countries, from 1789 to 1883, Inclusive,* [US, Congress, 49th Cong., 1st Sess., House Miscellaneous Documents, vol. no. 24, doc. no. 49, pt ii, Serial Set no. 2236] (Washington, DC, 1884); and Emory R. Johnson *et al.,* *History of Domestic and Foreign Commerce of the United States,* Carnegie Institution of Washington, Publication no. 215A, 2 vols in 1 pt (Washington, DC, 1915), I, 120–121. The earliest published colonial series – English exports to Pennsylvania, 1723–1747 – had been sent to Lewis Evans, engineer and geographer of Philadelphia, at his request by a friend in London. Evans gave a copy of the data to Swedish botanist Pehr Kalm who visited him in 1748 and Kalm later printed them in his account of his journey: *En resa till Norra America, på Kongl[igt] Swenska Wetenskaps Academiens befallning, och Publici*

Nevertheless many historians remain unaware that Whitworth's annual series of English trade figures did not and *do not record the actual value of trade* with other countries of the world. We have in Whitworth's book not the current value of English imports and exports but rather a series of figures that express the volume of trade in money terms of constant value. As they stand, the data bear only an incidental relationship to the English balance of trade – with the Thirteen Continental Colonies or anywhere else. (Even if the ledgers did serve their intended function for England, they cannot be used to establish a colonial balance of trade, because they show a colony's trade only with England and Wales.) The purpose of this discussion is to offer a systematic conversion of the constant value series of exports from England, Wales, and Scotland into a current value series through the mechanism of a commodity price index. The result is a closer approximation of the actual annual value of British exports during the eighteenth century.[3]

♦ ♦ ♦ ♦ ♦

To determine the character of the series that Whitworth printed and to understand the uses to which we may put it, we must first consider what it was that the compilers of these figures were attempting to measure and then assess the methods that they employed. Twentieth-century economists recognize the balance of trade as only one aspect of a nation's international balance of payments, which overall includes three main sectors: the balance on current account, the bullion account, and the capital account. The capital account deals with the long- and short-term overseas investments by residents of one area in the enterprises of another. English money used to underwrite an ironworks in Massachusetts or a sugar plantation in Barbados represents such a

---

kostnad, 3 vols (Stockholm, 1753–1761), III, 187–188, 526. Compare *The America of 1750: Peter Kalm's Travels in North America – The English Version of 1770*, [trans John Reinhold Foster], rev. edn, ed. Adolph B. Benson, 2 vols (New York, 1937), I, 28–29. Kalm also contributed part of the series to the dissertation of one of his students at Åbo University (modern Turku University). See Daniel [E.] Lithander, *Oförgripeliga Tancker om Nödwändigheten of Skogarnas Bettre Wård och Ans i Finland* [Certain Considerations about the Necessity of Better Maintaining and Improving the Forests in Finland] (Åbo [Turku], [Finland], 1753), p. 17. What might well be Evans's, original series still survives. See "An Accot. of the Value of Exports from England to Pennsylvania," 1723–1747, Custom House, London, 4 Apr. 1749, in the Penn Family Papers, 1629–1834, vol. VII: Philadelphia Land Grants, 1684–1772, item 67, HSP. See also Lawrence Henry Gipson, *Louis Evans* (Philadelphia, 1939), p. 7. The dating of the compilation suggests that Evans sent the table on to Kalm after his visit. The most extensive and authoritative published version of these data is that prepared by Lawrence A. Harper, revised and extended by Jacob M. Price, and presented in [US, Department of Commerce, Bureau of the Census], *Historical Statistics of the United States: Colonial Times to 1970*, 2 vols (Washington, DC, 1975), II, 1176–1177 (ser. Z 213–226). See also Jacob M. Price, "New Time Series for Scotland's and Britain's Trade with the Thirteen Colonies and States, 1740 to 1791," *WMQ*, 3rd ser., XXXII (April 1975), 307–325.

3 For a considered comment on this attempt, see S[imon] D. Smith, *A Note on the Current and Constant Value of Eighteenth-Century English Exports*, University of York, Discussion Papers in Economics, no. 93/7 (York, [1993]).

movement of capital, as does colonial investment in securities of the East India Company or the Bank of England. The bullion account measures the flow of hard currency between one area and another. Here we would enter the value of gold and silver coin that individual merchants shipped from the Thirteen Continental Colonies to Great Britain in payment of debts. The balance on current account concerns the value of goods imported and exported as well as the value of the "invisibles," the costs that these exchanges of commodities incurred such as the cost of shipping services. The balance of trade, which deals solely with merchandise, thus constitutes only part of the last of these three categories. Yet its calculation provides an important starting point in the accounting of international indebtedness. We do well to examine it, as long as we remember that there is much more besides.

Regular recording of the English balance of trade began only in the last decades of the seventeenth century but it had its origins much earlier. Starting, apparently, in the reign of King James I, or perhaps even earlier in the reign of Queen Elizabeth I, a variety of national and international pressures impelled Englishmen into a recognition of how useful it would be to have a more accurate record of their trade with the rest of the world. English mercantilism cried out for such an accounting; abortive and fragmentary attempts to strike the balance of trade litter the seventeenth century.[4] Government had required the formal entry of goods coming and going at each English port from as early as the fifteenth century. The documents generated in the process provided the basis not only for the collection of the customs and the publication of a daily newspaper that reported on the state of London's imports and exports but also for a more orderly check on the

---

4   G[eorge] N. Clark, *Guide to English Commercial Statistics 1696–1782*, Royal Historical Society, Guides and Handbooks, no. 1 (London, 1938), pp. xi–xvi. The earliest such attempt may have been what produced the two extant tables of English imports and exports for the year 1570 that survive in Titus B. IV, fols 225–226, Cotton MSS, BL; they have been printed – without attribution – in Hubert Hall, *A History of the Custom-Revenue in England from the Earliest Times to the Year 1827*, 2 vols (London, 1885), II, 243–244. The data compiled by and for the Surveyor-General of the Customs, Lionel Cranfield, dated between 1605 and 1614 seem not to have survived except for the summary table reproduced in E[dward] M[isselden], *The Circle of Commerce. Or the Balance of Trade, in Defence of Free Trade . . .* (London, 1623), pp. 121–122. Compare the materials from the papers of Lionel Cranfield as calendared in [GB, Historical Manuscripts Commission], *Calendar of the Manuscripts of . . . Lord Sackville . . .*, ed. A[rthur] P. Newton and F[rederick] J. Fisher, 2 vols (London, 1940–1966), passim. Concerning these data, see also John J. McCusker, "The Business Press in England before 1775," *The Library: Transactions of the Bibliographical Society*, 6th ser., VIII (Sept. 1986), 205–231 – revised as chapter seven of the present book (see esp. n. 9). The two compilations done for London for 1663 and 1669 are in Add. MS 36785, BL. Concerning them, see also Margaret Priestly, "Anglo-French Trade and the 'Unfavourable Balance' Controversy, 1660–1685," *EcHR*, 2nd ser., IV (No. 1, 1951), 36–52. For further discussion of the state of England's foreign trade over these years, see A[nnie] M. Millard, "The Import Trade of London, 1600–1640," 3 vols (Ph.D. diss., University of London, 1956); and Ralph Davis, "English Foreign Trade, 1660–1700," *EcHR*, 2nd ser., VII (Dec. 1954), 150–166.

entire kingdom's trade.[5] Not until the late 1680s, however, did the government begin regularly to compile national trade statistics on an annual basis.[6]

5   John J. McCusker, *European Bills of Entry and Marine Lists: Early Commercial Publications and the Origins of the Business Press* (Cambridge, Mass., 1985), pp. 15–16, describes the entry procedures that created these records. See also Clark, *English Commercial Statistics*, pp. 52–56. Most of the extant port books are in Port Books, 1565–1798, E 190, PRO. There is more information about them, in the introduction to [GB, PRO], *Descriptive List of Exchequer . . . Port Books*, [by Neville J. Williams], 3 vols (London, 1960–1972), I, v–ix; Williams, "The London Port Books," *Transactions of the London and Middlesex Archaeological Society*, XVIII (1955), 13–26; and D[onald] M. Woodward, "Port Books," *History: The Journal of the Historical Association*, LV (June 1970), 207–210. One of them has been published; it recorded the imports into London by English citizens (and those foreigners who paid native rates) for the year from 30 Sept. 1567–30 Sept. 1568: *The Port and Trade of Early Elizabethan London: Documents*, ed. Brian Dietz, London Record Society Publications, vol. VIII ([London], 1972). See also Sven-Erik Åström, "The Reliability of the English Port Books," *Scandinavian Economic History Review*, XVI (no. 2, 1968), 126–136. After 1619 (and, perhaps, even earlier), a compilation of each day's record of the goods entered at the customhouse as imports and exports began to be published, printed and sold "about the City to any merchant or other, that will pay for them forty shillings the year." John Houghton described the service, ["Custom-House Bills"], *Collection for Improvement of Husbandry and Trade* (London), [I] (no. 6, 27 Apr. 1692), [p. 1]. In the "Inventory of Books and Papers of the Late Plantation Office" prepared by the outgoing Secretary to the Commissioners for Trade and Plantations, John Povey, for his successor, William Popple, in Aug. 1696 Povey listed eleven vols of "Bills of Entry." CO 326/1, p. 150, PRO. It would appear that the Commissioners for Trade and Plantations had been among the subscribers to this newspaper and that it had preserved and bound the daily issues. The bound volumes do not appear to have survived, however. Compare C[harles] S. S. Higham, *The Colonial Entry-Books: A Brief Guide to the Colonial Records in the Public Record Office before 1696*, Helps for Students of History, no. 45 (London, 1921), p. 43. For more about these published bills of entry, see McCusker, op. cit., pp. 15–51; and McCusker, "Business Press in England," pp. 209–214 – revised as chapter seven of the present book.

6   Clark, *English Commercial Statistics*, p. xvi. On 30 Dec. 1695 Parliament ordered and – after a labor of fourteen months – the Customs produced compilations for the three years 1693–1695 that pre-figured the Customs 3 accounts. [Charles Davenant], *The Political and Commercial Works of That Celebrated Writer Charles D'Avenant, LL.D. . . .*, ed. Charles Whitworth, 5 vols (London, 1771), I, 95; [GB, Parl., Lords], *The Manuscripts of the House of Lords*, in progress (London, 1871 to date), new ser., II, 7, 24–27, 411, 419–422, VI, 221. The "Account of Exports and Imports, London and the Outports," 1693–1695, in twelve books, is in the Parchment Collection, Sessional Papers, House of Lords, HLRO. See, especially, the covering letter from the Commissioners of the Customs to the Committee of the House of Lords, 16 Feb. 1696/97. I am very grateful to Dwyryd Jones for pointing out their location to me. See his *War and Trade in the Age of William III and Marlborough* ([Oxford, 1988]).
    Similar pressures had an impact upon other European nations and led to the compilation of comparable balance of trade statistics in Ireland (from 1681), France (1716), Sweden (1738), and Scotland (1755). Irish records for 1698 to 1829 survive as Customs 15/1–140, PRO. Four earlier ledgers for 1683 to 1686 are Add. MS 4759, BL. Arthur Dobbs, in *An Essay on the Trade and Improvement of Ireland*, 2 vols (Dublin, 1729–1731), I, 4–6, drew evidence from ledgers for 1681, 1695, 1696, 1697, and 1698, of which only the last is extant.
    For the compilation of the French statistics, see [Ambroise Marie] Arnould, *De la balance du commerce et des relations commerciales extérieures de la France, dans toutes les parties du globe, particulièrement à la fin du règne de Louis XIV, et au moment de la Révolution . . . avec la valeur de ses importations et exportations progressives depuis 1716 jusqu'en 1788 inclusivement*, 3 vols (Paris, 1791–1795), I, viii, II, 121–133, and elsewhere. See also

The office of Inspector-General of Imports and Exports came into being in 1696 as a division of the Customs.[7] The first Inspector-General, William Culliford, set his clerks to work immediately. Over a year later they completed volume one in the series of the annual great folio ledgers of imports and exports that make up the set known today as "Customs 3" in the Public Record Office in London.[8] Each volume contained six major sections:

Ruggiero Romano, "Documenti e prime considerazioni intorno alla 'Balance du commerce' della Francia dal 1716 al 1780," in *Studi in onore di Armando Sapori*, 2 vols (Milan, [1957]), II, 1265–1300. For very valuable, critical comments about those statistics, see Bertrand Gille, *Les Sources statistiques de l'histoire de France. Des enquêtes du XVIIe siècle à 1870* (Paris, 1964), pp. 96–97; and David S. Landes, "Statistics as a Source for the History of Economic Development in Western Europe: The Protostatistical Era," in *The Dimensions of the Past: Materials, Problems, and Opportunities for Quantitative Work in History*, ed. Val R. Lorwin and Jacob M. Price (New Haven, Conn., 1972), pp. 63–64, 85, n. 33. For the Swedish series, see Bertil Boëthius and Eli F. Heckscher, *Svensk handelsstatistik, 1637–1717* (Stockholm, 1938), p. xlvi. For Scotland, see n. 9 of this chapter and Price, "New Time Series for Scotland's and Britain's Trade."

7   Clark, *English Commercial Statistics*, pp. 1–44, treats in detail the antecedents to the office, its establishment, and its subsequent history down to the end of the 18th century. Very helpful also is [Romaine] E[lizabeth] B[oody] Firuski [Schumpeter], "Trade Statistics and Cycles in England, 1697–1825" (Ph.D. diss., Radcliffe College, Harvard University, 1934). For the context of these developments, see Elizabeth Evelynola Hoon*, The Organization of the English Customs System 1696–1786* (New York, 1938); and Dora Mae Clark, *The Rise of the British Treasury: Colonial Administration in the Eighteenth Century* (New Haven, Conn., 1960). For the administration of the Customs from the perspective of a Commissioner of the Customs during the 1680s, see Richard [B.] Grassby, *The English Gentleman in Trade: The Life and Works of Sir Dudley North, 1641–1691* (Oxford, 1994), pp. 157–176.

8   Customs 3/1–82, PRO. Customs 2/1–10, PRO, duplicate Customs 3 up to 1702 and add an earlier volume for 1697. Ledgers for 1705 and 1712 no longer survive in the Public Record Office. A copy of the 1727 ledger, which was also once absent from the set in PRO, did exist among the many duplicate volumes in the Departmental Archives, HM Customs and Excise, Library, New King's Beam House, London, and has been transferred to the PRO. It is now designated Customs 3/82, PRO. Some data for the years 1705 and 1712 can be retrieved from contemporary accounts made up from the ledgers while the set was still intact. The Customs 3 ledgers were for a time complemented by, and later supplanted by, another series: the States of Navigation, Commerce and Revenue, 1772 to 1808, Customs 17/1–30, PRO.

The "year" used in the Customs 3 ledgers changed twice between 1697 and 1780. The accounts for 1697 and 1698 – Customs 2/1–4 and 3/1, PRO – were based on the 12 months from Michaelmas to Michaelmas, Sept. 29 through 28 Sept. The next ledger – Customs 2/5 and 3/2, PRO – included only the 3 months from Michaelmas to Christmas 1698; figures from this ledger have been ignored in the present discussion because of the statistical difficulties in dealing with a quarter year. All later accounts incorporated data for a full 12 months. The year ran from Christmas to Christmas, 25 Dec. to 24 Dec., until 1752 when, as a result of the calendar reform, Treasury accounts for that year were extended to include 11 additional days through 5 Jan. 1753, to compensate for the loss of 11 days in Sept. (the 3rd through the 13th). After that, the Treasury year ran from 6 Jan. through 5 Jan. See, for instance, the accounts of payments into the Exchequer from the 4½% Duty, in E 351/1265, PRO, and in T 38/340, PRO. Since the Ledgers of Imports and Exports were compiled under the jurisdiction of the Treasury, they must surely have followed suit, even though the annual ledgers continued to state that they included data from Christmas to Christmas. A comparison of the data from a volume of the Customs 3 ledgers and the volume for the same year from the Customs 17 ledgers, which were explicitly stated to be based on the new accounting year, shows them to be

226

imports, reexports, and exports for both London and "the Outports" (i.e., the remainder of England and Wales). Within each section trade was further broken down by the areas to or from which goods were shipped: the foreign nations of the world listed roughly alphabetically, then the three Channel Islands, Alderney, Guernsey, and Jersey, and finally, the colonies of Great Britain. Under a separate heading for each area the clerk wrote across the page the name of the item traded, the quantity traded that year, the valuation per unit, and the total value. Item followed item down the page in an arrangement that was, again, basically alphabetical but that grouped some commodities under inclusive headings such as "grocery" or "drugs." At the end of each sub-category the clerk summed up the total for that part of that particular section. The grand totals from each of the six sections provided an annual summary of England's "balance of trade" on the final folio of the ledger.[9] Whitworth, in effect, printed the summary table from each of the Customs 3 ledgers through to the year 1773.

the same. See similar conclusions reached by Rupert C. Jarvis, "Official Trade and Revenue Statistics," *EcHR*, 2nd ser., XVII (Aug. 1964), 45, 47; and Phyllis Deane and W[illiam] A. Cole. *British Economic Growth, 1688–1959: Trends and Structure*, 2nd edn (Cambridge, Eng., 1969), p. 321, n. 4. See also Clark, *English Commercial Statistics*, pp. 11–12, 37.

   In addition to Whitworth, David Macpherson, *Annals of Commerce, Manufactures, Fisheries and Navigation, with Brief Notices of the Arts and Sciences Connected with Them . . . to . . . 1801* (London, 1805), III–IV, passim, printed the annual summaries of English trade from 1760 through 1800. The Customs 3 ledgers and Customs 17 accounts also provided the source for [Romaine] Elizabeth Boody Schumpeter, *English Overseas Trade Statistics 1697–1808* (Oxford, 1960).

9   Clark, *English Commercial Statistics*, pp. 8–10, describes the internal arrangement of the ledgers. See also Schumpeter, *English Overseas Trade Statistics*, pp. 1–2.

   Ledgers of Imports and Exports for Scotland, 1755–1827, are in Customs 14/1–39, PRO. The accounts for the years 1763 and 1769 have not survived. There are contemporary extracts from these ledgers for the years 1755–1801 in BT 6/185, fols 168–197, PRO. The Scottish ledgers used the 6 Jan. through 5 Jan. Treasury year, thus adding weight to the supposition that the English ledgers did also. No Scottish customhouse returns were deposited with the British Customs authorities before 1761. See, e.g., the statement by Thomas Irving, 5 Feb. 1787, in [GB, Parl., Commons], *An Account of the British Produce and Manufactures Exported from England to France between . . . 1714 and . . . 1761*, HC Sessional Papers to 1801, Accounts and Papers, vol. XIX, no. 426 [Lambert 3867] ([London], 1787), p. 1. Compare [GB, Parl., Commons], *Customs Tariffs of the United Kingdom from 1800 to 1897, with Some Notes upon the History of the More Important Branches of Receipts from the Year 1660*, HC Sessional Papers, 1898, vol. LXXXV (Accounts and Papers, vol. XXXIV), [Cmd. 8706] (London, 1897), p. 24, where T. J. Pittar implied that the gap in the records was because of their accidental destruction by fire. See also T 64/274, no. 131, PRO. (For the British sessional papers and the mode of their citation, see John J. McCusker, "New Guides to Primary Sources for the History of Early British America," *W&MQ*, 3rd ser., XLI (Apr. 1984), 277–295 – revised as chapter one of the present book.) Earlier records survive in Scotland. See the Scottish 17th-century port books (E. 72), similar to those of England, and the Scottish Customs accounts dating from 1742 (E. 504) in the Exchequer Records, Scottish Record Office, Edinburgh, as well as the various records in the several major 18th-century ports. Summaries of the annual Scottish figures in Customs 14, PRO, can be found in BT 6/185, fols 168–197, PRO; the data were printed in Macpherson, *Annals of Commerce*, II–IV, passim. For Thomas Irving, see John J. McCusker, "Colonial Civil Servant and Counter-Revolutionary: Thomas Irving (1738?–1800) in Boston, Charleston, and London," *Perspectives in American History*, XII

Although there is little doubt about what Culliford and his successors were attempting to produce with the Customs 3 ledgers, we may legitimately question how successful they were. Moreover, we must do so before we as economic historians set out to use their figures.[10] To begin with, as in any project of such scope, the room for simple clerical errors was abundant. Some we can find by checking calculations, but there are certainly others that we have yet to detect (or cannot). The presumption must be that they are not statistically important. Random errors have a tendency to balance out and can reasonably be assumed to do so.[11] To quote Deane and Cole: "It is generally agreed that the physical quantities recorded in the statistics are as accurate as eighteenth-century officials could make them."[12]

By contrast, systematic distortions affecting both the quantities of goods recorded and the unit values used pose more serious difficulties. Imports were taxed in England, sometimes at very high rates, and this created an impetus to smuggle. As a result, the official figures for certain imports understate the actual volume, although some work has been done to repair this defect.[13] Obviously, therefore, we must be alert to such possible defects on a commodity-by-commodity basis.

According to contemporaries, figures for exports suffered much less from the problem of smuggling than from a certain upward bias caused by the

(1979), 314–350 – revised as chapter nine of the present book. For more information about the Scottish data, see Price, "New Time Series for Scotland's and Britain's Trade."

10 Compare what follows with the nicely balanced judgment in *The British Merchant; or, Commerce Preserv'd* (London), no. 63, 12 Mar. 1713/14.

11 The figures used as the basis for table 10.3 differ in several instances from other published versions of the same data. The revisions in the *Historical Statistics of the United States*, II, 1176–1177, incorporated corrections to earlier mistakes in transcription from Whitworth and the original ledgers. See the corrections to Ser. Z 220 for 1715 and ser. Z 217 for 1763. Both of these mistakes were carried through to the totals; they have also to be corrected. Harper himself silently corrected an error of Whitworth's for New York in 1767. The original ledgers contain much more significant mistakes. The sum of London's exports of English goods to Virginia and Maryland for 1773 was incorrectly cast; the total should be £428,904 (not £328,904). See Customs 3/73, fols 87–89, PRO. Ralph Davis detected this error. See his "English Foreign Trade, 1700–1774," *EcHR*, 2nd ser., XV (Dec. 1962), 285–286, n. 2, where he also points out other similar problems. Table 10.2 and table 10.3 of this chapter take these alterations into account. Note, importantly, that a very significant typographical mistake occurred in the most recent edition of *Historical Statistics of the United States*, II, 1177–1178. The columns headed "exports" from Scotland should be labeled "imports" and vice versa. The "Correction Sheet" that accompanied the original edition of the work was not included with – nor was the mistake corrected in – a commercial edition of the same work: [US, Department of Commerce, Bureau of the Census], *The Statistical History of the United States, from Colonial Times to the Present*, ed. Ben J. Wattenberg (New York, 1976).

12 Deane and Cole, *British Economic Growth*, p. 44. Compare Davis, "English Foreign Trade, 1660–1700," p. 156, concerning the values assigned the 1663 and 1669 compilations: "it might be supposed that these revised values would be as accurate as near-contemporaries in close contact with the world of commerce could achieve."

13 See W[illiam] A. Cole, "Trends in Eighteenth Century Smuggling," *EcHR*, 2nd ser., X (Apr. 1958), 395–409; and Deane and Cole, *British Economic Growth*, pp. 44–45. Compare Hoh-Cheung Mui and Lorna H. Mui, "Smuggling and the British Tea Trade before 1784," *AHR*, LXXIV (Oct. 1968), 44–73.

practice among merchants of overstating the quantities of merchandise shipped abroad in the hope of both inflating their own reputations and of discouraging competition. The customhouse records were open to public scrutiny and summaries of the bills of entry were published daily.[14] At London, merchants were quick to correct mistakes that appeared in the published bills.[15] Modern analyses have played down the significance of such over-entries to the point that they are no longer considered a serious threat to analyses built upon these statistics.[16] Far more important is the problem created by the unchanging unit values, to the resolution of which this study is devoted.

The English ledgers of imports and exports failed in their purpose of "ascertaining the real values of trade,"[17] the actual market value of the goods traded, because the unit values that the Inspectors-General assigned the commodities were not the current market prices of a given year but formalized official values derived at the beginning of the eighteenth century and applied, practically unchanged, throughout that century and beyond down to 1870. At the start Culliford and his clerks, in establishing unit values for

---

14 McCusker, *European Bills of Entry*, pp. 15–51.

15 [John Lewis, at London], to [Arthur Onslow, at Liverpool], 30 June 1783, "Papers Relating to the Bills of Entry," No. 2016, Harpton Court Deeds and Documents, Department of Manuscripts and Records, National Library of Wales, Aberystwyth.

16 Schumpeter, *English Overseas Trade Statistics*, pp. 5–6, felt that the practice had considerably less effect on trade returns "than might be inferred from the attention given to it in public debates and treatises on overseas trade." Writing in 1692, John Houghton agreed: "I presume, such doings, if any, are very trivial to the bulk of things." *Collection for Improvement of Husbandry and Trade* (London), 27 Apr. 1692. Compare [Robert Paul], *The Business of the Comptroller-General of the Accounts of His Majesty's Customs* (London, 1723), pp. 20–21. See also [Schumpeter], "Trade Statistics," pp. 130–144. Compare John J. McCusker, *Rum and the American Revolution: The Rum Trade and the Balance of Payments of the Thirteen Continental Colonies, 1650–1775*, 2 vols (New York, 1989 [Ph.D. diss., University of Pittsburgh, 1970]), II, 881–882, 986–987, nn. 11–12, where I advance conclusions similar to Schumpeter's after examining the statistics for selected trades. It is significant that the complaints of 18th-century authors ascribing such a defect to the Customs 3, PRO, figures simply copy earlier writers' complaints about figures derived from London port books. Compare Josiah Child, *A New Discourse of Trade* . . . (London, 1693), p. 137; and Joshua Gee, *The Trade and Navigation of Great-Britain Considered* . . . (London, 1729), pp. 117–118. See, especially, "Copies of all Entries of Goods and Merchandise Outwards for North America . . . from 22d. December 1775, to the 13th May 1776 . . . and also the several Quantities of Goods actually Shipped . . . in consequence of such Entries . . .," endorsed Custom House, London, 8 Nov. 1776, MS North b. 69 (SC 49490), Papers of Frederick, Lord North, 2nd Earl of Guildford, North Family Papers, Bodleian Library, Department of Western Manuscripts, University of Oxford. This account demonstrates that the Customs was well aware of the situation and prepared to adjust for it. Houghton was correct in his judgment.

17 Clark, *English Commercial Statistics*, p. 39. Here Clark used "real value" to mean the actual market value of the goods traded. This is just the opposite of the way in which economists use the word "real"; by "real" they mean the value adjusted for inflation. The contrast is between the current, actual market value of goods, valued using market prices, and the official, constant or "real" value of the commodities, priced using fixed or nominal values. The original version of this chapter published in 1971 occasionally and confusingly used the word "real" in the way that Clark did.

their calculations, sought out the actual market price in England of goods exported and reexported; for imported goods, they used estimates of the "first cost" of commodities, that is price at the place from which they were shipped to England.[18] During the earliest years this exercise was repeated annually and, thus, during the earliest years the official values in the ledgers varied with the market. For these years the totals consequently reflect the actual value of England's trade with the world. But after about 1702, when the values finally became fixed, the Customs 3 ledgers, whatever their accuracy in the amount of goods imported and exported, ceased being an accurate record of England's balance of trade.[19]

These statements contain no revelation. Eighteenth-century writers were aware from the beginning of the unchanging nature of the official values and the effect they had upon the annual summaries.[20] Nineteenth- and twentieth-

18 The entries were valued, for imported goods, "according to their current price abroad," and for exported goods, "according to their current price here at home." Davenant in his *Political and Commercial Works*, ed. Whitworth, V, 350. Compare Clark, *English Commercial Statistics*, pp. 10, 59; Schumpeter, *English Overseas Trade Statistics*, p. 8, based upon William Irving's data in [GB, Parl., Commons], *An Account of the Official and Likewise of the Real or Current Value, at which Each Article of the Imports and Exports of Great Britain to and from Ireland during the Three Years Ending the 5th Jan. 1803, Has Been Estimated*, HC Sessional Papers, 1803–1804, vol. VIII (Accounts and Papers, vol. II), [no. 190] ([London], 1804). For the origins of this practice, see Henry S. Cobb, "'Books of Rates' and the London Customs, 1507–1558," *The Guildhall Miscellany*, IV (Oct. 1971), 1–3. This means that the figures for the Thirteen Continental Colonies' imports from and exports to England included no freight or insurance costs; each was valued FOB at the point of export.

For English market prices, the staff of the Inspector-General most likely turned to the London commodity price currents that were published in the City several times weekly. Such recourse was neither difficult nor exceptional. It is precisely what a contemporary writer did who, in 1714, had access to and quoted from "several London Price Courants" for the years 1676–1682. *The British Merchant; or, Commerce Preserv'd* (London), no. 85, 28 May 1714. For the London commodity price currents (and other business newspapers), see John J. McCusker and Cora Gravesteijn, *The Beginnings of Commercial and Financial Journalism: The Commodity Price Currents, Exchange Rate Currents, and Money Currents of Early Modern Europe*, Nederlandsch Economisch-Historisch Archief, ser. III, no. 11 (Amsterdam, 1991), pp. 291–311.

19 The prices of some commodities, notably wool, continued to be adjusted sporadically during the next two decades. See below.

20 The earliest authors to expound upon this subject were, naturally, the Inspectors-General of Imports and Exports. See the comments, in 1711, of the second Inspector-General, Charles Davenant, in his *Political and Commercial Works*, ed. Whitworth, V, 350; the comments, in 1718, of the third Inspector-General, Henry Martin, CO 390/12, fols 9–10, PRO; and the comments, in 1791, of the twelfth Inspector-General, Thomas Irving, Customs 17/12, pp. 3–4, PRO. Martin's observations have been printed by Clark, *English Commercial Statistics*, pp. 62–69, but with some significant omissions. Compare CO 390/12, fol. 10r, PRO, with p. 63, and fol. 17r with p. 66. Irving's conclusions can be found reprinted in part by John Ehrman, *The British Government and Commercial Negotiations with Europe 1783–1793* (Cambridge, Eng., 1962), pp. 212–214. See also John Oxenford, at London, to Commissioners for Trade and Plantations, 31 Aug. 1720, CO 388/22, no. Q 75, PRO; George Chalmers, *An Estimate of the Comparative Strength of Great Britain, during the Present and Four Preceding Reigns; and of the Losses of Her Trade from Every War Since the Revolution*, [1st edn] (London, 1782), pp. 35–36; and Macpherson, *Annals of Commerce*, III, 340, IV, 464.

century scholars have long shared this knowledge.[21] The reactions have varied but can be classified broadly into two kinds: some writers have appreciated the potential of the ledgers as a constant value series of trade figures and used them as such; others have seen them only as a distorted approximation of the balance of trade, the defects of which might be repaired if possible or, if not, ignored.

As a constant value series, Customs 3 ledgers can be used both in national income accounting and in measuring the changing volume of trade. Analysis of changes in an economy through a study of alterations in the levels of consumer living or in the size of the gross national product requires a constant value series. Long-term trends in the volume of trade can best be traced by removing from consideration the changes due solely to varying price levels. "Thus it is simpler to describe the fluctuations of woollen exports in money than to give the number of short cloths and Spanish cloths, double bays, Colchester bays, perpetuanas, says, serges, worsted stuffs."[22] A constant value index, by removing the potentially distorting factor of changing prices, stands other key elements in relief.[23] So advantageous is it to have a constant value series that, had the Customs 3 ledgers been prepared in current value terms, it is safe to say that some economic historian would by now have reduced them to constant value terms.[24]

---

21 Warnings in the 19th century were sounded by, among others, J[ohn] Marshall, *A Digest of All the Accounts, Relating to the Population, Productions, Revenues, Financial Operations, Manufactures, Shipping, Colonies, Commerce, etc., etc., of the United Kingdom of Great Britain and Ireland, Diffused Through More Than 600 Volumes of Journals, Reports, and Papers, Presented to Parliament during the Last Thirty-Five Years*, 2 vols (London, 1833), I, 120a; Stephen Bourne, "The Official Trade and Navigation Statistics," *Journal of the Statistical Society of London*, XXXV (June 1872), 206–208; and T. J. Pittar, in *Customs Tariffs of the United Kingdom from 1800 to 1897*, pp. 16, 51. In the 20th century the most authoritative voices have been E[phraim] Lipson, *The Economic History of England*, 6th edn, 3 vols (London, 1956), III, 93–94; Clark, *English Commercial Statistics*, pp. 33–39; T[homas] S. Ashton, who followed Clark, in his introduction to Schumpeter, *English Overseas Trade Statistics*, pp. 2–4; and Deane and Cole, *British Economic Growth*, pp. 42–43. Compare *Historical Statistics of the United States*, II, 1157.

22 Clark, *English Commercial Statistics*, p. 37.

23 Almost every writer cited above in n. 20 of this chapter not only warned that the Customs 3, PRO, figures were not a current value series but also pointed out their potential as a constant value series. Henry Martin was among the first to realize the significance of the changes that had taken place in the series and argued in 1718 that it was particularly well adapted "to discover at one view the increase or decrease of the quantitys of goods, imported or exported." CO 390/12, fols 9–10, PRO. Deane and Cole, *British Economic Growth*, pp. 40–97, employ the evidence of the Customs 3, PRO, ledgers as an index to the volume of trade in discussing the 18th century. See also Lawrence A. Harper, *The English Navigation Laws: A Seventeenth-Century Experiment in Social Engineering* (New York, 1939), passim. Schumpeter, *English Overseas Trade Statistics*, sought to make the Customs 3, PRO, series more usable by revaluing all the major commodities to the official value for one year. But Deane and Cole discovered that the series was a perfectly satisfactory volume index just as it stood. *British Economic Growth*, pp. 43–44. Compare W[alter] E. Minchinton, "Editor's Introduction," in *Growth of English Overseas Trade in the Seventeenth and Eighteenth Centuries*, ed. Minchinton (London, 1969), pp. 54–55, n. 5, whose argument is simply fallacious.

24 A current value series is converted to a constant value series by dividing the former through with a commodity price index (CPI). This division has the effect of reducing the value

Yet anyone who sought the actual, current value of English trade could not use the series as it existed. The necessity of converting to current value has been recognized by many in the past, not the least of whom was Benjamin Franklin, who endeavored to bring the official values for the 1760s into accord with current market prices.[25] Others, contemporary with Franklin and later, have sought similar solutions.[26] Nevertheless some economic historians

factor in a series to a common unvarying unit. Obviously the process can also be reversed and a constant value series converted to a current value series by introducing (or reintroducing) the changes in value through multiplication by a CPI. The interrelated character of these three elements is emphasized when we appreciate that one CPI, the Paasche index (after its inventor), is defined as the quotient resulting from the division of the current value of a series by its value in constant prices. It has the formula:

$$\text{Paasche price index} = \frac{\sum p_1 q_1}{\sum p_0 q_1}$$

This is a current weight CPI as opposed to a Laspeyres or fixed weight CPI. For a basic discussion of these considerations, see any manual of economic statistics, for instance, Daniel B. Suits, Statistics: *An Introduction to Quantitative Economic Research* (Chicago, 1963), pp. 230–238. Compare Walter R. Crowe, *Index Numbers: Theory and Applications* (London, 1969), pp. 56–65. The classic treatise on price indices is Irving Fisher, *The Making of Index-Numbers: A Study of Their Varieties, Tests, and Reliability* (Boston, 1922). Also important is Wesley C. Mitchell, *The Making and Using of Index Numbers*, US, Department of Labor, Bureau of Labor Statistics, Bulletin no. 656, pt i (Washington, DC, 1938). Compare John J. McCusker, *How Much Is That in Real Money? A Historical Price Index for Use as a Deflator of Money Values in the Economy of the United States* (Worcester, Mass., 1992).

25   See the two letters, signed "F. B.," that appeared in the *London Chronicle*, 3 Nov. and 8 Dec. 1768, and were reprinted in the *Pennsylvania Journal, and the Weekly Advertiser* (Philadelphia), 26 Jan. 1769, the *Pennsylvania Chronicle, and Universal Advertiser* (Philadelphia), 6 Mar. 1769, and elsewhere. Franklin suggested an increase of one-third over the official values. His data, and perhaps his correction factor, came from John Huske, an American-born merchant and member of Parliament. See *Benjamin Franklin's Letters to the Press 1758–1775*, ed. Verner W. Crane (Chapel Hill, NC, 1950), pp. 141–151; *The Papers of Benjamin Franklin*, ed. Leonard W. Labaree *et al.*, in progress (New Haven, Conn., 1959 to date), XV, 249–255, 280–282. For Huske (1724–1773), "a tough, unscrupulous adventurer," see Lewis [B.] Namier and John Brooke, *The History of Parliament: The House of Commons, 1754–1790*, 3 vols (London, 1964), II, 658–662. Compare Franklin's attempt with that of Bryan Edwards, *The History, Civil and Commercial, of the British Colonies in the West Indies*, 2 vols (London, 1793), I, 236, n. 1, II, 383–384.

26   César Moreau, an early 19th-century French writer on economic matters, at one time the Vice-Consul of France at London, and, in 1829, the founder of the "Société Française de Statistique Universelle," attempted a revaluation of the official figures for several selected sets of years. Moreau, *Chronological Records of the British Royal and Commercial Navy, from the Earliest Period (A.D. 827) to the Present Time (1827)* (London, 1827), pp. 13, 15, 17, 18, 23, 30 (note his "Observations," p. 17). For Moreau, see Fernand Faure, *Les Précurseurs de la Société de Statistique de Paris* (Nancy, 1909), p. 45.
       Since World War II several economic historians have used various means to try to reach the same goal. Albert H. Imlah, "Real Values in British Foreign Trade, 1798–1853," *JEcH*, VIII (Nov. 1948), 133–152, broke new ground when he corrected 19th-century figures using a rather involved process made necessary by the great length of time between the choice of the official values and the date of his series. See also Imlah, *Economic Elements in the "Pax Britannia": Studies in British Foreign Trade in the Nineteenth Century* (Cambridge, Mass., 1958), esp. pp. 20–31. Gordon Carl Bjork, "Stagnation and Growth in the American Economy, 1784–1792" (Ph.D. diss., University of Washington, 1963),

have doubted that it could be done. G. N. Clark, Chichele Professor of Economic History in the University of Oxford, wrote that "it appears to be impossible to invent a formula of any practicable use for converting them, from year to year, to approximate real value," to an approximation of the actual, current value.[27] With all deference to Professor Clark, I should like to try just that. Much work done during the first third of this century in both the history of prices and in the theory of index numbers supplies the elements for a solution of the problem. The key, of course, is the nature of the series as a constant value index.

By its very nature, a constant value series can be converted to a current value series through the use of a commodity price index. The CPI expresses the percentage variation over time in the level of prices relative to a base period. One merely multiplies each annual Customs 3 total by the appropriate figure from the CPI. The method assumes that the percentage variations of the CPI equal the percentage variations experienced by the net current value of the Customs 3 series over time compared with the same base period. The very nature of the construct is the best support for the correctness of this procedure, but there are also objective tests of the results, as we shall see.

Obviously much depends on the choice of the CPI and base period. There are two very serviceable indices for England in the eighteenth century. The E. H. Phelps Brown and S. V. Hopkins series, which spans about three-quarters of the second millennium AD (1264–1954), has the advantage of

pp. 115–118, converted the official value of British imports from the United States in the years 1770–1775 and 1784–1792 into dollars using a weighted price index. Following the suggestion of James Shepherd, Robert Paul Thomas, in "A Quantitative Approach to the Study of the Effects of British Imperial Policy upon Colonial Welfare: Some Preliminary Findings," *JEcH*, XXV (Dec. 1965), 616 and n. 5, "adjusted" the prices of colonial imports "by the Schumpeter–Gilboy price index" in order "to make them more accurate." In what way and to what extent he fails to say. James Floyd Shepherd, Jr, "A Balance of Payments for the Thirteen Colonies, 1768–1772" (Ph.D. diss., University of Washington, 1966), p. 80, concluded that the official values during his period were "95 percent of the actual value" and corrected for this deficiency.

Many others either have been ignorant of or have ignored the injunctions against using these figures as if they were a current value series and, blithely accepting the ledgers at face value, have proceeded to write about an apocryphal balance of trade. Most notably they have been historians of colonial America. Even so careful and conscientious an economic historian as Michel Morineau has been caught in a pointless, specious comparison by failing to grasp the essential character of these data. See Morineau, *Incroyables Gazettes et fabuleux métaux: Les retours des trésors américains d'après les gazettes hollandaises (XVIe–XVIIIe siècles)* (London and Paris, 1985), pp. 166–173, where he discusses these numbers as if they were current values rather than constant values.

27 Clark, *English Commercial Statistics*, p. 39. It should be noted that Clark considered his "criticism of the British trade statistics of the seventeenth and eighteenth centuries . . . [as] merely directives for effective work, not warnings against expecting useful results" (ibid., p. 41).

reflecting long-term trends quite adequately.[28] On the other hand, to section out a century from their figures risks incurring distortions induced a hundred years earlier or later. Fortunately we need not debate the issue but can, instead, turn to a CPI constructed for precisely the period of interest to us here, 1697–1800. Prepared in the 1930s by E. B. Schumpeter and E. W. Gilboy, this unweighted CPI of English wholesale prices has two series, one for producers' goods and another for consumers' goods.[29] The average of the two series, recomputed to the required base period (1700–1702 = 100), appears in table 10.1.[30]

During the base period the official values for the Customs 3 ledgers were established at the levels they were to maintain well into the nineteenth century. Although some historians have thought that the values were all chosen in 1696, the year in which the first volume was begun, we now know that during the earliest years the Inspector-General and his clerks attempted to keep pace with changing prices.[31] In fact, for those commodities the prices of which we can check in contemporary published business newspapers, the success of the endeavor is most impressive.[32] Each new ledger brought fewer and fewer changes, however, with the period 1700–1702, Culliford's last years in office, marking the end of the effort to keep prices current. A few variations continued to be introduced, particularly during the next decade in the value of exported woollens,[33] and in 1724 a change in the collection of the customs

---

28 E[rnest] H. Phelps Brown and Sheila V. Hopkins, "Seven Centuries of the Prices of Consumables, compared with Builders' Wage-Rates," *Economica*, n.s., XXIII (Nov. 1956), 296–314. Much of the material used to compile the Phelps Brown–Hopkins series came from William [H.] Beveridge, *Prices and Wages in England from the Twelfth to the Nineteenth Century* (London, 1939). For a discussion of the Phelps Brown–Hopkins index, see McCusker, *How Much Is That in Real Money?*, pp. 334–335.

29 [Romaine] Elizabeth Boody Schumpeter, "English Prices and Public Finance, 1660–1822," *Review of Economic Statistics*, XX (Feb. 1938), 21–37; Elizabeth W. Gilboy, "The Cost of Living and Real Wages in Eighteenth Century England," *Review of Economic Statistics*, XVIII (1936), 134–143. The series is reprinted in B[rian] R. Mitchell, *British Historical Statistics* (Cambridge, Eng., [1988]), pp. 719–720. Note that the use of the harvest year by Schumpeter and Gilboy and its application here to trade data based on the calendar year creates potential statistical difficulties. Another index of English prices, 1729–1800, appeared as Chart I in Earl J. Hamilton, "Prices, Wages, and the Industrial Revolution," in *Studies in Economics and Industrial Relations*, ed. Wesley C. Mitchell *et al.* (Philadelphia, 1941), p. 101. Compare, as well, the work of François Simiand, *Recherches anciennes et nouvelles sur le mouvement général des prix du XVIe au XIXe siècle* (Paris, 1932).

30 This same averaging of the two Schumpeter–Gilboy series provided the CPI used by Deane and Cole, *British Economic Growth*, fig. 7 (pullout at end of book). See also, ibid., p. 14.

31 Clark, *English Commercial Statistics*, pp. 10–11, traced the mistake back to Macpherson, *Annals of Commerce*, III, 340. See also Schumpeter, *English Overseas Trade Statistics*, tables XLVI, XLVII.

32 Based on a comparison of the Customs 3, PRO, valuations for the years 1697 through 1702 with prices from extant London commodity price currents. The former, from the ledgers themselves, are summarized in Schumpeter, *English Overseas Trade Statistics*, pp. 70–71. Copies of commodity price currents survive in several places. For their locations, see McCusker and Gravesteijn, *Beginnings of Commercial and Financial Journalism*, pp. 291–311.

33 Clark, *English Commercial Statistics*, pp. 10–23, discussed the evidence thoroughly.

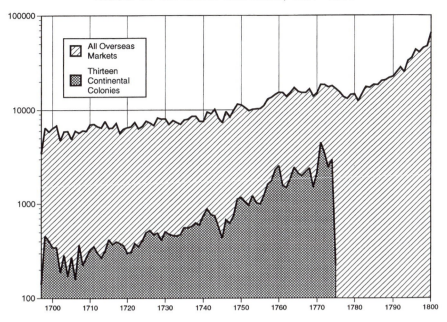

Figure 10.1 Current value of exports from England and Wales (after 1755, Great Britain), 1697–1800. Upper chart: to all overseas markets. Lower chart: to the Thirteen Continental Colonies. (In hundreds of thousands of pounds sterling.)

Source: table 10.2 and table 10.3.
Note: This graph is a semilogarithmic projection.
Concerning this format see n. 35 of this chapter.
Courtesy of the author.

reduced the number of items in the ad valorem category and substituted official values for some minor imported goods.[34] Even so, since the vast majority of the official values were set in the years 1700–1702, this period must be the base.

The reinflation of annual totals from Customs 3 ledgers upon which tables 10.2 and 10.3 are based is an aggregate procedure. (See figure 10.1.[35]) The CPI from table 10.1 becomes the percentage through which the constant values of the ledger are converted into the current values of these tables. As an aggregate procedure, two considerations restrict the correction to export values alone. Such a process obviously assumes that the CPI represents the

34 See Customs 3/26–28A, PRO. Rum is an example of such a commodity. See McCusker, *Rum and the American Revolution*, II, 1071–1072.
35 The graph is a semilogarithmic projection or log-normal format. The vertical or y-axis is logarithmic; the horizontal or x-axis is arithmetic (i.e., "normal"). It permits us both to see the general direction of the trend lines and to compare the rates of increase and decrease of each series. The steeper the slope of a line in a semilog graph, the sharper the rate of increase (or decrease) it describes.

value of all the commodities entered into the ledgers. A CPI need not be based on prices for all commodities but only be broadly enough grounded to reflect changes in the price levels of all commodities; one constructed on selected key commodities can quite adequately trace the variations of an entire market.[36] But the Schumpeter–Gilboy index includes prices for only a few imported goods and, with reference to the Customs 3 ledgers, is more representative of the price levels internal to England and, therefore, of exports. For this reason, table 10.2 corrects only the values of goods exported from England.

When this aggregate procedure is applied to the official values for the trade of the Thirteen Continental Colonies in the Customs ledgers, the potential for distortion depends directly on the breadth of the range of products that entered into the trade. Little or no problem arises with English exports to the Thirteen Continental Colonies since the records reveal that England and Wales sent a reasonably representative sampling of their goods westward across the Atlantic. By contrast, imports into England from the same colonies, dependent as they were on a rather narrow range of products salable in the mother country, offer just the opposite case. A large margin of error would result should we attempt to ascertain the current value of imports into Britain from Maryland and Virginia by adjusting to constant value according to the English CPI because the price of one commodity, tobacco, was of overriding importance. The same would be true with regard to the sugar colonies. For this reason table 10.3 corrects only the values of exports to the Thirteen Continental Colonies.

◆ ◆ ◆ ◆ ◆

In conclusion, although the statistical interrelationships between a current value series, a CPI, and a constant value series demonstrate sufficiently the validity of the procedures adopted here, two tests of the computed current value series offer further support of the results achieved. The first test compares the corrected series with the most authoritative eighteenth-century revaluation of England's balance of trade. The second test compares the corrected series with the best modern attempt to calculate the balance of trade of the Thirteen Continental Colonies. In neither instance is the difference statistically significant.

At the end of the 1790s Thomas Irving, Inspector-General of Imports and Exports, sought to demonstrate the great divergence that had grown up between the official and the actual value of British trade. He computed the latter by replacing the official unit values in the ledgers with current market

---

36 For a discussion of these considerations, see Mitchell, *Making and Using Index Numbers*, pp. 33–59. Compare McCusker, *How Much Is That in Real Money?* pp. 304–305. The point seems to have escaped Ralph Davis, *The Industrial Revolution and British Overseas Trade* (Leicester, 1979), p. 79, who then, in his error, influenced others. See, e.g., Julian Hoppit, *Risks and Failure in English Business, 1700–1800* (Cambridge, Eng., 1987), p. 97.

prices. According to his calculations, the annual value of all goods exported from Great Britain in terms of actual market prices during the years 1796 to 1798 averaged £43,138,000.[37] The average current value for 1796 to 1798 from table 10.2(B), column (5), comes to £43,069,000. The difference, £69,000, falls shy of Irving's figures by less than two-tenths of 1 percent.

In the 1960s James F. Shepherd reconstructed the balance of payments of the Thirteen Continental Colonies on the eve of the American Revolution. He estimated that British exports averaged £2,790,000 per year during the period 1768 to 1772.[38] The comparable figure calculated from table 10.3(C), column (7) is £2,790,403. The difference, less than £500, is one one-hundredth of 1 percent of Shepherd's estimate.

37 "Commercial Accounts of Great Britain," pp. 5, 9–11, in [GB, Parl., Commons], *Accounts and Papers Relative to the Commerce, Revenue, and Expenditure of the Kingdoms of Great Britain and Ireland*, HC Sessional Papers to 1801, Accounts and Papers, vol. XLIX, no. 981 [Lambert 5010] ([London], 1800). Deane and Cole, *British Economic Growth*, pp. 43, 315, compared the values that Irving used with actual, contemporary market prices and reported them "remarkably accurate." They had reference to Thomas Tooke, *Thoughts and Details on the High and Low Prices of the Last Thirty Years* (London, 1823), IV, Appendix, 1–69; and Thomas Tooke and William Newmarch, *A History of Prices, and of the State of the Circulation, from 1793 to [1856]*, 6 vols (London, 1838–1857).

For a similar accounting for the year 1788 in which Irving compared the current value and the constant value of imports into Great Britain from the British West Indies, see [GB, Parl., Commons], *Report of the Lords of the Committee of [the Privy] Council . . . [for] Trade and Foreign Plantations . . . Concerning the Present State of the Trade to Africa*, HC Sessional Papers to 1801, Accounts and Papers, vols XXVI, no. 646a, 6 pts [Lambert 4132] ([London, 1789]), pt iv: "Accounts," "Supplement to Account No 10." In this instance he used an average of the prices reported in the London commodity price currents compiled "at Six different Periods of the Year, when the greatest Quantity of each Commodity was at Market." He made no allowance for freight costs but did deduct 5 percent for "Insurance and Expenses of Landing." For Thomas Irving, see John J. McCusker, "Colonial Civil Servant and Counter-Revolutionary: Thomas Irving (1738?–1800) in Boston, Charleston, and London," *Perspectives in American History*, XII (1979), 314–350 – revised as chapter nine of the present book. For the London commodity price currents, see n. 18 of this chapter.

38 Shepherd, "Balance of Payments," p. 90 (table 3–14). The figure given in the text is the result of subtracting from Shepherd's total the 10 percent he added as an approximation of shipping costs in order for him to estimate the value as landed (CIF) in North America (ibid., pp. 80–83, 87). See also Shepherd, "A Balance of Payments for the Thirteen Colonies, 1768–1772: A Summary," *JEcH*, XXV (Dec. 1965), 691–695; Shepherd and Gary M. Walton, "Estimates of 'Invisible' Earnings in the Balance of Payments of the British North American Colonies, 1768–1772," *JEcH*, XXIX (June 1969), 230–263.

Table 10.1 English wholesale commodity price index, 1697–1801
(Base: 1700–1702 = 100)

Year	CPI	Year	CPI	Year	CPI
1697	112.3	1732	87.0	1767	101.1
1698	111.3	1733	83.1	1768	100.2
1699	113.8	1734	84.6	1769	92.9
1700	104.1	1735	83.6	1770	94.3
1701	97.2	1736	82.2	1771	97.7
1702	98.7	1737	84.6	1772	104.5
1703	96.3	1738	83.6	1773	106.0
1704	97.2	1739	85.6	1774	104.1
1705	92.9	1740	91.9	1775	102.6
1706	96.8	1741	99.7	1776	104.5
1707	89.0	1742	95.3	1777	102.1
1708	91.9	1743	90.0	1778	107.5
1709	100.6	1744	88.5	1779	107.5
1710	110.9	1745	80.7	1780	108.4
1711	118.6	1746	89.5	1781	109.4
1712	96.8	1747	85.6	1782	114.7
1713	93.8	1748	89.0	1783	119.6
1714	94.3	1749	90.9	1784	113.8
1715	92.4	1750	89.0	1785	110.4
1716	91.4	1751	85.1	1786	112.8
1717	90.0	1752	84.6	1787	110.9
1718	89.5	1753	83.1	1788	113.8
1719	91.9	1754	87.0	1789	108.9
1720	93.8	1755	89.0	1790	112.3
1721	91.9	1756	90.0	1791	110.9
1722	89.0	1757	98.7	1792	113.3
1723	85.1	1758	100.6	1793	123.0
1724	88.0	1759	97.7	1794	124.0
1725	89.5	1760	97.2	1795	130.8
1726	94.3	1761	94.8	1796	142.0
1727	93.8	1762	95.3	1797	140.5
1728	94.3	1763	98.2	1798	134.7
1729	96.8	1764	98.7	1799	140.0
1730	93.8	1765	99.7	1800	173.1
1731	89.0	1766	100.2	1801	189.6

Notes and sources:
John J. McCusker, *How Much Is That in Real Money? A Historical Price Index for Use as a Deflator of Money Values in the Economy of the United States* (Worcester, Mass., 1992), pp. 340–343, column (2). Note the correction introduced here for 1799.

Table 10.2 Official[a] and current[b] value of all goods exported from England, Wales, and Scotland[c] (thousands £'s sterling)

(A) From England and Wales, 1697–1754

Year	Official value	Current value	Year	Official value	Current value	Year	Official value	Current value
1697[d]	3,453	3,453	1716	7,050	6,444	1735	9,329	7,802
1698[d]	6,464	6,464	1717	7,997	7,193	1736	9,702	7,972
1699[d]	5,871	5,871	1718	6,361	5,691	1737	10,082	8,530
1700[d]	6,384	6,384	1719	6,835	6,281	1738	10,196	8,527
1701[d]	6,813	6,813	1720	6,911	6,485	1739	8,844	7,568
1702[d]	4,739	4,739	1721	7,201	6,618	1740	8,198	7,533
1703	6,133	5,885	1722	8,265	7,354	1741	9,570	9,539
1704	6,099	5,931	1723	7,396	6,293	1742	9,574	9,124
1705	5,259	4,884	1724	7,601	6,689	1743	11,310	10,174
1706	6,191	5,990	1725	8,482	7,588	1744	9,190	8,132
1707	6,392	5,688	1726	7,693	7,257	1745	9,072	7,322
1708	6,564	6,032	1727	7,275	6,827	1746	10,767	9,633
1709	5,913	5,951	1728	8,707	8,213	1747	9,775	8,365
1710	6,295	6,979	1729	8,240	7,973	1748	11,141	9,913
1711	5,693	7,074	1730	8,549	8,022	1749	12,679	11,528
1712	6,869	6,646	1731	7,852	6,996	1750	12,699	11,299
1713	6,892	6,467	1732	8,870	7,721	1751	12,420	10,568
1714	8,004	7,550	1733	8,838	7,348	1752	11,595	9,810
1715	6,922	6,395	1734	8,299	7,021	1753	12,244	10,180
						1754	11,788	10,259

(B) From England, Wales, and Scotland, 1755–1800

	From England and Wales		From Scotland		Total
Year	Official value (1)	Current value (2)	Official value (3)	Current value (4)	current value[e] (5)
1755	11,065	9,846	536	477	10,323
1756	11,721	10,543	626	563	11,106
1757	12,339	12,179	829	818	12,997
1758	12,618	12,700	831	836	13,536
1759	13,948	13,631	940	919	14,550
1760	14,695	14,290	1,086	1,056	15,346
1761	14,873	14,102	1,166	1,106	15,207
1762	13,545	12,908	998	951	13,859
1763	14,488	14,230	1,091	1,072	15,301
1764	16,202	15,992	1,244	1,228	17,220
1765	14,550	14,503	1,181	1,177	15,680
1766	14,025	14,048	1,164	1,166	15,214
1767	13,844	14,001	1,246	1,260	15,261
1768	15,118	15,143	1,502	1,504	16,647
1769	13,438	12,480	1,563	1,452	13,931
1770	14,267	13,458	1,728	1,630	15,088
1771	17,161	16,772	1,857	1,815	18,586
1772	16,159	16,892	1,561	1,632	18,524

Table 10.2 continued

| | From England and Wales | | From Scotland | | Total |
Year	Official value (1)	Current value (2)	Official value (3)	Current value (4)	current value^c (5)
1773	14,863	15,755	1,612	1,709	17,463
1774	15,916	16,561	1,372	1,428	17,989
1775	15,202	15,596	1,124	1,153	16,749
1776	13,730	14,353	1,026	1,073	15,426
1777	12,653	12,920	838	856	13,775
1778	11,551	12,412	703	755	13,168
1779	12,693	13,639	837	899	14,539
1780	12,552	13,610	1,002	1,086	14,696
1781	10,569	11,563	763	835	12,397
1782	12,356	14,178	654	750	14,929
1783	13,852	16,569	830	993	17,561
1784	14,171	16,123	930	1,058	17,181
1785	15,763	17,398	1,008	1,113	18,510
1786	15,386	17,356	915	1,032	18,388
1787	17,181	19,047	1,115	1,236	20,283
1788	16,935	19,268	1,189	1,353	20,621
1789	18,843	20,523	1,170	1,274	21,797
1790	18,885	21,211	1,235	1,387	22,598
1791	21,436	23,764	1,294	1,435	25,198
1792	23,674	26,820	1,231	1,395	28,215
1793	19,364	23,821	1,025	1,261	25,081
1794	25,663	31,819	1,085	1,345	33,164
1795	26,146	34,197	977	1,278	35,475
1796	29,196	41,452	1,323	1,878	43,330
1797	27,700	38,924	1,217	1,710	40,634
1798	31,923	42,995	1,669	2,248	45,243
1799	31,724	44,423	1,917	2,684	47,108
1800	35,774	61,923	2,346	4,061	65,984

Notes and sources:
The sources for this table are discussed in the text of this chapter.
a Included are exports, reexports, and prize goods shipped from England and Wales to all markets except Scotland, and from Scotland to all markets except England and Wales. Omitted are English and Welsh exports to Scotland before the Act of Union of 1707 and all exports of gold and silver bullion. Compare [Romaine] Elizabeth Boody Schumpeter, *English Overseas Trade Statistics 1697–1808* (Oxford, 1960), pp. 7–9.
b Annual total values of all goods exported as recorded in the Customs ledgers, Customs 2, 3, 14, and 17, PRO, multiplied by the revised Schumpeter–Gilboy CPI from table 10.1 expressed as a percentage. For 1705 and 1712 the total values are as found in Charles Whitworth, *State of the Trade of Great Britain in Its Imports and Exports . . . 1697 [to 1773]* (London, 1776), pt i, pp. 9, 16. For 1763 and 1769 the Scottish values are as found in BT 6/185, fols 168–197, PRO. See also n. 9 of this chapter.
c Scottish official values for each commodity differed from the English. Nevertheless, Scottish annual export figures have been made to vary with the English CPI on the assumption that the annual fluctuations in the Scottish market roughly paralleled those of English prices. A[lex] J. S. Gibson and T[homas] C[hristopher] Smout, *Prices, Food and Wages in Scotland, 1550–1780* ([Cambridge, Eng.], 1995), p. 4, consider these valuations to have been "broadly realistic" meaning, presumably, that they reflected Scottish market values. Any error induced

in the totals by these assumptions is thought to be insignificant if only because the Scottish portion of the whole was so small.

d For the year 1702 and earlier, when the official value was still being computed using actual market prices, no correction is required. Schumpeter, op. cit., p. 4.

e Totals may not equal the sum of their component parts because of rounding.

Table 10.3 Current value of goods exported to the Thirteen Continental Colonies (thousands £'s sterling)

(A) From England and Wales, 1697 to 1754

Year	To New England (1)	To New York (2)	To Pennsylvania (3)	To Maryland and Virginia (4)	To North and South Carolina (5)	To Georgia (6)	Total to all colonies[a] (7)
1697[b]	68	5	3	59	5		140
1698[b]	94	25	11	310	18		458
1699[b]	127	43	17	205	11		404
1700[b]	92	49	19	173	11		344
1701[b]	86	32	12	200	14		344
1702[b]	65	30	9	72	10		187
1703	57	17	10	189	12		285
1704	73	22	11	59	6		171
1705	58	26	7	162	18		271
1706	55	31	11	56	4		156
1707	107	27	13	212	9		368
1708	106	25	6	73	11		221
1709	121	35	6	81	29		271
1710	118	35	10	141	22		326
1711	163	34	23	109	24		353
1712	124	18	8	130	19		300
1713	113	44	16	72	22		267
1714	114	42	14	122	22		315
1715	152	50	15	184	15		417
1716	111	48	20	164	25		368
1717	119	40	20	194	23		395
1718	118	56	20	172	14		381
1719	115	52	25	151	18		361
1720	121	35	23	104	17		300
1721	105	47	20	117	16		305
1722	119	51	23	154	31		378
1723	150	45	14	105	36		350
1724	148	55	27	142	33		406
1725	181	63	38	175	35		492
1726	189	80	35	175	41		522
1727	176	63	30	181	22		472
1728	184	77	35	161	31		488
1729	156	63	29	105	56		409
1730	195	60	46	142	61		504
1731	163	59	39	152	63		477
1732	189	57	36	129	51	1	462
1733	153	54	34	155	59	1	456
1734	124	69	46	146	84	2	471

241

Table 10.3 continued

Year	To New England (1)	To New York (2)	To Pennsylvania (3)	To Maryland and Virginia (4)	To North and South Carolina (5)	To Georgia (6)	Total to all colonies[a] (7)
1735	158	67	41	184	99	10	559
1736	183	71	51	168	83	2	557
1737	189	106	48	179	50	5	577
1738	170	112	51	216	73	5	628
1739	189	91	47	186	81	3	595
1740	157	109	52	259	167	3	747
1741	198	140	91	248	204	3	883
1742	142	160	72	252	121	16	762
1743	155	122	71	295	100	2	746
1744	127	106	55	208	70	1	567
1745	113	44	44	160	70	1	432
1746	187	78	66	253	92	1	676
1747	180	118	71	171	82	c	622
1748	176	128	67	225	143	1	739
1749	217	242	217	294	149	c	1,119
1750	306	238	194	311	118	2	1,168
1751	260	212	162	295	118	2	1,049
1752	231	164	171	275	128	3	971
1753	287	231	204	297	177	12	1,208
1754	287	111	213	282	130	2	1,024
1755	304	134	129	254	167	2	990
1756	346	225	180	301	164	c	1,216
1757	359	349	265	421	211	3	1,607
1758	469	359	263	441	182	10	1,724
1759	515	616	487	449	210	15	2,292
1760	583	467	688	589	212		2,540
1761	317	275	193	517	241	23	1,566
1762	236	275	197	398	185	23	1,313
1763	254	234	279	545	246	44	1,603
1764	454	509	430	509	302	18	2,221
1765	450	381	362	382	334	29	1,938
1766	410	331	328	373	297	67	1,807
1767	411	423	376	443	247	24	1,922
1768	420	484	433	477	290	57	2,161
1769	193	70	186	454	285	54	1,241
1770	372	449	127	677	138	53	1,816
1771	1,388	639	712	899	400	69	4,107
1772	862	360	531	830	470	97	3,149
1773	559	307	452	455	366	67	2,204
1774	585	456	651	550	393	60	2,695
1775	73	1	1	2	6	117	201

(B) From Scotland, 1762 to 1775[d]

Year	To New England (1)	To New York (2)	To Penn-sylvania (3)	To Maryland (4)	To Virginia (5)	To North Carolina (6)	To South Carolina (7)	To Georgia	Total to all colonies[a]
1762	14	22		19	100	2	6		162
1763	20	17	12	21	172	5	10		256
1764	28	9	3	18	153	4	6		222
1765	17	5	6	27	108	7	5		175
1766	10	2	7	38	110	7	5		178
1767	10	6	11	31	187	15	10	c	270
1768	11	8	10	41	153	6	5		233
1769	15	1	5	48	163	11	8		250
1770	21	4	4	51	212	17	4	3	317
1771	15	1	18	52	245	14	19	1	366
1772	20	6	19	53	179	19	12	3	312
1773	17	7	10	17	153	21	17	4	247
1774	15	23	21	25	142	30	6	2	263
1775	14	c				c	c	10	25

(C) Total from Great Britain, 1762 to 1775

Year	To New England (1)	To New York (2)	To Pennsylvania (3)	To Maryland and Virginia (4)	To North and South Carolina (5)	To Georgia (6)	Total to all colonies[a] (7)
1762	250	296	197	517	193	23	1,475
1763	274	252	291	738	260	44	1,859
1764	482	518	433	680	312	18	2,443
1765	467	386	368	517	346	29	2,113
1766	420	333	335	521	309	67	1,985
1767	421	429	387	660	272	24	2,193
1768	432	491	443	671	301	57	2,394
1769	208	71	190	664	304	54	1,491
1770	393	453	132	941	159	56	2,133
1771	1,403	640	731	1,196	433	70	4,473
1772	883	365	550	1,062	501	100	3,461
1773	576	314	462	625	404	71	2,451
1774	600	478	672	718	429	61	2,959
1775	87	2	1	2	7	127	226

Notes and sources:
The sources for this table are discussed in the text of this chapter.
a Totals may not equal the sum of their component parts because of rounding.
b See table 10.2, n. (d).
c Less than £550.
d See table 10.2, n. (c). Scottish ledgers did not distinguish between exports to the Thirteen Continental Colonies and the rest of "America" until 1762. In the first five-year period after that date (1762–1766), exports to the Continental Colonies constituted 74.8% of the total exports to "America." A crude estimate of the annual current value of exports to the Thirteen

Table 10.3 continued

Continental Colonies between 1755 and 1761 is possible, if we assume that during that period they formed the same proportion of the total export they did later, viz.:

Year	Value	Year	Value
1755	91	1759	235
1756	116	1760	248
1757	207	1761	216
1758	221		

SOURCES OF INVESTMENT CAPITAL IN THE COLONIAL PHILADELPHIA SHIPPING INDUSTRY

As economic historians delve ever more deeply into the economy of the Thirteen Continental Colonies, they become increasingly aware of its considerable growth and development over time. Enjoying, as the colonists did, both the example of the Mother Country and the considerable advantages of its economic, political, and military power, they forged an economy that paralleled that of a Mother Country which was itself, by the 1770s, on the eve of an industrial revolution. British interests, noting both the fact and the nature of the emerging economic strength of the Continental Colonies, complained of colonial competition in most every sphere of activity. The considerable tensions that resulted were one of the causes of the American Revolution.[1]

One aspect of the economy of the Thirteen Continental Colonies about which little is known is the source of the capital that fueled its development. Capital invested in enterprises in the colonies could have come from two sources. Capital invested from abroad, almost exclusively Great Britain, had been important from the very founding of the colonies, just as foreign capital continues to be even into our own day a major component of the funds invested in American enterprises. Domestic capital, theoretically cheaper than foreign capital, played some role but just how much a role it played and how, if any, that changed over time is not known. While there has not been any real debate about the importance of domestic versus foreign capital to colonial economic development, different opinions have been expressed. James F. Shepherd and Gary M. Walton, for instance, consider long-term foreign investments in the Thirteen Continental Colonies to have been

1   The original version of this chapter was published in *The Journal of Economic History*, XXXII (Mar. 1972), 146–157. Copyright © 1972 by the Economic History Association. This revision is presented here with the permission of the publishers of the journal.

I continue to be grateful for the help and support given me by the Council on Research in Economic History, the Smithsonian Institution, the American Philosophical Society, and both the General Research Board and the Computer Science Center of the University of Maryland.

trifling. Thus they can be seen as suggesting that much, if not all of invested capital was domestic in origin. By contrast, John G. B. Hutchins argued that much, if not most of the capital invested in the colonial shipping industry was British.[2] It is now possible to test these conflicting opinions and to say something more concrete about the accumulation and mobilization of colonial domestic savings, at least for the shipping industry.[3]

Long recognized as of some importance, the colonial shipping industry has more recently come to assume a greater significance as central to the export sector of the colonial economy. In terms of credits in the colonial balance of payments, one study has determined that, in the late colonial period, shipping charges assessed for freight carried on board colonial-owned vessels "were larger than the value of any commodity export with the one exception of tobacco."[4] Contemporaries evidently understood some of this: colonial merchants sought to expand their involvement in the carrying trade; and English merchants railed mightily against the incursion of colonial-owned vessels into what they considered their exclusive preserves. "Colonial-owned vessels" is the key here because, in order for the profits earned in the shipping industry to become credits in the colonial balance of payment, the vessels had to belong to residents of the Thirteen Continental Colonies and not to London merchants or other "foreigners." To own a ship meant to have bought it, and to buy it required the acquisition and the investment of capital. In the 1770s the colonists had ordered constructed, and no doubt owned, almost one-third of the shipping of the British Empire, 500,000 out of 1,500,000 measured tons, worth an estimated £2,500,000 sterling.[5] As

2 James F. Shepherd and Gary M. Walton, "Estimates of 'Invisible' Earnings in the Balance of Payments of the British North American Colonies, 1768–1772," *JEcH*, XXIV (June 1969), 230–263; John G. B. Hutchins, *The American Maritime Industries and Public Policy, 1789–1914: An Economic History*, Harvard Economic Studies, vol. LXXI (Cambridge, Mass., 1941), pp. 158–159.

3 This chapter is an outgrowth of a larger study – John J. McCusker, "The Pennsylvania Shipping Industry in the Eighteenth Century" (unpublished typescript, 1972) – to which the reader may turn for a fuller development of some points, a greater elucidation of sources used, and a more detailed support for most arguments. A copy has been deposited with the HSP, as has a copy of the compilation upon which the study is based: "Ships Registered at the Port of Philadelphia before 1776: A Computerized Listing" (unpublished computer printout, 1970). Jane E. Allen, "Lying at the Port of Philadelphia: Vessel Types, 1725–1775," *American Neptune*, LIII (Fall 1993), 149–176, is a summary in tabular form of and an exegesis upon some of the material in that compilation. Unfortunately, in her appendices (ibid., pp. 166–176), the author makes an extremely significant error when she presents the data for the tonnage registered in each of several years under a heading purporting to indicate the "tons *carried*" (my emphasis).

4 Shepherd and Walton, "Estimates of 'Invisible' Earnings," p. 235. Their rather more impressionistic treatment of the subject was soon superseded by Jacob M. Price, "A Note on the Value of Colonial Exports of Shipping," *JEcH*, XXXVI (Sept. 1976), 704–724, who was able to demonstrate that they had considerably underestimated the export value of colonial shipping.

5 This estimate, developed at length in McCusker, "Pennsylvania Shipping Industry in the Eighteenth Century," pp. 107–112 and elsewhere, rests ultimately on contemporary analyses of the vessels listed in *Lloyd's Register of Shipping . . . 1776* ([London, 1776]). See

much as 20 percent of the colonial third belonged to the shipowners of Pennsylvania.[6]

The source of this and subsequent assertions is a document compiled for this study and deposited in the manuscript collections of the Historical Society of Pennsylvania in September 1970; it is entitled "Ships Registered at the Port of Philadelphia before 1776: A Computerized Listing." The compilation assembles data from a variety of eighteenth-century sources in an attempt to reconstruct as fully as possible an account of all the vessels registered at Philadelphia from 1698 through 1776. Although there are only scattered returns before 1722 and partial returns until 1726, the document includes at least some record of every vessel registered between March 1726 and March 1776, the fifty years prior to the American Revolution.[7]

The individual register certificates, which the compilation seeks to duplicate in detail, contained considerable information about a vessel and its owners.

[West India Planters and Merchants, London], *Considerations on the Present State of the Intercourse between His Majesty's Sugar Colonies and the Dominions of the United States of America*, [ed. James Allen] ([London, 1784]), p. 53; [Richard Champion], *Considerations on the Present Situation of Great Britain and the United States of North America, with a View to Their Future Commercial Connections*, [1st ed.] (London, 1784), pp. 13–14; George Chalmers, *Opinions on Interesting Subjects of Public Law and Commercial Policy Arising from American Independence*, [1st edn] (London, 1784), p. 99; Thomas Irving, Inspector-General of Imports and Exports, at London, to the Commissioners of the Land Revenue, 7 Jan. 1792, as printed in [GB, Parl., Commons], *Journals of the House of Commons*, in progress (London, 1742 to date), XLVII, 357; Ralph Davis, *The Rise of the English Shipping Industry in the Seventeenth and Eighteenth Centuries* (London, 1962), pp. 66–68, 374–375, and passim; and Price, "Colonial Exports of Shipping," pp. 704–717. Irving, upon whose work much of the contemporary opinion actually rested, had held the same post in North America before the American Revolution and is, therefore, to be considered especially reliable. For more about him, see John J. McCusker, "Colonial Civil Servant and Counter-Revolutionary: Thomas Irving (1738?–1800) in Boston, Charleston, and London," *Perspectives in American History*, XII (1979), 314–350 – revised as chapter nine of the present book.

The colonial portion, some 500,000 measured tons, is here valued at £5.00 sterling a ton, or two-thirds of the cost of new vessels (see table 11.1). Second-hand vessels sold for between two-thirds and three-quarters of the cost per ton of new vessels. Compare Robert [S.] Craig, "Shipping and Shipbuilding in the Port of Chester in the Eighteenth and Early Nineteenth Centuries," *Transactions of the Historic Society of Lancashire and Cheshire*, CXVI (1965), 52.

6 We need to make an initial distinction that is important but somewhat difficult to observe in practice. The shipping industry discussed herein is part of the economy of the colony of Pennsylvania of which Philadelphia was the seat of government and the port of entry where ships were registered and at which they cleared inwards and outwards. Thus "Philadelphia," as in my title, is – and was – frequently but not unjustifiably used synecdochically where Pennsylvania is meant, and vice versa. Again, just as did the colonists themselves, the distinction is observed where it is significant. See McCusker, "Pennsylvania Shipping Industry in the Eighteenth Century," pp. 20–28.

7 My study owes an obvious debt of gratitude to Bernard Bailyn and Lotte Bailyn's *Massachusetts Shipping, 1697–1714: A Statistical Study* (Cambridge, Mass., 1959), which was based on a similar compilation. Compare similar studies by Bruce M. Wilkenfeld, "The New York City Shipowning Community, 1715–1764," *American Neptune*, XXXVII (Jan. 1977), 50–65, and Converse D. Clowse, "Shipowning and Shipbuilding in Colonial South Carolina: An Overview," *American Neptune*, XLIV (Fall 1984), 221–244.

By the end of the seventeenth century every vessel that engaged in trade with any of the colonies of Great Britain had by law to secure a register. Much like the certificate of registration for a modern motor car or the deed of ownership for a house, it became, in practice, a vessel's license to trade within the empire.[8] Vessels were most often registered at the port in which their controlling owner or owners resided. The law required the owner who sought the register to provide various items of information that served to identify the vessel as British and to indicate the name and place of residence of each of its owners.[9] This last bit of data, the residence of each owner, provides the basis for determining the source of the capital invested. Vessels could be bought and sold several times over, but each sale was the occasion for a new register, even if only one owner sold his or her share. Over 6,000 "shares" in some 3,200 vessels were traded at Philadelphia between 1726 and 1776. The register certificates offer a detailed insight into the point of origin of the capital used to purchase these shares.[10]

A person bought a certain fraction of a vessel of a particular tonnage and the price paid depended both on the size of the vessel and the proportion that the buyer chose to purchase. For purposes of construction and sale, eighteenth-century vessels were measured by formula to determine their ship-wright's or carpenter's tonnage. (This figure was later discounted – by an average of about 40 percent at Philadelphia – when the owner registered it in order to diminish the impact of duties assessed on its tonnage.[11]) The share to be purchased could be in theory any proportion of that measured tonnage. Because the register records do not indicate the proportion owned by each individual, we must here assume that every buyer purchased an equal part.[12] Thus, one of three owners of a 300 ton ship will be here considered as having had a one-third share and to have invested to the cost of 100 tons.

---

8   For British vessels that never ventured into the colonial trade there was no need until much later in the 18th century to have a certificate of registration. See Rupert [C.] Jarvis, "Ship Registry – to 1707," *Maritime History*, I (Apr. 1971), 29–45, and Jarvis, "Ship Registry – 1707–86," *Maritime History*, II (Sept. 1972), 151–167.

9   The certificate of registration traveled with each vessel. A transcript of the certificate was copied into a book kept at the port; copies of these volumes were sent to London. For the later period, see the description of these records in Grahame Farr, "Custom House Ship Registers," *MM*, LV (Feb. 1969), 3–15.

10 Compare S[arah] R. Palmer, "Investors in London Shipping, 1820–50," *Maritime History*, II (Apr. 1972), 46–67.

11 John J. McCusker, "Colonial Tonnage Measurement: Five Philadelphia Merchant Ships as a Sample," *JEcH*, XXVII (Mar. 1967), 82–91; McCusker, "The Tonnage of Ships Engaged in British Colonial Trade during the Eighteenth Century," *Research in Economic History*, VI (1981), 73–105 – revised as chapter three of the present book; and Christopher J. French, "Eighteenth-Century Shipping Tonnage Measurements," *JEcH*, XXXIII (June 1973), 434–443.

12 This is an assumption common to studies that use registry records. Compare Harrold E. Gillingham, "Some Colonial Ships Built in Philadelphia," *Pennsylvania Magazine of History and Biography*, LVI (Apr. 1932), 182; Bailyn and Bailyn *Massachusetts Shipping*, pp. 10–11; Rupert C. Jarvis, "Fractional Shareholding in British Merchant Ships with Special Reference to the 64ths," *MM*, XLV (Nov. 1959), 311; and Jarvis, "Eighteenth-Century

Such an assumption overstates the part of the whole owned by the smaller shareholders, and understates the part owned by the larger shareholders. Where it has been possible to perform tests of this assumption, they reveal that it has induced no significant distortion for the purposes of this discussion.[13]

Several factors determined the cost of vessels built at eighteenth-century Philadelphia. One was the size of the vessel, because larger vessels cost more per ton to build than smaller vessels. (Larger vessels made up for any higher initial cost by being more efficient.) Solely for reasons of expediency, made necessary by very scanty data, the distinction between larger and smaller vessels here is assumed to have been the same as the distinction between square-rigged vessels (ships, snows, and brigantines) and fore-and-aft-rigged vessels (sloops and schooners). Another factor in its cost was the vessel's readiness for sea. One could buy just a hull and pay less, or buy a fully rigged vessel ready for sea and pay more. Still a final factor was changes in supply and demand over time. The price per measured ton rose and fell during the fifty years in question, no doubt even more than is indicated by the crude data that provide the basis for table 11.1.[14]

Those who purchased the ships registered at Philadelphia juggled all of these variables, as well as several more, when making an investment decision. In sum, a trend is discernible in the nature of these decisions. Larger vessels were more efficient in carrying cargo and they cost less to operate since they required fewer crewmen per unit of cargo than did smaller vessels.[15] Philadelphia shipowners seemed to have appreciated this; as time went on they not only bought larger square-rigged vessels of every type but they also purchased more and more frequently the largest type of square-rigged vessel, the ocean-going ship.

The greater efficiencies of larger vessels offered themselves at the same time as did opportunities to make use of them. The larger the vessel, the larger had to be the volume of the trade in which it was employed in order to overcome problems of underutilization and delays in loading that lengthened

London Shipping," in *Studies in London History Presented to Philip Edmund Jones,* ed. A[lbert] E. J. Hollander and William Kellaway ([London], 1969), pp. 415–416.

13 One reason is that one-third of the vessels had only one owner and another one-third just two owners. See also Bailyn and Bailyn, *Massachusetts Shipping,* p. 11.

14 Compare a discussion of these several factors by R[obert S.] Craig, "Capital Formation in Shipping," in *Aspects of Capital Investment in Great Britain, 1750–1850: A Preliminary Survey,* ed. J. P. P. Higgins and Sidney Pollard (London, 1971), pp. 131–157.

15 Davis, *Rise of the English Shipping Industry,* pp. 72–75, discusses this consideration at length. Compare Gary Max Walton, "A Quantitative Study of American Colonial Shipping" (Ph.D. diss., University of Washington, 1966), pp. 129–131; and John J. McCusker and Russell R. Menard, *The Economy of British America, 1607–1789,* [2nd edn] (Chapel Hill, NC, [1991]), p. 266, n. 10. Note also the argument that a parallel productivity gain occurring for similar reasons reduced transportation costs in the fur trade. Fernand Ouellet, review of *Structure and Change: An Economic History of Quebec,* by Robert Armstrong, *Business History Review,* LXIX (Winter 1985), 707.

Table 11.1 Estimated cost per measured ton of vessels built in Pennsylvania, 1725–1774 (£'s sterling)

Period	Fore-and-aft-rigged		Square-rigged	
	Hull only (1)	Completed vessel (2)	Hull only (3)	Completed vessel (4)
1725–1734	2.20	4.90	3.00	6.60
1735–1744	1.80	3.80	2.40	5.00
1745–1754	2.20	5.30	3.00	7.10
1755–1764	2.20	4.90	2.90	6.50
1765–1774	2.80	6.40	3.80	8.50

Notes and sources:
The data are from scattered references in the letters and accounts of various Philadelphia merchants including the following: Letter Book of Jonathan Dickinson, Library Company of Philadelphia Collection, HSP; Coates and Reynell Papers, 1702–1843, HSP; John Reynell Papers, 1729–1783, HSP; Robert Ellis Letter Book, 1736–1748, HSP; Alexander Wooddrop Account Books, 1719–1734, LC; Davey and Carson Letter Book, 1745–1750, LC; and Wharton and Humphreys Shipyard Accounts, 1773–1795, Joshua Humphreys Papers, 1682–1835, HSP. See the discussion of their collection and compilation in John J. McCusker, "The Pennsylvania Shipping Industry in the Eighteenth Century" (unpublished typescript, 1972), pp. 127–134.

turn-around time. Moreover the traditional West Indian and coastwise markets of Philadelphia merchants could easily be glutted by too large a shipment of goods. Table 11.2, based on a comparison covering only the last half of the period 1726 through 1776 is revealing of several developments reflecting these considerations. Note that the average size of the vessels that engaged in the traditional trades from Philadelphia not only did not increase, but actually declined slightly over this period. On the other hand vessels clearing from Philadelphia for transatlantic trades grew greatly in their average size.[16] And it was in these same transatlantic trades that Philadelphia shipowners came more and more to engage their vessels in the decades before the American Revolution. Tonnage clearing to Great Britain increased 167 percent and to Southern Europe, 418 percent, while total tonnage cleared grew only 80 percent.[17]

It made no matter to the colonials that Great Britain's merchants felt that the transatlantic trade of the empire belonged to them – the Atlantic was their *mare nostrum*. The growing numbers of American-owned vessels

16 There was a parallel growth in the average size of square-rigged vessels built at Philadelphia during the period. Between 1726–1735 and 1765–1774 ships increased from 77 registered tons, on the average, to 134 registered tons; snows, from 51 to 86; and brigantines from 30 to 72. At the same time Philadelphia shipbuilders concentrated more of their production in the largest of these types, the ships. In the earlier period, 57.3 percent of all tonnage launched at Philadelphia was in ships but at the later period the proportion was 70.4 percent. McCusker, "Pennsylvania Shipping Industry in the Eighteenth Century," pp. 147–149.
17 Compare Wilkenfeld, "New York City Shipowning Community," pp. 62–64.

Table 11.2 The export trade of Philadelphia, 1750–1754 and 1770–1774: clearances from Philadelphia to each of five trading areas

Destination	1750–1754			1770–1774		
	Average number of vessels per year (1)	*Average registered tonnage per vessel* (2)	*Total registered tonnage* (3)	*Average number of vessels per year* (4)	*Average registered tonnage per vessel* (5)	*Total registered tonnage* (6)
Great Britain	16	71.0	1,136	26	116.7	3,034
Ireland	36	69.2	2,491	28	103.6	2,901
Southern Europe	36	48.3	1,739	101	88.7	8,959
West Indies	191	66.4	12,682	340	57.5	19,550
Coastwise	166	43.4	7,204	262	42.1	11,030
Total clearances	444		25,252	757		45,474

Notes and sources:
The numbers of vessels that cleared Philadelphia (columns [1] and [4]) are taken from the weekly shipping reports in the *Pennsylvania Gazette* (Philadelphia) as compiled in Arthur L. Jensen, *The Maritime Commerce of Colonial Philadelphia* (Madison, Wis., 1963), p. 290. The average tonnages (columns [2] and [5]) are calculated from two sets of sources. For 1750–1754 they are from the NOSL, POE Philadelphia, 1741–1742, which are catalogued as the Register of Ships Entering Port of Philadelphia, 1741–1742, and the Ships' Register [of Vessels Clearing Outward from the Port of Philadelphia], 1742, HSP. Note that these two items are not records of the registry of ships at the port but are Naval Office shipping lists showing the ships and their cargoes as they entered inward and cleared outward. For 1770–1774 they are from the Ledger of Imports and Exports, British North America, 1768–1772, pp. 3–4, 39–40, 101–2, 167–68, 227–28, Customs 16/1, PRO.

competing for the trade from London and Bristol to Boston and Philadelphia constituted a direct economic challenge to the merchants of the Mother Country. So, too, did the vastly increased trade of the colonies with Portugal,[18] the Mediterranean,[19] and the Wine Islands.[20] The merchants of London and the "Outports" were aware of the challenge and aware, too, that Philadelphia was the seat of much of this activity.

18 This is a subject that is still largely unexplored but for which the evidence exists in numerous documentary collections. See, e.g., the references to such correspondence in John J. McCusker, *Money and Exchange in Europe and America, 1600–1775: A Handbook,* [2nd edn] (Chapel Hill, NC, [1992]), p. 114.
19 For the trade to Leghorn (Livorno), for instance, see Guido Sonnino, *Saggio sulle Industrie, Marina e Commercio in Livorno sotto i primi due Lorensi (1737–1790)* (Cortona, 1909); and E[lizabeth] R. Poyser, "Anglo-Italian Trade from the Reign of Elizabeth to the French Revolution with Special Reference to the Port of Leghorn" (M.Litt. thesis, University of Cambridge, 1951). For the trade with Naples, see Luigi de Rosa, "Navi, merci, nazion-alità, itinerari in un porto dell'età preindustriale: Il porto di Napoli nel 1760," in *Saggi e Richerche sul Settecento* (Naples, 1968), pp. 332–370.
20 For this trade see, among others, Edward Delos Beechert, Jr, "The Wine Trade of the Thirteen Colonies" (M.A. thesis, University of California, Berkeley, 1949); Jorge Martins Ribeiro, "Alguns aspectos do comércio da Madeira com a América do Norte na segunda metade so século XVIII," in [Colóquio Internacional de História da Madeira, 3rd, 1993, Funchal], *Actas. III Colóquio Internacional de História da Madeira* (Funchal, 1993), pp. 389–401.

Table 11.3 The sources of capital invested in the shipping industry of colonial Philadelphia, 1726–1729 and 1770–1775

Source	1726–1729 *Annual average investment*		1770–1775 *Annual average investment*	
	Measured tonnage (1)	Value (£ sterling) (2)	Measured tonnage (3)	Value (£ sterling) (4)
Pennsylvania	1,007	5,790	8,276	61,653
Great Britain	513	2,950	926	6,898
Ireland	253	1,455	442	3,293
Europe and Africa	0	0	75	561
British North America	0	0	16	118
British West Indies	147	845	352	2,624
New Jersey	43	247	92	688
Delaware	117	673	239	1,781
Other Continental Colonies	60	345	389	2,901
Totals	2,140	12,305	10,807	80,515

Notes and sources:
John J. McCusker, "The Pennsylvania Shipping Industry in the Eighteenth Century" (unpublished typescript, 1972), pp. 222–226.

Nor did they just sit idly by. Although what the colonists were doing was all quite legal – it breached no tenets of the navigation laws – British merchants wanted to restrict it. Particularly in the 1760s and 1770s, when Parliament was increasingly active in mercantile matters,[21] numerous suggestions were discussed in England, including discriminatory taxes on colonial shipping and even the outright banning of colonial vessels from transatlantic trade.[22] Colonial merchants, at Philadelphia and elsewhere, can be forgiven if they felt their basic commercial rights threatened in the era of King George III.

This was all the more important to them because the size of the colonists' investment in the shipping industry had grown markedly in the fifty years before 1776. Table 11.3 indicates the relative input of capital invested in the vessels registered at Philadelphia at the two ends of the period for which we have data, 1726–1729 and 1770–1775. In the 1720s Pennsylvanians

21 Michael Kammen has concluded that "the two decades separating 1763 and 1783 may properly be called an age of interests, for they [that is, the interests] so dominated [British] politics that men observed that mercantilism had changed from the control of trade in the interest of national policy, to the control of national policy in the interest of trade." Kammen, *Empire and Interest: The American Colonies and the Politics of Mercantilism* (Philadelphia, 1970), p. 95.

22 See the letters of Benjamin Franklin, at London, to Joseph Galloway, Speaker of the Pennsylvania Assembly, at Philadelphia, 14 Apr. 1767, in *The Papers of Benjamin Franklin*, ed. Leonard W. Labaree *et al.*, in progress (New Haven, Conn., 1959 to date), XIV, 125; and Thomas Whately, one of George Grenville's close allies, at London, to John Temple, the Surveyor-General of Customs for the Northern District of America and one of the

purchased less than half of the tonnage registered at Philadelphia; in the 1770s they purchased more than three-quarters, an increase of almost 60 percent.[23] The merchants of Great Britain and Ireland purchased just over a third of the tonnage registered in the 1720s but by the 1770s their proportion was down to little more than an eighth, a drop of about 62.6 percent. Still, the relative decline masks an absolute increase in the size of the investment because of the great boom at Philadelphia. In the late 1720s roughly 2,100 measured tons of shipping were registered each year, while in the 1770s the quantity had grown over five times to more than 10,800 measured tons per year. Credits attributable to all "foreign" (that is, non-Pennsylvanian) capital

five Commissioners of the Board of Customs of North America, at Boston, 2 May 1767, in *The Bowdoin and Temple Papers [1756-1812]*, Massachusetts Historical Society Collections, 6th ser., vol. IX, and 7th ser., vol. VI, 2 vols (Boston, 1897–1907), I, 81. For an example of the impact of such rumors and reports, see William Lux, at Baltimore, to James, Russell and Molleson, at London, 17 Nov. 1764, William Lux Letter Book, 1763–1768, New-York Historical Society, New York City, and as edited in Pamela [B.] Satek, "William Lux of Baltimore, 18th-Century Merchant" (M.A. thesis, University of Maryland, 1974), p. 414.

The suggested restriction of American vessels to the coasting trade came most powerfully from Charles Jenkinson (later, Earl of Liverpool), also of Grenville's circle, joint secretary to the Treasury with Whately from 1763 to 1765, and "one of George III's chief favorites," as we are reminded by Lewis [B.] Namier, *England in the Age of the American Revolution*, 2nd edn (London, 1961), p. 76. For Jenkinson's suggestion that colonial vessels be restricted to that coastal trades, see Jenkinson, at Aix-la-Chapelle, to Frederick, Lord North, at London, 9 July 1777, Letter Book of Charles Jenkinson, 1775–1779, fols 72–74, Add. MS 38306, BL, and as discussed by Dora Mae Clark, *The Rise of the British Treasury: Colonial Administration in the Eighteenth* Century (New Haven, Conn., 1960), pp. 170–71. Jenkinson was blunt about his purpose: "it will restrain [their] growth . . . in that branch of trade in which they are most likely to become our rivals." If the Americans complained about these restrictions, then "suffer them not to have any shipping." Clark concluded: "It may be that American merchants avoided this calamity only by achieving independence" (ibid., p. 171).

Precisely these restrictions had been imposed as part of the punitive measures that Parliament passed in the spring of 1775 (Act of 15 George III, c. 10; Act of 15 George III, c. 18). They were said to be temporary and coercive in nature, but that did not prevent John Montagu, the Earl of Sandwich, First Lord of the Admiralty, from arguing during the debate over the second bill's passage that it should be made "a perpetual law of commercial regulation, operating to extend our trade, to increase our seamen, and to strengthen our naval power." [GB, Parl.], *The Parliamentary History of England from the Earliest Period to the Year 1803*, edited by William Cobbett, 36 vols (London, 1806–1820), XVIII, 448.

Compare the nearly contemporary comment by Charles Whitworth, *State of the Trade of Great Britain in Its Imports and Exports Progressively from the Year 1697 [to 1773]* . . . (London, 1776), p. lv, on the reason for the establishment of the colony of Georgia: "to turn the industry of this new people from the timber and provision trade, which the other colonies had prosecuted too largely, into channels more advantageous to the public." His view, from 1776, was that the "other colonies," had been engaging in trade "too largely," which he deemed not to be "advantageous to the public"! One or both of these expressions of opinion may have been the source of Jenkinson's notions.

23 Compare Anne Bezanson, "Inflation and Controls, Pennsylvania, 1774–1779," in *The Tasks of Economic History: Papers Presented at the Eighth Annual Meeting of the Economic History Association – A Supplement to the "Journal of Economic History"* (New York, 1948), p. 4.

invested in its shipping industry earned Pennsylvania £6,500 sterling annually in the 1720s, of which £4,400 sterling came from Great Britain and Ireland and £845 sterling from the British West Indies. A half-century later such "foreign" credits had increased almost three times to £18,900 sterling annually, of which £10,800 sterling came from British and Irish merchants residing in the British Isles, major European ports, and Africa. Another £2,600 sterling came from the British West Indies and the remainder from colonial investors in the other British colonies in North America.

The growth in the total of local capital invested in the shipping industry of colonial Pennsylvania was even more impressive. In the late 1720s Pennsylvanians mustered an annual average investment of £5,800 sterling while in the early 1770s the sum per year equaled £61,600 sterling, an increase of almost eleven times over four decades. With the average useful life of a vessel at twelve and one-half years,[24] Pennsylvanians held an investment worth in the neighborhood of £500,000 sterling in their shipping industry at the end of the colonial era.[25] As we might expect, a large proportion of the total came from the overseas merchants of the city of Philadelphia, although there seems to have been no significant segment of the business community without some interest in the colony's shipping industry.[26]

W. W. Rostow and others have proposed that the mobilization of domestic capital becomes stimulative of self-sustained economic growth when it begins to exceed roughly 10 percent of national income or net national product (NNP).[27] We are only beginning to develop estimates of national income for the Thirteen Continental Colonies and we have no idea of the total amount of domestic capital generated therein, but we can at least gather some sense

---

24 McCusker, "Pennsylvania Shipping Industry in the Eighteenth Century," pp. 121–127. Price, "Colonial Exports of Shipping,"p. 718, estimated "the life-expectancy of an average American-built topsailed ship ca. 1768–1776" at 13.3 years. Compare Marshall Smelser and William I. Davisson, "The Longevity of Colonial Ships," *American Neptune*, XXXIII (Jan. 1973), 16–19; Daniel Scott Smith, "A Note on the Longevity of Colonial Ships," *American Neptune*, XXXIV (Jan. 1974), 68–69; and Christopher J. French, "The Longevity of Ships in Colonial Trade: Some Further Evidence," *International Journal of Maritime History*, III (June 1991), 155–163. Smith's point is a critical one and has not been adequately acknowledged in the discussion. See also William J. Hausman, "Size and Profitability of English Colliers in the Eighteenth Century," *Business History Review*, LI (Winter 1977), 472.

25 Important because, as Robert Craig ("Shipping Records of the Nineteenth and Twentieth Centuries," *Archives*, VII [1965–1966], 192) noted of Great Britain, "in the eighteenth and nineteenth centuries . . . ships were the most important form of fixed (although floating and movable) capital investment . . . after land and housing."

26 McCusker, "Pennsylvania Shipping Industry in the Eighteenth Century," pp. 226–272.

27 W[alt] W. Rostow, *The Process of Economic Growth*, 2nd edn (New York, 1959), pp. 281–286; Rostow, *The Stages of Economic Growth: A Non-Communist Manifesto* (Cambridge, Eng., 1960), p. 37; W[illiam] Arthur Lewis, *The Theory of Economic Growth* (London, 1955), pp. 225–226; and A[lexander] K. Cairncross, "Capital Formation in the Take-Off," in *The Economics of Take-Off into Sustained Growth: Proceedings of a Conference Held by the International Economics Association*, ed. W[alt] W. Rostow (New York, 1963), pp. 248–253.

of the rate of increase in the growth of colonial NNP if we are prepared to accept certain assumptions. For instance, we might assume that the leading determinant of colonial income was the foreign sector of the economy and that the rate of increase in Pennsylvania's trade with England is representative of the rate of growth of its international trade in general. We could then compare this surrogate for the rate of increase of Pennsylvania's NNP and the rate of increase of the colony's accumulation of domestic savings, even though we would still be unable to stipulate the ratio of savings to NNP.[28] The sum of Pennsylvania's imports from and exports to England increased from an annual average of £46,500 sterling in 1725–1729 to £523,800 sterling in 1770–1774.[29] The population of the colony over the four decades 1730 to 1770 grew from 61,000 to 276,000.[30] The annual compound rate of growth on a per capita basis was just over 2.0 percent, here postulated as a proxy for the rate of increase in the colony's NNP.[31] The average annual per capita compound rate of growth in the investment of local capital in the Philadelphia shipping industry over the same period was just under 2.2 percent, roughly 6 percent more than that of NNP. In other words, according to these data, colonial investment in the shipping industry advanced slightly faster than did the economy itself. Yet there are problems with these figures. The crudeness of the estimates necessitates that we pay less attention to the numbers themselves than to the trends they indicate. Moreover, for this comparison to have any meaning, we have to assume that the patterns of growth of Pennsylvania's investments in the shipping industry were representative of the colonists' investments in all other enterprises. Still, given all of our assumptions, the results are significant.

While Pennsylvania's rate of economic growth is considerable, the ability of the colony's economy to generate increasing amounts of investment capital is even more striking. The suggestion of prosperity in the Thirteen

---

28 A similar initial assumption – "that the whole industrial and commercial sector grew at the same rate as international trade" – provided two British economic historians with an opportunity "to fix an upper limit" to the rate of growth of the economy of Great Britain. Phyllis Deane and W[illiam] A. Cole, *British Economic Growth, 1688–1959: Trends and Structure*, 2nd edn (Cambridge, Eng., 1969), pp. 79–81.

National income is the product of the operation of both the foreign and the domestic sectors. For a comparable extension of the Deane and Cole model to the economy of the early United States – and the additional assumptions involved – see Douglass C. North, *Growth and Welfare in the American Past: A New Economic History*, [1st edn] (Englewood Cliffs, NJ, 1966), pp. 59–63. See also North, *The Economic Growth of the United States, 1790–1860* (Englewood Cliffs, NJ, 1961), p. 2.

29 The data are as in Whitworth, *State of the Trade of Great Britain*, and Customs 3/74, PRO. The figures as found are effectively a constant value series. See John J. McCusker, "The Current Value of English Exports, 1697 to 1800," *W&MQ*, 3rd ser., XXVIII (Oct. 1971), 607–628 – revised as chapter ten of the present book.

30 John J. McCusker, *Rum and the American Revolution: The Rum Trade and the Balance of Payments of the Thirteen Continental Colonies, 1650–1775*, 2 vols (New York, 1989 [Ph.D. diss., University of Pittsburgh, 1970]), II, 568.

31 Compare McCusker and Menard, *Economy of British America*, pp. 53–60.

Continental Colonies that such growth poses raises important questions about the nature of the relationship between the colonists and the Mother Country.[32] The ramifications of one of Alice Hanson Jones's early conclusions are indeed far-reaching: "le niveau de vie américain, en 1774, était vraiment élevé en termes absolus aussi bien que relatifs'[33] [the standard of living in America in 1774 was truly high in both absolute and relative terms].[34] We are moved to agree with all of those who have sought and not found reasons for revolution in a colonial economy historically confined and crushed by English mercantilism and its navigation laws. Whatever else it might have been, the American Revolution was not a rising of impoverished masses – or merchants – in search of their share of the wealth. The "predicament of poverty," in Hannah Arendt's phrase, "was absent from the American

32 For the argument that the colonial economy grew over time and that this growth bene-fited all levels of society, see McCusker and Menard, *Economy of British America*, passim. Early efforts that developed this idea included three important dissertations and the published works that have grown out of them.: James Floyd Shepherd, Jr, "A Balance of Payments for the Thirteen Colonies, 1768–1772" (Ph.D. diss., University of Washington, 1966); Walton, "A Quantitative Study of American Colonial Shipping"; and Alice Hanson Jones, "Wealth Estimates for the American Middle Colonies, 1774" (Ph.D. diss., University of Chicago, 1968). Jones expanded her dissertation into a major book: *Wealth of a Nation to Be: The American Colonies on the Eve of Revolution* (New York, 1980). Shepherd and Walton subsequently published a book that gathered their articles, which were, in turn, based on their dissertations: *Shipping Maritime Trade, and the Economic Development of Colonial America* (Cambridge, Eng., 1972).

33 Jones, "La Fortune privée en Pennsylvanie, New Jersey, Delaware (1774)," *Annales: Histoire, Sciences Sociales,* XXIV (Mar.–Apr. 1969), 248. This article drew upon her more broadly based work that was later summarized in Jones, *Wealth of a Nation to Be.*

34 The problem of defining prosperity is always a comparative one. Suffice it to say that the citizens of the Thirteen Continental Colonies in the years immediately preceding 1775 seem from this study and those of Jones, Walton, Shepherd, and others to have been better off than people in other countries at the same time and in their own country at both an earlier and a later time. Besides the works of Walton, Shepherd, and Jones cited in the preceding note, see Curtis P. Nettels, *The Money Supply of the American Colonies before 1720*, University of Wisconsin, Studies in the Social Sciences and History, no. 20 (Madison, Wis., 1934), p. 278; George R. Taylor, "American Economic Growth before 1840: An Exploratory Essay," *JEcH*, XXIV (Dec. 1964), 427–444; and North, *Growth and Welfare*, p. 40. Even though there were distinct levels of economic attainment in colo-nial society, and even if we find that the secular trend in the concentration of wealth created an increasing gulf between the rich and the poor over the years separating 1607 and 1775, the fact remains that not only were the rich getting richer but the poor were also, albeit at a slower rate. See the very suggestive studies addressed to the changes in the structure of income distribution by James T. Lemon and Gary B. Nash, "The Distribution of Wealth in Eighteenth Century America: A Century of Change in Chester County, Pennsylvania, 1693–1802," *Journal of Social History*, II (1968–1969), 1–24; James A. Henretta, "Economic Development and Social Structure in Colonial Boston," *W&MQ*, 3rd ser., XXII (Jan. 1965), 75–92; and Alan Kulikoff, "The Progress of Inequality in Revolutionary Boston," *W&MQ*, 3rd ser., XXVIII (July 1971), 375–412.

The shift in income distribution that concentrates wealth in groups with a higher propensity to save is, of course, the classical mechanism for generating domestic savings and economic development. W[illiam] Arthur Lewis, "Economic Development with Unlimited Supplies of Labour," *Manchester School of Economic and Social Studies*, XXII (May 1954), 155–160; Rostow, *Process of Economic Growth*, pp. 292–296. This would appear to have been what happened in colonial Pennsylvania.

scene";[35] the colonists were already quite prosperous. Perhaps then in this broad sense, the Americans might be seen as having waited until they could afford a revolution.

Not only did the colonists find a potential for revolution in their prosperity, but they also found some causes. They could see that the prosperity that they had created was threatened, in much the same way that their political processes seemed threatened. Parliament's attempts to tighten the bonds of empire during and after the Seven Years War challenged established modes of economic behavior just as they struck at colonial political prerogatives. Lord Sheffield told us more than he might have realized about the coming of the Revolution when he complained in 1784 that, prior to 1775, "the Americans were rapidly engrossing the carrying trade," for his predecessors had tried to correct that anomaly.[36] One can think further of the imposition of a monopoly in the tea trade,[37] but there was more, much of it beyond the area of statute law. Between 1760 and 1775, for instance, the London West India merchants, with the help of the Crown, seized for themselves control of the rum trade into Great Britain, into Ireland, and even into Quebec![38] With these attempts and others to restructure the trade *within* the empire after the accession of King George III, Great Britain in effect told the colonists that they could expect to have preempted whatever avenue to economic success they chose that had proven successful enough to be competitive. The American Revolution came as a response to colonial fears of losing both political and economic rights. The American Revolutionary War might thus be seen as the ultimate employment of colonial risk capital.

35 Hannah Arendt, *On Revolution* (New York, 1963), pp. 61–68. Note her qualification that "what were absent from the American scene were misery and want rather than poverty." Compare Kulikoff, "Progress of Inequality in Revolutionary Boston," p. 383. See also the work of Billy G. Smith, esp. *The "Lower Sort": Philadelphia's Laboring People, 1750–1800* (Ithaca, NY, [1990]).

36 John [Baker Holroyd], Lord Sheffield, *Observations on the Commerce of the American States*, 6th edn, enl. (London, 1784), p. 100. Most interestingly, his example is Philadelphia!

37 See Arthur Meier Schlesinger, *The Colonial Merchants and the American Revolution, 1763–1776*, Columbia University Studies in History, Economics and Public Law, vol. LXXVIII, no. 182 (New York, 1918), pp. 265–278, for colonial reactions to the tea affair.

38 McCusker, *Rum and the American Revolution*, I, 479–504.

12

THE AMERICAN
INVASION OF NASSAU
IN THE BAHAMAS

On 16 May 1778 the French Toulon squadron under Comte d'Estaing sailed out of the Mediterranean Sea, unchallenged through the Straits of Gibraltar, into the Atlantic Ocean.[1] In London soon thereafter the House of Lords and the House of Commons rang with denunciations of the government for permitting this to happen, calling such disregard of traditional strategy irresponsible and near treason.[2] Modern students have agreed with Parliament that to have allowed the French to sail was a mistake and one writer believes it to have been perhaps "the most serious mistake that was made by the British in the course of the war."[3] Certainly without the powerful French fleet blockading Chesapeake Bay there would have been no American victory at Yorktown.[4] What is too rarely realized is the important role the Continental Navy of the United Colonies played in helping to draw the Royal Navy to the Western Hemisphere and thus so dividing its forces as to make any

1   The original version of this chapter was published in *American Neptune*, XXV (July 1965), 189–217. Copyright © 1965 by the *American Neptune* Inc. Copyright © renewed 1994 by John J. McCusker.
       I continue to be grateful for the help and support given me in the preparation of the original essay by both Edward L. Towle and Emory G. Evans.
       Jean-Baptiste-Charles-Henri-Hector, Comte d'Estaing (1729–1794), commanded the French fleet in American waters from 1778 to 1780.
2   [GB, Parl.], *The Parliamentary History of England from the Earliest Period to the Year 1803*, ed. William Cobbett, 36 vols (London, 1806–1820), XIX, 1145–1175, especially 1146–1147, 1155. See, too, George Germain to Lord North, 27 Apr. 1778, in [GB, Sovereign (1760–1820: George III)], *The Correspondence of George III from 1760 to December 1783*, ed. John [W.] Fortescue, 6 vols (London, 1927–1928), IV, 121–122. Compare Gerald S. Brown, "The Anglo-French Naval Crisis, 1778: A Study of Conflict in the North Cabinet," *W&MQ*, 3rd ser., XIII (Jan. 1956), 3–25.
3   Clifford August Morrison, "The Earl of Sandwich and British Naval Administration in the War of the American Revolution" (Ph.D. diss., Ohio State University, 1950), p. 205. Alfred Thayer Mahan called it an "unpardonable fault," *Major Operations of the Navies in the War of American Independence* (Boston, 1913), p. 79. See also, William M. James, *The British Navy in Adversity: A Study of the War of American Independence* (London, 1926), p. 87: and Brown, "Anglo-French Naval Crisis," pp. 12, 13. Compare N[icholas] A. M. Rodger, *The Insatiable Earl: A Life of John Montagu, Fourth Earl of Sandwich, 1718–1792* ([London, 1993]), pp. 274–279.
4   Washington himself recognized this, calling the French naval contribution to the revolutionary cause "the pivet upon which every thing turned." See Washington, at "Head

effective confrontation of the French in 1778 tactically impossible. The Earl of Sandwich, the First Lord of the Admiralty, lamented in April 1778, that: "there are not ships enough as yet in readiness to form a squadron fit to meet the Toulon fleet under Monsieur d'Estaing unless we were to sacrifice every other intended service to this object."[5] To do so would "expose our own coast and Ireland . . . as the Brest fleet would be superior to anything we shall have ready for sea." The reason why, as King George III himself bemoaned shortly thereafter in his message calling for "every effort to fit out the fleet," was that "having been obliged to send . . . everything we had to America, has crippled us."[6] The cream of the Royal Navy then cruised in the waters of the Western Hemisphere, thousands of miles from home, sent there in part to answer the challenge of the Continental Navy of the United Colonies.

The first engagement of the Continental Navy with British forces came with the amphibious attack from a fleet of eight ships upon the island of New Providence in the Bahamas in March 1776 (see figure 12.1). Naval warfare of a sort had begun almost immediately with the start of the Revolution. Within two months of his arrival at Cambridge in July 1775, General George Washington had organized a very small "navy" in an attempt to cut off supplies from the besieged British in Boston.[7] The Continental Congress soon recognized the need for the interception of all British supplies destined for the New World and undertook the formation of a united navy for the United Colonies.[8] From its initial action, with which we are here concerned, through a short history to its rapid but never quite complete demise, the Continental Navy continued to harass the British. The amphibious assault against Nassau was the first and most ambitious American challenge to the colonial empire of Great Britain during the Revolution. For a variety of reasons it was less than completely successful but it portended

Quarters," to Benjamin Franklin, 20 Dec. 1780, in *The Writings of George Washington*, ed. John C. Fitzpatrick, 39 vols (Washington, DC, 1931–1944), XX, 507. Compare Washington, at Mount Vernon, to Marquis de Lafayette, 15 Nov. 1781, ibid., XXIII, 341. See also William James Morgan, "'The Pivot upon Which Everything Turned': French Naval Superiority that Ensured Victory at Yorktown," *The Iron Worker* [Lynchburg, Va.], XXII (Spring 1958), 1–9.

5 "Lord Sandwich's Opinion, 6 April 1778," in *The Private Papers of John, Earl of Sandwich, First Lord of the Admiralty, 1771–1782*, ed. G[eorge] R. Barnes and J[ohn] H. Owen, Publications of the Navy Records Society, vols LXIX, LXXI, LXXV, LXXVIII, 4 vols (London, 1932–1938), II, 23.

6 George III to Lord Sandwich, 29 Apr. 1778, *Private Papers . . . Earl of Sandwich*, ed. Barnes and Owen, II, 38–39. Sandwich and others in the government also realized the strain the American war was placing upon the Royal Navy, ibid., I, 90, 201, 243, 249–250.

7 William Bell Clark, *George Washington's Navy: Being an Account of His Excellency's Fleet in New England Waters* (Baton Rouge, La., [1960]).

8 For the earliest beginnings of the Continental Navy, see entries for 3 and 5 Oct. 1775, in the handwriting of Charles Thomson, Secretary to the Continental Congress, The Secret Journals of Congress, 1774–1780, pt i (1774–1775), p. 9, Charles Thomson Papers, 1774–1811, HSP; and Gardner Weld Allen, *A Naval History of the American Revolution*, 2 vols (Boston and New York, 1913), I, 21–25, as well as the references he cites there.

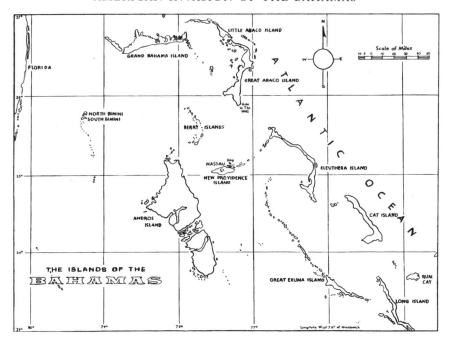

Figure 12.1 The Islands of the Bahamas.
Courtesy of the author.

more than it accomplished. The threat inherent in this surprise attack for the trade-rich West Indies and, more strategically and logistically important, to Great Britain's very ability to carry on a victorious war 3,000 miles from home, struck forcibly. Caron de Beaumarchais reported from London to the French Minister of Foreign Affairs, Comte de Vergennes, that the North government was so perplexed upon learning of the news of the American descent upon Nassau that it did not know which way to turn. "Le Ministère ne fait d'honneur plus de quel côte se tourner."[9] Great Britain reacted to this and subsequent challenges by dispatching the majority of its fighting ships to duty in the waters of the Western Hemisphere, leaving the way open for the undisputed sailing of the Toulon fleet in 1778.[10] Had not the Royal

9   [Pierre Augustin, Caron de Beaumarchais], at London, to [Charles Gravier], Comte de Vergennes, 11 May 1776, Correspondance Politique, Angleterre, vol. 516, fol. 121, Archives du Ministère des Relations Extérieures, Paris, and as reproduced in *Facsimiles of Manuscripts in European Archives Relating to America, 1776–1783*, ed. B[enjamin] F[ranklin] Stevens, 25 vols (London, 1889–1898), XIII, no. 1334, [p. 4].

10   As of 1 Jan. 1778, according to the best figures available, Great Britain had at the most 274 operative vessels of all types; 53 percent (146) were stationed in American waters; 34 percent (94) at home; and 13 percent (34) at other points around the globe ("American waters" is here used in the commonly accepted sense to mean the four Western Hemisphere

Navy been so occupied in the Western Atlantic as a consequence of the actions of the American forces, the freedom of the seas could have been denied to the French and perhaps the course of the war materially altered as a result.

◆ ◆ ◆ ◆ ◆

The invasion of Nassau came only a few months after the establishment of the Continental Navy.[11] The value of an organized naval force had been

stations of the Royal Navy: Newfoundland, North America [Halifax], Jamaica, and Leeward Islands). Even these figures are deceptively optimistic for over 80 percent of the vitally important frigate-class vessels (5th- and 6th-rate ships, mounting 20 to 44 guns) were in the Western Atlantic, at least 10 percent more were scattered at other duties, with only 8 out of the total of 77 frigates (10 percent) at home doing guard duty at "the principal trading towns" (*Private Papers . . . Earl of Sandwich*, ed. Barnes and Owen, I, 350). This disproportionate distribution of frigates caused no end of difficulties at home (ibid., I, 201–202). Still more indicative of the plight of the Royal Navy was the sorry state of its main battle fleet, the ships of the line (1st-, 2nd-, and 3rd-rate, 64 to 100 guns). The total of 274 vessels included 102 of these capital ships but a very strong case can be made that only 55 were in any condition for use (ibid., I, 350–351, 422; *Parliamentary History*, ed. Cobbett, XIX, 376). Supportable also is the contention that a mere 19 of these were actually fit for immediate duty, 8 of which (42 percent) were in American waters. This is based on Admiral Keppel's oft-quoted remark upon viewing the 42 ships of the line promised him for a Channel Fleet early in 1778 that he found only 6 ships "fit to meet a seaman's eye." *Parliamentary History*, ed. Cobbett, XX, 184, and XIX, 371, 450. See also, Thomas R. Keppel, *The Life of August, Viscount Keppel, Admiral of the White and First Lord of the Admiralty in 1782–3*, 2 vols (London, 1842), II, 19–20. His partisan position is supported, first, by the scramble for ships that ensued when Admiral Byron was finally ordered to pursue d'Estaing in early May, a situation that delayed his departure until 9 June, and, second, by the equally vocal complaints about the horrible condition of the navy from government supporters like Admirals Rodney and Palliser. See Keppel, *Life of . . . Viscount Keppel*, II, 22–23; Robert Greenhalgh Albion, *Forests and Sea Power: The Timber Problem of the Royal Navy, 1652–1862*, Harvard Economic Studies, vol. XXIX (Cambridge, Mass., 1926), p. 293. With no more than 8 frigates, at the most 4 ships of the 4th rate and perhaps as few as 11 ships of the line at his disposal, Sandwich might well have been worried about facing d'Estaing. See also Robert Beatson, *Naval and Military Memoirs of Great Britain from the Earliest Period to the Year 1803*, 6 vols (London, 1804), VI, 87–88, 91–94, 101–103, 110–111, 120–121; David Hannay, *A Short History of the Royal Navy, 1217–1815*, 2 vols (London, 1898–[1909]), II, 211–214; Piers Mackesy, *The War for America, 1775–1783* ([London, 1964]), pp. 162–179, 190–211 and passim; Daniel A. Baugh, "The Politics of British Naval Failure, 1775–1777," *American Neptune*, LII (Fall 1992), 221–246; and Rodger, *Insatiable Earl*, passim.

　　Charles M. Andrews summed up the point neatly near the end of a long disquisition on corruption in the British navy (*The Colonial Period of American History*, 4 vols [New Haven, Conn., 1934–1938], IV, 317): "When war broke out with France in 1778 the number of ships in the navy was insufficient . . ." With the force thus depleted, "operations in America simply ate up the strength of the Royal Navy" according to David Syrett, "Defeat at Sea: The Impact of American Naval Operations upon the British, 1775–1778," in *Maritime Dimensions of the American Revolution* (Washington, DC, 1977), p. 14.

11　The American attack upon the island of New Providence has been treated by a number of authors. One group has seemingly followed the imperfect account in *The Annual Register . . . for the Year 1776* (London, 1777), p. 158*, with its important mistake in the chronology of the invasion (Capt. Chambers is said to have sailed the night before the landing, a significant error; see below). Included here are Edward Field, *Esek Hopkins, Commander-in-Chief of the United States Navy, 1775–1777* (Providence, RI, 1898), pp.

recognized by the Continental Congress only in October 1775, when it saw the necessity of cutting off supplies from about-to-be-invaded Canada. The

98–118, and Carlos C. Hanks, "A Cruise for Gunpowder," *United States Naval Institute Proceedings*, LXV (Mar. 1939), 324–327. Others who have dealt with the invasion include [Robert Charles Sands, ed.], *Life and Correspondence of John Paul Jones Including His Narrative of the Campaign of the Liman* (New York, 1830), pp. 35–36; James Fenimore Cooper, *History of the Navy of the United States*, 2nd edn, rev., 2 vols (Philadelphia, 1840), I, 76–77; Allen, *Naval History*, I, 94–100; Lincoln Lorenz, *John Paul Jones: Fighter for Freedom and Glory* (Annapolis, Md., 1943), pp. 61–67; William Bell Clark, *Captain Dauntless: The Story of Nicholas Biddle of the Continental Navy* ([Baton Rouge, La.], 1949), pp. 102–108; and William James Morgan, *Captains to the Northward: The New England Captains in the Continental Navy* (Barre, Mass., 1959), pp. 33–42.

All of the above secondary treatments of the subject suffer for not having looked widely enough at the materials in the PRO. On the other hand, the analysis by Michael [J.] Craton, *A History of the Bahamas* (London, 1962), pp. 153–156, could have been much better had he used sources available in the United States. Compare Craton, *A History of the Bahamas*, 3rd edn ([Waterloo, Ontario], 1986), pp. 139–142. References hereafter are to Craton's 3rd edn.

The present discussion is based upon both British and United States sources. In the PRO is the correspondence to and from the North American Station of the Royal Navy, 1775–1776, Adm. 1/484, PRO, and Adm. 2/555, PRO; the general correspondence between the colonies and London, 1780–1783, CO 5/8, PRO; the correspondence concerning East Florida, 1775–1776, CO 5/556, PRO; concerning New York, 1775–1776, CO 5/1107, PRO; concerning the Bahamas, 1774–1781, CO 23/23, PRO, CO 23/24, PRO and CO 24/7, PRO; and concerning Jamaica, 1775–1776, CO 137/71, PRO. Copies of some of these documents are available in the form of transcripts, photostats, or microfilms in the Manuscript Division of the Library of Congress, Washington, DC. Especially important are the Benjamin Franklin Stevens Transcripts of Manuscripts in the Archives of England, France, Holland, and Spain Relating to America, 1763–1783, LC. See Grace Gardner Griffin, *A Guide to Manuscripts Relating to American History in British Depositories Reproduced for the Division of Manuscripts of the Library of Congress* (Washington, DC, 1946); and John R. Sellers, Gerard W. Gawalt, Paul H. Smith, and Patricia Molen van Ee, *Manuscript Sources in the Library of Congress for Research on the American Revolution* (Washington, DC, 1975), pp. 193–303. Some of the Bahamas letters descriptive of the invasion – Atwood to Germain, 22 Mar. 1776; Brown to Germain, 2 May 1776 and 10 May 1777; Browne to Germain, 17 Mar. and 5 Nov. 1776; and Germain to Browne, 14 Jan. 1777 – were printed in Malcolm Lloyd, Jr, "The Taking of the Bahamas by the Continental Navy in 1776," *Pennsylvania Magazine of History and Biography*, XLIX (Oct. 1925), 349–366. Robert Wilden Neeser edited some of the papers in Adm. 1/484, PRO, and published them in *The Despatches of Molyneux Shuldham, Vice-Admiral of the Blue and Commander-in-Chief of His Britannic Majesty's Ships in North America, January–July 1776*, Publications of the Naval History Society, vol. III (New York, 1913). (For the records in the PRO and the mode of their citation, see John J. McCusker, "New Guides to Primary Sources for the History of Early British America," *W&MQ*, 3rd ser., XLI (Apr. 1984), 277–295 – revised as chapter one of the present book.) For information about Royal Navy ships mentioned herein, see J[ames] J. Colledge, *Ships of the Royal Navy: An Historical Index*, [2nd edn, rev.], 2 vols ([Annapolis, 1987–1989]), and David [J.] Lyon, *The Sailing Navy List: All the Ships of the Royal Navy – Built, Purchased, Captured – 1688–1860* ([London, 1993]); for information about its officers, see [David Bonner-Smith et al.], *The Commissioned Sea Officers of the Royal Navy, 1660–1815*, ed. David Syrett and R[ichard] L. DiNardo, Occasional Publications of the Navy Records Society, vol. 1, [2nd edn, rev. and enl.] ([Aldershot, Eng.], 1994).

Sources found in repositories in the United States will be cited as they are used.

Many of the items from both United States and British archives cited herein have been reproduced in the *Naval Documents of the American Revolution*, ed. William Bell Clark and William J. Morgan, in progress (Washington, DC, 1964 to date).

hurried nature of this need dictated speed and, since it would take time to construct warships, the first authorization was for the purchase of several merchantmen to be converted into naval vessels. Two large ships and several smaller ones were bought, their decks strengthened and sides pierced for cannon, manned, provisioned, and made ready to sail. Difficulties abounded for the Naval Committee but by the end of December most of the ships had been assembled at Philadelphia, officers assigned to the vessels, and a Commander in Chief appointed. Captain Samuel Nicholas was put in charge of the marines and Commodore Esek Hopkins, an old sea dog from Providence, Rhode Island, was given overall command of this first fleet of the Continental Navy. They were but awaiting sailing orders during the first week of the new year when it became necessary to drop down-river to avoid being icebound.[12]

Commodore Hopkins' orders soon arrived. The states below the Mason-Dixon Line had had to be convinced of the desirability of a navy and one of the best arguments seems to have been, if the orders given Hopkins are any guide, that the Southern coasts could benefit from the new navy as much as Northern shores. Not only could the navy aid in the capture of Boston and Canada, but it could relieve the hard-pressed South, too. The Continental Congress was optimistic in its designs for the fleet and the orders that the Naval Committee dispatched to Hopkins on 5 January 1776 show their great hopes as well as the effects of Southern pressure. He was first directed to sail for "Chesepeak Bay in Virginia" and to "attack, take or destroy all the Naval force of our Enemies that . . . [he might] find there." John Murray, the Fourth Earl of Dunmore and Royal Governor of Virginia, had organized a few small vessels – a "mosquito fleet" – with which he had been harrying the rebellious segments of his colony. It was against him that the first blow was to be aimed and it was against Dunmore's imitators further south that Hopkins' orders directed him next. After having dealt successfully with Dunmore, he was, with his fleet, to make himself "Master of such forces as the Enemy may have both in North and South Carolina." This second phase accomplished, Hopkins was then "to proceed Northward directly to Rhode Island, and attack, take and destroy all the Enemies naval force" there. It was a large order for Hopkins, with his men untrained in naval warfare and his ships as yet untried.[13]

---

12 The best discussion of the early development of the Continental Navy is still Allen, *Naval History*, I, 1–58. See also, Gardner Weld Allen, "Esek Hopkins," *New England Quarterly*, IX (Sept. 1936), 483–485. For the composition of the fleet, see table 12.1. For details of the purchase, conversion, and outfit of the flagship of the first fleet, see John J. McCusker, "The Continental Ship *Alfred*," *Nautical Research Journal*, XIII (Autumn 1965), 39–68.

   The narrative in Charles R. Smith, *Marines in the Revolution: A History of the Continental Marines in the American Revolution, 1775–1783* (Washington, DC, 1975), pp. 41–57, follows very closely the account in the original version of this chapter.

13 "Orders given by the Naval Committee to Commodore Hopkins," in [US, Continental Congress], *Journals of the Continental Congress, 1774–1789*, ed. Worthington Chauncey Ford *et al.*, 34 vols (Washington, DC, 1904–1937), IV, 335.

Commodore Hopkins had a good deal of time to reread his orders and ponder his situation, for the river closed in on him and, despite the precaution taken, the fleet found itself frozen in the ice, unable to make it to sea for another six weeks. At least two important factors must have weighed heavily in his thoughts as he looked again at his instructions. When the fleet had left Philadelphia, conversation everywhere had centered around the crying need for gunpowder. Letters had been arriving almost daily from General Washington telling of the sad state of the army around Boston and begging for supplies. "Our want of powder is inconceivable," he wrote to Joseph Hewes on 25 December 1775.[14] Hopkins was certainly aware of this and, since his brother Stephen was a member of the Congress, he must also have known of the report that had reached the Secret Committee of Congress the previous November bringing word of the large supply of gunpowder in the Bahamas as well as of the resolution that committee had adopted.

> [Wednesday, 29 November 1775]
> Information being given to Con-
> gress that there is a large quan-
> tity of powder in the Island of
> Providence
> Resolved That the foregoing Comee take
> Measures for securing & bringing
> away the said powder.[15]

The "foregoing Com[mitt]ee" was the Naval Committee which a month later was to author Hopkins' orders.

Of equal weight in the decision Commodore Hopkins was about to make was the news that reached Philadelphia in mid-January of the reinforcement of Lord Dunmore's "mosquito fleet" by the addition of HMS *Liverpool*, a frigate of twenty-eight guns. On New Year's Day Dunmore's squadron had shelled and burned Norfolk, a rebel stronghold. What had appeared an easy campaign along the Southern coast now took on uncertain overtones. Hopkins dwelt even more deeply on the makeshift nature of his fleet. He finally came to the conclusion, as he later testified, that the "altered . . . Stacion of the Enemy Priticler as to the Strength of the fleet at Virginia"

---

14 Washington, at Cambridge, to Hewes, in *Writings of George Washington*, ed. Fitzpatrick, IV, 185. See also Orlando W. Stephenson, "The Supply of Gunpowder in 1776," *AHR*, XXX (Jan. 1925), 271–281, and Theodore George Thayer, *Nathaniel Greene: Strategist of the American Revolution* (New York, 1960), p. 79. Compare Elizabeth Miles Nuxoll, *Congress and the Munitions Merchants: The Secret Committee of Trade during the American Revolution, 1775–1777* (New York, 1985 [Ph.D. dissertation. City University of New York, 1979]).

15 Entry for 29 Nov. 1775, Secret Journals of Congress, pt ii (1775–1776), p. 3, HSP, and as printed in [US, Continental Congress], *The Secret Journals of the Acts and Proceedings of Congress, From the First Meeting Thereof to the Dissolution of the Confederation, by the Adoption of the Constitution of the United States*, 4 vols (Boston, 1820–1821), I, 35–36.

permitted him to use the clause in his instructions that allowed him to deal with unforeseen contingencies as he felt proper. "If bad Winds or Stormy Weather, or any other unforeseen accident or disaster disable you so to do," directed the last part of his orders from Congress, "You are then to follow such course as your best judgment shall suggest to you as most useful to the American Cause." This is what he attempted.[16]

When, on Saturday afternoon, 17 February 1776, the first American fleet stood out from Delaware Bay, past Cape Henlopen, it was outward bound not for Virginia or the Carolinas or Rhode Island but for the Bahamas (see table 12.1). Commodore Hopkins, as Commander in Chief of the Fleet, had designated in the sailing orders to his eight captains that they were to stay close to the flagship, *Alfred*, but if they became separated from the fleet on the way, they should rendezvous off "the Southern part of [Great] Abacco [Island]" in the Bahamas, some seventeen leagues north of the island of New Providence. He clearly seems to have had in mind a descent upon the town and forts of Nassau where the powder was located.[17]

Whether any factors beyond those already narrated influenced Commodore Hopkins in his decision is difficult to determine and thus impossible to evaluate. Particularly tantalizing is the possibility that he was encouraged by the Bahamians themselves. After the French and Indian War the Bahamas, as well as Bermuda and the whole of the British West Indies, were subject to the same pressures that Parliament applied to the Continental Colonies and they tended to react in much the same way. For example, *The Annual Register* reported that, in opposition to the Stamp Act of 1765, the people of St Kitts and Nevis went "to even greater lengths than the New-Englanders themselves."[18]

When war broke out in North America this sympathy remained and engendered support for the American cause. Protests were sent to the home government arguing that the American colonists (and thus the West Indians also) had the right to legislate for themselves. The legislatures of Grenada and Tobago passed motions of support for the rebel cause, as did the Barbados House of Assembly, and were suspended for so doing. The Assembly of Bermuda actually sent delegates to the Philadelphia Congress. Throughout this whole period, according to Lewis Namier, West Indians in the British Parliament "were prominent among the few Members who from the very outset upheld the American [constitutional] thesis." Some took to more active forms of assistance and Bermuda supplied the Americans with arms and ships

16 "Extract of a letter from Col. [Robert] Howe, to the Hon. the President of the Convention," Norfolk, 2 Jan. 1776, *New-York Journal; or, the General Advertiser*, 25 Jan. 1776. Notes prepared by Hopkins for the Congressional inquiry into the invasion in Aug. 1776, in *The Letter Book of Esek Hopkins, Commander-in-Chief of the United States Navy, 1775–1777*, ed. Alverda S. Beck (Providence, RI, 1932), pp. 56–57. Compare *Journal of the Continental Congress*, ed. Ford *et al.*, IV, 336.

17 "Orders given the Several Captains in the Fleet at Sailing from the Capes of Delaware Feby. 1776," in *Letter Book of Esek Hopkins*, ed. Beck, p. 44.

18 Act of 5 George III, c. 12. *The Annual Register . . . for the Year 1765* (London, 1766), p. 56.

Table 12.1 The first United States navy fleet, as it sailed, 17 February 1776

| Vessel | Guns (1) | Crew | | Captain (4) |
		Sailors (2)	Marines (3)	
Ship *Alfred*	20 9-pounders 10 6-pounders	160	63	"Commander-in-Chief of the Fleet," Esek Hopkins Captain Dudley Saltonstall
Ship *Columbus*	18 9-pounders 10 6-pounders	160	63	Captain Abraham Whipple
Brigantine *Cabot*	14 6-pounders	90	43	Captain John B. Hopkins
Brigantine *Andrew Doria*	16 6-pounders	67	37	Captain Nicholas Biddle
Sloop *Providence*	12 4-pounders	62	21	Captain John Hazard
Schooner *Fly*	6 9-pounders	30	–	Lieutenant Hoysteed Hacker
Sloop *Hornet*	10 4-pounders	70	–	Captain William Stone
Schooner *Wasp*	8 2-pounders	48	–	Captain William Hallock
Totals		687	226	

Notes and sources:
This table draws upon the following sources: "Intelligence," in Gov. William Tryon of New York to William Legge, 2nd Earl of Dartmouth, Sec. of State for the Colonies, 11 Feb. 1776, CO 5/1107, PRO (Stevens Trans.); "Arrangement of Officers and Men, of the Marines, on board the American Fleet," *The Correspondence of Esek Hopkins, Commander-in-Chief of the United States Navy,* ed. Alverda S. Beck (Providence, RI, 1933), p. 85; Nicholas Biddle to James Biddle, 15 Feb. 1776, Nicholas Biddle Papers, 1771–1776, HSP, as published in "The Letters of Nicholas Biddle," ed. William Bell Clark, *Pennsylvania Magazine of History and Biography,* LXXIV (July 1950), 381; "A Journal of a Cruize in the Brig *Andrew Doria* Nicholas Biddle Esqr. Commander from the Port of Philadelphia, Begun January 4th 1776," 18 Feb. 1776, enclosure in Vice Admiral Molyneux Shuldham to Philip Stevens, 8 July 1776, Adm. 1/484, pt ii, PRO (Stevens Trans.); Commodore Esek Hopkins to John Hancock, 8 Apr. 1776, *The Letter Book of Esek Hopkins, Commander-in-Chief of the United States Navy, 1775–1777,* ed. Alverda S. Beck (Providence, RI, 1932), p. 47; Letter of Capt. Samuel Nicholas, New London, 10 Apr. 1776, in *Thomas's Massachusetts Spy Or, American Oracle of Liberty* (Worcester), 10 May 1776; "A List of Ships and Vessels fitted out by the Rebels at Philadelphia," in Basil Keith, at Jamaica, to Lord George Germain, 14 Apr. 1776, CO 137/71, PRO (photostat, LC). The figures for the number of sailors and marines involved are, and can only be, approximations based on, in some cases, vastly contradictory statements.

until the arrival of British troops in 1779 forced them to stop.[19] However short-lived such stances may have been, at least at first there seems to have been some support for the American cause among many island residents.[20]

Whether, in the Bahamas, such sympathy extended to include an explicit

19 *The Annual Register . . . for the Year 1775* (London, 1776), pp. 62, 102; Alan Burns, *History of the British West Indies* (London, 1954), p. 518; Wilfred Breton Kerr, *Bermuda and the American Revolution, 1760–1783* (Princeton, NJ, 1936), pp. 38–50; Lewis [B.] Namier, *England in the Age of the American Revolution,* 2nd edn (London, 1961), p. 240; J[ohn] [W.] Fortescue, *A History of the British Army,* 13 vols in 19 pts (London, 1899–1930), III, 260, and Kerr, op. cit., p. 86.
20 See in this regard the work of Andrew J. O"Shaughnessy growing out of his thesis, "The Politics of the Leeward Islands, 1763–1783" (Ph.D. diss., University of Oxford, 1987).

invitation to the Americans to come to Nassau for the gunpowder and stores there, as the Bermudans had done in August of 1775, remains unsettled. Both the Chief Justice and the Governor of the Bahamas charged that certain individuals had invited invasion, Thomas Atwood complaining "that this whole affair has been brought upon us by the treachery of some few individuals" and Governor Montfort Browne stating that "the Americans were invited here," but neither offered proof of his accusations. From the American side, there were numerous possible ways for Congress to have learned about the gunpowder supply other than from Bahamian sources. Yet the welcome reception afforded the invaders by the people of Nassau leaves them open to charges of complicity. While the presently available evidence is not sufficient to justify unqualified acceptance of Browne's accusation, still the possibility of Bahamian connivance is very likely.[21]

Invited or not, the Americans were sailing southward toward New Providence during the final two weeks of February 1776. Commodore Hopkins' orders for reorganizing the squadron after the voyage show at least that he was considering an attack upon the island. When he directed the captains of any of his ships that might become separated from the fleet "to make the best of your way to the Southern part of Abacco (one of the Bahama Islands)," it is likely that he was thinking of the anchorage called then "Hole-in-the-Rock" and today "Hole-in-the-Wall," which he probably remembered from previous voyages into the area. Situated at 25° 51' north, 77° 10' west, Hole-in-the-Wall "is an archway" in "a small narrow tongue of low flat rock" that projects "about 300 yards from the southeast end" of Great Abaco Island, approximately fifty miles north of the town of Nassau (see figure 12.2). This was a logical rendezvous point for a fleet intent upon a descent upon New Providence, for it provided a well-known landmark and a semi-protected anchorage quite close by his destination. From there to Nassau harbor was but a short, direct sail.[22]

There is also strong evidence to suggest that Commodore Hopkins had an attack upon New Providence as his object right from the time he left the Delaware. Some authors have taken the position that Hopkins was merely

---

21 Kerr, *Bermuda and the American Revolution*, pp. 42–54; Atwood to Dartmouth, 22 Mar. 1776, Browne to Germain, 5 Nov. 1776 and 1 Apr. 1777, CO 23/23, PRO; Browne to the Council and General Assembly of the Bahamas, 15 Mar. 1779, CO 23/24, PRO. (William Legge, 2nd Earl of Dartmouth, was Sec. of State for the Colonies from Aug. 1772 to Nov. 1775; Lord George [Sackville] Germain succeeded him until 1782.) Browne's later accusations came when he was trying to reestablish his own authority over the islands. Opinions on Bahamian culpability vary from the statement of Michael Craton that "with certainty ... there is no evidence at this end of Hopkins being summoned by disloyal Bahamians" (letter to the author, Nassau, NP, 9 Aug. 1961) to Alan Burns's ready acceptance of Browne's charge (*History of the British West Indies*, p. 519).

22 *Letter Book of Esek Hopkins*, ed. Beck, p. 44; Samuel Eliot Morison, *John Paul Jones: A Sailor's Biography* (Boston, 1959), p. 45; Field, *Hopkins*, pp. 11, 113; [US, Department of the Navy], *Sailing Directions for the West Indies, Hydrographic Office Publications*, no. 128, 2 vols (Washington, DC, 1951), I, 55. See fig. 12.2.

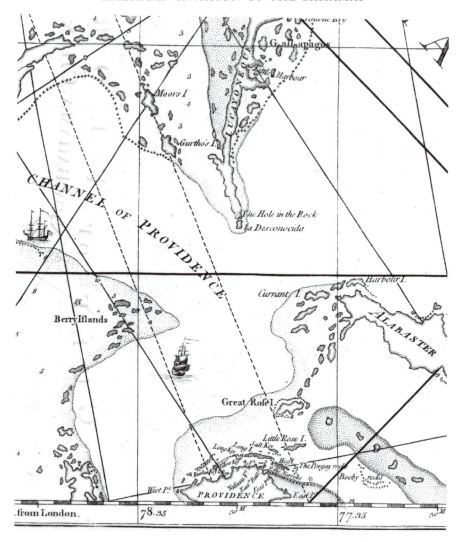

Figure 12.2 "Channel of Providence."

Note: The names of Hog Island (modern Paradise Island) and Long Island (modern Athol Island) are interchanged. Both "Nassau Ft." and the "East[er]n Batt[er]y" (Fort Montagu) are indicated; the depth of water off the latter is given as eight feet.

Source: The portion of the map illustrated is from Plate 4, "The Peninsula and Gulf of Florida, and the Bahama Islands," in Thomas Jefferys, *The West-India Atlas: or, A Compendious Description of the West Indies: Illustrated with Forty Correct Charts and Maps, Taken from Actual Surveys. Together with an Historical Account of the Several Countries and Islands Which Compose that Part of the World* (London, 1775). By permission of the British Library, London.

"an old privateering freebooter" out for "plunder rather than strategic objects and futile glory."[23] The actions of Lieutenant Hoysteed Hacker of the schooner *Fly* subsequent to getting to sea clearly show, however, that when Hopkins found it impossible to obey the commands of Congress, he definitely resolved upon a new and very strategic goal, the gunpowder and stores in the forts on New Providence. Soon after leaving Delaware Bay two of the smaller ships under Hopkins' command became separated from the fleet. On Monday, 19 February, two days out from Cape Henlopen, the sloop *Hornet* and the schooner *Fly* collided in "Hard gales and thick Weather," forcing *Hornet* to return to port for repairs. Lieutenant Hacker continued south after a delay but was too late for the rendezvous at Hole-in-the-Wall. Unable to find the fleet there, on 11 March he sailed *Fly* into Nassau harbor, indicating rather certainly that the ship commanders knew from the time they left Delaware Bay that Nassau was the objective of their cruise.[24]

Knowledge of the destination of this first American fleet was not limited to the captains of Commodore Hopkins' ships, however. Eight days after they had sailed and precisely a week before Hopkins' marines were to splash ashore, on 25 February, Captain Andrew Law, "an officer in His Majesty's Land Service," arrived at Nassau with the news that off Cape Delaware a fleet of eight warships was assembling whose "destination was against this Island."[25] The British had been aware of the preparations going on at Philadelphia for some time but each succeeding rumor varied the destination of Hopkin's fleet. It was as often reported to be going to New York City or Boston as anywhere else. The arrival of such news seems to have caused little stir and absolutely no preparations at Nassau.[26]

23 Fletcher Pratt, *The Navy: A History* (Garden City, NY, 1938), p. 6.
24 Esek Hopkins to John Hancock, 8 Apr. 1776, in *Letter Book of Esek Hopkins*, ed. Beck, p. 47; "A Journal of a Cruise In the Brig *Andrew Doria* Nicholas Biddle Esqr Commander from the Port of Philadelphia, Begun January 4th, 1776," 18 Feb. 1776, enclosure in Vice Admiral Molyneux Shuldham to Philip Stevens, 8 July 1776, Adm. 1/484, pt ii, PRO (Stevens Trans.) – hereafter cited as "Journal of the *Andrew Doria*." This journal was kept by Lt. James Josiah of *Andrew Doria*, it was retained by him when he later shipped aboard another vessel, and was captured with him when that ship fell into British hands later in the year. It is printed in Neeser, ed., *Despatches of Molyneux Shuldham*, pp. 275–305. Philip Stephens was Secretary to the Admiralty from 1763 to 1795.

   For the story of the *Hornet* after it separated from the fleet, see William Bell Clark, *Gallant John Barry, 1745–1803: The Story of a Naval Hero of Two Wars* (New York, 1938), pp. 77–78, 84, 88–92.
25 This information, and much besides, is recorded in "A Narrative of the Transactions &c, on the Invasion of the Island of New Providence by the Rebels in 1776," that was included in a letter sent from Nassau to George Germain by John Gambier, and four members of the Council, John Brown, Samuel Gambier, Robert Hunt, and Robert Sterling, on 31 Mar. 1779, CO 23/24, PRO. The letter and its enclosures were intended to vindicate the role of the Nassauvians during the invasion in reply to the charges leveled by Gov. Montfort Browne. Craton, *History of the Bahamas*, p. 139, reports the man's name as "Shaw."
26 Intelligence reports in Shuldham to Stephens, 19 Jan. and 8 Mar. 1776, Adm. 1/484, pt ii, PRO (Stevens Trans.), and in Gov. William Tryon of New York to Dartmouth, 5 Jan.

Not that one would have expected much activity in this remote colonial capital. Nassau was, as it is today, the administrative center of the Bahama Islands. It was home for most of the approximately 1,500 inhabitants of the island, about half of whom were of African origin if the colony-wide proportion held true for New Providence. It had had a checkered history, the frequent base of pirate squadrons and the goal of many a Spanish raiding party. Its chroniclers can tell of Blackbeard's well and how the Spanish are supposed to have roasted Governor Robert Clark "on a Spit after they had killed him."[27] The German doctor, Johann David Schöpf, who visited the

1776, and Tryon to Germain, 28 Apr. 1776, CO 5/1107, PRO (Stevens Trans.); see also, Lord North to Sandwich, 9 Jan. 1776, *Private Papers . . . Earl of Sandwich*, ed. Barnes and Owen, I, 207. Perhaps this inaction resulted from what had happened the previous fall. In Aug. 1775, General Thomas Gage, probably inspired by rumors of the disloyal behavior of the Bermudans, had sent to have the powder and stores removed from the Bahamas to Boston. Gov. Browne was away when Capt. John Linzie of HMS *Falcon* presented Gage's order and the Bahamas Council protested loudly that such an action would leave the colony defenseless. Besides, they declared, being loyal subjects they were prepared to defend His Majesty's forts and stores "against any lawless Attacks whatsoever." Gage must have been convinced or at least he thought all danger passed for not only did he not insist, but that same fall he ordered the Bahamian detachment of the Fourteenth Regiment to Boston. Brown to Dartmouth, 7 Nov. 1775, enclosing Gage to Browne, 29 Aug. 1775, the Minutes of the Bahama Islands Council, 26–27 Sept. 1775, and Brown to Gage, 29 Sept. 1775, CO 23/23, PRO. John Brown was President of His Majesty's Council.

This whole incident was later to be cast in a more sinister light by George Germain. Yet Germain's easy reasoning from "the refusal of the President and Council to deliver the ordinance to General Gage's order" to his conclusion that this was part "of a plot they had concerted with the rebels for putting . . . [the stores] into their hands" fails to convince. Not only is his logic faulty but his charges do not stand up in the face of the loyal efforts of the Council President after the invasion to restore royal government to the colony. Brown kept London informed on the state of the islands, tried several times to have a navy ship stationed at Nassau, and even went so far as to pay for repairs for the forts out of his own pocket. Germain to Browne, 14 July 1777, CO 23/23, PRO; Brown to Germain, 2 May 1776 and 10 May 1777, CO 23/23, PRO, 6 Sept. and 22 Jan. 1778, CO 23/24, PRO; Brown to Vice-Admiral Richard Howe, 10 July and 31 July 1777, CO 23/24, PRO; Brown to Vice-Admiral Clark Gayton, 22 Mar. 1776, in Basil Keith to Germain, 14 Apr. 1776, CO 137/71, PRO (photostat, LC); John Gambier to Germain, 12 Dec. 1778, CO 23/24, PRO. Howe was Commander of the North American Station, Gayton was Commander of the Jamaica Station, Keith was the Governor of Jamaica, and Gambier was Lieutenant Governor of the Bahamas from Jan. to Dec. 1778.

Gov. Browne, when he returned to the island late in 1778, tried to capitalize on Germain's earlier suspicions and stirred up a hornet's nest by accusing everyone in sight, including Brown and Gambier, of treason. The Bahamians countered by charging him with criminal negligence in the surrender to the Americans. Browne's efforts reaped only his own summary recall to London. Gambier to Germain, 27 Feb. 1779, and Gambier *et al.* to Germain, 31 Mar. 1779, CO 23/24, PRO; Germain to Browne, 28 Aug. 1779, CO 5/8, PRO.

27 Browne to Dartmouth, 6 May 1775, CO 23/23, PRO; Evarts B. Greene and Virginia D. Harrington, *American Population before the Federal Census of 1790* (New York, 1932), [p. xxiii]; total population of the colony in 1773 was 2,052 whites and 2,241 blacks. Thomas Southey, *Chronological History of the West Indies*, 3 vols (London, 1827), II, 414, 415, 417; John Oldmixon, *The British Empire in America, Containing the History . . . of All the British Colonies on the Continent and Islands of America*, 2nd edn, 2 vols (London, 1741), II, 424 (quotation). See also Burns, *History of the British West Indies*, p. 361, n. 3.

island in 1784 and left about the only early account of a trip there, described it as the "little town Nassau which hugs the hilly shore." In true Baedeker-like fashion, Schöpf went into great detail about the harbor, the town, the buildings, and the inhabitants of this sleepy island settlement (see figure 12.3).

> The houses are of wood, all lightly built and of simple construction; according to the needs of the climate here, attention has been given only to roof, shade, space, and air . . . There is but one tolerably regular street, or line of houses, which runs next to the water. . . . A church, a goal, and an Assembly-house make up the public buildings of the town . . . There is no pavement in the town, but none is needed, since the streets, like the island, are almost wholly stone. The inhabitants of the town of Nassau are a few royal officials, divers merchants, ship-builders and carpenters, skippers, pilots, fishermen, and what laborers are needed . . . The real planters . . . live near the town on their estates.

Schöpf had difficulty finding accommodations because of the recent influx of a new group, the "*Refugies*" from North America. These were, of course, the Loyalists, arriving to start a new life in the Bahamas. Had the Bahamians been more prepared for their American visitors in 1776, they might have afforded their German tourist better housing eight years later. As it was, their week of grace went to no avail. The Americans were at hand.[28]

On 1 March 1776 the six remaining ships of Commodore Hopkins' fleet (less *Hornet* and *Fly*) assembled some fifty miles to the north northeast of Nassau, off Hole-in-the-Wall. Sharing the anchorage were two sloops from Nassau that *Alfred* had captured earlier near Great Abaco. The two captains of these vessels were impressed as pilots and brought on board the flagship at Hopkins' command where they were questioned about affairs on New Providence Island. Hopkins was probably told both of the recent departure from Nassau of His Majesty's sloop of war *Savage*, eighteen guns, that had been called to New York, and of General Gage's withdrawal to Boston of the detachment of the Fourteenth Regiment formerly stationed in Fort Nassau. They could also have told him of the sorry state of the one vestige of the royal armed forces left at Nassau, His Majesty's schooner *St. John*, eight guns, Lieutenant William Grant commanding, which was in desperate need of an overhaul. *St. John* was in no shape to put up any resistance and the forts which a year earlier the Governor Montfort Browne had estimated would require 140 men to defend adequately were now deserted. If there

---

28 Johann David Schöpf, *Travels in the Confederation,* trans. Alfred J. Morrison, 2 vols (Philadelphia, 1911), II, 262–265, from Schöpf, *Reise durch Einige der mittlern und südlichen Vereinigten Nordamerikanischen Staten, nach Ost-Florida und den Bahama Inslem Unternommen in den Jahren 1783 und 1784,* 2 vols (Erlangen, 1788), II, 412–415. See the detailed "Plan of the Town and Harbour of New Providence in the Bahamas," by John Montresor, dated 1770, CO 5/88, fol. 252, PRO. It shows every property in the town and indicates the name of every owner.

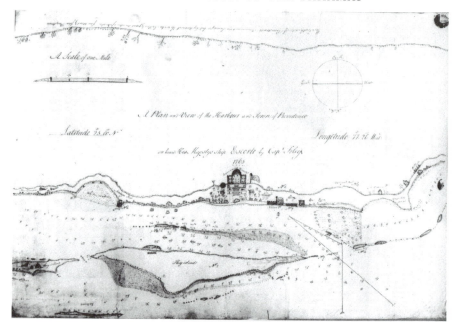

Figure 12.3 "A Plan and view of the harbour and town of Providence." This was made as part of a hydrographic survey of the Bahamas by Captain Thomas Foley in 1765. North is to the bottom of the map. The building given such prominence is Government House, the Governor's residence. Notice the location of "Nassau Fo.", "Montagu Fort", and "New Guinea."
Courtesy of the United Kingdom, Ministry of Defence, Hydrographic Office, Taunton, Somerset.

had been any doubts lingering in Hopkins' mind, such news must surely have dispersed them.[29]

Commodore Hopkins would have been further encouraged had he known of the unenergetic and indecisive character of Bahamian leadership. On the day that the fleet rendezvoused off Great Abaco, Governor Browne was made aware, for the second time, of their approach, and once again he did nothing.

29 "Journal of the *Andrew Doria*," 18 Feb. 1776; Sands, ed., *Life . . . of . . . Jones*, p. 35; letter of "Capt. of Marines, on board the ship *Alfred*," [Samuel Nicholas], at New London, Conn., 10 Apr. 1776, in *Thomas's Massachusetts Spy Or, American Oracle of Liberty* (Worcester), 10 May 1776, and as printed in *American Archives: . . . a Documentary History of . . . the North American Colonies; of . . . the American Revolution; and of the Constitution of the Government of the United States . . .*, ed. Peter Force, 9 vols ([Washington, DC, 1837–1853]), 4th ser., V, 846–847 – hereafter cited as "Samuel Nicholas Letter"; Browne to Germain, 5 Nov. 1776, CO 23/23, PRO. See also, "Disposition of His Majesty's Ships and Vessels in North America under the Command of Rear Admiral Shuldham," in Shuldham to Stephens, 23 Mar. 1776, Adm. 1/484, pt ii, PRO (Stevens Trans.). A year earlier the "Monthly Return of Capt Wm Blackells Company of his Majesty's 14th Regt"

In the afternoon of 1 March Captain George Dorsett brought the news of the presence of the fleet near "the Island of Abaco" but Browne, curiously, asked Dorsett to keep his information to himself. As he had already been told that the destination of the fleet was Nassau, why he acted in such an irresponsible manner is hard to understand. Certainly, as his critics later charged, had Browne reacted properly to this information "Martial Law might have been proclaimed, the Arms & Accouterments of the Militia examined, and there defects remedied; the Forts put in a condition of defense, & supplied with those Articles which from a long Peace were deficient, and a mode of defense considered and determined upon." Yet perhaps Browne feared that if he armed the militia too soon he might invite a rising of American sympathizers. Or maybe, as Michael Craton speculates, Browne "hoped that if he ignored trouble it would go away." In any case, Browne's later complaints that some of his fellow Bahamians in this time of emergency were "Backward in their assistance" appear ludicrous in the light of his own ostrich-like attitude.[30]

The next day, Saturday, 2 March, the fleet began preparations for the attack. The guns were exercised, the rigging checked, and muskets and ammunition issued to the marines who were then transferred from on board their several ships to the two captured sloops and *Providence*. Some time during that night the whole fleet weighed anchor and made sail for New Providence. The plan was for the fleet proper, except for the three sloops with the marines on board, to hang back and stay out of sight of land. Meanwhile the other three ships, as day dawned, were to sail right into the harbor of Nassau with the marines hidden below deck until they "got in Close to the Fort – and then they were to land Instantly & take possession before the Island could be alarmed."[31]

The island of New Providence had two forts at this period (see figure 12.3). As Schöpf pointed out, "the harbor of Providence is formed and protected by a small island, called Hog island, lying to the north." Because of this, he continued, "there are two approaches to the harbor, one to the east, and the other to the west." As Schöpf went on to mention, and as the Bahamians themselves were only too aware, these two entrances to the harbor of Nassau had proved a problem in defense. A fort, Fort Nassau, which had

---

for 1 May 1775, listed one captain, one surgeon, two "Sergeants," and 18 privates (14 present, 4 absent), CO 23/23, PRO. Shuldham to Stephens, 16 Apr. 1776, Adm. 1/484, pt ii, PRO (Stevens Trans.); Browne to Dartmouth, 6 May 1775, CO 23/23, PRO.

30 "Deposition by George Dorsett," in Gambier *et al.* to Germain, 31 Mar. 1779, CO 23/24, PRO; Gambier *et al.* to Germain, 31 Mar. 1779, CO 23/24, PRO; Craton, *History of the Bahamas*, p. 140; Browne to Germain, 5 Nov. 1776, CO 23/23, PRO.

31 "Journal of the *Andrew Doria*," 18 Feb. 1776; Clark, *Captain Dauntless*, p. 105; Brown to Germain, 2 May 1776, CO 23/23, PRO; quotation from John Paul Jones, [on board *Alfred*, New London, Conn.], to Joseph Hewes, 14 Apr. 1776, John Paul Jones Manuscripts, 1775–1788, Peter Force Papers, LC, and as printed in John Henry Sherburne, *The Life and Character of the Chevalier John Paul Jones* (Washington, DC, 1825), pp. 11–14.

been first built in 1697, protected the western entrance to the harbor. Subsequently the islanders had been attacked many times from the east and as a result a second fort, Fort Montagu, was built in 1742. Peter Henry Bruce, its architect, stated that its purpose was to shut up "the back door through which the place often had been surprised." Since 1744, when Fort Nassau was considerably rebuilt by Bruce, little had been done to keep the fortification in repair. Governor Browne had reported in 1775 that even though Fort Nassau was well supplied with cannon – "46 pieces of twelve and eighteen pounders" – it was indefensible for practical purposes because the walls were so weak that he dared not fire the guns. It was even necessary, he stated, to employ a small cannon at the main gate as a signal gun. At that time he estimated that the necessary "Repair may be made & the Forts supplied with what they want, for £1000 Sterling."[32]

Fort Nassau suffered even more seriously from a very poor strategic location. High hills to the south overlooked the fort "within Musquet shot." The Governor's house, located upon this commanding ridge, was so prominent that it served "as a landmark to in-coming ships," and the small cannon there could be played with telling effect upon Fort Nassau, as Browne himself noted (see figure 12.3). The Americans in 1776 were quick to realize this, as was the British Colonel Andrew Deveaux when, in April 1783, he recaptured New Providence from the Spanish by gaining control of this very ridge.[33]

Fort Montagu suffered from no such topographical disadvantage. In fact it had, and has still today, a rather beautiful setting, situated at the eastern end of the harbor on a deep cove guarding that entrance to the port. A small square structure, built of native stone, at the time of Commodore Hopkins' arrival it was fitted with seventeen cannon, twelve- and eighteen-pounders. Governor John Tinker, in 1742, was eminently pleased with the new Fort Montagu and he felt that, properly defended, it would make the Bahamas "the strongest possession in British America."[34]

32 Schöpf, *Travels*, II, 262, 263; [Bede Clifford], *Historic Forts of Nassau in the Bahamas*, 2nd edn (Nassau, NP, 1952), pp. 8, 27; Peter Henry Bruce, *The Memoirs of Peter Henry Bruce* (London, 1782), p. 398; Browne to Dartmouth, 6 May 1775, CO 23/23, PRO. For the armaments of Fort Nassau, see also *The Correspondence of Esek Hopkins, Commander-in-Chief of the United States Navy*, ed. Alverda S. Beck (Providence, RI, 1933), p. 35, *American Archives*, ed. Force, 4th ser., V, 824, and *Correspondence of George III*, ed. Fortescue, III, 213.

33 "Directions to Sail into Providence Harbour," no. 8, to accompany "A Plan and View of the Harbour and Town of Providence," Capt. Thomas Foley, 1765, Vz 10/24, Hydrographic Office, The Admiralty Library, Ministry of Defence, Taunton, Somerset; "Samuel Nicholas Letter"; "Extract of a letter from Colonel [Andrew] Deveaux, to Sir Guy Carleton dated New Providence, June 6, 1783," *The Annual Register . . . for the Year 1783* (London, 1784), pp. 260–262. See also Craton, *History of the Bahamas*, pp. 146–147. There are slightly variant copies of the Foley materials in MPG 14, 15, 16, and 1066, PRO (extracted from CO 23/18, PRO). See also "A Particular Plan of the Forts Nassau and Montagu," by John Montresor, dated 18 Aug. 1770, at CO 5/88, fol. 255, PRO.

34 "Samuel Nicholas Letter"; "Return of Ordinance & Military Stores at Fort Montague New Providence 5th May 1775," CO 23/23, PRO. Compare *Correspondence of Esek Hopkins*,

Commodore Hopkins' original plan for attacking these forts was a good one given his knowledge of affairs on New Providence. Through some miscalculation, however, instead of just the sloops approaching Nassau harbor, the whole fleet suddenly appeared "a little to the windward of the Bar" quite early on Sunday morning, 3 March 1776. Governor Browne was quickly roused from his bed and hurried to the door of Government House still dressed in his sleeping gown. What he saw on the morning horizon caused him to have the alarm sounded immediately – three cannon shots – and the drum beat to call out the militia. He also sent word to the various members of the council, summoning them to meet him at Fort Nassau without delay. About seven o'clock, Samuel Gambier, brother of the Nassauvian John Gambier who had been acting Governor of the colony from 1758 to 1760 and a twenty-year member of the council, rode into the fort to find Browne still, presumably, in his nightshirt and near panic. Fearing its capture, Browne was considering sending off the gunpowder in the fast sloop of Captain William Chambers, *Mississippi Packet*, which was sitting partly loaded with Bahamian lumber in the nearby harbor. Gambier wondered out loud if the powder would not be needed in the defense of the town? The Governor looked around at the assembling but mostly unarmed militia, at the one crumbling bastion of the fort and at the two cannon that had fired his alarm earlier and that had been blown off their mountings in the process and hesitatingly agreed. Meanwhile, he suggested, Captain Chambers could be sent out to scout the ships in an attempt to learn their intentions. Adverse winds kept Chambers from getting too far, however, and he was forced to return no wiser than when he had set out. By this time it was obvious that the fleet was not about to storm the harbor and so, after ordering thirty of the assembled militia to Fort Montagu, Browne, "saying that he would just go home, & make himself a little decent," retired again to Government House.[35]

The sound of Governor Browne's signal cannon had echoed across the water and Commodore Hopkins realized that his ships had been spotted. The chance for a surprise attack had been lost, probably because the very winds that kept Captain Chambers close to shore had, in the false light of dawn, propelled the Americans faster and farther than they had planned. To attempt now to force their way over the bar, down the channel, and into the harbor under the guns of the fort would be foolhardy. So, at Hopkins' signal, the fleet "suddenly tacked, and stood toward the East." "At 10 A.M.

---

ed. Beck, p. 35; and John Tinker to the Duke of Montagu, 28 Aug. 1742, printed in Bruce, *Memoirs*, pp. 398–399. See the "Particular Plan of the Forts Nassau and Montagu," by John Montresor, dated 1770, at CO 5/88, fol. 255, PRO.

35 Brown to Gayton, 22 Mar. 1776, in Keith to Germain, 14 Apr. 1776, CO 137/71, PRO (photostat, LC); Atwood to Dartmouth, 22 Mar. 1776, CO 23/23, PRO; "Narrative of . . . the Invasion," in Gambier *et al.* to Germain, 31 Mar. 1779, CO 23/24, PRO.

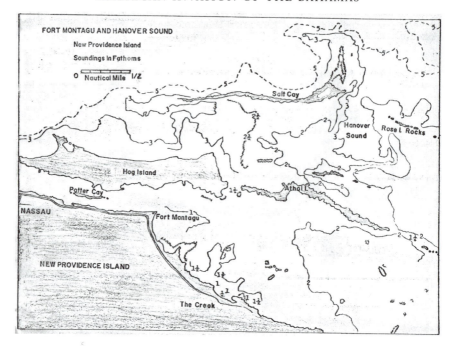

Figure 12.4 Fort Montagu and Hanover Sound, New Providence Island. This map shows the eastern end of New Providence and the surrounding islands with Hanover Sound. It is based on [United States, Department of the Navy, Hydrographic Office], *New Providence Island*, H[ydrographic] O[ffice] [Chart no.] 1377, 21st edn, revised (Washington, DC, 1961). Courtesy of the author.

[they] came too under Roze Island," at an anchorage called Hanover Sound, about six miles east of Nassau harbor (see figure 12.4).[36]

At first Commodore Hopkins had considered proceeding to the west end of the island and attempting to march the marines from there to the rear of the town. The lack of a suitable place to anchor, the fact that there was no road from that end of the island to town, and the time such a maneuver would give the defenders to prepare deterred him. Instead, apparently on the basis of information that John Paul Jones, who was then First Lieutenant on board the flagship, had acquired from the captured pilots, Hopkins chose to go to Hanover Sound. According to Jones, it was he who guided the fleet into the anchorage from the "fore-topmast-head" of *Alfred*.[37]

36 Brown to Gayton, 22 Mar. 1776, in Keith to Germain, 14 Apr. 1776, CO 137/71, PRO (photostat, LC); Atwood to Dartmouth, 22 Mar. 1776, CO 23/23, PRO; "Narrative of the Invasion," in Gambier *et al.* to Germain, 31 Mar. 1779, CO 23/24, PRO; Gambier to Germain, 27 Feb. 1779, CO 23/24, PRO. See fig. 12.2.
37 Sands, ed., *Life . . . of . . . Jones*, pp. 35–36; Morison, *Jones*, p. 46; Clark, *Captain Dauntless*, p. 105; Field, *Hopkins*, pp. 11, 113.

Having reached Hanover Sound it became necessary to resolve upon a new plan of action. After some consultation on board the flagship, no doubt involving Second Lieutenant Thomas Weaver of *Cabot* who was familiar with New Providence, a decision was made to try a landing on the east shore of the island and to attempt to storm Fort Montagu there. The "back door" to Nassau was to be tried, probably at the suggestion of Lieutenant Weaver, who certainly could have recalled earlier Spanish attacks on the island by this means. Commodore Hopkins gave Weaver command of fifty sailors to augment Captain Samuel Nicholas's force of some 220 marines and he sent the schooner *Wasp* to help cover with its eight guns, this first amphibious assault in Marine Corps history. The rest of the fleet remained anchored in Hanover Sound.[38]

Sometime around noon the sailors and marines splashed ashore on a beach about a mile and a half south and east of Fort Montagu at a place called "the Creek." Nearby, to the north, stood a small cluster of shacks, the homes of some of the free blacks and mulattos of New Providence, appropriately named New Guinea. At first these poor people thought the invading Americans to be the perennial Spanish raiders and they grew quite excited, expecting most likely to be taken prisoner and sold into slavery. Except for the residents of New Guinea the landing was unopposed and Captain Nicholas had all his men on shore by about two o'clock. This absence of immediate opposition was fortunate for the Americans, since Nicholas's marines had by this time been cooped up aboard the three sloops for almost a whole day without, as he said, either "a convenience to sleep or cook in."[39]

Word of the invasion was brought to Fort Nassau soon thereafter but Governor Browne still had not returned. When he did arrive about noon, "presumably now dressed out in his full uniform," he complained "that he had had a violent fit of Cholick, which had detained him so long." He was told that it appeared that men were coming ashore in large numbers somewhere below Fort Montagu, and he then sent word there ordering Lieutenant Burke out "to reconnoitre and if possible to prevent" the landing. The original force of thirty men sent to Fort Montagu early in the morning had been reinforced about ten o'clock by another detachment of equal size in response to a report that ships had been seen in the distance. Half of this total complement was now formed up into a small scouting party under Lieutenants Burke and Judkin. They left the fort and advanced toward the enemy beachhead, somewhat less than two miles below, to meet the foe. Just about the whole of the American force must have been drawn up on the beach when

38 Hopkins to Hancock, 8 Apr. 1776, *Letter Book of Esek Hopkins*, ed. Beck, p. 47; "Samuel Nicholas Letter"; table 12.1.
39 Atwood to Dartmouth, 22 Mar. 1776, CO 23/23, PRO; "Samuel Nicholas Letter"; Schöpf, *Travels*, II, 264. See also fig. 12.2.
    Southey, *Chronological History of the West Indies*, II, 417, noted that the population count in 1773 had omitted any indication of free African-Americans, even though the one in 1734 had mentioned 77 of them among the population. A report in 1787 stated that the colony's population included 100 free blacks. CO 318/2, fol. 24r, PRO.

they arrived, however, and there was little that they could do. The size of the contingent already ashore precluded little more than reconnaissance. A man was sent under a flag of truce to inquire who the invaders were and what their object was. When the reply came back that "they were sent by the Congress of the United Colonies in order to possess themselves of the powder and stores belonging to his Majesty," Lieutenant Burke returned with the militia in the direction of the fort without either side firing a shot.[40]

Governor Browne, in the meanwhile, had arrived at Fort Montagu, with about eighty more of his militia to reinforce the garrison. He immediately ordered Captain Walker, Lieutenant Pratt, and Ensign Barrett forward with forty more men to reinforce Burke and Judkin. This second group met the first retreating, however, and they all retired to the fort. The return of his two detachments and Lieutenants Burke and Judkin's reports about the size of the enemy force, which Governor Browne could see in the distance massing on the beach, finally convinced him that his position was precarious. With the Americans beginning to move in the direction of Fort Montagu he realized that unless he acted quickly he could be outflanked and cut off from town. Even if he and his men could withstand a siege in Fort Montagu, the town and the fort there would be the Americans' for the taking. As the last of his returning militia entered the fort, Browne instructed that three cannon be fired in the direction of the approaching enemy. He then marched the entire company to Fort Nassau, leaving two men behind in the now deserted fort with orders to spike the cannon at the first sign of the Americans' approach.[41]

Here Governor Browne lost his best opportunity to stop the Americans and foil the invasion – or, at least, so ran Bahamian charges against him later. As one Nassauvian recalled it, "the Rebels disembarked their Men . . . on a spot the most disadvantageous for them that can be conceived as there is but one passage [from there] to the Town." This path ran "thro a rugged narrow way, one side open to the Sea, & within range of the Guns of Fort Montagu, and on the other closed by an impenetrable Wood." Browne's critic felt that

> had a few Breast Works been thrown up across this road (the materials proper for which, vizt. loose stones & high Trees are always at hand) this Pass might have been defended with a very inconsiderable number of men against double the force of the Rebels.

As we have seen, however, matters were not that simple and by the time Browne arrived at Fort Montagu the weather gauge had been lost to the

---

40 Craton, *History of the Bahamas*, p. 141; "Narrative of . . . the Invasion," in Gambier *et al.* to Germain, 31 Mar. 1779, CO 23/24, PRO; Atwood to Dartmouth, 22 Mar. 1776, CO 23/23, PRO; "Samuel Nicholas Letter"; Brown to Gayton, 22 Mar. 1776, in Keith to Germain, 14 Apr. 1776, CO 137/71, PRO (photostat, LC).

41 Atwood to Dartmouth, 22 Mar. 1776, CO 23/23, PRO; Brown to Gayton, 22 Mar. 1776, in Keith to Germain, 14 Apr. 1776, CO 137/71, PRO (photostat, LC); "Narrative of . . . the Invasion," in Gambier *et al.* to Germain, 31 Mar. 1779, CO 23/24, PRO.

enemy. Faced with the probability that the Americans would bypass him and march directly to the town, Browne had little choice but to do as he did. Certainly it was his late arrival at the fort that lost the initiative for the Nassauvians and for this he can be blamed. Nevertheless his tactics once there seem sound. Any attempt to build earthworks at that late hour would surely have been met with overwhelming resistance from the Americans. In this instance, anyhow, retreat was the better part of valor.[42]

Whatever the wisdom in Governor Browne's decision to pull back to Fort Nassau, the immediate result was the almost total dispersion of his militia. The men must all have realized that their removal to the western garrison left the town open to the enemy. Each had to look to his own and that was what they did. Man after man scurried to his home, packed up the family treasure and the family too, and bundled all on their way to the interior of the island and safety. Yet remarkably few men followed their families. In a short time most of the militia had reassembled at Fort Nassau. By three o'clock, however, the crisis had past, and Browne had recovered his composure enough to take command again.[43]

At this juncture Governor Browne's most pressing need was to discover the disposition and plans of the enemy. Almost naïvely forthright, he chose the most direct way to find out. He sent a man to inquire. What is even more difficult to believe is that the Americans obliged him.

Captain Nicholas had cautiously halted his column at the firing of the three cannon from Fort Montagu and, thinking it still occupied, consulted with his officers and Lieutenant Weaver "what was to be done." They were apparently still conferring when Lieutenant Burke again approached, about four o'clock in the afternoon. He came this time at Governor Browne's explicit order "to wait on the Commanding Officer of the Enemy to know his Errand and on what account he had landed his troops." Burke met with John Trevett, the First Lieutenant of the marines from on board *Columbus*, who acted as Nicholas's emissary. He delivered the Governor's message, adding, almost apologetically, evidently in reply to an American remonstrance, "that it was by the Governor's order" that the cannon had been fired. Fort Montagu, he hastened to continue, now stood deserted and defenseless, and was the Americans' merely for the marching. Nicholas had Trevett tell Burke that they were only after the military stores on the island and announce to him that he would be seeing the Governor in the morning. With that the weary Americans took possession of Fort Montagu and prepared to spend the night there.[44]

Thus made aware of the enemy's plans, Governor Browne could more leisurely

42 Gambier *et al.* to Germain, 31 Mar. 1779, CO 23/24, PRO.
43 "Narrative of . . . the Invasion," in Gambier *et al.* to Germain, 31 Mar. 1779, CO 23/24, PRO.
44 "Samuel Nicholas Letter"; Atwood to Dartmouth, 22 Mar. 1776, CO 23/23, PRO; John Trevett, "Journal of John Trevett, U.S.N., 1774–1782," *Rhode Island Historical Magazine*, VI (July 1885), 73.

contemplate his next move. The threat of immediate assault had disappeared with the welcome addition of at least twelve hours' grace. He remembered the vulnerability of Fort Nassau to an enemy in control of the commanding ridge above and behind it and he despatched Captain Thomas Hodgson and Ensign Barrett with forty men to Government House to retain possession of that vantage point and not incidentally to protect his personal property and his "Dear wife and aged Aunt." His fears for this ridge were well founded for one of Captain Nicholas's first objectives the next morning would be that very spot, which, Nicholas quickly realized, "with [its] two four pounders . . . commands the garrison and town." The Governor also attempted to augment his militia force, which numbered that day between 150 and 160 men, by issuing a "Proclamation by beat of Drum offering a Reward of a Pistole to every free Negroe and others that wod. imediately enter the fort properly armed." In a further effort to rally support he called another meeting of the most important men of the community at Fort Nassau for eight o'clock that evening.[45]

In the meanwhile, Captain Nicholas appears to have been in contact with Commodore Hopkins on board *Alfred*. Hopkins, upon hearing of the relatively peaceful development of affairs so far, seems to have sensed an opportunity to continue his vicarious conquest in the same bloodless manner, and he decided to issue a manifesto stating his intentions to the people of Nassau. This document was dated on Sunday, the day of the invasion, and there is reason to believe that it was published early enough for word of its nature to have reached Fort Nassau that evening. Hopkins offered to ensure the safety of town and populace in exchange for no resistance and no interference.

To the Gentlemen, Freemen, and Inhabitants of the Island of New Providence

The Reasons of my Landing an armed force on the Island is in Order to take Possession of the Powder and Warlike Stores belonging to the Crown, and if I am not Opposed in putting my design in Execution the Persons and Property of the Inhabitants Shall be Safe, Neither shall they be Suffered to be hurt in Case they make no Resistance.

Given under my hand onboard the Ship Alfred March 3rd. 1776.

E. H. Cr. in Chief.[46]

45 Atwood to Dartmouth, 22 Mar. 1776, CO 23/23, PRO; "Samuel Nicholas Letter." A year earlier Gov. Browne had written that

the Militia . . . is formed of white Men, free Mulattoes, and free Negroes, from the age of sixteen to sixty. The whole number consists of about 300 Men and are divided into three Companys. It seldom happens that half of them are home at the same time, as they are seafaring men.

Browne to Dartmouth, 6 May 1775, CO 23/23, PRO. The militia "Field Return Nassau January 2d 1775" included 299 privates of which only 134 were present; CO 23/23, PRO. The *pistole* or *doblon* (in English the doubloon) was a gold coin of Spanish origin, the equivalent of $4.00. Adjusted for inflation, it was worth roughly $84 in 1997 terms.

46 *Letter Book of Esek Hopkins*, ed. Beck, p. 44; Browne to Germain, 5 Nov. 1776, CO 23/23, PRO. The original document is at CO 23/10, fol. 246r, PRO.

Commodore Hopkins' attempt to deplete the militia force by written manifesto appears to have been more successful than Governor Browne's attempt to augment it by spoken proclamation for this "paper was handed about amongst the people to the eastward of the Town . . . [and] induced many of the Inhabitants to refuse coming to defend the Fort, and others to join the Rebels." Even before the eight o'clock meeting at the fort some of the militia had left and more were asking permission to go.[47]

The reluctance of the inhabitants to fight the Americans seems confirmed in the attitude of the council, the officers of the militia, and some of the more consequential citizens when they met with Governor Browne that evening. The Governor asked them "whether from the Force the Rebels were supposed to be, and the Condition Fort Nassau was then found to be in, with what strength was then in the Fort, if it was defensible or not?" They replied, fourteen to ten, that in their opinion it was not. The next question, then, was what to do with the nearly 200 barrels of gunpowder in Fort Nassau? Browne did not want to leave it for the Americans, but, almost echoing Hopkins' manifesto, he worried that "sending away the whole of it might enrage a disappointed enemy, and induce them to burn the town." The council concurred, though, that the bulk of the powder should be shipped to safety.[48]

Captain William Chambers was again called upon and again responded with commendable patriotism. This native of England was "A Man truly attached to Government" for he unhesitatingly placed himself and his vessel at the Governor's disposal and threw overboard the load of lumber stowed in the hold of *Mississippi Packet* for delivery to Jamaica. Around midnight, Chambers began supervising the careful loading of the 162 barrels of gunpowder that the militiamen brought out of Fort Nassau. They put 119 barrels on board Chambers' vessel and another 42 barrels in HMS *St. John*. Governor Browne, who was superintending the whole operation, took a few moments hastily to pen a short note to Governor Patrick Tonyn of East Florida and the two ships cast off for St Augustine about two o'clock Monday morning, 4 March 1776.[49]

For some unknown reason Commodore Hopkins left the main entrance to Nassau harbor unguarded, and thus the departure of the two ships was unhampered. *Providence, Wasp*, and the two captured sloops had, of course,

---

47 Brown to Gayton, 22 Mar. 1776, in Keith to Germain, 14 Apr. 1776, CO 137/71, PRO (photostat, LC); Brown to Germain, 2 May 1776; CO 23/23, PRO; Gambier *et al.* to Germain, 31 Mar. 1779, CO 23/24, PRO.

48 Atwood to Dartmouth, 22 Mar. 1776, CO 23/23, PRO; Browne to Germain, 5 Nov. 1776, CO 23/23, PRO; Browne to Germain, 2 May 1776, CO 23/23, PRO; "Narrative of . . . the Invasion," in Gambier *et al.* to Germain, 31 Mar. 1779, CO 23/24, PRO.

49 Grant to Tonyn, 8 Mar. 1776, in Tonyn to Germain, 8 Mar. 1776, CO 5/556, PRO (Stevens Trans.); Browne to Germain, 5 Nov. 1776, CO 23/23, PRO; Atwood to Dartmouth, 22 Mar. 1776, CO 23/23, PRO; Buckley to Gayton, 21 Mar. 1776, in Keith to Germain, 14 Apr. 1776, CO 137/71, PRO (photostat, LC); Browne to Tonyn, 4 Mar. 1776, CO 5/556, PRO (Stevens Trans.). Some 24 barrels of powder were left behind, presumably to appease the Americans. See "Inventory of Stores &c. taken at Fort Nassau – March 3 [*sic*, for 4], 1776," in *Correspondence of Esek Hopkins*, ed. Beck, p. 35.

moved in to disembark the invasion force that afternoon and were presumably still close by Fort Montagu to render any assistance needed by Captain Nicholas and his men. All the while, however, the main elements of the fleet, *Alfred, Columbus, Cabot,* and *Andrew Doria,* were kept safely anchored in the deep waters of Hanover Sound. Thus the loss of the precious powder, the prime object of the whole voyage, could have been avoided. John Paul Jones, writing long afterwards, suggested rather cryptically that the removal of the powder "was forseen" and pointed out that this "might have been prevented, by sending the two brigantines [*Cabot* and *Andrew Doria*] to lie off the bar." Although Jones was writing with the obvious benefit of hindsight, there is no known reason why what he stated could not have been done. The blame must lie entirely with Hopkins. The harbor had two entrances; both of them should have been sealed (see figure 12.3).[50]

Even with the two ships safely under way, Governor Browne had little sleep that night. The departure of the powder had "almost instantaneously produced a desertion of three fourths of the Men and Negroes." Browne asked his council whether, in the light of this mass departure, it might not be advisable to recall the detachment he had sent to Government House. Evidently he was still hoping to be able to put up at least a token defense. When the council agreed with him, Browne himself went up to Government House to bring the forty-some men back to Fort Nassau, but when they heard what had transpired, "not conceiving themselves a suffict Force . . ., [they] solicited that they might not remain" either. The belief seems to have been general that the fort and what stores remained should be left to the Americans; there were too few men left to fight and not much left to fight for. Why risk the destruction of the town for a few "unserviceable" cannon? As the situation worsened, Browne expostulated that he would not "leave the Fort while any One wod. stand by him," but to no avail. "At day break, the Governor, Council, and Officers, finding themselves almost entirely deserted, were at last obliged to leave the Fort."[51]

Morning found Fort Nassau empty and Governor Browne at Government House awaiting the arrival of the Americans. They were on their way. Captain Nicholas had had his men up before dawn and by sunrise they had covered the mile and a half or so from Fort Montagu to the first of the "line of houses" along the "one tolerably regular street" of the town of Nassau. Before they were actually in the town, however, another messenger arrived from the Governor asking the intentions of the Americans. Nicholas wearily sent Browne "the same answer as before." The messenger went back to the Governor and soon returned to tell Nicholas that "the western garrison [Fort Nassau] was ready for his reception and that he might march his force in as soon as he pleased." There would be no battle. Nicholas had waited with

50 Sands, ed., *Life . . . of . . . Jones,* p. 36.
51 Atwood to Dartmouth, 22 Mar. 1776, CO 23/23, PRO; Brown to Gayton, 22 Mar. 1776, in Keith to Germain, 14 Apr. 1776, CO 137/71, PRO (photostat, LC); Brown to Germain, 2 May 1776, CO 23/23, PRO.

his troops about an hour on the outskirts of Nassau while this exchange was taking place, and now he began to move his men forward into the town. As the marines and sailors were marching down the main street, Nicholas chose for himself a special guard and went up the hill to Government House where he demanded and received the keys to Fort Nassau. He then rejoined his men and the Americans took possession of the fort about eight o'clock that morning. The British colors were hauled down and the Grand Union flag of the United Colonies run up in their stead.[52]

A report was then sent to Commodore Hopkins, who had been waiting off Hog Island with part of the fleet perhaps for a combined land-sea assault on Fort Nassau, if it should have come to that, telling him that the fort had been taken and that it was safe to bring the ships into the harbor. Only part of the fleet entered the port area at that time; the others stayed at Hanover Sound with *Andrew Doria* and *Wasp* until early Wednesday morning, 6 March, when they came over also. At that time the schooner *Wasp* was left outside the bar "to serve as a lookout." Although this latter maneuver is understandable and certainly commendable, it stands as the only completely comprehensible disposition of his ships that Hopkins undertook during the entire cruise.[53]

While they were waiting for Commodore Hopkins to come ashore, the marines at Fort Nassau noticed "Gov. Brown and his council walking his piazza and his servants below with hosses." Evidently assuming that Browne was up to no good and was perhaps about to escape to the interior of the island, Captain Nicholas, although he had as yet no orders from Hopkins concerning the Governor, sent Lieutenant Trevett, Lieutenant Henry Dayton of *Providence*, and "a young officer from Philadelphia" to bring Browne down to the fort. Browne's reaction betrayed his intentions. In Trevett's words:

> [We] informed him he must go with us to the fort. He made reply that it was beneath his dignity, as Governor, to go to the fort. We replied he must go. Then he said it must be by force of arms; and he walked down with us to the fort.

52 Schöpf, *Travels*, II, 162; "Samuel Nicholas Letter"; message as quoted by Jones in Jones to Joseph Hewes, 14 Apr. 1776, Jones Manuscripts, LC; "Journal of John Trevett," p. 73; Gambier *et al.* to Germain, 31 Mar. 1779, CO 23/24, PRO. The question of what flag the fleet actually flew has been a matter of controversy for a long time; see Hugh F. Rankin, "The Naval Flag of the American Revolution," *W&MQ*, 3rd ser., XI (July 1954), 339–353. The conclusion that it was the Grand Union flag is verified and the question over the color of the stripes is settled in the report on Hopkins' fleet sent by Capt. Andrew Buckley at Savannah to Admiral Clark Gayton at Jamaica and through him to London. In the description "Of their Colours," the flag is said to be one with "a union Jack in a Canton with a Fly consisting of 13 Stripes, Red and White, or Blue and White." See "A List of Ships and Vessels fitted out by the Rebels at Philadelphia, to cruize against the English, which were ready to sail on the 12th of February 1776," Buckley to Gayton, 21 Mar. 1776, in Keith to Germain, 14 Apr. 1776, CO 137/71, PRO (photostat, LC).

53 "Journal of John Trevett," p. 73; "Journal of the *Andrew Doria*," 18 Feb. 1776; Log of the *Wasp*, 9 Mar. 1776, HCA 30/733/10, fol. 1r [fol. 4r], PRO, and as cited in Clark, *Captain Dauntless*, p. 107.

Why he had not left before the Americans even arrived cannot be understood. He had both sufficient time to escape, a place to go, and the freedom to depart at his convenience. As a later critic of Governor Browne's pose as maligned and deserted servant of the Crown pointed out, his capture was unnecessary. He claimed that his recent behavior demonstrated that he had no intention of running and hiding. He had had an "interval of near 5 hours, vizt. from four o'clock, the time of . . . [the] coming out of the Fort . . . till 9"; "the Country was open"; and Browne's "family [was] out of town" already.[54] Yet he remained at his post.

Presumably Governor Browne and Commodore Hopkins met for the first time soon thereafter in Fort Nassau. We can only imagine Hopkins' frame of mind when he learned of the loss of the gunpowder, yet it is likely that his addiction to "profane swearing" was much in evidence when he was told that Browne had shipped almost all of it to St Augustine. Hopkins was not at all happy as Browne quickly learned. The Governor was confined for a short time in Fort Nassau, "in a place without food, water, bed, table or chair" and then, under Hopkins' order, he was removed to Government House, as he later complained, "for the better convenience of their officers and men." There he was kept under close guard for four days, and the following Sunday, 10 March, he was, to use his own words, "seized, Collered, and Dragged away like a fellon to the Gallows," and put aboard the flagship *Alfred*. Later, when Hopkins returned to the ship, Browne demanded to know why he was being so treated. Hopkins replied tersely, "for presuming to fire upon [my] troops from Fort Montagu." The real reason was surely Browne's spiriting away of the gunpowder.[55]

Two other men were incarcerated aboard *Alfred* along with Governor Browne. One was a close friend of the Governor, Lieutenant James Babbidge, a half-pay officer of the British Army, who had been acting as Browne's secretary and whom he had been trying to have appointed lieutenant governor. The other man was Thomas Irving, formerly the Inspector-General of Imports and Exports of North America, more recently the Receiver-General of the Quit Rents of South Carolina, and a good Tory. One could almost get the impression that the Nassauvians were taking this opportunity to rid themselves of pesky colonial officials. Hopkins' officers' mess must surely have been the scene of lively conversations on the return voyage.[56]

---

54 "Journal of John Trevett," p. 73; "Samuel Nicholas Letter"; Gambier *et al.* to Germain, 31 Mar. 1779, CO 23/24, PRO. The "young officer" may have been Marine Lt. Isaac Craig of *Andrew Doria*, who was from Philadelphia.

55 Field, *Hopkins*, p. 190. See also Francis S. Drake, *The Life and Correspondence of Henry Knox* (Boston, 1873), p. 27; Browne to Germain, 5 Nov. 1776, CO 23/23, PRO; "Journal of John Trevett," pp. 73–74; Atwood to Dartmouth, 22 Mar. 1776, CO 23/23, PRO; Morgan, *Captains to the Northward*, p. 42; Lorenz, *Jones*, p. 67.

56 Browne to Germain, 5 Nov. 1776, CO 23/23, PRO; Hopkins to Hancock, 8 Apr. 1776, *Letter Book of Esek Hopkins*, ed. Beck, p. 47; Browne to Dartmouth, 6 May 1775, CO 23/23, PRO. It was not "Thomas Arwin" as both Hopkins and Craton, *History of the*

Complain as Governor Browne did, Commodore Hopkins could afford to pay little attention to his loud protestations during the two weeks following the initial landing, for he was a very busy man. An inventory of the captured military stores found in both of the forts was immediately undertaken and was completed the very day Hopkins stepped ashore. The marines and sailors soon thereafter started loading the cannon and shells aboard the several ships. The little *Andrew Doria*, for instance, "receiv'd on board 4780 Shott and Sheels of Different Sizes" that were put in its hold replacing its ballast. Similar cargo was moved on board the other vessels of the fleet. In fact there was not room enough to hold all the loot and Hopkins contracted with the master of the sloop *Endeavor* Captain Charles Walker, to carry away the remainder of the captured material.[57]

Besides supervising the loading of the military stores, Commodore Hopkins had to be concerned with the administration of the captured town and the disposition of his own men. Although there was probably a steady stream of townspeople to see him, they do not appear to have given him much trouble. If anything they were overly hospitable, something that probably accounted for much of Governor Browne's later pique. Hopkins and his officers were, he later complained, "countenanced by many of the principal inhabitants, and elegantly entertained at the House of some of the officers of the Government." Significantly there is no record of a deputation of leading citizens coming to ask that their beloved Governor be returned to them.[58]

His own men proved to be the greatest source of worry for Commodore Hopkins. They were unused to the climate and the country, and a fever began to spread among them, so much so that by the time the fleet got to New London, Connecticut, in the early part of April, several men had died and 140 had to be placed in makeshift hospitals. It has been charged that excessive drinking was what ailed the majority, and drink to excess many certainly did, but it seems likely that malaria or some related disease was the real cause. Those men who did not get sick at Nassau became greedy and were equally a cause of trouble for Hopkins. Here they were the conquering army and they could have no spoils. Even "some of the leading Officers," it appears, pressured Hopkins to allow some pillaging, but he had given his

---

Bahamas, p. 142, mistakenly report. For Irving, see John J. McCusker, "Colonial Civil Servant and Counter-Revolutionary: Thomas Irving (1738?–1800) in Boston, Charleston, and London," *Perspectives in American History*, XII (1979), 314–350 – revised as chapter nine of the present book.

57 See "Stores &c taken at Fort Montague March 3, 1776," and "Inventory of Stores &c, taken at Fort Nassau – March 3 [4], 1776," in *Correspondence of Esek Hopkins*, ed. Beck, p. 35, and *American Archives*, ed. Force, 4th ser., V, 824; "Journal of the *Andrew Doria*," 18 Feb. 1776. Walker was subsequently paid $2,000 by the Continental Congress "for the hire of" *Endeavor* and was given the even more rewarding privilege of being allowed to purchase produce to that sum for resale in the Bahamas; *American Archives*, ed. Force, 5th ser., I, 1576. Adjusted for inflation $2,000 in 1776 was worth nearly $37,000 in 1997 terms.

58 See *Letter Book of Esek Hopkins*, ed. Beck, p. 45: Browne to the Council and General Assembly of the Bahamas, 15 Mar. 1779, CO 23/24, PRO; Log of the *Wasp,* 9–16 Mar. 1776, HCA 30/733/10, fol. 1r [fol. 4r], PRO.

word. There would be no "injury to private property." This resolution raised Hopkins' stock in the eyes of the Nassauvians, one of whom wrote that he feared for the island's fate in the hands of a "Commander of less humanity."[59]

No other major problems developed during the two weeks and everything was finally loaded and secured by Saturday, 16 March. The marines were then embarked and the order was given to prepare to sail. While Commodore Hopkins would not let Governor Browne go ashore to say goodbye to his "Dear wife and aged Aunt," he must have let someone come on board *Alfred* the next day just before sailing, for Browne, even though by his own testimony watched by "innumerable Senterys," was able to dispatch a note to England protesting his self-sacrifice and fidelity to duty. About four o'clock in the afternoon, when all was ready, Hopkins ordered that the signal be given "for weighing & coming to sail." The crew of *Alfred* then answered to the command to "Loose all the Topsails and Sheet them home," and, with billowing canvas catching the "Moderate Breeze" of that overcast Sunday afternoon, 17 March 1776, this first American fleet made it swiftly again to sea.[60]

◆ ◆ ◆ ◆ ◆

The American invasion of Nassau in the Bahamas left but another British colony in the New World in a precarious state of imbalance. Invited or not, the descent of the Americans destroyed effective government and thus exposed New Providence to external harassment and internal dissension throughout the war. A decade of anarchy followed in the wake of their departure.[61]

The effects of the invasion of Nassau were not restricted to the Bahamas alone. With this attack, what, until that time, had been a serious but rather

---

59 "Journal of the *Andrew Doria*," 18 Feb. 1776; Esek Hopkins to Stephen Hopkins, 21 Apr. 1776, *Letter Book of Esek Hopkins*, ed. Beck, p. 52; Brown to Gayton, 22 Mar. 1776, in Keith to Germain, 14 Apr. 1776, CO 137/71, PRO (photostat, LC).

60 "Journal of the *Andrew Doria*," 18 Feb. 1776 and 17 Mar. 1776; Browne to Germain, 5 Nov. 1776, CO 23/23, PRO; Browne to Dartmouth, 17 Mar. 1776, CO 23/23, PRO; Log of the *Wasp*, 17 Mar. 1776, HCA 30/733/10, fol. 1r [fol. 4r], PRO; "Signals for the American Fleet," *Letter Book of Esek Hopkins*, ed. Beck, p. 40. The fleet arrived at New London, Connecticut, 8 Apr. 1776, after an eventful voyage involving the first battle between the Continental Navy and the Royal Navy. See Morison, *Jones*, pp. 47–51; and John J. McCusker, *"Alfred": The First Continental Flagship, 1775–1778*, Smithsonian Studies in History and Technology, no. 20 (Washington, DC, 1973).

61 Craton, *History of the Bahamas*, pp. 141–157. New Providence was captured twice more during the war, and the second time remained in enemy hands for almost a year before being retaken (see the discussion earlier in this chapter). On 27 Jan. 1778, Lt. John Trevett led twenty-eight men ashore in the middle of the night from the sloop *Providence*, Capt. John Peck Rathburne in command. They overpowered the sentinels at Fort Nassau and aimed the guns of the fort at the town and the ships in the harbor. Acting Gov. John Gambier found himself confronted with a *fait accompli* and two days later *Providence* sailed away with 1,600 barrels of gunpowder and several prizes. Allen, *Naval History*, I, 292–295, the references he cited there, and Gambier to Germain, 25 Feb. 1778, CO 23/24, PRO.

John Trevett had taken the occasion of his first stay on New Providence to prepare the way for a future visit. When he led the American attack on the island in 1778 he "recollected that when I was at the taking of New Providence with Com. Hopkins, I left

localized rebellion in one of the New England colonies, took on hemispheric proportions. While often verging for the modern reader on the comic and the ludicrous and involving much that was inept and inexcusable, the invasion not only challenged the Mistress of the Seas in her own element but promised a series of many more such raids ranging down the British West Indies. Panic-inspired rumors raced to London reporting that Commodore Hopkins' fleet had been seen in the harbor at Charleston, South Carolina, that it was expected soon at St Augustine, that it "would endeavour to intercept the Jamaica Fleet of Merchantmen, homeward bound," that it had "totally defeated" a British fleet – perhaps the same fleet – "after a dreadful slaughter."[62] No wonder that the North government did not know which way to turn. They could meet this threat in but one way. To protect the empire Great Britain was forced to send the fleet across the Atlantic.

Soon the war became an international affair and Britain suddenly found its own shores unprotected. In the face of a bellicose France, England could mount but a feeble force because the bulk of the Royal Navy was elsewhere. The defense of the home islands threatened to collapse as combined Franco-Spanish fleets roamed the Channel at their pleasure.[63] The French navy was free to sail where it would – to the Chesapeake, for instance, off Yorktown. The divisive effects of the Continental Navy's early endeavors had been sufficient to disperse Royal Navy power and to allow France the freedom to concentrate its forces where it would. Had there been no Continental Navy, this might well have not been the case and the role of the French navy might have been seriously curtailed. Had there been no Continental Navy of the United Colonies, ultimate victory in the American Revolution might have been British.[64]

---

out one of the pickets of the fort, and I thought this might prove fortunate if it has not been replaced . . . and [I] found it as I left it, still." Employing this gap in the outer defenses of the fort, Gambier took his men up to and over the walls, into the fort. "Journal of John Trevett," p. 39.

What one ship accomplished by stealth in 1778, 59 did in strength in 1782, when a combined Spanish–American force appeared off the bar in the evening of 5 May. Gov. John Maxwell held out for two days, but, in the face of the inevitable, he surrendered to the ultimatum of no less a personage than Don Juan Manuel de Cagigal y Montserrat de la Vega y Adames, the Governor of Cuba. Allen, *Naval History,* II, 583–584; James A. Lewis, *The Final Campaign of the American Revolution: Rise and Fall of the Spanish Bahamas* ([Columbia, SC, 1991]).

62 Information of Andrew Breedon, 20 Mar. 1776, in Buckley to Gayton, 21 Mar. 1776, enclosed in Keith to Germain, 14 Apr. 1776, CO 137/71, PRO (photostat, LC), and Capt. Buckley's comments and additions in his covering letter, ibid. The last quote is from the *Public Advertiser* (London), 29 July 1776. Compare the report that Hopkins' fleet had attacked Bermuda. *London Chronicle,* 20 June 1776. And that it was "hovering among these Windward Islands." Gov. Morris Valentine to Germain, St Vincent, 1 Aug. 1776, CO 260/4, fol. 26, PRO. See also [Beaumarchais] to Vergennes, 11 May 1776, as cited above in n. 9 of this chapter.

63 See A[lfred] Temple Patterson, *The Other Armada: The Franco-Spanish Attempt to Invade Britain in 1779* (Manchester, [1960]).

64 "American naval operations in the Atlantic during the first years of the War for Independence were crucial to the success of the American effort." Syrett, "Defeat at Sea," p. 13.

13

MONEY SUPPLY, ECONOMIC GROWTH, AND THE QUANTITY THEORY OF MONEY

France, 1650–1788

Co-authored with James C. Riley

In the early modern era the European money stock grew rapidly.[1] Part of the growth has been explained by a larger supply of metals usable as coin or bullion.[2] More gold and more silver were produced, especially in South America, and much of this output was minted in Europe or for use in Europe. Part of the growth, indeed an increasing part of it, can be explained by a growing supply of other means of payment. Governments, merchants, and others produced a variety of paper supplements for coin. While the stock of money did not grow in the same way throughout Europe, all the continent shared in the phenomenon of an enlarged money supply.

Following Earl Hamilton's study of money supply and prices in sixteenth-century Spain, it has been customary in French historiography to expect

---

1 The original version of this chapter was published in *Explorations in Economic History*, XX (July 1983), 274–293. Copyright © 1983 by Academic Press Inc. This revision is presented here with the permission of the publishers of the journal and the blessings of my original co-author. See also John J. McCusker and James C. Riley, "The French Economy, 1650–1788: Economic Growth, the Money Supply, and Monetarist Theory – A Summary," *Business and Economic History*, 2nd ser., XI (1982), 102–104; and McCusker and Riley, "Money Supply, Economic Growth, and the Quantity Theory of Money: France, 1650–1788," in [International Economic History Congress, 8th, 1982, Budapest], *Münzprägung, Geldumlauf und Wechselkurse / Minting, Monetary Circulation and Exchange Rates: Akten des 8th International Economic History Congress, Section C 7, Budapest, 1982*, ed. Eddy van Cauwenberghe and Franz Irsigler, Trierer Historische Forschungen, Band 7 (Trier, 1984), pp. 255–289.

We continue to be grateful for the help and support given us in the preparation of this chapter by Rondo Cameron, Stanley Engerman, Huston McCulloch, Angus Maddison, Toshio Ogahara, L. S. Presnell, N. J. Simler, F. C. Spooner, Richard Sylla, Herman van der Wee, Elmus Wicker, and two anonymous referees.

2 Pierre Vilar, *A History of Gold and Money, 1450–1920*, trans. Judith White (London, 1976), pp. 76–79, 197–199. See also Adolph Soetbeer, *Edelmetall-Produktion und Wertverhältnis zwischen Gold und Silber seit der Entdeckung Amerikas bis zur Gegenwart [Petermanns Geographische Mittheilungen*, Band XIII, Erganzungsheft no. 57] (Gotha, 1879).

growth in the money stock to have been accompanied by growth in prices.[3] This linkage between the money stock and prices is characteristic of the quantity theory of money, although this theory has been presented in several different forms. "What quantity theorists have held in common is the belief that ... qualifications [about factors influencing price change] are of secondary importance for substantial changes in either prices or the quantity of money, so that the one will not in fact occur without the other."[4] Thinking more generally about the historical record, Anna J. Schwartz has hazarded the view that "long-run price changes consistently parallel ... monetary changes," moving up with increasing stocks and down with diminishing stocks.[5]

Schwartz noticed one exception to this price/money growth relationship – sixteenth-century England. She interpreted it as something like the exception that proves the rule in an essay arguing that historical experience from classical antiquity to the more recent past shares the feature of showing that price change can be explained by monetary factors and, more simply, by the rate of change in the money stock.[6] Like most students of the price/money relationship, Schwartz identified periods of price movement – usually inflation – and then sought an explanation. Perhaps price inflation can usually be explained by monetary influences. But is change in the stock of money usually associated with price movement? Moreover, does the phenomenon to be discussed here – the long-run experience of a major economy undergoing considerable growth without industrial modernization – support the modern quantity theory, or monetarist expectation of a long-run stable velocity of (and demand for) money? Ordinarily, unstable velocities are related only to such factors as major innovations in financial institutions.[7] In this essay we examine the evidence about a long period in French history in which the

3 Earl J. Hamilton, *American Treasure and the Price Revolution in Spain, 1501–1650*, Harvard Economic Studies, vol. XLIII (Cambridge, Mass., 1934). Compare [Camille] Ernest Labrousse, "Les 'bons prix' agricoles du XVIIIe siècle," in *Des derniers temps de l'âge seigneurial aux préludes de l'âge industriel (1660-1789)*, ed. [Camille] Ernest Labrousse *et al.*, vol. II of *Histoire économique et sociale de la France* (Paris, [1970]), pp. 367–416; Fernand [P.] Braudel, *Civilization and Capitalism, 15th–18th Century*, trans. [Miriam Kochan and] Siân Reynolds, 3 vols (New York, 1981–1984), I, 466–468; Pierre Goubert, *L'Ancien Régime*, [7th edn], 2 vols (Paris, 1982); and Emmanuel Le Roy Ladurie, *Les Paysans de Languedoc*, [2nd edn], 2 vols (Paris, [1974]), I, 533.
4 Milton Friedman, "Money: Quantity Theory," in *International Encyclopedia of the Social Sciences*, ed. David L. Sills and Robert K. Merton, 19 vols ([New York, 1968]), X, 433.
5 Anna J. Schwartz, "Secular Price Change in Historical Perspective," *Journal of Money, Credit, and Banking*, V (Feb. 1973), 264.
6 Ibid.
7 Richard T. Selden, "Monetary Velocity in the United States," in *Studies in the Quantity Theory of Money*, ed. Milton Friedman (Chicago, [1956]), pp. 179–257; [Jon] Lars [B.] Jonung, "The Long Run Demand for Money – A Wicksellian Approach," *Scandinavian Journal of Economics*, LXXX (no. 2, 1978), 216–230; and Michael David Bordo and [Jon] Lars [B.] Jonung, "The Long Run Behavior of the Income Velocity of Money in Five Advanced Countries, 1870–1975: An Institutional Approach," *Economic Inquiry*, XIX (Jan. 1981), 96–116.

money stock grew most rapidly when prices were stable, and least rapidly when prices were rising. In this period, it seems, within the equation of exchange, that $M \neq P$ or Y.[8] Indeed, the discrepancy between M and Y is, for the period as a whole and for certain sub-periods, so large as to make V appear the most volatile of other elements (besides M) in the equation of exchange.

Several features make this period especially interesting. First, while French experience was certainly singular in some respects, the general scheme outlined here – monetary growth considerably, and erratically, in excess of growth in prices and output – can be expected to apply also to other European economies in the same period. Second, this scheme calls attention to the importance of several questions seldom posed in early modern economic history. Given that the equation of exchange, in any of its full forms, is an identity, how is the discrepancy between the ordinary expectations of quantity theory and French experience to be explained? Part of it may be owing to an inadequate description and measurement of transactions, output, or income. Another issue often omitted in the historical literature is discussion of the demand for money. The evidence to be presented here will imply that the demand for money rose very appreciably during much of this period and, through the first century or so, most rapidly in a part of the period when little change in output or income is likely.

In terms of theory, this case study not only raises some interesting issues but also involves some qualifications. First, in quantity theory it is customary to distinguish between short- and long-run effects. In periods of business expansion, V is expected to increase, although gradually; in periods of business contraction, V is expected to decline. Exactly the opposite is forecast for long-run experience. In secular eras of growth in income, V is expected to decline; in secular eras of decline in income, V is expected to rise. Here we are unable to comment profitably about short-run expectations because it is not clear that the French economy of 1650–1788 experienced business cycles.[9] But we can examine the behavior of V in the long run to see whether

---

8   Here we refer both to Irving Fisher's form of the equation of exchange, $MV = PT$, and to the Cambridge cash balances reformulation, $M = kY$, where

    M = the money stock,
    V = the transactions velocity of circulation,
    P = the price level,
    T = the volume of monetary transactions within the economy,
    k = cash balances held by the public (the inverse of V, defined, however, in
        terms of monetary income y rather than transactions T),
    Y = $P \times y$.

9   But see the evidence of such cycles in the economy of Great Britain and British America, in John J. McCusker and Russell R. Menard, *The Economy of British America, 1607–1789*, [2nd edn] (Chapel Hill, NC, [1991]), pp. 60–67, as revised in McCusker, *How Much Is That in Real Money? A Historical Price Index for Use as a Deflator of Money Values in the Economy of the United States* (Worcester, Mass., 1992).

these and other expectations hold up for an economy that was not yet modern but that nevertheless was undergoing considerable growth in an early modern context.

ESTIMATES OF MONEY, PRICES, OUTPUT, AND VELOCITY

There are several things to notice about the data cited here. The first is that they represent best-informed estimates. Measurement errors are likely, but in our judgment corrections will not significantly change the basic trends of M, P, y, and V that are observed and inferred here. Sources for these estimates are discussed in more detail in appendix 13.2. Price and monetary comparisons for this period involve both adjustments from current to constant values and adjustments to a standard silver equivalent for the money of account, the *livre tournois* (table 13.1, columns [2] and [3][10] and Appendix 13.1).[11]

Second, French population growth, according to the most careful estimates, would substantially influence the interpretation of output and money stock estimates. Thus we present per capita estimates of these figures. However, since both sides of the equation of exchange are adjusted to reflect population growth, this procedure produces estimates of V that vary only slightly from those that would be calculated from aggregate figures alone.

---

10 By law, on 7 Apr. 1803, the franc became the new French monetary unit, supplanting the *livre tournois* (*l.t.*). While in theory the *franc* was supposed to be worth a bit less than the *livre tournois,* in practice it turned out to be of the same value because the *livre* had never contained its full weight equivalent of silver. The difference was minor, 4.5 grams as opposed to the stipulated 4.505 grams. J[acques] Peuchet, *Dictionnaire universel de la géographie commerçante* ..., 5 vols (Paris, VII–VIII [1799–1800]), IV, 380; F[rederic] Braesch, *La Livre tournois et le Franc de germinal (Essai sur la monnaie métallique),* vol. V of *Finances et Monnaie Révolutionnaires (Recherches Études et Documents)* (Paris, 1936); René Sédillot, *Le Franc: Histoire d'une monnaie des origines à nos jours* (Paris, 1953); and Vilar, *History of Gold and Money,* trans. White, p. 307.

It is necessary to express a general caution about monetary conversions over such long periods of time. At best, the resulting figures are merely suggestive of trends. The appearance of precision in numbers expressed to a third decimal place should not mislead the reader; such seeming precision is an artifact of our mathematical procedures. For a discussion of the caution necessary in dealing with these data, see Pierre Goubert, *Beauvais et le Beauvaisis de 1600 à 1730: Contribution à l'histoire sociale de la France,* 2 vols (Paris, [1960]), I, 375–377, 399–400. For comment on the reasons for converting from nominal to constant values, which has been controversial in French historiography, see Jean Meuvret, "Simple mise au point," *Annales: Histoire, Sciences Sociales,* X (Jan.–Mar. 1955), 48–54. On the appropriateness of the concept of "real" prices or "real" values for historical analyses, see Robert William Fogel, *Without Consent or Contract: The Rise and Fall of American Slavery* (New York, 1989), p. 432, n. 7.

11 Micheline Baulant and Jean Meuvret, *Prix des céréales extraits de la Mercuriale de Paris (1520-1698),* 2 vols (Paris, 1960–1962), I, 249; Labrousse, "Les 'bons prix' agricoles du XVIIIe siècle," pp. 383–396; Georges Frêche and Geneviève Frêche, *Les Prix des grains, des vins et des légumes à Toulouse (1486–1868): Extraits des Mercuriales, suivis d'une bibliographie d'histoire des prix,* Travaux et Recherches de la Faculté de Droit et des Sciences Économiques de Paris, Série "Sciences Historiques," no. 10 (Paris, 1967), p. 131.

Table 13.1 Estimates of the population, the value of *livres tournois*, the money stock and prices, France, 1650–1788

Date	Population (millions) (1)	Changing value of the livre tournois — Value (grams of silver) (2)	Changing value of the livre tournois — Index (1788=100) (3)	Estimated Money Stock — Total (millions of livres tournois) Original estimate (4)	Estimated Money Stock — Total (millions of livres tournois) Adjusted estimate (5)	Estimated Money Stock — Per capita (livres tournois) Original estimate (6)	Estimated Money Stock — Per capita (livres tournois) Adjusted estimate (7)	Indexes of Commodity Prices — Baulant/Meuvret Index (1788=100) (8)	Indexes of Commodity Prices — Baulant/Meuvret Rate of change (9)	Labrousse All prices Index (1788=100) (10)	Labrousse All prices Rate of change (11)	Labrousse Wheat prices Index (1788=100) (12)	Labrousse Wheat prices Rate of change (13)
1650	20.0	8.33	187.2	167 to 201	344 to 376	9.63	18.00	129.50	-0.187	–	–	–	–
1683	21.5	8.33	187.2	500	936	23.26	43.53	108.46	-0.077				
1700	21.5	7.27	163.4	271 to 573	690 to 936	23.14	37.81	106.38	-0.070				
1754	24.9	4.45	100.0	1,500	1,500	60.24	60.24	80.96	+0.623	69.73	+1.066	72.38	+0.955
1763	25.9	4.45	100.0	1,500 to 1,600	1,500 to 1,600	59.85	59.85	80.63	+0.865	72.52	+1.294	72.05	+1.320
1774	26.9	4.45	100.0	1,800 to 1,900	1,800 to 1,900	68.77	68.77	113.67	– 0911	93.37	+0.491	94.19	+0.428
1784 to 1788		–	4.45	2,000 / 2,200 / 2,600	2,000 / 2,200 / 2,600	–	–	–	–	–	–	–	–
1788	27.9	4.45	100.0	(2,100)	(2,100)	75.27	75.27	100.0	–	100.0	–	100.0	–

Notes and sources:
See the discussion of the sources for these figures in appendix 13.1.
The rates of change in columns (9), (11), and (13) are calculated over the period between the specified dates and 1788.

Third, in measuring the French money stock, we have sought to include only the supply of specie – coins made of precious and non-precious metals (gold, silver, copper, and billon [a mixture of copper with silver or nickel]) – and to exclude paper money. On several occasions between 1650 and 1788 (e.g., 1693–1697 and 1701–1720) the central government and its agencies issued and then retired paper money. We have omitted these issues here because they fall wholly inside the benchmark data or because, for the latter decades of the period, central government issues of paper money comprised small parts of the specie money stock and took the form of paper with special purposes and uses. A wide variety of other paper also circulated, including bills of exchange, promissory notes, and similar instruments. The quantity of such paper money is known to have increased during this period, and is believed, during the eighteenth century at least, to have increased more rapidly than the specie stock.[12] Because of this more rapid rate of growth, and because of the unavailability of estimates of the volume of such paper, we have been content to provide estimates of the specie stock.

These figures will bias downward the rate of monetary growth and lend an element of caution to our results. Adherence to this procedure will also lead to a conservative definition of money. This seems appropriate in light of the very personal quality of value in most paper instruments: people valued bills of exchange and promissory notes and were willing to accept them in lieu of specie because they respected the integrity of the endorsers or, rather, because they had no grounds for suspicion about the endorsers. But the principal reason for adhering to this narrow definition of money is that this approach diminishes the gap between M and P, and between M and Y, and thus presents a modest rather than a radical version of the problem.

DATA AND CALCULATIONS

The index numbers in table 13.1, column (3), may now be used to revise estimates of the money stock to *livres tournois* of a constant silver equivalent (table 13.1, column [5]). To calculate per capita rates of increase, we turn to population data provided chiefly by Jacques Dupâquier (table 13.1, column [1]).[13] Columns (6) and (7) utilize the data from columns (2) and (4) to provide per capita estimates of the French money stock in both current and constant silver equivalent *livres*.

12 Labrousse, "Les 'bons prix' agricoles du XVIIIe siècle," pp. 394–395.
13 Jacques Dupâquier, "Révolution française et révolution démographique," in *Vom Ancien Régime zur Französischen Revolution: Forschungen und Perspektiven/De l'Ancien Régime à la Révolution Française: Recherches et Perspectives*, ed. Ernst Hinrichs, Eberhard Schmitt, and Richard Vierhaus, Veröffentlichungen des Max-Planck-Instituts für Geschichte, 55 (Göttingen, 1978), p. 236; Marcel R. Reinhard, André Armengaud and Jacques Dupâquier, *Histoire générale de la population mondiale*, 3rd edn (Paris [1968]), p. 179; and Jacques Dupâquier, *La Population française aux XVIIe et XVIIIe siècles* (Paris, 1979), pp. 34, 81. See also Jacques Dupâquier, *Histoire de la population française*, 4 vols (Paris, 1995).

Lacking a general index for prices in France during these years, we provide two substitutes. In columns (8) through (13) multi-year averages from the indices developed by Micheline Baulant and Jean Meuvret and by C.-E. Labrousse are provided for benchmark years.[14] The Baulant–Meuvret series – columns (8) and (9) – spans the entire period for Paris wheat prices, and the Labrousse series provides information about agricultural prices across France during 1726–1789 while leaving the components of the series unweighted.[15] Because Parisian and national wheat prices increased somewhat less after 1726 than did general agricultural prices, we have calculated minimum and maximum versions of the level of price change for the later benchmark years (using columns [11] and [13]). (See also appendix 13.1 for information about the data in table 13.1.)

To gauge the rate of change in income, we have employed two types of estimates, both of which produce similar results. For table 13.2 a lower bound figure for growth is derived from Paul Bairoch's backward projection of growth between 1500 and 1800 that, in his view, provides a ceiling rate of growth in income (0.3 percent) based on an estimate of how much growth is feasible in early modern economies.[16] In an era in which it is reasonable to expect some increase in the level of monetization, Bairoch's method diminishes the problem of comparing less monetized with more monetized economies by trying to gauge the market value of all necessary consumables. Other scholars provide data suggesting higher estimates of growth in income, and these figures are incorporated in table 13.2 by an alternative, higher-bound growth estimate of 0.5 percent per annum.[17] This rate, suggested by the work of Tihomir J. Markovitch and Angus Maddison, more satisfactorily combines growth in income and increased monetization.[18]

14 Micheline Baulant, "Le Prix des grains à Paris de 1431 à 1789," *Annales: Histoire, Sciences Sociales*, XXIII (May–June 1968), 539–540; Labrousse, " 'Les Bons Prix' agricoles du XVIIIe siècle," pp. 386–387; C[amille]-E[rnest] Labrousse, *Esquisse du mouvement des prix et des revenus en France au XVIIIe siècle*, 2 vols (Paris, 1933), I, 103–104.
15 Labrousse, " 'Les Bons Prix' agricoles du XVIIIe siècle," p. 387; Labrousse, *Esquisse du mouvement des prix et des revenus en France*, I, 103–104. Labrousse also presents other calculations showing that an unweighted agricultural price series moved less erratically than weighted indices, and that, after 1728, agricultural prices increased more than prices in general.
16 Paul Bairoch, "Europe's Gross National Product, 1800–1975," *Journal of European Economic History*, V (Fall 1976), 277.
17 Compare with the estimates of contemporary British and American economic growth in, respectively, C[harles] Knick Harley, "British Industrialization before 1841: Evidence of Slower Growth during the Industrial Revolution," *JEcH*, XLII (June 1982), 286, and McCusker and Menard, *Economy of British America*, pp. 53–60. The former develops an argument that per capita income in Great Britain grew at the rate of 0.27 percent between 1700 and 1770 and at 0.33 percent from 1770 to 1815; the latter suggests that the average annual rate of growth in the Thirteen Continental Colonies from 1650 to 1770 was probably between 0.3 percent and 0.6 percent. Harley's estimates constitute a revision, downwards, of those presented by Phyllis Deane and W[illiam] A. Cole. *British Economic Growth, 1688–1959: Trends and Structure*, 2nd edn (Cambridge, Eng., 1969), pp. 75–82 and elsewhere.
18 Tihomir J. Markovitch, "L'Évolution industrielle de la France au XVIIIe siècle," *Revue d'Histoire Économique et Sociale*, LIII (nos 2–3, 1975), 277–279; Tihomir J. Markovitch,

Table 13.2 Comparison of rates of change in the per capita money supply, price levels, and per capita output with the velocity of circulation of money for France for five periods, 1650–1788

Periods	Categories	Annual average rate of increase (%)	
		Output at 0.3% (1)	*Output at 0.5%* (2)
1650	Money stock	1.042	1.042
to	Output	0.3	0.5
1788	Prices	−0.187	−0.187
	Estimated velocity	−0.929	−0.729
1683	Money stock	0.523	0.523
to	Output	0.3	0.5
1788	Prices	−0.077	−0.077
	Estimated velocity	−0.300	−0.100
1700	Money stock	0.786	0.786
to	Output	0.3	0.5
1788	Prices	−0.070	−0.070
	Estimated velocity	−0.555	−0.355
1754	Money stock	0.657	0.657
to	Output	0.3	0.5
1788	Prices (min.)	0.623	0.623
	Prices (max.)	1.066	1.066
	Estimated velocity (min.)	0.266	0.466
	Estimated velocity (max.)	0.709	0.909
1763	Money supply	0.921	0.921
to	Output	0.3	0.5
1788	Prices (min.)	0.865	0.865
	Prices (max.)	1.294	1.294
	Estimated velocity (min.)	0.244	0.444
	Estimated velocity (max.)	0.673	0.873
1774	Money supply	0.647	0.647
to	Output	0.3	0.5
1788	Prices (min.)	−0.911	−0.911
	Prices (max.)	0.491	0.491
	Estimated velocity (min.)	−1.258	−1.058
	Estimated velocity (max.)	0.144	0.344

Notes and sources:
Derived from table 13.1.

Les Industries lainières de Colbert à la Révolution, vol. I of *Histoire des industries françaises*, Travaux de Droit, d'Économie, de Sociologie et des Sciences Politiques, no. 104 (Geneva, 1976), pp. 457–495; and Angus Maddison, *Phases of Capitalist Development* (Oxford, 1982), pp. 163, 169.

In the chart in figure 13.1 we have adopted another approach, using estimates of aggregate income from the beginning and end of this period. The figure for the beginning of the period is drawn from F. P. Braudel and Frank Spooner's estimate of per capita income at 100 *l.t.*[19] In a population now estimated to have totaled 20 million, this figure provides an aggregate income estimate of 2,000 million *l.t.* For the end of the period, Christian Morrisson estimates total output at 4,300 million francs or 154 *l.t.* per capita.[20] Taking population into account, the Braudel–Spooner and Morrisson estimates produce a per capita growth rate of 0.32 percent; this estimate falls between the rates used in table 13.2, 0.3 percent and 0.5 percent.[21] A somewhat higher rate (0.59 percent) is suggested by the combination of Morrisson's end figure with a retrospective estimate by Pierre Le Pesant, sieur de Boisguillebert, of 1,400 million *l.t.* in income in 1661.[22]

RESULTS

These data provide the figures necessary for calculations reported in table 13.2 and for the chart in figure 13.1. The table takes estimates of three variables – money stock, prices, and output – and combines them in the equation of exchange to gauge V (or, in the income version of the equation, $1/k$). Because we are working in these tables with compound rates of change, the formula as it applies is

$$\hat{M} + \hat{V} = \hat{P} + \hat{y}$$

19 F[ernand] P. Braudel and Frank C. Spooner, "Prices in Europe from 1450 to 1750," in *The Economy of Expanding Europe in the Sixteenth and Seventeenth Centuries*, edited by E[dwin] E. Rich and C[harles] H. Wilson, vol. IV of *The Cambridge Economic History of Europe* (Cambridge, Eng., 1967), p. 446. Compare [Charles Davenant], *Discourses on the Publick Revenues, and on the Trade of England* . . ., 2 vols (London, 1698), I, 24, 174, 183, 188; Fr[ançois] Gerboux, *Discussion sur les effets de la démonétisation de l'or, relativement à la France* ([Paris, 1803]), pp. 33 and after.

20 In Christian Morrisson and Robert Goffin, *Questions financières aux XVIIIe et XIXe siècles*, Travaux et Recherches de la Faculté de Droit et des Sciences Économiques de Paris, Série "Sciences Historiques," no. 2 (Paris, 1967), p. 76.

21 In this calculation the income estimate applies to 1650 and the rate of change is calculated from 1650 to 1784. The year 1784 is the end date because price data for the years after 1788 are not used under the assumption that 1789 and 1790 prices are among the three highest prices of the period. Thus 1784 is the last year for which a truncated 13-year average can be calculated. The method of truncation employed here involved deleting the three lowest and three highest prices within each 13-year period before calculating the average. This procedure was adopted as a way to dampen the effect of prices from exceptional periods like the Fronde that produced very high prices during 1650–1652.

22 As reported and adjusted to 1700–1710 prices by Jan Marczewski in "Some Aspects of the Economic Growth of France, 1660–1958," *Economic Development and Cultural Change*, IX (Apr. 1961), 371–372. For a critique of Boisguillebert's (1646–1714) works, see Walter Braeuer, *Frankreichs wirtschaftliche und soziale Lage um 1700: Dargestellt unter besonderer Berücksichtigung der Werke von Vauban und Boisguillebert*, Marburger Rechts- und Staatswissenschaftliche Abhandlungen, Reihe B: Staatswissenschaftliche Abhandlungen, vol. 1 (Marburg, 1968). See also, below, n. 46.

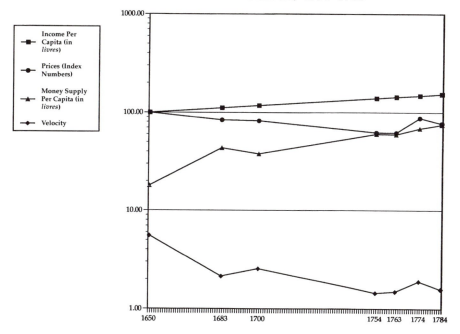

Figure 13.1 Changes in money supply, prices, income and velocity,
France, 1650–1788.

Source: Table 13.1.

Note: This graph is a semilogarithmic projection. Concerning this format see n. 35 of chapter 10.
Courtesy of the author.

with the superscript circumflex (^) denoting the annual percentage rate of
change for each variable. This computation is repeated six times for each of
six overlapping sets of years, beginning 1650–1788 and ending 1774–1788.
The rate of increase in the money stock has been calculated from data in
table 13.1, column (7); the rate of increase in output, discussed above, is
the range of the estimated ceiling figure for the entire period, 0.3 percent
to 0.5 percent; and the rates of change in prices are calculated from the
series provided in table 13.1, columns (9), (11), and (13). Beginning with
1754–1788, we do the computation twice using the minimum and maximum
versions of agricultural price change provided in table 13.1 to derive
minimum and maximum estimates of V.

The chart in figure 13.1 employs the data developed in table 13.1 and
the Braudel–Spooner/Morrisson estimates of aggregate output to derive a
different picture of results. Using benchmark year figures, the chart provides
curves of the index numbers for prices, the per capita money supply, and
the per capita income, and then sketches the value of V implied by these
figures. It is noteworthy that the V values computed from M and Y estimates

297

are much lower than those estimated for some underdeveloped nineteenth-century economies, for example Brazil.[23]

It is advisable to consult both table 13.2 and figure 13.1 because of the difficult nature of the data. Annual data are available for prices but not for other variables. To establish the calculations on the same terms, we have used only benchmark estimates of all variables in figure 13.1. In figure 13.1 the rates of change for all variables are estimated around the benchmark years, whereas in table 13.2 these variables are estimated for overlapping segments of the same long period, 1650–1788. Figure 13.1 suggests more clearly the shorter-run shifts in these variables, while table 13.2 provides a longer-run frame of reference.

Because the benchmark years do not coincide, except by chance, with shifts in the level of prices, output, the money stock, or population, the charts do not necessarily relate very closely to the timing of changes in the actual performance of the economy. No authority would accept a depiction of the period 1650–1788 as one of steady if slow growth in income, as implied by figure 13.1. (As an artifact of the semilog scale, income appears to expand more rapidly between 1683–1700 than at other periods. Our calculations are based on straight line interpolations between the Braudel–Spooner and Morrisson income estimates.) Most seem to believe that the era up to ca. 1730 was one of contraction – a phase B in François Simiand's language – with, however, periods of expansion (e.g., ca. 1660–1680).[24] Most regard the period after 1730 as an era of aggregate expansion, with, however, a slowing down in the rate of growth around 1770.[25] And all authorities recognize the peculiar difficulties of estimating M and P, if not also y, between about 1705 and 1726. (We have included those years in our charts with reservations since, because of John Law's programs, monetary manipulations, and other factors, the pattern of gradual change certainly reflects reality more poorly for those years than for any other period within 1650–1788.)

Benchmark years adhering more closely to judgments about the timing of shifts in economic performance would, of course, provide a different scheme of change in V. But they would not, in our judgment, change the nature of the problem noticed here. Looking at table 13.1 and the chart in figure 13.1, we notice two things. First, for the period 1650–1788 as a whole and for

23 Nathaniel H. Leff, "A Technique for Estimating Income Trends from Currency Data and an Application to Nineteenth-Century Brazil," *Review of Income and Wealth*, XVIII (Dec. 1972), 357–358 and n. 11.

24 François Simiand, *Recherches anciennes et nouvelles sur le mouvement général des prix du XVIe au XIX siècle* (Paris, 1932).

25 James C. Riley, *The Seven Years War and the Old Regime in France: The Economic and Financial Toll* (Princeton, NJ, 1986), pp. 3–37.
    Compare the similar periodization of the cycles of expansion and contraction in the Anglo-American economy discussed in McCusker and Menard, *Economy of British America*, pp. 60–67, especially p. 67, and for the Scottish economy in A[lex] J. S. Gibson and T[homas] C[hristopher] Smout, *Prices, Food and Wages in Scotland, 1550–1780* ([Cambridge, Eng.], 1995), pp. 164–167.

most sub-periods within it, the French money stock increased much more rapidly than P or $P + y$. For this place and period "what quantity theorists have held in common" is not borne out, either in the traditional form of the quantity theory (crudely, $M = P$) or the more modern form of it (crudely, $M = Y$). Second, table 13.2 and figure 13.1, interpreted in the light of more impressionistic evidence about the timing of shifts in the direction of output, also imply a scheme of unstable rather than stable velocities. The sign of V shifts from period to period within wide parameters: conceivably from -1.258 to $+0.867$, although more probably within -0.929 and $+0.709$ (omitting the extreme estimate for 1774–1788). Nor does a higher estimate of the rate of growth in monetized income (0.5 percent) smooth out the curve (table 13.2, column [2]). In figure 13.1 the instability of V is understated because of the use of straight-line interpolations to estimate income values from the beginning to the end of the period and because M and P values both are reported in the form of smoothed averages. Nevertheless, this chart calls attention to a very substantial, and apparently irregular, scheme of change in the demand for money.

CONCLUSION

Where do these calculations leave us? In the first place, they point to an inconsistency between the best-informed evidence now available about the French economy and monetary experience in this period and the theory most commonly used by scholars to interpret that experience. This is the case even though we have sought to adopt estimates of these variables that will tend to underestimate the size of this gap and, thereby, to leave less room to criticize putative measurement errors, and more room to consider the incongruity. Certainly the evidence can be improved, and perhaps improvements will change the interpretation put upon it. However, only radical changes in the trends suggested by the evidence will remove the problem noticed here: the money stock did not grow and diminish in the scheme ordinarily expected from experience with prices and output.

In our judgment the evidence is of a high enough quality to prompt a search for an explanation of this incongruity within the equation of exchange, and indeed within quantity theory, rather than in measurement error. Our reasons for this have to do both with confidence in the trends revealed by the data presented here (rather than in the specific numbers) and with the simple fact that very little thought has been given to the influences affecting the demand for money and changes in that function in traditional economies. Yet it is apparent that other forces besides new financial institutions, or increased monetization, can be expected to influence the demand for cash balances. Among those forces that will constitute subjects for future research are changes in the distribution of cash holdings within the populace and a more refined development of the problem of what constitutes monetization.

For the moment, however, it is enough to comment on the nature – rather than the resolution – of this problem.

As would be expected in quantity theory, figure 13.1 indicates that velocity declined (i.e., the demand for money increased) in the long run during an era of growth in output and income. But the proportions of change are out of balance. Velocity declined on a much more massive scale than income increased. Further, the timing of changes in the trend of V does not coincide closely with what is known about the timing of changes in the trend of income. To begin, the first period (1650–1683) is generally seen as a period of growth in Y, but on a modest scale. However, during those years velocity fell sharply. From 1680 or so to about 1730 is ordinarily depicted as an era of contraction, but in figure 13.1 we notice a reversal in trend (one that might have been influenced by especially weak data for 1683 or 1700) within a strong overall continuation in the decline of V. The remainder of the eighteenth century, up to some time between 1760 and 1780, is ordinarily depicted as an era of economic growth and expanding output, one ending in the 1780s in a crisis of employment, trade, and, in 1788, agricultural output. In a long-run framework, velocity should be expected to decline from 1730 to 1788. But in fact it is observed to move erratically. One way of explaining this scheme is to hypothesize that financial sophistication and added economic stability led to some increase in V toward the end of the century.[26] But it is difficult to find either feature in an era of increasing strain in agricultural output (1775–1789), war (1778–1784), and high and volatile interest rates.

In a short-run framework, assuming now for the moment that we notice, after about 1760, the appearance of fairly robust business cycles, one would expect V to rise in the expansionary phase (as it does to about 1774) and decline in the phase of contraction. Evidently the fit between modern quantity theory and French experience in these years improves as one approaches 1788. But an addition to the money stock estimates of data on fiduciary money, which is believed to have expanded much more rapidly than specie in this period, would call even that fit into question.

In the final analysis the discrepancies we have noticed ($\hat{M} \neq \hat{V}$, $\hat{P} \neq \hat{y}$) seem to point to the need for a more careful examination of the demand for money during a period of monetization and very substantial increases in average per capita cash balances. Possibly the quantity theory may still serve as a functional theoretical tool, but if so it must serve in a form that focuses more attention on the behavior of the demand for money and less on prices and income.

---

26 Jonung, "Long Run Demand for Money," pp. 216–230; Bordo and Jonung, "Long Run Behavior of the Income Velocity of Money," pp. 96–116.

APPENDIX 13.1

Notes on the data in table 13.1

Population estimates in column (1) for 1754, 1763, 1774, and 1788 are straight-line interpolations based on Dupâquier's quinquennial estimates. The figure for 1683 is dated to 1690 in the source. These estimates are for population within the modern boundaries of France.

The basis for the figures in columns (2) and (3) is the materials published by Natalis de Wailly.[27] Several authors have expressed reservations about Wailly's tables. Goubert regarded them as especially inadequate for the time of John Law because Wailly did not take into account either paper money or small denomination coinage.[28] Nevertheless everyone, including the authorities cited here, continues to use Wailly – as we do. In light of the very close fit between Wailly's silver equivalents and *livre* exchange rates at Amsterdam, more confidence in Wailly's table appears to be warranted.[29] For 1700, during which four monetary revaluations occurred, we calculated a weighted average based on the time during which valuations were current within the year.

Except for the years 1650 and 1700, the figures in column (5) are those in column (4) adjusted using index numbers from column (3). For reasons explained in appendix 13.2 of this essay, the adjusted estimates for 1650 and 1700 are based on an average of the middle and higher values. In subsequent calculations, where the data in column (5) show a range, we have used this midpoint.

The figures in columns (8) and (12) are index numbers for a truncated thirteen-year average of the prices for grain in *livres tournois,* with the average centered on the date shown in every instance but 1788. The index number shown for 1788 is for the price of that year itself. We abandoned our averaging procedure in this instance because of the distortions that would have been introduced into any average by the impact of the French Revolution.[30] The mean value of the prices in the series during 1780–1788 is 22.02; the value for 1788 alone is 24.00. The value used here is thus somewhat higher than the mean for preceding years, which has the effect of lowering our index number slightly.

27 Natalis de Wailly, *Mémoire sur les variations de la livre tournois depuis le règne de Saint Louis jusqu'à l'établissement de la monnaie décimale,* Institut Impérial de France, Académie des Inscriptions et Belles-Lettres, Mémoires. vol 21, pt ii. (Paris, 1857), pp. 177–427. Compare the "Tableau représentant la valeur de 20 sous pour un livre tournois, depuis Charlemagne jusqu'à nos jours . . .," in C.-F[rançois] Martin, *Les Tables de Martin, ou le régulateur universel des calculs en parties-doubles . . .* (Paris, 1817), pp. 802–803.
28 Goubert, *Beauvais et le Beauvaisis,* I, 376 and 399. For a broader discussion of the problems in monetary conversions, see Jean Meuvret, "L'Histoire des prix des céréales en France dans la seconde moitié du XVIIe siècle," *Mélanges d'Histoire Sociale,* V (1944), 27–44.
29 N[icolaas] W. Posthumus, *Inquiry into the History of Prices in Holland,* 2 vols (Leiden, 1946–1964), I, 590–610, 651–655.
30 See also n. 21 of this chapter.

APPENDIX 13.2

Additional notes on sources

Money supply: table 13.1, column (4)

In this column we estimate France's money stock (through 1700) from figures of production of French mints gathered and aggregated into multi-year moving averages by Spooner.[31] The seventeenth- and eighteenth-century literature also provides some observations and estimates.[32] Like many early modern estimates, the means by which figures were derived are seldom explained with any care. It is obvious that the people who compiled the contemporary estimates employed here – from Jean Baptiste Colbert to Jacques Necker – utilized both the mint output figures and other sources. Their figures provide the only independent means available to verify the mint output data. Such estimates can be found only for a few random years and some estimates are obviously uninformed. We have discarded extreme figures and focused on those totals provided by knowledgeable observers and on years for which Spooner's reconstruction can be matched with estimates from independent observers.

1650

The estimates in Spooner are based on mint figures.[33] His rather sophisticated computations allow for the probable effects of wear, clipping, and similar things; for exports and imports; and for re-mintings. Nevertheless, as Michel Morineau has pointed out, Spooner failed to take into account the circulation in France of foreign coins.[34] Hence Morineau believes that even the high range of Spooner's estimate may have been too low. Spooner would probably retort that mint production did not determine specie supply but was highly correlated with it. Mohamed el Kordi found through his study of large loan contracts a mix of French and Spanish coins in Bayeux during the period 1600–1640, mostly French coins from 1640–1670, and only French coins after 1670.[35] Note also the statement in the 1781 edition of Samuel Ricard's *Traité général du commerce*: "les espèces étrangères ne peuvent pas avoir cours en France, en qualité de monnaies."[36]

---

31 Frank C. Spooner, *International Economy and Monetary Movements in France, 1493–1725* (Cambridge, Mass., 1972), passim (esp. pp. 302, 306–309, 334–340).
32 Compare Fernand [P.] Braudel, *L'Identité de la France*, 2 vols in 3 pts ([Paris, 1986]), II, pt ii, pp. 355–359.
33 Spooner, *International Economy and Monetary Movements*, p. 339 and elsewhere (esp. pp. 306–309).
34 Michel Morineau, "Des métaux précieux américains au XVIIe et au XVIIIe siècle et de leur influence," *Bulletin de la Société d'Histoire Moderne*, LXXVII (1977), 21, 25–26.
35 Mohamed el Kordi, *Bayeux aux XVIIe et XVIIIe siècles: Contribution à l'histoire urbaine de la France* (Paris, [1970]), p. 254.
36 Samuel Ricard, *Traité général du commerce . . .*, rev. edn, [ed. Tomás Antonio de Marien y Arrospide], 2 vols (Amsterdam, 1781), I, 106.

Since the initial estimate in our series is especially important for any subsequent calculations, it is worthwhile to compare Spooner's estimates, and Morineau's criticisms of them, with other estimates for approximately the same period. According to Colbert, France's specie stock during the period 1630–1670 totaled only some 150 million *l.t.*[37] Braudel and Spooner estimated that around 1660 the French specie stock was 16 to 17 *l.t.* per person (current value).[38] Using their figure for the country's population, 16 million people, the total specie stock would have been between 256 and 272 million *l.t.* They based their estimate (as Spooner had based his own earlier figure) on a study of the output of the French mint over the preceding thirty years, which they think amounted to some 267.7 million *l.t.* But the mint data Spooner presented show extraordinarily high levels of mint activity for some years after 1650 (i.e., 1651, 1652, and 1653) that may have substantially augmented the French money supply, perhaps by as much as 100 million *l.t.*, between 1650 and 1660.[39]

As we see the immediate problem, it is to discover whether more foreign coins circulated in France than French coins circulated abroad, or vice versa. Because we believe the former more likely than the latter, we have based our own calculations on the mean of Spooner's estimates and on the larger of his two numbers; we have not used the smaller one.

1683

François Véron Duverger de Forbonnais suggested the figure for this year – 500 million *l.t.* – based both on memoirs from the period and on the recoinage of 1689.[40] His estimate was higher than the one Spooner made, which Spooner based on thirty-year and sixty-year moving averages of mint output, but lower than the one for 1689 offered by the contemporary French banker, Jean Henri Huguetan, at 534 million *l.t.*[41] Meuvret also used the figure 500 million *l.t.* for 1683.[42] The contemporary commentator Gregory

---

37 "Mémoire au Roi sur les finances [1670]," in *Lettres, instructions, et mémoires de Colbert*, ed. [Jean] Pierre Clément, 8 vols in 10 pts (Paris, 1859–1882), VII, 235, 237, 239: " ... 150 millions de livres d'argent monnoyé qui roule dans le royaume" (p. 235). Compare Charles Woolsey Cole, *Colbert and a Century of French Mercantilism*, 2 vols (New York, 1939), I, 337.

38 Braudel and Spooner, "Prices in Europe from 1450 to 1750," p. 446.

39 Spooner, *International Economy and Monetary Movements*, p. 339.

40 [François Véron Duverger de Forbonnais], *Recherches et considérations sur les finances de France, depuis l'année 1595 jusqu'à l'année 1721*, [2nd edn], 2 vols (Basle, 1758), I, 297.

41 Spooner, *International Economy and Monetary Movements*, pp. 305–309; P[eter] G. M. Dickson and John Sperling, "War Finance, 1698–1714," in *The Rise of Great Britain and Russia, 1688–1715/25*, ed. J[ohn] S. Bromley, vol. VI of *The New Cambridge Modern History* (Cambridge, Eng., 1970), p. 303, citing Huguetan, "Mémoire touchant les finances de France," July, 1705.

42 Jean Meuvret, "Les Français et l'argent," in *La France et les Français*, ed. Michel François ([Paris, 1972]), pp. 1409–1410.

King estimated the French supply of gold and silver in 1688 at £39.4 million sterling, or about 522 million *l.t.* at the current exchange rate.[43] However, the reliability of any of King's efforts has been seriously challenged by G. S. Holmes.[44]

1700

The source here is, once again, Spooner's work; our calculations are based on the midpoint of his range and his upper limit.[45] Sébastien Le Prestre de Vauban implied an estimate of slightly more than 480 million *l.t.* during the War of the League of Augsburg which ended in 1697.[46] Ambroise Marie Arnould later estimated the specie stock in 1697 at 489 million *l.t.*[47] Thus, once again, we think that the higher end of Spooner's range is more plausible. After 1700 the French specie stock seems to have decreased considerably; issues of paper money are thought to have driven specie abroad or into hiding. P. G. M. Dickson and John Sperling repeat Huguetan's estimate for 1705 of only 125 million *l.t.*[48] The stock had increased again by 1715, but the available estimates vary so widely (by up to 1,200 million *l.t.*) that using any one of them here seemed unwise.

---

43 *Two Tracts, by Gregory King*, ed. George E. Barnett (Baltimore, 1936), p. 34; John J. McCusker, *Money and Exchange in Europe and America, 1600–1775: A Handbook*, [2nd edn] (Chapel Hill, NC, [1992]), pp. 93, 308. The exchange rate used is the average for the three years 1687–1689.

44 G[eoffrey] S. Holmes, "Gregory King and the Social Structure of Pre-Industrial England," *Transactions of the Royal Historical Society*, 5th ser., XXVII (1977), 41–68.

45 Spooner, *International Economy and Monetary Movements*, p. 307.

46 [Sébastien Le Prestre de Vauban], *Projet d'une dixme royale: Qui supprimant la taille . . . & tous autres impôts onereux . . .*, [1st edn] (n.p. [Paris], 1707), pp. 103–104. Vauban wrote his essay in 1698 but it was only published in 1707, the year of his death; King Louis XIV ordered it suppressed, to no effect – other than encouraging publishers and printers to hide behind false imprints; there was a second printing in 1707 (with his name on the title page) and many more the following year. Later editions include a modern one, edited by Jean-François Pernot, with an introduction by Emmanuel Le Roy Ladurie: Vauban, *La Dîme royale* (Paris, 1992). For more about Vauban and his work, see Braeuer, *Frankreichs wirtschaftliche und soziale Lage um 1700*, pp. 77–101 and passim. A contemporary critic of Vauban's proposals argued, first, that they were poor and not his anyway but belonged to Boisguillebert and, second, that in reality, in 1704, France had a total of 460 million *l.t.* [Jean Pottier de la Hestroye], *Réflexions sur la Traité de la dîme royale de Mr. le Mareschal de Vauban*, 2 vols in 1 pt (n.p. [Paris ?], 1716), passim.

47 [Ambroise Marie] Arnould, *De la balance du commerce et des relations commerciales extérieures de la France, dans toutes les parties du globe, particulièrement à la fin du règne de Louis XIV, et au moment de la Révolution . . . avec la valeur de ses importations et exportations progressives depuis 1716 jusqu'en 1788 inclusivement*, 3 vols (Paris, 1791–1795), II, 195–205.

48 Dickson and Sperling, "War Finance, 1698–1714," p. 303, again citing Huguetan, "Mémoire touchant les finances de France," July, 1705. Contrast the report, "sans doute de l'année 1706," discussed by Braudel, *L'Identité de la France*, II, pt 2, p. 357 – citing G7 1622, AN – that put the money stock at 300 million *l.t.*, of which 50 million *l.t.* was in paper money.

1754

Forbonnais based this estimate – 1,500 million *l.t.* – on the mint output after 1726, being careful to reduce it in order to take into account the export of specie.[49] We believe that his allowance may have been insufficient and that his figure probably overstated the specie stock. Note, too, that in 1757, the year of Forbonnais' first edition, Jean Baptiste Naveau gave the same figure, 1,500 million *l.t.*[50]

1763

At the close of the Seven Years War considerable complaint arose in France about the nation's financial situation. Contributors to the debate over how to reform the finances often considered the subject of the money supply and suggested estimates of the specie stock that ranged from 800 million *l.t.* to 1,600 million *l.t.*[51] We think the higher end of this range to be the more accurate.

1774

Although we have used the Count d'Albon's figure, we believe that the French money stock grew somewhat less than would appear when comparing his figure with those we show for 1788.[52] This was so in large measure because of the costs of French participation in the American War of Independence and because of a probable decrease during the 1780s of French credits in the current and capital accounts of the balance of payments. In 1773 Necker estimated the money stock at nearly 2,000 million *l.t.*[53]

49 [Forbonnais], *Recherches et considérations sur les finances de France*, I, 297–298.
50 [Jean Baptiste Naveau], *Le Financier citoyen* (n.p. (Paris), 1757), I, 414. In the preface to his work he stated that he had worked 28 years as a revenue officer (ibid., I, ix).
51 M. B., "Mes Rêveries sur les *Doutes modestes*, à la occasion des *Richesse de l'État*," in *Richesse de l'État, à laquelle on a ajouté les pièces qui ont paru pour & contre*, [comp. Roussel de La Tour] (Amsterdam, 1764), p. 102; [Jacob Nicolas Moreau], *Doutes modestes sur la "Richesse de l'État," ou Lettre écrite à l'auteur de ce systesme, par un de ses confrères* [Paris, 1763], p. 5; *Ressource actuelle pour les besoins de l'état, ou supplément à la brochure intitulée "Richesse de l'État"* (n.p. [Paris] [1763]), p. 5, n.; and [Roussel de La Tour], *La Richesse de l'État* (n.p. [Paris] [1763]), pp. 3–4. It is quite possible that "M[onsieur] B." was Nicolas Baudeau, who also contributed to the debate his *Ideés d'un citoyen sur l'administration des finances du roi* (Amsterdam, 1763). All of the works in this controversy that have no place of publication on their title pages or that were published at Amsterdam were most likely published at Paris, "Amsterdam" in this instance being a false imprint. For Roussel de La Tour's work, "la popularité" of which "fut extraordinaire," see René Stourm, *Bibliographie historique des finances de la France au dix-huitième siècle* (Paris, 1895), pp. 105–106. For the debate his proposals engendered, see [Friedrich Melchior] Grimm, *Correspondance littéraire, philosophique et critique, adressée à un souverain d'Allemagne*, 16 vols (Paris, 1812–1813), III, 410–419, 428–439, 502–503.
52 [Claude Camille François d'Albon], *Observations d'un citoyen sur le nouveau plan d'imposition* (Amsterdam, 1774), p. 23.
53 [Jacques Necker] *Éloge de Jean-Baptiste Colbert, discours qui a remporté le prix de l'Académie Française, en 1773* (Paris, 1773), p. 120.

1788

These figures are for one of the years 1784–1788; in our calculations we have assigned them all to 1788. The effect is, of course, to lend a slight downward bias to some of our estimates of the rate of growth of the money stock. There are many estimates of the specie stock for this period. Necker preferred a figure of 2,200 million *l.t.*, which he arrived at after adjusting mint output figures downward to account for specie exports.[54] (He seems not to have taken into account the import of foreign coins.) Necker's is the figure most frequently cited by later authorities.[55] Arnould preferred a figure of 2,000 million *l.t.*[56] Guy Thuillier reports a French mint output over 1726–1791 of 2,979 million *l.t.*, including an allowance for some 240 million *l.t.* in gold coins not brought in for recasting in 1785. He suggested an estimate of 2,300 million *l.t.* to 2,600 million *l.t.* for the money stock on the eve of the Revolution. In defense of this higher figure, Thuillier calls attention to and incorporates estimates to account for two means by which specie and precious metals entered the country, means that others seem to have neglected, that is smuggling and importing during foreign wars.[57] Louis Dermigny has offered two estimates of the specie stock in this period. Originally he gave an estimate of 1,200 million *l.t.*[58] Later he increased this figure to 1,600 million *l.t.*, which Labrousse reported from private correspondence.[59] Meuvret suggests a figure of 2,500 million *l.t.* as of 1784.[60]

Rondo Cameron offers some intriguing points of comparison. He estimated that the specie stock in England and Wales increased from £10 million

54 [Jacques] Necker, *De l'administration des finances de la France*, 3 vols ([Paris], 1784), III, 66, 67–76 ("Sur l'augmentation progressive du numéraire en France"). For a contemporary comment on Necker's figures, see [August Ludwig von Schlözer], "Berechnung des Französischen Nationals Capitals," *Stats-Anzeigen*, IV (1784), 331–339. The commentary is here attributed to Von Schlözer, the publisher of this monthly journal, on the strength of [Clarita] Renate [Frowein] Zelger's calling the publication "eine Einmann-Zeitschrift" in her study "Der historisch-politische Briefwechsel und die Staatsanzeigen August Ludwig v. Schlözers als Zeitschrift und Zeitbild" (Ph.D. diss., University of Munich, 1953), p. 66.
55 For instance, the discussion in Finances, III, pt ii, pp. 232 and following, in the *Encyclopédie méthodique* . . ., 10 vols in 17 pts (Paris and Liege, 1783–1784). Meuvret reports Necker's figure as 2,500 million *l.t.* Meuvret, "Les Français et l'argent," p. 1410.
56 Arnould, *De la balance du commerce . . . de la France*, II, 206–213. Braudel, *L'Identité de la France*, II, pt 2, p. 357: "Pour une estimation grossière, disons 2 milliards."
57 Guy Thuillier, "Le Stock monétaire de la France en l'an X," *Revue d'Histoire Économique et Sociale*, LII (no. 2, 1974), 247–248, 252.
58 Louis Dermigny, "Circuits de l'argent et milieux d'affaires au XVIIIe siècle," *Revue Historique*, no. 212 (Oct.-Dec. 1954), 263; Dermigny, "La France à la fin de l'Ancien Régime: Une carte monétaire," *Annales: Histoire, Sciences Sociales*, X (Oct.-Dec. 1955), 489 and n. 2.
59 Labrousse, "Les 'bons prix' agricoles du XVIIIe siècle," p. 394.
60 Meuvret, "Les Français et l'argent," pp. 1409–1410. See also Maurice Lévy-Leboyer, "Le Crédit et la monnaie: L'Apprentissage du marché," in *L'Avènement de l'ère industrielle (1789–années 1880)*, ed. by Patrick Léon *et al.*, vol III of *Histoire économique et sociale de la France* (Paris, [1976]), pt i, p. 405, who, citing Thuillier, stated that the money supply in 1786 "était de 2,3 à 2,6 milliards."

sterling in 1688–1689 to £16 million in 1775 or, on a per capita basis, from £1.82 to £2.15.[61] At the prevailing London/Paris exchange rates, these figures were the equivalent of 24 *l.t.* in 1688–1689 and 51 *l.t.* in 1775.[62] If the latter per capita figure had appertained in France in 1775, the total money supply would have been roughly 1,360 million *l.t.* or considerably less than the 1,800 *l.t.* to 1,900 million *l.t.* reported for 1774 in table 13.1.

Since France produced very little in precious metals from mines within the kingdom, the overall growth of the money supply must be explained by a balance of payments situation in which net credits in the current and capital accounts produced inflows of bullion. A favorable current account was the consequence of more exports than imports and more foreigners visiting France than Frenchmen going abroad. The capital account inflow may also have been related to larger investment from abroad in French government loans, trade, industry, and land than the quantity of French capital exports for these and other purposes. Others have noticed the rapid rate of increase in France's specie stock.[63]

Prices: table 13.1, columns (8) through (13)

Three price series have been consulted to estimate the trend between 1650 and 1788. Labrousse provides an index for 1726–1789 stretching across French markets but limited in the range of commodities to agricultural goods.[64] Meuvret and Baulant's series, which extends over the entire period, provides only wheat quotations on the Paris market.[65] Louise Tilly's examination of prices in three French markets during a longer period that included 1650–1788 shows that grain prices in other markets converged with those in Paris by 1650, and thus establishes Paris prices as representative of grain prices for at least these markets.[66] To check how well Paris wheat prices speak for French prices in general, we have consulted a third series, Nicolaas Posthumus's index of commodity prices on the Amsterdam market. This series reminds us of the growing integration of European markets during the seventeenth century. And, because Posthumus deals with both harvest and non-harvest items, his index provides an idea of relative price shifts during

61 Rondo [E.] Cameron, "England, 1750–1844," in *Banking in the Early Stages of Industrialization: A Study in Comparative Economic History*, edited by Rondo [E.] Cameron (New York, 1967), p. 42. The per capita figures are here calculated using the population numbers implicit in his table.

62 McCusker, *Money and Exchange*, pp. 93, 97, 308, 312.

63 Jean Bouvier, "Vers le capitalisme bancaire: L'Expansion du crédit après Law," in *Des derniers temps de l'âge seigneurial*, ed. Labrousse *et al.*, pp. 307–308; Labrousse, "Les 'bons prix' agricoles du XVIIIe siècle," p. 394; Morrisson and Goffin, *Questions financières aux XVIIe et XVIIIe siècles*, pp. 76–78.

64 Labrousse, "Les 'bons prix' agricoles du XVIIIe siècle," p. 387.

65 Baulant, "Le Prix des grains à Paris," pp. 539–540.

66 Louise A. Tilly, "The Food Riot as a Form of Political Conflict in France," *Journal of Interdisciplinary History*, II (Summer 1971), 37–38, 40.

this period. Posthumus's data indicate the higher relative price of non-harvest goods at the beginning of this period, a more rapid decline of non-harvest than harvest goods toward approximate parity between 1715 and 1770, and then a more rapid pace of increase in harvest item prices.[67] If it is reasonable to assume that Amsterdam prices for non-harvest items reflect trends in the same goods in French markets, then this series indicates that a grain price series, such as used here, will tend to overstate price increases.

The curve of grain prices suggested by Posthumus's data departs from the Paris curve during the 1780s, when Amsterdam grain prices continued to rise, and Paris wheat prices declined from highs in the 1770s. In part this divergence must be due to the poor French harvests of the mid-1770s, but it may also reflect interrupted grain shipments to Amsterdam during the Fourth Anglo-Dutch War (1780–1784). In a sketch of the general price scheme, one notices the high level of prices at the middle of the seventeenth century, the trend of decline during ca. 1650–1730, the slight rise of ca. 1730–1760, and the strongly rising trend after 1760.

Income and output: table 13.2, columns (1) and (2), and figure 13.1

Current scholarly opinion is in agreement that the French economy expanded in real terms during the seventeenth century but is in disagreement about the rate of growth. The highest rate yet suggested, an annual average of 1.0 percent between 1701–1710 and 1781–1790, requires an implausibly low estimate of output at the beginning of this period.[68] It also stands at odds with impressionistic depictions of economic life in the eighteenth century, which call attention to gradual change rather than dynamic growth at a pace exceeding that of any other economy of the day. Other work suggests considerably lower growth rates. Investigating the woollen industry, a major industry believed to have grown markedly, Markovitch found production to have expanded at rates between 0.57 percent and 0.66 percent per annum.[69] Adjusting the Marczewski–Toutain–Markovitch estimates, Angus Maddison suggests an aggregate growth in gross domestic product between 1700 and 1820 that works out to an annual rate of 0.551 percent.[70] It should be noted that the growth rate suggested by Maddison's numbers extends into a later

67 Posthumus, *Inquiry into the History of Prices in Holland*, passim.
68 Patrick [K.] O'Brien and Caglar Keyder, *Economic Growth in Britain and France, 1780–1914: Two Paths to the Twentieth Century* (London, [1978]), p. 57, using the data developed in Marczewski, "Some Aspects of the Economic Growth of France," pp. 371–378.
69 Markovitch, "L'Évolution industrielle de la France," pp. 277–279; Markovitch, *Histoire des industries françaises*, pp. 457–495.
70 Maddison, *Phases of Capitalist Development*, pp. 163, 169. See Marczewski, "Some Aspects of the Economic Growth of France," pp. 369–386; and Jean Marczewski, *Le Produit physique de l'économie française de 1789 à 1913 (Comparison avec la Grande-Bretagne)*, Cahiers de l'Institut de Science Économique Appliquée, ser. AF: "Histoire Quantitative de l'Économie Française," no. 4 (Paris, 1965), pp. lxxviii–lxxxiv and elsewhere.

period than dealt with here, a period during part of which higher rates of growth are believed to have prevailed.

Christian Morrisson has offered an estimate of total output toward the end of the century which, at 4,300 million *francs,* is lower than the figures suggested by the inquiry sponsored by the Institut de Science Économique Appliquée, reported on by Marczewski.[71] Comparing this figure with estimates of output between 1660 and 1700, which range from 1,400 million *l.t.* in 1661 by Boisguillebert to 100 *l.t.* per capita – and, thus, with a population of 20 million, some 2,000 million *l.t.* – by Braudel and Spooner, furnishes a lower and more plausible estimate of the rate of expansion in this economy.[72] Taking population into account (table 13.1, column [1]), these estimates produce a growth rate of between 0.32 percent and 0.59 percent per annum.

Reflecting on how much growth is feasible for early modern economies, and thinking in terms of backward projection, Paul Bairoch has ventured the opinion that "it is unlikely that [European] per capita income increased by more than 0.2–0.3 percent [per annum] between 1500 and 1800."[73] As a rate of increase continuously compounded over three centuries, this rate still seems excessive. We have taken Bairoch's higher-bound estimate of 0.3 percent as a lower-bound estimate of growth in eighteenth-century France. Our higher-bound estimate in table 13.2 – 0.5 percent per annum – derives from other evaluations of the performance of the French economy, as discussed above, and from the recognition that some estimates of growth incorporate increased monetization, which Bairoch's technique does not. This figure is an appropriate ceiling to use in the equation of exchange, in which either T or y is meant to refer to a level of monetary dealings.

71 In Morrisson and Goffin, *Questions financières aux XVIIe et XVIIIe siècles,* p. 76.
72 Braudel and Spooner, "Prices in Europe from 1450 to 1750," p. 446. See also [Davenant], *Discourses on the Publick Revenues,* I, 24, 174, 183, 188; Marczewski, "Some Aspects of the Economic Growth of France," pp. 369–386; and Gerboux, *Discussion sur les effets de la démonétisation de l'or,* p. 35.
73 Bairoch, "Europe's Gross National Product," p. 277.

14

THE ECONOMY OF THE BRITISH WEST INDIES, 1763–1790

Growth, stagnation, or decline?

The islands of the West Indies have been compared to a necklace of jewels strung in a curving line along the outer edge of the Caribbean Sea.[1] Anchored at the north end by Jamaica and at the south by Barbados, the chain of the British West Indies was interspersed with other islands variously held by France, Spain, The Netherlands, Denmark, and even Sweden. Jamaica and Barbados stood apart. The other British islands belonged to one or another of two geographical groups: to the north, the Leeward Islands; to the south, the Windward Islands. In the first group were four chief islands – Antigua, Montserrat, St Christopher (colloquially called St Kitts), and Nevis – and a subgroup of smaller islands, the British Virgin Islands. In the Windward Islands were Dominica, St Vincent, Tobago, and Grenada and the Grenadines. The Windward Islands were also called the Ceded Islands because they had been turned over to Great Britain by France in 1763 as part of the

1   The original version of this chapter was published under a different title in *The Economy of Early America: The Revolutionary Era, 1763–1790*, ed. Ronald Hoffman, John J. McCusker, Russell R. Menard, and Peter J. Albert (Charlottesville, Va., 1988), pp. 275–302. Copyright © 1988 by the Rector and Visitors of the University of Virginia. This revision is presented here with the permission of the University Press of Virginia.
    I continue to be thankful for the help and support given me by Paul G. E. Clemens, Stanley L. Engerman, the other participants in the conference on the Economy of Early America: The Revolutionary Period, 1763–1790, and by the members of the Indiana University Economic History Workshop, the University of Illinois Economic History and Comparative Systems Workshop, the seminar on the Histoire Économique sur l'Atlantique et Ses Rivages of the Université de Bordeaux III, the Quantitative Economic History Discussion Group of the London School of Economics, and the Forsker- og Hoved-fagsseminar i Økonomisk Historie of Universitetet i Bergen. I am also pleased to acknowledge the assistance of the Institute of Early American History and Culture, Harvard University, the National Endowment for the Humanities, the American Council of Learned Societies, the American Enterprise Institute, the American Historical Association, the American Philosophical Society, the University of Maryland, the fellows of St Catherine's College, Oxford, and the John Simon Guggenheim Memorial Foundation. The original essay was completed while I was a visiting research fellow at the Centrum voor Economische Studiën, Katholieke Universiteit Leuven, Belgium, to the faculty and students of which I am especially grateful.

settlement ending the Seven Years War. All of the British West Indies are listed, with their estimated populations, 1760–1790, in table 14.1.

There were other changes in the ownership of the individual islands during the seventeenth and eighteenth centuries for all but the two most important British islands, Jamaica and Barbados. From the time these two had been first occupied by Englishmen, they continued without interruption to be productive members of the old empire. Sugar manufacture started on Barbados in the 1630s underwent a period of very rapid expansion in the 1640s and 1650s, and continued to grow during the next two decades, though at a much slower rate. Decline had set in by the 1680s and lasted for the next half century. The recovery that began in the 1720s persisted until the time of the Revolutionary War. The Leeward Islands followed a path similar to that of Barbados, differing only in the timing and intensity of their own "sugar revolutions." None experienced this transformation as early, as suddenly, or as completely as Barbados. Jamaica, captured from Spain in 1654, benefited from a steady growth that continued until the Revolutionary War, merely slowing somewhat between the 1680s and the 1730s.

The economies of all of the British sugar islands were similar in structure, and one can easily talk about them as one entity. The chief difference in sugar growing between Barbados and Jamaica was the restriction imposed on the former by the limited supply of land available to its planters – and even that difference was muted somewhat by the availability of new lands for sugar in neighboring colonies. Jamaica suffered from no such restriction, its land being effectively limitless, at least in this era. As a result of this difference the planters of Barbados (and the Leeward Islands) tended to farm more intensively, whereas Jamaican planters engaged in land-extensive agriculture. Nevertheless, all the British West Indies were prosperous places by the time of the War for American Independence.[2]

◆ ◆ ◆ ◆ ◆

The American Revolution ended that period of prosperity not only in the British West Indies but throughout British America. All will agree that the years immediately following 1776 were not as good, economically speaking, for the colonies in rebellion as the years preceding the war. One study of

2 For an account of the economic history of the British sugar islands, see Richard B. Sheridan, *Sugar and Slavery: An Economic History of the British West Indies, 1623–1775* (St Lawrence, Barbados, 1974). For a more recent, shorter synthesis, see John J. McCusker and Russell R. Menard, *The Economy of British America, 1607–1789,* [2nd edn] (Chapel Hill, NC, [1991]), pp. 144–168. Older but still valuable treatments are Frank Wesley Pitman, *The Development of the British West Indies, 1700–1763,* Yale Historical Publications, Study 4 (New Haven, Conn., 1917), and Lowell Joseph Ragatz, *The Fall of the Planter Class in the British Caribbean, 1763–1833: A Study in Social and Economic History* (New York, 1928). For general histories, see Alan Burns, *History of the British West Indies* (London, 1954), and J[ohn] H. Parry, P[hillip] M. Sherlock, and A[nthony] P. Maingot, *A Short History of the West Indies,* 4th edn (London, 1987).

Table 14.1 Population estimates for the British West Indies, 1760–1790 (thousands)

Colony	Category	1760 (1)	1770 (2)	1780 (3)	1790 (4)
Jamaica	White	10.0	12.2	17.9	18.3
	Black	172.9	201.7	243.2	275.6
	Total	182.9	213.9	261.1	293.9
Barbados	White	17.8	17.2	16.9	16.2
	Black	86.6	92.0	82.4	75.4
	Total	104.4	109.2	99.3	91.6
Antigua	White	3.2	2.8	2.3	5.0
	Black	35.2	38.6	37.9	45.0
	Total	38.4	41.4	40.2	50.0
Montserrat	White	1.4	1.3	1.1	0.8
	Black	9.1	9.9	9.3	8.0
	Total	10.5	11.2	10.4	8.8
Nevis	White	1.2	1.6	2.0	1.5
	Black	8.5	8.8	9.0	8.4
	Total	9.7	10.4	11.0	9.9
St Christopher	White	2.6	2.1	2.1	4.0
	Black	22.3	23.4	24.6	26.3
	Total	24.9	25.5	26.7	30.3
British Virgin Islands	White	1.2	1.2	(1.2)	(1.2)
	Black	6.8	8.5	10.2	(10.2)
	Total	8.0	9.7	11.4	11.4
Dominica	White	1.6	3.1	1.2	1.2
	Black	5.7	14.8	18.8	15.4
	Total	7.3	17.9	20.0	16.6
St Vincent	White	0.8	2.0	1.5	1.4
	Black	5.4	8.3	11.9	11.8
	Total	6.2	10.3	13.4	13.2
Grenada	White	1.3	1.6	1.1	1.0
	Black	12.4	24.7	31.5	27.0
	Total	13.7	26.3	32.6	28.0
Tobago	White	–	0.2	0.8	0.5
	Black	–	3.2	12.0	15.4
	Total	–	3.4	12.8	15.9
SUBTOTALS					
Leeward Islands	White	9.6	9.0	8.7	12.5
	Black	81.9	89.2	91.0	97.9
	Total	91.5	98.2	99.7	110.4
Windward Islands	White	3.7	6.9	4.6	4.1
	Black	23.5	51.0	74.2	69.6
	Total	27.2	57.9	78.8	73.7
TOTALS					
British West Indies	White	41.1	45.3	48.1	51.1
	Black	364.9	433.9	490.8	518.5
	Total	406.0	479.2	538.9	569.6

Notes and sources:
Estimates are based on materials assembled and methods discussed in John J. McCusker, *Rum and the American Revolution: The Rum Trade and the Balance of Payments of the Thirteen Continental Colonies, 1650–1775*, 2 vols (New York, 1989, [Ph.D. diss., University of

Pittsburgh, 1970]), II, 548–767, supplemented by additional research. Data for the period after 1790 are especially fragmentary and the estimates for 1790 are based on figures for 1785–1789, thus understating somewhat the actual population levels for 1790.

"Black" includes slaves, free blacks, maroons, and Amerindians; the last three groups constituted an insignificant percentage of the total.

Not all totals agree because of rounding. Figures in parentheses are essentially guesses. The subtotals for the Leeward Islands add together the figures for Antigua, Montserrat, Nevis, St Christopher, and the British Virgin Islands (Anguilla, Tortola, and others). The subtotals for the Ceded Islands, or Windward Islands, add together the figures for Dominica, Grenada and the Grenadines, St Vincent, and Tobago. The Windward Islands did not become British until 1763. It is therefore technically incorrect to add the population of this group to the total of the British West Indies for 1760 though not to have done so in this instance would have distorted unacceptably any calculations of the changes between 1760 and 1770. The figures presented in Alex[andre] Moreau de Jonnès, *Recherches statistiques sur l'esclavage colonial et sur les moyens de le supprimer* (Paris, 1842), pp. 36–45, are not strictly comparable to the above estimates since his numbers were not subjected to the same adjustments to correct for undercounting and other problems with the raw data. See the discussions in the text and notes in McCusker, *Rum and the American Revolution*, II, 548–767. Contrast the wildly inaccurate, even mythical figures in Avalle, *Tableau comparatif des productions colonies françaises aux Antilles, avec celles des colonies anglaises, espagnoles et hollandaises, de l'année 1787 à 1788* (Paris, [1799]), table IX: "Relevé général de la population . . ."

the period's economic history has even suggested that the decline in the United States during the War of Independence approached the levels recorded during the Great Depression of the 1930s.[3] Nevertheless, renewal had set in by the middle of the 1780s. It is probable that, for the United States, economic historians will eventually agree to characterize the whole era of the American Revolution in terms of three sub-periods: 1763–1775, a time of general prosperity; 1776–1783, a time of severe depression; and 1783–1790, a time of slow recovery.[4]

However apropos that characterization may be of the economy of the United States, we cannot be sure it serves equally well for the other British colonies in the New World – Canada and the West Indies. Indeed, for the West Indies there is reason to think that it is much too sanguine a picture. The standard works on the subject – in so far as there are any works on the subject of the economy of the British West Indies in the late eighteenth century – designate the whole period after 1763 as one of decline. Alan Burns, in his *History of the British West Indies*, entitled his chapter on the two decades after 1764 the "years of disaster."[5] Lowell Joseph Ragatz also

3 McCusker and Menard, *Economy of British America*, pp. 373–374. Compare Stanley L. Engerman and Robert E. Gallman, "U.S. Economic Growth, 1783–1860," *Research in Economic History*, VIII (1983), 19.

4 This is not to say that there were no fluctuations within these sub-periods. See ibid., pp. 60–65. The standard work on the latter two sub-periods (and beyond) is still Curtis P. Nettels, *The Emergence of a National Economy, 1775–1815*, vol. II of *The Economic History of the United States*, ed. Henry David et al. (New York, [1962]).

5 Burns, *History of the British West Indies*, pp. 501–535. Compare Robert Livingston Schuyler, *The Fall of the Old Colonial System: A Study in British Free Trade, 1770–1870* (London, 1945), for whom "the fall" began in 1770 and the somber tone in Perry and Sherlock, *History of the West Indies*, pp. 127–141.

dated the long-term decline of the British Caribbean as having begun with the Treaty of Paris that ended the Seven Years War.[6]

Yet much of the evidence that the economic fortunes of the West Indian possessions of Great Britain peaked before that war and fell steadily thereafter is at least worthy of reexamination. Most of what Ragatz and others have relied on to demonstrate their case is simply a repetition of contemporary fears and complaints uttered in petitions and papers presented before Parliament pleading the particular purposes of the sugar lobby. The island planters had a good deal to fear and, indeed, they had been complaining mightily for years. But their jaundiced views of their expectations during the decades after 1763, and especially after 1783, have become accepted by many as historically accurate. What the economic situation of the British West Indies actually was over these years remains to be established.

◆ ◆ ◆ ◆ ◆

The British West Indian sugar planters traditionally pursued two interrelated goals as they sought to maximize the returns from their enterprises. On the one hand, they tried to keep high the prices they received for things they sold; on the other hand, they tried to keep low the prices they paid for the things they purchased. They exported sugar, molasses, rum, and other, less important, tropical commodities. In order to maintain high prices for their exports, they strove both to preserve their monopoly on the supply of these goods to Great Britain and Ireland and to extend it to the entirety of the British Empire. One such attempt produced the Molasses Act of 1733, but it proved less than effective. Another of their efforts resulted in the return

---

6 Ragatz, *Fall of the Planter Class.* Compare Eric Williams, *Capitalism and Slavery* (Chapel Hill, NC, 1944). For the broader historiographical traditions of which these works are a part, especially Williams's work, see Elsa V. Goveia, A *Study on the Historiography of the British West Indies to the End of the Nineteenth Century*, Instituto Panamericano de Geografía e Historia, publicación no. 78 (Mexico, 1956); Seymour Drescher, *Econocide: British Slavery in the Era of Abolition* (Pittsburgh, 1977), pp. 3–9; William A. Green, "Caribbean Historiography, 1600–1900: The Recent Tide," *Journal of Interdisciplinary History*, VII (Winter 1977), 509–530; Richard B. Sheridan, "Eric Williams and Capitalism and Slavery: A Biographical and Historiographical Essay," in *British Capitalism and Caribbean Slavery: The Legacy of Eric Williams*, ed. Barbara L. Solow and Stanley L. Engerman (Cambridge, Eng., 1987), pp. 317–345; and McCusker and Menard, *Economy of British America*, pp. 17–50 (especially pp. 41–45) and 144–168.

  Ragatz's book began where the other standard book on the subject (Pitman, *Development of the British West Indies*) left off. In contrast, Richard Pares, the fine historian of the West Indies, called the period ending with the War of Independence a "silver age," a view concurred in by Richard B. Sheridan. Pares, *Merchants and Planters*, Supplement no. 4 to *The Economic History Review* (Cambridge, Eng., 1960), p. 40; Sheridan, *The Development of the Plantations to 1750; An Era of West Indian Prosperity, 1750–1775*, Chapters in Caribbean History, pt i ([St Lawrence, Barbados, 1970]), p. 74. The "golden age" is supposed to have been the halcyon days of the 1640s. Compare Jacques Godechot, "La Période révolutionnaire et impériale," *Revue Historique*, no. 539 (July–Sept. 1981), 225, summing up Michel Devèze, *Antilles, Guyanes, la mer des Caraïbes de 1492 à 1789* (Paris, 1977): "Les Antilles françaises connaissent, entre 1763 et 1789, l'apogée de leur prospérité."

to France after the Seven Years War of Martinique and Guadeloupe – but not the Windward Islands.

Just as the sugar planters tried to extend their monopoly on supply to maintain high prices for their exports, they also tried to keep their costs low. The planters needed to purchase and import almost all their supplies – food, timber products, livestock – and they tried to keep these costs down by limiting the markets to which their suppliers could sell such items. The Molasses Act was designed to do that, too, by preventing the North American colonists from trading with the West Indian colonies of the French, the Danes, the Dutch, or the Spanish. It surprised no one, then or later, that the North Americans were not comfortable with attempts to prevent them from buying or selling in the "foreign" West Indies. But the British West Indian sugar planters were not overconcerned about the plight of the North Americans. In pursuit of their own profits, in ways as mercantilistic as those of the mother country, they tried every device they could to maximize returns and minimize costs.[7]

They persisted in these efforts after the Seven Years War. We are all more or less familiar with the events of the period 1763–1790 as seen from the perspective of the British sugar planters. They continued to be unhappy that the Treaty of Paris had introduced four new sugar islands into the old select circle of British producers, thus diluting the monopoly on supply previously enjoyed by the older colonies. They were unhappy with the events of the War of Independence because it cut off their trade with the Thirteen Continental Colonies, disrupted their trade with Europe, and introduced foreign produce into the British market as captured cargoes, the prizes of war. And they were particularly unhappy after the war when the British government, enforcing the Navigation Acts with new orders and acts, tried to close down for good most of the trade with the United States. Each of these developments threatened the position of the sugar producers of the

---

7   For the details of all this, see Pitman, *Development of the British West Indies*. See also Richard B. Sheridan, "The Molasses Act and the Market Strategy of the British Planters," *JEcH*, XVII (Mar. 1957), 62–83. The law was the Act of 6 George II, c. 13. However aggrieved the West Indians may have felt, it is important to appreciate the preferential treatment accorded them within the old empire. Just as the passage of the Molasses Act attests to Parliament's willingness to give special help to the planters, so also did the government cater to West Indian commercial interests. As Jacob M. Price has put it:

> The original laws [of trade] too, whatever they said on paper, were never seriously intended to apply to the West Indies where "international trade" remained the rule rather than the exception. How really serious were the British ministers after 1763 in wishing to alter the trade [between the British and the non-British colonies]? The establishment of free ports, *inter alia,* suggests a greater interest in legitimating rather than stopping it.

Price, Review of *Trade and Empire: The British Customs Service in Colonial America, 1660–1775* by Thomas C. Barrow, *JEcH*, XXVII (Sept. 1967), 400. The West Indians' complaints were intended simply to induce a continuation or expansion of such privileged treatment.

British West Indies, either by weakening the market for their produce or by increasing the cost of their provisions and supplies. They complained before the fact that such actions would harm them. They complained over the years that these actions were harming them. And they complained later that they had suffered greatly as a result of these actions.[8] Given the obvious self-serving content of the complaints, the questions to be answered are: "Were they harmed?" and, if so, "How much were they harmed?" Ragatz and others, by relying almost exclusively on the public petitions and protests of the complainants, have answered just as did the complainants themselves. We might want to have another look.

Ideally, of course, we could turn to a range of data to answer these questions, but in reality we cannot. Economic data are much less abundant for the British West Indies than they are for Great Britain itself or even for the Thirteen Continental Colonies. And economic data for the British West Indies, however difficult to find for the period before 1775, are still more difficult to find for the years afterwards. The last two phases of the Second Hundred Years War between Great Britain and France – 1776–1783, 1793–1815 – disrupted and destroyed the records and record keeping of the British West Indies. We are left with limited evidence to answer our questions.[9]

Despite such constraints, several considerations suggest that the effort is worthwhile. It is clear that the British West Indies were the most important colonial possessions of Great Britain's first empire. British economic growth in the eighteenth century depended on all its colonies as producers and consumers, and the West Indies fulfilled both functions superbly, far better per capita than did their neighbors in the Thirteen Continental Colonies. Over the period 1763–1775, the British West Indies were the destination of 7.6 percent of all British exports and accounted for 22.1 percent of all British imports. They were the largest supplier of imports and the fourth largest overseas consumer of British produce and manufactures. A good portion of the commodities imported into Great Britain from the British West Indies were reexported for sale abroad. Much of British overseas trade depended on its Caribbean colonies, as did, therefore, a good part of British government revenues. Anything that harmed Great Britain's trade with the West Indies threatened the soundness of the metropolitan government and, indeed, the stability of the nation itself.[10]

8   For the details of all this, see Ragatz, *Fall of the Planter Class*, esp. pp. 81–201. Compare Alice B. Keith, "Relaxations in the British Restrictions on the American Trade with the British West Indies, 1783–1802," *Journal of Modern History*, XX (Mar. 1948), 1–18.

9   Even the records kept in England are deficient for this period; a fire in the customhouse in London in 1814 destroyed many of the English Ledgers of Imports and Exports for the 1780s and later. See John J. McCusker, "Colonial Civil Servant and Counter-Revolutionary: Thomas Irving (1738?–1800), in Boston, Charleston, and London," *Perspectives in American History*, XII (1979), 344 – revised as chapter nine of the present book. For these materials, see also McCusker and Menard, *Economy of British America*, pp. 73–78.

10   These data are from BT 6/185, PRO. In this volume are some contemporary extracts from the English and Scottish Ledgers of Imports and Exports mentioned in the notes

It is clear, too, that a major change in the economy of the British West Indies did occur sometime between the middle of the eighteenth century and the middle of the nineteenth century, just as Ragatz has said. Islands that had been lively, viable contributors to an imperial economy in 1750 were dead in the water by 1850. In order to discover the causes of the change and to identify the particular results of what happened, we need first to find out when things started to go wrong. If the decline began about 1763, then perhaps Ragatz is right in relating it to the difficulty that the older sugar islands encountered in competing with the newly ceded Windward Islands. As he argued, poor farming practices and an inability or unwillingness to innovate may have been the reason for the decline of Barbados, Jamaica, and the Leeward Islands. If the decline began about 1776, then perhaps it was the disruption and devastation of the War of Independence that caused it. The war at first cut off the Thirteen Continental Colonies as suppliers and as markets. After 1778, when the French entered the war on the side of the United States, their naval forces upset trade still further and then captured several British islands. Maybe the War of Independence, as in the words of David H. Makinson, "cost the British West Indies their economic life."[11]

But if the economy of the British West Indies came through the war years without too much damage, then maybe the causes of the decline have to be sought in the 1780s. Perhaps, as the West Indians feared, continued restrictions on their trade with the United States wrought irreparable harm to their economy. The Orders in Council of 1783 and the subsequent laws that prevented the post-war resumption of the old patterns of trade certainly raised the ire of both the sugar planters and the Americans. Arranging for the resumption of free trade with the British West Indies became a major goal of United States foreign policy over the next fifty years. Whether the closing

to table 14.2. See also the notes to table 14.4, where this same source has been used. The base for these constant-value figures is 1700–1702. See John J. McCusker, "The Current Value of English Exports, 1697–1800," *W&MQ*, 3rd ser., XXVIII (Oct. 1971), 618 – revised as chapter ten of the present book. The importance of the West Indies to British economic growth has long been recognized in the literature. See Phyllis Deane and W[illiam] A. Cole, *British Economic Growth, 1688–1959*, 2nd edn (Cambridge, Eng., 1969), pp. 86–88, and, especially, Jacob M. Price, "Colonial Trade and British Economic Development, 1660–1775," *Lex et Scientia: The International Journal of Law and Science*, XIV (July–Sept. 1978), 106–126. Compare Stanley L. Engerman, "Notes on Patterns of Economic Growth in the British Colonies in the Seventeenth, Eighteenth, and Nineteenth Centuries," in *Disparities in Economic Development since the Industrial Revolution,* ed. Paul Bairoch and Maurice Lévy-Leboyer (New York, 1981), pp. 46–57. It was originally presented as a paper at the Seventh International Economic History Congress at Edinburgh in 1978. See also McCusker and Menard, *Economy of British America*, pp. 35–50.

11 David H. Makinson, *Barbados: A Study of North-American–West-Indian Relations, 1739–1789,* Studies in American History, no. 3 (The Hague, 1964), p. 132. Richard B. Sheridan would seem to agree: "The Crisis of Slave Subsistence in the British West Indies during and after the American Revolution," *W&MQ*, 3rd ser. XXXIII (Oct. 1976), 615–641, and "The Slave Trade to Jamaica, 1702–1808," in *Trade, Government and Society in Caribbean History, 1700–1920: Essays Presented to Douglas Hall,* ed. B[arry] W. Higman (Kingston, Jamaica, 1983), pp. 1–16.

of these ports to most American vessels harmed the British West Indies – and, if so, to what extent – is, however, still an unsettled issue. If it did not, if the economy of the British West Indies made it through the 1780s relatively unharmed, maybe the causes of their ultimate decline need to be sought later, perhaps in the Napoleonic Wars or even in the abolition of the slave trade and the emancipation of the slaves. Perhaps, as Seymour Drescher has suggested, Great Britain killed off the British West Indies in the nineteenth century by an act of "econocide." We need to find out when the turning point in the economic fortunes of the British West Indies happened before we can start to look for its causes.

♦ ♦ ♦ ♦ ♦

The argument presented here is that Ragatz was wrong in his choice of 1763 as marking the beginning of the economic deterioration of the British West Indies and that any decline started only after 1790.[12] Up to that point the economy of the British Caribbean continued to grow and change in several significant ways. While the data discussed herein do not address fully the issues of development or decline, they do reflect the state of the economy well enough to support these contentions. In particular they challenge any ideas that the British West Indies began a downward slide in the 1760s from which they never recovered. Rather, as we shall see, the dozen years after the

12 Engerman, "Economic Growth in the British Colonies," has already established that the decline only began with the changes attendant upon emancipation, and not before. Drescher, *Econocide*, reached a similar conclusion in an analysis of the West Indies that borrowed heavily both in method and in content from John J. McCusker, *Rum and the American Revolution: The Rum Trade and the Balance of Payments of the Thirteen Continental Colonies, 1650–1775*, 2 vols (New York, 1989 [Ph.D. diss., University of Pittsburgh, 1970]). Compare Seymour Drescher, "Le'Déclin' du système esclavagiste britannique et l'abolition de la traité," trans. C[laude] Carlier, *Annales: Histoire, Sciences Sociales*, XXXI (Mar.–Apr. 1976), 414–435. Nevertheless Engerman's message – and, more importantly, its implications – have not been fully appreciated by some historians. See, for example, Selwyn H. H. Carrington, "Teaching and Research of United States History in the English-Speaking West Indies," in Lewis Hanke, *Guide to the Study of United States History outside the U.S., 1945–1980*, 5 vols (White Plains, NY, 1985), I, 423–432. Compare his "Economic and Political Development in the British West Indies during the Period of the American Revolution" (Ph.D. diss., University of London, 1975), "The American Revolution and the British West Indies' Economy," *Journal of Interdisciplinary History*, XVII (Spring 1987), 823–850, and *The British West Indies during the American Revolution*, Koninklijk Instituut voor Taal-, Land- en Volkenkunde, Caribbean ser., no. 8. (Dordrecht, 1988). Unfortunately they are all of a piece, all of them poorly done, all of them driven by an idée fixe for which the sources offer no support. See also Herbert C. Bell, "British Commercial Policy in the West Indies, 1783–93," *English Historical Review*, XXXI (July 1916), 429–441; Charles R. Ritcheson, *Aftermath of Revolution: British Policy toward the United States, 1783–1787* (Dallas, 1969); and John Philip Wise, "British Commercial Policy, 1783–1794: The Aftermath of American Independence" (Ph.D. diss., University of London, 1972). Jack Greene, in his review of Carrington's book, made the key point about it and, by extension, the other works in the same vein: "the author has not provided the evidence necessary to verify . . . [his] conclusion." Jack P. Greene, review of *The British West Indies during the American Revolution*, by Selwyn H. H. Carrington, *Nieuwe West-Indische Gids*, LXIII (nos 3–4, 1989), 251–253.

Treaty of Paris in 1763 witnessed a major expansion in the islands. The period of the War of Independence was one of depression for the British West Indies, as it was in the United States, but one of less severity in the islands than on the North American continent. Moreover, in the post-1783 era the West Indies recovered more quickly and more fully than did their continental cousins. By every available measure, the British West Indies were in better shape in 1790 than they had been in 1770 – and that was distinctly not true of the United States. Whenever the planter class of the British West Indies began to fall, it was not before 1790.

We begin by formulating and analyzing estimates of the population of the British West Indies. While no one would argue that short-term changes in human population necessarily relate causally and directly to parallel changes in an economy, there are several reasons to examine these figures for the British Caribbean. Primarily this is indicated because over 90 percent of the West Indians were black slaves. They were the workforce of the plantations, a term much too dry to convey the reality of their economic exploitation or their human suffering. "Work animals" better describes how they were treated and how we can view their role in the economy. As plantation slaves, they were fed, clothed, and housed only well enough to keep them in the fields during their prime working years. They were literally worked to death and then replaced with new slaves from Africa. Thus there are some economic inferences to be drawn from short-term changes in the size of the black population of the islands.

Certainly some of the West Indian planters thought so. They argued, especially in the 1780s, that the war just over had nearly devastated them and that the changed trade regulations about to come into effect would finish the job. Numbers of slaves had died during the war from malnutrition and other causes and the expected continuation of high prices for provisions would only exacerbate the problem. In other words, they implied that the depressed state of the economy could be read in the population figures for their colonies, at least in the black population figures.[13] We are interested in population statistics for the British West Indies not only because they allow us to test these notions but also because they provide us with the necessary capability of reducing other economic data to a per capita basis, thus rendering comparisons more valid.

A critical point to be made about the decennial estimates of population in table 14.1 is their relatively unreliable or "fragile" character, especially those for the year 1790. They are probably all in the right order of magnitude, and those for each decade are all of roughly equal fragility so that comparisons among them are valid, but that is the best that can be said for them.

---

13   See, for example, Bryan Edwards, *The History, Civil and Commercial, of the British Colonies in the West Indies*, 2 vols (London, 1793), II, 415. See also the "extracts of two letters from Jamaica," 21 Sept. 1786, BT 6/76, PRO. Compare Ragatz, *Fall of the Planter Class*, pp. 142–153, and Sheridan, "Crisis of Slave Subsistence," pp. 615–641.

Data collection in the British West Indies, which had been poor before the 1780s, seems to have broken down completely after 1790. As a result these figures are at their worst when we need them most. In so far as the figures for 1790 are wrong, however, it is most likely as underestimates.[14] Nevertheless these data do allow us to make a point or two – points that, of course, take into account the weakness of the data.

First, and most significantly, the population of the British West Indies continued to grow throughout the period. In forty years the total population of the islands increased 40 percent. Although growth was not uniform across all the colonies – and, indeed, the population declined on some of the older islands, notably Barbados – the number of both whites and blacks grew during the period. Because many of the complaints mentioned before emanated from Barbados, it is significant that Barbados lost nearly 20 percent of its own black population between 1770 and 1790.[15] But the decay of the older islands relative to islands with newer lands was a continuing process in the Caribbean. Involved was the shift in resources from less productive to more productive fields of endeavor, a development most often effected by the actual migration of planters, equipment, and slaves. Whatever this may have meant for any one island, it can hardly be equated with the economic decline of the British West Indies.[16]

While the total population of the islands did grow, the second fact to emerge from table 14.1 is that the rate of growth decreased over the era. But this deceleration in the growth rates of the white and black populations is

14 Any underestimation of the data on population for 1790 in table 14.1 would result in an overstatement of the per capita figures in column (3) of table 14.4. That undesirable effect is offset by using data from somewhat earlier in the decade (1784–1790) to compile the estimates for 1790.

15 See Makinson, *Barbados*, pp. 83–136. The nadir was reached in 1784; the slave population of Barbados increased slowly and unevenly after that date. See "An Account of the Number of Slaves [in Barbados] returned to the Treasurer's Office . . . from . . . 1780 to 1787," CO 28/61, fol. 204, PRO. Compare "Barbados. Report of a Committee of the General Assembly, upon the several Heads of Enquiry, &c., relative to the Slave Trade," dated 18 and 23 Feb. 1788, pp. 2–3, in [GB, Parl., Commons], *Minutes of the Evidence . . . Respecting the African Slave Trade*, HC Sessional Papers to 1801, Accounts and Papers, vol. XXIX, no. 697 (1) [Lambert 4187] ([London, 1790]); and "An Account [from the] . . . British West India Islands [of] . . . the Number of Negroes Imported [and] . . . Exported [in 1787 and 1788]," 17 Mar. 1790, in *Minutes of the Evidence . . . Respecting the African Slave Trade.*, HC Sessional Papers to 1801, Accounts and Papers, vol. XXXI, no. 705 (4) [Lambert 4201] ([London, 1790]). For a discussion of the slave trade during this period, see Philip D. Curtin, *The Atlantic Slave Trade: A Census* (Madison, Wis., 1969), pp. 127–162.

16 In much the same way, we need to be wary of statements that the number of sugar plantations declined when, indeed, the acreage under cultivation and/or the quantity of sugar grown and manufactured increased. Any "decline" in the number of plantations may be explained by consolidation, for example. See the report in [Jamaica, Assembly], *Proceedings of the Hon[ourable] House of Assembly of Jamaica, on the Sugar and Slave Trade* (St Jago de la Vega, 1792), appendix 12, which contrasts the 775 plantations on the island in 1772 with the 767 there in 1791. Patented acreage in Jamaica grew from 1,671,569 acres in 1754 to 1,907,589 acres in 1789 (McCusker, *Rum and the American Revolution*, I, 242,

probably not very significant. To begin with, the decennial estimates for 1790 are most likely underestimates, and the growth rates for the decade of the 1780s are therefore lower than was in fact the case. Even so, the white population grew at a slightly faster rate in the 1780s (0.63 percent) than it had in the 1770s (0.58 percent), though not as rapidly as it had in the 1760s (0.98 percent).[17] The rate of growth of the black population in the 1780s was much slower than in earlier decades – 0.57 percent as opposed to a rate that averaged 1.33 percent between 1750 and 1780.[18] Nevertheless, just as these figures suggest, the declining rate of growth was a continuing phenomenon and not something that we can necessarily blame on anything that pertained to this particular decade. Even more to the point of this analysis, however, is the importance of changing population size on the economy. Increases or decreases in the size of the labor force were less important than were changes in output.

The produce of the sugar islands was, of course, sugar – or, more accurately, sugar and its by-products, molasses and rum. We have no precise figures on the quantity of sugar harvested and manufactured annually in the British West Indies; our best data are the amounts of sugar exported from the islands that were imported elsewhere.[19] Data on sugar exports are reasonable proxies for sugar production only if the product mix – the relative proportion of sugar, molasses, and rum made from a given quantity of raw cane juice – stayed the same. Assuming no significant change in product mix over the

n. 21). Even the Assembly's figures for the number of plantations is questionable. Among the additional materials collected for the projected, but never published revision of his "History of Jamaica," Edward Long recorded a detailed report showing 1,061 Jamaican sugar plantations in 1784. Add. MS 12404, fol. 194r, BL. The number continued to grow through the 1790s, despite the great difficulties created for the industry by the war with France. Between 1792 and 1799 at least 84 new sugar plantations were established on the island. [Jamaica, Assembly], *Journals of the Assembly of Jamaica from January 20th, 1663–4 . . . [to 1826],* 15 vols (Jamaica, 1795–1829), X, 438.

17 See in this regard the caution in the notes to table 14.1. Some of this growth was due to immigration. Many of those who immigrated into the British West Indies in the 1780s were Loyalists fleeing from the United States. See Ragatz, *Fall of the Planter Class,* pp. 194–199.

18 The estimated black population in the British West Indies in 1750 was 330,000 people. McCusker, *Rum and the American Revolution,* II, 712. The average annual rate of increase in the black population in the 1750s was 1.01 percent, in the 1760s, 1.75 percent, and 1.22 percent in the 1770s.

19 Many of these and subsequent points about the nature of the West Indies sugar industry are developed more fully in the appendices and text of McCusker, *Rum and the American Revolution.* The standard English language treatise on the sugar industry, Noel Deerr, *The History of Sugar,* 2 vols (London, 1949–1950), I, 193–203, presents the figures for sugar imported into England as if these data showed the quantities produced in each island. Even such careful scholars as Engerman ("Economic Growth in the British Colonies," table 3) have been misled by Deerr's work. Compare [Romaine] Elizabeth Boody Schumpeter, *English Overseas Trade Statistics, 1697–1808* (Oxford, 1960), pp. 61–62, and McCusker, *Rum and the American Revolution,* II, 885–887, 891–929, esp. p. 991, n. 24. The most authoritative work on sugar is still Edmund O. von Lippmann, *Geschichte des Zuckers seit den ältesten Zeiten bis zum Beginn der Rübenzucker-Fabrikation: Ein Beiträge zur Kulturgeschichte,* 2nd edn (1929; repr., enl., Niederwalluf [Wiesbaden], 1970).

Table 14.2 Sugar and rum exports from the British West Indies, 1770–1773 and 1784–1787

| Year | Imported from the British West Indies into | | | |
	England (1)	United States (2)	Canada (3)	Total (4)
SUGAR (hundredweight)				
1770	1,818,229	65,489	653	1,884,371
1771	1,492,096	46,994	840	1,539,930
1772	1,786,045	44,456	979	1,831,480
1773	1,762,387	39,365	393	1,802,145
1784	1,815,510	47,595	14,744	1,877,849
1785	2,173,468	46,116	12,214	2,231,798
1786	1,813,098	35,801	18,836	1,867,735
1787	1,926,121	19,921	9,891	1,955,933
RUM (gallons)				
1770	2,631,210	3,250,060	38,310	5,919,580
1771	2,728,565	2,180,060	67,588	4,976,213
1772	2,284,163	3,332,750	85,715	5,702,628
1773	2,282,544	3,049,298	82,505	5,414,347
1784	1,981,308	2,742,271	888,170	5,611,749
1785	3,558,380	2,188,000	677,412	6,423,792
1786	2,229,231	1,399,040	953,743	4,582,014
1787	2,251,341	1,620,205	874,580	4,746,126

Notes and sources:
The data for England are from the Customs Ledgers of Imports and Exports for these years. Not all totals agree because of rounding. For the data cited here, only the ledgers for 1770–1773 survive. See Customs 3/70–73, PRO. The data continued to be collected and the ledgers compiled, and even though the later ledgers are lost, contemporaries who had access to them sometimes published extracts from them. See, for example, Bryan Edwards, *The History, Civil and Commercial, of the British Colonies in the West Indies*, 2 vols (London, 1793), II, 509–510. Compare "An Account of the Quantity of Sugar Imported into Britain between 1772 and 1791," 8 Nov. 1792, Add. MS. 12432, fol. 18, BL, and the data presented by Thomas Irving, the Inspector-General of Imports and Exports, in Apr. 1791 to the "Select Committee appointed to take Examination of Witnesses on the Slave Trade," as printed in [G.B., Parl., Commons], *Minutes of the Evidence . . . Respecting the African Slave Trade*, HC, Sessional Papers to 1801, Accounts and Papers, vol. XXXIV, no. 748 (3), [Lambert 4281] ([London], 1791), pp. [269a], [271a]. Irving used the two four-year periods 1772–1775 and 1787–1790 for his comparisons; he "selected those years as exhibiting the fairest state of the produce of the sugar colonies"; "I am of opinion, that the Islands did not recover [from] the . . . consequences of war, sooner than about the year 1787" (ibid., p. 265). For the origins and basis of the compilation of these data, see G[eorge] N. Clark, *Guide to English Commercial Statistics, 1696–1782*, Royal Historical Society, Guides and Handbooks, no. 1 (London, 1938); John J. McCusker, "The Current Value of English Exports, 1697 to 1800," *W&MQ*, 3rd ser., XXVIII (Oct. 1971), 607–628 – revised as chapter 10 of the present book; McCusker, "Colonial Civil Servant and Counter-Revolutionary: Thomas Irving (1738?–1800), in Boston, Charleston, and London," *Perspectives in American History*, XII (1979), 314–350 – revised as chapter 9 of the present book; and McCusker, *European Bills of Entry and Marine Lists: Early Commercial Publications and the Origins of the Business Press* (Cambridge, Mass., 1985).
The data for the Thirteen Continental Colonies (United States) and for Canada are from local customhouse records, compiled at the time. See the "Account of the Quantity of British West Indies products imported into the thirteen colonies and British North America," 1770–1774, Add. MS 38342, fol. 51, BL; and the two accounts of the exports from the British

West Indies to the current and the former British colonies in North America, 1783–1787, in [G.B., Parl., Commons], *Report of the Lords of the Committee of [the Privy] Council ... [for] Trade and Foreign Plantations ... Concerning the Present State of the Trade to Africa*, HC, Sessional Papers to 1801, Accounts and Papers, vols XXVI, no. 646a, 6 pts, [Lambert 4132] ([London, 1789]), pt iv: "Accounts," accounts no. 13 and no. 21. Compare the "State of the Trade with America from 1783–1789," CO 325/6, PRO; David Macpherson, *Annals of Commerce, Manufactures, Fisheries and Navigation, with Brief Notices of the Arts and Sciences Connected with Them ... to ... 1801*, 4 vols (London, 1805), IV, 161; and the accounts William Irving submitted, 15 Apr. 1807, in [G.B., Parl., Commons, Committee on the Commercial State of the West India Colonies], *Report from the Committee on the Commercial State of the West India Colonies*, HC, Sessional Papers, 1807, vol. III (Reports), no. 65 ([London], 1807), pp. 73–74. For rum, one can compare the British Customs figures with those generated by the Excise Office. See "An Account of the Amount of Excise Duties received yearly on Rum imported from the British West India Islands into England," 1734–1788, Excise Office, 15 Aug. 1788, T 38/363, PRO. Comparable data for Scotland and Ireland have yet to be compiled, but see John J. McCusker, *Rum and the American Revolution: The Rum Trade and the Balance of Payments of the Thirteen Continental Colonies, 1650–1775*, 2 vols (New York, 1989 [Ph.D. diss., University of Pittsburgh, 1970]), II, 886, 894–895, 942–943. See also the discussion of all these data by Thomas Irving in several reports and letters dated the fall of 1787 and spring of 1788 in the Grenville Papers, Add. MS 59238, fols 62–76, 91–95, 107, 122–123, BL.
    Note that as a general policy, the statistics drawn from these data have been weighted against the argument.

short term (a fair assumption), we can attempt an assessment of changes in the economy of the sugar islands by comparing the quantities of sugar exported from the British West Indies.[20]

    An intensive analysis of the British West Indian economy has shown than the quantity of sugar produced and exported from the British Caribbean grew steadily from the 1730s through to the end of the first of the three periods that interest us here, 1763–1775.[21] The growth was shared by all of the British islands and continued until the beginning of the War of Independence. We do not know what happened during the war – although we can expect that there was some falling off – but, as table 14.2 shows, the increase in production resumed in the 1780s. A comparison of the two four-year periods 1770–1773 and 1784–1787 shows that the quantity of sugar produced and shipped from the British West Indies expanded by over 12 percent. The quantity of rum produced and exported actually fell by slightly less than 3 percent. Even though the war had disrupted considerably the production and marketing of sugar and its by-products, sugar output in the British islands during the decade of the 1780s nevertheless ran ahead of what it had been before the war.

20 However reasonable this assumption is over the short term – and the data for rum "exported" tend to support such a proposition – this is a questionable statement about the long-term behavior of the planters who, for instance, on Barbados did move increasingly over the 18th century into the production of clayed sugar. See the subsequent discussion. Indeed, I argue not only that, over the long term, quite significant shifts did occur in the product mix but also that this transformation was the reason for the continuing success of the sugar island economies. McCusker, *Rum and the American Revolution*, I, passim.
21 McCusker, *Rum and the American Revolution*, I, 128–301, esp. p. 230.

This is revealed all the more clearly if we value the quantities of produce exported in each period by the London price for raw muscovado sugar (table 14.3). The annual average crop in the early 1770s was worth about £3,200,000 sterling (in current pounds), in the mid-1780s about £4,200,000. We can reduce this to an estimate of output per worker by dividing the value produced by the number of blacks in the colonies. On that basis, each West Indian black worker can be credited with producing £6.89 worth of sugar in the early 1770s and £8.38 worth of sugar in the mid-1780s. Between the 1770s and the 1780s labor productivity in sugar went up by over 21 percent.[22]

These figures for value of output per worker probably underestimate the increase in productivity in the sugar industry. Any such underestimate is an artifact of the premise implicit in using the total black population as the divisor for both periods – that is, that the proportion of black workers involved in sugar production was the same in the 1770s and the 1780s.[23] However, the proportion did change. Despite the suggestions by Ragatz and others that the West Indian planters were tradition-bound and unusually adverse to adopting new methods, there were many innovations introduced into West Indian agriculture during the last half of the eighteenth century.

Some of those innovations had to do with the sugar crop itself. There was a very early (and technologically quite significant) attempt to adapt the steam engine to the sugar mill: one example of an ongoing interest in making milling more efficient. A new variety of sugar cane was introduced, experimented with, and eventually widely adopted; it yielded more juice of a higher sugar content.[24] Planters appear to have varied the product mix over time, producing more crystalline sugar or more molasses and rum as the relative prices of each shifted. Over the eighteenth century the Barbadian planters turned increasing quantities of their raw muscovado sugar into white clayed

22 From table 14.3, the average price for muscovado sugar for 1770–1773 was 36s. 9½d. (£1.81) per cwt.; for 1784–1787, 42s. 7½d. (£2.13). From table 14.1, the population figures that are used are the mid-points between those for 1770 and 1780 and those for 1780 and 1790. The Phelps Brown and Hopkins commodity price index records a 5.75 percent rise between 1770–1773 and 1784–1787 (John J. McCusker, *How Much Is That in Real Money? A Historical Price Index for Use as a Deflator of Money Values in the Economy of the United States* [Worcester, Mass., 1992], pp. 342–343.). On a constant value basis, productivity in sugar alone rose almost 15 percent. If one factors in the value of exported rum (at 6s. 1d. per gallon in the earlier period and 7s. 4d. per gallon in the later period; see T. 38/363, PRO), the productivity of the entire sugar sector rose in real terms at an annual average rate of 0.7 percent.

23 Another potential cause of distortion might have arisen if there had been a significant change in the age structure of the black population. There is no evidence for any such change nor any reason to believe it took place.

24 "The Otaheite Cane . . . is said to afford one-sixth more sugar than the Creole variety, besides having the advantage of yielding four crops in the same time required for three of the Creole." [Benjamin Silliman, Sr.], *Manual on the Cultivation of the Sugar Cane, and the Fabrication and Refinement of Sugar* (Washington, DC, 1833), p. 10.

Table 14.3 The price of muscovado sugar at London, 1760–1787 (shillings sterling per hundredweight)

Year	Price	Year	Price
1760	32–47	1774	27–44
1761	32–50	1775	25–39
1762	28–49	1776	29–47
1763	25–37	1777	39–67
1764	27–40	1778	45–68
1765	32–44	1779	50–59
1766	29–42	1780	45–59
1767	33–42	1781	56–73
1768	32–41	1782	40–73
1769	33–42	1783	28–45
1770	31–42	1784	26–46
1771	32–44	1785	35–45
1772	24–43	1786	40–56
1773	28–45	1787	41–52

Notes and sources:
Bryan Edwards, *The History, Civil and Commercial, of the British Colonies in the West Indies*, 2 vols (London, 1793), II, 267. These are the prices of the lowest grade of raw, muscovado sugar on the London market. The sugar was paid to the Customs on the islands for the 4½% duty. The Customs then transported it to London and sold it there at auction. See John J. McCusker, *Rum and the American Revolution: The Rum Trade and the Balance of Payments of the Thirteen Continental Colonies, 1650–1775*, 2 vols (New York, 1989 [Ph.D. diss., University of Pittsburgh, 1970]), II, 1142, 1187, n. 273. English sugar brokers believed that, because they were of lower quality, these sugars averaged 3s. (15p) per cwt. less than the average price paid for the planters' sugars sold in the same market. See *An Account of the Late Application to Parliament from the Sugar Refiners, Grocers, &c. of the Cities of London and Westminster, the Borough of Southwark and the City of Bristol* (London, 1753), p. 2n. Compare the comments on the sales of the "King's Sugars" in the letters of the London firm Lascelles and Maxwell to various West Indian planters. Letter to Samuel Redhead, at Antigua, 29 Jan. 1747/48, Lascelles and Maxwell Letter Book, 1746–1748, fol. 242; and to Gedney Clarke, at Barbados, 14 Oct. 1758, Letter Book, 1756–1759, fol. 243, Wilkinson and Gaviller, Ltd., Papers, vols III and VII, as transcribed in Richard Pares Papers, Box IV, Rhodes House Library, University of Oxford.

sugar. The British planters on Grenada, taking their cue from their French predecessors, concentrated on clayed sugar from the first.[25]

Other innovations had to do with the development of new crops, among them cocoa, coffee, indigo, and cotton being notable additions to the increased output of the several islands. Such crops had traditionally occupied a role subservient to sugar and its by-products but, during the years after 1763 and, especially after 1783, these commodities assumed somewhat greater

25 Despite his conclusions, Ragatz, *Fall of the Planter Class*, esp. pp. 37–80, 199–202, is the source himself of much of the information about the developments mentioned in this and next paragraph. For clayed sugar on Barbados and Grenada, see McCusker, *Rum and the American Revolution*, I, 198–220, 221–224. Compare the argument in W[illiam] A. Green, "The Planter Class and British West Indian Sugar Production, before and after Emancipation," *EcHR*, 2nd ser., XXVI (Aug. 1973), 448–463. For the steam engine and

importance. Whereas such goods had constituted perhaps 6 percent by value of the exports of the British West Indies in the 1760s, the percentage had probably doubled to around 12 percent by value by the late 1780s.[26] It would go higher later.

All of these developments suggest that a smaller proportion of the black population was involved in making the sugar produced in the mid-1780s than in the early 1770s. If a relatively smaller number of black laborers worked at sugar production in the 1780s than in the 1770s, then the output per worker rose in the period by even more than the 20 percent suggested above. The diminishing rate of increase in the black population of the British West Indies might simply have reflected this increase in productivity. To the degree that agricultural and technological innovations improved labor productivity, they worked as well to decrease the need for fresh supplies of slaves and, thus, to diminish demand in the slave trade.

A growing population, increasing sugar production, and greater productivity, even given a hiatus during the war years, suggest the possibility that the economy of the British West Indies was not yet in decline by the 1780s. Other data support this contention. Table 14.4 presents figures showing the level of imports into Great Britain from the British West Indies (in other words, British West Indian exports) and exports from Great Britain to the British West Indies (or British West Indian imports) in constant value terms on a per capita basis for the three sub-periods of the era after 1763: 1763–1775, 1776–1783, and 1784–1790.

In table 14.4 British exports to the West Indies and imports from the islands are reduced to a per capita basis in two ways, either by using the total population of the several islands or by using only a part of that total population. In the second series of reductions, British imports/West Indian exports are reduced to a per capita basis using the figures for just the black

---

sugar milling, see McCusker and Menard, *Economy of British America*, p. 324. For innovation in sugar production over the centuries, see the work of J[ohn] H. Galloway, especially his "Tradition and Innovation in the American Sugar Industry, c. 1500–1800: An Explanation," *Annals of the Association of American Geographers*, LXXV (Sept. 1985), 334–351, and *The Sugar Cane Industry: An Historical Geography from Its Origins to 1914* (Cambridge, Eng., 1989), pp. 84–119 and passim. For the interest generally among sugar plantation owners in technological improvements, see David [J.] Hancock, *Citizens of the World: London Merchants and the Integration of the British Atlantic Community, 1735–1785* ([Cambridge, Eng., 1995]), pp. 150, 163–164, 390.

26 The figure for the 1760s is based on *American Husbandry* (1775), ed. Harry J. Carman, Columbia University Studies in the History of American Agriculture, no. 6 (New York, 1939), pp. 429, 439, 445–446, 448–449, 462, and elsewhere; that for the 1780s is a guess founded on impressions gained from reading, among others, Edwards, *History of the British West Indies*, II, 268 and after. D[avid] J. Pope, "Shipping and Trade in the Port of Liverpool, 1783–1793," 2 vols (Ph.D. diss., University of Liverpool, 1970), II, 153–161, developed figures for cotton imports into Liverpool from the British West Indies that show a fourfold increase between 1770 and 1791–1792 although, as the author is careful to point out, some of that cotton had been grown in the non-British islands and imported into them for reexport to the British market.

Table 14.4 Average annual value of goods exported and imported between Great Britain and the British West Indies and between Great Britain and the United States, 1763–1789 (constant £'s sterling)

	1763–1775 (1)	1776–1783 (2)	1784–1789 (3)
EXPORTS TO THE BRITISH WEST INDIES			
From England and Wales	1,189,698	1,185,148	1,295,992
From Scotland	72,017	167,610	182,283
From Great Britain, total value	1,261,715	1,352,758	1,478,275
Per capita value, based on:			
White British West Indian population	27.85	28.12	28.93
Total British West Indian population	2.63	2.51	2.60
IMPORTS FROM THE BRITISH WEST INDIES			
Into England and Wales	2,763,593	2,511,998	3,515,218
Into Scotland	150,985	154,603	279,335
Into Great Britain, total value	2,914,578	2,666,601	3,794,553
Per capita value, based on:			
Black British West Indian population	6.72	5.43	7.32
Total British West Indian population	6.08	4.95	6.66
EXPORTS TO THE UNITED STATES			
From Great Britain, total value	2,563,397	699,521	2,333,171
Per capita value, based on:			
Total United States population	1.19	0.25	0.59
IMPORTS FROM THE UNITED STATES			
Into Great Britain, total value	1,702,309	160,473	928,097
Per capita value, based on:			
Total United States population	0.79	0.06	0.24

Notes and sources:
These data are from BT 6/185, PRO. In that volume are contemporary extracts from the English and Scottish Ledgers of Imports and Exports as discussed in the notes to table 10.2. These are not current values; the base for these constant value figures is 1700–1702. See John J. McCusker, "The Current Value of English Exports, 1697 to 1800," *W&MQ*, 3rd ser., XXVIII (Oct. 1971), 618 – revised as chapter ten of the present book. Compare B[rian] R. Mitchell, *British Historical Statistics* (Cambridge, Eng., [1988]), pp. 448–450; [U.S., Department of Commerce, Bureau of the Census], *Historical Statistics of the United States: Colonial Times to 1970*, 2 vols (Washington, DC, 1975), II, 1176–1178 (ser. Z 213–244, incorporating the corrections for ser. Z 227–234; see n. 11 in chapter ten of this book). In order to include more of the wartime trade between the United States and Great Britain, Florida is accounted part of the Continental Colonies/United States. The population data for the British West Indies are from table 14.1, using 1770 for the 1763–1775 calculation, 1780 for the 1776–1783 calculation, and 1790 for the 1784–1789 calculation (see also n. 14 of this chapter). Population data for the Thirteen Continental Colonies for the same decennial years are from *Historical Statistics of the United States*, I, 8, II, 1168 (ser. A 1, Z 1). On including 1783 as a "war year," see Richard Pares, *War and Trade in the West Indies, 1739–1763* (London, 1936), pp. 474–475, n. 1.

population of the islands in 1770, 1780, and 1790; and West Indian imports/British exports are reduced using the figures for just the white population. This second series of reductions is the more revealing because production of West Indian exports is more likely to have varied significantly with the black population, the producers, than with total population, and because consumption of imports from Great Britain is more likely to have varied significantly with the white population, the consumers. The per capita level of consumption – the standard of living – of the black population, especially as it was reflected in imports from Great Britain, is unlikely to have changed much, if at all, over a short space of time, especially in constant value terms.[27]

As we might have expected, both imports into the islands and exports from them were lower in constant value terms during the war than they were before the war, according to three out of four of these per capita measures (table 14.4, column [2]). (Using constant values discounts for any wartime-induced price differences.[28]) Less expected, but in line with the general argument presented here, all three measures rose again after the war to levels nearly the same as or higher than they had been before. Only the level of British exports/West Indian imports measured against the number of white consumers failed to conform to the general pattern of decrease then increase. Instead it increased during *both* periods. During the war it rose 1 percent over its pre-war level. And it grew again after the war by almost 3 percent. On a per capita basis, the white inhabitants of the British West Indies were steady customers of the mother country.[29]

At a constant value, West Indian exports/British imports measured per capita against the black population exhibited the same general three-part pattern but with a much wider variation than West Indian imports/British exports. The figures for West Indian exports/British imports combine the total value of all goods shipped, sugar included. The decrease during the war was sharp – exports fell 19 percent, and the post-war increase was even steeper – exports rose again by nearly 35 percent. West Indian exports to Great Britain in the 1780s, on a per capita constant value basis, were 9.5 percent higher than they had been in the 1760s and early 1770s. In so far

27 The subject of changes in the standard of living of blacks in the British West Indies (and elsewhere in the Western Hemisphere) is a topic of lively debate. For a summary of this debate, see McCusker and Menard, *Economy of British America*, p. 58, n. 8, and pp. 295–296. This all needs to be understood within the context of the discussions engendered by Robert William Fogel and Stanley L. Engerman, *Time on the Cross: The Economics of American Negro Slavery*, 2 vols (Boston, 1974). The point here is merely that any change is unlikely to have been reflected over the short term by variations in the value of goods imported from Great Britain if only because so very small a proportion of those things that blacks in the British West Indies consumed was imported from Great Britain.

28 See McCusker, "Current Value of English Exports." The base for this series is 1700–1702=100.

29 Some of the British goods imported into the British West Indies were, of course, destined for reexportation to other markets. Traditionally these had been in the non-British Caribbean, especially the Spanish settlements on the Main. During and after the War of Independence some of these goods were also reexported to North America.

For the impact of the importation of English cloth into Mexico by way of Jamaica, especially after the end of the mid-1760s, see Richard J. Salvucci, *Textiles and Capitalism in Mexico: An Economic History of the Obrajes, 1539–1840* ([Princeton, NJ, 1987]), esp. pp. 153–157.

as either or both imports or exports approximated the changing levels of West Indian gross national product, the economy of the islands certainly did not suffer materially over this period. Indeed, it seems by these data to have improved. Measured by the total value of exports (table 14.4), real per capita gross national product in the British West Indies advanced at an annual rate of 0.52 percent between the late 1760s and the mid-1780s – despite the war.[30]

This is all the more striking by contrast with the United States, where the struggle for independence cost the mainland colonists dearly. According to James F. Shepherd and Gary M. Walton, exports per capita from the United States were 25 percent lower in 1791–1792 than they had been in 1768–1772.[31] Table 14.4 shows that per capita exports from the United States to Great Britain were 70 percent less in 1784–1789 than they had been in 1763–1775. Estimates of gross national product for 1774 and 1790 indicate a 46 percent lower figure for the latter year over the former one.[32] Per capita wealth data comparing 1805 with 1774 argue that citizens were 14 percent worse off.[33] Yet all of these figures were generated by an economy that had experienced years of recovery. Wartime levels at the depths of the depression must have been very much lower. Stanley L. Engerman and Robert E. Gallman conclude that, if these estimates are found to be accurate, then something "truly disastrous" happened to the economy of the United States between 1775 and 1790.[34]

To the extent that we can rely on the data offered here, we can say that, in comparison with the experience of the United States, the West Indies did very well indeed over this period. For the British West Indian planters, the

30 Compare McCusker and Menard, *Economy of British America*, pp. 52–58, 373–376. David Eltis, "The Total Productivity of Barbados, 1664–1701," *JEcH*, LV (June 1995), 312–338, presented data showing a growth rate for the Barbadian economy over the last third of the 17th century averaging 0.54 percent.

31 James F. Shepherd and Gary M. Walton, "Economic Change after the American Revolution: Pre- and Post-War Comparisons of Maritime Shipping and Trade," *Explorations in Economic History* XIII (Oct. 1976), 397–422.

32 McCusker and Menard, *Eeonomy of British America*, pp. 373–376. Between 1929 and 1933, during the Great Depression, real per capita GNP fell by 48 percent. [US, Department of Commerce, Bureau of the Census], *Historical Statistics of the United States: Colonial Times to 1970*, 2 vols (Washington, DC, 1975), I, 224 (ser. F 2).

33 As developed in Alice Hanson Jones, *Wealth of a Nation to Be: The American Colonies on the Eve of the Revolution* (New York, 1980), p. 81, in comparison with data assembled in Samuel Blodget, *Economica: A Statistical Manual for the United States of America* (Washington, DC, 1806), p. 196.

34 Engerman and Gallman, "U.S. Economic Growth," p. 19. Compare Nettels, *Emergence of a National Economy*, pp. 45–88, and elsewhere.
    Sheridan, *Sugar and Slavery*, pp. 229–232, presented data for 1771–1775 that suggested a total wealth for the island of Jamaica of £18,000,000. On average, therefore, each of the estimated 15,000 white inhabitants was worth £1,200 sterling. (The population

years 1763–1775 were a time of prosperity; 1776–1783 was a time of disruption, even depression; but 1783–1790 was a time of considerable recovery to levels of prosperity that exceeded 1763–1775. Over the whole era, imports in real, per capita terms stayed constant. Exports in real, per capita terms increased markedly. The output of sugar, the West Indies' major crop, stayed steady in terms of volume and increased in market value both absolutely and on a per capita basis. The economy of the British West Indies was not an economy in decline – yet. The decline and fall of the British West Indies began sometime after 1790.

estimate is from table 14.1.) Compare Engerman, "Economic Growth in the British Colonies," table 4, where he excluded the value of slaves from the total wealth and included the slaves among the wealth holders. Sheridan's calculations originally appeared in his article "The Wealth of Jamaica in the Eighteenth Century," *EcHR*, 2nd ser., XVIII (Aug. 1965), 292–311. Michael [J.] Craton, *Sinews of Empire: A Short History of British Slavery* (London, 1974), pp. 132–156, offered an alternative, lower set of estimates that Engerman, "Economic Growth in the British Colonies," n. 4, argued was too low. Jamaican probate inventories could be used to develop better wealth estimates. Estate Inventories, 1675–1839, Jamaica Archives, Island Record Office, Spanish Town.

BIBLIOGRAPHY
Primary sources: manuscripts

BELGIUM

Antwerp

- Plantin-Moretus Museum
  * Collection des Manuscrits

CANADA

Ottawa, Ontario

- Public Archives of Canada
  * Sir Guy Carleton Papers: British Army Headquarters in America Papers, 1747–1783 (transcripts)
  * Ermatinger Estate Papers, 1758–1874, MG 19 A28
    Lawrence Ermatinger Papers, 1765–1780

Winnipeg, Manitoba

- Provincial Archives of Manitoba
  * Hudson's Bay Company Archives

Victoria, British Columbia

- McPherson Library, University of Victoria
  * Jan Kupp. "Dutch Documents Taken from the Notarial Archives of Holland Relating to the Fur Trade and Cod Fisheries of North America." MS C. 433. 18 vols. Unpublished typescript

DENMARK

Copenhagen

- Rigsarkivet
  * Dansk-Vestindiske Lokalarkiver

Generalguvernørens Arkiv
   Placat Bog, St. Croix, 1744–1791
- Københavns Universitets-bibliotek

FRANCE

Aix-en-Provence

- Archives Nationales, Centre des Archives d'Outre-Mer (AN-CAOM)
  - * Pierre de Vaissière [and Yvonne Bézard]. "Répertoire numérique provisoire du fonds des Archives Colonies conservé[es] aux Archives Nationales." Unpublished typescript, 1914
  - * Fonds des Colonies, Archives Ministérelles Anciennes
    Série A, Actes du Pouvoir Souverain
    Série B, Correspondance au Départ
    Série C, Correspondance à l'Arrivée
      C8 Martinique et Îles du Vent
       C8A Série principle
       C8B Supplément
       C9A Saint-Domingue et Îles Sous le Vent
       C10E Île de Tabago

Marseilles

- Chambre de Commerce et d'Industrie
  - * Archives
    Fonds Annexes de la Chambre
      Série L. IX.: Fonds Roux, 1728–1843

Paris

- Archives Nationales (AN)
  - * Pierre de Vaissière [and Yvonne Bézard]. "Répertoire numérique provisoire du fonds des Archives Colonies conservé[es] aux Archives Nationales." Unpublished typescript, 1914
  - * Fonds de la Marine
    Séries Anciennes
- Bibliothèque Nationale de France
  - * Département des Imprimés
  - * Département des Manuscrits
    Fonds Français
    Nouvelles Acquisitions Françaises
    Mélanges de Colbert
  - * Département des Médailles et Antiques
- Ministère des Relations Extérieures (formerly Ministère des Affaires Étrangères)
  - * Archives (Quai d'Orsay)
    Correspondance des Postes
      Série Correspondance Politique
       Fonds Angleterre

GREAT BRITAIN

ENGLAND

Bristol

- Avon County Reference Library
  * Jeffries Collection
    Isaac Hobhouse Letters, 1722–1736
- Bristol Record Office
  * Ashton Court Papers, The Woolnough Papers
    Spring Plantation Papers

Kingston-upon-Thames

- Surrey Record Office, County Hall
  * Goulburn Papers
    Amity Hall Plantation Records

Liverpool

- National Museums and Galleries on Merseyside
  * Merseyside Maritime Museum
    National Museum of H.M. Customs and Excise
    Maritime Records Centre
    Archives of the Liverpool Dock Trust
       Customs Bills of Entry

London

- Bank of England
  * Reference Library
    Elizabeth A. Buckman. "Course of the Exchange, 1705–1888: Bibliographical
    Notes." Unpublished typescript, 1977
- British Library (BL)
  * Charles Burney Collection of Newspapers
  * Department of Manuscripts
    Cotton Manuscripts
    Titus B. IV
    Egerton Manuscripts
    Egerton MSS. 2643–2651, Correspondence and Papers of the Family of
    Barrington, 1490–1713
    King's Manuscripts
    King's MS 205, Reports on the State of the British Colonies, 1721–1766
    Royal Manuscripts
    Royal MS 18 A. XII, Flavius Vegecius Renatus, De re Militari
    Additional Manuscripts (Add. MSS.)
    Add. MS 4759, Imports and Exports of Ireland, 1683–1686
    Add. MS 6180, Papers Relating to the Royal Society
    Add. MSS. 12402–12440, Charles Edward Long Manuscripts
    Add. MS 14252, Ranulphi de Glanvilla Tractatus, de Legibus Angliæ. . . .

Add. MS 22183, Sir Henry Johnson Papers

Add. MSS. 34412–34471, Auckland Papers

Add. MSS. 35349–36278, Hardwicke Papers

   Add. MSS. 36208–36215, Prize Appeal Causes before the Commissioners for Prize Appeals, 1762–1763

Add. MS 36785, London Trade Statistics, 1663 and 1669

Add. MSS. 38190–38489, Liverpool Papers

   Add. MSS. 38197–38236, Correspondence of Charles Jenkinson, 1718–1807

   Add. MS 38306, Letter Book of Charles Jenkinson, 1775–1779

   Add. MSS. 38329–38356, Papers of the First Earl of Liverpool, 1643–1808

   Add. MSS. 38388–38394, Minutes of Committee of Trade of the Privy Council, 1784–1793

   Add. MS 39683, The Memorandum Book of Messrs. John Cooke and Co., 1761–1793

Add. MSS. 41346–41475, Martin Papers

   Add. MSS. 41349–41351, Letter Book of Samuel Martin, 1756–1776

   Add. MSS. 58855–59494, Dropmore Papers: Correspondence and Papers of William Wyndham, Baron Grenville

      Add. MSS. 59230–59250, Correspondence and Papers relating to the British Colonies, 1764–1817

      Add. MSS. 59238–59239, Correspondence and Papers of George Grenville . . . relating to the British West Indies, 1764–1817

   * Department of Printed Books

   * National Collection of Newspapers, Colindale

• Corporation of London Records Office

   * Liber Custumarum, ca. 1324

   * Liber Ordinationum, ca. 1300

   * Repertories of the Court of Aldermen, 1495 to date

• Guildhall Library

   * Printed Books Section

   * Manuscripts Section

      Archives of the City Livery Companies

         Fishmongers' Company Archives

            Register of Freedom Admissions, 1614–1860 (MS 5576/1–5)

            Indexes to Freedom Admissions, 1592–1752 (MS 5587/1–2)

      Lloyd's Marine Collection

      New England Company Archives

         Correspondence from Boston, 1677–1761 (MS 7955)

      Parish Registers

         St John at Hackney, 1546–1823

         Transcript of Baptisms, 1545–1741 (MS 478/1)

• H.M. Customs and Excise, Library, New King's Beam House

   * Departmental Archives

• House of Lords Record Office (HLRO)

   * Records of Proceedings in Committees of the House of Lords

      Committee Minute Books, 1661–1836

   * Sessional Papers, House of Lords

      Main Papers

      Parchment Collection

   * Parliament Office Papers

      Unpresented Papers, 1702–1911

- National Maritime Museum, Greenwich
  * Department of Ships' Plans and Technical Records
    Admiralty Sailing Navy Draughts, 1700–1830
- Office of Population Censuses and Surveys
  * Register of Deaths
- Post Office Archives and Records Centre
  * Post Office Archives
    Post Class 1, Financial: Treasury Letter Books, 1686–1955
    Post Class 48, Overseas
    Post Class 48/1–3, Packet Offices, Letter Book, 1703–1709
- Public Record Office (PRO)
  * Admiralty Records (Adm)
    Adm. 1, Admiralty Papers, 1660–1934
      Adm. 1/480–Adm. 1/509, Admiralty, In-Letters, Admirals' Despatches, North America, 1745–1815
      Adm. 1/3992–Adm. 1/3946, Admiralty, In-Letters, Letters from Lloyd's, 1793–1839
    Adm. 2, Admiralty Out-Letters, 1656–1859
    Adm. 51, Captains' Logs, 1669–1852
    Adm. 52, Masters' Logs, 1672–1840
    Adm. 68, Greenwich Hospital, Accounts, Various, 1696–1865
      Adm. 68/194–Adm. 68/219, Seamen's Sixpence Ledgers, 1725–1834
    Adm. 106, Navy Board Records, 1658–1837
      Adm. 106/1–Adm. 106/2065, Navy Board, In-Letters, 1660–1837
- Board of Customs and Excise Records (Customs)
  * Customs 2, Inspectors-General Accounts of Imports and Exports, 1696–1702
  * Customs 3, Ledgers of Imports and Exports, England and Wales, 1697–1780
  * Customs 4, Ledgers of Imports, England and Wales, by Countries, 1805–1899
  * Customs 5, Ledgers of Imports, England and Wales, by Articles, 1792–1899
  * Customs 8, Ledgers of Exports of British Merchandise, England and Wales, by Countries, 1812–1899
  * Customs 9, Ledgers of Exports of British Merchandise, England and Wales, by Articles, 1812–1899
  * Customs 10, Ledgers of Exports, of Foreign and Colonial Merchandise, England and Wales, by Countries, 1809–1899
  * Customs 11, Ledgers of Exports, of Foreign and Colonial Merchandise, England and Wales, by Articles, 1809–1899
  * Customs 14, Ledgers of Imports and Exports, Scotland, 1755–1827
  * Customs 15, Ledgers of Imports and Exports, Ireland, 1698–1829
  * Customs 16/1, Ledger of Imports and Exports, British North America, 1768–1772
  * Customs 17, State of Navigation, Commerce, and Revenue, 1772–1808
  * Customs 21, Miscellaneous Books, 1715–1857
    Customs 21/16, Letter Book of the Inspectors-General of Imports and Exports and Register of Shipping in North America, 1768–1775
- Board of Trade Records (BT)
  * BT 5, Minutes, 1784–1850
  * BT 6, Miscellanea, 1697–1867
- Records of the Chancery (C)
  * C 66, Patent Rolls, 1201–1945
  * C 103–C 116, C171, Chancery Masters' Exhibits, ca. 1620– ca. 1860
- Colonial Office Records (CO)
  * CO 5 America and West Indies, Original Correspondence, 1606–1807

CO 5/3–CO 5/285, Secretary of State
  CO 5/3–CO 5/8, Despatches and Miscellaneous, 1702–1783
  CO 5/83–CO 5/111, Military Despatches, 1763–1784
  CO 5/176, North Carolina, South Carolina, Georgia, 1778–1783
  CO 5/358–CO 5/535, South Carolina, Original Correspondence, 1663–1784
  CO 5/540–CO 5/573, East Florida, Original Correspondence, 1746–1789
  CO 5/924–CO 5/969, New Hampshire, Original Correspondence, 1679–1777
  CO 5/1037–CO 5/1232, New York, Original Correspondence, 1664–1799
  CO 5/1305–CO 5/1450, Virginia, Original Correspondence, 1606–1777
* CO 23–CO 27, Bahamas, Original Correspondence, etc., 1696–1940
* CO 28–CO 33, Barbados, Original Correspondence, etc., 1627–1941
* CO 42–CO 47, Canada, Original Correspondence, etc., 1700–1927
* CO 111–CO 116, British Guiana, Original Correspondence, etc., 1681–1940
* CO 137–CO 142, Jamaica, Original Correspondence, etc., 1658–1940
* CO 260, St. Vincent, Original Correspondence, 1668–1873
* CO 323–CO 325, Colonies General, 1662–1858
* CO 318, West Indies, Original Correspondence, 1624–1940
* CO 326, Board of Trade, General Registers, 1623–1849
* CO 388–CO 391, Board of Trade Papers, 1654–1803
● Exchequer and Audit Department Records (AO)
* AO 1, Audit Office, Declared Accounts (In Rolls), 1536–1828
* AO 3, Audit Office, Accounts, Various, 1539–1886
  AO 3/305, Audit Office, Accounts, Customs, Receipts, American Plantations, 1677–1787
* AO 12, Loyalist Claims Commission, 1776–1831, Series I: Commission Records
* AO 13, Loyalist Claims Commission, 1780–1835, Series II: Original Claims
● Records of the Exchequer, King's Remembrancer (E)
* E 112, Bills, Answers, and Depositions, Elizabeth I to 1841
* E 134, Depositions Taken under Commission, Elizabeth I to Victoria
* E 190, Port Books, 1565–1798
* E 219, Exchequer Office, Clerks' Papers
● Records of the Exchequer, Treasurer's Remembrancer (E)
* E 351, Declared Accounts (Pipe Office), 1500–1810
  E 351/607–E 351/1268, Customs Accounts
● Records of the Court of King's Bench (KB)
● Foreign Office Records (FO)
* FO 4, General Correspondence, United States of America, 1780–1792
● High Court of Admiralty Records (HCA)
* HCA 13, Depositions Taken under Commission, 1536–1826
* HCA 30, Miscellanea, 1531–1888
* HCA 32, Prize Papers, 1661–1855
* HCA 42, Prize Appeal Papers, 1689–1833
● Maps and Plans (MP)
● Prerogative Court of Canterbury Records (PROB)
* PROB 11, Registered Copies of Wills, 1383–1858
● Public Record Office Documents (PRO)
* PRO 30, Documents Acquired by Gift, Deposit, or Purchase
  PRO 30/8, Chatham Papers
  PRO 30/55, Sir Guy Carleton Papers: British Army Headquarters in America Papers, 1747–1783
● State Paper Office Records (SP)

* SP 9, State Papers, Domestic, Miscellaneous, 1463–19th Century
* SP 14, State Papers, Domestic, James I, 1603–1625
* SP 46 State Papers, Domestic, Supplementary, 14th? Century–George III
* SP 110, State Papers Foreign, Supplementary, 1616–1825
* SP 113–SP 128, State Papers, Pamphlets, Gazettes, etc.
  SP 116, State Papers, Pamphlets, Gazettes, etc., England, 1591–1780
● Treasury Office Records (T)
* T 1, Treasury Board, In-Letters, 1557–1920
* T 11, Treasury, Out-Letters to Customs and Excise, 1667–1922
* T 28, Treasury, Out-Letters, Various, 1763–1885
  T 28/1–T 28/3, Out-Letters to America, 1763–1823
* T 29, Treasury, Minute Books, 1667–1870
* T 38, Treasury Accounts, Departmental, 1558–1881
  T 38/339–T 38/366, Treasury Accounts, Customs, Elizabeth I–1835
* T 64, Treasury, Miscellanea, Various, 1547–1874
  T 64/88–T 64/90, Journal of William Blathwayt, Surveyor and Auditor
  General of Plantation Revenues, 1680–1717
  T 64/273–T 64/289, Trade Returns, England, 1674–1802
* T 70, Treasury, Expired Commissions, African Companies, 1660–1833
  T 70/76–T 70/99, Royal African Company, Court of Assistants, Minute
  Books, 1673–1752
  T 70/936–T 70/961, Royal African Company, Accounts, Invoice Books,
  Homewards, 1673–1743
● University of London
* Senate House, Library
  Goldsmiths' Library
  Palaeography Room
    "Answers from James Glenn, Governor of South Carolina, to Queries from
    the Lords Commissioners for Trade and Plantations," 1749, MS 114
    "State of the Navigation, Revenues and Commerce of Great Britain in the
    Year 1790," MS 140
* London School of Economics and Political Science, British Library of Political
  and Economic Science
  Manuscript Department
  G. A. Falla. "A Catalogue of the Papers of William Henry Beveridge, 1st
  Baron Beveridge." Unpublished typescript, 1981
  Beveridge Wages and Prices Collection

Maidstone, Kent

● Centre for Kentish Studies, County Hall
* Sackville (Knole) Manuscripts
  Cranfield Papers

Oxford

● Bodleian Library, University of Oxford
* Hope Collection of Newspapers
* John Nichols Newspaper Collection
* Department of Western Manuscripts
  North Family Papers

Papers of Frederick, Lord North, 2nd Earl of Guildford
* Rhodes House Library
Richard Pares Papers

Taunton, Somerset

- The Admiralty Library, Ministry of Defence
  * Hydrographic Office
    Vz 10/24. Captain Thomas Foley. "A Plan and View of the Harbour and Town of Providence," 1765

SCOTLAND

Dumfries

- Ewart Public Library
  * Alastair T. M. Maxwell-Irving. "The Irvings of Dumfries (Senior Cadets of the Irvings of Bonshaw)." Unpublished typescript, 1968

Edinburgh

- National Library of Scotland
  * Manuscript Department
    Alastair T. M. Maxwell-Irving. "The Irvings of Dumfries (Senior Cadets of the Irvings of Bonshaw)." Unpublished typescript, 1968
    MSS. 8793–8800, Houston Papers, 1729–1798
    MSS. 5027–5046, Charters 3887, 4006, Charles Steuart Papers, 1758–1797
- Scottish Record Office
  * Court of Sessions Productions (CS)
    CS 96/2147–2162, 4912–4193, James Corbet Papers, 1745–1762
  * Exchequer Records (E)
  * Lanark Commissary Court Records (CC)
  * Miscellaneous Gifts and Deposits (GD)
    GD 237, Collections Deposited by Messrs. Tods, Murray and Jamieson, W.S.
    GD 237/139, Accounts and Papers Relating to the South Sugar House, Glasgow
  * Register House Records (RH)
    RH 15, Miscellaneous Bundles
    RH 15/92/13, Robert Menzies Papers

WALES

Aberystwyth

- National Library of Wales
  * Department of Manuscripts and Records
    Bute Papers
    Harpton Court Deeds and Documents

ITALY

Florence

- Archivio di Stato

Milan

- Università Commerciale Luigi Bocconi, Istituto di Storia Economica
  * Archivio Saminiati

Parma

- Archivio di Stato
  * Archivio Fiere de' Cambi

Prato

- Archivio di Stato
  * Archivio Datini

JAMAICA

Spanish Town

- Island Record Office
  * Jamaica Archives
    Estate Inventories, 1675–1839

MEXICO

Mexico City

- Archivo General de la Nación
  * Archivo del Hospital de Jesús

THE NETHERLANDS

Amsterdam

- Gemeente Archief
  * Archives of the Holland Land Company, 1789–1869
  * Notariële Archieven, 1569–1895
- Internationaal Instituut voor Sociale Geschiedenis
  * Economisch-Historische Archief
    Collectie Commerciële Couranten, 1580–1870
    Collectie Jozef Antoon Lodewijk Velle, 1400–1925
    Wissels uit de 17e, 18e, en 19e Eeuw

*   Economisch-Historische Bibliotheek

Leiden

● Gemeente Archief

SPAIN

Valladolid

● Archivo Histórico Provincial y Universitario, Universidad de Valladolid
  *   Archivo Simón Ruiz

TRINIDAD

St Augustine

● University of the West Indies Library
  *   West India Committee Records

UNITED STATES OF AMERICA
CONNECTICUT

Hartford

● Connecticut State Library
  *   Connecticut Archives, 1636–1820
     Revolutionary Series

New Haven

● Yale University
  *   Beinecke Rare Book and Manuscript Library

DELAWARE

Wilmington

● Eleutherian Mills Historical Library, Greenville
  *   William Henry Russell Collection of Morris Family Papers, 1684–1935
     Samuel Morris, Jr., Letter Book, 1757–1763

DISTRICT OF COLUMBIA

Washington

- Library of Congress (LC)
  - * Geography and Map Division
  - * Law Library
  - * Manuscript Division
    - "Dictionary Catalog of Collections." 4 vols. Unpublished computer printout, 1986
    - "Reference Index for the Dictionary Catalog of Collections." 4 vols. Unpublished computer printout, 1986
    - Sir Guy Carleton Papers: British Army Headquarters in America Papers, 1747–1783 (microfilm)
    - Davey and Carson Letter Book, 1745–1750
    - Peter Force Papers
      - John Paul Jones Manuscripts, 1775–1788
      - Samuel and Jonathan Smith Letter Book, 1765–1770
      - Charles Whitworth. *State of the Trade of Great Britain in Its Imports and Exports. . . 1697 [to 1773]* (London, 1776)
    - Foreign Reproductions
    - Neil Jamieson Papers, 1757–1789
    - Thomas Jefferson Papers, 1651–1856
    - Benjamin Franklin Stevens Transcripts of Manuscripts in the Archives of England, France, Holland, and Spain Relating to America, 1763–1783
    - Alexander Wooddrop Account Books, 1719–1734
  - * Newspapers and Current Periodicals Room
  - * Division of Rare Books and Special Collections
- National Archives
  - * Record Group 55, Records of the Government of the Virgin Islands, 1672–1950
    - Customs Journals for Christiansted, 1757–1762
    - Customs Journals for Fredericksted, 1760, 1763
  - * Record Group 360, Records of the Continental and Confederation Congresses and the Constitutional Convention, 1765–1821
    - Intercepted Letters, 1775–1781
- Smithsonian Institution
  - * National Postal Museum

ILLINOIS

Chicago

- Joseph Regenstein Library, University of Chicago
  - * Department of Special Collections
    - MS 1030, Imports and Exports of North America, 1770

MARYLAND

Baltimore

- Maryland Historical Society
  * Annapolis Port of Entry Record Books, 1756–1775 (MS 21)
  * Smith Letter Books, 1774–1821 (MS 1152)
    Letter Book of John Smith and Sons, 1775–1784

MASSACHUSETTS

Boston

- Baker Library, Graduate School of Business Administration, Harvard University
  * Kress Library of Business and Economics
  * Manuscripts and Archives Department
    Henry Lloyd Letter Book, 1765–1767
- Massachusetts Historical Society
  * Daniel Axtell Account Book, 1699–1707
  * Great Britain, Commissioners of the Customs in America, Customs Papers, 1765–1774
  * James Murray Papers, 1766–1781
- Massachusetts State Archives Facility, Columbia Point
  * Archives of the Commonwealth of Massachusetts
    Judicial Archives
      Records of the Inferior Court of Common Pleas

Cambridge

- Harvard University Library, Harvard University
  * Harvard College Library
    Houghton Library
    Jared Sparks Manuscripts
    IV Bernard Papers
    X Papers Relating to New England

Worcester

- American Antiquarian Society
  * Manuscripts and Archives
    Thomas Fitch Letterbook, 1703–1711
  * Newspapers and Serials

MICHIGAN

Ann Arbor

- William L. Clements Library, University of Michigan
  * Germain Papers, 1683–1785
  * Shelburne Papers, 1665–1797

NEW HAMPSHIRE

Concord

- New Hampshire Historical Society
  * New Hampshire Provincial Deeds

NEW YORK

Clinton

- Hamilton College Library
  * Beinecke Collection of Manuscripts

New York City

- New-York Historical Society
  * William Lux Letter Book, 1763–1768
- New York Public Library
  * Manuscript and Archives Division
    Sir Guy Carleton Papers: British Army Headquarters in America Papers, 1747–1783 (photostats)
    Transcripts of the Manuscript Books and Papers of the Commission of Enquiry into the Losses and Services of the American Loyalists, 1783–1790
    Van Cortlandt Account Books, 1700–1875
    John Van Cortlandt Daybook, Journals, and Ledgers, 1757–1772
      Journal C, 1764–1772
  * Map Division

North Tarrytown

- Rockefeller Archive Center, Pocantico Hills
  * English Translations of Notarial Documents Pertaining to North America in the Gemeente Archief, Amsterdam

OHIO

Cincinnati

- American Jewish Archives
  * Nathan Simson Papers, 1710–1725

PENNSYLVANIA

Philadelphia

- American Philosophical Society
  * Burd-Shippen Papers, 1708–1792
    Miscellaneous Items, 1708–1757

- Barry Hayes Hepburn, Private Collection
  * Journal of the *Black Prince*
- City of Philadelphia, Department of Records
  * Archives of the City of Philadelphia
      City Council Records (Record Group 120)
      Common Council, Minutes, 1704–1776
- Historical Society of Pennsylvania (HSP)
  * Nicholas Biddle Papers, 1771–1776
  * John and Peter Chevalier Day Book and Journals, 1757–1783
  * Coates and Reynell Papers, 1702–1843
      John Reynell Day Book, 1741–1745
      John Reynell Day Book, 1748–1752
      John Reynell Ledger C, 1741–1758
      John Reynell Ledger D, 1745–1767
      John Reynell Letter Books, 1729–1774
  * Custom House Papers, 1704–1789
      Custom House Papers, 1750–1774
  * Henry Drinker Papers, 1756–1869
      Abel James and Henry Drinker Letter Books, 1762–1786
  * Robert Ellis Letter Book, 1736–1748
  * Joshua Humphreys Papers, 1682–1835
      Joshua Humphreys Note Book, 1719–1832
      Wharton and Humphreys Shipyard Accounts, 1773–1795
  * Logan Papers, 1664–1871
      James Logan, Copies of Letters Sent, 1712–1715
  * John J. McCusker. "The Pennsylvania Shipping Industry in the Eighteenth Century." Unpublished typescript, 1972
  * John J. McCusker. "Ships Registered at the Port of Philadelphia before 1776: A Computerized Listing." Unpublished computer printout, 1970
  * Library Company of Philadelphia Collection
      Letter Book of Jonathan Dickinson
  * Norris Family Papers, 1705–1860
      Isaac Norris Letter Book, 1716–1730
  * Penn Family Papers, 1629–1834
      Vol. VII: Philadelphia Land Grants, 1684–1772
  * Register of Ships Entering Port of Philadelphia, 1741–1742
  * John Reynell Papers, 1729–1761
      John Reynell Correspondence, 1740–1741, Coates and Reynell Papers
  * Ship Register Books of the Province of Pennsylvania, 1722–1776
  * Ships' Register [of Vessels Clearing Outward from the Port of Philadelphia], 1742
  * Charles Steuart Letter Books, 1751–1763
  * Charles Thomson Papers, 1774–1811
      The Secret Journals of Congress, 1774–1780
  * Willing and Morris Letter Book, 1754–1761
- Wharton School of Finance and Commerce, University of Pennsylvania
  * Department of Economics, Library
      Papers of the "I[ndustrial] R[esearch] D[epartment], Wholesale Prices"[1]

---

[1] When I consulted this collection – essentially the papers of Dr. Anne Bezanson and her colleagues – in May 1971, it was in the care of Prof. Dorothy S. Brady (†1977) of the Department of Economics of the Wharton School. Attempts (in 1994 and 1995) to

BIBLIOGRAPHY
RHODE ISLAND

Providence

- John Carter Brown Library, Brown University
  * Brown Papers
  * Map Drawers

SOUTH CAROLINA

Charleston

- South Carolina Historical Society
  * Henry Laurens Papers, 1747–1801

VIRGINIA

Charlottesville

- Alderman Library, University of Virginia
  * Roger Atkinson Letter Book, 1769–1776
  * Virginia Colonial Records Project
    Survey Reports

Richmond

- Library of Virginia
  * Virginia Colonial Records Project
    Survey Reports
- Virginia Historical Society
  * Adams Family Papers, 1672–1792

Williamsburg

- Colonial Williamsburg Foundation Library
  * Sir Guy Carleton Papers: British Army Headquarters in America Papers, 1747–1783 (photostats)
  * Charles Steuart Papers, 1762–1789
  * Virginia Colonial Records Project
    Survey Reports
  * William Blathwayt Papers, 1631–1722

establish the current location of the collection have proven fruitless despite the enthusiastic efforts of such people as Stephen Lehmann of the Van Pelt Library and Sue Torelli of the Center for Human Resources of the Wharton School, to both of whom I extend my thanks.

345

Primary sources: newspapers and other serials

Annual Register; or, A View of the History, Politics, and Literature for the Year ...
  (London)
Avis Divers et Petites Affiches Américaines (Au Cap, Saint-Domingue)
Barbados Gazette (Bridgetown)
Boston Chronicle
Boston-Gazette, and Country Journal
Boston News-Letter
The British Merchant; or, Commerce Preserv'd (London)
Collection for Improvement of Husbandry and Trade (London)
Connecticut Gazette (New London)
Correspondance Maritime de Bordeaux
[Corso de' Cambij], Napoli
[Corso de Cambio], Bergamo
[Corso del Cambio], Firenze
[Corso del Cambio], in Genova
[Corso del Cambio], Livorno
[Corso del Cambio], Venetia
Corso di Mercanzie, Venezia
[Corso de Pretii de Mercantie] in Fiorenza
Cours van Negotie (Amsterdam)
Course of the Exchange (London)
Daily Official List (London)
Dumfries Courier
The Financial Times (London)
Freke's Prices of Stocks (London)
Gazette de la Martinique (Saint-Pierre)
Gentleman's Magazine (London)
Georgia Gazette (Savannah)
*Great Britain's Weekly Pacquet: Containing the Prices of Goods, with their Neat Duties
  and Draw-Backs; And a Collection of Sundry Goods Imported and Exported Weekly.
  With an Account of News Foreign and Domestic* (London)
In Genova. Prezzi correnti in questa Piazza delle sottonotate Mercantie
The Jewish Chronicle (London)
De Koopman, of Bijdragen ten Opbouw van Neerlands Koophandel en Zeevaard
  (Amsterdam)
Lloyd's List (London)
London Chronicle
London Course of the Exchange
London Price Current
London Price Current on The Royal Exchange
[Manifesto del Carico], Livorno
Massachusetts Gazette. And Boston News-Letter
Le Mémorial des Marchands (London)
Merchants Remembrancer (London)
Mercury (London)
Le Négociant, ou, Annonces et Avis Divers sur le Commerce (Paris)
Newcastle Journal (Newcastle upon Tyne)
New-York Gazette; and the Weekly Mercury
New-York Journal; or, the General Advertiser
The New York Times

Nota de prezzi di Mercanzie, . . . in Fiera . . . di Bolgzano
Nouvelles Extraordinaires de Divers Endroits (Leiden)
Pennsylvania Chronicle, and Universal Advertiser (Philadelphia)
Pennsylvania Gazette (Philadelphia)
Pennsylvania Journal: and the Weekly Advertiser (Philadelphia)
Pretij de' Cambij seguiti in Bologna
Prezzi Correnti delle Seguenti Mercanzie, Livorno
Prezzi de Cambi Posti Nella Fiera de Verona
Prezzi de Cambij fatti in pagamenti di fiera . . . fatta in Novi
Prezzi de Cambij fatti in pagamenti di fiera . . . fatta in Piacenza
Prezzi de Cambij fatti in pagamenti di fiera . . . fatta in Rapallo
Prezzi de Cambij fatti in pagamenti di fiera . . . fatta in Santa Margherita
Prezzi de Cambij fatti in pagamenti di fiera . . . fatta in Sestri Levante
Prezzi di Cambi, corsi in Fiera . . Bolzano
Prices of Merchandise in London
Pris au Commerce qui ce Fait à Bordeaux
Pris courrant des Marchandises à Londres
Pris des marchandises en Londres
Prix Courant de S. Proctor (London)
Prix courant de marchandises à Londres
Proctor's Price-Courant: The Prices of Merchandise in London
Proctor's Price-Courant Improv'd (London)
Proctor's Price-Courant Reviv'd (London)
Public Advertiser (London)
Robinson's Merchants Weekly Remembrancer, of the Present-Money-Prices of their Goods Ashoar in London
Royal Danish American Gazette (Christiansted, St. Croix)
Royal Georgia Gazette (Savannah)
Scots Magazine (Edinburgh)
South Carolina Gazette (Charleston)
Stats-Anzeigen (Göttingen)
Thomas's Massachusetts Spy Or, American Oracle of Liberty (Worcester)
The Times (London)
Vervolg van den Surinaamschen Landman (Paramaribo)
Virginia Gazette (Williamsburg)
The Wall Street Journal (New York)
A Weekly Account of Goods Imported Into, and Exported Out Of the Port of Dublin
Weekly Courant or, British Advertiser (London)
Weekly Register (Baltimore)
Whiston's Merchants Weekly Remembrancer, of the Present-Money-Prices of their Goods Ashoar in London (London)

Secondary sources

Åkerlund, Harald. *Fartygsfynden i den forna hamnen i Kalmar.* Uppsala, 1951
Åkerlund, Harald. "Galtabäcksbåtens ålder och härstamning." *Göteborgs och Bohusläns Fornminnes Förenings Tidskrift, 1942,* 22–49
Åström, Sven-Erik. "The Reliability of the English Port Books." *Scandinavian Economic History Review,* XVI (no. 2, 1968), 126–136
[Abeille, Louis Paul, and Mathieu Tillet.] *Observations de la Société Royale d'Agriculture sur l'uniformité des poids et des mesures.* [Paris, 1790]

Abell, Westcott [S.] *The Shipwrights' Trade.* Cambridge, Eng., 1948

An Account of Her Majesty's Revenue in the Province of New York, 1701–1709: The Customs Records of Early Colonial New York. Edited by Julius M. Bloch. Ridgewood, NJ, [1966]

An Account of the Late Application to Parliament from the Sugar Refiners, Grocers, &c. of the Cities of London and Westminster, the Borough of Southwark and the City of Bristol. London, 1753

Ackerman, Robert K. *South Carolina Land Policies.* Columbia, SC, 1977

Adams, Thomas R. *The American Controversy: A Bibliographical Study of the British Pamphlets about the American Disputes, 1764–1783.* Providence, RI, 1980

Adams, Thomas R. *American Independence, the Growth of an Idea: A Bibliographical Study of the American Political Pamphlets Printed between 1764 and 1776 Dealing with the Dispute between Great Britain and Her Colonies.* Providence, RI, 1965

Addison, W[illiam] Innes, ed. *The Matriculation Albums of the University of Glasgow from 1728 to 1858.* Glasgow, 1913

Albert, of Aix (Albertus Aquensis). *Liber Christianae Expeditionis pro ereptione, emundatione et restitutione Sanctae Hierosolymitanae Ecclesiae.* [Edited by Paul Meyer]. In *Historiens occidentaux,* IV, 265–713. Recueil des historiens des Croisades. Paris, 1879

Alberti, Hans-Joachim v[on]. *Mass und Gewicht: Geschichtliche und tabellarische Darstellungen von den Anfängen bis zur Gegenwart.* Berlin, 1957

Albion, Robert Greenhalgh. *Forests and Sea Power: The Timber Problem of the Royal Navy, 1652–1862.* Harvard Economic Studies, vol. XXIX. Cambridge, Mass., 1926

Albion, Robert Greenhalgh. *The Rise of New York Port, 1815–1860.* New York, 1939

[Albon, Claude Camille François d'.] *Observations d'un citoyen sur le nouveau plan d'imposition.* Amsterdam, 1774

Alden, John Eliot. "John Mein, Publisher: An Essay in Bibliographic Detection." *Papers of the Bibliographical Society of America,* XXVI (1942), 199–214

Alden, John E. "John Mein: Scourge of Patriots." *Publications of the Colonial Society of Massachusetts,* XXXVI (*Transactions,* 1937–1942), 571–599

Alden, John [E.], and Dennis Channing Landis. *European Americana. A Chronological Guide to Works Printed in Europe Relating to the Americas, 1493–1776 [i.e., 1750].* 6 vols. New York, 1980–1995

Allen, Eric W. "International Origins of the Newspaper: The Establishment of Periodicity in Print." *Journalism Quarterly,* VII (December 1930), 307–319

Allen, Gardner Weld. "Esek Hopkins." *New England Quarterly,* IX (September 1936), 483–485

Allen, Gardner Weld. *A Naval History of the American Revolution.* 2 vols. Boston and New York, 1913

Allen, Jane E. "Lying at the Port of Philadelphia: Vessel Types, 1725–1775." *American Neptune,* LIII (Fall 1993), 149–176

Almgren, Bertil. "Vikingatåg och vikingaskepp." *Tor: Meddelanden från Institutionen för Nordisk Fornkunskap vid Uppsala Universitet,* VIII (1962), 186–200

Alston, R[obin] C., and M[ervyn] J. Jannetta. *Bibliography, Machine Readable Cataloguing and the ESTC: A Summary History of the Eighteenth Century Short Title Catalogue.* London, 1978

Die althochdeutschen Glossen. Edited by [Emil] Elias [von] Steinmeyer and Eduart Sievers. 5 vols. Berlin, 1879–1922

Altnordische Saga-Bibliothek. Edited by Gustaf Cederschiöld, Hugo Gering, and Eugen Mogk. 17 vols. Halle a.S., 1892–1929

American Antiquarian Society, Worcester, Massachusetts. *Catalogue of the Manuscript Collections of the American Antiquarian Society.* 4 vols. Boston, 1979

American Archives: ... a Documentary History of ... the North American Colonies; of ... the American Revolution; and of the Constitution of the Government of the United States ... Edited by Peter Force. 9 vols. [Washington, DC, 1837–1853]

American Husbandry. Containing an Account of the Agriculture of the British Colonies in North-America and the West Indies ... 2 vols. London, 1775

American Husbandry. Edited by Harry J. Carman. Columbia University Studies in the History of American Agriculture, no. 6. New York, 1939

American Stampless Cover Catalog: The Standard Reference Catalog of American Postal History. 3rd edn Edited by E[dward] N. Sampson *et al.* North Miami, Fla., [1978]

Les Anciens Systèmes des mesures: Projet d'enquête métrologique – Table ronde du 17 octobre 1981. [Paris, 1982]

[Anderson, John.] "Douglas, Duke of Queensbury." In *The Scots Peerage*, edited by James Balfour Paul, VII, 112–156. Edinburgh, 1910

Anderson, R[oger] C. *Oared Fighting Ships from Classical Times to the Coming of Steam.* London, 1962

Anderson, Romola, and R[oger] C. Anderson. *The Sailing-Ship, Six Thousand Years of History.* [New edn] New York, 1963

Anderson, Sven Axel. *Viking Enterprise.* Columbia University Studies in History, Economics and Public Law, no. 424. New York, 1936

Andrews, Charles M. "The Boston Merchants and the Non-Importation Movement." *Publications of the Colonial Society of Massachusetts,* XIX *(Transactions,* 1916–1917), 159–259

Andrews, Charles M. *The Colonial Period of American History.* 4 vols. New Haven, Conn., 1934–1938

Andrews, Charles M. *Guide to the Materials for American History, to 1783, in the Public Record Office of Great Britain.* Carnegie Institution of Washington, Publication no. 90A. 2 vols. Washington, DC, 1912–1914

Andrews, Charles M., and Frances G. Davenport. *Guide to the Manuscript Materials for the History of the United States to 1783, in the British Museum, in Minor London Archives, and in the Libraries of Oxford and Cambridge.* Carnegie Institution of Washington, Publication no. 90. Washington, DC, 1908

Anglo-Jewish Notabilities: Their Arms and Testamentary Dispositions. London, 1949

The Anglo-Saxon Chronicle: According to the Several Original Authorities. Edited and translated by Benjamin Thorpe. [Rolls Series, no. 23.] 2 vols. London, 1861

The Anglo-Saxon Minor Poems. Edited by Elliott Van Kirk Dobbie. Vol. VI of *The Anglo-Saxon Poetic Records: A Collective Edition.* Edited by George Philip Krapp and Elliott Van Kirk Dobbie. New York, 1942

The Anglo-Saxon Poetic Records: A Collective Edition. Edited by George Philip Krapp and Elliott Van Kirk Dobbie. 6 vols. New York, 1931–1953

Anno. *Das Annolied.* Edited by Max Roediger. In *Monumenta Germaniae Historica ..., Scriptores qui Vernacula Lingua Usi Sunt: Deutsche Chroniken und andere Geschichtsbucher des Mittelalters,* vol. I, pt ii, pp. 63–144. Hanover, 1895

Antúnez y Acevedo, Rafel. *Memorias históricas sobre la legislación y gobierno del comercio de los españoles con sus colonias en las Indias occidentales.* Madrid, 1797

Appianus, of Alexandria. *Appiani Historia Romana.* Edited by Ludwig Mendelssohn. 2 vols. Leipzig, 1879–1881

[Arango y Parreño, Francisco de.] *Resultan grandes perjuicios de que en Europa se haga la fabricación del refino.* Havana, [1796]

De archieven in Amsterdam. Edited by J. H. van den Hoek Ostende, P. H. J. van der Laan, and E. Lievense-Pelser. Vol. VIII of *Overzichten van de archieven en verzamelingen in de openbare archiefbewaarplaatsen in Nederland.* Alphen aan den Rijn, 1981

Archives of Maryland. Edited by William Hand Browne *et al.* In progress. Baltimore, 1883 to date

Archives USA. Alexandria, Va., forthcoming

Arendt, Hannah. *On Revolution*. New York, 1963

Armytage, Frances. *The Free Port System in the British West Indies: A Study in Commercial Policy, 1766–1792*. New York and London, 1953

Arneth, Alfred. *Prinz Eugen von Savoyen*. [2nd edn.] 3 vols. Vienna, 1864

Arnold, Arthur P. "Anglo-Jewish Wills and Letters of Administration (Registered at the Principal Probate Registry, Somerset House, London)." In *Anglo-Jewish Notabilities: Their Arms and Testamentary Dispositions*, pp. 129–225. London, 1949

Arnould, [Ambroise Marie]. *De la balance du commerce et des relations commerciales extérieures de la France, dans toutes les parties du globe, particulièrement à la fin du règne de Louis XIV, et au moment de la Révolution ... avec la valeur de ses importations et exportations progressives depuis 1716 jusqu'en 1788 inclusivement*. 3 vols. Paris, 1791–1795

Astorquia, Madeline, *et al. Guide des sources de l'histoire des États-Unis dans les archives françaises*. Paris, 1976

Aubin, Hermann. "Der Rheinhandel in römischer Zeit." *Bonner Jahrbücher: Jahrbücher des Vereins von Altertumsfreunden im Rheinlande*, CXXX (1925), 1–37

Austria. Handels-Ministerium. *Über das Verhältnis des Bergkrystall-Kilogrammes, welches bei Einführung des metrischen Maasses und Gewichtes das Urgewicht in Österreich bilden soll, zum Kilogramme der Kaiserlicher Archive in Paris ...* Vienna, 1870

Avalle. *Tableau comparatif des productions colonies françaises aux Antilles, avec celles des colonies anglaises, espagnoles et hollandaises, de l'année 1787 à 1788*. Paris, [1799]

L'Avènement de l'ère industrielle (1789–années 1880). Edited by Patrick Léon *et al.* Vol. III of *Histoire économique et sociale de la France*. Paris, 1970

Avequin, [Jean-Baptiste (?)] "Suite du mémoire sur la canne d'Otaïti et la canne à rubans." *Journal de Chimie Médicale, de Pharmacie, de Toxicologie, et Revue des Nouvelles Scientifiques Nationales et Etrangères*, 2nd ser., II (1836), 132–135

B., M. "Mes Rêveries sur les *Doutes modestes*, à la occasion des *Richesse de l'État*." In *Richesse de l'État, à laquelle on a ajouté les pièces qui ont paru pour & contre*. [Compiled by Roussel de La Tour.] Amsterdam, 1764

Bachrach, Bernard S. "On the Origins of William the Conqueror's Horse Transports." *Technology and Culture*, XXVI (July 1985), 505–531

Bächtold, Hermann. *Der norddeutsche Handel im 12. und beginnenden 13. Jahrhundert*. Abhandlungen zur Mittleren und Neueren Geschichte, vol. XXI. Edited by Georg v[on] Below, Heinrich Finke, and Friedrich Meinecke. Berlin and Leipzig, 1910

Baerten, Jean, and Léone Liagre. *Guide des sources de l'histoire d'Amérique Latine conservées en Belgique*. Brussels, 1967

Baetjer, Katharine, and J. G. Links. *Canaletto*. New Yorks 1989

Bailyn, Bernard, and Lotte Bailyn. *Massachusetts Shipping, 1697–1714: A Statistical Study*. Cambridge, Mass., 1959

Bairoch, Paul. "Europe's Gross National Product, 1800–1975." *Journal of European Economic History*, V (Fall 1976), 273–340

Baker, E[dward] C. *A Guide to Records in the Leeward Islands*. Oxford, 1965

Baker, E[dward] C. *A Guide to Records in the Windward Islands*. Oxford, 1968

Baldasseroni, Pompeo. *Leggi e costumi del cambio che si osservano nelle principali piazze di Europa e singolarmente in quella di Livorno*. Pescia, 1784

Banking in the Early Stages of Industrialization: A Study in Comparative Economic History. Edited by Rondo [E.] Cameron. New York, 1967

Barbados. Laws and Statutes. *Acts and Statutes of the Island of Barbados ...* [Edited by John Jennings.] London, [1654]

Barbados. Laws and Statutes. *Acts, Passed in the Island of Barbados. From 1643, to 1762, Inclusive*. Edited by Richard Hall and Richard Hall. London, 1764

[Barker, Theodore C., ed.] "Consular Reports: A Rich but Neglected Historical Source." *Business History*, XXIII (July 1981), 265

Barrett, Ward. *The Sugar Hacienda of the Marquesses del Valle*. Minneapolis, Minn., 1970

Barth, Christian Karl. *Teutschlands Urgeschichte*. 2 vols. Bayreuth and Hof, 1817–1820

Bates, Frederick J., *et al. Polarimetry, Saccharimetry and the Sugars*. United States, Department of Commerce, National Bureau of Standards, Circular C 440. Washington, DC, 1942

Bateson, Mary "A London Municipal Collection of the Reign of John." *English Historical Review*, XVII (July, September 1902), 480–511, 707–730

Baudeau, Nicolas. *Idées d'un citoyen sur l'administration des finances du roi*. Amsterdam, 1763

Baugh, Daniel A. "The Politics of British Naval Failure, 1775–1777." *American Neptune*, LII (Fall 1992), 221–246

Baulant, Micheline. "Le Prix des grains à Paris de 1431 à 1789." *Annales: Histoire, Sciences Sociales*, XXIII (May–June 1968), 520–540

Baulant, Micheline, and Jean Meuvret. *Prix des céréales extraits de la Mercuriale de Paris (1520–1698)*. 2 vols. Paris, 1960–1962

Bautier, Robert-Henri. "Les Foires de Champagne: Recherches sur une évolution historique." *Recueils de la Société Jean Bodin pour l'Histoire Comparative des Institutions*, V (1953), 97–147

Beatson, Robert. *Naval and Military Memoirs of Great Britain from the Earliest Period to the Year 1803*. 6 vols. London, 1804

Beawes, Wyndham. *Lex Mercatoria Rediviva; or, the Merchants Directory*. London, 1751

Bede (Beda Venerabilis). *The Old English Version of Bede's Ecclesiastical History of the English People*. Edited and translated by Thomas Miller. Early English Text Society, nos. 95, 96, 110, 111. 4 vols. London, 1890–1898

Beechert, Edward Delos, Jr. "The Wine Trade of the Thirteen Colonies." M.A. thesis, University of California, Berkeley, 1949

The Beekman Mercantile Papers, 1746–1799. Edited by Philip L. White. 3 vols. New York, 1956

[Beelen-Bertholff, Fréderick Eugène François, baron de.] *Die Berichte des ersten Agenten Österreichs in den Vereinigten Staaten von Amerika, Baron de Beelen-Bertholff an Die Regierung der Österreichischen Niederlande in Brüssel, 1784–1789*. Edited by Hanns Schlitter. Fontes Rerum Austriacarum/Œsterreichische Geschichts-Quellen, Zwiete Abtheilung: Diplomataria et Acta, XLV. Band, Zweite Hälfte. Vienna, 1891

Belgrave, William. *A Treatise upon Husbandry or Planting*. Boston, 1755

Bell, Herbert C. "British Commercial Policy in the West Indies, 1783–93." *English Historical Review*, XXXI (July 1916), 429–441

Bell, Herbert C., David W. Parker, *et al. Guide to British West Indian Archive Materials, in London and in the Islands, for the History of the United States*. Carnegie Institution of Washington, Publication no. 372. Washington, DC, 1926

Bell, Whitfield J., Jr, and Murphy D. Smith. *Guide to the Archives and Manuscript Collections of the American Philosophical Society*. Memoirs of the American Philosophical Society, vol. LXVI. Philadelphia, 1966

Bellocchi, Ugo. *Storia del Giornalismo Italiano*. 8 vols. Bologna, 1974–1980

Bellot, H[ugh] Hale. "Parliamentary Printing, 1660–1837." *Bulletin of the Institute of Historical Research*, XI (November 1933), 85–98

Benaven, Jean Michel. *Le Caissier italien, ou l'art de connoitre les monnoies actuelles d'Italie . . .* 2 vols. [Lyons], 1797–1789.

Bénézit, Emmanuel. *Dictionnaire critique et documentaire des peintres, sculpteurs, dessinateurs et graveurs de tous les temps et tous les pays.* Revised edn. 10 vols. [Paris], 1976

Beowulf and Judith. Edited by Elliott Van Kirk Dobbie. Vol. IV of *The Anglo-Saxon Poetic Records: A Collective Edition.* Edited by George Philip Krapp and Elliott Van Kirk Dobbie. New York, 1953

Berkeley, Edmund, Jr. "The Naval Office in Virginia, 1776–1789." *American Neptune,* XXXIII (January 1973), 20–33

Bernard, Annick. *Guide de l'utilisateur des catalogues de livres imprimés de la Bibliothèque Nationale.* Paris, 1986

Bernocchi, Mario *Le monete della Repubblica Fiorentina.* Arte e Archeologia, Studi e Documenti, vols V–VII, XI. 4 vols. Florence, 1974–1978

Beveridge, William [H.] *Prices and Wages in England from the Twelfth to the Nineteenth Century.* London, 1939

Bezanson, Anne. "Inflation and Controls, Pennsylvania, 1774–1779." In *The Tasks of Economic History: Papers Presented at the Eighth Annual Meeting of the Economic History Association – A Supplement to the "Journal of Economic History,"* pp. 1–28. New York, 1948

Bianco, Stefano. *Proportioni della quantità' discreta ridotte in prattica.* Naples, 1653

Biddle, Nicholas. "The Letters of Nicholas Biddle [1771–1777]." Edited by William Bell Clark. *Pennsylvania Magazine of History and Biography,* LXXIV (July 1950), 348–405

Billington, Ray Allen, ed. *The Reinterpretation of Early American History: Essays in Honor of John Edwin Pomfret.* San Marino, Calif., 1966

Binney, J[ohn] E. D. *British Public Finance and Administration, 1774–92.* Oxford, 1962

Biskupa Sögur, gefnar út af hinu Íslenzka Bókmentafélagi. [Edited by Jón Sigurthsson and Guthgrandur Vigfússon.] 2 vols. Copenhagen, 1856–1878

Bjork, Gordon Carl. "Stagnation and Growth in the American Economy, 1784–1792." Ph.D. dissertation, University of Washington, 1963

Black, Jeremy [M.] *The English Press in the Eighteenth Century.* London, 1987

Black, R[obert] D[enis] Collison. *A Catalogue of Pamphlets on Economic Subjects Published between 1750 and 1900 and Now Housed in Irish Libraries.* Belfast and New York, 1969

Black, William. "Journal of William Black, 1744." Edited by R[obert] Alonzo Brock. *Pennsylvania Magazine of History and Biography,* I (April, July, October 1877), 117–132, 233–249, 404–419, II (January 1878), 40–49

Blake, George. *Lloyd's Register of Shipping, 1760–1960.* [London, 1960]

Blocksidge, Ernest W. *Hints on the Register Tonnage of Merchant Ships.* 2nd edn. Liverpool, 1942

Blodget, Samuel. *Economica: A Statistical Manual for the United States of America.* Washington, DC, 1806

Blom, Anthony. *Verhandeling van den Landbouw in de Colonie Suriname.* Amsterdam, 1787

Bloomberg-Rissmann, John. "Pre-1701 Records in the English Short-Title Catalogue: A Description and Explanation." *Factotum: Newsletter of the XVIIIth Century STC,* XXXVIII (February 1994), 3–5

Bloomberg-Rissmann, John. *Searching ESTC on RLIN. Factotum,* Occasional Paper 7. [London], 1996

Bode, Hermann [P.] *Die Anfänge wirtschaftlicher Berichterstattung in der Presse: Eine volkswirtschaftliche Studie als Beitrag zur Geschichte des Zeitungswesens.* Pforzheim, 1908

Boehmer, George H. "Prehistoric Naval Architecture of the North of Europe." In

Report of the United States National Museum . . . of the Smithsonian Institution for . . . 1891, pp. 527–647. Vol. II of the *Annual Report of the Board of Regents of the Smithsonian Institution . . . for . . . 1891*. [United States. Congress. 52nd Congress, 1st Session, House Miscellaneous Documents, vol. no. 44, doc. no. 344, pt ii. Serial Set no. 3002.] Washington, DC, 1892

Boëthius, Bertil, and Eli F. Heckscher. *Svensk handelsstatistik, 1637–1717*. Stockholm, 1938

Bogel, Else, Elger Blühm *et al. Die deutschen Zeitungen des 17. Jahrhunderts*. 3 vols. Bremen, 1971–1985

Boizard, Jean. *Traité des monoyes, de leurs circonstances et dépendances*. Paris, 1692

Bolton, Herbert E. *Guide to Materials for the History of the United States in the Principal Archives of Mexico*. Carnegie Institution of Washington, Publication no. 163. Washington, DC, 1913

Bond, Beverley W., Jr. *The Quit-Rent System in the American Colonies*. New Haven, Conn., 1919

Bond, Maurice F. *Guide to the Records of Parliament*. London, 1971

Bond, Phineas. "Letters of Phineas Bond, British Consul at Philadelphia, to the Foreign Office of Great Britain, 1787, 1788, 1789." Edited by J[ohn] Franklin Jameson. In American Historical Association, *Annual Report for the Year 1896*, I, 513–659. Washington, DC, 1897

Bond, Phineas. "Letters of Phineas Bond, British Consul at Philadelphia, to the Foreign Office of Great Britain, 1790, 1791, 1792, 1793, 1794." Edited by J[ohn] Franklin Jameson. In American Historical Association *Annual Report for the Year 1897*, pp. 454–568. Washington, DC, 1898

Bond, Thomas. *A Digest of Foreign Exchanges*. Dublin, 1795

[Bonner-Smith, David, *et al.*] *The Commissioned Sea Officers of the Royal Navy, 1660–1815*. Edited by David Syrett and R[ichard] L. DiNardo. Occasional Publications of the Navy Records Society, vol. 1. [2nd edn, rev. and enl.] [Aldershot, Eng.], 1994

Bordo, Michael David, and [Jon] Lars [B.] Jonung. "The Long Run Behavior of the Income Velocity of Money in Five Advanced Countries, 1870–1975: An Institutional Approach." *Economic Inquiry*, XIX (January 1981), 96–116

Born, Lester K. *British Manuscripts Project: A Checklist of the Microfilms Prepared in England and Wales for the American Council of Learned Societies, 1941–1945*. Washington, DC, 1955

Bosch, J[ohannes] van den. *Nederlandsche Bezittingen in Azia, Amerika en Afrika*. The Hague, 1818

Bosch-Gompera, P. "Phéniciens et Grecs dans l'Extrême-Occident." *La Nouvelle Clio: Revue Mensuelle de la Découverte Historique*, III (October–December 1959), 282–283

Bosworth, Joseph. *An Anglo-Saxon Dictionary*. Edited by T[homas] Northcote Toller. 4 vols. Oxford, 1882–1898

[Bourgoing, Jean François.] *Nouveau voyage en Espagne, ou tableau de l'état actuel de cette monarchie . . . depuis 1782 jusqu'à présent*. 3 vols. Paris, 1789

Bourne, Stephen. "The Official Trade and Navigation Statistics." *Journal of the Statistical Society of London*, XXXV (June 1872), 196–217

Bouthillier, Le Sieur. *Le Banquier français. Ou, la pratique des lettres de change suivant l'usage des principales places de France*. 2nd edn, revised. Paris, 1727

Bouvier, Jean. "Vers le capitalisme bancaire: L'Expansion du crédit après Law." In *Des derniers temps de l'âge seigneurial aux préludes de l'âge industries (1660–1789)*. Edited by [Camille] Ernest Labrousse *et al.*, pp. 301–321. Vol. II of *Histoire économique et sociale de la France*. Paris, [1970]

Bowden, Peter J. *Economic Change: Prices, Wages, Profits and Rents, 1500–1750*. Vol.

I of *Chapters from The Cambridge Agricultural History of England*. Edited by Joan Thirsk. Cambridge, Eng., [1990]

The Bowdoin and Temple Papers [1756–1812]. Massachusetts Historical Society Collections, 6th ser., vol. IX, and 7th ser., vol. VI. 2 vols. Boston, 1897–1907

Bowen, Frank C. *A Century of Atlantic Travel, 1830–1930*. Boston, 1930

Boxer, C[harles] R. "English Shipping in the Brazil Trade, 1640–65." *Mariner's Mirror*, XXXVII (July 1951), 197–230

Boyd, Julian P. "A New Guide to the Indispensable Sources of Virginia History." *William and Mary Quarterly*, 3rd ser., XV (January 1958), 3–13

Braesch, F[rederic]. *La Livre tournois et le Franc de germinal (Essai sur la monnaie métallique)*. Vol. V of *Finances et Monnaie Revolutionnaires (Recherches, Études et Documents*. Paris, 1936

Braeuer, Walter. *Frankreichs wirtschaftliche und soziale Lage um 1700: Dargestellt unter besonderer Berücksichtigung der Werke von Vauban und Boisguillebert*. Marburger Rechts- und Staatswissenschaftliche Abhandlungen, Reihe B: Staatswissenschaftliche Abhandlungen, vol. 1. Marburg, 1968

Brathwait, Richard. *Whimzies: Or, a New Cast of Characters*. London, 1631

Braudel, Fernand [P.] *Civilization and Capitalism, 15th–18th Century*. Translated by [Miriam Kochan and] Siân Reynolds. 3 vols. New York, 1981–1984

Braudel, Fernand [P.] *L'Identité de la France*. 2 vols in 3 pts. [Paris, 1986]

Braudel, Fernand [P.], and Ruggiero Romano. *Navires et marchandises à l'entrée du port de Livourne (1547–1611)*. Paris, 1951

Braudel, F[ernand] P., and Frank C. Spooner. "Prices in Europe from 1450 to 1750." In *The Economy of Expanding Europe in the Sixteenth and Seventeenth Centuries*, edited by E[dwin] E. Rich and C[harles] H. Wilson, pp. 374–486. Vol. IV of *The Cambridge Economic History of Europe*. Cambridge, Eng., 1967

Breton, Arthur J. *A Guide to the Manuscript Collections of the New-York Historical Society*. Westport, Conn., 1972

Brewington, M[arion] V. "A Boston Shipbuilding Contract of 1747." *American Neptune*, V (October 1945), 328

Briganti, Guiliano. *The View Painters of Europe*. [Translated by Pamela Waley.] London, 1970

Brigham, Clarence S. "Additions and Corrections to *History and Bibliography of American Newspapers, 1690–1820*." *Proceedings of the American Antiquarian Society*, n.s., LXXI (April 1961), 15–62

Brigham, Clarence S. *History and Bibliography of American Newspapers, 1690–1820*. 2 vols. Worcester, Mass., 1947

Bristol, Roger P. *Supplement to Charles Evans' American Bibliography*. Charlottesville, Va., 1970

British Borough Charters, 1042–1216. Edited by Adolphus Ballard. Cambridge, Eng., 1913

British Capitalism and Caribbean Slavery: The Legacy of Eric Williams. Edited by Barbara L. Solow and Stanley L. Engerman. Cambridge, Eng., 1987

British Library. Department of Manuscripts. *The British Library Catalogue of Additions to the Manuscripts, New Series, 1986–1990*. 3 vols. London, 1993

British Library. Department of Manuscripts. *Index of Manuscripts in the British Library*. 10 vols. Cambridge, Eng., 1984–1985

British Library. Department of Printed Books. *The British Library General Catalogue of Printed Books to 1975*. 360 vols. London, 1979–1987

British Library. Department of Printed Books. *The British Library General Catalogue of Printed Books to 1975*. 5 CD-Roms. London and Cambridge, Eng., 1989–1992

British Library. Newspaper Library. *Catalogue of the Newspaper Library, Colindale*. 8 vols. London, 1975

The British Merchant: A Collection of Papers Relating to the Trade and Commerce of Great Britain and Ireland. [Edited by Charles King.] 2nd edn. 3 vols. London, 1743

The British Public Record Office: History, Description, Record Groups, Finding Aids, and Materials for American History, with Special Reference to Virginia. Special Reports 25, 26, 27, and 28 of the Virginia Colonial Records Project. Virginia State Library Publications, no. 12. Richmond, Va., 1960

British Records Relating to America. In progress. East Ardsley, Wakefield, West Yorkshire, Eng., 1963 (?) to date

Britnor, L[eonard] E. *British West Indies Postal Rates to 1900.* [England], 1977

Britnor, L[eonard] E. "Edmund Dummer and His Packet Service." *B.W.I. Study Circle Bulletin,* no. 44 (March 1965), 2–7, 10–12

Britnor, L[eonard] E. *The History of the Sailing Packets to the West Indies.* British West Indies Study Circle, Paper no. 5 [England], 1973

Britnor, L[eonard] E. *An Introduction to the Postal History of the West Indies.* British West Indies Study Circle, Paper no. 1 [England], 1959

Brock, William R. *Scotus Americanus: A Survey of the Sources for Links between Scotland and America in the Eighteenth Century.* Edinburgh, 1982

Brøgger, A[nton] W., and Haakon Shetelig. *The Viking Ships: Their Ancestry and Evolution.* [Translated by Katherine John.] Oslo, [1951]

Bro-Jørgensen, J[ohannes] O., and Aa[ge] Rasch. *Asiatiske, vestindiske og guineiske handelskompagnien.* [Denmark. Rigsarkivet.] Vejledende Arkivregistraturen, vol. XIV. Copenhagen, 1969

Bromley, J[ohn] S., ed. *The Rise of Great Britain and Russia, 1688–1715/25.* Vol. VI of *The New Cambridge Modern History.* Cambridge, Eng., 1970

Brooks, F[rederick] W. *The English Naval Forces, 1199–1272.* London, [1932]

Brooks, N[icholas] P., and H. E. Walker. "The Authority and Interpretation of the Bayeux Tapestry." *Anglo-Norman Studies: Proceedings of the Battle Conference,* I (1978), 1–34

Brown, Gerald S. "The Anglo-French Naval Crisis, 1778: A Study of Conflict in the North Cabinet." *William and Mary Quarterly,* 3rd ser., XIII (January 1956), 3–25

Browne, Patrick. *The Civil and Natural History of Jamaica.* London, 1756

Bruce, Peter Henry. *The Memoirs of Peter Henry Bruce.* London, 1782

Brugmans, H[ajo]. "De Koopman: Mercurius als Spectator." *Jaarboek van het Genootschap Amstelodamum,* X (1912), 61–135

Brutails, J[ean] A. "Recherches sur l'équivalence des anciennes mesures de la Gironde." *Actes de l'Académie des Sciences, Belles-Lettres et Arts de Bordeaux* (1911), 5–155

Buckland, P. C., and Jon Sadler. "Ballast and Building Stone: A Discussion." In *Stone: Quarrying and Building in England, AD 43–1525,* edited by David Parsons, pp. 114–125. [Chichester, Sussex, 1990]

Buckman, Elizabeth A. "Course of the Exchange, 1705–1888: Bibliographical Notes." Unpublished typescript, 1977. Copy on deposit in the Bank of England, Reference Library, London

Budel, René. *De monetis, et re numaria . . .* Cologne, 1591

Buoninsegni, Tommaso. *De i cambi: Trattato risolutissimo et utilissimo, nel quale con molta brevità, & chiarezza si dichiarano i modi hoggi, usitati ne i cambi.* Florence 1573

Burke, [John] Bernard. *A Genealogical and Heraldic History of the Landed Gentry of Great Britain and Ireland.* 6th edn. 2 vols. London, 1879

Burke, [John] Bernard. *Burke's Genealogical and Heraldic History of the Landed Gentry.* Edited by Peter Townend. 18th edn. 2 vols. London, 1965–1969

Burnaby, Andrew. *Travels through the Middle Settlements in North-America, In the Years 1759–1760 with Observations upon the State of the Colonies.* 3rd edn. London, 1790

Burns, Alan. *History of the British West Indies.* London, 1954

Burwash, [Hazel] Dorothy. *English Merchant Shipping, 1460–1540.* Toronto, 1947

Bushnell, Edmund. *The Complete Ship-Wright . . . Teaching the Proportions Used by Experienced Ship-Wrights.* 5th edn. London, 1688

Cain, Robert J. *Preliminary Guide to the British Records Collection.* Archives Information Circular, no. 16. Raleigh, NC, 1979

Cairncross, A[lexander] K. "Capital Formation in the Take-Off." In *The Economics of Take-Off into Sustained Growth: Proceedings of a Conference Held by the International Economics Association,* edited by W[alt] W. Rostow, pp. 248–53. New York, 1963

Calendar of Letters from Canada, Newfoundland, Pennsylvania, Barbados and the Bahamas, 1721–1793, Preserved at the United Society for the Propagation of the Gospel. List and Index Society, [Publications], special ser., vol. 5. London, 1972

The Cambridge Economic History of Europe. Edited by M[ichael] [M.] Postan *et al.* 8 vols in 10 pts. Cambridge, Eng., 1941–1989

Cameron, Rondo [E.] "England, 1750–1844." In *Banking in the Early Stages of Industrialization: A Study in Comparative Economic History,* edited by Rondo [E.] Cameron, pp. 15–59. New York, 1967

Cappon, Lester J. "'The Historian's Day' – From Archives to History." In *The Reinterpretation of Early American History: Essays in Honor of John Edwin Pomfret,* edited by Ray Allen Billington, pp. 233–251. San Marino, Calif., 1966

Cappon, Lester J., and Stella F. Duff. *Virginia Gazette Index, 1736–1780.* 2 vols. Williamsburg, Va., 1950

Cappon, Lester J., *et al. Atlas of Early American History: The Revolutionary Era, 1760–1790.* Princeton, NJ, 1976

Caribbeana: Containing Letters and Dissertations . . . Chiefly Wrote by Several Hands in the West Indies. [Edited by Samuel Keimer.] London, 1741

Carrera Stampa, Manuel. "The Evolution of Weights and Measures in New Spain." [Translated by Robert S. Smith.] *Hispanic American Historical Review,* XXXIX (February 1949), 2–24

Carrera Stampa, Manuel. "El sistema de pesos y medidas colonial." *Memorias de la Academia Mexicana de la Historia,* XXVI (January–March 1967), 1–37

Carrington, Selwyn H. H. "The American Revolution and the British West Indies' Economy." *Journal of Interdisciplinary History,* XVII (Spring 1987), 823–850

Carrington, Selwyn H. H. *The British West Indies during the American Revolution.* Koninklijk Instituut voor Taal-, Land- en Volkenkunde, Caribbean ser., no. 8. Dordrecht, 1988

Carrington, Selwyn Hawthorne Harrington. "Economic and Political Development in the British West Indies during the Period of the American Revolution." Ph.D. dissertation, University of London, 1975

Carrington, Selwyn H. H. "Teaching and Research of United States History in the English-Speaking West Indies." In *Guide to the Study of United States History outside the U.S., 1945–1980,* edited by Lewis Hanke, I, 423–432. White Plains, NY, 1985

Carroll, Charles. "Extracts from Account and Letter Books of Dr. Charles Carroll, of Annapolis." *Maryland Historical Magazine,* XVIII (September 1923), 197–233

Carson, Edward [A.]. *The Ancient and Rightful Customs: A History of the English Customs Service.* London, 1972

Carson, Helen Craig. *Records in the British Public Record Office Relating to South Carolina, 1663–1782.* Columbia, SC, [1973]

Carter, Alice [C.] "The Dutch Notarial Archives." *Bulletin of the Institute of Historical Research*, XXVI (May 1953), 86–91

[Casaux, Charles.] *Essai sur l'art de cultiver la canne et d'en extraire le sucre.* Paris, 1781

Cash, Philip, Shirley Gordon, and [Diane] Gail Saunders. *Sources of Bahamian History.* London, 1991

Casson, Lionel. *The Ancient Mariners: Seafarers and Sea Fighters of the Mediterranean in Ancient Times.* New York, 1959

Casson, Lionel. "Harbour and River Boats of Ancient Rome." *Journal of Roman Studies*, LV (pts 1 and 2, 1965), 31–39

A Catalogue of the Bradshaw Collection of Irish Books in the University Library Cambridge. [Edited by Charles E. Sayle.] 3 vols. Cambridge, Eng., 1916

[Chalmers, George.] ["Biographical Account of Charles Steuart, Esqr."] *Gentleman's Magazine*, LXVIII (May 1798), 442–444

Chalmers, George. *Considerations on Commerce, Bullion and Coin, Circulation and Exchanges; with a View to Our Present Circumstances.* London, 1811

Chalmers, George. *An Estimate of the Comparative Strength of Great Britain, during the Present and Four Preceding Reigns; and of the Losses of Her Trade from Every War Since the Revolution.* [1st edn.] London, 1782

Chalmers, George. *Opinions on Interesting Subjects of Public Law and Commercial Policy Arising from American Independence.* [1st edn.] London, 1784

Chalmers, George. [*Works.*] 26 vols in 8 pts. [London, 1777–1799]

Chalmers, Robert F. "Straight Line Postal Markings." *American Philatelist*, XLII (September 1929), 781–791

Champion, Richard. *The American Correspondence of a Bristol Merchant, 1766–1776: Letters of Richard Champion.* Edited by G[eorge] H. Gutteridge. University of California, Publications in History, vol. XXII, no. 1. Berkeley, Calif., 1934

[Champion, Richard.] *Considerations on the Present Situation of Great Britain and the United States of North America, with a View to Their Future Commercial Connections.* [1st edn.] London, 1784

Chandler, M[ichael] J. *A Guide to Records in Barbados.* Oxford, 1965

Chapelle, Howard I. *The Search for Speed Under Sail, 1700–1855.* New York, 1967

Chapin, Howard M. *Rhode Island Privateers in King George's War, 1739–1748.* Providence, RI, 1926

Charnock, John. *Biographia Navalis; or, Impartial Memoirs of the Lives and Characters of the Officers of the Navy of Great Britain, from the Year 1660 to the Present Time.* 6 vols. London, 1794–1798

Chassaigne, Philippe. "L'Économie des îles sucrières dans les conflits maritimes de la seconde moitié du XVIIIème siècle: L'exemple de Saint-Domingue." *Histoire, Économie et Société*, VII (no. 1, 1988), 93–105   .

Chaunu, Huguette, and Chaunu, Pierre. *Séville et l'Atlantique (1504–1650).* 8 vols in 11 pts. Paris, 1955–1960

Chaunu, Pierre. "La Tonelada espanole aux XVIe et XVIIe siècles." In [Colloque International d'Histoire Maritime. 1st. Paris. 1956.] *Le Navire et l'économie maritime du XVe au XVIIIe siècles*, edited by Michel Mollat, pp. 71–81. Paris, 1957

Cheney, C[hristopher] R. *Handbook of Dates for Students of English History*, Royal Historical Society, Guides and Handbooks, no. 4. London, 1961

Chevalier, François. *La Formation des grands domaines au Mexique: Terre et société aux XVIe–XVIIe siècles.* Travaux et Mémoires de l'Institut d'Ethnologie de Paris, no. 56. Paris, 1952

Chevalier, François. *Land and Society in Colonial Mexico: The Great Hacienda.* Translated by Alvin Eustis. Edited by Lesley Byrd Simpson. Berkeley and Los Angeles, 1966

Chiavari, Fabiano. *Tractatus de Cambijs*. Rome, 1557

Child, Josiah. *A New Discourse of Trade . . .* London, 1693

Churchill, W[illiam] A. *Watermarks in Paper in Holland, England, France, etc., in the XVII and XVIII Centuries and Their Interconnection*. Amsterdam, 1935

Ciano, Cesare. *La sanità marittima nell'età medicea*. Biblioteca del "Bollettino Storico Pisano," Collana Storica, no. 15. [Pisa, 1976]

Cinq études lyonnaises. Edited by H[enri]-J[ean] Martin. Histoire et Civilisation du Livre, no. 1. Geneva and Paris, 1966

Clark, Dora Mae. "The American Board of Customs, 1767–1783." *American Historical Review*, XLV (July 1940), 777–806

Clark, Dora Mae. *The Rise of the British Treasury: Colonial Administration in the Eighteenth Century*. New Haven, Conn., 1960

Clark, G[eorge] N. *Guide to English Commercial Statistics, 1696–1782*. Royal Historical Society, Guides and Handbooks, no. 1. London, 1938

Clark, William Bell. *Captain Dauntless: The Story of Nicholas Biddle of the Continental Navy*. [Baton Rouge, La.], 1949

Clark, William Bell. *Gallant John Barry, 1745–1803: The Story of a Naval Hero of Two Wars*. New York, 1938

Clark, William Bell. *George Washington's Navy: Being an Account of His Excellency's Fleet in New England Waters*. Baton Rouge, La., [1960]

Claypoole, James. *James Claypoole's Letter Book, London and Philadelphia, 1681–1684*. Edited by Marion Balderston. San Marino, Calif., 1967

[Clifford, Bede E. H.] *Historic Forts of Nassau in the Bahamas*. 2nd edn. Nassau, New Providence, 1952

Clowes, G[eoffrey] S. Laird. *British Fishing and Coastal Craft: Historical Review and Descriptive Catalogue*. London, 1937

Clowes, G[eoffrey] S. Laird. *Sailing Ships: Their History and Development as Illustrated by the Collection of Ship-Models in the Science Museum*. 5th edn. London, 1932

Clowse, Converse D. "Shipowning and Shipbuilding in Colonial South Carolina: An Overview." *American Neptune*, XLIV (Fall 1984), 221–244

Cobb, Henry S. "'Books of Rates' and the London Customs, 1507–1558." *The Guildhall Miscellany*, IV (October 1971), 1–13

Codignola, Luca. *Calendar of Documents Relating to French and British North America in the Archives of the Sacred Congregation "de Propaganda Fide" in Rome, 1622–1799*. 6 vols. Ottawa, Ontario, 1983

Codignola, Luca. *Guide to Documents Relating to French and British North America in the Archives of the Sacred Congregation "de Propaganda Fide" in Rome, 1622–1799*. Ottawa, Ontario, 1991

Colbert, Jean Baptiste. *Lettres, instructions et mémoires de Colbert*. Edited by [Jean] Pierre Clément. 8 vols in 10 pts. Paris, 1859–1882

Cole, Arthur Harrison. *Wholesale Commodity Prices in the United States 1700–1861*. 2 vols. Cambridge, Mass., 1938

Cole, Charles Woolsey. *Colbert and a Century of French Mercantilism*. 2 vols. New York, 1939

Cole, W[illiam] A. "Trends in Eighteenth Century Smuggling." *Economic History Review*, 2nd ser., X (April 1958), 395–409

A Collection of Tracts Relative to the Law of England. Edited by Francis Hargrave. Dublin, 1781

Colledge, J[ames] J. *Ships of the Royal Navy: An Historical Index*. [2nd edn, rev.] 2 vols. [Annapolis, 1987–1989]

Colloque International d'Histoire Maritime. 1st. 1956. Paris. *Le Navire et l'économie maritime du XVe au XVIIIe siècles*. Edited by Michel Mollat. Paris, 1957

Colloque International d'Histoire Maritime. 2nd. 1957. Paris. *Le Navire et l'économie maritime du Moyen Age au XVIIIe siècle principalement en Méditerranée.* Edited by Michel Mollat. Paris, 1958

Colloque International d'Histoire Maritime. 3rd. 1958. Paris. *Le Navire et l'économie maritime du Nord de l'Europe du Moyen Âge au XVIIIe siècle.* Edited by Michel Mollat. [Paris], 1960

Colóquio Internacional de História da Madeira. 3rd. 1993. Funchal. *Actas. III Colóquio Internacional de História da Madeira.* Funchal, 1993

Commerce of Rhode Island, 1726–1800. [Edited by Worthington Chauncey Ford.] *Collections of the Massachusetts Historical Society,* 7th ser., vols IX–X. 2 vols. Boston, 1914–1915

The Compleat Compting-House Companion; or, Young Merchant and Tradesman's Sure Guide . . . London, 1763

Congrès National des Sociétés Savantes. 92nd. 1967. Strasbourg and Colmar, France. Section d'Histoire Moderne et Contemporaine. *Actes du Quatre-Vingt-Douzième Congrès National des Sociétés Savantes.* 3 vols. Paris, 1970

Connecticut (Colony). *The Public Records of the Colony of Connecticut.* Edited by James Hammond Trumbull and Charles Jeremy Hoadly. 15 vols. Hartford, Conn., 1850–1890

Connor, R[obert] D. *The Weights and Measures of England.* London, 1987

Cook, James. *The Journals of Captain James Cook on His Voyages of Discovery.* Edited by J[ohn] C. Beaglehole. 5 vols in 6 pts. Cambridge, Eng., 1955–1974

Coolhaas, W[illem] Ph. *A Critical Survey of Studies on Dutch Colonial History.* Edited by G. J. Schutte. Koninklijk Instituut voor Taal-, Land- en Volkenkunde, Bibliographical ser., no. 4. 2nd edn, revised. The Hague, 1980

Cooper, James Fenimore. *History of the Navy of the United States.* 2nd edn, revised. 2 vols. Philadelphia, 1840

Córdoba, Pedro Tomás de. *Memorias geográficas, históricas, económicas y estadísticas de la isla de Puerto-Rico.* 6 vols. [Puerto Rico], 1831–1838

Cornwall County and Diocesan Record Office. *The United States of America: Maps, Letters, Diaries.* Handlist no. 1. Truro, Eng., 1981

The Court and City Register. 42 vols. London, 1742–1813

Cox, Richard J., and Larry E. Sullivan. *Research Collections of the Maryland Historical Society: Historical and Genealogical Manuscripts and Oral History Interviews.* Baltimore, 1981

Coxe, Tench. *A View of the United States of America . . .* Philadelphia, 1794

Craig, R[obert S.] "Capital Formation in Shipping." In *Aspects of Capital Investment in Great Britain, 1750–1850; A Preliminary Survey,* edited by J. P. P. Higgins and Sidney Pollard, pp. 131–148. London, 1971

Craig, Robert [S.] "Shipping and Shipbuilding in the Port of Chester in the Eighteenth and Early Nineteenth Centuries." *Transactions of the Historic Society of Lancashire and Cheshire,* CXVI (1965), 39–68

Craig, Robert [S.] "Shipping Records of the Nineteenth and Twentieth Centuries." *Archives,* VII (1965–1966), 191–198

Craton, Michael John. "The Caribbean Vice Admiralty Courts, 1763–1815: Indispensable Agents of an Imperial System." Ph.D. dissertation, McMaster University, 1968

Craton, Michael [J.] *A History of the Bahamas.* London, 1962

Craton, Michael [J.] *A History of the Bahamas.* 3rd edn. [Waterloo, Ontario], 1986

Craton, Michael [J.] *Sinews of Empire: A Short History of British Slavery.* London, 1974

Cressy, David. *Coming Over: Migration and Communication between England and New England in the Seventeenth Century.* Cambridge, Eng., 1986

Crick, Bernard R. "First List of Addenda to a Guide to Manuscripts Relating to America in Great Britain and Ireland." *Bulletin of the British Association for American Studies*, n.s., V (December 1962), 47–63

Crick, Bernard R. "Second List of Addenda to a Guide to Manuscripts Relating to America in Great Britain and Ireland." *Bulletin of the British Association for American Studies*, n.s., VII (December 1963), 55–64

Crick, Bernard R., and Miriam Alman. *A Guide to Manuscripts Relating to America in Great Britain and Ireland*. London, 1961

Crimmin, P[atricia] K. "A Distilling Machine of 1772." *Mariner's Mirror*, LII (November 1966), 392

Crowe, Walter R. *Index Numbers: Theory and Applications*. London, 1969

Crowhurst, R. P[atrick]. "The Admiralty and the Convoy System." *Mariner's Mirror*, LVII (November 1971), 163–173

Crumlin-Pedersen, Ole. "Cog-Kogge-Kaag: Træk af en frisisk skibstypes historie." *Årbog Handels- og Søfartsmuseet på Kronborg*, XXIV (1965), 81–144

Crumlin-Pedersen, Ole. "En Kogge i Roskilde." *Årbog Handels- og Søfartsmuseet på Kronborg*, XXV (1966), 39–57

Curtin, Philip D. *The Atlantic Slave Trade: A Census*. Madison, Wis., 1969

Dabney, William M., and Marion Dargan. *William Henry Drayton and American Revolution*. Albuquerque, NM, 1962

Dalton, Michael. *The Countrey Justice, Containing the Practice of the Justices of the Peace*. 5th edn. London, 1635

Daly, John. *Descriptive Inventory of the Archives of the City and County of Philadelphia*. Philadelphia, 1970

Da Silva, José-Gentil. *Banque et crédit en Italie au XVIIe siècle*. 2 vols. Paris, [1969]

Da Silva, José-Gentil, and Rugierro Romano. "L'Histoire des changes: Les foires de 'Bisenzone' de 1600 à 1650," in *Annales: Histoire, Sciences Sociales*, XVII (July–August 1962), 715–721

Dauphin, V[ictor]. "Tableau des mesures ou expressions de mesures usitées en Anjou avant l'introduction du système métrique." *Revue d'Histoire Économique et Sociale*, XIX (no. 1, 1931), 77–96

[Davenant, Charles.] *Discourses on the Publick Revenues, and on the Trade of England* . . . 2 vols. London, 1698

Davenant, Charles. *The Political and Commercial Works of That Celebrated Writer Charles D'Avenant, LL.D* . . . Edited by Charles Whitworth. 5 vols. London, 1771

Davies, D[avid] W. *A Primer of Dutch Seventeenth Century Overseas Trade*. The Hague, 1961

Davies, K[enneth] G. *The Royal African Company*. London, 1957

Davis, L[ance] E., and J[onathan] R. T. Hughes. "A Dollar–Sterling Exchange, 1803–1894." *Economic History Review*, 2nd ser., XIII (August 1960), 52–78

Davis, Ralph. "English Foreign Trade, 1660–1700." *Economic History Review*, 2nd ser., VII (December 1954), 150–166

Davis, Ralph. "English Foreign Trade, 1700–1774." *Economic History Review*, 2nd ser., XV (December 1962), 285–303

Davis, Ralph. *The Industrial Revolution and British Overseas Trade*. Leicester, 1979

Davis, Ralph. "The Organization and Finance of the English Shipping Industry in the Late Seventeenth Century." Ph.D. dissertation, University of London, 1955

Davis, Ralph. *The Rise of the English Shipping Industry in the Seventeenth and Eighteenth Centuries*. London, 1962

Day, John. *The Modest Vindication of John Day of London, Merchant*. London, 1646

Deadman, Hugo, and Elizabeth Scudder. *An Introductory Guide to the Corporation of London Records Office*. [London, 1994]

Deane, Phyllis, and W[illiam] A. Cole. *British Economic Growth, 1688–1959: Trends and Structure.* 2nd edn. Cambridge, Eng., 1969

Debien, G[abriel]. "Comptes, profits, esclaves et travaux de deux sucreries de Saint-Domingue (1774–1798)." *Revue de la Société d'Histoire et de Geographie d'Haïti,* XV (October 1944), 1–62, XVI (January 1945), 1–51

Debien, G[abriel]. *Plantations et esclaves à Saint-Domingue.* Université de Dakar, Faculté des Lettres et Sciences Humaine, Publication de la Section d'Histoire, no. 3. Dakar, Senegal, 1962

Debures, P. *Tableau complet des poids et mesure anciennement en usage à Marseille et à Paris, comparés avec les poids et mesure de la République.* Marseilles, XI [1802–1803]

Deerr, Noel. *The History of Sugar.* 2 vols. London, 1949–1950

Denmark. Nationalmuseet. *Vikingeskibene i Roskilde Fjord.* Copenhagen, 1963

Dermigny, Louis. "Circuits de l'argent et milieux d'affaires au XVIIIe siècle." *Revue Historique,* no. 212 (October–December 1954), 239–278

Dermigny, Louis. "La France à la fin de l'Ancien Régime: Une carte monétaire." *Annales: Histoire, Sciences Sociales,* X (October–December 1955), 480–493

Des derniers temps de l'âge seigneurial aux préludes de l'âge industriel (1660–1789). Edited by [Camille] Ernest Labrousse *et al.* Vol. II of *Histoire économique et sociale de la France.* Paris, [1970]

De Roover, Raymond [A.] "On the Authorship and Dating of 'For the Understanding of the Exchange'." *Economic History Review,* XX (April 1967), 150–152

De Roover, Raymond [A.] *Gresham on Foreign Exchange: An Essay on Early English Mercantilism with the Text of Sir Thomas Gresham's Memorandum for the Understanding of the Exchange.* Cambridge, Mass., 1949

Devèze, Michel. *Antilles, Guyanes, la mer des Caraïbes de 1492 à 1789.* Paris, 1977

Dewar, M[ary]. "The Memorandum 'For the Understanding of the Exchange': Its Authorship and Dating." *Economic History Review,* 2nd ser., XVIII (April 1967), 476–487

DeWitt, Donald L. *Guides to Archives and Manuscript Collections in the United States: An Annotated Bibliography.* Westport, Conn., [1994]

Diccionario universal de historia y de geografía ... sobre las Americas en general y Especialmente sobre la Republica Mexicana. 10 vols. Mexico, 1853–1856

Dick, Alexander. *Curiosities of a Scots Charta Chest, 1600–1800, with the Travels and Memoranda of Sir Alexander Dick, Baronet, of Prestonfield, Midlothian Written by Himself.* Edited by Margaret Alice Forbes. Edinburgh, 1897

Dickerson, Oliver M. *The Navigation Acts and the American Revolution.* Philadelphia, 1951

Dickson, P[eter] G. M., and John Sperling. "War Finance, 1698–1714." In *The Rise of Great Britain and Russia, 1688–1715/25,* edited by J[ohn] S. Bromley, pp. 284–315. Vol. VI of *The New Cambridge Modern History.* Cambridge, Eng., 1970

Dickson, R[obert] J. *Ulster Emigration to Colonial America, 1718–1775.* Publications of the Ulster–Scot Historical Society, no. 1. London, 1966

Dictionary of Canadian Biography. Edited by George W. Brown *et al.* 13 vols. Toronto, 1966–1991

Dictionary of National Biography. Edited by Leslie Stephen and Sidney Lee. 63 vols. London, 1885–1901

Dietrich [Franz Eduard Christoph]. "Die Räthsel des Exeterbuchs: Würdingung, Lösing und Herstellung." *Zeitschrift für Deutsches Altertum,* XI (1859), 448–490

[Digges, Dudley.] *The Defence of Trade. In a Letter to Sir Thomas Smith Knight, Governour of the East-India Companie, &c. From One of that Societie.* London, 1615

Dillen, J[ohannes] G. van. *Bronnen tot de geschiedenis der Wisselbanken (Amsterdam, Middelburg, Delft, Rotterdam).* Rijks Geschiedkundige Publicatiën, 59–60. 2 vols. The Hague, 1925

The Dimensions of the Past: Materials, Problems, and Opportunities for Quantitative Work in History. Edited by Val R. Lorwin and Jacob M. Price. New Haven, Conn., 1972

Disparities in Economic Development since the Industrial Revolution. Edited by Paul Bairoch and Maurice Lévy-Leboyer. New York, 1981

[Dixon, J. T.] "The Problem of Imperial Communications during the Eighteenth Century, with Special Reference to the Post Office." [M.A. thesis, University of Leeds, 1964]

Dobbelaar, Jan Pieter. *De branderijn in Holland tot het begin der negentiende eeuw.* Rotterdam, 1930

Dobbs, Arthur. *An Essay on the Trade and Improvement of Ireland.* 2 vols. Dublin, 1729–1731

Documentos relativos a la independencia de Norteamérica existentes en archivos españoles. 11 vols in 14 pts. Madrid, 1976–1985

Documents Illustrative of the History of the Slave Trade to America. Edited by Elizabeth Donnan. Carnegie Institution of Washington, Publication no. 409. 4 vols. [Washington, DC], 1930–1935

Documents of the American Revolution, 1770–1783, (Colonial Office Series). Edited by K[enneth] G. Davies. 21 vols. Shannon, Ireland, 1972–1981

Documents Relating to New Netherland, 1624–1626, in the Henry E. Huntington Library. Translated and edited by A[rnold] J. F. van Laer. San Marino, Calif., 1924

Donaldson, Gordon. *The Scots Overseas.* London, 1966

Doursther, Horace. *Dictionnaire universel des poids et mesures anciens et modernes* . . . Brussels, 1840

Dowden, John. *The Church Year and Kalendar.* Cambridge, Eng., 1910

Dowell, Stephen. *A History of Taxation and Taxes in England from the Earliest Times to the Year 1885.* 2nd edn, revised. 4 vols. London, 1888

Drake, Francis S. *The Life and Correspondence of Henry Knox.* Boston, 1873

Drayton, John. *Memoirs of the American Revolution, from Its Commencement to the Year 1776, Inclusive; as Relating to the State of South-Carolina.* Charleston, 1821

Drescher, Seymour. "Le 'Déclin' du système esclavagiste britannique et l'abolition de la traité." Translated by C. Carlier. *Annales: Histoire, Sciences Sociales*, XXXI (March–April 1976), 414–435

Drescher, Seymour. *Econocide: British Slavery in the Era of Abolition.* Pittsburgh, 1977

Driel, A. van. *Tonnage Measurement: Historical and Critical Essay.* The Hague, 1925

Duncan, T[homas] Bentley. *Atlantic Islands: Madeira, the Azores and the Cape Verdes in Seventeenth-Century Commerce and Navigation.* Chicago, [1972]

Dunn, Richard S. Review of *English America and the Restoration Monarchy of Charles II: Transitional Politics, Commerce, and Kinship*, by J[ack] M. Sosin. *American Historical Review*, LXXXVII (October 1982), 1150–1151

Dupâquier, Jacques. *Histoire de la Population française.* 4 vols. Paris, 1995

Dupâquier, Jacques. *La population française aux XVIIe et XVIIIe siècles.* Paris, 1979

Dupâquier, Jacques. "Révolution française et révolution démographique." In *Vom Ancien Régime zur Französischen Revolution: Forschungen und Perspektiven/De l'Ancien Régime à la Révolution Française: Recherches et Perspectives*, edited by Ernst Hinrichs, Eberhard Schmitt, and Richard Vierhaus, pp. 233–260. Veröffentlichungen des Max-Planck-Instituts für Geschichte, 55. Göttingen, 1978

The Economic Organization of Early Modern Europe. Edited by E[dwin] E. Rich and C[harles] H. Wilson. Vol. V of *The Cambridge Economic History of Europe.* Cambridge, Eng., 1977

The Economics of Take-Off into Sustained Growth: Proceedings of a Conference Held by the International Economics Association. Edited by W[alt] W. Rostow. New York, 1963

The Economy of Early America: The Revolutionary Period, 1763–1790. Edited by Ronald Hoffman, John J. McCusker, Russell R. Menard, and Peter J. Albert. Charlottesville, Va., 1988

The Economy of Expanding Europe in the Sixteenth and Seventeenth Centuries. Edited by E[dwin] E. Rich and C[harles] H. Wilson. Vol. IV of *The Cambridge Economic History of Europe.* Cambridge, Eng., 1967

Edinburgh. *Register of Marriages of the City of Edinburgh, 1751–1800.* Edited by Francis J. Grant. Publications of the Scottish Record Society, [o.s.], vol. 53. 1 vol. in 11 pts. Edinburgh, 1917–1922

Edinburgh (Parish). *The Register of Marriages for the Parish of Edinburgh, 1585–1750.* Edited by Henry Paton. Publications of the Scottish Record Society, [o.s.], vols 27, 35, 2 vols in 11 pts. Edinburgh, 1905–1908

Edinburgh. Scottish Record Office. *List of American Documents [in the Scottish Record Office].* Edinburgh, 1976

Edinburgh. Scottish Record Office. *Source List of Manuscripts Relating to the U.S.A. and Canada in Private Archives Preserved in the Scottish Record Office.* List and Index Society, [Publications], special ser., vol. 3. London, 1970

Edwards, Bryan. *The History, Civil and Commercial, of the British Colonies in the West Indies.* 2 vols. London, 1793

Egils Saga Skallagrímssonar. Edited by Finnur Jónsson. Vol. III of *Altnordische Saga-Bibliothek.* Edited by Gustaf Cederschiöld, Hugo Gering, and Eugen Mogk. Halle a.S., 1894

Ehrenberg, Richard. *Das Zeitalter der Fugger: Geldkapital und Creditverkehr im 16. Jahrhundert.* 2 vols. Jena, 1896

Ehrman, John. *The British Government and Commercial Negotiations with Europe, 1783–1793.* Cambridge, Eng., 1962

Ehrman, John. *The Younger Pitt: The Years of Acclaim.* London, 1969

The Eighteenth Century. In progress. Woodbridge, Conn., 1982 to date

The Eighteenth Century Short Title Catalogue: The British Library Collections. Edited by R[obin] C. Alston. 113 microfiche. London, 1983

The Eighteenth Century Short Title Catalogue. [2nd edn, rev.] 220 microfiche. London, 1990

[Eike, von Repgow.] *Sachsenspiegel: Landrecht.* Edited by Karl August Eckhardt. *Monumenta Germaniae historica . . ., Fontes juris Germanici antiqui,* n.s., vol. I, pt i. 2nd edn. Göttingen, [1955]

Einzig, Paul. *The History of Foreign Exchange.* 2nd edn, revised. New York, 1970

Eisenstein, Elizabeth. *The Printing Press as an Agent of Change: Communications and Cultural Transformation in Early Modern Europe.* 2 vols. Cambridge, Eng., 1979

el Kordi, Mohamed. *Bayeux aux XVIIe et XVIIIe siècles: Contribution à l'histoire urbaine de la France.* Paris, [1970]

Ellis, Kenneth. *The Post Office in the Eighteenth Century: A Study in Administrative History.* Oxford, 1958

Eltis, David. "The Total Productivity of Barbados, 1664–1701." *Journal of Economic History,* LV (June 1995), 312–338

Encyclopédie méthodique. . . . 10 vols in 17 pts. Paris and Liege, 1783–1784

Engerman, Stanley L. "Notes on Patterns of Economic Growth in the British Colonies in the Seventeenth, Eighteenth, and Nineteenth Centuries." In *Disparities in Economic Development since the Industrial Revolution,* edited by Paul Bairoch and Maurice Lévy-Leboyer, pp. 46–57. New York, 1981

Engerman, Stanley L., and Robert E. Gallman. "U.S. Economic Growth, 1783–1860." *Research in Economic History,* VIII (1983), 1–46

Ennius. *The Annals of Quintus Ennius.* Edited by Ethel Mary Stewart. Cambridge, Eng., 1925

Ennius. *Ennianae Poesis reliquiae iteratis curis.* Edited by John Vahlen. [2nd edn.] Leipzig, 1903

Erickson, Edgar L. "The Sessional Papers." *Library Journal*, LXXVIII (1 January 1953), 13–17

Erickson, Edgar L. "The Sessional Papers: Last Phase." *College and Research Libraries*, XXI (September 1960), 343–358

Erwin, Joseph. ["Present State of the Trade and Navigation of Pennsylvania."] *American Museum*, VIII (September 1790), 114–118

ESTC on CD-ROM: The Eighteenth Century Short Title Catalogue. London, 1992

Evans, Charles. *American Bibliography: A Chronological Dictionary of All Books, Pamphlets and Periodical Publications Printed in the United States of America, 1639–1800.* 14 vols. Chicago, New York, and Worcester, Mass., 1903–1959

Evans, Charles H. *Exports, Domestic and Foreign, from the American Colonies to Great Britain, from 1697 to 1789, Inclusive. Exports, Domestic, from the United States to All Countries, from 1789 to 1883, Inclusive.* [United States. Congress. 48th Congress, 1st Session. House Miscellaneous Documents, vol. no. 24, doc. no. 49, pt ii. Serial Set no. 2236.] Washington, DC, 1884

The Exeter Book. Edited by George Philip Krapp and Elliott Van Kirk Dobbie. Vol. III of *The Anglo-Saxon Poetic Records: A Collective Edition.* Edited by George Philip Krapp and Elliott Van Kirk Dobbie. New York, 1936

Facsimiles of Manuscripts in European Archives Relating to America, 1776–1783. Edited by B[enjamin] F[ranklin] Stevens. 25 vols. London, 1889–1898

Færøyvik, Bernard. "Leivder av eit kaupskip på Holmen, Bergenhus." *Bergens Sjøfartsmuseum Årshefte 1948*, pp. 12–43

Falconer, William. *An Universal Dictionary of the Marine . . .* [4th edn.] London, 1780

Falk, Hjalmar [S.] *Altnordisches Seewesen.* Heidelberg, 1912

Farr, Grahame. "Custom House Ship Registers." *Mariner's Mirror*, LV (February 1969), 3–15

Faure, Fernand. *Les Préecurseurs de la Société de Statistique de Paris.* Nancy, 1909

Faust, Albert B. *Guide to the Materials for American History in Swiss and Austrian Archives.* Carnegie Institution of Washington, Publication no. 220. Washington, DC, 1916

Fayle, C[harles] Ernst. "Shipowning and Marine Insurance." In *The Trade Winds: A Study of British Overseas Trade during the French Wars, 1793–1815*, edited by C[yril] Northcote Parkinson, pp. 25–48. London, [1948]

Febvre, Lucien [P. V.], and Henri-Jean Martin. *The Coming of the Book: The Impact of Printing, 1450–1800.* Translated by David Gerard. Edited by Geoffrey Nowell-Smith and David Wootton. London, 1976

Fédou, René. "Imprimerie et culture: La vie intellectuelle à Lyon avant l'apparition du livre." In *Cinq études lyonnaises*, edited by H[enri]-J[ean] Martin, pp. 9–25. Histoire et Civilisation du Livre, no. 1. Geneva and Paris, 1966

Félix, Joël. *Économie et finances sous l'Ancien Régime: Guide du chercheur, 1523–1789.* Paris, [1994]

Fernández, Manuel Salustio. *Instrucción breve sencilla sobre el sistema métrico decimal . . .* 2nd edn. Santiago, 1859

Field, Edward. *Esek Hopkins: Commander-in-Chief of the Continental Navy during the American Revolution.* Providence, RI, 1898

Fish, Carl Russell. *Guide to the Materials for American History in Roman and Other Italian Archives.* Carnegie Institution of Washington, Publication no. 128. Washington, DC, 1911

Fisher, H[arold] E. S. *The Portugal Trade: A Study of Anglo-Portuguese Commerce, 1700–1770.* London, 1971

Fisher, Irving. *The Making of Index-Numbers: A Study of Their Varieties, Tests, and Reliability*. Boston, 1922

Fitzhugh, William. *William Fitzhugh and His Chesapeake World, 1676–1701: The Fitzhugh Letters and Other Documents*. Edited by Richard Beale Davis. Virginia Historical Society, Documents, vol. 3. Chapel Hill, NC, 1963

Fleischmann, Charles L. ["Report on Sugar Cane and Its Culture in Louisiana."] In [United States. Patent Office.] *Annual Report of the Commissioner of Patents, for the Year 1848*, pp. 274–336. [United States. Congress. 30th Congress, 2nd Session. House Executive Documents, vol. no. 6, doc. no. 59. Serial Set no. 542.] Washington, DC, 1849

Fogel, Robert William. *Without Consent or Contract: The Rise and Fall of American Slavery*. New York, 1989

Fogel, Robert William, and Stanley L. Engerman. *Time on the Cross: The Economics of American Negro Slavery*. 2 vols. Boston, 1974

[Forbonnais, François Véron Duverger de.] *Recherches et considérations sur les finances de France, depuis l'année 1595 jusqu'à l'année 1721*. [2nd edn.] 2 vols. Basle, 1758

Fornmanna Sögur, eptir gömlum handritum útgefnar ath tilhutun hins konúngliga Norræna fornfrætha fèlags. 12 vols. Copenhagen, 1825–1837

Fortescue, J[ohn] [W.] *A History of the British Army*. 13 vols in 19 pts. London, 1899–1930

Foster, Janet, and Julia Sheppard. *British Archives: A Guide to Archive Resources in the United Kingdom*. 3rd edn. [London, 1995]

France. Archives Nationales. *Les Archives Nationales: État général des fonds*. Edited by Jean Favier. 5 vols. Paris, 1978–1988

France. Archives Nationales. *États des inventaires*. Edited by Jean Favier. 4 vols. Paris, 1985–1994

France. Archives Nationales. *Guide des sources de l'histoire de l'Amérique latine et des Antilles dans les archives françaises*. Paris, 1984

France. Archives Nationales. *Inventaire analytique de la correspondance générale avec les colonies: Départ, Série B*. Edited by Étienne Taillemite. Paris, 1959

France. Archives Nationales. *Inventaire de la série Colonies C8: Martinique (Correspondance à l'arrivée)*. Edited by Étienne Taillemite, Odile Krakovitch, and Michele Bimbenet[-Privat]. 3 vols. Paris, 1967–1984

France. Archives Nationales. *Inventaire des archives Colonies, sous-série C13: Correspondance à l'arrivée en provenance de la Louisiane*. Edited by Marie-Antionette Menier, Étienne Taillemite, and Gilberte de Forges. 2 vols. Paris, 1976–1983

France. Archives Nationales. *Inventaire des archives Colonies, sous-série C14: Correspondance à l'arrivée en provenance de la Guyane Française*. Edited by C. Bougard-Cordier *et al.* 2 vols. Paris, 1974–1977

France. Archives Nationales. *Inventaire des archives de la Marine, sous-série B7 (Pays étrangers, commerce, consulats) déposée aux Archives Nationales*. Edited by Étienne Taillemite and Philippe Henrat. 6 vols. Paris, 1964–1980

France. Archives Nationales. *Les Inventaires des Archives Nationales*. 8,388 microfiche. Paris, 1989

France. Archives Nationales. "Répertoire numérique provisoire du fonds des Archives Colonies conservé[es] aux Archives Nationales." Compiled by Pierre de Vaissière [and Yvonne Bézard]. Unpublished typescript, 1914. Copy on deposit in the Archives Nationales.

La France et les Français. Edited by Michel François. [Paris, 1972]

Franklin, Benjamin. *Benjamin Franklin's Letters to the Press 1758–1775*. Edited by Verner W. Crane. Chapel Hill, NC, 1950

Franklin, Benjamin. *The Papers of Benjamin Franklin*. Edited by Leonard W. Labaree *et al.* In progress. New Haven, Conn., 1959 to date

Frêche, Georges, and Geneviève Frêche. *Les Prix des grains, des vins et des légumes à Toulouse (1486–1868): Extraits des Mercuriales, suivis d'une bibliographie d'histoire des prix.* Travaux et Recherches de la Faculté de Droit et des Sciences Économiques de Paris. Série "Sciences Historiques," no. 10. Paris, 1967

Freidel, Frank, and Richard K. Showman. *Harvard Guide to American History.* Rev. edn. 2 vols. Cambridge, Mass., 1974

French, Christopher J. "Eighteenth-Century Shipping Tonnage Measurements." *Journal of Economic History,* XXXIII (June 1973), 434–443

French, Christopher J. "The Longevity of Ships in Colonial Trade: Some Further Evidence." *International Journal of Maritime History,* III (June 1991), 155–163

Frese, Joseph R. "The Greenwich Hospital Tax, Continued." *Essex Institute Historical Collections,* CVI (January 1970), 46–53

Frese, Joseph R. "Henry Hutton and the Greenwich Hospital Tax." *American Neptune,* XXXI (July 1971), 192–216

Frese, Joseph R. "The Royal Customs Service in the Chesapeake, 1770: The Reports of John Williams, Inspector General." *Virginia Magazine of History and Biography,* LXXXI (July 1973), 280–318

Frese, Joseph R. "Some Observations on the American Board of Customs Commissioners." Massachusetts Historical Society, *Proceedings,* LXXXI (1969), 3–30

Fridenberg, Albert M. "The Simson Trust." *Publications of the American Jewish Historical Society,* XXVIII (1922), 246–248

Friedman, Milton. "Money: Quantity Theory." In *International Encyclopedia of the Social Sciences,* edited by David L. Sills and Robert K. Merton, X, 432–447. [New York, 1968]

Friedman, Milton, and Rose [D.] Friedman. *Free to Choose: A Personal Statement.* New York and London, 1980

Friis, Astrid, and Kristof Glamann. *A History of Prices and Wages in Denmark, 1660–1800.* London, 1958

Fusfeld, Daniel R. "On the Authorship and Dating of 'For the Understanding of the Exchange'." *Economic History Review,* XX (April 1967), 145–150

[Galfridus.] *Promptorium parvulorum sive clericorum lexicon anglo-latinum princeps* . . . Edited by Albert Way. Royal Historical Society, Camden Society, [o.s.], nos. 25, 54, 89. 3 vols. London, 1843–1865

Galloway, J[ohn] H. *The Sugar Cane Industry: An Historical Geography from Its Origins to 1914.* Cambridge, Eng., 1989

Galloway, J[ohn] H. "Tradition and Innovation in the American Sugar Industry, c. 1500–1800: An Explanation." *Annals of the Association of American Geographers,* LXXV (September 1985), 334–351

Gates, Paul W. *The Farmer's Age: Agriculture, 1815–1860.* Vol. III of *The Economic History of the United States,* edited by Henry David *et al.* New York, [1962]

Gee, Joshua. *The Trade and Navigation of Great-Britain Considered* . . . London, 1729

Gehlen, A. Fl. *Notariële Akten uit de 17e en 18e eeuw: Handleiding voor gebruikers.* Werken der Stichting tot Uitgaaf van de Bronnen van het Oud-Vaderlandse Recht, no. 12. Zutphen, 1986

Gehring, Charles. *A Guide to Dutch Manuscripts Relating to New Netherland in United States Repositories.* Albany, N.Y., 1978

Gelder, H. E. van. *Notarieele Protocollen van 1597 tot 1811, opgenomen in het Archiefdepot der Gemeente's-Gravenhage.* The Hague, 1911

General Index to the Contents of Savannah, Georgia, Newspapers, 1763–1799. 10 vols. [Savannah, 1937]

Gerboux, Fr[ançois]. *Discussion sur les effets de la démonétisation de l'or, relativement à la France.* [Paris, 1803]

[Gerhard, Dietrich, Egmont Zechlen, and Erich Angermann.] *Americana in deutschen Sammlungen (ADS): Ein Verzeichnis von Materialien zur Geschichte der Vereinigten Staaten von Amerika in Archiven und Bibliothek der Bundesrepublik Deutschland und West-Berlin.* 11 vols in 5 pts. n.p. [Heidelberg (?)], 1967

Gibb, D[avid] E. W. *Lloyd's of London: A Study in Individualism.* [2nd edn.] London, 1972

Gibson, A[lex] J. S., and T[homas] C[hristopher] Smout. *Prices, Food and Wages in Scotland, 1550–1780.* [Cambridge, Eng.], 1995

Gilboy, Elizabeth W. "The Cost of Living and Real Wages in Eighteenth Century England." *Review of Economic Statistics,* XVIII (1936), 134–143

Gildas. *Gildae Sapientis de excidio et conquestu Britanniae, ac flebili castigatione in reges, princips, et sacerdotes epistola.* In *Chronica Minora Saec. IV. V. VI. VII,* edited by Theodor Mommsen, vol. III, pt. i, pp. 1–110. Vol. XIII of *Monumenta Germaniae historica . . ., auctores antiquissimi.* Berlin, 1898

Gille, Bertrand. *Les Sources statistiques de l'histoire de France. Des enquêtes du XVIIe siècle à 1870.* Paris, 1964

Gille, Paul. "Jauge et tonnage des navires." In [Colloque International d'Histoire Maritime. 1st. Paris. 1956]. *Le Navire et l'économie maritime du XVe au XVIIIe siècles,* edited by Michel Mollat, pp. 85–100. Paris, 1957

Gillingham, Harrold E. "Some Colonial Ships Built in Philadelphia." *Pennsylvania Magazine of History and Biography,* LVI (April 1932), 156–186

Gipson, Lawrence Henry. *A Guide to Manuscripts Relating to the History of the British Empire, 1748–1776.* Vol. XV of *The British Empire before the American Revolution.* New York, 1970

Gipson, Lawrence Henry. *Louis Evans.* Philadelphia, 1939

Glamann, Kristof. *European Trade, 1500–1700.* Translated by Geoffrey French. [London, 1971]

[Glen, James.] *A Description of South Carolina, Containing Many Interesting and Curious Particulars.* London, 1761

Glete, Jan. *Navies and Nations: Warships, Navies and State Building in Europe and America, 1500–1860.* Acta Universitatis Stockholmiensis: Stockholm Studies in History, vol. 48. Stockholm, [1993]

Godechot, Jacques. "La Période révolutionnaire et impériale." *Revue Historique,* DXXXIII (January–March 1980), 101–147, DXXXVI (October–December 1980), 399–469, no. 539 (July–September 1981), 161–126

Godefroy, Fréderic. *Dictionnaire de l'ancienne langue française et tous ses dialectes du IXe au XVe siècle.* 10 vols. Paris, 1881–1902

Goldenberg, Joseph A. "An Analysis of Shipbuilding Sites in *Lloyd's Register* of 1776." *Mariner's Mirror,* LIX (November 1973), 419–435

Golder, Frank A. *Guide to Materials for American History in Russian Archives.* Carnegie Institution of Washington, Publication no. 239. 2 vols. Washington, DC, 1917–1937

Goldsmiths'-Kress Library of Economic Literature. In progress. Woodbridge, Conn., 1974 to date

Goldsmiths'-Kress Library of Economic Literature: A Consolidated Guide to . . . the Microfilm Collection. 9 vols. Woodbridge, Conn., 1976–1989

González de los Rios, Pelayo. *Prontuario del sistema legal de pesas, medidas y monedas, o sea el sistema metrico decimal . . .* Havana, 1862

Gordon, William. *The Universal Accountant and Complete Merchant.* 3rd edn. Edinburgh, 1770

Goubert, Pierre. *L'Ancien Régime.* [7th edn.] 2 vols. Paris, [1982]

Goubert, Pierre. *Beauvais et le Beauvaisis de 1600 à 1730: Contribution à l'histoire sociale de la France.* 2 vols. Paris, [1960]

Gould, John D. *The Great Debasement: Currency and the Economy in Mid-Tudor England.* Oxford, 1970

Gould, J[ohn] D. "The Trade Depression of the Early 1620s." *Economic History Review,* 2d ser., VII (August 1954), 81–88

Goveia, Elsa V. *A Study on the Historiography of the British West Indies to the End of the Nineteenth Century.* Instituto Panamericano de Geografía e Historia, publicación no. 78. Mexico, 1956

Grafton, Anthony T. "The Importance of Being Printed." *Journal of Interdisciplinary History,* XI (Autumn 1980), 265–286

Graham, Gerald S. "The Ascendancy of the Sailing Ship." *Economic History Review,* 2nd ser., IX (August 1956), 74–88

Graham, Gerald S. *British Policy and Canada, 1774–1791: A Study in 18th Century Trade Policy.* London, 1930

Gras, Norman Scott Brien. *The Early English Customs System: A Documentary Study of the Institutional and Economic History of the Customs from the Thirteenth to the Sixteenth Century.* Cambridge, Mass., 1918

Gras, Norman Scott Brien. *The Evolution of the English Corn Market from the Twelfth to the Eighteenth Century.* Harvard Economic Studies, vol. XIII. Cambridge, Mass., 1915

Grassby, Richard [B.] *The English Gentleman in Trade: The Life and Works of Sir Dudley North, 1641–1691.* Oxford, 1994

Gravesteijn, C[ora], J[acobus] J. Seegers, and R[iekie] van Sijtveld-Verhoeven. *Handel in Theorie en Pratijk. Katalogus betreffende werken gepubliceerd voor 1830 aanwezig in de Economisch-Historische Bibliotheek, Amsterdam.* Amsterdam, 1981

Gray, Lewis Cecil. *History of Agriculture in the Southern United States to 1860.* Carnegie Institution of Washington, Publication no. 430. 2 vols. [Washington, DC], 1933

Great Britain. Commissioners for Taking, Examining and Stating the Public Accounts. *The Reports of the Commissioners Appointed to Examine, Take, and State the Public Accounts of the Kingdom.* Edited by William Molleson and John Lane. 3 vols. London, 1783–1787

Great Britain. Commissioners for Trade and Plantations. *Journal of the Commissioners for Trade and Plantations [1704–1782].* 14 vols. London, 1920–1938

Great Britain. Commissioners for Trade and Plantations. *Report of a Committee of the Lords of the Privy Council on the Trade of Great Britain with the United States, January 1791.* [Edited by Worthington C. Ford.] Washington, DC, 1888

Great Britain. Commissioners for Trade and Plantations. *A Report of the Lords of the Committee of Privy Council, Appointed for All Matters Relating to Trade and Foreign Plantations, on the Commerce and Navigation between His Majesty's Dominions, and the Territories belonging to the United States of America.* [London], 1791

Great Britain. Court of Chancery. *Chancery Masters' Exhibits.* List and Index Society, [Publications], vols 13–14. 2 vols. London, 1966

Great Britain. Court of Chancery. *Reports of Cases Argued and Determined in the High Court of Chancery, during the Time of Lord Chancellor Eldon.* Compiled by Francis Vesey and John Beames. 1st American edn. Edited by Edward D. Ingraham. 3 vols in 2 pts. Philadelphia, 1822

Great Britain. High Court of Admiralty. *Select Pleas in the Court of Admiralty [1390–1602].* Edited by Reginald G. Marsden. Selden Society Publications, vols 6 and 11. 2 vols. London, 1894–1897

Great Britain. Historical Manuscripts Commission. *Calendar of the Manuscripts of . . . Lord Sackville . . .* Edited by A[rthur] P. Newton and F[rederick] J. Fisher. 2 vols. London, 1940–1966

Great Britain. Historical Manuscripts Commission. *Manuscripts of the Earl of Egmont:*

Diary of Viscount Percival, Afterwards First Earl of Egmont. 3 vols. London, 1920–1923

Great Britain. Historical Manuscripts Commission. *Record Repositories in Great Britain: A Geographical Directory.* 9th edn, revised. London, 1991

Great Britain. Historical Manuscripts Commission. *Seventh Reports of the Royal Commission on Historical Manuscripts.* 2 vols. London, 1879

Great Britain. Laws and Statutes. *A Collection in English, of the Statutes Now in Force, Continued from the Beginning of Magna Carta . . . Until . . . [1610].* London, 1615

Great Britain. Laws and Statutes. *Die Gesetze der Angelsachsen.* Edited and translated by F[elix] Liebermann. 3 vols in 4 pts. Halle a.S., 1903–1916

Great Britain. Laws and Statutes. *The Laws of the Kings of England from Edmund to Henry I.* Edited and translated by A[gnes] J. Robertson. Cambridge, Eng., 1925

Great Britain. Laws and Statutes. *The Statutes at Large . . . of Great Britain [1225–1806].* [Edited by Danby Pickering *et al.*] 46 vols. Cambridge, Eng., 1762–1807

Great Britain. Laws and Statutes. *The Statutes of the Realm. Printed . . . from Original Records and Authentic Manuscripts [1225–1713].* [Edited by Alexander Luders *et al.*] London: Record Commission, 1810–1828

Great Britain. Laws and Statutes. *The Statutes of the United Kingdom of Great Britain and Ireland [1801–1869].* [Edited by Thomas Edlyne Tomlins *et al.*] 29 vols. London, 1804–1869

Great Britain. Laws and Statutes (1649–1660, Commonwealth). *Acts and Ordinances of the Interregnum, 1642–1660.* Edited by C[harles] H. Firth and R[obert] S. Raith. 3 vols. London, 1911

Great Britain. Laws and Statutes. Customs. *The Rates of Merchandise . . . As They are Rated and Agreed on by the Common House of Parliament . . . Saturday July 28. 1660.* London, 1660

Great Britain. Parliament. *The Parliamentary History of England from the Earliest Period to the Year 1803.* Edited by William Cobbett. 36 vols. London, 1806–1820

Great Britain. Parliament. 1621. House of Commons. *Commons Debates, 1621.* Edited by Wallace Notestein, Frances Helen Relf, and Hartleys Simpson. 7 vols. New Haven, Conn., 1935

Great Britain. Parliament. 1766. House of Commons. *The Examination of Doctor Benjamin Franklin, before an August Assembly, Relating to the Repeal of the Stamp Act.* Philadelphia, 1766

Great Britain. Parliament. House of Commons. *Journals of the House of Commons.* In progress. London, 1742 to date

Great Britain. Parliament. House of Commons. *An Account of the British Produce and Manufactures Exported from England to France between . . . 1714 and . . . 1761.* House of Commons, Sessional Papers to 1801, Accounts and Papers, vol. XIX, no. 426. [London], 1787

Great Britain. Parliament. House of Commons. *An Account of the Official and Likewise of the Real or Current Value, at which Each Article of the Imports and Exports of Great Britain to and from Ireland during the Three Years Ending the 5th Jan. 1803, Has Been Estimated.* House of Commons, Sessional Papers, 1803–1804, vol. VIII (Accounts and Papers, vol. II), [no. 190]. [London], 1804

Great Britain. Parliament. House of Commons. *Accounts and Papers Relative to the Commerce, Revenue, and Expenditure of the Kingdoms of Great Britain and Ireland.* House of Commons, Sessional Papers to 1801, Accounts and Papers, vol. XLIX, no. 981. [London], 1800

Great Britain. Parliament. House of Commons. *Customs Tariffs of the United Kingdom from 1800 to 1897, with Some Notes upon the History of the More Important Branches of Receipts from the Year 1660.* House of Commons, Sessional Papers,

1898, vol. LXXXV (Accounts and Papers, vol. XXXIV). [Cmd 8706.] London, 1897

Great Britain. Parliament. House of Commons. *House of Commons Sessional Papers of the Eighteenth Century.* Edited by Sheila Lambert. 147 vols. Wilmington, Del., 1975

Great Britain. Parliament. House of Commons. *Minutes of the Evidence . . . Respecting the African Slave Trade.* House of Commons, Sessional Papers to 1801, Accounts and Papers, vols XXIV, XXV, XXIX, XXX, XXXI, XXXIV, nos 626–646, 697–699, 705, 745–748. 6 vols. [London], 1789–1791

Great Britain. Parliament. House of Commons. *A Report from the Committee Appointed to Enquire into the Original Standards of Weights and Measures in This Kingdom, and to Consider the Laws Relating Thereto.* London, 1758

Great Britain. Parliament. House of Commons. *Report of the Lords of the Committee of [the Privy] Council . . . [for] Trade and Foreign Plantations . . . Concerning the Present State of the Trade to Africa.* House of Commons, Sessional Papers to 1801, Accounts and Papers, vol. XXVI, no. 646a. 6 pts. [London, 1789]

Great Britain. Parliament. House of Commons. *Reports from Committees of the House of Commons, Reprinted by Order of the House.* 15 vols. London, 1773–1803

Great Britain. Parliament. House of Commons. Committee of Secrecy. *Third Report from the Committee of Secrecy [on the Outstanding Demands on the Bank of England].* [London], 1797

Great Britain. Parliament. House of Commons. Committee on the Commercial State of the West India Colonies. *Report from the Committee on the Commercial State of the West India Colonies.* House of Commons, Sessional Papers, 1807, vol. III (Reports), no. 65. [London], 1807

Great Britain. Parliament. House of Commons. Select Committee on Finance. *First [–Thirty-sixth] Report from the Select Committee on Finance: Collection of the Public Revenue, Customs.* 36 vols in 5 pts. [London], 1797–1798

Great Britain. Parliament. House of Commons. Select Committee on the High Price of Gold Bullion. *Report, Together with Minutes of Evidence, and Accounts, from the Select Committee on the High Price of Gold Bullion.* House of Commons, Sessional Papers, 1810, vol. III (Reports). [London, 1810]

Great Britain. Parliament. House of Lords. *Journals of the House of Lords.* In progress. London, 1767 to date

Great Britain. Parliament. House of Lords. *The Manuscripts of the House of Lords.* In progress. London, 1871 to date

Great Britain. Parliament. House of Lords. Select Committee Appointed to Consider the Petition of the . . . City of Glasgow. . . . *Report from the Select Committee of the House of Lords Appointed to Consider the Petition of the . . . City of Glasgow Taking Notice of the Bill Entitled "An Act for Ascertaining and Establishing Uniformity of Weights and Measures etc."* House of Commons, Sessional Papers, 1824, vol. VII (Reports), no. 94. [London, 1824]

Great Britain. Public Record Office. *America and the West Indies.* Vol. II of *Maps and Plans in the Public Record Office.* London, 1975

Great Britain. Public Record Office. *Calendar of Documents Preserved in France Illustrative of the History of Great Britain and Ireland . . . A.D. 918–1206.* By J[ohn] Horace Round. London, 1899

Great Britain. Public Record Office. *Calendar of State Papers, Colonial Series, America and West Indies [1574–1739].* By W[illiam] Noel Sainsbury *et al.* 45 vols in 46 pts. London, 1860–1994

Great Britain. Public Record Office. *Calendar of Treasury Books and Papers Preserved in Her Majesty's Public Record Office, 1729–1745.* By William A. Shaw. 5 vols. London, 1898–1903

Great Britain. Public Record Office. *Calendar of Treasury Books Preserved in Her Majesty's Public Record Office*. By William A. Shaw. In progress. London, 1904 to date

Great Britain. Public Record Office. *Calendar of Treasury Papers Preserved in Her Majesty's Public Record Office, 1557–1728*. By Joseph Redington. 6 vols. London, 1868–1899

Great Britain. Public Record Office. *Current Guide*. [3rd edn.] 27 microfiche. London, 1996

Great Britain. Public Record Office. *Descriptive List of Exchequer . . . Port Books*. [By Neville J. Williams.] 3 vols. London, [1960–1972]

Great Britain. Public Record Office. *Guide to the Contents of the Public Record Office*. 3 vols. London, 1963–1968

Great Britain. Public Record Office. *Kew Lists: The Microfiche Edition*. 3,483 microfiche. [London, 1988]

Great Britain. Public Record Office. *Kew Lists: Microfiche Supplement, 1987–1991*. 278 microfiche. [London, 1991]

Great Britain. Public Record Office. *Maps and Plans in the Public Record Office*. In progress. London, 1967 to date

Great Britain. Public Record Office. *Treasury Board Papers (T. 1/319–364): Descriptive List and Index, Mainly 1745–1755*. List and Index Society, [Publications], vol. 120. London, 1975

Great Britain. Public Record Office. *Treasury Board Papers (T. 1/365–388): Descriptive List and Index, Mainly 1756–1758*. List and Index Society, [Publications], vol. 125. London, 1976

Great Britain. Public Record Office. *Treasury Board: Papers, 1759–1764 (T 1/389–436), with an Index to T 1/429–436*. List and Index Society, [Publications], vol. 240. [London], 1990

Great Britain. Royal Commission on Public Records. *Report of the Royal Commission on Public Records Appointed to Enquire into and Report on the State of the Public Records and Local Records of a Public Nature of England and Wales*. [House of Commons, Sessional Papers. Cmd 6361, 6395, 6396, 7544–7546, 367–369.] 3 vols in 9 pts. London, 1912–1919

Great Britain. Sovereigns (1760–1820: George III). *The Correspondence of King George the Third from 1760 to December 1783*. Edited by John [W.] Fortescue. 6 vols. London, 1927–1928

Green, William A. "Caribbean Historiography, 1600–1900: The Recent Tide." *Journal of Interdisciplinary History*, VII (Winter 1977), 509–530

Green, W[illiam] A. "The Planter Class and British West Indian Sugar Production, before and after Emancipation." *Economic History Review*, 2nd ser., XXVI (August 1973), 448–463

Greene, Evarts B., and Virginia D. Harrington. *American Population before the Federal Census of 1790*. New York, 1932

Greene, Jack P. Review of *The British West Indies during the American Revolution*, by Selwyn H. H. Carrington. *Nieuwe West-Indische Gids*, LXIII (nos 3–4, 1989), 251–253

Gremigni, Elena. *Periodici almanacchi livornesi secoli XVIIe–XVIIIe*. [Quaderni della Labronica, no. 69.] Livorno, 1996

Grimm, [Friedrich Melchior]. *Correspondance littéraire, philosophique et critique, adressée à un Souverain d'Allemagne*. 16 vols. Paris, 1812–1813

Grimm, Jakob [Ludwig Karl]. *Teutonic Mythology*. Edited and translated by James Steven Stallybrass. 4 vols. London, 1882–1888

[Grimm, Jakob Ludwig Karl, and Wilhelm Karl Grimm.] *Deutsche sagen*. Edited by Herman [Friedrich] Grimm. 3rd edn. 2 vols in 1 pt. Berlin, 1891

Grimsted, Patricia K. *Archives and Manuscript Repositories in the USSR: Estonia, Latvia, Lithuania, and Belorussia*. Princeton, NJ, 1981

Grimsted, Patricia K. *Archives and Manuscript Repositories in the USSR: Moscow and Leningrad.* Princeton, NJ, 1972

Grimsted, Patricia Kennedy *et al. Archives in Russia, 1993: A Brief Directory – Part 1, Moscow and St. Petersburg.* Edited by Patricia Kennedy Grimsted *et al.* Washington, DC, [1993]

Gronovius, Jacobus. *Thesaurus Graecarum antiquitatum . . .* 12 vols in 13 pts. Leiden, 1697–1702

Groome, Francis H. *Ordnance Gazetteer of Scotland: A Survey of Scottish Topography, Statistical, Biographical, and Historical.* Edinburgh, 1886

Groth, Otto. *Die Zeitung: Ein System der Zeitungskunde (Journalistik).* 4 vols. Mannheim, 1928–1930

The Growth of English Overseas Trade in the Seventeenth and Eighteenth Centuries. Edited by W[alter] E. Minchinton. London, 1969

Guilleux La Roërie, [Louis]. Comment on "Dimensions et caractéristiques des 'Koggen' hanséatiques dans le commerce Baltique," by Paul Heinsius. In [Colloque International d'Histoire Maritime. 3rd. Paris. 1958.] *Le Navire et l'économie maritime du Nord de l'Europe du Moyen Âge au XVIIIe siècle,* edited by Michel Mollat, pp. 20–21. Paris, 1960

Guilleux La Roërie, [Louis], and J[ean] Vivielle. *Navires et marins: De la rame à l'hélice.* [2nd edn.] 2 vols. Paris, 1946

Hagedorn, Bernard. *Die Entwickelung der wichtigsten Schiffstypen bis ins 19. Jahrhundert.* Veröffentlichungen des Verein für Hamburgische Geschichte, vol. 1. Berlin, 1914

Hale, Matthew. "A Treatise in Three Parts." In *A Collection of Tracts Relative to the Law of England,* edited by Francis Hargrave, pp. 1–248. Dublin, 1787

Hall, Hubert. *A History of the Custom-Revenue in England from the Earliest Times to the Year 1827.* 2 vols. London, 1885

Hall, Hubert, and Freida J. Nicholas. *Select Tracts and Table Books Relating to English Weights and Measures (1100–1742).* Royal Historical Society, Camden, 3rd ser., no. 41, *Camden Miscellany,* vol. XV. London, 1929

Hamer, Philip M. *A Guide to Archives and Manuscripts in the United States.* New Haven, Conn., 1961

Hamilton, Alexander. *The Papers of Alexander Hamilton.* Edited by Harold C. Syrett *et al.* 26 vols. New York, 1961–1979

Hamilton, Earl J. *American Treasure and the Price Revolution in Spain, 1501–1650.* Harvard Economic Studies, vol. XLIII. Cambridge, Mass., 1934

Hamilton, Earl J. "Prices, Wages, and the Industrial Revolution." In *Studies in Economics and Industrial Relations,* edited by Wesley C. Mitchell *et al.,* pp. 99–112. Philadelphia, 1941

Hamilton, Earl J. *War and Prices in Spain, 1651–1800.* Harvard Economic Studies, vol. LXXXI. Cambridge, Mass., 1947

Hancock, David [J.] *Citizens of the World: London Merchants and the Integration of the British Atlantic Community, 1735–1785.* [Cambridge, Eng., 1995]

Handler, Jerome S. *A Guide to Source Materials for the Study of Barbados History, 1627–1834.* Carbondale, Ill., 1971

Handler, Jerome S. *Supplement to "A Guide to Source Materials for the Study of Barbados History, 1627–1834."* Providence, RI, 1991

Handler, Jerome S., and Samuel J. Hough. "Addenda to *A Guide to Source Materials for the Study of Barbados History, 1627–1834.*" *Journal of the Barbados Museum and Historical Society,* XXXVI–XXXVIII (1980–1987), 172–177, 279–285, 385–397, 82–92, 296–307, 107–116

Hanke, Lewis. *Guide to the Study of United States History outside the U.S., 1945–1980.* 5 vols. White Plains, NY, 1985

Hanks, Carlos C. "A Cruise for Gunpowder." *United States Naval Institute Proceedings*, LXV (March 1939), 324–327

Hanna, Mary Alice. *Trade of the Delaware District before the Revolution*. Northampton, Mass., 1917

Hannay, David. *A Short History of the Royal Navy, 1217–1815*. 2 vols. London, 1898–[1909]

Die Hanse-Kogge von 1380. Edited by Klaus-Peter Kiedel and Uwe Schnall. Bremerhaven, 1982

Hansisches Urkundenbuch. Edited by [Johann Mathias] Konstantin Höhlbaum, K[arl] Kunze, and W[alther] Stein. 11 vols. Halle a.S. and Leipzig, 1876–1939

Hanson, L[aurence] W. *Contemporary Printed Sources for British and Irish Economic History, 1701–1750*. Cambridge, Eng., 1963

Harden, Donald [B.] *The Phoenicians*. London, 1962

Hardy, Charles. *A Register of Ships, Employed in the Service of the Honourable the East India Company, from the Year 1760 to 1810* . . . [2nd edn], rev. and enl. Edited by Horatio Charles Hardy. London, 1811

Harley, C[harles] Knick. "British Industrialization before 1841: Evidence of Slower Growth during the Industrial Revolution." *Journal of Economic History*, XLII (June 1982), 267–289

Harper, Lawrence A. *The English Navigation Laws: A Seventeenth-Century Experiment in Social Engineering*. New York, 1939

[Harris, Joseph.] *An Essay upon Money and Coins*. 2 vols in 1 pt. London, 1757–1758

Harris, Michael. *London Newspapers in the Age of Walpole: A Study of the Origins of the Modern English Press*. London, 1986

Harris, P. M. G. "Inflation and Deflation in Early America, 1634–1860: Patterns of Change in the British-American Economy." *Social Science History*, XX (Winter 1996), 469–505

Harris, Walter. "Of the Weights and Measures used in Ireland; and of Denomination Given to Lands There." In *The Whole Works of Sir James Ware Concerning Ireland*, translated and edited by Walter Harris, II, 222–227. Dublin, 1745 [*sic*, for 1746]

Hart, Simon. "Amsterdam Shipping and Trade to Northern Russia in the Seventeenth Century." *Mededelingen van de Nederlandse Verening voor Zeegeschiedenis*, XXVI (March 1973), 5–30, 105–116

Hart, Simon. *Geschrift en Getal: Een keuze uit de demografisch-, economisch- en sociaal-historische studiën op grond van Amsterdamse en Zaanse archivalia, 1600–1800*. Hollandse Studiën, 9. Dordrecht, 1976

Harvard University. Graduate School of Business Administration. Baker Library. Kress Library of Business and Economics. *Catalogue, with Data upon Cognate Items in Other Harvard Libraries*. 5 vols. Boston, 1940–1967

Harvard University. Graduate School of Business Administration. Baker Library. Manuscripts and Archives Department. *Manuscripts in Baker Library: A Guide to Sources for Business, Economic, and Social History*. By Robert W. Lovett and Eleanor C. Bishop. 4th edn. Boston, 1978

Hatton, Edward *The Merchant's Magazine: or, Trade-Man's Treasury*. [2nd edn.] London, 1697

Hauschild-Thiessen, Renate, and Elfriede Bachmann. *Führer durch die Quellen zur Geschichte Lateinamerikas in der Bundesrepublik Deutschland*. Veröffentlichungen aus dem Staatsarchiv der Freien Hansestadt Bremen, vol. 38. Bremen, 1972

Hauser, Henri. *Recherches et documents sur l'histoire des prix en France, de 1500 à 1800*. Paris, 1936

Hausman, William J. "Size and Profitability of English Colliers in the Eighteenth Century." *Business History Review*, LI (Winter 1977), 460–473

Haviland, E[dward] K. "Classification Society Registers from the Point of View of the Maritime Historian." *American Neptune*, XXX (January 1970), 9–39

Hayes, Richard. *The Negociator's Magazine*. 4th edn. London, 1739

Hayes, Richard. *The Negociator's Magazine*. 9th edn. Revised by Benjamin Webb. London, 1764

Hayes, Richard J. *Manuscript Sources for the History of Irish Civilization*. 11 vols. Boston, 1965

Heckscher, Eli F. *Mercantilism*. Translated by Mendel Shapiro. 2nd edn, revised. Edited by E[rnst] F. Söderlund. 2 vols. London, [1955]

Hedges, James B. *The Browns of Providence Plantations*, 2 vols. Cambridge, Mass., 1952–1968

Heers, Jacques. "Types de navires et spécialisation des trafics en Méditerranée à la fin du Moyen Âge." In [Colloque International d'Histoire Maritime. 2nd. Paris. 1957.] *Le Navire et l'économie maritime du Moyen Âge au XVIIIe siècle principalement en Méditerranée*, edited by Michel Mollat, pp. 107–117. Paris, 1958

Heinsius, Paul. "Dimensions et caractéristiques des 'Koggen' hanséatiques dans le commerce Baltique." In [Colloque International d'Histoire Maritime. 3rd. Paris. 1958.] *Le Navire et l'économie maritime du Nord de l'Europe du Moyen Âge au XVIIIe siècle*, edited by Michel Mollat, pp. 7–23. Paris, 1960

Heinsius, Paul. *Das Schiff der hansischen Frühzeit*. Quellen und Darstellungen zur Hansischen Geschichte, n.s., vol. XII. 2nd edn, revised. Cologne, 1986

Helferty, Seamus, and Raymond Refaussé. *Directory of Irish Archives*. 2nd edn. [Blackrock, Co. Dublin, 1993]

Hemphill, John M., II. "Freight Rates in the Maryland Tobacco Trade, 1705–1762." *Maryland Historical Magazine*, LIV (March, June 1959), 36–58, 153–187

Henderson, J[ames] M. *Scottish Reckonings of Time, Money, Weights and Measures*. Historical Association of Scotland [Pamphlets], n.s., no. 4. [Edinburgh], 1926

Henige, David P. *Colonial Governors from the Fifteenth Century to the Present: A Comprehensive List*. Madison, Wis., 1970

Henning, Richard. *Terrae Incognitae: Eine Zusammenstellung und kritische Bewertung der wichtigsten vorcolumbischen Entdeckungsreisen an Hand der darüber vorliegenden Originalberichte*. 2nd edn, revised 4 vols. Leiden, 1944–1950

Henretta, James A. "Economic Development and Social Structure in Colonial Boston." *William and Mary Quarterly*, 3rd ser., XXII (January 1965), 75–92

Herbach, Johann Caspar. *Europäische Wechselhandlung . . . auch eine General-Wechsel-Reduction*. Nuremberg, 1757

H[er]l[ein], J[an] D. *Beschryvinge van de Volk-Plantinge Zariname*. [2nd edn.] Leeuwarden, 1718

Higgins, J. P. P., and Sidney Pollard. *Aspects of Capital Investment in Great Britain, 1750–1850: A Preliminary Survey*. London, 1971

Higgs, Henry. *Bibliography of Economics, 1751–1775*. Cambridge, Eng., 1935

Higham, C[harles] S. S. *The Colonial Entry-Books: A Brief Guide to the Colonial Records in the Public Record Office before 1696*. Helps for Students of History, no. 45. London, 1921

Histoire économique et sociale de la France. Edited by Fernand [P.] Braudel and [Camille] Ernest Labrousse. 4 vols in 8 pts. Paris, 1970–1982

Historical Society of Pennsylvania. *Guide to the Manuscript Collections of the Historical Society of Pennsylvania*. 3rd edn. Philadelphia, 1991

Hocquet, Jean-Claude. "Pesos y medidos y la historia de los precios en México: Algunas consideraciones metodológicas." [Translated by Ana Claudia Morales Viramontes.] In *Los precios de alimentos y manufacturas novohispanos*, edited by Virginia García Acosta, pp. 72–85. [Mexico City, 1995]

Hocquet, Jean-Claude. "Tonnages ancien et moderne: Botte de Venise et tonneau anglais." *Revue Historique*, no. 550 (April–June 1989), 349–360

Hoes, H. J. "Voorgeschiedenis en ontstaan van het *Financieele Dagblad, 1796–1943.*" *Economisch- en Sociaal-Historisch Jaarboek*, XLIX (1986), 1–43

Holmes, G[eoffrey] S. "Gregory King and the Social Structure of Pre-Industrial England." *Transactions of the Royal Historical Society*, 5th ser., XXVII (1977), 41–68

Holroyd, Maria Josepha. *The Girlhood of Maria Josepha Holroyd (Lady Stanley of Aderley). Recorded in Letters of a Hundred Years Ago: From 1776 to 1796.* Edited by J[ane] H. Adeane. London, 1896

Homans, Isaac Smith, Jr. *An Historical and Statistical Account of the Foreign Commerce of the United States.* New York, 1857

Hoon, Elizabeth Evelynola. *The Organization of the English Customs System 1696–1786.* New York, 1938

Hopkins, Esek. *The Correspondence of Esek Hopkins, Commander-in-Chief of the United States Navy.* Edited by Alverda S. Beck. Providence, RI, 1933

Hopkins, Esek. *The Letter Book of Esek Hopkins, Commander-in-Chief of the United States Navy, 1775–1777.* Edited by Alverda S. Beck. Providence, RI, 1932

Hoppit, Julian. "Reforming Britain's Weights and Measures, 1660–1824." *English Historical Review*, CVIII (January 1993), 82–104

Hoppit, Julian. *Risks and Failure in English Business, 1700–1800.* Cambridge, Eng., 1987

Horowicz, Kay, and Robson Lowe. *The Colonial Posts in the United States of America, 1606–1783.* London, 1967

Horwitz, Henry. *Chancery Equity Records and Proceedings, 1600–1800: A Guide to Documents in the Public Record Office.* Public Record Office Handbook 27. London, 1995

Houghton, John. ["Custom-House Bills."] *Collection for Improvement of Husbandry and Trade* (London), I (no. 6, 27 April 1692), 1

Hulton, Ann. *Letters of a Loyalist Lady: Being the Letters of Ann Hulton, Sister of Henry Hulton Commissioner of Customs at Boston, 1767–1776.* Cambridge, Eng., 1927

Hulton, Henry. "An Englishman Views the American Revolution: The Letters of Henry Hulton, 1769–1776." Edited by Wallace Brown. *Huntington Library Quarterly*, XXXVI (November 1972, February 1973), 1–26, 139–151

Humbla, [Knut] Philibert. "Båtfyndet vid Åskekärr." *Göteborgs och Bohusläns Fornminnes Förenings Tidskrift 1934*, pp. 1–21

Humbla, [Knut] Philibert, and Lennart von Post. "Galtabäcksbåten och tidgit båtbyggeri i Norden." *Göteborgs Kungl[ig] Vetenskaps- och Vitterhets-samhälles Handlingar*, 5th ser., pt A: Humanistiska Skrifter, VI (1937), 1–148

Hutchins, John G. B. *The American Maritime Industries and Public Policy, 1789–1914: An Economic History.* Harvard Economic Studies, vol. LXXI. Cambridge, Mass., 1941

Huvelin, P[aul]. *Essai historique sur le droit des marchés & des foires.* Paris, 1897

Hyamson, Albert M. "Plan of a Dictionary of Anglo-Jewish Biography." In *Anglo-Jewish Notabilities: Their Arms and Testamentary Dispositions*, pp. 1–73. London, 1949

Imlah, Albert H. *Economic Elements in the "Pax Britannia": Studies in British Foreign Trade in the Nineteenth Century.* Cambridge, Mass., 1958

Imlah, Albert H. "Real Values in British Foreign Trade, 1798–1853." *Journal of Economic History*, VIII (November 1948), 133–152

Index to Personal Names in the National Union Catalog of Manuscript Collections, 1959–1984. 2 vols. Alexandria, Va., 1988

Index to Subjects and Corporate Names in the National Union Catalog of Manuscript Collections, 1959–1984. 3 vols. Alexandria, Va., 1994

Ingram, K[enneth] E. *Manuscripts Relating to Commonwealth Caribbean Countries in United States and Canadian Repositories.* St. Lawrence, Barbados, 1975

Ingram, K[enneth] E. *Sources for West Indian Studies: A Supplementary Listing, with Particular Reference to Manuscript Sources.* Zug, Switzerland, 1983

Ingram, K[enneth] E. *Sources of Jamaican History, 1655–1838: A Bibliographical Survey with Particular Reference to Manuscript Sources.* 2 vols. Zug, Switzerland, 1976 [M.Phil. thesis, University of London, 1970]

International Economic History Congress. 8th. 1982. Budapest. *Münzprägung, Geldumlauf und Wechselkurse / Minting, Monetary Circulation and Exchange Rates: Akten des 8th International Economic History Congress, Section C 7, Budapest, 1982.* Edited by Eddy van Cauwenberghe and Franz Irsigler. Trierer Historische Forschungen, Band 7. Trier, 1984

International Encyclopedia of the Social Sciences. Edited by David L. Sills and Robert K. Merton. 19 vols. [New York, 1968–1991]

International Genealogical Index: IGI. [2nd edn.] 11,712 microfiche. [Salt Lake City, Utah], 1992

In the Time of Harvest: Essays in Honor of Abba Hillel Silver on the Occasion of His 70th Birthday. Edited by Daniel Jeremy Silver. New York, [1963]

Introduction à la métrologie historique. Edited by Bernard Garnier, J[ean]-C[laude] Hocquet, and D[enis] Woronoff. Paris, 1989

Ireland (Eire). Laws and Statutes. *The Statutes at Large, Passed in the Parliaments Held in Ireland: from . . . 1310 . . . to . . . 1800.* [Edited by James Goddard Butler.] 20 vols. Dublin, 1786–1801

Ireland (Eire). Parliament. House of Commons. *The Journals of the House of Commons of the Kingdom of Ireland, 1613–1776.* 19 vols. Dublin, 1753–1776

Irving, John Beaufin. *The Irvings, Irwins, Irvines, or Erinveines, or Any Other Spelling of the Name: An Old Scots Border Clan.* Aberdeen, 1907

[Irving, Thomas.] *A State of the Importations from Great-Britain into the Port of Boston, From the beginning of Jan. 1769 to Aug. 17th 1769. . . .* Boston, 1769

[Irving, Thomas.] *A State of Importations from Great-Britain, into the Port of Boston, From the beginning of January, 1770. . . .* [1st edn.] Boston, 1770

[Irving, Thomas.] *A State of Importations from Great-Britain, into the Port of Boston, From the beginning of January, 1770. . . .* [2nd edn.] Boston, 1770

[Irving, Thomas.] *A State of Importations from Great-Britain, into the Port of Boston, From the beginning of January, 1770. . . .* [3rd edn.] Boston, 1770

Isidore, of Seville. *Isidori Hispalensis episcopi Etymologiarium sive Originum libri XX.* Edited by W[allace] M. Lindsay. 2 vols. Oxford, [1911]

Israel, Jonathan I. "The Amsterdam Stock Exchange and the English Revolution of 1688." *Tijdschrift voor Geschiedenis,* CIII (1990), 412–440

Jal, A[ugustin]. *Archéologie navale.* 2 vols. Paris, 1840

Jal, A[ugustin]. *Glossaire nautique: Répertoire polyglotte de termes de marine anciens et modernes.* Paris, 1848

Jal, A[ugustin]. *Nouveau glossaire nautique.* New edn. [Edited by Michel Mollat.] In progress. Paris and The Hague, 1970 to date

Jamaica. Assembly. *Journals of the Assembly of Jamaica from January 20th, 1663–4 . . . [to 1826].* 15 vols. Jamaica, 1795–1829

Jamaica. Assembly. *Proceedings of the Hon[ourable] House of Assembly of Jamaica, on the Sugar and Slave Trade.* St. Jago de la Vega, 1792

Jamaica. Laws and Statutes. *Acts of Assembly Passed in the Island of Jamaica; From the Year 1681, to the Year 1769.* 2 vols. St. Jago de la Vega, 1769–1771

James, William M. *The British Navy in Adversity: A Study of the War of American Independence.* London, 1926

Jameson, J[ohn] Franklin. "Guide to the Items Relating to American History in the

Reports of the English Historical Manuscripts Commission and Their Appendices." In American Historical Association. *Annual Report for the Year 1898*, pp. 611–708. Washington, DC, 1899

Jarvis, Rupert C. "The Archival History of the Customs Records." *Journal of the Society of Archivists*, I (April 1959), 239–250

Jarvis, Rupert C. "Eighteenth-Century London Shipping." In *Studies in London History Presented to Philip Edmund Jones*, edited by A[lbert] E. J. Hollander and William Kellaway, pp. 403–425. [London], 1969

Jarvis, Rupert C. "Fractional Shareholding in British Merchant Ships with Special Reference to the 64ths." *Mariner's Mirror*, XLV (November 1959), 301–319

Jarvis, Rupert C. "Official Trade and Revenue Statistics." *Economic History Review*, 2nd ser., XVII (August 1964), 43–62

Jarvis, Rupert [C.] "Ship Registry – to 1707." *Maritime History*, I (April 1971), 29–45

Jarvis, Rupert C. "Ship Registry – 1707–86." *Maritime History*, II (September 1972), 151–167

Jarvis, Rupert C. "The Sources of Transport History: Sources for the History of Ships and Shipping." *Journal of Transport History*, III (Nov. 1958), 212–234

Jefferson, Thomas. *The Papers of Thomas Jefferson*. Edited by Julian P. Boyd *et al.* In progress. Princeton, NJ, 1950 to date

Jefferys, Thomas. *The West-India Atlas: or, A Compendious Description of the West Indies: Illustrated with Forty Correct Charts and Maps, Taken from Actual Surveys. Together with an Historical Account of the Several Countries and Islands Which Compose that Part of the World*. London, 1775

Jellema, Dirk. "Frisian Trade in the Dark Ages." *Speculum*, XXX (January 1955), 15–36

Jellema, Dirk. "Frisian Trade to 1100." Ph.D. diss, University of Wisconsin, 1951

Jenkins, L[awrence] W. "Contract to Build a Brigantine . . . 1750." *American Neptune*, XXI (June 1961), 15

Jenkins, William Sumner. A *Guide to the Microfilm Collection of Early State Records: Supplement*. [Washington, DC], 1951

Jenkins, William Sumner. *Records of the States of the United States of America: A Microfilm Compilation*. [Washington, DC], 1949

Jenkins, William Sumner, and Lillian A. Hamrick. A *Guide to the Microfilm Collection of Early State Records*. [Washington, DC], 1950

Jensen, Arthur L. "The Inspection of Exports in Colonial Pennsylvania." *Pennsylvania Magazine of History and Biography*, LXXVIII (July 1954), 275–297

Jensen, Arthur L. *The Maritime Commerce of Colonial Philadelphia*. Madison, Wis., 1963

Jensen, Merrill. *The Founding of a Nation: A History of the American Revolution, 1763–1776*. New York, 1968

Jensen, Merrill. *The New Nation: A History of the United States during the Confederation, 1781–1789*. New York, 1950

Johnson, Cecil. *British West Florida, 1763–1783*. New Haven, Conn., 1943

Johnson, Emory R. *et al. History of Domestic and Foreign Commerce of the United States*. Carnegie Institution of Washington, Publication no. 215A. 2 vols in 1 pt. Washington, DC, 1915

Johnson, Herbert Alan. *The Law Merchant and Negotiable Instruments in Colonial New York, 1664 to 1730*. Chicago, 1963

Jones, Alice Hanson. "La Fortune privée en Pennsylvanie, New Jersey, Delaware (1774)." *Annales: Histoire, Sciences Sociales*, XXIV (March–April 1969), 235–249

Jones, Alice Hanson. *Wealth of a Nation to Be: The American Colonies on the Eve of Revolution*. New York, 1980

Jones, D[wyryd] W. *War and Trade in the Age of William III and Marlborough.* [Oxford, 1988]

Jones, John Paul. *Life and Correspondence of John Paul Jones Including His Narrative of the Campaign of the Liman.* [Edited by Robert Charles Sands.] New York, 1830

Jones, Newton B. "Weights, Measures, and Mercantilism: The Inspection of Exports in Virginia, 1742–1820." In *The Old Dominion: Essays for Thomas Perkins Abernethy,* edited by Darrett B. Rutman, pp. 122–134. Charlottesville, Va., 1964

Jonung, [Jon] Lars [B.] "The Long Run Demand for Money – A Wicksellian Approach." *Scandinavian Journal of Economics,* LXXX (no. 2, 1978), 216–230

Josa, Guy. *Les Industries du sucre et du rhum à la Martinique (1639–1913).* Paris, 1931

Joyce, Herbert. *The History of the Post Office from Its Establishment down to 1836.* London, 1893

Kålund, P[eter] E. Kristian. *Bidrag til en historisk-topografisk Beskrivelse af Island.* 2 vols. Copenhagen, 1877–1882

Kalm, Pehr. *The America of 1750: Peter Kalm's Travels in North America – The English Version of 1770.* [Translated by John Reinhold Foster.] Revised and edited by Adolph B. Benson. 2 vols. New York, 1937

Kalm, Pehr. *En resa till Norra America, på Kongl[igt] Swenska Wetenskaps Academiens befallning, och Publici kostnad.* 3 vols. Stockholm, 1753–1761

Kammen, Michael. *Empire and Interest: The American Colonies and the Politics of Mercantilism.* Philadelphia, 1970

Karras, Alan L. *Sojourners in the Sun: Scottish Migrants in Jamaica and the Chesapeake, 1740–1800.* Ithaca, NY, [1992]

Keevil, John J., Christopher [C.] Lloyd, and Jack L. S. Coulter. *Medicine and the Navy, 1200–1900.* 4 vols. Edinburgh and London, 1956–1963

Keith, Alice B. "Relaxations in the British Restrictions on the American Trade with the British West Indies, 1783–1802." *Journal of Modern History,* XX (March 1948), 1–18

Kelly, Patrick. *Metrology; or An Exposition of Weights and Measures, Chiefly Those of Great Britain and France.* London, 1816

Kelly, Patrick. *The Universal Cambist, and Commercial Instructor.* [1st edn.] 2 vols. London, 1811

Kelly, P[atrick]. *The Universal Cambist and Commercial Instructor.* 2nd edn. 2 vols. London, 1835

Kemble, John Haskell. "England's First Atlantic Mail Line." *Mariner's Mirror,* XXVI (January, April 1940), 33–54, 184–198

Kenneally, Finbar, *et al. United States Documents in the Propaganda Fide Archive: A Calendar.* 9 vols. Washington, DC, 1966–1982

Keppel, Thomas R. *The Life of August, Viscount Keppel, Admiral of the White and First Lord of the Admiralty in 1782–3.* 2 vols. London, 1842

Ker, Neil R. "*Liber Custumarum,* and Other Manuscripts Formerly at the Guildhall." *The Guildhall Miscellany,* I (no. 3, February 1954), 37–45

Kerr, Wilfred Breton. *Bermuda and the American Revolution, 1760–1783.* Princeton, NJ, 1936

Ketner, F[rans], ed. "Bijdrage tot de kennis van de Utrechtse maten en gewichten." *Bijdragen en Medelingen van het Historisch Genootsch,* LXVI (1948), 190–198

King, Gregory. *Two Tracts, by Gregory King.* Edited by George E. Barnett. Baltimore, 1936

Kisch, Bruno. *Scales and Weights: A Historical Outline.* Yale Studies in the History of Science and Medicine, no. 1. New Haven, Conn., 1965

Klein, Herbert S. "The English Slave Trade to Jamaica, 1782–1808." *Economic History Review,* 2nd ser., XXXI (February 1978), 25–45

Klopfer, Helen Louise. "Statistics of the Foreign Trade of Philadelphia, 1700–1860." Ph.D. dissertation, University of Pennsylvania, 1936

Koen, E[lly] M., *et al.* "Notarial Records relating to the Portuguese Jews in Amsterdam." *Studia Rosenthaliana: Tijdschrift voor Joodse Wetenschap en Geschiedenis in Nederland,* IV (January 1970), 106–124

Koenig, W[illiam] J., and S[ydney] L. Mayer. *European Manuscript Sources of the American Revolution.* London and New York, 1974

Konwiser, Harry M. *Colonial and Revolutionary Posts: A History of the American Postal Systems, Colonial and Revolutionary Periods.* Richmond, Va., 1931

Konwiser, Harry M. *United States Stampless Cover Catalogue.* Batavia, NY, 1936

Kruse, Jürgen Elert. *Allgemeiner und besonders Hamburgischer Contorist.* Hamburg, 1753

Kula, Witold. *Miary i ludzie.* Warsaw, 1970

Kulikoff, Alan. "The Progress of Inequality in Revolutionary Boston." *William and Mary Quarterly,* 3rd ser., XXVIII (July 1971), 375–412

Kupp, Jan. "Dutch Notarial Acts Relating to the Tobacco Trade of Virginia, 1608–1653." *William and Mary Quarterly,* 3rd ser., XXX (October 1973), 653–655

Kynaston, David. *"The Financial Times": A Centenary History.* London, 1988

Labrousse, [Camille] Ernest. "Les 'bon prix' agricoles du XVIIIe siècle." In *Des derniers temps de l'âge seigneurial aux préludes de l'âge industriel (1660–1789),* edited by [Camille] Ernest Labrousse *et al.,* pp. 367–416. Vol. II of *Histoire économique et sociale de la France.* Paris, [1970]

Labrousse, C[amille]-E[rnest]. *Esquisse du movement des prix et des revenues en France au XVIIIe siècle.* 2 vols. Paris, 1933

Lamb, D. P. "Volume and Tonnage of the Liverpool Slave Trade." In *Liverpool and the African Slave Trade, and Abolition: Essays to Illustrate Current Knowledge and Research,* edited by Roger [T.] Anstey and P[aul] E. H. Hair, pp. 91–112. Historic Society of Lancashire and Cheshire, Occasional Series, vol. 2. [Liverpool], 1976

Landes, David S. "Statistics as a Source for the History of Economic Development in Western Europe: The Protostatistical Era." In *The Dimensions of the Past: Materials, Problems, and Opportunities for Quantitative Work in History,* edited by Val R. Lorwin and Jacob M. Price, pp. 53–91. New Haven, Conn., 1972

Lane, Frederic C. "Stowage Factors in the Maritime Statutes of Venice." *Mariner's Mirror,* LXIII (August 1977), 293–294

Lane, Frederic C. "Tonnages, Medieval and Modern." *Economic History Review,* 2nd ser., XVII (December 1964), 213–233

Lane, Frederic Chapin. *Venetian Ships and Shipbuilders of the Renaissance.* Baltimore, 1934

Lanner, Allen H. *A Critical Edition of Richard Brathwait's "Whimzies."* New York, 1991. Ph.D. diss., New York University, 1966

Laurence, of Verona (Laurentius Veronensis). *De Bello Balerico sive rerum in Majorica Pesanorum ac de eorum triumphano Pisis habito anno salutis 1115.* In *Patrologiae Cursus Completus . . . Series Latinae,* edited by J[acques] P[aul] Migne, CLXIII, 513–576. Paris, 1859

Laurens, Henry. *The Papers of Henry Laurens,* edited by Philip M. Hamer *et al.* In progress. Columbia, SC 1968 to date

The Law in America, 1607–1861. Edited by William Pencak and Wythe W. Holt, Jr. [New York, 1989]

Learned, Marion Dexter. *Guide to the Manuscript Materials Relating to American History in the German State Archives.* Carnegie Institution of Washington, Publication no. 150. Washington, DC, 1912

Leff, Nathaniel H. "A Technique for Estimating Income Trends from Currency Data and an Application to Nineteenth-Century Brazil." *Review of Income and Wealth,* XVIII (Dec. 1972), 355–368

Lehmann, Hannelore. "Paul Jacob Marperger (1656 bis 1730), ein Vergessener Ökonom der deutschen Frühaufklärung: Versuch einer Übersicht über sein Leben und Wirken." *Jahrbuch für Wirtschaftsgeschichte*, [XI] (no. 4, 1971), 125–157

Leland, John. *The Itinerary of John Leland in or about the Years 1535–1543*, edited by Lucy Toulmin Smith. 5 vols. London, 1907–1910

Leland, Waldo G., John J. Meng, and Abel Doysié. *Guide to Materials for American History in the Libraries and Archives of Paris*. Carnegie Institution of Washington, Publication no. 392. 2 vols. Washington, DC, 1932–1943

Lemon, James T., and Gary B. Nash. "The Distribution of Wealth in Eighteenth Century America: A Century of Change in Chester County, Pennsylvania, 1693–1802." *Journal of Social History*, II (1968–1969), 1–24

Leroy, Charles. "Mesures de capacité en usage en Haute-Normandie aux XVIIe et XVIIIe siècles." *Bulletin de la Société Libre d'Émulation, du Commerce et de l'Industrie de la Seine-Inférieure* (1936), 49–97, and (1937), 155–218

Le Roy Ladurie, Emmanuel. *Les Paysans de Languedoc*. [2nd edn.] 2 vols. Paris, [1966]

Letters of Delegates to Congress, 1774–1789, edited by Paul H. Smith. In progress. Washington, DC, 1976 to date

Levitt, Ian, and [Thomas] Christopher Smout. "Some Weights and Measures in Scotland, 1843." *Scottish Historical Review*, LVI (October 1977), 146–152

Levy, Matthias. "Jews in the English Press." *The Jewish Chronicle* (London), 19 August 1904

Lévy-Leboyer, Maurice. "Le Crédit et la monnaie: L'Apprentissage du marché." In *L'Avènement de l'ère industrielle (1789–années 1880)*, edited by Patrick Léon et al., pt i, pp. 391–429. Vol. III of *Histoire économique et sociale de la France*. Paris, [1976]

Lewis, James A. *The Final Campaign of the American Revolution: Rise and Fall of the Spanish Bahamas*. [Columbia, SC, 1991]

Lewis, W[illiam] Arthur. "Economic Development with Unlimited Supplies of Labour." *Manchester School of Economic and Social Studies*, XXII (May 1954), 139–191

Lewis, W[illiam] Arthur. *The Theory of Economic Growth*. London, 1955

Lincoln, Waldo. "List of Newspapers of the West Indies and Bermuda in the Library of the American Antiquarian Society." *Proceedings of the American Antiquarian Society*, n.s., XXXVI (1926), 130–155

Lind, James. *An Essay on the Most Effectual Means of Preserving the Health of Seamen in the Royal Navy*. New edn, enlarged. London, 1774

Lindqvist, Sune. "Birkamynten." *Fornvännen: Meddelanden från K[ungliga] Vitterhets Historie och Antikvitets Akademien*, XXI (1926), 307–334

Lippmann, Edmund O. von. *Geschichte des Zuckers seit den ältesten Zeiten bis zum Beginn der Rübenzucker-Fabrikation: Ein Beiträge zur Kulturgeschichte*. 2nd edn. 1929. Reprinted and enlarged. Niederwalluf (bei Wiesbaden), 1970

Lipson, E[phraim]. *The Economic History of England*. 6th edn. 3 vols. London, 1931

A List of Persons Concerned in the Rebellion, Transmitted to the Commissioners of the Excise by the Several Supervisors in Scotland, in Obedience to a General Letter of the 7th May 1746 with a Supplementary List with Evidences to Prove the Same, edited by Walter Macleod. Publications of the Scottish History Society, [1st ser.], vol. 8. Edinburgh, 1890

Lithander, Daniel [E.] *Oförgripeliga Tancker om Nödwändigheten of Skogarnas Bettre Wård och Ans i Finland*. Åbo, [Finland], 1753

Liverpool and the African Slave Trade, and Abolition: Essays to Illustrate Current Knowledge and Research, edited by Roger [T.] Anstey and P[aul] E. H. Hair. Historic Society of Lancashire and Cheshire, Occasional Series, vol. 2. [Liverpool], 1976

Lloyd, Christopher [C.], and Jack L. S. Coulter. *Medicine and the Royal Navy, 1714–1815.* Vol. III of John J. Keevil *et al. Medicine and the Royal Navy, 1200–1900.* Edinburgh and London, 1961

Lloyd, Malcolm, Jr. "The Taking of the Bahamas by the Continental Navy in 1776." *Pennsylvania Magazine of History and Biography,* XLIX (October 1925), 349–366

Lloyd's Register of Shipping . . . 1764. [London, 1764]

Lloyd's Register of Shipping . . . 1768. [London, 1768]

Lloyd's Register of Shipping . . . 1776. [London, 1776]

Lobo Cabrera, Manuel. *Monedas, pesas y medidas en Canarias en el siglo XVI.* Las Palmas, 1989

Lodolini, Elio. *Guida delle fonti per la storia dell'America Latina esistenti in Italia.* Pubblicazioni degli Archivi di Stato, LXXXVIII. Rome, 1976

London. Customhouse. Clerks. *An Abstract of the Grievances of the Poore Clerks of His Majesties Custome-house London, by Reason of Letters Pattents Lately Obtained for the Erecting of a New Office called the Office of the Clerke of the Bills.* [London, 1621]

London. Sugar Refiners. *Epitome of the Sugar Trade.* [London, 1781]

London. University. British Library of Political and Economic Science. "A Catalogue of the Papers of William Henry Beveridge, 1st Baron Beveridge." Compiled by G. A. Falla. Unpublished typescript, 1981. Copy on deposit in the Manuscript Department

London. University. Goldsmiths' Company's Library of Economic Literature. *Catalogue of the Goldsmiths' Library of Economic Literature.* By M[argaret B. C.] Canney *et al.* 5 vols. Cambridge, Eng., and London, 1970–1995

The London Gold Market. [London], 1980

[Long, Edward.] *The History of Jamaica or, General Survey of the Antient and Modern State of that Island . . .* 3 vols. London, 1774

Looyenga, A. J. "Business and Urban Scenery: Illustrations in Eighteenth-Century Commercial Newspapers." Unpublished paper, in progress

López Dóminguez, F[rancisco] A. "Origin and Development of the Sugar Industry in Porto Rico." *The [Louisiana] Planter and Sugar Manufacturer,* LXXIX (23 July–13 August 1927), 61–63, 83–85, 103–105, 123–125

Lorenz, Lincoln. *John Paul Jones: Fighter for Freedom and Glory.* Annapolis, 1943

Lowe, Robson. *Handstruck Postage Stamps of the Empire, 1680–1900.* 2nd edn. London, [1938]

Lubbock, Basil. "Ships of the Period and Developments in Rig." In *The Trade Winds: A Study of British Overseas Trade during the French Wars, 1793–1815,* edited by C[yril] Northcote Parkinson, pp. 87–101. London, [1948]

Luca, Hieronymus da. *Tractato de Cambi e de Marchi per Lione.* Florence, 1517

Luebeck, Emil. *Das Seewesen der Griechen und Römer.* 2 vols. Hamburg, 1890–1891

Luzzatto, Gino. "Vi furono fiere a Venezia?" *Recueils de la Société Jean Bodin pour l'Histoire Comparative des Institutions,"* V (1953), 267–279

Lydon, James G. "New York and the Slave Trade, 1700 to 1774." *William and Mary Quarterly,* 3rd ser., XXXV (April 1978), 375–394

Lyman, John. "Carpenter's Measurement." *American Neptune,* XXIII (April 1963), 141–142

Lyman, John. "Early Tonnage Measurement in England." *Mariner's Mirror,* LIV (May 1968), 114

Lyman, John. "A Philadelphia Shipbuilding Contract of 1746." *American Neptune,* V (July 1945), 243

Lyman, John. "Register Tonnage and Its Measurements." *American Neptune,* V (July, October 1945), 223–234, 311–325

Lynsky, Myer. *Sugar Economics, Statistics, and Documents.* [New York], 1938

Lyon, David [J.] *The Sailing Navy List: All the Ships of the Royal Navy – Built, Purchased, Captured – 1688–1860.* [London, 1993]

[Lyons, J. J.] "Items Relating to the Simson Family, New York." *Publications of the American Jewish Historical Society,* XXVII (1920), 371–375

Mackay, Henry. *An Abridgment of the Excise-Laws, and of the Customs-Laws Therewith Connected, Now in Force in Great Britain.* Edinburgh, 1779

Mackesy, Piers. *The War for America, 1775–1783.* [London, 1964]

Macpherson, David. *Annals of Commerce, Manufactures, Fisheries and Navigation, with Brief Notices of the Arts and Sciences Connected with Them . . . to . . . 1801.* 4 vols. London, 1805

Maddison, Angus. *Phases of Capitalist Development.* Oxford, 1982

Madison, James. *The Papers of James Madison.* Edited by William T. Hutchinson *et al.* In progress. Chicago, 1962 to date

Madox, Thomas. *The History and Antiquities of the Exchequer of the Kings of England . . .* 2nd edn. 2 vols. London, 1769

Magalhães Godinho, Vitorino [de]. *Prix et monnaies au Portugal, 1750–1850.* [Paris], 1955

Mahan, Alfred Thayer. *Major Operations of the Navies in the War of American Independence.* Boston, 1913

Mair, John. *Book-keeping Methodiz'd; or A Methodical Treatise of Merchant-Accompts, According to the Italian Form,* 5th edn. Edinburgh, 1757

Makinson, David H. *Barbados: A Study of North-American–West-Indian Relations, 1739–1789,* Studies in American History, no. 3. The Hague, 1964

Malmesbury, William of. *Willelmi Malmesbiriensis monachi de gestis regum Anglorum libri qunique: Historiae novellae libri tres.* Edited by William Stubbs. [Rolls Series, no. 90.] 2 vols. London, 1887–1889

Malvezin, Théophile. *Histoire du commerce de Bordeaux depuis les origines jusqu'à nos jours.* Bordeaux, 1892

Malynes, Gerald [de]. *Consuetudo, vel Lex Mercatoria; or the Ancient Law-Merchant.* [1st edn.] London, 1622

Manross, William Wilson. *The Fulham Papers in the Lambeth Palace Library. American Colonial Section: Calendar and Indexes.* Oxford, 1965

Manross, William Wilson. *S.P.G. Papers in the Lambeth Palace Library: Calendar and Indexes.* Oxford, 1974

Maracchi Biagiarelli, Berta. "Il privilegio di stampatore ducale nella Firenze Medicea." *Archivio Storico Italiano,* CXXIII (no. 3, 1965), 304–370

Marcus, G[eoffry] J. "The Evolution of the Knörr." *Mariner's Mirror,* XLI (May 1955), 115–122

Marcus, G[eoffry] J. "The Greenland Trade-Route." *Economic History Review,* 2nd ser., VII (August 1954), 71–80

Marcus, G[eoffry] J. "The Navigation of the Norsemen." *Mariner's Mirror,* XXXIX, (May 1953), 112–131

Marcus, G[eoffry] J. "The Norse Emigration to the Faeroe Islands." *English Historical Review,* LXXI (January 1956), 56–61

Marcus, Jacob Rader. *Early American Jewry.* 2 vols. Philadelphia, 1951–1953

Marcus, Jacob R. "The Oldest Known Synagogue Record Book of Continental North America, 1720–1721." In *In the Time of Harvest: Essays in Honor of Abba Hillel Silver on the Occasion of His 70th Birthday,* edited by Daniel Jeremy Silver, pp. 227–234. New York, [1963]

Marczewski, Jan [sic]. "Some Aspects of the Economic Growth of France, 1660–1958." *Economic Development and Cultural Change,* IX (April 1961), 369–386

Marczewski, Jean [sic]. *Le Produit physique de l'économie française de 1789 à 1913*

(Comparison avec la Grande-Bretagne). Cahiers de l'Institut de Science Économique Appliquée, sér. AF: "Histoire Quantitative de l'Économie Française," no. 4. Paris, 1965

Marin, Pieter. *Groot Nederdiutsch en Fransch Woordenboek . . . Grand dictionnaire hollandais & français*. 3rd edn. Dordrecht and Amsterdam, 1752

Maritime Dimensions of the American Revolution. Washington, DC, 1977

Markovitch, Tihomir J. "L'Évolution industrielle de la France au XVIIIe siècle: Une première analyse." *Revue d'Histoire Économique et Sociale*, LIII (no. 2–3, 1975), 266–288

Markovitch, Tihomir J. *Les Industries lainières de Colbert à la Révolution*. Vol. I of *Histoire des industries françaises*. Travaux de Droit, d'Économie, de Sociologie et des Sciences Politiques, no. 104. Geneva, 1976

Marperger, Paul Jacob. *Anleitung zum rechten Verstand und nußbarer Allerhand so wohl gedrucker als geschreibener . . . Zeitungen oder Avisen*. n.p. [Leipzig (?), n.d. 1726 (?)]

M[arperger], P[aul] J. *Erläuterung der Hamburger und Amsterdamer Waaren-Preiß-Couranten*. [Dresden, 1725]

M[arperger], P[aul] J. *Erläuterung der Holländischen und sonderlich der Amsterdamer Waaren-, Geld- und Wechsel-Preiß-Couranten*. [Dresden, 1726]

Marshall, J[ohn]. *A Digest of All the Accounts, Relating to the Population, Productions, Revenues, Financial Operations, Manufactures, Shipping, Colonies, Commerce, etc., etc., of the United Kingdom of Great Britain and Ireland, Diffused Through More Than 600 Volumes of Journals, Reports, and Papers, Presented to Parliament during the Last Thirty-Five Years*. 2 vols. London, 1833

Martin, Alfred S. "The King's Customs: Philadelphia, 1703–1774." *William and Mary Quarterly*, 3rd ser., V (April 1948), 201–216

Martini, Angelo. *Manuale di Metrologia: Ossia Misure, Pesi e Monete in Uso Attualmente e Anticamente Presso Tutti i Popoli*. Turin, 1883

Martin, C.-F[rançois]. *Les Tables de Martin, ou le Régulateur Universel des Calculs en Parties-Doubles. . . .* Paris, 1817

Maryland (Colony). Laws and Statutes. *Laws of Maryland, at Large, with Proper Indexes*. Edited by Thomas Bacon. Annapolis, 1765

Massachusetts (Colony). Laws and Statutes. *The Acts and Resolves, Public and Private, of the Province of the Massachusetts Bay*. [Edited by Abner Cheney Goodell *et al.*] 21 vols. Boston, 1869–1922

Massachusetts Historical Society, Boston. *Catalog of Manuscripts of the Massachusetts Historical Society*. 7 vols. Boston, 1969

Massie, J[oseph]. *Calculations and Observations Relating to an Additional Duty upon Sugar*. [London], 1759

Massie, J[oseph]. *A State of the Exports to and Imports from the British Sugar Colonies*. [London, 1760]

Mathews, Alizon M. "Editions of the Court and City Register, 1742–1813." *Bulletin of the Institute of Historical Research*, XIX (1942–1943), 9–12

Matteson, David M. *List of Manuscripts Concerning American History Preserved in European Libraries and Noted in Their Published Catalogues and Similar Printed Lists*. Carnegie Institution of Washington, Publication no. 359. Washington, DC, 1925

Mauro, Frédéric. *Le Portugal et l'Atlantique, au XVIIe siècle (1570–1670): Étude économique*. Paris, 1960

Maxwell, Herbert. *A History of Dumfries and Galloway*. 2nd edn. Edinburgh, 1900

Maxwell-Irving, Alastair T. M. *The Irvings of Bonshaw: Chiefs of the Noble and Ancient Scots Border Family of Irving*. Bletchley, 1968

Maxwell-Irving, Alastair T. M. "The Irvings of Dumfries (Senior Cadets of the Irvings of Bonshaw)" Unpublished typescript, 1968. Copies on deposit in the National Library of Scotland, Edinburgh, and Ewart Public Library, Dumfries

May, Louis-Philippe. *Histoire économique de la Martinique (1635–1763)*. Paris, 1930

McCowen, George Smith, Jr. *The British Occupation of Charleston, 1780–82*. Columbia, SC, 1972

McCusker, John J. *"Alfred": The First Continental Flagship, 1775–1778*. Smithsonian Studies in History and Technology, no. 20. Washington, DC, 1973

McCusker, John J. "The American Invasion of Nassau in the Bahamas." *American Neptune*, XXV (July 1965), 189–217

McCusker, John J. "The Business Press and Transaction Costs in Early Modern Europe, 1530–1775." Paper presented at the conference on "The Rise of Merchant Empires: Changing Patterns of Long-Distance Trade, 1360–1750," Center for Early Modern History, University of Minnesota, 1987

McCusker, John J. "The Business Press in England before 1775." *The Library: Transactions of the Bibliographical Society*, 6th ser., VIII (September 1986), 205–231

McCusker, John J. "Colonial Civil Servant and Counter-Revolutionary: Thomas Irving (1738–1800) in Boston, Charleston, and London." *Perspectives in American History*, XII (1979), 314–350

McCusker, John J. "Colonial Tonnage Measurement: Five Philadelphia Merchant Ships as a Sample." *Journal of Economic History*, XXVII (March 1967), 82–91

McCusker, John J. "The Continental Ship *Alfred*." *Nautical Research Journal*, XIII (Autumn 1965), 39–68

McCusker, John J. "Correction." *William and Mary Quarterly*, 3rd ser., XXXI (January 1974), 164

McCusker, John J. "The Current Value of English Exports, 1697 to 1800." *William and Mary Quarterly*, 3rd ser., XXVIII (October 1971), 607–628

McCusker, John J. "The Early History of 'Lloyd's List.'" *Historical Research: The Bulletin of the Institute of Historical Research*, LXIV (October 1991), 427–431

McCusker, John J. "Les Équivalents métriques des poids et mesures du commerce colonial aux XVIIe et XVIIIe siècles." *Revue Française d'Histoire d'Outre-Mer*, LXI (no. 3, 1974), 349–365

McCusker, John J. *European Bills of Entry and Marine Lists: Early Commercial Publications and the Origins of the Business Press*. Cambridge, Mass., 1985

McCusker, John J. "Growth, Stagnation, or Decline? The Economy of the British West Indies, 1763–1790." In *The Economy of Early America: The Revolutionary Period, 1763–1790*, edited by Ronald Hoffman, John J. McCusker, Russell R. Menard, and Peter J. Albert, pp. 275–302. Charlottesville, Va., 1988

McCusker, John J. *How Much Is That in Real Money? A Historical Price Index for Use as a Deflator of Money Values in the Economy of the United States*. Worcester, Mass., 1992

McCusker, John J. "How Much Is That in Real Money? A Historical Price Index for Use as a Deflator of Money Values in the Economy of the United States: Addenda et Corrigenda." *Proceedings of the American Antiquarian Society*, CVI (October 1996), 315–322

McCusker, John J. *An Introduction to the Naval Office Shipping Lists*. In progress

McCusker, John J. *Money and Exchange in Europe and America, 1600–1775: A Handbook*. [2nd edn.] Chapel Hill, NC, [1992]

McCusker, John J. "New York City and the Bristol Packet: A Chapter in 18th Century Postal History." *Postal History Journal*, XIII (July 1968), 15–24

McCusker, John J. "The Pennsylvania Shipping Industry in the Eighteenth Century." Unpublished typescript, 1972. Copy on deposit in the Historical Society of Pennsylvania, Philadelphia

McCusker, John J. "Price History: The International Context, Old and New." Paper presented at the conference on "Wage and Price History: The View from the Nordic Countries," Institutt for Økonomisk Historie, Universiteit i Bergen, 1988

McCusker, John J. "The Role of Antwerp in the Emergence of Commercial and Financial Newspapers in Early Modern Europe." In *La Ville et la transmission des valeurs culturelles au bas Moyen Âge et aux temps modernes – Die Stade und die Übertragung von kulturelles Werten im Spätmittelalter und in die Neuzeit – Cities and the Transmission of Cultural Values in the Late Middle Ages and Early Modern Period*, Gemeentekrediet van België/Crédit Communal de Belgique, Collection Histoire, no. 96. Brussels, 1996

McCusker, John J. *Rum and the American Revolution: The Rum Trade and the Balance of Payments of the Thirteen Continental Colonies, 1650–1775*. 2 vols. New York, 1989. Ph.D. dissertation, University of Pittsburgh, 1970

McCusker, John J. "Ships Registered at the Port of Philadelphia before 1776: A Computerized Listing." Unpublished computer printout, 1970. Copy on deposit in the Historical Society of Pennsylvania, Philadelphia

McCusker, John J. "Sources of Investment Capital in the Colonial Philadelphia Shipping Industry." *Journal of Economic History*, XXXII (March 1972), 146–157

McCusker, John J. "The Tonnage of Ships Engaged in British Colonial Trade during the Eighteenth Century." *Research in Economic History*, VI (1981), 73–105

McCusker, John J. "The Tonnage of the Continental Ship *Alfred*." *Pennsylvania Magazine of History and Biography*, XC (April 1966), 227–232

McCusker, John J. "Weights and Measures in the Colonial Sugar Trade: The Gallon and the Pound and Their International Equivalents." *William and Mary Quarterly*, 3rd ser., XXX (October 1973), 599–624

McCusker, John J. "The Wine Prise and Medieval Mercantile Shipping." *Speculum: A Journal of Medieval Studies*, XLI (April 1966), 279–296

McCusker, John J., and Cora Gravesteijn. *The Beginnings of Commercial and Financial Journalism: The Commodity Price Currents, Exchange Rate Currents, and Money Currents of Early Modern Europe*. Nederlandsch Economisch-Historisch Archief, ser. III, no. 11. Amsterdam, 1991

McCusker, John J., and Simon Hart. "The Rate of Exchange on Amsterdam in London, 1590–1660." *The Journal of European Economic History*, VII (Winter 1979), 689–705

McCusker, John J., and Russell R. Menard. *The Economy of British America, 1607–1789*. [2nd edn.] Chapel Hill, NC, [1991]

McCusker, John J., and James C. Riley. "The French Economy, 1650–1788: Economic Growth, the Money Supply, and Monetarist Theory – A Summary." *Business and Economic History*, 2nd ser., XI (1982), 102–104

McCusker, John J., and James C. Riley. "Money Supply, Economic Growth, and the Quantity Theory of Money: France, 1650–1788." In [International Economic History Congress. 8th. 1982. Budapest]. *Münzprägung, Geldumlauf und Wechselkurse / Minting, Monetary Circulation and Exchange Rates: Akten des 8th International Economic History Congress, Section C 7, Budapest, 1982*, edited by Eddy van Cauwenberghe and Franz Irsigler, pp. 255–289. Trierer Historische Forschungen, Band 7. Trier, 1984

McDowall, William. *History of the Burgh of Dumfries, with Notices of Nithsdale, Annadale, and the Western Border*. 3rd edn. Dumfries, 1906

McDowall, William. *Memorials of St. Michael's, the Old Parish Churchyard of Dumfries*. Edinburgh, 1876

Mead, H[ilary] P. "Obituary: Captaine de Corvette de Reserve Louis Guilleux." *Mariner's Mirror*, XLVII (May 1961), 160

Medieval Trade in the Mediterranean World. Edited by Robert S. Lopez and Irving W. Raymond. New York, 1955

Melis, Federigo. *Documenti per la storia economica dei secoli XIII–XVI.* Istituto Internazionale di Storia Economica "F. Datini." Pubblicazioni. Serie I: Documenti, no. 1. Florence, 1972

Menand, Catherine [S.] "Juries, Judges, and the Politics of Justice in Pre-Revolutionary Boston." In *The Law in America, 1607–1861,* edited by William Pencak and Wythe W. Holt, Jr, pp. 155–185. [New York, 1989]

A Metric America: A Decision Whose Time Has Come. Washington, DC, 1971

Meuvret, Jean. "Les Français et l'argent." In *La France et les Français,* edited by Michel François, pp. 1398–1420. Paris, 1972

Meuvret, Jean. "L'Histoire des prix des céréales en France dans la seconde moitié du XVIIe siècle." *Mélanges d'Histoire Sociale,* V (1944), 27–44

Meuvret, Jean. "Manuels et traités à l'usage des négociants aux premières époques de l'âge moderne." *Études d'Histoire Moderne et Contemporaine,* V (1953), 5–29

Meuvret, Jean. "Simple mise au point." *Annales: Histoire, Sciences Sociales,* X (January–March 1955), 48–54

Mews, Siegfried. *Gotlands Handel und Verkehr bis zum Auftreten der Hansen (12. Jahrhundert).* Berlin, 1937

Mexico. Archivo General de la Nación. "Inventario del Archivo del Hospital de Jesús." [Compiled by C. Emilio Quintanar.] *Boletín del Archivo General de la Nación,* VII (April–June, July–September, October–December 1936), 273–299, 437–459, 600–618, VII (April–June, July–September 1937), 233–302, 406–471

Middleton, Arthur Pierce. *Tobacco Coast: A Maritime History of Chesapeake Bay in the Colonial Era.* Newport News, Va., 1953

Migne, J[acques] P[aul]. *Patrologiae cursus completus, sive bibliotheca universalis . . . omium SS. patrum, doctorum, scriptorum ecclesiasticorum . . . Series Latina.* 221 vols in 222 pts. Paris, 1844–1864

Millard, A[nnie] M. "The Import Trade of London, 1600–1640." 3 vols. Ph.D. dissertation, University of London, 1956

Milner, Anita Cheek. *Newspaper Indexes: A Location and Subject Guide for Researchers.* 3 vols. Metuchen, NJ, 1977–1982

Minchinton, W[alter] E. "Editor's Introduction." In *The Growth of English Overseas Trade in the Seventeenth and Eighteenth Centuries,* edited by W[alter] E. Minchinton, pp. 1–63. London, 1969

M[isselden], E[dward]. *The Circle of Commerce. Or the Balance of Trade, in Defence of Free Trade . . .* London, 1623

Mitchell, B[rian] R. *British Historical Statistics.* Cambridge, Eng., [1988]

Mitchell, Wesley C. *The Making and Using of Index Numbers.* United States, Department of Labor, Bureau of Labor Statistics, Bulletin no. 656, pt i. Washington, DC, 1938

Mitchison, Rosalind. *Agricultural Sir John: The Life of Sir John Sinclair of Ulbster, 1754–1835.* London, 1962

Mörner, Magnus. *Fuentes para la historia de Ibero-América [conservadas en] Escandinavia.* Translated by Ester Pastor Lopez. Stockholm, 1968

Montagu, John. Fourth Earl of Sandwich. *The Private Papers of John, Earl of Sandwich, First Lord of the Admiralty, 1771–1782.* Edited by G[eorge] R. Barnes and J[ohn] H. Owen. Publications of the Navy Records Society, vols LXIX, LXXI, LXXV, LXXVIII. 4 vols. London, 1932–1938

Monumenta Germaniae historica inde ab anno Christi quinguentesimo usque ad annum millesimum et quinguentesimum. Edited George Henry Pertz *et al.* In progress. Hanover *et al.,* 1826 to date

Mooney, James E. "Loyalist Imprints Printed in America, 1774–1785." *Proceedings of the American Antiquarian Society*, n.s., LXXXIV (1975), 105–128

Moore, Alexander. "Daniel Axtell's Account Book and the Economy of Early South Carolina." *South Carolina Historical Magazine*, XCV (October 1994), 280–301

Moore, Caroline T., and Agatha Aimar Simmons. *Abstracts of the Wills of the State of South Carolina, 1670–1784*. 3 vols. Columbia, SC, 1960–1969

Moore, Jonas. *A New Systeme of the Mathematicks*. 2 vols. London, 1681

Moorsom, G[eorge] "On the New Tonnage-Law, as Established in the Merchant Shipping Act of 1854." *Transactions of the [Royal] Institution of Naval Architects*, I (1860), 128–142

Morcken, Roald. *Langskip, knaar or kogge: Nye synspunkter på sagatidens skipsbygging in Norge og Nordeuropa*. 2nd edn, revised. Bergen, 1983

Moreau, César. *Chronological Records of the British Royal and Commercial Navy, from the Earliest Period (A.D. 827) to the Present Time (1827)*. London, 1827

[Moreau, Jacob Nicolas.] *Doutes modestes sur la "Richesse de l'État," ou Lettre écrite à l'auteur de ce systeme, par un de ses confrères*. [Paris, 1763]

Moreau de Jonnès, Alex[andre]. *Recherches statistiques sur l'esclavage colonial et sur les moyens de le supprimer*. Paris, 1842

Moreau de Saint Méry, M[édéric] L. É. *Description topographique, physique, civile, politique et historique de la partie française de l'isle Saint-Domingue*. Revised edn. Edited by Blanche Maurel and Étienne Taillemite. 3 vols. Paris, 1958

Moreau de Saint-Méry, [Médéric L. É.] *Loix et constitutions des colonies françaises de l'Amérique sous le vent*. 6 vols. Paris, [1784–1790]

Morelli [Timpanaro], Maria Augusta. *Delle prime gazette fiorentine*. Florence, [1963]

Morelli [Timpanaro], Maria Augusta "Gli inizi della stampa periodica a Firenze nella prima metà del XVII secolo." *Critica Storia: Bollettino dell'Associazione degli Storici Europei*, VI (May 1968), 288–323

Morgan, Kenneth [J.] *Bristol and the Atlantic Trade in the Eighteenth Century*. Cambridge, Eng., 1993

Morgan, William James. *Captains to the Northward: The New England Captains in the Continental Navy*. Barre, Mass., 1959

Morgan, William James. "'The Pivot Upon Which Everything Turned': French Naval Superiority That Ensured Victory at Yorktown." *The Iron Worker* [Lynchburg, Va.], XXII (Spring 1958), 1–9

Moriarty, G[eorge] Andrew[s]. "Articles of Agreement, 1747." *The Mariner: The Quarterly Journal of the Ship Model Society of Rhode Island*, VII (January 1933), 10–11

Morineau, Michel. *Incroyables Gazettes et fabuleux métaux: Les retours des trésors américains d'après les gazettes hollandaises (XVIe–XVIIIe siècles)*. London and Paris, 1985

Morineau, Michel. *Jauges et méthodes de jauge anciennes et modernes*. Cahiers des Annales, no. 24. Paris, 1966

Morineau, Michel. "Des métaux précieux américains au XVIIe et au XVIIIe siècle et de leur influence." *Bulletin de la Société d'Histoire Moderne*, LXXVII (1977), 17–27

Morison, Samuel Eliot. "The Commerce of Boston on the Eve of the Revolution." *Proceedings of the American Antiquarian Society*, n.s., XXXII (April 1922), 24–51

Morison, Samuel Eliot. *John Paul Jones: A Sailor's Biography*. Boston, 1959

Morris, Gouverneur. *The Diary and Letters of Gouverneur Morris, Minister of the United States to France . . .* Edited by Anne Cary Morris. 2 vols. New York, 1888

Morris, Robert. *The Papers of Robert Morris, 1781–1784*. Edited by E[dgar] James Ferguson *et al.* In progress. Pittsburgh, 1973 to date

Morrison, Clifford August. "The Earl of Sandwich and British Naval Administration in the War of the American Revolution." Ph.D. dissertation, Ohio State University, 1950

Morrisson, Christian, and Robert Goffin. *Questions financières aux XVIIIe et XIXe siècles*. Travaux et Recherches de la Faculté de Droit et des Sciences Économiques de Paris. Série "Sciences Historiques," no. 2. Paris, 1967

Mortimer, [Thomas]. *Every Man His Own Broker: or, A Guide to Exchange-Alley*. [5th edn.] London, 1762

[Morton, Becky.] *ESTC: An Eighteenth-Century Short Title Catalog*. Research Libraries Group 82–42. Stanford, Calif., 1982

Mowat, Charles Loch. *East Florida as a British Province, 1763–1784*. University of California, Publications in History, vol. XXXII. Berkeley and Los Angeles, Calif., 1943

Mui, Hoh-Cheung, and Lorna H. Mui. "Smuggling and the British Tea Trade before 1784." *American Historical Review*, LXXIV (October 1968), 44–73

Munimenta Gildhallae Londoniensis: Liber Albus, Liber Custumarum, et Liber Horn. Edited by Henry Thomas Riley. [Rolls Series, no. 12.] 3 vols in 4 pts. London, 1859–1862

Munter, Robert. *A Dictionary of the Print Trade in Ireland, 1550–1775*. New York, 1988

Murray, James. *Letters of James Murray, Loyalist*. Edited by Nina Moore Tiffany and Susan I. Lesley. Boston, 1901

Naft, Stephen, and Ralph de Sola. *International Conversion Tables*. Revised and enlarged. Edited by P[hilip] H. Bigg. London, [1965]

Namier, Lewis [B.] *England in the Age of the American Revolution*. 2nd edn. London, 1961

Namier, Lewis [B.], and John Brooke. *The History of Parliament: The House of Commons, 1754–1790*. 3 vols. London, 1964

Nansen, Fridtjof. *In Northern Mists: Arctic Exploration in Early Times*. Translated by Arthur G. Chater. 2 vols. London, 1911

Nardin, J[ean]-C. "Les Archives anciennes de la Grenade." *Revue Française d'Histoire d'Outre-Mer*, XLIV (1962), 117–140

Nardin, Jean-Claude. *La Mise en valeur de l'Isle de Tabago (1763–1783)*. Paris and The Hague, 1969

Nasatir, Abraham P., and Gary Elwyn Monell. *French Consuls in the United States: A Calendar of Their Correspondence in the Archives Nationales*. Washington, DC, 1967

National Inventory of Documentary Sources in Canada. In progress. Alexandria, Va., 1991 to date

National Inventory of Documentary Sources in the United Kingdom and Ireland. In progress. Cambridge, Eng., 1984 to date

National Inventory of Documentary Sources in the United States. In progress. Teaneck, NJ, 1983 to date

Naval Documents of the American Revolution. Edited by William Bell Clark and William J. Morgan. In progress. Washington, DC, 1964 to date

[Naveau, Jean Baptiste.] *Le Financier citoyen*. n.p. [Paris], 1757

[Necker, Jacques.] *Éloge de Jean-Baptiste Colbert, discours qui a remporté le prix de l'Académie Française, en 1773*. Paris, 1773

Necker, [Jacques]. *De l'administration des finances de la France*. 3 vols. [Paris], 1784

Nef, John U. *The Rise of the British Coal Industry*. 2 vols. London, 1932

Nelson, Carolyn. "American Readership of Early British Serials." In *Serials and Their Readers, 1620–1914*, edited by Robin Myers and Michael Harris, pp. 27–44. Winchester, 1993

Nelson, Carolyn, and Matthew Seccombe. *British Newspapers and Periodicals, 1641–1700: A Short-Title Catalogue of Serials Printed in England, Scotland, Ireland, and North America*. New York, 1987

Nelson, George A. "A Contract to Build a Sloop in 1694." *American Neptune*, II (October 1942), 338

Nennius. *Historia Brittonum* . . . In *Chronica minora saec. IV. V. VI. VII.*, edited by Theodor Mommsen, vol. III, pt i, pp. 111–222. Vol. XIII of *Monumenta Germaniae historica* . . ., *auctores antiquissimi*. Berlin, 1898

Netherlands Antilles. Laws and Statutes. *Publikaties en andere wetten alsmede de oudste resoluties betrekking hebbende op Curaçao, Aruba, Bonaire*. Edited by J[acobus] Th. de Smidt, T. van der Lee, and J[acob] A. Schiltkamp. West Indisch Plakaatboek, no. 2. Werken der Stichting tot Uitgaff der Bronnen van het Oud-Vaderlandse Recht, no. 2. 2 vols. Amsterdam, 1978

Netherlands Antilles. Laws and Statutes. *Publikaties en andere wetten betrekking hebbende op St. Maarten, St. Eustatius, Saba, 1648/1681–1816*. Edited by J[acobus] Th. de Smidt and T. van der Lee. West Indisch Plakaatboek, no. 3. Werken der Stichting tot Uitgaff der Bronnen van het Oud-Vaderlandse Recht, no. 4. Amsterdam, 1979

Nettels, Curtis P. *The Emergence of a National Economy, 1775–1815*. Vol. II of *The Economic History of the United States*, edited by Henry David *et al.* New York, [1962]

Nettels, Curtis [P.] "England's Trade with New England and New York, 1685–1720." *Publications of the Colonial Society of Massachusetts*, XXVII (*Transactions*, 1930–1933), 322–350

Nettels, Curtis P. *The Money Supply of the American Colonies before 1720*. University of Wisconsin, Studies in the Social Sciences and History, no. 20. Madison, Wis., 1934

Nevis. Laws and Statutes. *Acts of Assembly Passed in the Island of Nevis, from 1664, to 1739, Inclusive*. London, 1740

The New Cambridge Modern History. 14 vols. Cambridge, Eng., 1957–1979

New York (City). Chamber of Commerce. *Colonial Records of the New York Chamber of Commerce, 1768–1784; with Historical and Biographical Sketches*. Edited by John Austin Stevens, Jr. New York, 1867

New York (City). Mayor's Court. *Select Cases of the Mayor's Court of New York City, 1674–1784*. Edited by Richard B. Morris. American Legal Records, vol. II. Washington, DC, 1935

New York (Colony). Laws and Statutes. *The Colonial Laws of New York from the Year 1664 to the Revolution*. [Edited by Robert C. Cumming.] 5 vols. Albany, NY, 1894

New York (Colony). Laws and Statutes. *Laws and Ordinances of New Netherland, 1638–1674*. Translated and edited by E[dmund] B. O'Callaghan. Albany, NY, 1868

New York (Colony). Laws and Statutes. *Laws of New York, from the Year 1691 to [1762]*. [Edited by William Livingston and William Smith, Jr.] 2 vols. New York, 1752–1762

Nicolaysen, N[icolay]. *Langskibet fra Gokstad ved Sandefjord/The Viking-Ship Discovered at Gokstad in Norway*. [Translated by Thomas Krag.] Oslo, 1882

Norona, Delf. "The Earliest American Postmark." *American Philatelist*, XLI (August 1928), 725–726

North, Douglass C. *The Economic Growth of the United States, 1790–1860*. Englewood Cliffs, NJ, 1961

North, Douglass C. *Growth and Welfare in the American Past: A New Economic History*. [1st edn.] Englewood Cliffs, NJ, 1966

North, Douglass C. "Transaction Costs in History." *Journal of European Economic History*, XIV (September–December, 1985), 557–576

Norton, Mary Beth. *The British-Americans: The Loyalist Exiles in England, 1774–1789*. Boston, 1972

Nuxoll, Elizabeth Miles. *Congress and the Munitions Merchants: The Secret Committee of Trade during the American Revolution, 1775–1777*. New York, 1985. Ph.D. dissertation, City University of New York, 1979

O'Brien, Patrick [K.], and Caglar Keyder. *Economic Growth in Britain and France, 1780–1914: Two Paths to the Twentieth Century*. London, [1978]

O'Rourke, D[ermot] T. "John Houghton (1645–1705): Journalist, Apothecary and F.R.S." *Pharmaceutical Historian: Newsletter of the British Society for the History of Pharmacy*, IX (April 1979), 2–3

O'Shaughnessy, Andrew J. "The Politics of the Leeward Islands, 1763–1783." Ph.D. dissertation, University of Oxford, 1987

Observations des négocians de Bordeaux, sur l'arrest du Conseil, du 30 Août 1784, qui a été connu à Bordeaux le 20 Novembre. Paris, 1784

Ogilby, John. *America: Being the Latest and Most Accurate Description of the New World*. London, 1671

The Old Dominion: Essays for Thomas Perkins Abernethy. Edited by Darrett B. Rutman. Charlottesville, Va., 1964

Oldmixon, John. *The British Empire in America, Containing the History . . . of All the British Colonies on the Continent and Islands of America*. 2nd edn. 2 vols. London, 1741

Olsen, Olaf. "Die Kaufschiffe der Wikingerzeit in Lichte des Schiffsfundes bei Skuldelev im Roskilde Fjord." In *Die Zeit der Stadtgründung im Ostseeraum*, [edited by Mårten Stenberger], pp. 20–34. Acta Visbygensia I: Visby-Symposiet för Historiska Vetenskapen, 1963. Visby, 1965

Olsen, Olaf, and Ole Crumlin-Pedersen. "The Skuldelev Ships: A Preliminary Report on Underwater Excavations in Roskilde Fjord, Zealand." *Acta Archeologia* [Copenhagen], XXIX (1958), 161–175

Olsen, Olaf, and Ole Crumlin-Pedersen. "The Skuldelev Ships (II): A Report of the Final Underwater Excavations in 1959 and the Salvaging Operation in 1962." *Acta Archeologia* [Copenhagen], XXXVIII (1967), 73–174

Olsen, Olaf, and Ole Crumlin-Pedersen. *Vikingeskibene i Roskilde Fjord: Årets Fund*. [Copenhagen, 1963]

Olsen, Olaf, and Ole Crumlin-Pedersen. "The Viking Ships in Roskilde Fjord." *Mariner's Mirror*, XLIX (November 1963), 300–302

Oppenheim, M[ichael]. *A History of the Administration of the Royal Navy, and of Merchant Shipping in Relation to the Navy from 1509 to 1660*. London and New York, 1896

Oppenheim, Samuel. "Will of Nathan Simson, a Jewish Merchant of New York before 1722, and Genealogical Note Concerning Him and Joseph Simson." *Publications of the American Jewish Historical Society*, XXV (1917), 87–91

Orden, José Tudela de la. *Los manuscritos de América en las Bibliotecas de España*. Madrid, 1954

O[rozco] y B[erra], M[anuel]. "Medidas y pesos en la Republica Mexicana." In *Diccionario Universal de Historia y de Geografía . . . sobre las Americas en General y Especialmente sobre la Republica Mexicana*, V, 206–214. Mexico, 1854

Osebergfundet. Edited by A[nton] W. Brøgger *et al.* 5 vols. Oslo, 1917–1928

Ostlund, H. G[ote]. "Stockholm Natural Radiocarbon Measurements I." *Science*, CXXVI (13 September 1957), 493–497

Ouellet, Fernand. Review of *Structure and Change: An Economic History of Quebec*, by Robert Armstrong. *Business History Review*, LXIX (Winter 1985), 706–708

Overzichten van de archieven en verzamelingen in de openbare archiefbewaarplaatsen in Nederland. Edited by L. M. Th. L Hustinx *et al.* 14 vols. Alphen aan den Rijn, 1979–1992

The Oxford English Dictionary: Being a Corrected Re-Issue . . . of A New English

Dictionary on Historical Principles. Edited by James A[ugustus] H[enry] Murray *et al*. 10 vols in 13 pts. Oxford, 1933

Oxford University. Bodleian Library. Rhodes House Library. *Manuscript Collections (Africana and non-Africana) in Rhodes House Library, Oxford: Supplementary Accessions to the End of 1977, and Cumulative Index*. By Wendy S. Byrne. Oxford, 1978

Oxford University. Bodleian Library. Rhodes House Library. *Manuscript Collections (Excluding Africana) in Rhodes House Library, Oxford*. By Louis B. Frewer. Oxford, 1970

Oxholm, Peter Lotharius. *De Danske Vestindiske Øers: Tilstand Henseende til Population, Cultur og Finance-Forfatning*. Copenhagen, 1797

Paige, John. *The Letters of John Paige, London Merchant, 1648–1658*. Edited by George F. Steckley. London Record Society Publications, vol. XXI. London, 1984

Palatsky, Eugene H. "Danish Viking Ships." *Expedition: The Bulletin of the University Museum of the University of Pennsylvania*, IV (Winter 1962), 40–43

Palmer, Gregory. *A Bibliography of Loyalist Source Material in the United States, Canada, and Great Britain*. Westport, Conn., 1982

Palmer, S[arah] R. "Investors in London Shipping, 1820–50." *Maritime History*, II (April 1972), 46–67

Palmer, Stanley H. *Economic Arithmetic: A Guide to the Statistical Sources of English Commerce, Industry, and Finance, 1700–1850*. New York, 1977

Pampaloni, Guido. *Inventario sommario dell'Archivio di Stato di Prato*. Florence, 1958

Pares, Richard. *Merchants and Planters*. Supplement no. 4 to *The Economic History Review*. Cambridge, Eng., 1960

Pares, Richard. *War and Trade in the West Indies, 1739–1763*. London, 1936

Pares, Richard. *Yankees and Creoles: The Trade between North America and the West Indies before the American Revolution*. London, 1956

The Paris Psalter and the Meters of Boethius, edited by George Philip Krapp. Vol. V of *The Anglo-Saxon Poetic Records: A Collective Edition*, edited by George Philip Krapp and Elliott Van Kirk Dobbie. New York, 1932

Paris. Bibliothèque Nationale. Département des Imprimés. *Catalogue général des livres imprimés de la Bibliothèque Nationale: Auteurs [à 1959]*. 231 vols in 232 pts. Paris, 1897–1981

Paris. Bibliothèque Nationale. Département des Manuscrits. *Catalogue général des manuscrits français*. In progress. Paris, 1886 to date

Parker, David W. *Guide to the Materials for United States History in Canadian Archives*. Carnegie Institution of Washington, Publication no. 172. Washington, DC, 1913

Parkinson, C[yril] Northcote. "The East India Trade." In *The Trade Winds: A Study of British Overseas Trade during the French Wars, 1793–1815*, edited by C[yril] Northcote Parkinson, pp. 141–156. London, [1948]

Parry, J[ohn] H. "Transport and Trade Routes [1300–1700]." In *The Economy of Expanding Europe in the Sixteenth and Seventeenth Centuries*, edited by E[dwin] E. Rich and C[harles] H. Wilson, pp. 155–219. Vol. IV of *The Cambridge Economic History of Europe*. Cambridge, Eng., 1967

Parry J[ohn] H., P[hillip] M. Sherlock, and A[nthony] P. Maingot. *A Short History of the West Indies*. 4th edn. London, 1987

Parsons, Wayne. *The Power of the Financial Press: Journalism and Economic Opinion in Britain and America*. Aldershot, Hampshire, 1989

Pásztor, Lajos. *Guida delle fonti per la storia dell'America Latina negli archivi della Santa Sede e negli archivi ecclesiastici d'Italia*. Collectanea Archivi Vaticani, no. 2. Vatican City, 1970

Patterson, A[lfred] Temple. *The Other Armada: The Franco-Spanish Attempt to Invade Britain in 1779*. Manchester, [1960]

[Paul, Robert.] *The Business of the Comptroller-General of the Accounts of His Majesty's Customs.* London, 1723

Paullin, Charles O., and Frederic L. Paxson. *Guide to the Materials in London Archives for the History of the United States since 1783.* Carnegie Institution of Washington, Publication no. 90B. Washington, DC, 1914

Pedley, Avril J. M. *The Manuscript Collections of the Maryland Historical Society.* Baltimore, 1968

Pennsylvania. Laws and Statutes. *Statutes at Large of Pennsylvania from 1682 to 1801,* edited by James T. Mitchell and Henry Flanders. 18 vols. Harrisburg, Pa., 1896–1915

Perez, Luis Marino. *Guide to the Materials for American History in Cuban Archives.* Carnegie Institution of Washington, Publication no. 83. Washington, DC, 1907

Peri, Gio[vanni] Domenico. *Il Negotiante.* [3rd (?) edn.] 4 vols in 1 pt. Venice, 1682

Perini, David. Aurelius. *Bibliographia Augustiniana cum Notis Biographicis: Scriptores Itali.* 4 vols. Florence, [1929–1938]

Perkins, Edward J. "Foreign Interest Rates in American Financial Markets: A Revised Series of Dollar–Sterling Exchange Rates, 1835–1900." *Journal of Economic History,* XXXVIII (June 1978), 392–417

Perrat, Charles. "Barthélemy Buyer et les débuts de l'imprimerie à Lyon." *Humanisme et Renaissance,* II (1935), 103–121, 349–387

Peterkin, Joshua. *A Treatise on Planting, from the Origin of the Semen to Ebulliotion with a Correct Mode of Distillation . . .* 2nd edn, revised. Basseterre, St Christopher, 1790

Peuchet, J[acques]. *Dictionnaire universel de la géographie commerçante . . .* 5 vols. Paris, VII–VIII [1799–1800]

Phelps Brown, E[rnest] H., and Sheila V. Hopkins. *A Perspective of Wages and Prices.* London, 1981

Phelps Brown, E[rnest] H., and Sheila V. Hopkins. "Seven Centuries of the Prices of Consumables, compared with Builders' Wage-Rates." *Economica,* n.s., XXIII (November 1956), 296–314

Phipps, Constantine John. *A Voyage Towards the North Pole Undertaken by His Majesty's Command, 1773.* London, 1774

Pieterse, Wilhelmina C. *Inventory of the Archives of the Holland Land Company Including the Related Amsterdam Companies and Negotiations Dealing with the Purchase of Land and State Funds in the United States of America, 1789–1869.* Translated by Sytha Hart. Amsterdam, 1976

Pirenne, H[enri]. "Un Grand Commerce d'exportation au Moyen Âge: Le vins de France." *Annales d'Histoire Économique et Sociale,* V (May 1933), 225–243

Pitkin, Timothy. *A Statistical View of the Commerce of the United States of America.* 2nd edn. New Haven, Conn., 1835

Pitman, Frank Wesley. *The Development of the British West Indies, 1700–1763.* Yale Historical Publications, Studies, 4. New Haven, Conn., 1917

Plomer, Henry R. *A Dictionary of the Booksellers and Printers Who Were at Work in England, Scotland and Ireland from 1641 to 1667.* London, 1968

Poelman, H[uibert] A. *Geschiedenis van den Handel van Noord-Nederland gedurende het Merowinginsche en Karolingische Tijdperk.* The Hague, 1908

Pollard, A[lfred] W., and G[ilbert] R. Redgrave. *A Short-Title Catalogue of Books Printed in England, Scotland, & Ireland and of English Books Printed Abroad, 1475–1640.* 2nd edn, revised and enlarged. Edited by W[illiam] A. Jackson, F[rederic] S. Ferguson, and Katharine F. Pantzer. 3 vols. London, 1976–1991

Pope, D[avid] J. "Shipping and Trade in the Port of Liverpool, 1783–1793." 2 vols. Ph.D. dissertation, University of Liverpool, 1970

Popkin, Jeremy D. *News and Politics in the Age of Revolution: Jean Luzac's "Gazette de Leyde."* Ithaca, NY, [1989]

The Port and Trade of Early Elizabethan London: Documents. Edited by Brian Dietz. London Record Society Publications, vol. VIII. London, 1972

Posthumus, N[icolaas] W. *Inquiry into the History of Prices in Holland.* 2 vols. Leiden, 1946–1964

[Pottier de la Hestroye, Jean.] *Réflexions sur la traité de la dîme royale de Mr. le Mareschal de Vauban.* 2 vols in 1 pt, n.p. [Paris?], 1716

Poyser, E[lizabeth] R. "Anglo-Italian Trade from the Reign of Elizabeth to the French Revolution with Special Reference to the Port of Leghorn." M.Litt. thesis, University of Cambridge, 1951

Pratt, Fletcher. *The Navy: A History.* Garden City, NY, 1938

Los precios de alimentos y manufacturas novohispanos. Edited by Virginia García Acosta. [Mexico City, 1995]

Prestwich, Menna. *Cranfield: Politics and Profits under the Early Stuarts – The Career of Lionel Cranfield, Earl of Middlesex.* Oxford, 1966

Prevost, W[illiam] A. J. "Letters from Dumfries during the Jacobite Rebellion in 1745." Dumfriesshire and Galloway Natural History and Antiquarian Society, *Transactions and Journal of Proceedings,* 3rd ser., XL (1961–1962), 171–183

Price, Jacob M. "Colonial Trade and British Economic Development, 1660–1775." *Lex et Scientia: The International Journal of Law and Science,* XIV (July–September 1978), 106–126

Price, Jacob M. "New Time Series for Scotland's and Britain's Trade with the Thirteen Colonies and States, 1740 to 1791." *William and Mary Quarterly,* 3rd ser., XXXII (April 1975), 307–325

Price, Jacob M. "A Note on the Value of Colonial Exports of Shipping." *Journal of Economic History,* XXXVI (September 1976), 704–724

Price, J[acob] M. "Notes on Some London Price-Currents, 1667–1715." *Economic History Review,* 2nd ser., VII (December 1954), 240–250

Price, Jacob M. Review of *Trade and Empire: The British Customs Service in Colonial America, 1660–1775,* by Thomas C. Barrow. *Journal of Economic History,* XXVII (September 1967), 399–400

Price, Jacob M., and Paul G. E. Clemens. "A Revolution of Scale in Overseas Trade: British Firms in the Chesapeake Trade, 1675–1775." *Journal of Economic History,* XLVII (March 1987), 1–43

Priestly, Margaret. "Anglo-French Trade and the 'Unfavourable Balance' Controversy, 1660–1685." *Economic History Review,* 2nd ser., IV (no. 1, 1951), 36–52

Pringle, Robert. *The Letterbook of Robert Pringle, 1737–1745.* Edited by Walter B. Edgar. 2 vols. Columbia, SC, 1972

Proceedings of the Battle Conference 1978. Edited by R. Allen Brown. Ipswich, 1979

Prou, [Jean] Maurice. *Les Monnaies carolingiennes.* Paris, 1896

[Quélus, Christophe (?) de.] *Histoire naturelle du cacao et du sucre.* [Corrected and edited by Nicolas Mahudel.] Paris, 1719

Ragatz, Lowell Joseph. *The Fall of the Planter Class in the British Caribbean, 1763–1833: A Study in Social and Economic History.* New York, 1928

Raimo, John W. *A Guide to Manuscripts Relating to America in Great Britain and Ireland.* Westport, Conn., 1979

Ralph, Elizabeth. *Guide to the Archives of the Society of Merchant Venturers of Bristol.* [Bristol, 1988]

Ralph, Elizabeth. *Guide to the Bristol Archives Office.* Bristol, 1971

Ramage, Craufurd Tait. *Drumlanrig Castle and the Douglases: with the Early History and Ancient Remains of Durisdeer, Closeburn, and Morton.* Dumfries, 1876

Rankin, Hugh F. "The Naval Flag of the American Revolution." *William and Mary Quarterly,* 3rd ser., XI (July 1954), 339–353

Recueil des historiens des Croisades. 16 vols in 18 pts. Paris, 1841–1906

Reducción completa y recíproca de las monedas, pesos y medidas de Castilla con las de Cataluña, Aragón, Valencia, Mallorca, Navarra y otras provincias: Con una adición de valor de varias monedas estrangeras. Barcelona, 1823

Reesse, J[an] J. *De Suikerhandel van Amsterdam van het begin der 17de eeuw tot 1894.* 2 vols. Haarlem, 1908–1911

Reid, R[obert] C. "The Baronies of Enoch and Durisdeer." Dumfriesshire and Galloway Natural History and Antiquarian Society, *Transactions and Journal of Proceedings,* 3rd ser., VIII (1923), 142–183

Reinhard, Marcel R., André Armengaud, and Jacques Dupâquier. *Histoire générale de la population mondiale.* 3rd edn. Paris, [1968]

Remarks upon the Evidence given by Thomas Irving, Esq., Inspector General of the Exports and Imports to Great Britain before the Select Committee appointed to Take the Examination of Witnesses on the Slave Trade. London, 1791

Report of the Caribbean Archives Conference Held at the University of the West Indies, Mona, Jamaica, September 20–27, 1965. n.p. [Kingston, Jamaica (?)], 1965

Ressource actuelle pour les besoins de l'état, ou supplément à la brochure intitulée "Richesse de l'État." n.p. [Paris, 1763]

Ribeiro, Jorge Martins. "Alguns aspectos do comércio da Madeira com a América do Norte na segunda metade so século XVIII." In [Colóquio Internacional de História da Madeira. 3rd. 1993. Funchal]. *Actas. III Colóquio Internacional de História da Madeira,* pp. 389–401. Funchal, 1993

Ricard, Jean Pierre. *Le Négoce d'Amsterdam . . .* Amsterdam, 1722

Ricard, Samuel. *Traité général du commerce . . .* [1st edn.] Amsterdam, 1700

Ricard, Samuel. *Traité général du commerce . . .* 4th edn, revised. Amsterdam, 1721

Ricard, Samuel. *Traité général du commerce . . .* Revised edn. [Edited by Tomás Antonio de Marien y Arrospide.] 2 vols. Amsterdam, 1781

Rich, Wesley Everett. *The History of the United States Post Office to the Year 1829.* Harvard Economic Studies, vol. XXVII. Cambridge, Mass., 1924

Richesse de l'État, à laquelle on a ajouté les pièces qui ont paru pour & contre. [Compiled by Roussel de La Tour.] Amsterdam, 1764

Riley, James C. *The Seven Years War and the Old Regime in France: The Economic and Financial Toll.* Princeton, NJ, 1986

Riley, James C., and John J. McCusker. "Money Supply, Economic Growth, and the Quantity Theory of Money: France, 1650–1788." *Explorations in Economic History,* XX (July 1983), 274–293

Rimbert. *Vita Anskari auctore Rimberto. Scriptores rerum Germanicarum in usum scholarum ex Monumentis Germaniae historicis recusi,* [vol. 55]. Edited by G[eorg] Waitz. Hanover, 1884

Rinchon, Dieudonné. *Pierre-Ignace-Liévin Van Alstein: Captaine négrier, Gand 1733-Nantes 1793.* Mémoires de l'Institut français d'Afrique Noire, no. 71. Dakar, Senegal, 1964

Ritcheson, Charles R. *Aftermath of Revolution: British Policy toward the United States, 1783–1787.* Dallas, 1969

Robelo, Cecilio. A. *Diccionario de pesas y medidas Mexicanas, antiguas y modernas . . .* Cuernavaca, Mexico, 1908

Roberts, J. E. "Distillation of Water at Sea." *Mariner's Mirror,* LXIV (November 1978), 299–300

Roberts, Lewes. *The Merchants Mappe of Commerce . . .* [1st edn.] [London], 1638

Roberts, Lewes. *The Merchants Map of Commerce . . .* 3rd edn, revised. London, 1677

Robertson, Mary. *Guide to American Historical Manuscripts in the Huntington Library.* San Marino, Calif., 1979

[Robertson, Robert.] *A Detection of the State and Situation of the Present Sugar Planters of Barbadoes and the Leeward Islands.* London, 1732

[Robertson, Robert.] *A Supplement to the Detection . . .* London, 1732

Robinson, Howard. *Carrying British Mail Overseas.* London, [1964]

Rodger, N[icholas] A. M. *The Insatiable Earl: A Life of John Montagu, Fourth Earl of Sandwich, 1718–1792.* [London, 1993]

Rodger, N[icholas] A. M. *The Wooden World: An Anatomy of the Georgian Navy.* London, 1986

Roessingh, M[arius] P. H. *Guide to the Sources in the Netherlands for the History of Latin America.* The Hague, 1968

Rogers, Jr., George C. *The History of Georgetown County, South Carolina.* Columbia, SC, [1970]

Rohwer, Barbara [C.] *Der friesische Handel im frühen Mittelalter.* Leipzig, 1937

Rolt, [Richard]. *A New Dictionary of Trade and Commerce.* London, 1756

Romano, Ruggiero. "Documenti e prime considerazioni intorno alla 'Balance du commerce' della Francia dal 1716 al 1780." In *Studi in onore di Armando Sapori*, II, 1265–1300. Milan, [1957]

Rosa, Luigi de. "Navi, merci, nazionalità, itinerari in un porto dell'età preindustriale: Il porto di Napoli nel 1760." In *Saggi e Richerche sul Settecento*, pp. 332–370. Naples, 1968

Rostow, W[alt] W. *The Process of Economic Growth.* 2nd edn. New York, 1959

Rostow, W[alt] W. *The Stages of Economic Growth: A Non-Communist Manifesto.* 3rd edn. Cambridge, Eng., 1990

Rota, Pietro. *Storia delle Banche.* Milan, 1874

Roth, Cecil. *The Great Synagogue, London, 1690–1940.* London, [1950]

Roth, Cecil. "The Portsmouth Community and Its Historical Background." *Transactions of the Jewish Historical Society of England*, XIII (1932–1935), 157–187

Rotnem, V. W. "New York Straight Line Postmarks." *Collectors Club Philatelist*, XIII (April 1934), 84–86

Roubert, Jacqueline. "La Situation de l'imprimerie lyonnaise à la fin du XVIIe siècle." In *Cinq études lyonnaises*, edited by H[enri]-J[ean] Martin, pp. 77–111. Histoire et Civilisation du Livre, no. 1. Geneva and Paris, 1966

[Roussel de La Tour.] *La Richesse de l'État.* n.p. [Paris, 1763]

Rowe, Helen. *A Guide to the Records of Bermuda.* Hamilton, Bermuda, 1980

Rowe, John. *Letters and Diary of John Rowe, Boston Merchant, 1759–1762, 1764–1779.* Edited by Anne Rowe Cunningham. Boston, 1903

The Royal Kalendar; or, Complete and Correct Annual Register for England, Scotland, Ireland, and America for the Year 1800. London, [1800]

The Royal Kalendar; or, Complete and Correct Annual Register for England, Scotland, Ireland, and America for the Year 1801. London, [1801]

Rubens, Alfred. "Early Anglo-Jewish Artists." *Transactions of the Jewish Historical Society of England*, XIV (1935–1939), 102–103

Ruiters, Dierick. *Toortse der Zee-vaert* (1632). Edited by S[amuel] P. l'Honoré Naber. Werken Uitgegeven door de Linschoten-Vereeniging, VI. The Hague, 1913

De Rijksarchieven in Nederland: Overziect van de inhoud van de rijksarchiefbewaarplaatsen. Edited by L[ouis] P. L. Pirenne. 2 vols. The Hague, 1973

Rymer, Thomas. *Fædera, conventiones, literæ, et cujuscumque generis acta publica, inter reges Anglicæ.* 3rd edn. Edited by Jean LeClerc and Paul de Rapin. 10 vols. The Hague, 1737–1745

Saggi e Richerche sul Settecento. Naples, 1968

Salisbury, William. "Early Tonnage Measurement in England." *Mariner's Mirror,* LII (February, May, November 1966), 41–51, 173–180, 329–340, LIII (August 1967), 251–264, and LIV (February 1968), 69–76

Salomon, Ludwig. *Allgemeine Geschichte des Zeitungswesens.* Leipzig, 1907

Salvucci, Richard J. *Textiles and Capitalism in Mexico: An Economic History of the Obrajes, 1539–1840.* [Princeton, NJ, 1987]

Sanford, Peleg. *The Letter Book of Peleg Sanford of Newport, Merchant (later Governour of Rhode Island), 1666–1668.* Edited by Howard M. Chapin. Providence, RI, 1928

Satek, Pamela [B.] "William Lux of Baltimore, 18th-Century Merchant." M.A. thesis, University of Maryland, 1974

Savours, Ann. "The Parliamentary Award of 1772 to Dr. Charles Irving for Salt Water Distillation at Sea." *Mariner's Mirror,* LXXVI (November 1990), 362–365

Sawyer, P[eter] H. *The Age of the Vikings.* London, [1962]

Scaccia, Sigismund. *Tractatus de commerciis, et cambio.* Rome, 1619

Scammell, G[eoffrey] V. "English Merchant Shipping at the End of the Middle Ages: Some East Coast Evidence." *Economic History Review,* 2nd ser., XIII (no. 3, 1961), 327–341

Schäfer, [Johann Heinrich] Dietrich. *Die Hansestädte und König Waldemar [IV] von Dänemark: Hansische Geschichte bis 1376.* Jena, 1879

Schaube, Adolf. "Ein italienischer Coursbericht von der Messe von Troyes aus dem 13. Jahrhundert." *Zeitschrift für Social- und Wirtschaftsgeschichte,* V (1897), 248–308

Schefferus, Johannes Guilielmus. "De varietate navium dissertatio." In *Thesaurus Graecarum antiquitatum,* edited by Jacobus Gronovius, XI, 769–788. Leiden, 1701

Scheuchzer, Johann J. *Kupfer-Bible, in welcher de Physica Sacra, oder Beheiligte Natur-wissenschaft derer in Heil. Schrifft Vorkommenden Natürlichen Sachen . . .* 4 vols in 6 pts. Augsburg and Ulm, 1731–1735

Schlesinger, Arthur M. "Propaganda and the Boston Newspaper Press, 1767–1770." *Publications of the Colonial Society of Massachusetts,* XXXII (*Transactions,* 1933–1937), 396–416

Schlesinger, Arthur Meier. *The Colonial Merchants and the American Revolution, 1763–1776.* Columbia University Studies in History, Economics and Public Law, vol. LXXVIII, no. 182. New York, 1918

[Schlözer, August Ludwig von.] "Berechnung des Französischen Nationals Capitals," *Stats-Anzeigen,* IV (1784), 331–339

[Schmid, Gerhard.] *Übersicht über Quellen zur Geschichte Lateinamerikas in Archiven der Deutschen Demokratischen Republik.* Potsdam, 1971

Schneider, Jürgen, *et al. Währungen der Welt.* 11 vols in 14 pts. Stuttgart, 1991–1997

Schnepper, Heinrich. *Die Namen der Schiffe und Schiffsteile in Altenglischen: Eine kulturgeschichtlich-etymologische Untersuchung.* Kiel, 1908

Schöpf, Johann David. *Reise durch Einige der mittlern und südlichen Vereinigten Nordamerikanischen Staten, nach Ost-Florida und den Bahama Inslem Unternommen in den Jahren 1783 und 1784.* 2 vols. Erlangen, 1788

Schöpf, Johann David. *Travels in the Confederation.* Translated by Alfred J. Morrison. 2 vols. Philadelphia, 1911

Schumacher, Max George. *The Northern Farmer and His Markets during the Late Colonial Period.* New York, 1975. Ph.D. dissertation, University of California, Berkeley, 1948

Schumpeter, [Romaine] Elizabeth Boody. *English Overseas Trade Statistics 1697–1808.* Oxford, 1960

Schumpeter, [Romaine] Elizabeth Boody. "English Prices and Public Finance, 1660–1822." *Review of Economic Statistics,* XX (February 1938), 21–37

[Schumpeter], [Romaine] E[lizabeth] B[oody] Firuski. "Trade Statistics and Cycles in England, 1697–1825." Ph.D. dissertation, Radcliffe College, Harvard University, 1934

Schuyler, Robert Livingston. *The Fall of the Old Colonial System: A Study in British Free Trade, 1770–1870.* London, 1945

Schwartz, Anna J. "Secular Price Change in Historical Perspective." *Journal of Money, Credit, and Banking,* V (February 1973), 243–269

The Scots Peerage. Edited by James Balfour Paul. 9 vols. Edinburgh, 1904–1914

Sedgwick, Romney. *The History of Parliament: The House of Commons, 1715–1754.* 2 vols. London, 1970

Sédillot, René. *Le Franc: Histoire d'une monnaie des origines à nos jours.* Paris, 1953

Selden, Richard T. "Monetary Velocity in the United States." In *Studies in the Quantity Theory of Money,* edited by Milton Friedman, pp. 179–257. Chicago, [1956]

Serials and Their Readers, 1620–1914. Edited by Robin Myers and Michael Harris. Winchester, 1993

The Siege and Capture of Havana, 1762. Edited by David Syrett. Publications of the Navy Records Society, vol. CXIV. London, 1970

Seybert, Adam. *Statistical Annals . . . of the United States of America.* Philadelphia, 1818

Shaw, Ralph R., and Richard H. Shoemaker. *American Bibliography. A Preliminary Checklist for 1801–1819.* 22 vols. New York, 1958–1966

[Sheffield, John Baker Holroyd, Lord.] *Observations on the Commerce of the American States with Europe and the West Indies.* [1st edn.] London, 1783

Sheffield, John [Baker Holroyd], Lord. *Observations on the Commerce of the American States.* 6th edn, enlarged. London, 1784

Shepherd, James Floyd, Jr. "A Balance of Payments for the Thirteen Colonies, 1768–1772." Ph.D. dissertation, University of Washington, 1966

Shepherd, James F. "A Balance of Payments for the Thirteen Colonies, 1768–1772: A Summary." *Journal of Economic History,* XXV (December 1965), 691–695

Shepherd, James F., and Gary M. Walton. "Economic Change after the American Revolution: Pre- and Post-War Comparisons of Maritime Shipping and Trade." *Explorations in Economic History* XIII (October 1976), 397–422

Shepherd, James F., and Gary M. Walton. "Estimates of 'Invisible' Earnings in the Balance of Payments of the British North American Colonies, 1768–1772." *Journal of Economic History,* XXIV (June 1969), 230–263

Shepherd, James F., and Gary M. Walton. *Shipping Maritime Trade, and the Economic Development of Colonial America.* Cambridge, Eng., 1972

Shepherd, William R. *Guide to the Materials for the History of the United States in Spanish Archives.* Carnegie Institution of Washington, Publication no. 91. Washington, DC, 1907

Sherburne, John Henry. *The Life and Character of the Chevalier John Paul Jones.* Washington, DC, 1825

Sheridan, Richard B. "The Crisis of Slave Subsistence in the British West Indies during and after the American Revolution." *William and Mary Quarterly,* 3rd ser., XXXIII (October 1976), 615–641

Sheridan, Richard [B.] *The Development of the Plantations to 1750; An Era of West Indian Prosperity, 1750–1775.* Chapters in Caribbean History, pt i. [St. Lawrence, Barbados, 1970]

Sheridan, Richard B. "Eric Williams and Capitalism and Slavery: A Biographical and Historiographical Essay." In *British Capitalism and Caribbean Slavery: The Legacy of Eric Williams,* edited by Barbara L. Solow and Stanley L. Engerman, pp. 317–345. Cambridge, Eng., 1987

Sheridan, Richard B. "The Molasses Act and the Market Strategy of the British Planters." *Journal of Economic History,* XVII (March 1957), 62–83

Sheridan, R[ichard] B. "Samuel Martin, Innovating Sugar Planter of Antigua, 1750–1776." *Agricultural History,* XXXIV (July 1960), 126–139

Sheridan, Richard B. "The Slave Trade to Jamaica, 1702–1808." In *Trade, Government and Society in Caribbean History, 1700–1920: Essays Presented to Douglas Hall*, edited by B[arry] W. Higman, pp. 1–16. Kingston, Jamaica, 1983

Sheridan, Richard B. *Sugar and Slavery: An Economic History of the British West Indies, 1623–1775*. St. Lawrence, Barbados, 1974

Sheridan, R[ichard] B. "The Wealth of Jamaica in the Eighteenth Century." *Economic History Review*, 2nd ser. XVIII (August 1965), 292–311

Shetelig, Haakon. *Tuneskibet: [Skibsfundet paa nedre Haugen paa Rolvsøy, 1867]*. Norske Oldfund, vol. II. Oslo, 1917

"Ship Registers in the South Carolina Archives, 1734–1780." Edited by R. Nicholas Olsberg. *South Carolina Historical Magazine*, LXXIV (October 1973), 189–299

Shoemaker, Richard H., *et al. Checklist of American Imprints [1820–1875]*. In progress. New York and Metuchen, NJ, 1964 to date

Shuldham, Molyneux. *The Despatches of Molyneux Shuldham, Vice-Admiral of the Blue and Commander-in-Chief of His Britannic Majesty's Ships in North America, January–July 1776*. Edited by Robert Wilden Neeser. Publications of the Naval History Society, vol. III. New York, 1913

Shy, Arlene Phillips, and Barbara A. Mitchell. *Guide to the Manuscript Collections of the William L. Clements Library*. Revised edn. Boston, 1978

Siebert, Frederick Seaton. *Freedom of the Press in England, 1746–1766: The Rise and Decline of Government Controls*. Urbana, Ill., 1952

[Silliman, Benjamin, Sr.] *Manual on the Cultivation of the Sugar Cane, and the Fabrication and Refinement of Sugar*. Washington, DC, 1833

Simiand, François. *Recherches anciennes et nouvelles sur le mouvement général des prix du XVIe au XIXe siècle*. Paris, 1932

Sinclair, John. *The Correspondence of the Right Honourable Sir John Sinclair, Bart., with Reminiscences of the Most Distinguished Characters Who Have Appeared in Great Britain, and in Foreign Countries, during the Last Fifty Years*. [Edited by John Sinclair.] 2 vols. London, 1831

Sinclair, John. *The History of the Public Revenue of the British Empire*. [1st edn.] 3 vols. London, 1785–1790

Sinclair, John. *The Statistical Account of Scotland. Drawn Up from the Communications of the Ministers of the Different Parishes*. 21 vols. Edinburgh, 1791–1799

Sjøvold, Thorlief. *Vikingeskipne: En kort orientering on Tuneskipet, Gokstadskipet og Osebergskipet*. [Oslo, 1952]

Skinner, V[ernon] L., Jr. *Abstracts of the Inventories of the Prerogative Court [of Maryland, 1718–1777]*. 17 vols. [Westminster, Maryland], 1988–1991

Skorsetz, Ulrike, and Janine Micunek. *Guide to Inventories and Finding Aids at the German Historical Institute, Washington, D.C.* Reference Guides of the German Historical Institute, Washington DC, no. 5. Washington, DC, 1995

Skov, Sigvard. "Et middelaldert skibsfund fra Eltang Vig." *Kuml: Årbog for Jysk Arkaeologisk Selskab*, [II] (1952), 65–83

Slicher van Bath, B[ernard] H. "The Economic and Social Conditions in the Frisian Districts from 900 to 1500." *Afdeling Agrarische Geschiedenis Bijdragen*, XIII (1965), 97–133

Sluiter, Engel. "The Dutch Archives and American Historical Research." *Pacific Historical Review*, VI (March 1937), 21–35.

Smelser, Marshall, and William I. Davisson "The Longevity of Colonial Ships." *American Neptune*, XXXIII (January 1973), 16–19

Smith, Adam. *An Inquiry into the Nature and Causes of the Wealth of Nations* (1776). Edited by R[oy] H. Campbell, A[ndrew] S. Skinner, and W[illiam] B. Todd. 2 vols. Oxford, 1976

Smith, Anthony *The Newspaper: An International History*. London, 1979

Smith, Billy G. *The "Lower Sort": Philadelphia's Laboring People, 1750–1800*. Ithaca, NY, [1990]

Smith, Charles R. *Marines in the Revolution: A History of the Continental Marines in the American Revolution, 1775–1783*. Washington, DC, 1975

Smith, Daniel Scott. "A Note on the Longevity of Colonial Ships." *American Neptune*, XXXIV (January 1974), 68–69

Smith, George. *A Compleat Body of Distilling . . .* London, 1725

Smith, Paul H. Review of *Documents of the American Revolution, 1770–1783, Colonial Office Series*, edited by K[enneth] G. Davies. *American Historical Review*, LXXXVI (December 1981), 1146–1147

Smith, S[imon] D. *A Note on the Current and Constant Value of Eighteenth-Century English Exports*. University of York, Discussion Papers in Economics, no. 93/7. York, [1993]

Smith, William. "The Colonial Post-Office." *American Historical Review*, XXI (January 1916), 258–275

Smith, William. *The History of the Post Office in British North America, 1639–1870*. Cambridge, Eng., 1920

Smyth, J[ohn] F. D. *A Tour in the United States: Containing an Account of the Present Situation of that Country . . .* 2 vols. London, 1784

Snyder, Carl F., and L[ester] D. Hammond. *Determination of Weight per Gallon of Blackstrap Molasses*. United States, Department of Commerce, National Bureau of Standards, *Technologic Papers*, XXI, 409–412, no. 345. Washington, DC, 1927

Snyder, Carl F., and L[ester] D. Hammond. "Determination of Weight per Gallon of Blackstrap Molasses." *The [Louisiana] Planter and Sugar Manufacturer*, LXXIX (1 October 1927), 268

Snyder, Carl F., and L[ester] D. Hammond. *Weights per United States Gallon and Weights per Cubic Foot of Sugar Solutions*. United States, Department of Commerce, National Bureau of Standards, Circular C 457. Revised edn. Washington, DC, 1946

The Society of Ship-Owners of Great Britain. *Collection of Interesting and Important Reports and Papers on the Navigation and Trade of Great Britain, Ireland, and the British Colonies in the West Indies*. [Compiled by Nathaniel Atcheson.] [London], 1807

Sögur Magnúsar konúngs Góda, Haralds konúngs Hardráda ok sona hans. [Edited by Thorgier Gudmundsson and Rasmus Kristian Rask.] Vol. VI of *Fornmanna Sögur, eptir gömlum handritum útgefnar ath tilhutun hins konúngliga Norræna fornfrætha félags*. 12 vols. Copenhagen, 1825–1837

Sølver, Carl V. "Rabaekroret." *Årbog Handels- og Søfartsmuseet på Kronborg*, [III] (1944), 108–118

Sølver, Carl V. "The Rabaek Rudder." *Mariner's Mirror*, XXXII (April 1946), 115–120

Soetbeer, Adolph. *Edelmetall-Produktion und Wertverhältnis zwischen Gold und Silber seit der Entdeckung Amerikas bis zur Gegenwart*. [*Petermanns Geographische Mittheilungen*, Band XIII, Erganzungsheft no. 57.] Gotha, 1879

Sonnino, Guido. *Saggio sulle industrie, marina e commercio in Livorno sotto i primi due Lorensi (1737–1790)*. Cortona, 1909

Sosin, Jack M. *English America and the Restoration Monarchy of Charles II: Transitional Politics, Commerce, and Kinship*. Lincoln, Nebraska, 1980

South Carolina. Court of Chancery. *Records of the Court of Chancery of South Carolina, 1671–1779*. Edited by Anne King Gregorie. American Legal Records, vol. VI. Washington, DC, 1950

South Carolina. Laws and Statutes. *The Statutes at Large of South Carolina*. Edited by Thomas Cooper and David J. McCord. 10 vols. Columbia, 1836–1841

Southey, Robert. *History of Brazil*. 3 vols. London, 1810–1819

Southey, Thomas. *Chronological History of the West Indies*. 3 vols. London, 1827

Spain. Dirección General de Archivos y Bibliotecas. *Guía de fuentes para la historia de Ibero-América conservadas en España*. 2 vols. Madrid, 1966–1969

Spain. Laws and Statutes. *Informe de la imperial ciudad de Toledo al real, y Supremo Consejo de Castilla, sobre inqualácion de pesos y medidas en todos los reynos, y senorias de S[u] Mag[estad] segun las layes*. [Edited by Andrés Marcos Burriell.] [Madrid], 1758

Spain. Laws and Statutes. *Recopilación de layes de los reynos de las Indias*. 4 vols. Madrid, 1681

Spooner, Frank C. *International Economy and Monetary Movements in France, 1493–1725*. Cambridge, Mass., 1972

Spooner, Frank C. *Risks at Sea: Amsterdam Insurance and Maritime Europe, 1766–1780*. Cambridge, Eng., 1983

Spotswood, Alexander. *The Official Letters of Alexander Spotswood, Lieutenant-Governor of the Colony of Virginia, 1710–1722*. Edited by R[obert] A. Brock. Collections of the Virginia Historical Society, n.s., vols I and II. 2 vols. Richmond, Va., 1882–1885

Staff, Frank. *The Transatlantic Mail*. London and New York, [1956]

Staring, W[inand] C. H. *De Binnen- en Buitenlandsche Maten, Gewichten en Munten*. Edited by R. W. van Wieringen. 4th edn. Schoonhaven, [1902]

Starkey, Otis P. *Commercial Geography of Barbados*. Indiana University Department of Geography, Technical Report no. 9. [Bloomington, Ind.], 1961

[Starling, Samuel.] *The Cry of the Oppressed by Reason of False Measures: or, A Discovery of the True Standard-Gallon of England. . . .* London, 1659

[Starling, Samuel.] *A Discovery of the True Standard-Gallon of England*. London, 1658

Steele, Ian K. *The English Atlantic, 1675–1740: An Exploration of Communication and Continuity*. New York, 1986

Steele, Richard, and Joseph Gillmore. *An Account of the Fish-Pool: Consisting of a Description of the Vessel so Call'd . . .* London, 1718

Stenton, Frank, *et al. The Bayeux Tapestry: A Comprehensive Survey*. 2nd edn. London, 1965

Stephenson, Orlando W. "The Supply of Gunpowder in 1776." *American Historical Review*, XXX (January 1925), 271–281

Steuart, A[rchibald] Francis. "Letters from Virginia, 1774–1781." *Magazine of History*, III (March, April 1906), 151–161, 211–218

Stevens, Robert White. *On the Stowage of Ships and Their Cargoes*. [1st edn.] Plymouth and London, 1858

[Stieler, Kaspar von.] *Zeitungs-Lust und Nutz: oder, derer so genanten Novellen oder Zeitungen, wirkende Ergetzlichkeit . . .* Hamburg, 1695

Stone: Quarrying and Building in England, AD 43–1525. Edited by David Parsons. [Chichester, Sussex, 1990]

Stourm, René. *Bibliographie historique des finances de la France au dix-huitième siècle*. Paris, 1895

Stubbs, William. *The Constitutional History of England in Its Origins and Development*. 3rd edn. 3 vols. Oxford, 1883

Studi in onore di Armando Sapori. 2 vols. Milan, [1957]

Studies in Economics and Industrial Relations. Edited by Wesley C. Mitchell *et al.* Philadelphia, 1941

Studies in London History Presented to Philip Edmund Jones. Edited by A[lbert] E. J. Hollander and William Kellaway. [London], 1969

Studies in the Quantity Theory of Money. Edited by Milton Friedman. Chicago, [1956]

Suchtelen, N. J. van. "Maten en gewichten in Suriname." *De Surinaamse Landbouw*, X (1962), 214–216

Suits, Daniel B. *Statistics: An Introduction to Quantitative Economic Research*. Chicago, 1963

Sulivan, J. A. "The Distillation and Purification of Water at Sea." *Mariner's Mirror*, LXV (May 1979), 161–162

Supple, Barry. *Commercial Crisis and Change in England, 1600–1642: A Study in the Instability of a Mercantile Economy*. Cambridge, Eng., 1959

Surinam. Laws and Statutes. *Plakaten, ordonnantiën en andere wetten, uitgevaardigd in Suriname, 1667–1816*. Edited by J[acobus] Th. de Smidt and T. van der Lee. West Indisch Plakaatboek, no. 1. Werken der Vereniging tot Uitgaaf der Bronnen van het Oud-Vaderlandsche Recht, 3rd ser., no. 24. 2 vols. Amsterdam, 1973

Sutherland, William. *The Ship-Builders Assistant: or, Some Essays Towards Compleating the Art of Marine Architecture*. London, 1711

[Swinton, John.] *A Proposal for Uniformity of Weighs and Measures in Scotland, by Execution of the Laws Now in Force*. Edinburgh, 1779

Syrett, David. "Defeat at Sea: The Impact of American Naval Operations upon the British, 1775–1778." In *Maritime Dimensions of the American Revolution*, pp. 13–22. Washington, DC, 1977

Szymanski, Hans. *Deutsche Segelschiffe: Die Geschichte der hölzernen Frachtsegler an den deutschen Ost- und Nordseeküsten, vom Ende des 18. Jahrhunderts bis auf die Gegenwart*. Veröffentlichungen des Instituts für Meereskunde an der Universität Berlin, Neue Folge B: Historisch-volkswirtschaftliche Reihe, Heft 10. Berlin, 1934

Tawney, R[ichard] H. *Business and Politics under James I: Lionell Cranfield as Merchant and Minister*. Cambridge, Eng., 1958

Taylor, George R. "American Economic Growth before 1840: An Exploratory Essay." *Journal of Economic History*, XXIV (December 1964), 427–444

Teenstra, Marten D. *De Landbouw in de Kolonie Suriname*. Groningen, 1835

Thayer, Theodore George. *Nathaniel Greene: Strategist of the American Revolution*. New York, 1960

Thesée, Françoise. "Sur deux sucreries de Jacquezy (nord de Saint-Domingue), 1778–1802." In [Congrès National des Sociétés Savantes (92nd, 1967, Strasbourg and Colmar, France). Section d'Histoire Moderne et Contemporaine]. *Actes du Quatre-Vingt-Douzième Congrès National des Sociétés Savantes*, II, 217–295. Paris, 1970

Thestrup, Poul. *The Standard of Living in Copenhagen, 1730–1800 Some Methods of Measurement*. Københavns Universitet, Institut for Økonomisk Historie, Publikation no. 5. Copenhagen, 1971

Thirsk, Joan, and J[ohn] P. Cooper. *Seventeenth Century Economic Documents*. Oxford, 1972

[Thomas, Dalby.] *An Historical Account of the Rise and Growth of the West India Collonies*. London, 1690

Thomas, Isaiah. *The History of Printing in America*. 1810. New edn. Edited by Marcus A. McCorison. New York, 1970

Thomas, Robert Paul. "A Quantitative Approach to the Study of the Effects of British Imperial Policy upon Colonial Welfare: Some Preliminary Findings." *Journal of Economic History*, XXV (December 1965), 615–638

["Thomas Irving Obituary."] *Gentleman's Magazine*, LXX (August 1800), 798

Thomasson, H. "Äskekärrsbåtens ålder." *Göteborgs och Bohusläns Fornminnes Förenings Tidskrift 1934*, pp. 22–34

Thünen, Johann Heinrich von. *Der isolirte Staat in Beziehung auf Landwirtschaft und Nationalökonomie, oder Untersuchungen über den Einfluss, den die Getreidepreise, der Reichthum des Bodens und die Abgaben auf den Ackerbau ausüben*. 3rd edn. Edited by Hermann Schumacher-Zarchlin. 3 vols in 4 pts. Berlin, 1875

Thuillier, Guy. "Le Stock monétaire de la France en l'an X." *Revue d'Histoire Économique et Sociale,* LII (no. 2, 1974), 247–257

Tillet, [Mathieu]. *Essai sur le rapport des poids étrangers avec le marc de France* ... Paris, 1766

Tillet, [Mathieu]. *Saggio sul rapporto dei pesi stanieri con il marco di Franco* ... Florence, 1769

Tilly, Louise A. "The Food Riot as a Form of Political Conflict in France." *Journal of Interdisciplinary History,* II (Summer 1971), 23–57

Tinniswood, J. T. "English Galleys, 1272–1377." *Mariner's Mirror,* XXXV (October 1949), 276–315

Tooke, Thomas. *Thoughts and Details on the High and Low Prices of the Last Thirty Years.* London, 1823

Tooke, Thomas, and William Newmarch. A *History of Prices, and of the State of the Circulation, from 1793 to [1856].* 6 vols. London, 1838–1857

Torr, Cecil. *Ancient Ships.* Cambridge, Eng., 1894

Torre, Raffelle della. *Tractatus de cambiis.* [Genoa, 1641]

Trade, Government and Society in Caribbean History, 1700–1920: Essays Presented to Douglas Hall. Edited by B[arry] W. Higman. Kingston, Jamaica, 1983

The Trade of Bristol in the Eighteenth Century. Edited by W[alter] E. Minchinton. Bristol Record Society, Publications, vol. 20. [Bristol, 1957]

The Trade Winds: A Study of British Overseas Trade during the French Wars, 1793–1815. Edited by C[yril] Northcote Parkinson. London, [1948]

Tresoir van de Maten van Gewichten van Coorn, Lande, van Elle ende natte Mate, Oock van de Gelde en Wissel ... Amsterdam, 1590

Trevett, John. "Journal of John Trevett, U.S.N., 1774–1782." *Rhode Island Historical Magazine,* VI (July, October 1885, January, April 1886), 72–74, 106–110, 194–199, 271–278, VII (July, October 1886, January 1887), 38–45, 151–160, 205–208

Trinidad Almanac and Commercial Register for 1840. Trinidad, 1840

Tucker, Josiah. *Four Tracts, Together with Two Sermons, on Political and Commercial Subjects.* Gloucester, Eng., 1774

Tuxen, N[icolaï] E. "De Nordiske Langskibe." *Aarbøger for Nordisk Oldkyndighed og Historie,* [2nd ser., I] (1886), 49–134

Tyson, George F. *A Guide to Manuscript Sources in United States and West Indian Depositories Relating to the British West Indies during the Era of the American Revolution.* Wilmington, Del., 1978

Tyson, George F., Jr, and Carolyn Tyson. *Preliminary Report on Manuscript Materials in British Archives Relating to the American Revolution in the West Indian Islands.* St. Thomas, US Virgin Islands, 1974

Ulibarri, George S., and John P. Harrison. *Guide to Materials on Latin America in the National Archives of the United States.* Washington, DC, 1974

Unger, Richard W. *Dutch Shipbuilding before 1800: Ships and Guilds.* Assen and Amsterdam, 1978

Unger, Richard W. *The Ship in the Medieval Economy, 600–1600.* London, [1980]

United Nations. Food and Agricultural Organization. *The World Sugar Economy in Figures* ... *1880–1959.* Commodity Reference, Ser. 1. [Rome, 1961]

United Nations. Statistical Office. *World Weights and Measures: Handbook for Statisticians.* [Revised edn.] New York, [1966]

United States. Congress. Joint Economic Committee. *Employment, Growth, and Price Levels: Hearings before the Joint Economic Committee, Congress of the United States* ... *April 7, 8, 9, and 10, 1959.* [United States. Congress. 86th Congress, 1st Session.] 10 pts in 13 vols. Washington, DC, 1959–1960

United States. Continental Congress. *Journals of the Continental Congress, 1774–1789.*

Edited by Worthington Chauncey Ford *et al.* 34 vols. Washington, DC, 1904–1937

United States. Continental Congress. *The Secret Journals of the Acts and Proceedings of Congress, From the First Meeting Thereof to the Dissolution of the Confederation, by the Adoption of the Constitution of the United States.* 4 vols. Boston, 1820–1821

United States. Department of Commerce. Bureau of the Census. *Historical Statistics of the United States: Colonial Times to 1970.* [United States. Congress. 93rd Congress, 1st Session. House Documents, no. 93–78.] 2 vols. Washington, DC, 1975

United States. Department of Commerce. Bureau of the Census. *The Statistical History of the United States, from Colonial Times to the Present.* Edited by Ben J. Wattenberg. New York, 1976

United States. Department of Justice. *Official Opinions of the Attorney General of the United States.* Edited by Benjamin F. Hall *et al.* In progress. Washington, DC, 1852 to date

United States. Department of State. *Report of the Secretary of State, upon Weights and Measures.* [By John Quincy Adams.] [United States. Congress. 16th Congress, 2nd Session. Senate Documents, vol. no. 4, doc. no. 119. Serial Set no. 45. House Documents, vol. no. 8, doc. no. 109. Serial Set no. 55.] Washington, DC, 1821

United States. Department of the Navy. Hydrographic Office. *New Providence Island.* H[ydrographic] O[ffice], [Chart no.] 1377. 21st edn, revised. Washington, DC, 1961

United States. Department of the Navy. Hydrographic Office. *Sailing Directions for the West Indies.* Hydrographic Office Publications, no. 128. 2 vols. Washington, DC, 1951

United States. Laws and Statutes. *Laws and Regulations for the Government of the Post Office Department.* Washington, DC, 1843

United States. Laws and Statutes. *The Statutes at Large of the United States of America.* Edited by R[ichard] Peters *et al.* 17 vols. Boston, 1845–1873

United States. Library of Congress. *A Catalogue of Books Represented by Library of Congress Printed Cards.* 167 vols. Ann Arbor, Michigan, 1942–1946

United States. Library of Congress. *National Union Catalog, Pre-1956 Imprints.* 754 vols. [London], 1968–1981

United States. Library of Congress. Cataloging Publications Division. *Newspapers in Microform, United States, 1948–1972.* Washington, DC, 1973

United States. Library of Congress. Descriptive Cataloging Division. *The National Union Catalog of Manuscript Collections.* 29 vols. Ann Arbor, Mich., Hamden, Conn., and Washington, DC, 1962–1994

United States. Library of Congress. Geography and Map Division. *Maps and Charts of North America and the West Indies, 1750–1789: A Guide to the Collections in the Library of Congress.* By John R. Sellers and Patricia Molen Van Ee. Washington, DC, 1981

United States. Library of Congress. Manuscript Division. "Dictionary Catalog of Collections." 3 vols. Unpublished computer printout, 1986

United States. Library of Congress. Manuscript Division. *A Guide to Manuscripts Relating to American History in British Depositories Reproduced for the Division of Manuscripts of the Library of Congress.* By Grace Gardner Griffin. Washington, DC, 1946

United States. Library of Congress. Manuscript Division. *Handbook of Manuscripts in the Library of Congress.* Washington, DC, 1918

United States. Library of Congress. Manuscript Division. *Manuscript Sources in the Library of Congress for Research on the American Revolution.* By John R. Sellers, Gerard W. Gawalt, Paul H. Smith, and Patricia Molen van Ee. Washington, DC, 1975

United States. Library of Congress. Manuscript Division. *Manuscripts on Microfilm: A Checklist of the Holdings in the Manuscript Division [of the Library of Congress].* By Richard B. Bickel. Washington, DC, 1975

United States. Library of Congress. Manuscript Division. "Reference Index for the Dictionary Catalog of Collections." 4 vols. Unpublished computer printout, 1986

United States. National Archives and Records Administration. *Guide to Federal Records in the National Archives of the United States.* By Robert B. Machette *et al.* 3 vols. Washington, DC, 1995

United States. National Archives and Records Administration. *A Guide to Pre-Federal Records in the National Archives.* By Howard H. Wehmann, edited by Benjamin L. De Whitt. Washington, DC, 1989

United States. National Archives and Records Administration. *Guide to the National Archives of the United States.* Washington, DC, 1974

United States. Patent Office. *Annual Report of the Commissioner of Patents.* In progress. Washington, DC, 1837 to date

Usher, Abbott Payson. *The History of the Grain Trade in France, 1400–1710.* Harvard Economic Studies, vol. IX. Cambridge, Mass., 1913

Van der Wee, Herman. *The Growth of the Antwerp Market and the European Economy (Fourteenth–Sixteenth Centuries).* 3 vols. The Hague, 1963

Van der Wee, Herman. "Monetary, Credit and Banking Systems." In *The Economic Organization of Early Modern Europe.* Edited by E[dwin] E. Rich and C[harles] H. Wilson, pp. 290–392. Vol. V of *The Cambridge Economic History of Europe,* Cambridge, Eng., 1977

Vauban, [Sébastien Le Prestre de]. *La Dîme royale.* [Edited by Jean-François Pernot.] Paris, 1992

[Vauban, Sébastien Le Prestre de.] *Projet d'une dixme royale: Qui supprimant la taille . . . & tous autres impôts onereux . . .* [1st edn,] n.p. [Paris], 1707

Vegetius. *Flavi Vegeti Renati Epitoma Rei Militari.* Edited by Carl Lang. 2nd edn. Leipzig, 1885

Veitia Linage, Joseph de. *Norte de la contratación de las Indias Occidentales.* Seville, 1672

Veitia Linage, Joseph de. *The Spanish Rule of Trade to the West Indies.* Translated by John Stevens. London, 1702

Velden, M[atthijs] v[an]. *Fondament vande Wisselhandeling.* Amsterdam, 1629

The Vercelli Book. Edited by George Philip Krapp. Vol. II of *The Anglo-Saxon Poetic Records: A Collective Edition.* Edited by George Philip Krapp and Elliott Van Kirk Dobbie. New York, 1932

Verdenhalven, Fritz. *Alte Maße, Münzen und Gewichte aus dem deutschen Sprachgebiet.* Neustadt an der Aisch, 1968

Vernon, John. *The Compleat Comptinghouse: or, The Young Lad Taken from the Writing School, and Fully Instructed, by Way of Dialogue, in All the Mysteries of a Merchant.* London, 1678

Viall, H. R. "Tyne Keels." *Mariner's Mirror,* XXVIII (April 1942), 160–162

View of the Political State of Scotland in the Last Century: A Confidential Report of the Political Opinions, Family Connections, or Personal Circumstances of the 2662 County Voters in 1788. Edited by Charles Elphinstone Adam. Edinburgh, 1887

Vieweg, Richard. *Mass und Messen in kulturgeschichtlicher Sicht.* Beiträge zur Geschichte der Wissenschaft und der Technik, Heft 4. Wiesbaden, 1962

Vilar, Pierre. *A History of Gold and Money, 1450–1920.* Translated by Judith White. London, 1976

Villani, Giovanni. *Croniche . . . dopo la confusione della torre di Babello insino all' a 1338.* 8 vols in 4 pts. Florence, 1823

Virginia (Colony). Laws and Statutes. *A Collection of All the Acts of Assembly Now *in Force, in the Colony of Virginia.* [Edited by John Halloway *et al.*] Williamsburg, Va., 1733

Virginia. Laws and Statutes. *The Statutes at Large; Being a Collection of All the Laws of Virginia.* Edited by William Waller Hening. 13 vols. Richmond, Va., 1809–1823

Vogel, Walther. "Zur nord- und westeuropäischen Seeschiffahrt im früheren Mittelalter." *Hansische Geschichtsblätter,* [XXXV] (1907), 153–205

Vogel, Walther. *Geschichte der deutschen Seeschiffahrt . . . von der Urzeit bis zum Ende des XV. Jahrhunderts.* Berlin, 1915

Vogel, Walther. Review of *Die Entwicklung der wichtigsten Schiffstypen bis ins 19. Jahrhundert,* by Bernard Hagedorn. *Hansische Geschichtsblätter,* XX (1914), 375

Vom Ancien Régime zur Französischen Revolution: Forschungen und Perspektiven/De l'Ancien Régime à la Révolution Française: Recherches et Perspectives. Edited by Ernst Hinrichs, Eberhard Schmitt, and Richard Vierhaus. Veröffentlichungen des Max-Planck-Instituts für Geschichte, 55. Göttingen, 1978

Wadstein, Elis. "Friserns och forntida handelsvögar i Norden." *Götesborgs Kungl[ig] Vetenskaps- och Vitterhets-samhälles Handlingar,* 4th ser., XXI–XXII (1918–1919), 1–[25]

Wätjen, Herman. *Das holländische Kolonialreich in Brasilien: Ein Kapital aus der Kolonialgeschichte des 17. Jahrhunderts.* Gotha, 1921

Wailly, Natalis de. *Mémoire sur les variations de la livre tournois depuis le règne de Saint Louis jusqu'à l'établissement de la monnaie décimale.* Institut Impérial de France, Académie des Inscriptions et Belles-Lettres, *Mémoires.* Vol. 21, pt ii. Paris, 1857

Wal, G[errit] van der. *Rekeneenheid en Ruilmiddel.* Helder, 1940

Walde, Alois. *Vergleichendes Wörterbuch der indogermanischen Sprachen.* Edited by Julius Pokorny. 3 vols. Berlin and Leipzig, 1927–1932

Walne, Peter. *A Guide to Manuscript Sources for the History of Latin America and the Caribbean in the British Isles.* London, 1973

Walton, Gary M. "Colonial Tonnage Measurements: A Comment." *Journal of Economic History,* XXVII (September 1967), 392–397

Walton, Gary Max. "A Quantitative Study of American Colonial Shipping." Ph.D. dissertation, University of Washington, 1966

Walvin, James. *Black and White: The Negro and English Society, 1555–1945.* London, 1973

Wandalbert, of Prüm. *Vita [et miracula] sancti goaris.* In *Patrologiae cursus completus . . . series latinæ,* edited by J[acques] P[aul] Migne, CXXI, 639–674. Paris, 1852

Ward, John. *The Young Mathematicians Guide: Being a Plain and Easy Introduction to the Mathematicks.* 6th edn, revised. London, 1734

Wardle, Arthur C. "The Post Office Packets." In *The Trade Winds: A Study of British Overseas Trade during the French Wars, 1793–1815,* edited by C[yril] Northcote Parkinson, pp. 278–290. London, [1948]

Ware, James. *The Whole Works of Sir James Ware Concerning Ireland.* Translated and edited by Walter Harris. 3 pts in 2 vols. Dublin, 1739–1745

Warner, Sam Bass, Jr. *Writing Local History: The Use of Social Statistics.* American Association for State and Local History, Technical Leaflet 7. Revised edn. Nashville, Tenn., 1970

[Warren, William.] *Whereas the Queen has been Pleased to Direct, that a Monthly Correspondence be Established between this Kingdom, and Her Majesties Dominions on the Continent of America, by Packet-Boats, to Pass to, and from Bristol and New York . . .* [London, 1710]

Warren, Winslow. ["Loss of Boston Customs Records, 1776."] *Proceedings of the Massachusetts Historical Society,* XLIII (1909–1910), 423–428

Washington, George. *The Writings of George Washington*. Edited by John C. Fitzpatrick. 39 vols. Washington, DC, 1931–1944

Waters, David W. *The Art of Navigation in Elizabethan and Early Stuart Times*. 2nd edn, revised. Greenwich, Eng., 1978

Watson, Alan D. "Placemen in South Carolina: The Receiver Generals [*sic*] of the Quitrents." *South Carolina Historical Magazine*, LXXIV (January 1973), 18–30

Watson, Alan D. "The Quitrent System in Royal South Carolina." Ph.D. dissertation, University of South Carolina, 1971

Watts, John. *Letter Book of John Watts, Merchant and Councilor of New York, January 1, 1762–December 22, 1765*. [Edited by Dorothy C. Barck.] Collections of the New-York Historical Society, LXI. New York, 1928

Webb, Stephen Saunders. *The Governors-General: The English Army and the Definition of the Empire, 1569–1681*. Chapel Hill, NC, 1979

Weill, Georges [J.] *Le Journal: Origines, évolution et rôle de la presse périodique*. Paris, 1934

Weinbaum, Martin. *London unter Eduard I. und II.: Verfassungs- und Wirtschaftsgeschichtliche Studien*. Vierteljahrschrift für Sozial- und Wirschaftsgeschichte, Beihften 28–29. 2 vols. Stuttgart, 1933

Welch, Charles. "The City Printers." *Transactions of the Bibliographical Society*, XIV: 1915–1917 (1919), 175–241

[Welland, Dennis], Bernard R. Crick, and Naomi Connelly. "Third List of Addenda to a Guide to Manuscripts Relating to America in Great Britain and Ireland." *Bulletin of the British Association for American Studies*, n.s., XII/XIII (1966), 61–77

Werner, Johannes. *Børsen: En Fremstilling i Billeder og Text af Københavns Børsbygnings Historie, 1619–1915*. Copenhagen, 1915

West India Planters and Merchants. London. *Considerations on the Present State of the Intercourse between His Majesty's Sugar Colonies and the Dominions of the United States of America*. [Edited by James Allen.] [London, 1784]

Westergaard, Waldemar C. *The Danish West Indies under Company Rule (1671–1754), with a Supplementary Chapter, 1755–1917*. New York, 1917

[Wheelock, Arthur K., Jr., *et al.*] *Johannes Vermeer*. [Edited by Arthur K. Wheelock, Jr.] Washington, DC, [1995]

Whitbread, L[eslie G.] "The 'Frisian Sailor' Passage in Old English Gnomic Verses." *Review of English Studies*, [o.s.], XXII (1946), 215–219

Whitworth, Charles. *Commerce de la Grande-Bretagne, et tableaux de ses importations progressives, depuis l'année 1697 jusqu'à la fin de l'année 1773*. Paris, 1777

Whitworth, Charles. *State of the Trade of Great Britain in Its Imports and Exports . . . 1697 [to 1773]*. London, 1776

Widukind, of Korvey. *Widukindi rei gestae Saxonicae*. Edited by Georg Waitz. In *Monumenta Germaniae historica*. Edited by George Henry Pertz. *Scriptores rerum Germanicorum*. Hanover, 1839

Wilkenfeld, Bruce M. "The New York City Shipowning Community, 1715–1764." *American Neptune*, XXXVII (January 1977), 50–65

Wilkens, Hans. "Zur Geschichte des niederländischen Handels im Mittelalter." *Hansische Geschichtsblätter*, XIV (1908), 295–356, and XV (1909), 125–203

William, of Tyre. *Historia rerum in partibus transmarinis gestarum a tempore successorum Muhumeth usque ad annum Domini MCLXXIV*. [Edited by Arthur Auguste Beugnot and A. Langlois.] Vol. I, pts i–ii, of *Historiens occidentaux. Recueil des historiens des Croisades*. Paris, 1844

Williams, Eric. *Capitalism and Slavery*. Chapel Hill, NC, 1944

Williams, Neville [J.] "The London Port Books." *Transactions of the London and Middlesex Archaeological Society*, XVIII (1955), 13–26

Willis, Jean Louise. "The Trade between North America and the Danish West Indies,

1756–1807, with Special Reference to St. Croix." Ph.D. dissertation, Columbia University, 1963

"Wills of Early New York Jews [1704–1799]." Edited by Leo Herskowitz. *American Jewish Historical Quarterly*, LV–LVI (March, September, and December 1966), 319–363, 62–122, 163–207

Wilson, David M. *The Bayeux Tapestry: The Complete Tapestry in Colour.* [London, 1985]

Wing, Donald [G.] *Short-Title Catalogue of Books Printed in England, Scotland, Ireland, Wales, and British America and of English Books Printed in Other Countries, 1641–1700.* 2nd edn, revised and enlarged. Edited by John J. Morrison *et al.* 3 vols. New York, 1972–1988

Winter, P[ieter] J. van. *Het aandeel van den Amsterdamschen handel aan den opbouw van het Amerikaansche gemeenebest.* Werken Uitgegeven door de Vereenignig het Nederlandsch Economisch-Historisch Archief, nos 7, 9. 2 vols. The Hague, 1927–1933

Winthrop Papers. Edited by Malcolm Freiberg *et al.* In progress. Boston, 1929 to date

Wise, John Philip. "British Commercial Policy, 1783–1794: The Aftermath of American Independence." Ph.D. dissertation, University of London, 1972

Witsen, Nicolaas Corneliszoon. *Aeloude en hedendaagsche Scheeps-bouw en bestier* . . . Amsterdam, 1671

Woodward, D[onald] M. "Port Books." *History: The Journal of the Historical Association*, LV (June 1970), 207–210

Wright, Charles, and C[harles] Ernest Fayle. *A History of Lloyd's from the Founding of Lloyd's Coffee House to the Present Day.* London, 1928

Wright, I[rene] A. "The Coymans Asiento (1685–1689)." *Bijdragen voor Vaderlandsche Geschiedenis en Oudheidkunde*, 6th ser., I (nos 1–2, 1924), 23–62

Wright, Thomas. *Anglo-Saxon and Old-English Vocabularies.* 2nd edn. Edited by Richard Paul Wülcker. 2 vols. London, 1884

W[ybard], J[ohn]. *Tactometria. seu, Tetagmenometria. Or, the Geometry of Regulars* . . . London, 1650

Zampetti, Pietro. *I vedutisti veneziana del Settecento.* Venice, 1967

Die Zeit der Stadtgründung im Ostseeraum. [Edited by Mårten Stenberger.] Acta Visbygensia I: Visby-Symposiet för Historiska Vetenskapen, 1963. Visby, 1965

Zelger, [Clarita] Renate [Frowein]. "Der historisch-politische Briefwechsel und die Staatsanzeigen August Ludwig v. Schlözers als Zeitschrift und Zeitbild." Ph.D. dissertation, University of Munich, 1953

Zevenboom, K. M. C., and D[irk] A. Wittop Koning. *Nederlandse gewichten: Stelsels, ijkewezen, vormen makers en merken.* Rijksmuseum voor de Geschiedenis der Natuurwetenschappen te Leiden, Mededeling no. 86. Leiden, 1953

Zupko, Ronald Edward. *British Weights and Measures: A History from Antiquity to the Seventeenth Century.* Madison, Wis., 1977

Zupko, Ronald Edward. *A Dictionary of English Weights and Measures from Anglo-Saxon Times to the Nineteenth Century.* Madison, Wis., 1968

Zupko, Ronald Edward. *A Dictionary of Weights and Measures for the British Isles: The Middle Ages to the Twentieth Century.* Memoirs of the American Philosophical Society, vol. CLXVIII. Philadelphia, 1985

Zupko, Ronald Edward. *French Weights and Measures before the Revolution: A Dictionary of Provincial and Local Units.* Bloomington, Indiana, 1978

Zupko, Ronald Edward. *Revolution in Measurement: Western European Weights and Measures since the Age of Science.* Memoirs of the American Philosophical Society, vol. CLXXXVI. Philadelphia, 1990

Zupko, Ronald Edward. "The Weights and Measures of Scotland before the Union." *Scottish Historical Review*, LVI (October 1977), 119–145

INDEX